A CONCISE

HISTORY

of the

CATHOLIC

CHURCH

THOMAS
BOKENKOTTER

DOUBLEDAY

New York   London   Toronto   Sydney   Auckland

A CONCISE
HISTORY
of the
CATHOLIC
CHURCH

Revised and Expanded Edition

PUBLISHED BY DOUBLEDAY
a division of Random House, Inc.

DOUBLEDAY and the portrayal of an anchor with a dolphin are registered
trademarks of Random House, Inc.

Book design by Donna Sinisgalli

Excerpts from *The Jerusalem Bible,* © 1966 by Darton, Longman & Todd, Ltd., and
Doubleday, a Division of Random House, Inc. Used by permission of the publishers.

Library of Congress Cataloging-in-Publication Data
Bokenkotter, Thomas S.
A concise history of the Catholic Church / Thomas Bokenkotter.—Rev. and expanded ed.
p. cm.
Includes bibliographical references and index.
1. Catholic Church—History. 2. Church history. I. Title.
BX945.3 .B66 2002
282'.09—dc21
2002074124

ISBN 0-385-50584-1

To

my dear mother

and father

❧

CONTENTS

PREFACE TO THE
THIRD EDITION

It was good news indeed when Trace Murphy, my editor, informed me that
Doubleday and Image Books planned to issue an illustrated edition of the
Concise History. Intended to mark the twenty-fifth anniversary of its publication, the project raised my hopes that the book may outlive its author—an
abiding vanity of authors.

My intent was, and is, to provide a guide for Catholics who wanted to
know more about the complex history of their two-thousand-year-old
Church. And also to provide some perspective for those confused by all the
changes brought on by the Second Vatican Council. In other words, to show
how change has been a constant in the history of the Church. In doing so I
have focused on the main events and personalities that have made the Roman
Catholic Church what it is today.

There is no need to dwell on the obvious limitations inherent in this type
of book. To try and condense two millennia of history into one volume means
that much of even real importance will be left out. My hope is that the updated bibliography will help to fill in the gaps.

The crisis engendered by Vatican II still continues as the Church seeks to
incorporate the new insights of the Council into its life and thought: collegiality, ecumenism, religious freedom, theological and cultural pluralism, a
pluralist approach to moral issues, dialogue, and use of biblical and historical
criticism. As I said in the Preface to the previous edition, just how these new
insights could be fitted into the ancient, rock-ribbed structure of Catholic
doctrine and tradition was not, and could not, be spelled out in the few short

years of the Second Vatican Council. It is no wonder that fur is still flying as the work continues of reconciling new insights with the ancient traditions, especially as defined so rigidly by the Council of Trent.

I might add that I am most grateful to the critics who have been generous toward this book in spite of its many limitations.

My special thanks to the staff at Doubleday—Trace, Siobhan, and Andrew—for their diligence in seeing this illustrated edition through the press.

PREFACE TO THE
IMAGE EDITION

The publication of a revised paperback edition of my *Concise History* gives me
an opportunity to say a few things about my approach in writing this general
history of the Church. My object was to provide for the general reader a brief
compendium of the main facts of the Church's history, i.e., an account of the
main events, personalities, and movements that have made the Church of
Rome what it is today. To do this in one relatively short volume is indeed a
challenging task, and by sheer limitation of space I felt compelled to focus my
attention almost exclusively on the Churches united with Rome. In doing so
I certainly did not intend to pass judgment on the claims of the other
Churches to be part of the "one, holy, catholic, and apostolic" Church of the
Apostles' Creed. The same is true in my use of the term "Catholic," which I
employ as the ordinary popular designation for the Churches united with
Rome.

In spite of all my efforts I realize the book has its share of short-comings
and omissions, which are perhaps inevitable in a book of this scope. Some
critics, for instance, have noted, with a certain amount of justice perhaps, a
tendency to glide over the negative and dark aspects of the Church's history.
Others would like to see more attention given to the activities of the ordinary
Catholic as opposed to the doings of Popes, bishops, and councils. I can only
say that after writing this book I am more aware than ever of how difficult it
is to produce a balanced account of the complex concatenation of events,
ideas, and personalities that constitute historical reality. And I can only hope

that this book with all its imperfections will provide the reader with some insight into the Church's fascinating and incredibly complicated past.

In conclusion, I want to add some words of thanks to those who have helped me improve this revised edition of my book by their constructive criticism and suggestions. In particular, I wish to thank Monsignor John Tracy Ellis of the Catholic University of Washington, Reverend John Jay Hughes, Professor Adjunct of St. Louis University, Reverend Robert McNamara, Professor of Church History at St. Bernard's Seminary in Rochester, and Reverend M. Edmund Hussey, Professor of Historical Theology at Mount St. Mary's Seminary in Norwood, Ohio.

Thomas Bokenkotter
St. Gregory's Seminary
Cincinnati, Ohio
1978

PREFACE TO THE REVISED
AND EXPANDED EDITION

My intention in writing *A Concise History* was to provide the ordinary Catholic and others with a relatively brief account of the Catholic Church's tumultuous history. I especially hoped it would help Catholics cope with all the changes going on in the Church by showing them how much change had occurred in the past.

I have tried in this revised and expanded edition to bring it up to date by covering the major events of the Church's last fifteen years, years of extraordinary drama, years that saw the crisis engendered by Vatican II continue unabated as the Church sought to incorporate the new insights of the Council into its life and thought: collegiality, ecumenism, religious freedom, theological and cultural pluralism, a personalist approach to moral issues, dialogue, use of biblical and historical criticism. Just how they could be fitted into the ancient, rock-ribbed structure of Catholic doctrine and tradition was not, and could not, be spelled out in the few short years of the Council. It is no wonder that much fur started flying when the work began of reconciling these concepts with the tradition, especially as defined so rigidly by the Council of Trent.

One thing sorely lacking in the previous editions of this history has been a bibliography to help the student with a desire for further reading. I hope I have supplied this lack by the extensive bibliography I have provided. The books were selected on the basis of their scholarly value and their accessibility for the average reader.

Special thanks to Pat Kossmann, my editor, who has been so helpful in many ways over the many years we have worked together.

Thomas Bokenkotter
Assumption Church
Walnut Hills, Cincinnati, Ohio
1990

INTRODUCTION

The Catholic Church is the oldest institution in the Western world. It can trace its history back almost two thousand years. It began in Jerusalem as a small nucleus of disciples who shared faith in the resurrection of Jesus, their crucified leader, and it spread quickly to countless cities of the Roman Empire. Its inflexible opposition to Roman culture, morals, and religion aroused the savage fury of the state, and many of the Church's members perished when they refused to conform. But its spiritual power was only magnified by persecution, and its progress remained constant. Finally it won a decisive victory over the old paganism when it drew to its side the Emperor Constantine himself, who in 312 attached its emblem—the monogram of Christ—to the banners of his troops and granted it complete religious liberty.

Its fortunes were henceforth linked intimately with the state, as emperor after emperor showered it with privileges and favors. When the Western Empire itself fell apart before the onslaught of the barbarians, it remained the only power that was not totally disrupted by the collapse; and under the leadership of remarkable Popes like Gregory the Great (d. 604), it evangelized the barbarians and laid the foundations for a whole new Christian civilization in the West: Christendom.

For nearly a thousand years then, the Catholic Church presided over the total life of Christendom and animated its laws, institutions, customs, literature, art, and architecture with its faith in Jesus Christ, God and man. Its Popes gradually established their supreme authority over the whole of Western Christendom. These powerful papal monarchs—brilliantly epitomized in Innocent III (d. 1216)—controlled a vast ecclesiastical machinery that regulated in minute detail the moral and social behavior of medieval men—kings and princes as well as peasants and townspeople.

As modern times dawned with the Renaissance of the fourteenth and fifteenth centuries, the unity of papal Christendom was severely undermined by many forces—social, economic, religious, and cultural—that could no longer be contained within the framework of the papal theocracy. When Luther dealt the most devastating blow—his denial of papal absolute authority—much of the elaborate structure simply collapsed. The Church of Rome, however, was able to save itself by a thoroughgoing reform at Trent (1545–63), and with greatly diminished membership and influence but with rejuvenated spiritual energy—most evident in the newly founded Jesuit Order—it set about its new task of recovering its lost territories and preserving the faith of its members, who were now exposed to the spirit of radical doubt engendered by the rising forces of rationalism and liberalism.

During the next four centuries, the Church as reorganized at Trent set itself with grim determination against most of the trends of modern secular culture. Shaken by crisis after crisis—the most notable one being the French Revolution, which began in 1789—it managed to keep its ranks unbroken and its faith unchanged. After the Revolution it experienced a powerful spiritual revival that manifested itself in the conversion of numerous members of Europe's intellectual elite, in the foundation of many new religious orders, in a dynamic missionary movement that extended its presence to every corner of the globe, and in the development of a social ethic that offered a consistent set of answers to the moral problems raised by the Industrial Revolution.

However, its attitude to the modern world outside the Church remained doggedly negative and condemnatory. This attitude was given classic form in the pontificate of Pius IX (1846–78), whose *Syllabus of Errors* anathematized the ideology of modern secular liberalism. When the liberal Catholics and Modernists attempted to work out a reconciliation of its traditional faith with the demand of modern culture, they were decisively put down. And it entered our own century with a constantly increasing membership (nearly one fifth of the world's population) tightly disciplined under the highly centralized control of Rome. The Popes of the twentieth century enhanced its prestige by the able leadership they provided in an age of technological advance and spiritual chaos.

With the advent of Pope John XXIII (d. 1963), a turning point was reached in the Church's relations with the modern world. With incredible boldness, John resolutely turned his back on four centuries of sterile polemics and called for dialogue with all men of good will. The Second Vatican Council (1962–65) embraced his optimistic vision of a renewed Church seeking greater unity with all men. It subjected the Church to a penetrating self-scrutiny and carried through sweeping changes that radically transformed the Church in many aspects of its life and doctrine.

The suddenness and extent of the changes profoundly shocked the Church's lethargic members and plunged the whole Church into a period of such intense inner turmoil that few minds would dare to offer any firm predictions about the outcome of it all. The history recited here, however, should at least provide the necessary perspective for whatever judgments we might care to make.

Postscript: December 1978 The death of Pope Paul VI on August 6, 1978, at the age of eighty touched off a fascinating series of events that made Rome the center of world attention for many weeks. Paul may well go down in history as one of the great modern pontiffs who skillfully balanced tradition with innovation in guiding the Church steadily through one of its most critical transition periods. But during the last years of his reign he often appeared painfully weary and depressed and frequently gave vent to lamentations on the evils rife in the Church and the world. Nor at his death did those mentioned as *papabili* stir the imagination or promise much in the way of creative leadership for a troubled Church. But when the conclave was held and Albino Luciani, the man elected to succeed him, appeared on the balcony of St. Peter's smiling broadly, laughing and waving his arms, the huge crowd below seemed to sense instinctively that he was just what the Church needed and they responded with wild applause and enthusiasm.

Their instinct proved sound. John Paul reigned only thirty-four days but in that short span succeeded in revivifying the image of the papacy. Son of a glassworker who had to emigrate to Switzerland to support his family back in Belluno, John Paul was no stranger to hardship and poverty. This, plus his years of pastoral work, enabled him to speak with genuine sympathy and understanding about the concerns and problems of ordinary people. His simple and direct homilies spiced with jokes and personal reminiscences delighted the faithful who flocked to his audiences, while his love for people was obviously sincere and unaffected; and as he made his way through the crowds he would often stop to kiss the children and embrace their parents.

In his typical self-deprecating way he called himself a "poor wren" and though possessed of real intellectual gifts he left behind no important addresses or encyclicals. Even had he enjoyed a longer reign, it is unlikely that he would have made any major shifts in the direction already traced out by his two predecessors whose memory he honored by choosing their names. He was theologically conservative, a strong upholder of traditional formulations of morality and doctrine, and though deeply sympathetic to the cause of the poor and the oppressed, was not at all impressed by the current theologies of liberation.

His sudden death on September 28 cut short all speculations about the direction of his pontificate and, as the cardinals gathered in Rome for another conclave, people wondered about their chances of finding another man of the caliber of Albino Luciani. In view of the conservative composition of the college he would have to be unequivocally traditional as regards doctrine, acceptable to the more socially conscious cardinals of the Third World and Latin America, and, considering the enormous pressures of the office, which no doubt hastened the death of John Paul, he would have to be of robust health as well. In addition, they had to try to find a man who could maintain the spirit of optimism and hope that John Paul had restored to the Church in such an incredibly short time.

It was a formidable challenge and as everyone knows the cardinals electrified the world by their imaginative choice. Not only did they break with a tradition of more than four and a half centuries by electing a non-Italian, but they chose a cardinal from Communist Poland, Karol Wojtyla, at fifty-eight the youngest Pope in over a century.

Part One

THE CHURCH
TRIUMPHS OVER
PAGANISM

A.D. 30–600

Chapter 1

JESUS

The Catholic Church has always claimed Jesus of Nazareth as its founder, and nearly everyone is familiar with the basic facts about this dynamic Jewish preacher and healer who was born around the turn of the first century A.D. (probably between 6 B.C. and A.D. 6) and was crucified by the Romans between A.D. 28 and 30. His early years were spent at Nazareth in Galilee with parents who were of lowly origin. At some point in his early manhood he felt a call to preach the coming of God's kingdom and began to gather huge crowds from the villages and towns in the region northwest of the Lake of Galilee; they were spellbound by his marvelous sermons and extraordinary healings. Well versed in the written and oral traditions of his Jewish religion, he presupposed in his preaching the basic Jewish faith in one God, the Lord of history, God's special covenant with the Jews, and the sacredness of the moral precepts of the Torah or Law, which his people regarded as the revealed will of God. The climax of his ministry came when he entered Jerusalem in triumph, only to be apprehended and crucified by the Romans as a political agitator.

His early life is wrapped in almost complete obscurity. Our only important sources for his life—the Gospels of Mark, Matthew, Luke, and John—tell us very little about this period; Mark and John pass over it altogether; Matthew and Luke each devote their first two chapters to an account of his infancy, but we can't be sure how much of this is history. It is, in fact, difficult to fit these first chapters of Matthew and Luke into any definite literary category; many scholars regard them as a type of Jewish *Midrash*—a commentary on Scripture that often used imaginative invention of episodes in order to illustrate biblical themes.

One indication of their nonhistorical character is the important differences—if not outright contradictions—between Matthew and Luke's accounts. Matthew, for instance, dates the birth of Jesus during Herod's reign—that is, not later than 4 B.C. (the date of Herod's death), while Luke dates it during the period when Quirinius was legate of Syria, which according to the historian Josephus was from A.D. 6 to 9. Moreover, the two evangelists disagree in the names they list in the genealogy they attribute to Jesus. The theological insight they intend to convey, however, is clear: Jesus, the son of David and Son of God, was the long-awaited Messiah who came to bring salvation to all—both Jews and Gentiles.

When we come to the so-called public life of Jesus, which begins with his baptism by John at the River Jordan, we must admit that we do not have the kind of biographical details that readers look for today, such as descriptions of his physical appearance and personal habits, some idea of his psychological development, or the influences that shaped his personality.

But there is no need for skepticism. More than a century of rigorous critical analysis of the New Testament has in no way disproven the constant belief of Christians that their Scriptures are based on the actual words and deeds of a unique historical personage.

The Gospels, as we've said, constitute—practically speaking—our only source of historical facts about Jesus, and they were written from forty to seventy years after his death. Their authors drew on an oral tradition that disseminated stories about the deeds and words of Jesus in the form of sermons and catechetical and liturgical material. Mark, we believe, was the first to cast this oral tradition in the form of a Gospel—a unique literary genre which he invented. His Gospel appeared shortly before the fall of Jerusalem, which occurred in the year 70. Some ten years later, Matthew and Luke each produced a Gospel by using Mark's work plus a collection of the words of Jesus (often referred to by scholars as Q, for *Quelle*, German for "source") and also some special material that each evangelist had at hand. Finally, at the turn of the century, the author known as John produced the fourth Gospel, which differs considerably from the other three in its portrait of Jesus.

The Gospels were not meant to be a historical or biographical account of Jesus. They were written to convert unbelievers to faith in Jesus as the Messiah of God, risen and living now in his church and coming again to judge all men. Their authors did not deliberately invent or falsify facts about Jesus, but they were not primarily concerned with historical accuracy. They readily included material drawn from the Christian communities' experience of the risen Jesus. Words, for instance, were put in the mouth of Jesus and stories were told about him which, though not historical in the strict sense, nevertheless, in the minds of the evangelists, fittingly expressed the real meaning and intent of Jesus as faith had come to perceive him. For this reason, scholars have come to make a distinction between the Jesus of history and the Christ of faith.

To find the Jesus of history, we have to sift through the material presented in the Gospels and try to determine by internal evidence what Jesus actually did and said as distinguished from what represents later interpretation. As a general rule, scholars hold that whatever cannot be deduced or explained from the Judaism of Jesus' time or from primitive Christianity should be ascribed to the Jesus of history. What this means specifically is that while historical criticism makes it impossible to reconstruct a biography of Jesus in the ordinary sense, it does permit us to recover a considerable amount of authentic Jesus material. In fact, by adhering to the historical critical method we can determine "the typical basic features and outlines of Jesus' proclamation, behavior, and fate."[1]

All attempts to trace the origin of Jesus' call to his divine mission are hindered by the fragmentary nature of the records. But there is good reason to suppose that his baptism by John was decisive in this regard. At least all our accounts agree that at his baptism "the Spirit descended on him"—a biblical phrase denoting the call of someone to be God's messenger.

The message that Jesus proclaimed was simple in formula yet inexhaustible: "The kingdom of God is at hand, repent!" Matthew puts the same words on the lips of John, but there is no doubt that he regarded John as only the herald of Jesus, through whose ministry God actually broke into human history in an absolutely unprecedented and definitive way.

Some scholars argue that Jesus announced this incursion of God into history as a purely future thing involving a cosmic catastrophe and the end of the world. However, there is now growing agreement that there is both a present and a future reference in Jesus' teaching: The reign of God already at work in his ministry was moving toward a consummation in the future.[2] Some of his parables—like the one about the prodigal son who was welcomed back with love by the father whose bounty he had wasted—emphasize the point that

---

[1] H. Küng, *On Being a Christian* (Garden City, N.Y.: Doubleday, 1976), p. 159.
[2] N. Perrin, *The Kingdom of God in the Teaching of Jesus* (Philadelphia: Westminster Press, 1963), pp. 185–206.

God with fantastic goodness and generosity was already extending mercy to sinners. And when Jesus ate and drank with publicans and harlots, the meaning he intended was clear: Salvation is offered now to all, a gift in no way dependent on one's prior righteousness.

It is thus clear, as the Jewish scholar David Flusser says, that Jesus is the "only Jew known to us from ancient times" who proclaimed that the "new age of salvation had already begun."[3] On the other hand, there is a strong tension in Jesus' proclamation between the present salvific action of God and its fulfillment in the future. God would intervene to establish something radically new; it would be a cataclysm bringing an end to all earthly hopes and schemes. So Jesus spoke in terms of extreme urgency about the need to repent and to be ready for the inbreaking of God into history.

Jesus not only preached the good news of the kingdom, he also gathered his followers into a fellowship. They often took their meals together, celebrating joyfully their new covenant with God while they anticipated the glorious banquet to come in the kingdom of heaven. He called them the light of the world, the city of God, the salt of the earth. They were a family whose common devotion to God's will united them far more intensely than any bonds of flesh and blood.

In some ways all of this resembled other spiritual movements of his day. Another Jewish group—the Essenes, for instance—had, as the Dead Sea Scrolls show, the same sense of joy at the imminent advent of God's kingdom. They too practiced renunciation of personal possessions and their leader too advocated celibacy. And from them Jesus may have derived his doctrine of not resisting evildoers. But they held to a sharp separation from the common herd, and many of them secluded themselves in monasteries near the Dead Sea. Jesus, on the other hand, opposed any form of exclusivism; it would have been at odds with his main doctrine of the boundless nature of God's offer of grace. So he deliberately sought out the social outcasts and even showed them special signs of his favor.

The members of Jesus' kingdom felt a most intimate relationship with God, whom they loved to call Father. And he taught them to live sincerely as God's children. Though a tiny group, poor and despised, they had the greatest of conceivable treasures—the absolute assurance of salvation, a salvation

---

[3] *Jesus* (New York: Herder & Herder, 1969), p. 90.

not dependent on their own achievements but on the unlimited goodness of God. Nor must they worry about daily necessities; their heavenly Father's providence, which reached even to the tiniest sparrow, would surely not desert them. Not that they would be spared any of the manifold forms of suffering and anguish that life brings to everyone. But there was no need for them to comprehend the unfathomable mystery of evil; enough to know that suffering when accepted brings one closer to God, while death itself is only the prelude to union with him.

Life in God's kingdom inaugurated by Jesus found its purest expression in prayer, and Jesus stood before his followers as a constant example of prayerfulness. As a pious Jew he observed the three liturgical hours of prayer daily and took part in the worship of synagogue and Temple. But, as in other matters touching the formal religion of the day, he challenged tradition and custom. He warned his followers against the spirit of routine and formalism so often characteristic of public prayer; he urged them to pray in secret as well, and he himself spent whole nights in prayer. Moreover, he gave them a distinctive prayer of their own, the Lord's Prayer, whose brief petitions to the Father so perfectly express his own yearning for the ultimate fulfillment of the divine purpose in history.

Jesus did not make a radical break with the morality of the Torah. He still recognized the sacred law as the authentic voice of God, but he did not hesitate to modify it, as in his prohibition of divorce. The main thing he insisted on, however, was complete submission to the will of God in all things. It was all summed up in his command to love: God first and then all human beings without exception, foreigners as well as one's own. This double commandment of love already existed in ancient Judaism, but Jesus radicalized it by removing all restrictions: One must love even one's enemies. Moreover, Jesus emphasized the motive for loving: We were to love others out of gratitude for God's love of us.

His encounter with the harlot in the house of Simon the Pharisee gave Jesus an occasion to drive home this point. The woman came in with an alabaster jar of ointment while Jesus was reclining, and she began to bathe his feet with her tears and wipe them with her hair, kissing them and anointing them with her ointment. When Simon reacted strongly at the sight of Jesus accepting such ministrations from a woman of the street, Jesus remonstrated with him. Whereas the woman had lavished signs of her love upon him, he said to Simon, ". . . you poured no water over my feet . . . You gave me no kiss . . . You did not anoint my head with oil . . ." And Jesus concluded that the woman was so loving because she was conscious of how much she herself needed forgiveness; "It is the man who is forgiven little who shows little love." And he said to her, "Your sins are forgiven."[4]

Accepting the rule of God meant radically changing one's order of values. There must be no divided loyalty: Every form of attachment, whether to family, property, business, or whatever, must be relegated to second place in the heart of one who aspires to follow Jesus. And like the prophets, he warned them of the special danger of riches; money could so easily take the place of God in a man's soul—for "no man can serve two masters." Service of the kingdom might even mean the complete renunciation of all material goods; when Jesus sent out messengers to spread the good news he wanted them to go as poor men, and he recommended celibacy for the sake of the kingdom. In any case, every follower of Jesus must deny himself, for the kingdom could not be brought in without suffering.

Suffering and affliction, in fact, were to be seen in a totally new way. Not that they were desirable in themselves; but if one accepted the kingdom, then poverty, hunger, and bereavement were no longer the absolute evils they appeared to be, for they could not prevent one from enjoying the love of God and might even be of help in this regard, whereas the things men cherish most—riches, abundance of friends, comfort, and good times—were real evils if they hindered one from seeking the kingdom.

The originality of Jesus was found not so much in the novelty of his ideas (for most of them were already present in the traditions of his people) but in the way he brought them together, developed and harmonized them, and above all made them real in his own life with such unparalleled intensity.

Miracles and exorcisms play very prominent parts in the ministry of Jesus; to pass over them as a concession to "modern ideas" would be a serious omission. However, it is not easy to determine what actually happened, since an analysis of the tradition often shows that the brute historical fact was much reworked in the course of transmission. Moreover, parallels to the Gospel miracles have been found by scholars in contemporary pagan and rabbinic literature as well as in the Old Testament: storms quelled, water changed into

---

[4] Lk. 7:36–48, *The Jerusalem Bible* (Garden City, N.Y.: Doubleday, 1966). All scriptural citations will be from this edition.

Christ Institutes the Eucharist.
Nicolas Poussin (1594–1665).
Louvre, Paris.   © *Réunion des*
Musées Nationaux/Art Resource,
New York.

wine, demons expelled, and so on.[5] Nevertheless, the kernel of historical fact
that they contain would seem to be that Jesus did exercise extraordinary powers of healing. And in an age when demons were held responsible for every
form of evil afflicting man, he would inevitably be portrayed as a chaser of
demons, as one victorious over all the forces that degrade man.

The question of Jesus' authority soon became a prime issue, for instead
of appealing to traditional forms of authority, he invoked his own religious experience and urged his hearers to do the same. In the name of the primacy of
love over law, he even attacked sacred Jewish traditions like the rigorous Sab-
bath observance and spoke slightingly of the Temple. His whole performance,
in fact, constituted a tremendous challenge to the establishment, which it
could hardly have left unanswered.

With a premonition of his approaching end, Jesus gathered his faithful
for one last meal together—probably the night before the Jewish Passover—
and offered them bread and wine, his body and blood, which would be sacri-

---

[5] See, for instance, R. Bultmann, *The History of the Synoptic Tradition* (Oxford: Basil Blackwell,
1968), pp. 209–44.

ficed to establish the new covenant between God and humanity. Clearly his actions—the taking of bread and wine, the giving of thanks, the breaking of the bread, and the sharing of food and drink—were all well known and quite regular Jewish observances. But Jesus gave them an entirely new significance when he commanded them to be repeated as a memorial of his passion and as a pledge of his continuing presence with them and of his coming again.

According to the Gospels, that same night Jesus was arrested at the instigation of both Roman and Jewish officials, brought before a Jewish high court, the Sanhedrin, for a kind of grand-jury proceeding, and found guilty. The Gospels would have us believe that both political and religious motives were involved. In the eyes of the Jewish authorities, he appeared to be a messianic pretender who, like other would-be messiahs at the time, thought of the coming of God's kingdom as necessitating a political revolution. Hence the Jewish leaders feared he might provoke a brutal repression by the Romans and bring ruin on the whole Jewish nation. The Sanhedrin also had purely religious reasons for wanting the death of Jesus: His claim to unique authority they regarded as blasphemy, and his words against the Temple and his criticism of the Jewish Law they considered sacrilege.

Then according to the Gospels, Pilate upon investigation found the political charge untenable, being perhaps most impressed by the unwillingness of Jesus' followers to use force to defend him at the time of his capture. And so after interrogating him, he resolved to release him. But the Jewish leaders would not stand for this, and by threatening to report Pilate to Caesar, they forced him to have Jesus executed.

The question then occurs: Are the Gospel accounts of the arrest, trial, and execution of Jesus true to history? Many scholars today say no. They view the Gospel version of the tragedy as tendentious—reflecting the point of view that prevailed in the Church when they were written thirty to sixty years after the event. According to their theory, the authors of the Gospels aggravated the responsibility of the Jews for the death of Jesus and minimized Roman participation. Their intent would have been to allay any suspicions of the Romans that the Christian Church might be politically subversive by clearing the name of their founder of any such implication. So they falsely pictured Pilate as not taking the political charges against Jesus seriously and transferred the chief responsibility for Jesus' death to the Jews.

Some scholars even go so far as to completely exonerate the Jewish authorities and reduce the whole affair to a political conflict between Jesus and the Romans. But while granting some measure of truth to this hypothesis, other scholars would not completely exonerate all the Jewish leaders. We have to suppose, they maintain, that a strong antipathy did exist between Jesus and some of the leaders—notably the temple priests—since it is a fact too deeply embedded in the tradition to be easily dismissed; and these leaders would surely have played some role in his death. In their eyes he might well have been viewed as a messianic pretender. While not constituting the whole Sanhedrin, his enemies would still have been a powerful group and would have interrogated him about his messianic pretensions and then handed him over to Pilate. For his part, Pilate would have had no qualms about quickly dispatching anyone who was in any way suspect of political subversion, even though he might not have been impressed by the seriousness of the accusation.

In any case, it all should have ended on Calvary. But something strange occurred, an experience that convinced Jesus' followers that he was still alive and that radically changed their outlook.

What actually happened on that first Easter morning? We have a number of sources that attempt to describe the resurrection of Jesus: the Gospels, the Acts of the Apostles, and the epistles of St. Paul. But when we analyze them

Resurrection of Christ. Andrea Mantegna (1431–1506). Musée des Beaux-Arts, Tours, France.   © *Scala/Art Resource, New York.*

we find a considerable variety in the way they relate the event. Thus they do not agree as to where and to whom Jesus first appeared (in Matthew and John, for example, Jesus appears first to Mary Magdalene and her companions in Jerusalem, while according to Paul he appeared first to Peter; John and Luke place his first appearance to his disciples in Jerusalem, Matthew in Galilee). So it is very difficult to form a consistent historical sequence of events. This is in decided contrast with the Passion accounts, which fit all the details into a consistent intelligible sequence.

Basic, however, to all the accounts was an appearance of Jesus to his followers that inaugurated the Christian community but that each individual community related in a way that reflected its own mentality, local associations, and theological conceptions.

The methods of historical criticism now make it possible to go behind the divergencies and reconstruct the probable sequence of events. Joachim Jeremias offers the following:

Mary Magdalene went alone at dawn on Easter Day to the tomb to mourn there for Jesus. From a distance she could see that the stone sealing the tomb had been rolled back. Concluding immediately that someone had broken in to steal the body, she ran to give the alarm to Peter. He in turn raced to the tomb and found the linen burial cloths lying about and the tomb indeed empty. He rushed back to the disciples. Then the decisive event occurred: The risen Lord appeared to Peter.

Chapter 2

THE CHURCH SPREADS
ACROSS THE EMPIRE

The resurrection of Jesus was the starting point of Christian faith. The idea of resurrection had already appeared in Judaism during the second century B.C., but Christians found their faith in resurrection given new clarity and certitude through faith in the resurrection of Jesus. They first gave voice to this faith in the various brief formulas such as we find in the First Epistle of St. Paul to the Corinthians: "Christ died for our sins in accordance with the Scriptures . . . he was buried and, in accordance with the Scriptures, rose on the third day."

The Acts of the Apostles pictures the Church itself as only beginning with the Pentecostal explosion of the Spirit—that is, the event that occurred on the Jewish feast of Pentecost shortly after the resurrection, when the first believers were filled with the Holy Spirit, who confirmed them in their faith and ignited in them a zeal to witness publicly and urge others to believe, repent, and be baptized. They shared an intimate fellowship of love and prayer centered on the eucharistic breaking of the bread in their homes—in obedience to the Lord's command at the Last Supper to repeat his words and actions.

This small community of believers at Jerusalem was led by twelve men who were supposedly chosen by Jesus himself during his lifetime and were later named apostles. Their leader and spokesman, according to the Acts of the Apostles, was Peter (or, in Greek, Cephas). According to Paul, Peter was the first to see the risen Jesus, while Acts pictures him as the apostle who preaches the first sermon and works the first miracle. Two others who stand out at this period were John, who is closely associated with Peter in Acts; and James, who apparently succeeded Peter as leader of the Jerusalem community after Peter departed to do missionary work.

The story of how this tiny community of believers spread to many cities of the Roman Empire within less than a century is indeed a remarkable chapter in the history of humanity. In attempting to trace it here we must realize that our sources are limited and that we must tolerate many gaps in our information. Still it is possible to put together the basic story.

We must keep in mind that the first apostles were all Jews, and so were their first converts. For a time the Church remained completely Jewish, a sect within Israel of those who believed in the resurrection of Jesus and regarded him as the promised Messiah who was about to come again to definitively establish the reign of God.

Their new faith did not require them to break with the Temple or the Law. In fact, the Acts of the Apostles emphasizes how faithful they were to daily prayer in the Temple. Some Jewish leaders, notably the Sadducees, regarded the Christians as an alien group of nonconformists and wanted to suppress them. But the Jewish leaders were unable to because public opinion favored the Christians and admired their fervent piety and fidelity to Jewish custom.

The spread of the Church beyond Jerusalem occurred very gradually as the disciples carried their message to the numerous Jewish communities scattered along the Mediterranean coast. At first they confined their evangelizing efforts to their fellow Jews, no doubt in conformity with the practice of Jesus himself, who said he had come to preach only to "the lost sheep of the house of Israel." The first group to break with this custom were probably some Jewish dissidents with strong Hellenistic ties and unorthodox views on the Jewish Temple worship. Their leader Stephen, the deacon, was arrested and denounced to the Sanhedrin for speaking against the Temple. When questioned by the high priest, he launched into a polemic against his fellow Jews whom he blasted as "stubborn people, with . . . pagan hearts and pagan ears."[1] Stephen was stoned to death, and his martyrdom triggered a general persecution; his followers sought refuge elsewhere and began to preach the Gospel wherever they traveled.

It was at Antioch, it seems, that they took the revolutionary step that

[1] Acts 7:51.

would have momentous consequences for the spread of the Church and the history of the world. Here they first preached the Gospel to the Gentiles and dared to baptize them. And they made this city the center of missionary work among the Gentiles.

Such an innovation no doubt sorely troubled many of the pious who found no room in their faith for the idea of a mission to the pagan Gentiles. But at first they went along. A liberal attitude toward Gentile converts seemed to prevail in the Church: They were not required to be circumcised or otherwise to observe the Jewish Law. But as greater numbers of them began to stream into the Church, misgivings were felt by the more traditional-minded, who demanded they be circumcised and made to obey the Jewish Law. There was undoubtedly a fear that the Church would be swamped by these Gentiles and lose its Jewish character. And so the Church was plunged into its first great controversy, which shook it to its roots; at bottom it was the question of whether it was going to remain an exclusively Jewish affair or stretch out to encompass all of humanity.

The man who contributed most to the solution of the matter was Saul of Tarsus, known by his Roman name, Paul. It was Paul who stripped the Gospel of much of its Jewish character and adapted it to appeal to all humanity.

For him, in fact, the very essence of the Gospel was at stake in the controversy over circumcision; to require Gentiles to practice the Jewish Law would be tantamount to saying that faith in the risen Lord Jesus was not enough for salvation; observance of the Law was also necessary.

Paul's understanding of the Gospel as a liberation from the Law was not some academic theory he had worked out in a study; it was at the very heart of the conversion experience that had changed him from a dedicated devotee of the Law to an ardent disciple of Jesus. As a zealous rabbi, student of the great Gamaliel at Jerusalem and subsequently a figure of importance in the synagogues there, Paul could say, "I stood out among other Jews of my generation [in my enthusiasm] for the traditions of my ancestors" (bracketed portion is my paraphrase).[2] He had even become a chief persecutor of the disciples and was present at the stoning of Stephen.

But then spiritual lightning struck! He had an immediate experience of the risen Jesus. His spiritual universe turned upside down; he realized that with the coming of Jesus the era of the Law had passed. "I look on everything

[2] Ga. 1:14.

as so much rubbish if only I can have Christ and be given a place in him. I am no longer trying for perfection by my own efforts, the perfection that comes from the Law, but I want only the perfection that comes through faith in Christ, and is from God and based on faith."[3] This central intuition into the meaning of the coming of Christ was henceforth to govern all of his preaching and writing.

So when Paul heard the traditionalists saying the Gentiles must be circumcised, he insisted, "what makes a man righteous is not obedience to the Law, but faith in Jesus Christ. . . . if the Law can justify us, there is no point in the death of Christ. . . . When Christ freed us, he meant us to remain free. Stand firm, therefore, and do not submit again to the yoke of slavery."[4]

There is no doubt that the conflict became shrill and bitter and that the unity of the Church was severely strained, particularly at Antioch, where the Christian community was already in large part Gentile. Their Jewish Christian brethren who had previously felt no scruples about joining in the common meals taken with the Eucharist now withdrew due to pressure from those who wanted to maintain the link with Judaism. Even Peter, who shared Paul's views, momentarily wavered and deserted the common table. Paul was indignant and dressed him down publicly.

A resolution of the issue could not be postponed indefinitely, and so a council was held at Jerusalem, probably in the year 49. It was undoubtedly a long and stormy session. At the close Peter argued in favor of freedom for the Gentiles, appealing to experience, which showed that the uncircumcised Gentiles also possessed the Spirit. Peter concluded: "We believe that we are saved in the same way as they are: through the grace of the Lord Jesus."[5]

It was James, however, who summed up the debate and pronounced the verdict: Circumcision would not be required of the Gentiles. But to soothe the sensibilities of the traditionalists and preserve the unity of table fellowship, a compromise was arranged: All would be obliged to follow certain Jewish laws; abstinence was required from any food offered in sacrifice to idols; illicit sexual intercourse was forbidden, and certain Jewish dietary regulations were imposed, specifically those that forbade the taking of meat with blood still in it (blood was regarded as the seat of life and hence belonging to the

[3] Ph. 3:8–9.
[4] Ga. 2:16, 21; 5:1.
[5] Acts 15:11.

Lord). The meat of strangled animals—that is, animals not killed according to Jewish ritual—was also forbidden.

This did not immediately clear up all dissension; some recalcitrants refused to go along and were later to trouble Paul no end by visiting his churches in order to lead them back to strict Jewish observance. But these traditionalists were fighting a losing battle; the pillars of the Church had decided against them in an open debate in full assembly. Paul's understanding of the Gospel was accepted by the Church as her own. The Church officially shed her exclusively Jewish character and became potentially the Church of all humanity. It was a great turning point in the history of the Church and of the world.

It was with the Gentiles that the future of the Church lay and now that the door was wide open, Paul lost no time in going out to gather them in. His ambition was to take the Gospel to the whole world; extended missionary journeys took him across Asia Minor and into Greece, where he left behind congregations in Iconium, Lystra, Colossae, Philippi, Thessalonica, Beroea, Athens, Corinth, Ephesus, and many other places.

He went only to those towns where the Gospel had not yet been preached, and his usual method was to start in the synagogue, where he endeavored to show to the Jews and proselytes gathered for the service that Christ was the fulfillment of the promises of the Old Testament. Often, as at Corinth, the outcome was trouble. When they turned against him in the Corinthian synagogue and began to insult him, he said, "Your blood be on your own heads . . . from now on I will turn to the Gentiles." And as usual he had more success with the pagan Corinthians, many of whom heard him and became believers and were baptized. In this way he left behind churches where the distinction between Jew and Gentile was of no importance.

His letters to his fledgling communities show Paul as the first and greatest in the ranks of shapers of Church history: men who combined a profound depth of religious experience with an uncanny ability to organize—men like Augustine, Bernard, Loyola, Luther, and Wesley. Paul's letters contain deep theological insights that laid the groundwork for the future developments of theology and yet at the same time reveal his remarkable concern for every little detail in the life of his congregations.

Thanks then to the Jerusalem decision allowing freedom to the Gentiles and thanks to the incredible labors of Paul and other missionaries, the Church spread with remarkable rapidity. We know that by the year 59, for instance,

Paul felt that he had exhausted his possibilities in the eastern Mediterranean. "All the way along, from Jerusalem to Illyricum, I have preached Christ's Good News to the utmost of my capacity."[6] And we may reasonably infer that those regions mentioned that he himself had not evangelized were evangelized by others.

Paul now set his sights on Spain, the oldest Roman province, and the main center of Roman civilization in the western Mediterranean. But before he could set sail for the West, there was a matter of critical importance to attend to. He must visit Jerusalem again to deliver the collection for the poor that he had taken up among his churches. It would also provide the occasion, he hoped, for reaching full agreement with the Church there as he entered on a new phase of his missionary effort. It is with this in mind that he penned his great epistle to the Romans, which he intended for Jerusalem as much as for Rome and which contained his mature reflection on the central issue of the Law vs. the Gospel. Hopefully it would clear up any remaining doubts the Jewish Christians still entertained on this matter. The whole epistle reflects Paul's tremendous concern for the unity of the Church, which was as much an obsession with him as the worldwide spread of the Gospel. "One Lord, one faith, one baptism," was the way he put it. Hence he strove to stay in touch with Jerusalem—the acknowledged mother of all the churches—and with its leaders there.

When Paul arrived in Jerusalem, he was induced by James and the fellow elders to show his reverence for the Law by undertaking a ceremonial purification in the Temple. While there he was recognized by some Asian Jews, who raised a hue and cry against him as a notorious traitor. The fracas that followed almost cost him his life; he was rescued by the Roman tribune but imprisoned to await trial. Finally, after two years in the garrison at Caesarea—an eternity for one so hungry to spread the Gospel—he appealed to Emperor Nero and was sent to Rome and detained for two years under house arrest while awaiting trial.

What was the charge against him? Apparently Rome saw in him the ringleader of a sect preaching a revolutionary international form of Judaism that might undermine the social order. Was he tried then and executed immediately, or did this occur a few years later, in 64? Most scholars prefer the latter alternative. In any case he probably never achieved his ambition of evangeliz-

---

[6] Romans 15:19.

ing Spain. But when he died, his dream of a Church as wide as humanity it-self was well on the way to realization—thanks in great part to his own clear-sighted vision and tremendous organizing skill.

There were, of course, many other missionaries at the time whose expe-rience must have closely paralleled Paul's. Unfortunately, we know little about them. Even Peter's career after he left Jerusalem is for the most part a lost chapter, although we can readily believe the unanimous Christian tradition that testifies to his death at Rome under Nero. Nor do we know much about the other apostles, although second-century legend is quite willing to fill up the lacunae in our knowledge: It tells us that St. Thomas evangelized the Parthians, St. Andrew the Scythians, St. Bartholomew went as far as India and perhaps to southern Arabia, while Philip died at Hierapolis in Phrygia. We only know for certain that many traveling missionaries crisscrossed the Ro-man world preaching the Gospel with much success, so that by the end of the first century Christianity was well established there.

The great success of the Gospel among the Gentiles was in stark contrast to its fate among the Jews. Those Jewish Christians who tried to convert their fellow Jews met with continual hostility and rejection; around A.D. 85 a for-mal anathema of them was incorporated in the synagogue liturgy. Nor were matters helped by the attitude of Gentile Christians who denounced the Jews as stiff-necked apostates deservedly punished by God when the Romans de-stroyed Jerusalem and burned down their temple in A.D. 70. A critical stage was reached in the Epistle to the Hebrews, which made rejection of Judaism essential for Christians and characterized return to Judaism as apostasy. Left alone and unsupported, the Jewish Christians gradually slipped into oblivion.

The rapid spread of the Gospel among the pagans, on the other hand, constituted the greatest religious revival in the history of man. How do we ex-plain such a phenomenon? No doubt our explanation will vary according to our particular philosophical or religious bias, but certainly all would agree that the expansion of Christianity owed much to general political, social, and cultural trends.

First of all, there were the favorable material conditions afforded by Rome's dominance of the Mediterranean world. After four centuries of ex-pansion, the Roman Empire by this time completely encircled the Mediter-ranean Sea and stretched from the Euphrates River in Syria to the Thames in Britain, from the Rhine and the Danube to the sands of the Sahara. And it bound together this vast medley of peoples of many races and languages with

Plaque showing the expansion of the Roman Empire under Trajan (98–117 C.E.). Fori Imperiali, Forum Romanum, Rome. © *Scala/ Art Resource, New York.*

its marvelous system of roads and shipping. This greatly facilitated the work of the Christian missionaries, who were able to travel the length and breadth of the Empire with relative ease. Moreover, the Romans promoted the spread of a common culture derived from Hellenism. This meant that the missionaries could preach the Gospel in Greek in almost all the large cities and be understood.

Second, the world was largely at peace, thanks to the work of Emperor Octavian Augustus, who reigned at the time of Christ's birth and early youth. The designated heir of the assassinated Julius Caesar, he had been able to outmaneuver the other contenders for power, and finally in 31 B.C., by his defeat of Antony and Cleopatra, win supreme command of the Roman Empire. With astute political realism, he fashioned a new system—the principate—which concentrated most of the power into his own hands while outwardly preserving traditional Republican forms. This new constitution that he devised enabled him to rule unchallenged for more than forty years and outlasted him for several centuries, providing the Empire with a stable form of government that enabled it to keep the barbarian menace at bay and give a large measure of peace to the world for nearly two hundred years. The conditions of security afforded to travelers by this Roman peace were very beneficial to the Christian missionaries.

Third, it was spiritually a time of extraordinary unrest. In spite of increasing prosperity and the possibilities of enhanced enjoyment in the cities where theaters, stadia, amphitheaters, and baths provided a constant source of amusement for the inhabitants, there was a growing spiritual hunger. The rapid social change accompanying progress unsettled many minds, while the political climate was most depressing. The loss of political freedom was bad enough, but the successors of Augustus were themselves a strange lot. Tiberius (d. 37), Gaius Caligula (d. 41), Claudius (d. 54), and Nero (d. 68) were Emperors whose personal lives were darkened by bizarre, macabre incidents and crimes: The atmosphere of their courts was heavy with intrigue and foul suspicion. Tiberius, under whom Christ was crucified, was a competent soldier but an unhappy Emperor—crushed by the discovery that his son, Drusus, had been murdered by his own most trusted adviser, Sejanus. His nerves shattered, Tiberius retired to Capri, where he spent the last years of his reign. Caligula was a mentally deranged megalomaniac who was assassinated. Claudius, weak in body and will, was dominated by his wife, Agrippina, who finally poisoned him to make room for her son, Nero. Then Nero in turn murdered her and began a reign of terror that took the lives of many of Rome's outstanding leaders before he himself was forced to commit suicide.

The reaction of sensitive spirits to all of this and their mood of gloom and pessimism is reflected in much of the literature and art of the time—in the writings of Petronius, Martial, Juvenal, Seneca, Pliny, and perhaps most memorably in the writings of the grim and somber Tacitus, chief historian of the age.

This state of affairs provided a great opportunity for a religion that could help fill the spiritual vacuum experienced by so many. And it was Christianity that made the most of this opportunity.

Not that a seeker after salvation would necessarily turn to religion. Some found consolation in philosophy. The Stoic philosophers, for instance, won many followers by their doctrine that one could put oneself in harmony with the universe by attending to the underlying rationality of its laws; they also emphasized the need for self-discipline in order to attain inner peace and equilibrium of soul amid the vexing contingencies of life. Philosophy, however, as always, was only a refuge for an elite. The ordinary man searched for spiritual peace in some form of religion, astrology, or magic.

The old Roman religion provided little competition for Christianity. Faith in the ancient gods could not be revived, as Augustus and other Emperors found to their dismay. Nor could the average person take much comfort in the rites and ceremonies dedicated to the deified Emperors themselves.

Much more powerful as a rival to Christianity were the mystery religions that were quite numerous and rapidly spreading during this period. They were syncretistic kinds of faith that fused Hellenic and Oriental thought. The most important ones were the Dionysian and Orphic mysteries of Thrace; the Eleusinian from Eleusis, near Athens; the religion of the Great Mother, Cybele, from Anatolia in Asia Minor; the Persian religion of Mithra and the Egyptian cult of Isis and Osiris. They were called mysteries because their central rites were kept secret from all but initiates. In spite of various differences, they all had certain characteristics in common: a sublime view of the godhead, a profound sense of cleavage between spirit and flesh, and a great yearning for a redeemer who would deliver devotees from all guilt and confer on them eternal life.

One of the best-known mystery religions is that of Cybele, the Great Mother. Like the others it gives evidence of having originated in fertility rites associated with the vegetative rhythms of nature—death in winter and resurrection in the spring. Cybele, the mother of all gods and men, had as her companion the semidivine Attis, who betrayed her and then in remorse castrated himself and died. The Great Mother, however, restored him to life and deified him, making him immortal. This myth was celebrated in two main rituals: In the *taurobolium,* the faithful reenacted the death of Attis by slaying a bull, then baptizing themselves in his blood—smearing it over themselves and even drinking it; in the spring festival of Attis's resurrection, they engaged in frenzied dancing while lacerating themselves and sprinkling the blood on a pine tree symbolizing Attis, until in a final ecstasy some of the men would castrate themselves in imitation of their god. By participating in such rituals the devotee believed himself regenerated, liberated from guilt, and reborn as a new person, sharing in the divinity and immortality of his gods.

The mystery religion that proved to be the most serious rival of Christianity, however, was Mithraism, which was restricted to men and very popular with soldiers. Originating in Persia, it was apparently spread around the Mediterranean by the soldiers of Alexander the Great. Mithra was a Persian sun god who had slain the cosmic bull whose blood was the source of all life. His images always show him fighting for right against wrong—an appealing idea for soldiers. The cult promised immortality to its initiates. Its shrines have been uncovered in many places, a large one recently in London.

Certain similarities of doctrines and rites have led some scholars to claim that Christianity belongs in the same category as the mystery religions and, in fact, is derived to some extent from them. The evidence, however, does not support such theories. The fact that both the mysteries and the Christian Church used certain rites such as washings, anointings, and sacred meals does not necessarily indicate a dependency. Such primitive symbols are so basic to humanity that any religious person might use them to express an experience transcending this world.

Moreover, the Christian conception of salvation is worlds apart from that of the mysteries. The devotees of Cybele or Mithra saw their salvation as a magical liberation from the flesh. Christians, on the other hand, assumed the existence of sin and free will and conceived redemption as the forgiveness of sin. They preached sin and repentance with a frightening earnestness that had nothing in common with the orgiastic, sex-laden ceremonies of the mysteries. As Paul put it, "You broke with idolatry when you were converted to God and became servants of the real, living God and . . . are now waiting for Jesus, his Son, whom he raised from the dead, to come from heaven to save us from the retribution."[7]

Again, unlike the mystery religions with their timeless myths linked with the rhythms of nature, Christianity was founded on a historical person and connected with datable events.

As to the ethical demands made of the initiate, there is no comparison between Christianity and the mysteries. At their best, the mysteries manifested vague yearnings for a better life. The Church, on the other hand, laid down clear and precise norms of conduct for a Christian. Its emphasis on sexual control was a distinctive Church ideal that differentiated it from the pagan world; it insisted on monogamy and the indissoluble character of marriage and strictly forbade abortion and infanticide. It condemned all forms of greed and dishonesty in business life, all materialistic hedonism, double dealing, and falsehood. In short, a Christian was to be a pure person who did not cling to his possessions, was not self-seeking, and was truthful and brave. And most important, it taught the individual to rely not on his own strength in the moral struggle but on the power of God's grace.

Finally, a most important difference and a potent cause of the superiority of Christianity was the effective demonstration by Christians in their own lives of the power of love; it proved an irresistible magnet for many souls and caused the pagans to exclaim, "Look how they love one another!" This love found expression in a multitude of activities.

---

[7] 1 Thess. 1:9–10.

Christians saw to the support of teachers and officials, of widows and orphans, of the sick and infirm and the disabled. Christians dedicated themselves to prisoners and people languishing in the mines, to those hit by great calamities and to the care of poor people needing burial; they furnished work to the unemployed, took care of brethren on journeys, and saw to the need of churches in poverty or in any peril.[8] There is indeed no doubt that the Christian Gospel led the world to a higher stage of morality. Its social and ethical dynamism exerted a powerful influence on potential converts. Two of its greatest thinkers in the second century, Tatian and Justin, for instance, were converted, as they acknowledged, by the moral attractiveness of the Christians they knew.

To sum up then, the remarkable expansion of Christianity in the first century owed much to general political, social, and cultural trends. But the main reason for Christianity's success was the fact that it provided the best answers to the basic religious questions of the tortured soul: inculcating worship of the one God, creator of all, in opposition to the crass idolatry of the times. By its preaching of Jesus the divine savior, risen and about to return for judgment, it brought assurance of liberation from sin, eternal resurrection, and a motive to lead a life of faith, holiness, self-control, love, and brotherliness.

---

[8] A. Harnack, *The Mission and Expansion of Christianity in the First Three Centuries* (New York: Harper Torchbook Edition, 1961), pp. 147–98.

Chapter 3

A CHURCH WITH AUTHORITY

By the end of the second century, the Christian Church presents itself as an institution with a clearly defined system of authority based mainly on its sacred Scriptures, its creed, and its hierarchy of bishop, priest, and deacon.

The question of how this system developed constitutes one of the most controverted chapters in the history of the Church.

Whether or not we accept the view that Jesus himself founded the Church and conferred authority over it on his twelve apostles, history clearly shows that from the beginning the first believers formed a tightly knit community and were conscious of being members of a unique fellowship—still within Israel indeed but with a distinct sense of identity due to their belief in the risen Jesus. This awareness soon found expression in the terms they used of themselves: They called themselves the saints, the elect, the Church of God, the true remnant of Israel, the new Israel.

Profoundly conscious, as they were, that it was the resurrection of Jesus and not some human agency that created the Church, they saw their fellowship as a gift of the Spirit, a miraculous act of God. This sense of the supernatural origin of the Church is powerfully conveyed by Paul, who thought of the Church as the new Eve—the spouse of Christ. Paul also spoke of the Church as Christ's body; as a farm or garden planted and watered by the apostles; as a building erected by the apostles on the foundation of Jesus Christ; and as the temple of God.

This unique Christ-centered self-image of the early Church is revealed clearly in its two most important rituals. First was the Eucharist, which was celebrated by repeating Christ's words at the Last Supper over bread and wine in obedience to his command to remember him and in the firm conviction that he was present as their risen Lord. A wealth of meaning was attached to this simple rite: It was the proclamation of the Lord "until he comes"; it was a sharing in his body and blood; it was a sacrifice, the re-creation of Christ's sacrifice, which inaugurated a new covenant between God and man.

The second act was the initiation rite of baptism, a cleansing with water; this was regarded as an essential part of conversion to Christ and admission to the community.

All of this shows a distinct sense of the Church's sense of supernatural oneness in Christ—but little idea of organization. The traditional Catholic view of the organization of the Church is that Jesus himself organized it by appointing the twelve apostles and giving them authority to assume control of the Church after his death. This is the picture presupposed and developed by Luke particularly; but many scholars, including some Catholic ones, view this conception as a retrojection of the later-developed Church system into the primitive era. To mention only one objection to the traditional view: If the twelve apostles were put in charge by Jesus, why do they so completely disappear from the subsequent history of the Church?

Many historians, therefore, prefer the theory that the primitive Church only slowly organized itself and shaped its system of authority in response to a variety of situations that existed in different localities. And in their view it only gradually settled everywhere on the three-tiered structure—bishop, priest, and deacon—as the one most conducive to its mission.

Those who favor this developmental approach interpret Paul, the earliest witness, in this sense. They hold that for Paul the Spirit is the one who organizes the community; rule by the Spirit means that love is the unifying and organizing force, and freedom is its characteristic quality. The various ministries needed to carry on and order the community are given directly by the Spirit. And Paul lists these in his Epistle to the Corinthians: "God has given the first place to apostles, the second to prophets, the third to teachers; after them, miracles, and after them, the gift of healing; helpers, good leaders, those with many languages."[1]

Note that Paul does not limit apostleship to the original twelve; an apostle for Paul was anyone who had personally been commissioned to preach by the risen Jesus and, as a witness to the resurrection, authorized to found and

---

[1] 1 Co. 12:28.

Predella of the conversion of St. Paul: St. Paul on the road to Damascus. From *The Coronation of the Virgin.* Giovanni Bellini (1430–1516). Museo Civico, Pesaro, Italy.   © *Scala/Art Resource, New York.*

lead churches.[2] He was to see to their right ordering and command the obedience of the community; but he exercised his authority in fellowship with all the other members of the community. In this sense, the Church was founded on the apostolic ministry and witness.[3] As a ministry of personal witness based on the Lord's commission, the apostolate was a unique and unrepeatable office.

Note also that while Paul singles out prophecy and teaching as the noblest gifts, he does not envisage them in a hierarchical order but rather regards all the various ministries—working of miracles, healing, helping, administrating, speaking in tongues—as a loosely connected set that complement each other.

As to the order of the universal church, he stresses the importance of communion with the other apostles and with Jerusalem, and he is willing to recognize a certain primacy of the mother Church. But this implied "no sort of subordination of his own authority and person to any other of supposedly higher status."[4] The decisive event that determined Paul's mission, his Gospel, was meeting Christ on the Damascus road, and it was because of this that even the leading apostles at Jerusalem had to recognize his authority. It is clear, however, that for Paul it was his "Gospel" that mattered, not personal

[2] 2 Co. 10:13–16, 13:10; 1 Co. 11:34; 2 Th. 3:4.
[3] 1 Co. 14:37; Ep. 2:20.
[4] H. von Campenhausen, *Ecclesiastical Authority and Spiritual Power* (Stanford, Calif.: Stanford University Press, 1969), p. 53.

recognition for its own sake. And he would not yield an inch on the principle of the freedom from the Law involved in the Gospel.

Paul's system of charismatic leadership worked all right as long as the Church lived in expectation of the immediate end of the world and the second coming of Jesus, and as long as the original apostles were still alive who were able to guarantee the veracity of the oral tradition about Jesus. But two things happened that necessitated a change: First, the expectation of the End faded as awareness grew that the Church was destined to continue in history, perhaps for a long time; second, death began to carry off the apostles.

So the Church was faced with the problem of how to stay in touch with its origins and preserve its unity and continuity with the original apostolic witness. There was a real danger of its tradition being swamped in a mass of conflicting interpretations of the meaning of Christ's life and resurrection. A group called the Gnostics, for instance, put forth an interpretation of Jesus that subverted most of the basic doctrines of the Church: Christ for them was not a true man but a particle of divinity who had merely assumed a human costume. One of their leaders, Marcion, rejected the Old Testament as the work of an evil, inferior demigod and professed belief only in Paul's writings.

To meet this crisis, a threefold solution was gradually devised: A specially commissioned ministry was established; an authoritative list of apostolic writings was issued; and a rule of faith or creed was drawn up.

The specially commissioned ministry was based on a system of governance by elders and deacons such as had apparently prevailed in some churches from the beginning (at Jerusalem, for example). In this system, unlike Paul's, it was not the Spirit who conferred office; office was conferred by formal appointment, although it was presumed that the appointee was specially endowed with the gift of the Spirit. The recipient was ordained to his office by the laying on of hands. This system is already found in the pastoral epistles where Timothy and Titus have been appointed to the office of elder; they are to choose reliable men to succeed them, and these in turn will choose others. The First Epistle of Peter also shows such a system already in operation, with a definitively fixed circle of presbyters or elders engaged in an orderly ministry, though as yet there is no distinction between clergy and laity. The whole Church is called a royal priesthood.

An important stage in this development was reached around A.D. 96, when the apostolic origin of this presbyteral system was asserted in the First Epistle of Clement. This was a letter written by the Roman Church to the

Church in Corinth in an effort to heal a schism there that occurred when a group of elders were deposed. Clement urged their restoration to authority by arguing that the deposed elders stood in due succession from the apostles. But as is shown by a Syrian catechetical manual, the *Didache,* dating probably from the end of the first century, the system of elders was still not universal. In this work prophets and teachers were still regarded as exercising the most important ministries. The manual reflects, however, a state of transition to the institutional type of Church organization, for it instructs the congregation to elect bishops and deacons if prophets and teachers are in short supply.

This term "bishop" was originally a secular Greek expression, *episkopos,* meaning supervisor or overseer. It gradually came into Church usage and was nearly synonymous at first with the word for elder, presbyter. These elders or bishops governed the churches collectively at first. But gradually one man took over the power and concentrated the various ministries in his hands. He was now called "bishop" to distinguish him from the presbyters, who were his subordinates.

This system—the monarchical episcopate—is already clearly enunciated at the end of the first century in the letters of Ignatius, the bishop of Antioch, who wrote while on his way to trial and eventual martyrdom in Rome. For Ignatius, the bishop is the focal point of the congregation; all important functions are vested in him; he alone has the right to lead public worship and administer the sacraments. His authority is without limits, but it is to be completely at the service of the community.

By 150 or 160 this system of authority was established practically everywhere. Four factors seem to account for its triumph. First, there was a need for one presbyter—the senior of the college, often—to represent Christ at the Eucharist; the same one would often be deputed to ordain as well, and he gradually claimed this power by right. Second, one person would be charged normally with carrying on correspondence with the other churches. Third, one person would often be chosen to represent a church at a general gathering. Fourth, in view of the Gnostic disturbance, congregations realized the value of having a single person as a focus of unity and as an authoritative doctrinal spokesman.

The authority of this monarchical bishop as a guarantor of the oral tradition was based on the claim that he stood in legitimate succession in a line reaching back to the apostles themselves. The implication was that his teaching would therefore be in conformity with his predecessors. This concept was given its classic form by Irenaeus around A.D. 185. Irenaeus used Rome as the pre-eminent example of a church whose fidelity to the original deposit of faith was guaranteed by the fact that its bishops were the direct successors of Peter and Paul; moreover, they spoke in agreement with the bishops of other sees who were also successors of apostles.

The second measure taken by the Church to guarantee the integrity of its tradition and safeguard its identity with the Church of the Apostles was its decision to recognize a certain limited body of writings as "Scripture." This Canon of the New Testament was supposed to contain the authentic tradition about Jesus. The decision to set these writings apart as sacred was a momentous one, for it meant that the Church would forever be subject to them as an absolute norm of its life and faith.

This canon was based on a consensus of the Church that all the books listed were associated with an apostle in some way and were orthodox in doctrine. Judgment about the authenticity of the canonical writings was based on the idea that the tradition of the Church in this matter was trustworthy in general, although it could be wrong in detail. The scholars did not accept the tradition uncritically; they did their best to verify whether the books in question were actually written by apostles or by those in touch with apostles. As long as there was uncertainty about apostolic authorship, there was reluctance to accept books as canonical. Thus St. John's Gospel was not readily accepted at first, and it was only after Irenaeus gave what was thought sufficient proof of its authorship by John that its canonicity was established. The same thing occurred with the Epistle to the Hebrews, which writers in the Western churches refused to quote for nearly two hundred years.

The interplay of the living Church and the written Scriptures—a constant feature of Christian history—was thus in operation from the start. The living community was constantly checked and controlled by the basic testimony of the apostle. But at the same time, the written records were checked and controlled by the living community—as one scholar has written, "simply because by that time it contained within it, or among its leaders, a sufficiently firm and uniform tradition to constitute it corporately a preserver of tradition. . . ."[5]

The Canon was virtually complete by the early decades of the second

[5] C. F. D. Moule, *The Birth of the New Testament* (New York: Harper & Row, 1962), pp. 191–94.

century, with such exceptions as mentioned; but it was not definitely finalized in the West until 380–90, and even later in the East.

The third means used by the Church to uphold its authority and safeguard orthodoxy was by the formulation of a creed, the "rule of faith," a compendium of the main teachings of the bishops. The earliest example of such a rule is found in the writings of Irenaeus. It asserts the Church's faith in one God, the Father and Creator of all things; in the incarnation of God in Christ Jesus; and in the Holy Spirit, through whom the prophets were inspired to foretell the salvation events connected with the ministry of Jesus Christ.

In this threefold manner—through bishops claiming to be successors of the apostles, through a Canon of Scripture, and through an authoritative creed—the Church erected a durable structure of authority, a framework of steel that has enabled it to meet every conceivable crisis.

There still remains the question of how the individual churches were related to one another. From the beginning they were deeply conscious of their unity and oneness in Jesus Christ, and this sense of unity was fostered by the great amount of intercourse that took place among them. The missionaries and their converts kept the churches in touch with each other by frequent visits. It was only slowly and by degrees, however, that these informal and personal relations were translated into institutional and organizational ones.

The first steps in this direction occurred, it seems, when the bishops of a particular region began to meet in synods to discuss their common problems and adopt common solutions. The first synod of which we have knowledge took place in Asia between 160 and 175. Gradually certain churches assumed authority over other churches. Some of them acquired so-called metropolitan status, which elevated them over the churches of a province, while others— Rome, Alexandria, and Antioch, to be specific—acquired suprametropolitan status, by which they exercised a primacy over these metropolitan churches. Political factors were mainly responsible for these differentiations, the political preponderance of a town inevitably securing its ecclesiastical preponderance. So the bishop of the capital of a Roman province was granted a certain superiority over the other bishops of that province; he had the right to convoke synods and to preside over the debates. The fourth canon of the Council of Nicaea (325) officially sanctioned this principle when it recognized the primacy of Rome, Alexandria, and Antioch.

However, over and above sheer political preponderance, Rome enjoyed certain attributes that raised it above all the other churches and destined it for a unique role as a center of Church unity. First, it could claim special status as the see of the apostles Peter and Paul. Irenaeus cited Rome as the preeminent example of his principle of apostolic succession: "When the Blessed Apostles [Peter and Paul] had founded and built up the Church, they handed over the ministry of the Episcopate to Linus."[6] Therefore, Irenaeus concluded, all the other churches should agree with Rome as an unquestioned channel of pure apostolic doctrine. Second, as the capital of the Empire, it attracted churchmen of rival schools of thought who were extremely desirous of having the support of the bishop of Rome. Third, it became a very wealthy church, noted for its munificent charity; its willingness to be of assistance to other churches around the world considerably enhanced its influence.

---

[6] *Adversus Haereses*, III, 3, 3. Translation found in *Documents in Early Christian Thought*, ed. M. Wiles and M. Santer (New York: Cambridge University Press, 1975), p. 130

Chapter 4

CONSTANTINE FAVORS THE CHRISTIANS AND INAUGURATES A NEW ERA OF CHURCH HISTORY

The Catholic Church met the threat of disintegration from within by welding a system of authority out of bishop, canon, and creed. But an even more devastating threat came from without, in the form of the omnipotent Roman state. The persecution of the Church by Rome lasted over two centuries and contributed greatly to the spread of the Church—the blood of martyrs being the seed of Christians, as Tertullian said. The era of persecutions ended not with a whimper but with a bang when the Emperor himself, Constantine, went over to the side of the Christians.

ROME WAS TOLERANT in principle and allowed many religions to flourish. It only declared war on the Christians when it realized that their aim was total triumph over all other religions. The first recorded incident of persecution by the Roman Government was Nero's action in 64. There is no reason for supposing that the Emperor based himself on an edict drawn up to proscribe Christianity. He merely exploited public opinion, which saw Christians as atheists and moral monsters because of their refusal to join in pagan worship and because of the secrecy with which they surrounded their own services.

It was not until the third century that the Roman Government decided seriously to deal with the Christian menace. The issue was basically religious.

The Christian Gospel proclaimed the reality of the one true God and hence demanded absolute rejection of the gods worshiped by Rome. Moreover, Christians took a relative view of the authority of the Emperor and Empire, which were only to be obeyed when they were in harmony with the will of the one true God, which had been revealed to his Church.

Edicts were now issued that forced the provincial governors to persecute Christians. Septimius Severus (193–211) was the first to issue such an edict. Powerful written protests against the cruelty of this persecution were penned by Tertullian in his *Ad Nationes* (195) and *Ad Scapulam* (211). This persecution subsided with the advent of a new Emperor, Alexander, a gentle and virtuous person who placed Jesus in his domestic pantheon with the other Roman gods. Alexander's assassination and the accession of Maximin in 235 again kindled the fires, but when Philip the Arabian (244–49), an Emperor friendly to the Christians, came to power, peace again ensued.

It lasted only a few years, for Decius (249–51) succeeded to the throne. He was another harsh persecutor who saw the Christian sect as a terrible poison to the ancient Roman morals and ordered all suspects to make a public act of homage to the gods. Great numbers of Christians apostatized when faced with the rack, but many important Church leaders, including Pope Fabian, suffered heroically and died at the hands of their torturers. Once things cooled down, the apostates begged for readmission to communion—creating grave pastoral problems for bishops like Cyprian of Carthage.

Persecution flared again and numbered among its victims Cyprian as well as Pope Sixtus II and his deacon Lawrence. But the zeal of the persecutors slackened, and for nearly a half century the Church was left undisturbed.

The final persecution of the Church began with a devastating intellectual assault by the pagan intelligentsia led by Porphyry (d. 303). In his work *Against the Christians,* Porphyry held Christ up to scorn as a pitiful weakling, attacked the Scriptures as full of absurdities and patent contradictions, scoffed at the Eucharist, and ridiculed the Christian works of mercy. This was the prelude to the attack launched by Diocletian, a strong and industrious ruler who had carried through a radical reorganization of the Empire; he divided it into 101 provinces and 12 dioceses, placing two co-emperors in supreme command, with imperial headquarters at Milan in the West and Nicomedia in the East.

The new system was designed to meet the extreme peril now facing the Empire from the hordes of barbarians pounding at her gates. Insecurity had become a way of life; intercourse among the cities was no longer safe, taxes skyrocketed, larger armies were required, the amenities of life disappeared, and people tried to save their skins as best they might. It was very tempting to blame the Christians for all the trouble, since their very existence could be regarded as a standing insult to the gods. The fact that so many of them even held high posts in the government and the army aggravated the offense.

Then at a public sacrifice a pagan priest claimed that the presence of Christians at the ceremony invalidated the sacrifice and thus endangered the state. It was the final straw. By a decree of February 303, Diocletian ordered all Christian places of worship to be destroyed and their sacred books handed over; Christians were forbidden to assemble and were to be denied the protection of the laws.

The first church destroyed was an imposing edifice that stood adjacent to the royal palace itself in Nicomedia; the Emperor watched from a window as his soldiers broke down the church's doors and ransacked the place, burning the ornaments and holy Scriptures.

With this act the final agony of the Church began; it was to last from 303 to 312. A second, more severe decree singled out bishops, priests, and deacons for special attention, while later great numbers of Christians in all ranks were seized. They had their eyes and tongues gouged out, their feet sawed off; they died at the stake or in a red-hot chair. Some were thrown to wild beasts to entertain a holiday mob; others were starved to death or thrown into dungeons.

The struggle for the soul of the Empire raged on a vast scale, for though only a sprinkling in the West, Christians in the East numbered around 10 per cent of the population, and in some cities even formed the majority. And it was mainly in the East that the blood flowed—under Galerius (Diocletian's successor) and Maximinus Daia.

It all came to a halt suddenly when Galerius by decree of 311 permitted Christians to resume their religious assemblies. But a cruel reversal occurred when Galerius died and Maximinus Daia once more called for Christian blood. But then just as suddenly he ordered the whole business to cease again. It was puzzling until observers learned that pressure to stop persecuting had been put on Maximinus by the new conqueror of Italy and Africa, Constantine, who was now sole master of the Western world. The son of the co-Emperor Constantius Chlorus, Constantine was hailed as Emperor by his troops on the death of his father in 306 but immediately had to face a rival, Maxentius, who had managed to secure Rome as his stronghold.

When Constantine finally emerged victorious in 312, he attributed his victory to the help of the Christian God. According to the Christian writer Lactantius (d. 320), on the eve of Constantine's fateful battle with Maxentius, Constantine had a vision of Christ, who told him to ornament the shields of his soldiers with the Savior's monogram—the Greek letters *chi* and *rho*. Constantine obeyed and in the ensuing battle was victorious as promised. Writing somewhat later, Eusebius, in his *Life of Constantine,* gave a more sensational account: Constantine and his whole army saw a luminous cross appear in the afternoon sky with the message "in this conquer."

It seems probable that Constantine was moved by some unusual religious experience to turn to the God of the Christians, a move no doubt facilitated by the vague monotheism he embraced in his early years. It did not mean an immediate full-fledged conversion to Christianity—Constantine was not even baptized until his final illness. But during the next decade he showed increasing signs of favor to the Christians. He met with the ruler of the eastern half of the Empire at Milan in early 313, and in February the two reached agreement on a policy of complete religious tolerance; Christians were even to receive back their property.

At first Constantine observed an attitude of formal correctness toward paganism. He remained its Supreme Pontiff, paid homage to the sun god on the official coinage, and in general was careful not to alienate the pagan

Constantine and Helena. From a thirteenth-century mosaic. St. Mark's, Venice.
© *Giraudon/Art Resource, New York.*

masses and aristocracy of Rome. But he gradually revealed his true feelings. He imposed restrictions on pagan practice and publicly displayed the Christian symbols. He attached the standards of the army to a cross emblazoned with the monogram of Christ and issued coins picturing himself wearing a helmet stamped with the same monogram. Moreover, he increasingly identified the interests of the state with those of Christianity. Anxious to secure unity in the Church as well as the state, he did not hesitate to intervene in Church affairs and tried to use the power of the state to end the Donatist schism in Africa.

Constantine was faced with an even more serious question of Church unity in 324 on his assumption of rule over the whole Empire. It had to do with trouble in Alexandria, Egypt, where the presbyter Arius challenged his bishop, Alexander, on the question of God the Son's relation to God the Father. The Emperor at first tried to pacify the disputants by urging them to tolerate differences on minor points of doctrine, but as the controversy increased in violence, he finally gathered some 220 or so bishops together in the first general or ecumenical council, at Nicaea, on May 20, 325. The Emperor exhorted the bishops to maintain peace and unity and even took part, it seems, in the debates. But the matter could not be settled so easily; indeed, the controversy remained unsettled at the time of his death.

The Emperor showed great generosity to the Church in lavishing donations on it and erecting numerous sumptuous basilicas, including the magnificent one over the supposed site of the tomb of Peter at Rome and another over the tomb of Christ in Jerusalem. He surrendered his Lateran palace in Rome to the bishop of Rome for a residence, and it remained the papal residence until 1308. When in 324 he moved the capital of the Empire to Byzantium, which was renamed Constantinople after him, he erected numerous churches there, including the two great ones dedicated to peace and to the holy apostles.

Constantine bestowed important privileges on the Christian clergy: They were recognized as a distinct social class and exempted from military service and forced labor. He invested the judicial decisions of the bishop with civil authority. He modified the Roman Law in the direction of Christian values. Sunday, the day when Christians assembled, was made a day of rest. Sexual offenses, such as adultery, concubinage, and prostitution, were treated more severely. On the other hand, a more humane attitude was shown toward slaves (their families could not be broken up), children, orphans, and widows. Under Constantine the Church was firmly set on the road to union with the state. He was thus in a real sense the architect of the Middle Ages.

This alliance with the state profoundly influenced every aspect of the Church's thought and life. It carried many advantages, but it also entailed some serious drawbacks: infringements on the Church's freedom as civil authorities exploited the relationship for political purposes; mass conversions where social conformity was the chief motivating factor; the widening of the gap between clergy and laity thanks to the official status conferred on them; persecution of dissenters as a menace to the unity of the state. The Church would never be the same again—for better and for worse—and so Constantine's conversion is certainly one of the greatest turning points in the history of the Church and of the world.

Chapter 5

WORSHIP, FAITH, AND LIFE
IN THE EARLY CHURCH

The period from Constantine to Pope Leo the Great (d. 461) was one of decisive importance in the history of the Catholic Church. Many of the basic features of Catholicism were fixed during these years in the form they were to retain, with relatively few modifications, for the next fifteen hundred years. Its chief act of worship, the Mass, was highly standardized and ritualized. Its chief dogma, belief in Jesus Christ, God and man, was affirmed and clarified in lasting terms. Many practices henceforth fundamental to its discipline and life originated and were incorporated into its canon law. Its clergy took on the character of a sacred caste and began to submit themselves to the law of celibacy. Monasticism took root in Egypt and spread across Christendom. Finally, the basic principles of its code of social and personal ethics achieved nearly permanent form.

THE MASS, ORIGINALLY called the Lord's Supper, the breaking of bread, the Eucharist, was celebrated by the first Christians in the late afternoon and was joined with a regular meal of ritual character. Toward the middle of the second century, however, the sacramental meal had become an independent rite and was now celebrated on Sunday morning and combined with a service of reading and preaching.

Our earliest description of the Mass is from the pen of Justin Martyr (d. 165) and reflects this development. It is a simple service consisting of prayers by the whole assembly followed by a kiss of peace. Bread and wine were then brought to the president of the assembly, who recited a long prayer of thanksgiving, all present finally consuming the bread and consecrated wine. On some occasions, the Eucharist was preceded by a reading of the prophets and memoirs of the apostles, as well as a homily by the president.

The oldest liturgical form of the Mass (except the *Didache*, a different type) is found in the *Church Order* of Hippolytus (d. 236).[1] It is evidently the basis of all eucharistic prayers that have since been composed. The bishop lays his hands upon the bread and wine and water offered upon the altar table and begins the following dialogue:

> *Bishop*: The Lord be with you.
> *Congregation*: And with thy spirit.
> *Bishop*: Hearts up.
> *Congregation*: We have them to the Lord.
> *Bishop*: Let us give thanks to the Lord.
> *Congregation*: It is meet and right.
> *Bishop*: We thank thee, God, through Thy beloved Servant Jesus Christ, whom in the last times Thou hast sent us as Savior and Redeemer and Messenger of Thy counsel, the Logos who comes from Thee, through whom Thou hast made all things, whom Thou wast pleased to send from heaven into the womb of the virgin, and in her body he became flesh and was shown forth as Thy Son, born of the Holy Spirit and the virgin. To fulfill Thy will and to prepare Thee a holy people, he stretched out his hands, when he suffered, that he might release from suffering those who have believed on Thee.
>
> And when he delivered himself to a voluntary passion, to loose death and to break asunder the bands of the devil, and to trample hell and to enlighten the righteous and to set up the boundary stone and to manifest the resurrection, he took a loaf, gave thanks, and spake, "Take, eat, this is my body which is given for you." Likewise also the cup and said, "This is my blood which is poured out for you. As often as you do this, you make my commemoration."
>
> Remembering therefore his death and resurrection, we offer to Thee the loaf and the cup and give thanks to Thee that Thou hast

---

[1] Hippolytus, *Church Order*, 31, 11:21, ed. F. X. Funk (trans. *Cambridge Ancient History*, XII, II [New York: Cambridge University Press, 1956], pp. 524–25).

Fresco depicting the interior
of Old Saint Peter's, Rome.
San Martino ai Monti, Rome.
© Scala/Art Resource, New York.

counted us worthy to stand before Thee and to do Thee priestly
service.

And we beseech Thee, that Thou send down Thy holy Spirit
upon this offering of the church. Unite it and grant to all the saints
who partake of it to their fulfilling with holy Spirit, to their strengthening of faith in truth, that we may praise and glorify Thee through
Thy Servant Jesus Christ, through whom to Thee be glory and hon-
our in Thy holy Church now and ever. Amen.

In their attitude toward worship as in other respects, Christians stood
apart from the pagan world. They had no special holy places or temples; or in
the words of Minucius Felix, "We have no shrines or altars."[2] As St. Paul told
them, "You are the temple of the living God."[3] The place where they worshiped had no particular importance in itself—it was usually just a large room
in one of the member's homes; the whole focus was on the worshiping and
praying community itself. But as time passed and as their numbers grew,
large, spacious buildings took the place of the simple rooms. The Eucharist
was no longer consecrated on a simple table but on a massive and ornate altar made of precious marbles and studded with gems.

Church architecture came into being, Constantine being a prime mover

[2] *Octavius,* c. 32.
[3] 2 Co. 6:16.

in this regard. As Christianity flourished under his protection, simple, spacious buildings were no longer sufficient; they had to be "splendid, public and imposing" as well.[4] Here as in their other artistic endeavors at the time, the Christians were receptive rather than creative. As models they had at hand the various Roman basilicas or assembly halls of different shapes and sizes. The imperial audience hall, with its apse to accommodate the throne of the Emperor, proved to be most suitable for adaptation to liturgical purposes. Constantine himself set the pace, erecting many churches such as the great Roman basilica over the spot where St. Peter's bones were thought to rest; like many of his structures it combined the basilica-type church with a large forecourt or atrium.

The liturgy itself was considerably influenced by the Constantinian revolution. Millions of pagans suddenly entered the Church, and some of their customs inevitably crept into the liturgy: the use of the kiss as a sign of reverence for holy objects, the practice of genuflection, devotion to relics, and the use of candles, incense, and other ceremonial features derived from the imperial court. Under this pagan influence Christians began to face the east while praying, which made it necessary for the priest to lead prayers with his back to the congregation.

Belief in the real presence of Jesus—both body and blood—under the form of bread and wine continued to animate the faithful at Mass (as it was called from the fifth century on). No orthodox spokesman of the early Church, in fact, ever subscribed to a mere symbolic interpretation of the rite. But there was as yet no official formulation to describe the nature of the change that took place in the bread and wine. (This only happened in the Middle Ages, with the definition of the theory of transubstantiation.)

For a long time the celebrant was left considerable freedom to improvise in conducting the liturgy. Even the wording of the canon was left to his discretion. But as Church organization became more centralized and as the danger of heresy increased (especially after the rise of Arianism), some amount of conformity was gradually imposed, the liturgies of a particular linguistic area being standardized to conform to the norms set by the great ecclesiastical sees of that region. In this way five main liturgies rose to dominance: three in the East (the West-Syrian of Antioch, the Coptic of Alexandria, and the Byzantine of Constantinople); and two in the West (the Romano-African, which

[4] R. Markus, *Christianity in the Roman World* (New York: Charles Scribner's Sons, 1974), p. 103.

stemmed from Rome and North Africa; and the Gallican, which covered most of Western Europe until the ninth century and still survives in a few places, such as Milan, Italy).

The formation of the liturgical calendar began with the special significance accorded to Sunday as the day of Christ's resurrection and hence as the day Christians ordinarily gathered for their weekly liturgy. But it did not become a public day of rest until the fourth century, when Constantine forbade all official litigation on that day.

Easter was celebrated very early—by the beginning of the second century. But its date was calculated differently in the East and in the West. At Rome, it was observed on the Sunday after the Jewish Passover, but in Asia it immediately followed the fourteenth of the Jewish month of Nisan, the beginning of the Passover. Pope Victor (d. 198) tried to make the Asians conform to Western usage but failed. However, the Roman custom finally prevailed everywhere.

Pentecost and Epiphany were the next feasts added to the calendar; the latter, on January 6, coincided with pagan festivals celebrating the birth of the new year. Christmas originated in the fourth century, when Constantine joined it with a pagan feast celebrating the birthday of the sun on December 25.

Although the Eucharist and baptism were accorded special importance, other rites of the Church were also considered sacraments instituted by Christ. By the Middle Ages seven sacraments were officially listed. Of these none underwent as much change as the sacrament of penance. Its earliest form is obscure. There even seems to have been a reluctance on the part of the first Christians to entertain the idea that a person once converted to Christ could sin and be forgiven again. The Shepherd of Hermas (c. 150) speaks as though a second remission of sins was unthinkable. But the Church soon had to reckon with the sad fact that many did fall into sin even after baptism.

And so the Church gradually developed a system for handling the problem of the sinner in its midst. It was anticipated, it seems, in the practice of excommunication deemed necessary from the earliest days in dealing with notorious troublemakers. Another precedent was the procedure of arbitration used to settle disputes among members. With these practices as a starting point, a system was gradually evolved whereby one guilty of grave sin could be pardoned after undergoing penance.

Cyprian gives the fullest description of how the system worked by the middle of the third century.[5] A Christian guilty of a very grave sin, such as murder or apostasy, in some way made known his sin to the bishop, usually in private, or he was admonished as a public sinner to present himself in church. He was then publicly excommunicated by the bishop and relegated to a specially reserved section at the rear. He could no longer receive Communion and was obligated to lead a life of utmost austerity—wearing coarse garments, keeping his hair cropped, abstaining from sexual relations, and curtailing other pleasures. In this state of abject humiliation he might have to remain for years. Details would vary from province to province, but certain features were universal: Penance was always public; it was never administered more than once to the same person; if a sinner relapsed he was left totally to the mercy of God.

Those penitents who had completed their penance were sacramentally reconciled with the Church—on Holy Thursday, as a rule. They prostrated themselves before the bishop, who raised them up while placing his hands on them signifying their restoration to full communion with the Church. This act of absolution or reconciliation with the Church was the essential sacramental act and still is.

The system made extreme demands on human nature, for once enrolled in the ranks of the penitents, a person was condemned for life to an inferior status in the Church: He could never be admitted to the clerical state, run for public office, or even have marital relations. Even after absolution, he had to continue to live like a monk.

It is no wonder then that this system, the perfect reflection of the legalistic mind, broke down. The average Christian in the Constantinian Church was no longer in the heroic mold of the age of martyrs. Rather than subject himself to the rigors of penance, he simply deferred it until he was on his deathbed or even postponed baptism until late in life.

During the early Middle Ages, the Celtic monks took the lead in devising a new system, which was private, which extended generally to all sins, and which allowed frequent confession. It is only in our own day that this Celtic system is itself in process of revision.

---

[5] *The Fathers of the Church. St. Cyprian: Letters* (Washington, D.C.: Catholic University Press, 1964); *Ancient Christian Writers. St. Cyprian: The Lapsed* (Westminster, Md.: Newman Press, 1957).

LIKE ITS WORSHIP, the faith of the Church underwent some development, and, in fact, its chief dogma, belief in the divinity of Jesus Christ, was not defined until the Council of Nicaea in 325. This council was called to settle a controversy over Christ's divinity, which erupted with violent intensity during the reign of Constantine when the presbyter Arius of Alexandria challenged his bishop, Alexander, on the question of God the Son's relation to God the Father.

To understand the unfolding of this controversy we must begin with the Church's basic understanding of Jesus Christ as it is found in the New Testament. Almost every page of the New Testament speaks in some way or other of Jesus Christ. Underlying all the variety of expressions and terms applied to Jesus there is the basic conviction that because of Jesus Christ, God was now an indestructible, vivid reality in the consciousness of men, his kingdom was definitively established, and all men were invited to taste and enjoy the peace, forgiveness, love, and joy of his kingdom. Note that Jesus was regarded as the indispensable agent and instrument of this reign of God; his death by crucifixion and his resurrection were the means of salvation. So closely did they associate Jesus with the work of God that they regarded him no less than God the Father as the object of faith. Mercy, grace, and peace were gifts from Jesus as well as from God. This faith in Jesus they expressed especially in the various titles they attributed to him, such as Messiah or Christ, Son of God, Savior, Lord. This last term, Lord, is especially significant, for it denoted their devotion to him and recognition of his sovereignty—a sovereignty that they recognized when they worshiped him in their liturgy and invoked him as their Lord.

Council of Nicea. Fresco. Cesare Nebbia (1534–1614). Biblioteca Apostolica Vaticana, Vatican.   © *Scala/Art Resource, New York.*

It was on this New Testament foundation of virtual belief in Christ's divinity that theologians began their speculations and developed a science about Christ that we call Christology. The most popular of the Christologies in the first several centuries of the Church proved to be the one known as the Logos Christology, from the Greek term *logos,* meaning "the Word." In this Christology, elaborated by such men as Tertullian, Origen, and Novatian, Jesus was asserted to be the divine Son, or Word or Wisdom, who participated with the Father in the creation as well as in the redemption of the world. The term *logos* was found already in John's "And the Word became flesh" and also in the Book of Proverbs (8:22–31), with its reference to a personified Wisdom distinct from the Father and begotten by him as his firstborn and instrument of creation. It was also a prominent concept in the prevailing Neo-Platonic philosophy of the time and so provided the theologians with a means of correlating the Christian revelation not only with the Old Testament but also with the insights of the classical philosophers.

This concept of the pre-existent Word when applied to Christ made it possible to distinguish in the eternal Godhead between God the Creator and the Word, his agent in creating. As Word he was the principle of rationality in God and also the principle of revelation; and as Word he had become incarnate in Christ. The concept of the Word also helped to clarify the meaning of the scriptural term "Son of God"; in this sense it meant not only the historical person of Christ but also his pre-existent being.

But some misgivings were registered as it was realized that Proverbs 8:22–31 could also be interpreted to subordinate the personified Word to God. This tendency was found even in some of Origen's writings, and it seems, in fact, that Proverbs 8:22–31 was the starting point of Arianism—interpreted, as it was, by the Arians in the light of certain philosophical assumptions: "God," they said, "was absolutely one, the only unbegotten, the only eternal, the only one without beginning, the only true, the only one who had immortality, the only wise, the only good, the only potentate . . . the monad and the principle of creation of all things."[6] Nor did he share these prerogatives with anyone, not even with the Word.

Arius, a presbyter in the church district of Baucalis in Alexandria, systematized and popularized this point of view. Through preaching and the hymns he composed, he taught that the Word was created to be the instru-

[6] Arius, *Epistle to Alexander,* 2, 4 (Opitz 3:12–13).

ment of the Father's cosmic activity. Thus in explicating the passage from Proverbs 8:22 ff.: "The Lord begot me, the firstborn of his ways, the forerunner of his prodigies of long ago . . . ," Arius wrote: "Before he was begotten or created or ordained or established, he did not exist."[7] So for Arius the Word had a beginning, and was even liable to change and sin. This was tantamount to denying all finality to the revelation of Christ and opening the way to a resurgence of pagan polytheism, with its myriads of intermediate gods and demons.

This denial of the divinity of Christ plunged Alexandria into controversy, and Arius' bishop, Alexander, suspended him. With the unity of the Church at stake, Constantine convoked the first ecumenical council, which met at Nicaea in 325. Though the bishops for the most part were men of modest learning, it did not take them long to decide that Arianism was not what they had been teaching and preaching all their lives. The vote against it was virtually unanimous; the divinity of Christ was not to be an open question in the Church. The creed they issued is with some additions still recited at Sunday Mass. It unequivocally condemned Arianism, asserting that the Son was begotten, not created, and was "identical in substance" with the Father (Greek: *homoousios*). In other words, the Word shared the divine nature and was fully equal with the Father.

But peace was not to be had so easily. While the bishops agreed in rejecting Arianism, they were not all happy with the term used to formulate the orthodox position—*homoousios*—which apparently had been imposed on them under the eagle eye of Constantine.

So, after the council a controversy began over this term, which lasted until 381, when its use was once more sanctioned at the Council of Constantinople. On one side were the Nicenes, under their leader, Athanasius, bishop of Alexandria, who defended the term. Opposed were a mixed group, mainly Greek-speaking churchmen, some of whom were Arian, but the majority merely conservatives who simply preferred the traditional lack of definition and objected to the Nicene *homoousios* as a novelty and a departure from pure biblical terminology. They were also for the most part followers of Origen in emphasizing the distinctions in the Godhead.

Complicating the situation was the accession to power of Constantine's

[7] J. Pelikan, *The Emergence of the Catholic Tradition* (Chicago: University of Chicago Press, 1971), pp. 192–93.

son Constantius, who became sole ruler in 350; he favored the Arians and tried to crush the Nicenes. With his help the Arians were able to chase Athanasius from his diocese; call numerous synods, which repudiated the Nicene formula; and promulgate the Arian doctrine under the cover of various vague formulas. The peak of their success came at Constantinople in 360, when bishops from East and West subscribed to an anti-Nicene formula that concealed its Arianism under the vague words: "The Son was like the Father." (This phrase later became the official dogma of the Arians.)

For a time even Pope Liberius vacillated and signed one of these vague formularies. Through it all, however, Athanasius stood unyielding as rock while suffering exile five times. While the Arians were much indebted to the rationalist philosophy of the day, Athanasius argued his case from the Christian theology of redemption: Christ had to be divine in order to cause our divinization. Now, since the divine Son is eternally generated by the Father, they must share the same nature, for the Godhead is a unique, indivisible monad; but at the same time, they must be truly distinct, since the Father is Father and not Son, and the Son is Son and not Father. And Athanasius found that only the term *homoousios,* meaning "identical in substance," was adequate to convey both distinction and identity.

His main difficulty was winning over the Eastern bishops, who preferred the formula "of a substance like the Father" *(homoiousios).* But the gap between them was considerably narrowed by their memorandum of 359, which insisted that though Father and Son are separate, yet the Son having been begotten from the Father is like him and hence "one and the same" as he. Eventually these two parties, the Homoousions and the Homoiousions, were brought even closer together at the council held in Alexandria under the aegis of Athanasius.

In the meantime, theological reflection on the nature of the Holy Spirit was stimulated by the whole controversy. Here also Athanasius' contribution was decisive: The Spirit, he asserted, was consubstantial with Father and Son. His work was completed by the Cappadocian Fathers Basil the Great (d. 379), Gregory of Nazianzus (d. 389), and Gregory of Nyssa (d. 395). The difficult problem of how he was distinct from Father and Son while sharing the same essence was solved by differentiating between their modes of origin; the Son is generated, but the Spirit proceeds.

Unity was then restored to the Church at the Council of Constantinople in 381, which reaffirmed the Nicene faith and endorsed the consubstantiality of the Spirit, thus giving the doctrine of the Trinity its definitive form.

Another great doctrinal struggle, however, almost immediately erupted as regards the relation of the divinity of Christ to his humanity, for once it was clearly defined that Jesus Christ fully shared the divinity of the Creator and Lord of heaven and earth, another question was bound to occur: How was his humanity related to his divinity or how were the events of his life and death related to his divine nature? But this controversy we will consider in a later chapter.

THE MINISTRY OF the Church developed a high degree of organization. We know that Pope Fabian (d. 250) divided Rome into seven regions with, it seems, a deacon in charge of each region. This corresponds with the list of ministers of the Roman Church given us by the historian Eusebius (d. c. 340): forty-six presbyters; seven deacons; seven subdeacons; forty-two acolytes; and fifty-two readers, exorcists, and doorkeepers. Next to the bishop, the deacon for a long time played the most important role in the Church. Elected by the community, he was charged with administering Communion to the faithful, bringing alms to the poor, leading the prayer of the faithful at Mass, and in general acting as the bishop's right-hand man. His control of the funds assured him special influence, and many deacons passed directly to the episcopate without passing through the priesthood. But the deacon lost his prominence as the Church spread into the countryside and it was necessary to multiply outlying churches—now called parishes. The presbyter now assumed functions that were previously often monopolized by the bishop: presiding at the Eucharist, preaching, and absolving penitents. The office of the deacon then became just a ritual step leading to the priesthood.

The clergy at first were not sharply differentiated from the laity in their lifestyle: The clergy married, raised families, and earned their livelihood at some trade or profession. But as the practice grew of paying them for their clerical work, they withdrew more and more from secular pursuits, until by the fourth century such withdrawal was deemed obligatory.

An important factor in this change was the increasing stress laid on the cultic and ritualistic aspects of the ministry. At first the Christian presbyter or elder avoided any resemblance to the pagan or Jewish priests and, in fact, even deliberately refused to be called a priest. He saw his primary function as the ministry of the Word. The ritualistic features of his sacramental ministry were kept in a low key. Even as late as the fifth century, John Chrysostom still stressed preaching as the main task of the Christian minister. But the image of the Christian presbyter gradually took on a sacral character.

This sacralization of the clergy was brought about by various developments—theological, liturgical, and legal. The Old Testament priesthood, for instance, was seen as the type and model for the New Testament priesthood. The more elaborate liturgy of the post-Constantinian era, with its features borrowed from paganism, enhanced the image of the minister as a sacred personage. The ministry of the Word diminished in importance when infant baptism became the rule rather than the exception, for infants could not be preached to. Imperial legislation established the clergy as an independent corporation with its own rights and immunities.

In line with these developments, there was a big shift in the very idea of the sacred. Before Constantine the whole Church was considered the realm of the sacred as opposed to the profane world outside; after Constantine and the breakdown of the separation between Church and world, the polarity between sacred and profane was transformed into one between sacred clergy and profane laity.

A clear indication of this trend in the Western Church is found in the requirement of celibacy for the clergy, which was adopted mainly on the grounds that sexual intercourse was incompatible with the sacred character of the clerical state. Legislation to this effect was first passed at the local synod of Elvira, Spain, and taken up by the Popes beginning with Siricius (d. 399), who enforced clerical celibacy in their decretals.

Even before it became a necessity for the Western clergy, virginity and celibacy were held in high esteem. There is very early evidence for the existence of Christian ascetics—men and women who practiced a special form of asceticism, renounced marriage, and lived lives of seclusion from the world. At first they did not form distinct communities under a fixed rule; they usually lived with their families and kept their own property. However, their vows to live a life of continence were recognized by Church authorities. Origen regarded the life of asceticism as a kind of spiritual marriage with Christ, an idea that became very popular; Methodius likened ascetics to martyrs.

From this practice it was only a short step to monasticism, wherein the ascetic secluded himself completely from society by going out into the wilder-

St. Anthony. Francisco de
Zurbarán (1598–1664).
Palazzo Pitti, Florence, Italy,
Fondazione Contini
Bonacossi.   © *Scala/Art
Resource, New York.*

ness or desert. As far as we know, the first one to do this was St. Anthony of
Egypt, who was deeply moved when he happened to hear the text: "There is
one thing further you must do. Sell all you have and give to the poor. You will
have treasure in heaven. Then come and follow me." He took up an abode in
complete solitude on the east bank of the Nile. As others gathered around
him, a large populace of monks formed in the deserts south of Alexandria.
Some practiced lives of complete solitude except for a weekly assembly and
liturgy, while others lived in communities. Pachomius (b. c. 290), another
Egyptian, originated another form of monasticism characterized by a high degree of organization: work, study of Scripture, and prayer were integrated into
a balanced daily schedule.

The monk completely renounced sex, while the general Christian attitude toward sex was suspicious and even hostile. But Christians were not
alone in this regard. Dualism, a philosophy that saw the world as a place of
exile and the flesh as a prison of the soul, was widespread in late antiquity.

Neo-Platonism and the innumerable mystery religions were dualistic. And for many pagans as well as for many Christians, "the body became the chief locus of all the frustrating powers of the world."[8] The Christians were simply more emphatic in the abuse they heaped on the flesh. Justin and Clement reflect the common teaching of the Church in their view that sex and marriage were justified only by the intention to procreate. Most Church Fathers allowed marital intercourse only if procreation was directly intended. But the first Church legislation against contraception apparently was not passed until the Council of Braga in 572.[9] Augustine accentuated the Church's rigorous attitude toward sex by his fateful association of original sin and sexuality.

Roman law allowed abortion, imposed no criminal penalty for abandonment of a child, and even permitted infanticide. It was only through Christian influence that these crimes were eventually outlawed.

Divorce was consistently condemned by the Church, in keeping with its absolute prohibition by Jesus.

There was a strong body of opinion in the Church before the time of Constantine against Christians becoming soldiers. Manuals of Church discipline exist that rule out military service by Christians. But this view never won predominance. Many Christians, it seems, served in the Roman legions, and in 314 the Synod of Arles condemned Christians who deserted from the army. A half century later, Athanasius taught that it was lawful and even meritorious to kill enemies in time of war. Augustine finally formulated the theory of the just war which, as repeated by Aquinas in the Middle Ages, remained the standard Christian approach down to our times.

In their general view of social reform, the early Christians followed the lead of St. Paul, who pessimistically saw social evils—war, slavery, private property, poverty, oppression—as the result of sin and hence endemic to the human condition.

[8] R. Markus, p. 31.
[9] J. Noonan, *Contraception* (New York: New American Library [Mentor Book], 1967), p. 186.

Chapter 6

THE FINAL VICTORY
OVER PAGANISM

At the dawn of the fourth century, Christianity was still the religion of only a minority of Roman citizens, but by the end of the century it was embraced by the majority, and Emperor Theodosius proclaimed it the official religion of the Empire in the year 380. The story of its irresistible progress constitutes one of the most dramatic chapters in the history of the early Church.

One development that pointed to its eventual triumph over paganism was the mass influx of peasants into the fold during the latter part of the third century. Until the third century, Christianity was almost exclusively urban in character and rooted in the middle and lower urban classes. The countryside had remained stubbornly pagan, conservatively attached to their local deities and superstitions and their old ways of life. There was also a language barrier, for the peasants clung to their ancient Coptic, Berber, Syriac, Thracian, or Celtic tongues. It was quite normal, therefore, for missionaries to bypass the rural areas and simply move from city to city.

It was only in the second half of the third century that Christianity began to make considerable inroads into the rural lands. In many of the great provinces of the Empire, the peasants deserted the temples of their ancestral gods and turned to Christ. In one North African township, dedication tablets tell the tale: The last one dedicated to Saturn-Baal Hammon is dated 272; all subsequent ones uncovered have proven to be Christian. By the year 300, North Africa was largely Christian. In Asia Minor the story was similar. The most famous of the missionaries there was Gregory the Wonderworker. His well-known remark that he found only seventeen Christians when he arrived in Neo-Cesarea in 243 and left only seventeen pagans when he was ready to die thirty years later is probably close to the truth, since it is in accord with the general history of the province. Numerous tombstones found in the countryside, dating between 248 and 279, are patently Christian in their wording and often pay homage to the deceased as "a soldier of Christ." In Egypt and probably also in Syria, there was the same widespread turning to Christ by the peasants. Eusebius gives us an eyewitness account of the conversion of the Copts to Christianity when he was in Egypt in 311–12. Altars to Christ abounded, he reports, and the majority of the population were already Christian.

A big change in the complexion of the aristocracy also contributed greatly to the progress of Christianity. Like the peasants, but for different reasons, the aristocrats had remained pagan for the most part. Prejudices instilled in them by their education and their class made them hard to reach. Trained in a curriculum almost exclusively devoted to rhetoric, they learned to put a great premium on mere verbal elegance and so were snobbishly inclined to dismiss the holy books of the Christians as uncouth and barbarian. Moreover, as scions— supposedly—of the Gracchi and Scipios of the ancient Roman nobility, they were moved by a sense of pious family obligation in trying to maintain their religious traditions.

But this situation began to change in the fourth century. Circumstances fostered an upward social mobility, and numerous members of the middle classes were able to move into the equestrian or senatorial order; and many of these were already Christian or disposed to become Christian. This restructuring of the social order began with Diocletian's reorganization, which enabled many members of the lower classes to take high administrative offices. This smoothed the way for Constantine's pro-Christian policies, since it meant he was not hampered by an entrenched aristocracy in key offices who were hostile to religious innovation. He and his successors furthered this social mobility by greatly enlarging the senatorial order, particularly in the new Senate at Constantinople, where Constantine enrolled thousands of new members. Many of these came from the middle classes. Many were barristers of humble origins. Many of them were already Christian, while many of the others had no problem in converting to the new faith now favored by the imperial court. All of this had a profound impact on the religious situation; it meant that Constantine and his Christian successors were able to build up an aristocracy sympathetic to their religious policies.

In consequence, paganism in the East put up no serious political resistance to the pro-Christian policies of the fourth-century Emperors. The same was not true, however, of the West, where the senatorial order remained quite pagan, and as late as 380 stoutly resisted, though in vain, the Emperor's command to remove the pagan statue of Victory from their chamber.

This pro-Christian imperial policy, as we have seen, began with Constantine, who favored the Christians and only tolerated paganism, hoping to see it die a natural death. His three sons, however, who succeeded him at his death in 337, took a more resolute stance. This was especially true of Constantius, who was left sole ruler in 350. He aimed at the total extirpation of paganism; he ordered the temples closed and imposed the death penalty for participating in sacrifices. Some pagans still managed to carry on their worship at the great shrines in Heliopolis, Rome, and Alexandria, but they were caught in a tight squeeze.

This growing dominance of the Christians was severely challenged, however, when the new Emperor, Julian, took office in 360. Upon assuming the

Bust of the Roman Emperor Julian the Apostate (361–70 C.E.). Musei Capitolini, Rome. © *Giraudon/Art Resource, New York.*

imperial purple he marched into Constantinople, declared himself a pagan, and stated his intention of restoring the ancient religion. As a boy raised in the imperial household he was baptized Christian and forced to conform to his uncle's religion; but the bookish and dreamy lad secretly dedicated himself to the ancient gods, and once securely in power he tore off his mask and showed his true colors. No doubt his negative view of Christianity was influenced by his dolorous experiences in the professedly Christian imperial household, where the death of his Uncle Constantine was attended by a bloodbath, with the massacre of cousins and relatives and where his own life hung in the balance for a long time.

But his "apostasy" went much deeper than that. For Julian the religion of the gods was not merely a religion but also the very marrow of Romanitas—the highest level of cultural achievement possible to man and the source of Rome's sublime morality. Christianity, on the other hand, was merely a recurrence of the age-old barbarism, a silly religion based on fables about an illiterate peasant whose teachings were weak, impractical, and socially subversive.

Accordingly, Julian moved quickly to reverse the religious policies of his predecessors: The privileges and immunities granted to the Christian priests were revoked; the labarum (a military banner decorated with the monogram of Christ) and other Christian emblems were abolished. A great effort was made to revitalize the pagan religion by conferring favors on its priests, importing Oriental cultic rites, and developing its theology along the lines of Neo-Platonism. Julian issued minute directions for sacrificial rites and ordered all the gods to be invoked—Saturn, Jupiter, Apollo, Mars, Pluto, Bacchus, and Venus, and even the Oriental deities, Mithras and Isis. He exhorted his devotees to live lives of austere morality and to outdo the Christians in works of charity.

But Julian's anti-Christian reaction failed. His mechanical assemblage of outdated ideas and foreign importations could not be given the breath of life; it was no match for the simple but vital Christian message. It could not compete with a religion that freed man from rituals and statutory morality in order to serve and love his neighbor as himself in imitation of his divine master, Jesus Christ. After a brief reign Julian came to an inglorious end in 363 on the sands of Mesopotamia after being struck by a Persian arrow. His death marked the definitive triumph of Christianity in the Empire.

A clear indication of this was given when his own troops elected as his successor Jovian, a general conspicuous for his Christian faith; he immediately restored official status and privilege to the Christian Church. His reign was short (363–64), and the army then raised another Christian, Valentinian, to the throne, who ruled with his brother Valens. They spent most of their energies on the frontier trying to halt the barbarians, Valentinian facing the Franks and Saxons while fortifying the Rhine against the Alemanni, while Valens was on the Danube, against the Goths. It was Valens who brought the Empire to the brink of collapse by his defeat at Adrianople in 378, where the Goths slaughtered two thirds of the Roman army, including himself.

While the Empire continued on its downward path, the Church continued to gain in popular favor and official standing in spite of internal dissension. The Church gradually became the only true bastion of freedom within the totalitarian Roman state, where the collapse of the old civic institutions had deprived its citizens of their political rights and loaded them with heavy economic disabilities. In the Church, however, they still could have a sense of participation and of some control over their destiny. Here they found also not only spiritual liberty but material assistance as well.

One of the most potent reasons, in fact, for the appeal of the Church to the masses was its magnificent system of charity, which aroused the admiration even of Julian the Apostate. Eventually it broadened out to include a whole organism of institutions, including orphanages, hospitals, inns for travelers, foundling homes, and old-age homes—so much so that as the state became increasingly unable to cope with the immense burden of social distress brought about by the barbarian invasions of the fourth and fifth centuries, it relied more and more on the Church.

The bishop was even given public judicial authority in all matters concerning care of the poor and social welfare. He was supposed to eat daily with the poor, and he often did. Ambrose wanted no gold vessels on the altars when there were captives to be ransomed, while at a later period Gregory the Great felt personal guilt when a poor man was found dead of starvation in his city. The bishop, moreover, stood forth as the champion of the oppressed against the clumsy and insensitive imperial bureaucracy and gradually became the most important figure in the city. While clothed in an aura of supernatural prestige, he enjoyed at the same time a popular authority, since he was elected by the people.

The immense influence of the Church over the masses was recognized by Emperors Gratian and Theodosius, who finally established it as the basis of the

Marble head of Emperor
Theodosius I, the Great
(379–95 c.e.). Louvre, Paris.
© *Erich Lessing/Art Resource,
New York.*

whole social order. This is the intent of the epoch-making decree promulgated
by Theodosius from Thessalonica on February 27, 380, which began: "We desire that all peoples who fall beneath the sway of our imperial clemency should
profess the faith which we believe has been communicated by the Apostle Peter
to the Romans and maintained in its traditional form to the present day. . . ."[1]
Paganism was declared illegal, while privileges were granted to the Catholic
clergy; they were accorded immunity from trial except in ecclesiastical courts.
Roman law was revised in harmony with Christian principles: The Sunday observance laws of Constantine were revived and enlarged, with the banning of
public or private secular activities. The pagan calendar was revised and given a
Christian character; Christmas and Easter were made legal holidays. Various
forms of heresy were proscribed and the property of their adherents confiscated. Pagan rites and practices were outlawed and the pagan priesthood
abolished.

Gratian ordered the removal of the statue and altar of Victory from the

---

[1] *Codex Theodosianus,* XVI, 1, 2.

Senate house in Rome in 382; his successor, Valentinian II, influenced by Ambrose and Pope Damasus, turned a deaf ear to the embassy of pagan senators who demanded its restoration. The co-Emperor of the East, Theodosius, gave memorable witness to his personal respect for the authority of the Church when after ordering a horrible massacre of the citizens of Thessalonica (390) he accepted the rebuke of Bishop Ambrose and did public penance at the door of the cathedral in Milan. (This one act did more than tons of theology to illustrate the authority of the Church over the state and lay the foundations of the papal monarchy over medieval Christendom.)

What explains the triumph of the Church? Besides the factors already alluded to, we would point out, first, the simple force of the Church's incomparable organization with all its ramifications, from the wall of Hadrian to the Euphrates River. It had no rival in this regard. Then we must remember that in a time of extreme social decay, it provided a refuge for the oppressed and acted as an agent of social justice. And finally, in the words of one of the great historians of this period, "In its high ethical appeal, its banishment of the blood and sacrifice from worship, and adherence to a god at once transcendent and active in the universe Christianity presented in a coherent form ideas to which the pagan world was groping."[2]

---

[2] W. Frend, *The Early Church* (New York: J. B. Lippincott, 1966), p. 138.

Chapter 7

JEROME

The Western Church originally recognized four men as its doctors or teachers *par excellence:* Ambrose, Augustine, Jerome, and Gregory the Great. Each of them played a singular role in shaping the theology and spirituality of the Catholic Church. In this chapter we intend to focus on Jerome, whose long life spanned a good part of the fourth century and in many ways epitomizes the history of his times.

Jerome was born of wealthy Christian parents, probably in 331, in the town of Striden, in the Latin-speaking Roman province of Dalmatia, a part of modern Yugoslavia. While his early life is veiled in obscurity, we do know that he received an education that was superb for its time. He studied grammar at Rome under the celebrated Aelius Donatus, whose writings were used as textbooks throughout the Middle Ages. Under the great scholar's tutelage for some four or five years Jerome made an intensive study of the Roman classics—Vergil, Cicero, Terence, Sallust, Horace, and others—nurturing in this way the literary talent that was to make him the greatest stylist of Christian antiquity. Further studies in rhetoric prolonged his stay at Rome for possibly another four or five years, a period during which he also began accumulating the books that were to make his library the most important private collection of the day.[1] They were also years when he began to take his Christian faith more seriously; and in fact some time during this sojourn at Rome he sought the baptism which according to the custom of the day his parents had postponed. But his conversion to ascetical Christianity was still years away and there are indications that his ardent pursuit of learning was sometimes put

---

[1] J. N. D. Kelly, *Jerome* (New York: Harper & Row, 1975), p. 20.

St. Jerome and the Lion. Colantonio *(fl.* 1420–60). Museo Nazionale di Capodimonte, Naples, Italy.   © *Scala/Art Resource, New York.*

aside for pursuits no less ardent but less ennobling, sexual adventures that were to cause him much remorse of conscience.

Little is known about the next ten years or so of his life. It seems that at some point while traveling in Gaul he settled in Trier, a city often used as the western capital of the Empire during the fourth century. It was also one of the centers in the West of the new monastic movement that had just started to take hold there after firmly establishing itself in the East. While sojourning in Trier—possibly to find a career in government service—and influenced perhaps by this new movement, Jerome dedicated himself wholeheartedly to the Christian life and began a close study of the Bible and theology while practicing a high degree of prayer and detachment. He then returned to his native region to visit his family and friends, and he stopped at the city of Aquileia, which was also a center of the monastic movement. There he stayed with a priest friend, Chromatius, who had organized his household into a quasi-monastic community. Jerome found this environment most congenial and was soon bubbling over with enthusiasm for the kind of ascetic life practiced by his friends. It was a happy period for Jerome but it was not to last. He was a man of explosive temperament with an uncontrollable, nasty tongue. A quarrel broke out and Jerome packed up his books and took off for the East, intending to visit Jerusalem. His long overland journey through Greece and Asia Minor was, however, arduous in the extreme and when he arrived at his friend Evagrius' house in Antioch, he was broken in health and unable to continue on to Jerusalem.

It was at this point, it seems, while convalescing amid the comforts of Evagrius' mansion, surrounded by his cherished books and intellectual companions, that Jerome made his momentous decision to fully embrace the ascetic life. In a dream he saw himself dragged before the Last Judgment seat and accused by the Judge of being a disciple of Cicero, not of Christ, and then flogged until his shoulders were black and blue. So affected was he by the vividness of the dream that he resolved to put aside the pagan classics for good and devote himself exclusively to the things of Christ.

Completely converted to the ascetic ideal, he took up his abode in the Syrian desert not far from Antioch. Many hermits already lived there seeking communion with God by practicing austerities of the most bizarre kind. They slept on the bare ground, loaded themselves with chains, ate only dates or raw herbs. Some, like the famous Simeon, even perched themselves permanently on the top of the pillars still standing amid the ruins of antiquity. In this sun-scorched barren retreat he spent several years praying, studying, barely keeping body and soul together while fending off the evil fantasies spawned by his sex-haunted imagination. "Although my only companions were scorpions and wild beasts, time and again I was mingling with the dances of girls."[2] To quell the flames of lust, he found a singular remedy: the study of Hebrew! With a convert from Judaism as his tutor, he began studying this difficult tongue. Jerome was the first Latin Christian to learn Hebrew and "indeed the first Christian of note at all apart from Origen (c. 185-c. 254)."[3] His mastery of the tongue was far superior to Origen's or any other Christian writer for centuries to come and it exerted a decisive influence on the shape of his future career.

While not much given to theological speculation, Jerome could not ignore the great controversy over the nature of the Godhead that was still agitating the Church. Theological differences with the monks in fact drove him

[2] Kelly, *Jerome, Letter* 22, 7, trans. Kelly, p. 52.
[3] Ibid., p. 50.

from the desert back to Antioch, a city itself divided into a number of factions over the Arian issue. One of the factions was outright Arian, but even the orthodox were split between the followers of Paulinus who stuck to the formula mandated by the Council of Nicaea and the followers of Meletius who had adopted a theology which went beyond Nicaea in referring to the three members of the Trinity as the "three hypostases." The conservative Jerome sided with Paulinus, who ordained him a priest.

The Emperor Valens' death at Adrianople in 378 and the accession of the Nicene-minded co-emperors, Gratian in the West and Theodosius in the East, had great repercussions on the fortunes of the various parties. Under Theodosius' leadership a church council was held at Constantinople in 381 (the Second Ecumenical Council) which saw the definitive triumph of Nicene orthodoxy. While marred by unseemly disorders, it officially reaffirmed the Nicene creed while also recognizing the "three hypostases" theology in terms acceptable to the West. At the same time the council endorsed the Meletian party at Antioch much to the dismay, no doubt, of Jerome who, though resident at Constantinople at the time of the council, makes no mention of it in his writings.

In the meantime, Jerome had embarked on a literary career by publishing a number of works that gained him considerable notice. One of these was his translation from the Greek, with many additions and supplements, of the *Chronicle* of Eusebius of Caesarea (d. 340). It was the most successful attempt at a history of the world up to that time and through Jerome's endeavors it became one of the most popular books in the Middle Ages. Another project he undertook at this time—the translation of thirty-seven of Origen's homilies—points to an intellectual interest that was to profoundly influence his intellectual and spiritual development. Jerome was fascinated with Origen's writings for obvious reasons. As a biblical scholar, daring speculative theologian, and prolific polymath, Origen (d. c. 254) was the greatest mind produced by the Church before Constantine. Jerome's enthusiasm for Origen at first knew no bounds and he often borrowed freely from the master's writings. Later, when a strong anti-Origen movement surfaced in the Church, Jerome did a switch and played down his immense debt to the Alexandrian genius.

In 382 Jerome left Constantinople for Rome in the company of his bishop, Paulinus, and began one of the most important and most turbulent chapters in his life. It all started smoothly enough when the reigning Pope, Damasus (d. 384), took him into his service and made him a member of his intimate circle of advisers. This Pope, whose election in 382 was a rowdy affair marked by hand-to-hand fighting between rival factions, was himself a scholar of some distinction and a patron of learning. Damasus was much impressed by Jerome's erudition and command of Hebrew and often consulted him on problems of scriptural interpretation. It was in fact at the Pope's behest that Jerome began work on a project that was to constitute his most lasting achievement: a translation of the Bible from the original languages. Up to this point Christians had at their disposal a translation of the Bible called the Old Latin which in its Old Testament part was based not on the Hebrew original but on a Greek translation known as the Septuagint. This Old Latin version was in a great state of disorder with many variations that had crept into the text. The Pope did not want a completely new translation but only wanted Jerome to sort out the various readings and establish a standard version based on comparison with the original languages. It was a work that would take him more than twenty years to complete, and while in Rome he finished only the four gospels. Moreover, he soon abandoned the idea of simply revising the existing translation of the Old Testament. He decided to start fresh from the Hebrew original and produce an entirely new translation. This was a courageous undertaking, for his new rendering of many venerable readings of the Bible shocked the sensibilities of the faithful and he was roundly denounced throughout the Christian world. Even Augustine, as we shall see, found the new translation uncalled for. Jerome was pained but not surprised by the response and referred to his critics as "howling dogs who rage savagely against me."[4] But his translation slowly caught on and gradually achieved recognition as the standard, or "Vulgate," Latin text of the Bible. Its influence on the religious imagination and literature of the West was immeasurable.

While in the employ of the Pope, Jerome struck up an acquaintance with a number of high-born Roman ladies of wealth who were practicing a rudimentary form of what would later be called convent life. Nuns as yet in the strict sense did not exist but these women were their forerunners; they lived in seclusion, vowed themselves to celibacy, and dedicated themselves to study and prayer. Firm now in the conviction that asceticism was the most perfect form of Christian life, and at the same time feeling deeply the need of female companionship, Jerome was delighted to make friends with these ladies who

---

[4] *Preface to Samuel; to Isaiah; to Psalms* (Vulgate) (PL 28, 558; 772; 1125f.), trans. in Kelly, p. 168.

invited him to become their teacher and spiritual director. With two of them in particular, Paula and her daughter, Eustochium, he formed an extremely close and lasting friendship. To encourage them to persevere in their chosen way of life he composed some of his most eloquent treatises on the ascetic vocation. Jerome repeatedly exalts virginity in these treatises as the only appropriate state in life for the committed Christian; it was the original state willed by God before the Fall, while sexual intercourse and marriage should be regarded as an inferior choice, one of the unhappy consequences introduced by original sin. In one of his pamphlets, *Against Jovinian*, Jerome got so carried away and dwelt on the disagreeable aspects of marriage in such crude and excessive terms that even his friends were embarrassed and felt it necessary to remonstrate with him. Jerome's response was characteristic:

> In order to make my meaning quite clear,
> let me state that I should definitely like
> to see every man take a wife—the kind of
> man, that is, who perhaps is frightened of the
> dark and just cannot quite manage to lie down
> in his bed all alone.[5]

Many Roman Christians at the time were rather cool toward Jerome's crusade for asceticism and virginity which they regarded as extremist. One of them was a layman, Helvidius, who in his published refutation of Jerome strove to prove that even Mary after the birth of Jesus lived a normal married life with Joseph. This attack on the perpetual virginity of the Mother of God aroused Jerome to an absolute fury which he unleashed in his reply, *Against Helvidius*. Though sprinkled with the gratuitous insults that came so readily to Jerome's tongue, it was learned and persuasive enough to convince most of his contemporaries and demolish Helvidius. The perpetual virginity of Mary was henceforth to be an unassailable doctrine of Catholic Christianity. The pamphlet was also successful in converting many to Jerome's view of consecrated celibacy as a superior state of life—a doctrine that would have tremendous influence on the development of Catholic spirituality and its sexual ethic.

[5] *The Satirical Letters of St. Jerome.* Trans. Paul Carroll (Chicago: Henry Regnery Company, 1956), p. 108.

As long as his patron Pope Damasus lived, Jerome could carry on his campaign for asceticism without too much hindrance. But with the death of the pontiff his situation radically changed. Many members of the Church at Rome were repelled by his extreme views; they regarded his type of asceticism as an Oriental intrusion. He also made many enemies by his frequent attacks on the conventional Christians who with the coming of Constantinian mass Christianity were now so numerous around him. Jerome found many targets for his satirical talent and indulged it to the full, showing no mercy as he lashed out at the worldly bishops living in luxury, the priests fawning on the rich, and the pseudo-virgins parading around in the company of young fops. With the elevation of Siricius (384–399) to the throne of the apostles, his enemies struck back. Some kind of formal charge was brought against him by the authorities, involving among other things his relations with Paula, it seems; and Jerome, while indignantly rejecting the accusation, found it necessary or expedient to leave the eternal city for good.

Paula and Eustochium followed him and after joining his company—probably at Antioch—they started out on a pilgrimage to the Holy Land. Helena, the mother of Constantine, at a great age made a pilgrimage to Palestine in 326 and with the help of her son carried out a program of restoring the places sacred to the memory of Jesus and ornamenting two of them, on the Mount of Olives and at Bethlehem, with imposing basilicas. Her action gave a great impetus to the practice of visiting the Holy Land and by Jerome's time such pilgrimages were quite common. Jerome and his companions made an extensive tour of the holy places and the indefatigable scholar made a very detailed inventory of them, including a description of the Church of the Resurrection built by Constantine in Jerusalem over the cave associated with Jesus' resurrection and the Church of the Nativity built by Helena over the cave which ancient tradition regarded as his birthplace.

The three pilgrims were enthralled by what they saw in the Holy Land and after a brief journey to visit the monks in the Egyptian desert decided to make their stay a permanent one. Fascinated above all by Bethlehem with its grotto of the Nativity, they decided to settle there in 386 and follow a monastic way of life. Jerome's friends, Rufinus and Melania, had already established monasteries for Latin-speaking ascetics, separate ones for men and women, in Jerusalem on the Mount of Olives, and Jerome and Paula were eager to try out the same idea. Their two monasteries were eventually built and, thanks to the fame of their founders, soon attracted a number of recruits. As the basis for their rule of life they drew on their knowledge and experience of the Egyptian monks. Jerome freely adapted the type of monastic life inaugurated in Egypt by St. Pachomius, whose *Rule* he later translated. It prescribed an orderly routine of community life for the monks who, while living in individual cells, took their meals in common, engaged in manual labor to support themselves, and met for prayer at regular intervals throughout the day. Monasticism had by this time taken firm root in the East, but although publicized especially by the translation of St. Athanasius' *Life of St. Antony,* it had not yet taken much hold in the West. The monastic communities of Jerome and Rufinus, which adapted Egyptian monasticism to the Latin temperament, were well advertised especially through the writings and letters of Jerome and much visited by pilgrims from the West and no doubt they contributed greatly to the spread of monasticism in the West during the fifth century.

The founding of the monasteries was a dream come true for Jerome, and in spite of all the problems and worries—financial ones especially—he continued to rule and guide his monks for thirty years until his death. While doing so he poured out a huge assortment of writings which were to establish his reputation as the most learned of all the scholars in the early Church. He completed his monumental translation of the Bible from the Hebrew original while turning out commentaries on Scripture which alone constituted an enormous output—embracing a good number of the books of the Old and New Testaments. In addition, he translated numerous theological works, compiled several encyclopedic type reference works, penned biographies of notable Christian ascetics, and composed an outline history of Christian literature, *Famous Men,* which became the standard text on the subject. He also kept up a lively correspondence with many of the leading figures of the day and his letters are a major source for the history of his times.

Controversy was the breath of life to Jerome, and even while committed to the supposedly peaceful life of a monk, he plunged into a number of violent quarrels that filled the whole Church with their noise. One of these involved him with his boyhood friend, Rufinus, ruler of the neighboring Latin monastery in Jerusalem. Some preliminary tensions between the two no doubt occurred when Jerome took a high and mighty attitude toward the more relaxed spirit prevalent in Rufinus's and Melania's monasteries and when Rufinus complained about Jerome's audacity in putting out a totally new translation of the Bible. But the issue that led to a lasting break between the two monks was Origenism. Both were longtime admirers of the master; but when a strong anti-Origen movement surfaced in the Church, Jerome went over to the anti-Origen side and accused Rufinus and his bishop, John of Jerusalem, of conniving to spread Origen's heresies. John in turn excommunicated Jerome and in 397 even tried to have him removed from his diocese by force. A truce was arranged for a time but the war broke out again when Rufinus, now resident in Rome, put out a translation of Origen's *chef d'oeuvre, First Principles,* and covered it with a preface that recalled how Jerome himself had often lavished praise on Origen.

Jerome was appalled by the insinuation that he might in any way be sympathetic to Origen's heterodoxies and he drove his pen furiously into action. The two former friends now blasted each other in pamphlets that sizzled with charge and countercharge. Rufinus finally called it quits and ceased referring to Jerome in his writings, but Jerome was not the type to let up. He continued to level abuse at Rufinus and even when he heard of the man's death in 411 could not withhold a remark about the "Scorpion Rufinus . . . buried with his brother giants, Enceladus and Porphyrion—that multiple-headed Hydra has finally ceased hissing."[6]

Jerome also played an unseemly role in the quarrel between the crafty patriarch of Alexandria, Theophilus (d. 412) and the saintly patriarch of Constantinople, John, later known as Chrysostom ("Golden-tongued") (d. 407), who was renowned for his eloquence and mastery of Scripture. The unscrupulous Theophilus exploited Jerome's anti-Origen feelings and secured his assistance in his maneuvers to humiliate Alexandria's rival see of Constantinople by having its intransigent bishop deposed. John had already alienated a good segment of the populace, including the clergy, and the Empress Eudoxia by his outspoken denunciation of vice and was found guilty of Origenism and other charges at a farcical trial at the Synod of the Oak (403) presided over by Theophilus. John was sent into exile but was soon recalled. However, he soon fell afoul of Eudoxia again and his enemies secured his banishment to Pontus, where he was finally deliberately killed by enforced traveling on foot in wretched weather.

Jerome's quarrelsomeness and touchiness is also apparent in his correspondence with Augustine, the great African theologian and, later, like Jerome, a doctor of the Church. It began when the younger scholar—eager to make friends with the erudite Hebraist—wrote to Jerome for some advice on

---

[6] *The Satirical Letters of St. Jerome,* p. 197.

theological matters. He also had the temerity to differ with some of Jerome's biblical opinions and even worse to question the propriety of Jerome's great project—the translation of the Bible from the Hebrew original. Like so many of his contemporaries, Augustine thought that the authority of the Old Latin version should not be challenged since it was based on the Greek Septuagint, which was generally considered a divinely inspired translation. Moreover, it was consecrated by such long usage in the life and prayer of the Church that Augustine felt that any attempt to change it would seriously disturb the faithful. Jerome was quite irritated by what he thought was the younger man's brashness and accused him of trying to make a reputation for himself by challenging a well-known and established figure like himself. The two only slowly reached an understanding, in part because of confusion caused by mix-ups in the mail, with later letters arriving before earlier ones. But in the long run Augustine managed to disarm the irascible old Biblicist by masterful diplomacy and tact. He begged the older man's forgiveness, paid tribute to his unrivaled scriptural expertise, and asked only to be allowed to sit at his feet and learn from him. Jerome was deeply touched and responded with profuse words of affection and esteem for Augustine.

An interesting glimpse into the evolving piety of the Church of Jerome's day is provided by his pamphlet *Against Vigilantius,* in which he defends the increasingly popular custom of venerating relics of the martyrs and saints, of burning candles at their shrines, of seeking their intercession in prayer as well as the observance of vigils at the site of their burial. He nicknames his opponent "Dormitianus" (sleepyhead) and mingles serious scholarly arguments with scurrilous invective, which he hurls at his opponent's head. The pamphlet was widely read and made an important contribution to the general acceptance of these practices by the Church.

The last controversy Jerome took up had to do with the campaign waged by Pelagius, a British theologian and monk in favor of his views on grace, free will, and original sin. Like his colleague Augustine, Jerome was deeply disturbed by Pelagius' seeming denial of the crippling effects of original sin on our free will and by his denial of our need for divine help in avoiding sin and by his insistence that we could earn our salvation by our own efforts. Jerome and Augustine joined forces to combat Pelagius and their letters at this juncture show them now enjoying a warm friendship. The old monk of Bethlehem was now quite ready to defer to the brilliant bishop of Hippo, whose learning and orthodoxy he had come to fully respect and admire.

Jerome's declining years were darkened by the terrible series of events that betokened the end of the Roman Empire. On all sides, hordes of barbarians broke through the defenses and spread havoc with fire and sword. Picts, Scots, and Saxons overran Britain; Franks, Burgundians, Alemanni, Huns, Visigoths, and Vandals ravaged Gaul; Suevi, Vandals, and Visigoths, Spain; Vandals, Africa; Ostrogoths, Italy. Then Alaric and his Ostrogoths took the capital itself and pillaged Rome for three days. Jerome was numb with horror at the news: "The lamp of the world is extinguished, and it is the whole world which has perished in the ruins of this one city."[7]

Violence struck at Bethlehem too. In 416 Jerome was forced to flee for his life when his own monastery was seized by a band of ruffians—perhaps fanatical devotees of Pelagius—and burned to the ground. But his greatest sorrow was the death of the two people who meant the most to him. In 404 his dearest friend and coworker, Paula, died and left Jerome utterly prostrate with grief. And only a year before his own death in 420 Paula's daughter Eustochium, whom Jerome also loved beyond measure, fell ill and died—a blow that completely shattered him. The circumstances of his own death a year later are unknown. We only know that he was buried close to the tombs of Paula and Eustochium in their beloved Church of the Nativity a few yards away from the spot held sacred to Christ's birth.

In the memory of succeeding ages, Jerome's stature continued to grow until he was finally recognized as a Doctor and Father of the Church in view of the enormous contribution made by his translation of the Bible and his commentaries, by his multifaceted theological and historical writings, by his great influence on the development of Catholic mariology and spirituality, and by the impetus he gave to Western monasticism. The dark side of his personality—his ferocious intolerance and bigotry, his nasty explosions of temper, his uncouth displays of vanity, his delight in putting down his enemies by fair means or foul—was somehow glossed over; and posterity even accorded him the title "saint"—rightly perhaps, for at least no one could deny the burning sincerity and steadfast devotion he manifested in carrying out his commitment to Christ.

---

[7] *Commentary on Ezekiel, I, Prologue (CCL* 75:3–4). Trans. S. Katz, *The Decline of Rome and the Rise of Medieval Europe* (Ithaca, N.Y.: Cornell University Press, 1955), p. 92.

Chapter 8

AUGUSTINE

One of the decisive periods in the official suppression of paganism in Africa occurred during the years 399–401. A Roman mission arrived in Carthage in 399 with authority to close the temples. In the same year religious riots erupted that caused at least sixty deaths. By 401 the Catholic bishops in Council at Carthage had sent an embassy to Rome to appeal for even more legislation to uproot the remnants of idolatry. Among these bishops was Augustine of Hippo, the outstanding genius of the Western Church, who even in a short history of the Church deserves a chapter to himself.

Augustine was born in 354 in a small town, Thagaste, in Latin Africa (now part of modern Algeria). His father, a man of slender means, was a convert to Christianity late in life, while his mother, Monica, was a lifelong devout Christian.

At the cost of great sacrifice on the part of his parents, he managed to secure an education, which took him to Madaura first and finally to Carthage. It was narrow, exclusively literary, and consisted of the intense study of works of Vergil, Cicero, and a few other Latin classics. It left him ignorant of philosophy, science, and Greek. While a student in Carthage he plunged into the sensual excitements of the teeming city and was soon enthralled with a girl who bore him a son, Adeodatus; she remained his concubine for the next fifteen years. At the same time he underwent a kind of religious conversion: While reading Cicero's *Hortensius,* he was suddenly stirred by a passionate desire for wisdom. But where could he find it? Since he was reared in a Christian home, he naturally opened the Bible; but he soon found himself repelled by the clumsy translation, which offended his cultivated literary taste. Besides, the history of "God's people" with its record of violence and its image

St. Augustine (painted 1480).
Fresco. Sandro Botticelli
(1444–1510). Chiesa di
Ognissanti, Florence.
© *Scala/Art Resource, New York.*

of a vengeful God seemed in contradiction with the God of Jesus Christ. In his bewilderment he turned to the Manichaeans, whose rejection of the Old Testament and dualistic interpretation of the problem of evil (they attributed evil to a supreme principle) soothed his sense of guilt about his own sexual aberrations.

All the while, he pursued his successful career as a professor of rhetoric, at Carthage first and then at Rome, where influential friends brought him into touch with high imperial officials. This led to his appointment in 384 as professor of rhetoric to the court of the Emperor at Milan, the Western capital at the time.

His stay at Milan proved to be decisive for his intellectual and spiritual history. By the time he arrived there in the autumn of 384, he had become disillusioned with the Manichees and their doctrinaire claim to absolute certainty. He still believed truth might be attainable, but not in their simplistic fashion. Coming to Milan in this mood of uncertainty, he soon fell under the spell of the formidable Ambrose, chosen bishop eleven years before in a clamorous election by the people. The young professor began to attend the cathedral services and was greatly impressed by the prelate's powerful presentation of the Catholic faith, his easy familiarity with current intellectual trends, and his cogent answers to the Manichaean criticism of the Old Testament.

Augustine's circle of influential friends at Milan introduced him to the Neo-Platonic movement, which attracted many Christian intellectuals of the day. They found in this system a remarkable affinity with their faith. He studied Plotinus intensively and was able thereby to shake off a lingering materialism and to reach the concept of a purely spiritual reality.

The philosophy of Plotinus combined a profound sense of the spiritual unity of all things with an awareness of their innumerable gradations as emanations of a unique spiritual being. Thus each manifestation of the divine good was linked with all other manifestations to make the universe a continuous active whole, each stage of being deriving its awareness from a higher stage and in turn communicating it to an inferior one. The sublimity of this philosophy swept Augustine off his feet and decisively converted him from a literary career to a career in philosophy. He might have stopped there had it not been for the influence of St. Paul, who now also began to preoccupy his thoughts. It was the great apostle who helped him to realize that philosophy was not enough to overcome the moral contradictions of our nature; God alone incarnate in the flesh and revealed in the Scriptures could do so.

But still Augustine hesitated to seek Catholic baptism and make the renunciations it entailed. His divided soul would give him no rest, however, and finally in a moment of anguish, hearing a child's voice cry out, "Take and read," he reached for a copy of Paul's epistles, opened them at random, and glanced down: "no drunken orgies, no promiscuity or licentiousness," he read, "and no wrangling or jealousy. Let your armour be the Lord Jesus Christ"[1]; it was all finally settled in that moment; his doubts disappeared, his soul flooded with light and certainty.

Abandoning his plans for marriage (he had already dismissed his poor mistress), his public career, his hopes of financial security and social prestige,

---

[1] Rom. 13:13–14.

he retired to a country villa—Cassiciacum, near Lake Como—and there with
a little oddly assorted company of friends and relatives including his mother,
Monica, led a simple life of prayer and contemplation and began to sketch out
an ambitious program for a Christian philosophy while preparing himself for
baptism. This he received at the hands of Ambrose on the night of April
24–25 (Holy Saturday), 387. He then prepared to return to Thagaste, his
hometown, with his mother and friends in order to take up a quasimonastic
kind of life. But Monica died in the Roman seaport of Ostia, leaving him in
the throes of uncontrollable grief. The bereaved little party finally arrived in
Carthage in late 388; but death struck again, carrying off his son, Adeodatus.

A casual trip that he took a few years later to the ancient seaport of Hippo
to seek a recruit for his "monastery" had an unexpected result. While attending the liturgy in the cathedral, he was seized by the congregation and
brought before the bishop, Valerius, who ordained him on the spot. (This was
not an unusual occurrence in those days.) So Augustine took up residence
there, moved his community to the precincts of the cathedral in Hippo, and
soon came to the fore as the leading spokesman for the Catholic community.
In 393 he was honored with an invitation to address the African Catholic
bishops at one of their councils. In 395 Valerius chose him as his co-adjutor,
and a few years later Augustine succeeded him as bishop of Hippo. There he
remained for thirty-five years, until his death.

There were some three hundred or more Catholic bishops in Africa at the
time. Many, who were married men, could rival secular dignitaries by their
lavish displays of wealth. Augustine, in contrast, turned his episcopal house
into a monastery, gathered his priests around him, and required them to take
the vows of poverty, celibacy, and obedience to a strict rule. As bishops themselves later on, many of them disseminated his ideals throughout the Church
in Africa.

The victory of Christianity in Africa dated back to the latter half of the
third century. By the time of Augustine there were more than three hundred
sees in Africa. But—sadly—the Church in Africa was torn by dissension between Catholics and Donatists, a schism that dated back to the time of Constantine and that occurred when some of the bishops refused to recognize a
certain Caecilian as the legitimate bishop of Carthage on the grounds that he
had been consecrated by a "traditor"—that is, one who had handed over the
sacred Scriptures to the Roman persecutors under Diocletian. In spite of Constantine's effort to pressure the Donatists back into union with the Catholics,

the schism lasted, and by Augustine's time the two Churches faced each other in almost every town. The bishop of Hippo threw himself energetically into the controversy and by sermons and writings tried to heal the schism.

But at issue were two radically opposed conceptions of the nature of the Church: the Donatists claimed to be a pure Church, a Church of the elect, of the holy, of the martyrs, uncontaminated by and fiercely exclusive toward the world, an ark of refuge from evil society. By their practice of rebaptizing they claimed fidelity to the tradition of Cyprian and to true African Christianity as it was before Constantine.

The opposite tack was taken by Augustine and the Catholics who willingly acknowledged the co-existence of saints and sinners in their Church. A Church intended to embrace all of humanity could not be so sharply demarcated from the world, they argued. The final separation would only take place at the End. The Church's purpose was to be a sociological sign of God's presence in the world; its sacraments were holy, even if sometimes its ministers were not. Moreover, as Augustine was fond of pointing out, the Donatists were isolated from the worldwide Church, while the Catholics enjoyed communion with it by their agreement with overseas customs—such as the Roman ban on rebaptizing—and by their willingness to communicate with the overseas churches, an attitude that gained them the favor of the Emperor.

Arguments had little effect, however. Finally recourse was had to coercion. It was an easy step to take in the climate of opinion at the time—but a sad step for the Catholic Church. The current Emperor, Honorius, was a devout Catholic and had recently used force to suppress paganism, while some of the Donatists themselves were prone to violence. So in June 405, the *Edict of Unity* was published, which ordered the dissolution of the Donatist Church.

Although Augustine had endorsed the policy of the Empire in using coercion to repress paganism, he did not at first favor using it against the Donatists. The possibility of having his Church filled with counterfeit Catholics was too frightening. But when experience proved that many of these forcibly converted Donatists later made good Catholics, he gradually changed his mind, and in the course of justifying persecution of the Donatists wrote the only full treatise found in the history of the early Church on the right of the state to suppress non-Catholics—one that exercised tremendous influence on subsequent Church policy and provided a rationale for the medieval Inquisition.

The strands of his theology of persecution are numerous and subtly woven together: Augustine had a view of predestination that held that men were not ready to make free choice of salvation until God prepared them spiritually by many involuntary constraints and punishments as God dealt with his wayward children of the Old Testament; and so the persecution of the Donatists could be regarded as a divinely ordained castigation intended for their spiritual benefit. He believed that the majority of men, thanks to original sin, lived on such a low moral level that they could only be motivated by fear—and in this sense he interpreted the parable of the wedding banquet where the master forces the unwilling guests to attend his supper. Another factor was his experience with many of the coerced Donatists who later expressed their gratitude at being brought to see the light.

As the bishop of Hippo, Augustine was bound to a treadmill of ceaseless activity: as judge in the episcopal court arbitrating endless litigation, as administrator of the Church's vast property, as counselor of his priests, and as a leading member of the African hierarchy taking part in the great councils of the day. At the same time, as the shepherd of his flock he preached constantly before rapt and crowded congregations and left to posterity a collection of sermons that indicate his almost incredible knowledge of Scripture as well as a verbal dexterity that fascinated his uneducated audience and kept them interested even when he was expounding the most profound truths of the faith. Much of his success was due to an extraordinary sensitivity, by which he could identify with his people and so move them to identify completely with himself. With it all he managed to carry on a huge correspondence with a host of friends and acquaintances and to write innumerable treatises—thirty-three books alone between 395 and 410.

One of the most remarkable is his *Confessions,* a masterpiece of introspective autobiography, which he wrote shortly after becoming bishop. With marvelous literary artistry he charts the labyrinthine ways of his own spirit, and in a fiercely honest scrutiny of his whole past life analyzes the motives behind his spiritual evolution. It is a book concerned not so much with ideas as with feelings—the affections that really shaped his personality, the sins, the temptations, the love affairs, the motives, the ecstasies, the intellectual excitements. Always present is the sense of the mysterious abyss, the almost infinite depths of one's being and its continual yearning for more, which he felt could only be explained by supposing its source in the ineffably mysterious and all-loving Creator of the Christian revelation.

Two other great works of this period are the *De Genesi ad litteram,* a vast commentary on the book of Genesis, and *De Trinitate,* which reveal his genius for speculation.

His book *The City of God* breathes the atmosphere of Götterdämmerung that pervaded the world as the Roman Empire began to crumble. On August 24, 410, Alaric, with his Gothic army, laid Rome to a terrible sack for three days. This disaster, without parallel in her history, left the Empire in a state of absolute shock; Augustine with his flock meditated on the meaning of it all and in a sermon wondered aloud whether the end of the Empire was not at hand.

Later, in the same frame of mind, he began the huge *City of God,* which took thirteen years to write. With massive erudition and consummate artistry, he passes Christian judgment on the whole history, culture, and religion of pagan Rome and relates it to what he regards as the ultimate meaning of history itself.

History, he claims, can only be understood through the biblical revelation that discloses it as a continuing struggle between two cities, one made up of those who pursue only earthly goods and live under the curse of Adam. They constitute the City of Man and find their fitting symbol in the Roman Empire, which will probably decay, as signs already indicate, and as all other empires have. There is another city, however, destined to last forever: the City of God, whose history parallels the City of Man; the City of God embraces all those souls who live only as pilgrims in the midst of the world and have placed their hopes only in God.

Here and now, however, the two cities are not discernible as completely separate, nor can they be simply identified with any particular groups. The dividing line between them is invisible because ultimately it has to do with each man's commitment to final values. Rather, they are eschatological realities that overlap in history and will only be separated from each other at the end of time. The empirical Church, in particular, is not identical with the City of God; but in spite of the ambivalence the empirical Church shares with all human constructs, its mission is to act as a sociological sign of God's love for the world.

The sack of Rome drove many of its inhabitants to seek refuge in Africa. Among them was a theologian of genius, Pelagius, who came to Carthage with his disciple, Celestius, after spending some thirty years in Rome as a fashionable lecturer on religious and spiritual matters. In the cultivated and cosmopolitan atmosphere of Rome, Pelagius had disseminated his very personal ideas on free will, grace, and original sin without much opposition. But when he arrived in Africa, he almost immediately ran afoul of Augustine, who found these theories scandalous, heretical, and in direct contradiction with his own views on these matters. Fresh from victories over the Donatists, the bishop of Hippo jumped into the fray again.

The central idea of Pelagius was an intense conviction about human freedom: the certitude that man was in full control of his own moral destiny. However deeply wounded he was in his physical and spiritual condition by Adam's fall, it did not mean that man had lost his freedom; in spite of the evil influences of sin, he could out of his own resources choose the good. God's help was limited mainly to external means—the Commandments, the teaching and example of Christ, etc.—so that one could observe God's Commandments without sinning if one so chose. Celestius, his disciple, even denied the necessity of infant baptism.

Augustine, on the other hand, was profoundly impressed by the moral weakness of men and the deeply rooted character of their evil tendencies. It was clear proof for him that the whole human race was more intimately involved than Pelagius would allow in Adam's fall—that is, they shared his guilt and through him were deprived of the gifts originally bestowed to complete his faculties. Thus, Augustine taught, all humanity lost the gifts of immortality, immunity from physical decay, and strong inclination to virtue. Instead man was now subject to death and sickness, darkened in mind, and inclined toward sin. Henceforth he could not avoid sin without God's grace, which the bishop thought of as an interior experience of delight in spiritual things as God's own way of moving our will to choose the good.

This grace of God working in the very interior of our will is irresistible. But, Augustine argued, it does not take away our freedom, for the acts it elicits from our will are elicited with our consent. Only those who receive this grace are saved; those who do not are damned. Why some receive it and others do not is a mystery hidden in the inscrutable justice of God—the mystery of predestination.

While his opponent, Pelagius, moved to the Holy Land, where he found the bishops more receptive to his views, Augustine in Africa rallied the bishops to condemn the main teachings of Pelagius in 416. This stand was ratified by Pope Zosimus in his *Epistula tractoria* of 418. Nevertheless, the controversy was carried on by Julian, the bishop of Eclanum, who regarded Augustine's teaching as Manichaean. The controversy was also furthered by the so-called semi-Pelagians, found in the monasteries of southern Gaul, who approached the Pelagian heresy by their doctrine that the first beginnings of a good will can originate in man's own volition. They also denied the Augustinian predestination to hell.

The forensic triumph of Augustine, however, was all but total; his writings on grace were recognized as the best and most skillful interpretation of the Church's tradition on this matter and won him international renown, though a few of his ideas, such as his fatalistic theory of predestination, were not accepted. Posterity later ratified this judgment by granting him the title "Doctor Gratiae" (Teacher of grace). The Council of Orange (529) embodied the substance of his doctrine in the following propositions: 1. As a result of Adam's trespass, both death and sin were transmitted to all his descendants. 2. Man's will has been so vitiated by original sin that he can only love God if prompted and assisted by grace. 3. Baptismal grace enables all Christians with the help of Christ to do what is necessary for salvation. 4. In every good action, even the first impulse comes from God. But the council did not ratify his fatalistic theory of predestination to hell.

Augustine lived long enough to see the total collapse of Roman rule in Africa and the ruin of his diocese. In 429 and 430 the Vandals came pouring in; churches were burned, virgins and ascetics tortured and violated, bishops and clergy slaughtered, and his own city of Hippo packed to the walls with refugees. In the midst of all the turmoil and panic, Augustine fell ill with a fever; he asked to be left completely alone so that he could pray, and after several days of agony, he died. He was buried on August 28, 430.

A year later Hippo was taken and sacked.

Chapter 9

POPE LEO I WINS A GREAT
VICTORY FOR PAPAL
PRIMACY AT CHALCEDON

During the fourth and fifth centuries, the papacy made continual headway in advancing its claims to a primacy over the whole Church. It may be true, as some historians say, that the Council of Nicaea (325) "knew nothing of the doctrine of papal supremacy," yet T. Jalland, who quotes this opinion with approval, acknowledges that until the fourth quarter of the fourth century the Church had hardly yet accustomed itself to "speak in the language of jurisdiction whether papal or otherwise, and that in consequence the crucial question which see possessed its plenitude did not arise." And then Jalland goes on to say, "It is clear that the Church was moving in the direction of providing herself with the machinery for corporate action as an oecumenical society on an equal footing with an oecumenical State."[1] And as a matter of fact, we see the bishops of Rome defining their role as chief shepherds of the flock of Christ with growing consistency and precision. Pope Damasus (366–84) at a council in 382 seems to have claimed formally the possession of a primacy over all other churches in virtue not of conciliar decisions but of the Lord's promise to St. Peter. Pope Siricius (384–99) goes a step further: He not only hears appeals but even starts to take the initiative. In his letters—which for the first time are now called *decretals*—he implicitly claims the right to make decisions, with universal application in matters both doctrinal and disciplinary.

[1] *The Church and the Papacy* (London: S.P.C.K. [Society for Promoting Christian Knowledge], 1944), pp. 205–6.

It is true that these claims did not meet with perfect acquiescence on all sides. The attitude of the East was quite ambivalent, as we shall see a little later in connection with Pope Leo. But even in the West there was ambiguity. The African Church, for instance, was jealous of its independence, and the bishops there were quite ready to question Roman attempts to interfere with their doctrinal and disciplinary decisions. When Pope Zosimus (417–18) seemed on the point of reversing their condemnation of Pelagius, they reacted vigorously and persuaded Zosimus to join them in condemning Pelagius. On the other hand, we have to recognize with Jalland certain signs "of a conviction, in some measure shared by the Africans with the rest of the Church, that if a local decision . . . was to possess universal validity, it must in some way be supported by a verdict of the Roman see."[2] It is sometimes urged that Augustine himself was hostile to the exercise of Roman jurisdiction over the African Church. It is true that he gives various and conflicting interpretations of the famous text of Matthew, "Thou art Peter," at one time identifying Peter himself with the rock, while later interpreting it of Christ. And on several occasions he complained bitterly about Rome's exercise of its appellate powers— even threatening to resign if Rome reinstated a young priest whom Augustine had suspended. But we cannot say that he repudiated the appellate jurisdiction of the Roman see. And we must remember, in any case, that he never elaborated any carefully thought-out theory of authority in the Church. So we simply can't say what his final views on the primacy of Rome might have been.

When we come to the reign of Pope Leo I (440–61) we reach one of the momentous turning points in the history of the papacy. By common consent of historians, Leo was one of the greatest of ecclesiastical statesmen and deservedly surnamed "the Great." At a time when the world was cracking at the seams, Leo stood forth as a Pope of commanding character and genius who dramatically and successfully asserted the supreme authority of the papacy. Drawing on the rich heritage of papal experience and claims, he formulated a doctrine of papal primacy that was to weather all storms and guide the policy of all subsequent Popes. According to Leo, Peter was "the Rock" on which the Lord built his Church; his successors, the Popes, were merely his temporary and mystical personifications. In virtue of his office, the Pope had the plenitude of power over the universal Church: He was its supreme ruler, its

[2] Ibid., p. 282.

supreme teacher, and its supreme judge. All other bishops only shared in his responsibility for the whole Church.

It was most important for the history of the papacy that Leo not only enunciated this grandiose theory of papal primacy, but also that by and large he made its claims good. He exercised authority in Spain and North Africa; he frustrated the attempt to create an independent Gallic see in Arles—even going so far as to strip the saintly Hilary of his metropolitan authority there. In 445 he secured an edict from the Western Emperor, Valentinian III, who instructed the military commander in Gaul, the famous Aetius, that "the primacy of the Apostolic See as appropriate to St. Peter" must be observed.

Leo came to the papal office as twilight fell over the Roman Empire. His contemporary Aetius, the last effective Roman general in the West, strove valiantly to save Gaul and Italy from the universal doom, but he won his most notable victories only by using barbarian against barbarian. In 436 Aetius gained a resounding victory over the Visigoths with the help of the Huns and then defeated Attila and the Huns in 451 with the help of the Visigoths. Aetius himself was murdered later by the Emperor himself, the degenerate Valentinian III, who in a jealous pique cut him down with his sword; six months later Aetius' guards returned the favor by assassinating Valentinian. In the vacuum of secular leadership, it was Leo who virtually took charge of the city's fate. In 452 he traveled to Mantua to meet Attila and dissuade him from attacking Rome. Attila turned aside and Rome was saved—for the moment. A few years later Gaiseric the Vandal, having subdued Africa, launched his

Entry of King Etzel (Attila) into Vienna, a scene from *The Epos of the Nibelungs*. Albin Egger-Lienz (1868–1926). Landesmuseum, Ferdinandeum, Innsbruck, Austria. © *Erich Lessing/Art Resource, New York.*

fleet against Rome; again it was Leo who met the conqueror this time at the gates of the city itself. Gaiseric did not turn aside, but at the insistence of the Pope he limited himself to a peaceful sack.

Leo's most memorable exercise of authority, however, occurred in connection with an acute doctrinal crisis that faced the Church during his pontificate. It began in Constantinople when an old monk there named Eutyches, a dabbler rather than a real theologian, was summoned before a synod on the charge of teaching heresy. At issue were some of his statements regarding the relation of the human to the divine in Christ. He was duly found guilty and relieved of his office by Patriarch Flavian. There things might ordinarily have rested. But as it turned out, Eutyches was merely a pawn in the game of the scheming, ambitious patriarch of Alexandria, Dioscoros, who was searching for just such an incident to embarrass his rival Flavian. Dioscoros succeeded in turning the tables against Flavian. Dioscoros blew the whole matter up into a major crisis, leveled charges of heresy at Flavian himself, and with the help of his friend the chamberlain Chrysaphius, the chief adviser of the Emperor, persuaded the Emperor to call a council to settle the issue.

The question that pitted Dioscoros and Eutyches against Flavian was the continuation of a long-standing controversy over the relation of the human to the divine in Christ that divided the two major schools of theology in the East, Antioch and Alexandria. Antioch's greatest authority, Theodore of Mopsuestia, was influential in shaping its theology, which insisted on the full and genuine manhood of Christ. In describing how divinity and humanity were united in Christ, however, the Antiochenes left themselves open to the charge that the union was only moral rather than essential. Alexandria's most revered theologian, Cyril, on the other hand, so emphasized the unity of manhood and divinity in Christ that he was accused of submerging the humanity in the divinity.

One of the thorny questions raised in the controversy had to do with the various statements in the Scripture about Christ—some relative to his humanity, some of his divinity. More specifically, it was asked whether these statements could be predicted interchangeably of either his humanity or his divinity—in other words, whether one could say that God suffered on the cross (as some liturgies did) or that Jesus created the world. In accordance with their belief in the most intimate union conceivable of deity and humanity in Christ, the Alexandrians favored a complete exchange of subjects and predicates in statements about the God-man. The Antiochenes, on the other hand, shied away from what they thought were extremes in this practice. And Nestorius, Flavian's predecessor and a partisan of the Antiochene school, brought about his downfall when he took umbrage at the expression "Mother of God" (in Greek *Theotokos*), in reference to Christ's mother. Nestorius' demise took place at the Council of Ephesus in 431, which saw the triumph of the Alexandrian theology when *Theotokos* was endorsed by the bishops and approval was given to Cyril's expression: "The Logos himself suffered in the flesh." Nestorius was condemned as a heretic and exiled to Egypt.

Ephesus failed to bring peace between the two schools. A bloc of bishops under John of Antioch refused to subscribe to the decrees of Ephesus. A compromise was eventually arranged in 433, when the disputants signed a formula that spoke of a "union between two natures," but even this failed to satisfy the intransigents of both schools.

Dioscoros, the supporter of Eutyches and adversary of Flavian, was one of these intransigents. As patriarch of Alexandria, Dioscoros was looking for a way to secure a definitive triumph for the Alexandrian Christology and discredit the Antiochene school. So, as we have said, he found a perfect tool in Eutyches, a monk of Constantinople but a partisan of the Alexandrian theology. Dioscoros counted, moreover, on his friend Chrysaphius, the Emperor's trusted adviser, to bring matters to a favorable conclusion.

And so it turned out—at first. The Emperor called a council together at Ephesus in 449 and appointed Dioscoros to preside. Backed by an army of monks, favored by the Emperor and supported by most of the 130 bishops present, Dioscoros had everything his own way. Liberty of speech was sharply curtailed. The bishops listened to Eutyches recite his grievances against Flavian and then applauded his confession: "Two natures before the union; after the union, one nature."

Dioscoros then proceeded against Flavian, whom he accused of changing the faith of Nicaea and Ephesus by adding his doctrine of the "two natures." Sentence of deposition was passed against Flavian; those bishops who were reluctant to sign it were compelled to do so by soldiers amid scenes of violence and disorder. Flavian was treated as a prisoner, and if rumor is trustworthy, his death four days later was due to the rough handling he received.

Where was Pope Leo during all of this? At the inception of the struggle between Dioscoros and Flavian, the Pope studied the matter and decided in favor of Flavian. To him he addressed a letter dealing with the theological issue involved. Called the *Tome,* it set forth the principles of a solution to the dogmatic issue and is generally considered a masterpiece of dogmatic theology. As to Dioscoros' council, he was adamantly opposed but yielded to necessity and sent his legates.

When word finally reached Leo of the goings on at the Council of Ephesus, he was outraged. He dubbed Dioscoros' council a *latrocinium* or synod of robbers—a label that stuck to it. Leo then did his utmost to rally the Church against the heresy of Dioscoros and Eutyches. To Emperor Theodosius, Pope Leo wrote a strong letter asserting his power as successor of Peter to maintain the truth and calling on Theodosius to hold a general council to redress the injury inflicted on the Church's doctrine by the robber synod. The Pope had little success with the Emperor, who declared the question settled. But Leo was able to convince the Emperor's sister Pulcheria of the rightness of his cause.

She turned out to be a key personage. When Theodosius suffered a fatal fall from his horse, Pulcheria married his successor, Marcian, and the two reversed the policy of Theodosius. They decided to call another council to settle the issue along the lines of Leo's *Tome.* Leo, however, now had second thoughts about the wisdom of having a council. He felt that his *Tome*—which was read and applauded widely throughout the Church—could settle the dogmatic issue by itself given sufficient time for its dissemination, while he saw grave risks to the papal primacy if a council were held. It might tempt the patriarch of Constantinople—in league with Marcian—to arrogate increased ecclesiastical power to himself and so weaken papal primacy. But Leo was overruled by Marcian.

In obedience to the Emperor then, more than five hundred bishops—the largest such gathering in history so far—met at Chalcedon across the Bosphorus from the capital on October 8, 451. They filled the magnificent basilica of St. Euphemia under the watchful eyes of eighteen imperial commissioners. The only Western bishops, besides two refugees from Africa, were the papal legates, who were given the seats of honor at the left of the commissioners. At the insistence of the papal legates who presided, Dioscoros was seated among the accused. The Acts of Flavian's Synod of Constantinople were read, followed by the Acts of the "robber synod." The atmosphere was one of extreme tension—cheers, imprecations, and groans burst out spontaneously as the proceedings unfolded. The trial of Dioscoros lasted well into the night, and candles had to be brought in. As evidence piled up of the unseemly and even violent methods used by Dioscoros to gain his triumph at Ephesus, his supporters gradually deserted him until he was left with only twelve bishops. Sentence of deposition was finally leveled against him by the papal legates: "Leo, through us and the present holy Synod, together with St. Peter . . . deprives him of his episcopal office and of all sacerdotal dignity."[3] When Leo's *Tome* was read to them, they cried: "This is the faith of the Fathers and of the Apostles. This we all believe. Peter has spoken through Leo; thus Cyril taught; Leo and Cyril teach the same; anathema to him who teaches otherwise. . . ."

The bishops would have left matters rest there, having declared that orthodoxy on the question was adequately expressed in the creeds of Nicaea and Constantinople, the letters of Cyril, and the *Tome* of Leo. But the imperial commissioners wanted to close all loopholes and make an airtight definition that would secure the religious unity of the Empire. Or perhaps they feared that a simple ratification of Leo's *Tome* by the assembly would ascribe too much importance to papal authority. In any case, at their insistence a committee went to work to draft a definition. Their first proposal pleased the majority but not the papal legates, who demanded a definition more in harmony with Leo's *Tome;* in particular, they wanted Leo's phrase "two natures" to replace the one used, "out of two natures." But the majority refused to budge until finally the imperial commissioners confronted them with the pointed question: "Whom do you follow—Leo, or Dioscoros, who accepts 'out of two natures' but rejects [Leo's] 'two natures'?" "As Leo believes, so do we . . . ," they replied. "Then you must follow Leo in stating that 'two natures are united without change, and without division, and without confusion in Christ.' " So they went back to work and drew up a new formulary, which secured the adhesion of the whole council. Faithfully reflecting the thought of Leo, it says:

> One and the same Christ, Son, Lord, Only-begotten, made known in two natures [which exist] without confusion, without change, without division, without separation; the difference of the natures having been in no wise taken away by reason of the union, but rather

[3] Mansi, VI, 1048, quoted in R. V. Sellers, *The Council of Chalcedon* (London: S.P.C.K., 1961), p. 112.

the properties of each being preserved, and [both] concurring into one Person *(prosopon)* and one *hypostasis*—not parted or divided into two Persons *(prosopa)* but one and the same Son and Only-begotten, the divine Logos, the Lord Jesus Christ . . .[4]

Leo had won a great dogmatic victory, but he failed to unite Christendom. Two schisms occurred: The Nestorians rejected the formula of Chalcedon because they felt it confused the relations of the divine persons within the Trinity, the Monophysites denied that Christ's humanity was consubstantial with ours. Even the Byzantines themselves for a long time tended to interpret Chalcedon in a pro-Monophysite sense—mainly for political reasons.

Moreover, Leo's forebodings about the Council being used to set up Constantinople as a rival to Rome proved prophetic. Against the vehement protests of the papal legates, the Council passed Canon 28. It states:

Following in all things the decision of the holy Fathers and acknowledging the canon, which has just been read, of the One Hundred and Fifty Bishops beloved-of-God (who assembled in the Imperial city of Constantinople, which is New Rome, in the time of the Emperor Theodosius of happy memory), we also do enact and decree the same things concerning the privileges of the most holy Church of Constantinople, which is New Rome. For the Fathers rightly granted privileges to the throne of Old Rome, because it was the imperial city. And the One Hundred and Fifty most religious bishops, actuated by the same consideration, gave equal privileges to the most holy throne of New Rome, justly judging that the city which is honoured with the Sovereignty and the Senate, and enjoys equal privileges with the old imperial Rome, should in ecclesiastical matters also be magnified as she is, and rank next after her; so that in the Pontic, the Asian, and the Thracian Dioceses, the metropolitans only and such bishops also of the Dioceses aforesaid as are among the barbarians, should be ordained by the aforesaid most holy throne of the most holy Church of Constantinople; every metropolitan of the aforesaid dioceses, together with the bishops of his province, ordaining his own provincial bishops, as has been declared

---

[4] Sellers, *Council of Chalcedon*, p. 211.

by the divine canons; but that, as has been above said, the metropolitans of the aforesaid Dioceses should be ordained by the archbishop of Constantinople, after the proper elections have been held according to custom and have been reported to him.[5]

Pope Leo objected and refused to accept this canon. There were several reasons for his stand: First, Canon 3 of the Council of Constantinople (referred to at the beginning of Canon 28) had granted only an honorary precedence to the see of Constantinople; now Canon 28 of Chalcedon raised Constantinople to a position of such magnitude that when supported by the Emperors it might severely threaten the unity of the Church and endanger Rome's primacy. Second, Canon 28 was based exclusively on the principle of political accommodation; no reference was made to apostolicity, which by this time was generally accepted in the West as the "decisive factor in Church leadership."[6]

As a result Pope Leo rejected the canon as a defiance of ancient custom and defended the right of Alexandria to second place in the Church, as the see founded by St. Mark.

The dispute at bottom, as we can now see with the aid of much historical hindsight, was not only over two principles of Church organization but also a confusion over two types of primacy: directional vs. administrative. The directional primacy—the right to be the final court of appeal in matters of faith affecting the essential doctrinal unity of the Church—surely belonged to Rome as the apostolic see and the definitive see of Peter. But there was also need for the other type: a patriarchal or administrative primacy whereby certain sees because of their political and social importance had acquired the right to make final decisions in disciplinary questions affecting the churches within their sphere of influence so as to maintain the basic degree of liturgical and disciplinary uniformity. Like Alexandria and Antioch earlier, Constantinople had certainly won the right to such a primacy.

The inability of Rome and Constantinople to make such a distinction was a tragic matter. Even though things were temporarily patched up, with Leo accepting a conciliatory letter from the patriarch of Constantinople, who agreed not to officially promulgate Canon 28, the misunderstanding contin-

[5] *Cambridge Medieval History* (New York: Macmillan, 1936), vol. 1, pp. 510–11.
[6] F. Dvornik, *The Idea of Apostolicity in Byzantium and the Legend of the Apostle Andrew* (Cambridge, Mass.: Harvard University Press, 1958), p. 93.

ued to bedevil the relations between the two sees and finally played a major role in the final schism of the Middle Ages.

But Leo had done his work well for the future of Western Christendom. He left behind a papacy that was now fully conscious of its prerogatives and equipped with the prestige to carry them out; a papacy that was ready, when the empire totally collapsed, to embark on one of its greatest historic missions: taming the barbarians and salvaging for humanity the elements of the ancient civilization.

Part Two

THE MAKING OF CHRISTENDOM

A.D. 600–1300

Chapter 10

THE POPES AND FRANKS
JOIN FORCES TO CREATE A
NEW UNITY: CHRISTENDOM

There is no better illustration of the perennial vitality of the papacy than its behavior in the crisis engendered by the fall of Rome. Confronted by the collapse of the imperial administration in the West, the disintegration of the Roman social order, and its attendant chronic insecurity, the Popes refused to despair. Turning their backs on the past and all nostalgic yearnings for a golden age, they accepted the fact that the barbarians had come to stay. Their new mission was now obvious: to convert the barbarians and incorporate them into a peaceful Christian society. It was to be a labor of centuries, but eventually their persevering efforts were rewarded. Slowly their vision of the future began to take shape, and out of the wreckage of the Roman Empire in the West a new social order came into being: Christendom. It was preeminently the creation of the Popes, but also owed much to the anonymous labors of the peaceful monks and the political prowess of the bellicose Franks. Gregory the Great laid its foundation at the end of the sixth century, but its full realization only occurred when Charlemagne accepted a crown from the hands of Pope Leo III on Christmas Day in the year 800.

Before describing in detail the work of papacy, monks, and Franks in the construction of Christendom, let us first review the main stages in the downfall of the Roman Empire in the West. The Empire's frontiers were finalized in the second century: to the North, the wall of Hadrian in Britain (on a line from Tyne to Solway) and the Rhine and Danube rivers; to the East, the Euphrates River in Syria; to the South, the natural frontiers of the Sahara Desert and the mountains of interior Africa; and to the West, the Atlantic Ocean. Constant pressure was put on the barriers in the North by the various restless Germanic tribes: the Franks on the lower Rhine, the Alemanni in southern Germany, the Vandals in Silesia, and the Visigoths in the Ukraine and southern Russia. Surging forward in wave after wave, they forced Rome to consume a large part of her economic resources in defense of her sagging walls.

It was finally the Ostrogoths who struck the fatal blow. Frightened by the hordes of Huns pouring out of the steppes of Russia, they stampeded and sought refuge behind the walls of the Empire. The Romans were not strong enough to hold them back. Once they were inside, hostility soon flared between the hosts and their unwelcome guests. A full-scale war ensued, and at Hadrianople in 378 the Goths massacred the imperial forces and left the Emperor, Valens, dead on the battlefield. His death foreshadowed the doom of the Empire in the West.

Henceforth the barbarian tribes were free to move within the imperial boundaries and strike almost at will. The Vandals and Suevi crossed the Rhine in 406, and Rome itself was sacked by Alaric in 410. His successor established a Gothic kingdom in southern Gaul; the Vandals conquered Africa; while the Franks, the Burgundians, and the Alemanni occupied the west bank of the Rhine and northern and central Gaul. Western Europe became a mosaic of Germanic kingdoms.

With the coming of these barbarians the Catholic Church fell on evil days, since the Goths and Vandals were Arians, having been converted by the Arian Bishop Ulfilas (d. 383). Wherever they took over, they persecuted the Catholics. Huneric, the Vandal ruler in Africa in 484, summoned the 466 Catholic bishops to a meeting with their Arian colleagues; at its conclusion his edict was read, which prohibited all assemblies of Catholics, confiscated their churches, and drove the bishops out of their sees. The Visigoths in Spain also severely restricted the freedom of the subjugated Gallo-Roman populace. Everywhere, in fact, the Gallo-Roman Catholic populace was under the sway of persecuting Arian conquerors.

But Providence smiled on the Church in the person of Clovis, ruler of the Salian Franks. This belligerent prince had defeated the Roman ruler of northern Gaul in 486 and had established himself as the monarch of all Gallic territory north of the Loire River. A heathen rather than an Arian and by that very fact more acceptable to the Catholics of Gaul, he married a Catholic princess, Clotilda, and finally embraced the faith himself in 496, when he and three thousand of his men were baptized. It is difficult to exaggerate the importance of this baptism, for the Franks would "found the pontifical state, raise the Pope to royal rank, and by establishing the Carolingian empire, constitute the Christianity of the Middle Ages."[1]

Clovis was an insatiable warrior. By a series of conquests he was able to push his frontiers to the Alps, the Pyrenees, and the Rhine. His success was due not only to his military prowess but also to the Catholic bishops of many towns, who even before his baptism opened their gates to him, since he was preferable to their Arian rulers.

In 511, shortly before his death, Clovis called a Council of the Gallic bishops at Orléans. He could take satisfaction in the completion of his life's work: Barbarians and Gallo-Romans were now united in one faith and one kingdom. With the help of the bishops he had subjugated nearly the whole of Gaul, except the kingdoms of Burgundy, Provence, and Septimania. His codification of law, the *Law of the Salian Franks,* reflected his wisdom and the dominant influence of the Catholic bishops.

In the meantime, however, the Church and the papacy still suffered under the alien grip of the Arian Ostrogoths who had conquered Italy. A grand effort was made by Justinian, the ruler of the still independent Eastern Roman Empire, to reconquer the western territories. He began with Africa, where his great general, Belisarius, quickly overthrew the Vandals and liberated the Catholics. Turning toward Italy, he crossed over to Sicily in 535 and soon had Rome under his control. But the Ostrogoths showed more fire and determination than the Vandals, and under their leader, Totila (d. 552), rallied and fought tenaciously for twenty years. By the time they were subdued, pillage, rapine, and famine had devastated the peninsula. It was the beginning of the Dark Ages for Rome and Italy.

Catastrophe struck again when in 568 the Lombards, another migrating Germanic tribe, crossed the Alps, seized Milan, and forced the archbishop to flee. They terrorized the populace and occupied northern Italy and gradually advanced southward, where they unsuccessfully besieged Rome in 579. It was the final blow for the declining Roman civilization. No wonder many thought the end of the world was at hand.

Against this dark background there came to the throne of St. Peter one

[1] J. Wand, *A History of the Early Church,* 4th ed. (London: Methuen, 1963), p. 263.

of its noblest occupants, later known as St. Gregory the Great (d. 604). A man of true genius, profound spirituality, and unflagging energy, he confirmed and defined long-standing trends and gave the papacy a direction it was to follow throughout the Middle Ages.

Gregory was born and reared in Rome with every possible advantage of birth and wealth. Rising to Rome's highest post, prefect of the city, he suddenly abandoned the world altogether, spent his vast wealth in founding monasteries, and converted his own palatial home into a monastery, where he lived a life of asceticism and study. He left his seclusion to serve as papal envoy to Constantinople, but after six years returned home to his monastery. He was forced into public life again, however, when the papal office fell vacant in 590 and the people of Rome clamored for him to become Pope.

It was Gregory, as we said, who laid the foundations of medieval Christendom. To judge the truth of this statement we have only to consider the lasting influence of his four historic achievements: He established the Popes as de facto rulers of central Italy; he strengthened the papal primacy over the churches of the West; he immensely furthered the work of converting the bar-

The Baptism of Clovis at Rheims on December 25, 496 (1837). François-Louis Dejuinne (1786–1844). Châteaux de Versailles et de Trianon, Versailles, France.   © *Réunion des Músees Nationaux/Art Resource, New York.*

barians and initiated the conversion of the Anglo-Saxons; and he left behind a corpus of theological and spiritual writings that had a tremendous influence on the shaping of medieval thought. Let us consider them in order.

In view of the inability of the Eastern Roman Empire to stop the pillaging Lombards in the West, Gregory assumed the responsibility of feeding the Roman populace, of repairing the walls, and of mustering the troops. Several times by diplomatic maneuvers, he saved Rome from sack by the Lombards, and he finally led the way in bringing about a general peace. In this way in default of any strong leadership from the civil authorities, he became the ruler of central Italy and prepared the way for papal control of the papal states.

While recognizing the rights of the other patriarchates—Antioch, Constantinople, Alexandria, and Jerusalem—he vigorously intervened in the life of the other churches of his own Western patriarchate. In accordance with his dictum, "I know of no bishop who is not subject to the Apostolic See when fault has been committed," he corresponded incessantly with bishops and monks, advising them about their administrations and the enforcement of discipline. And though churches like those of Gaul and Spain still maintained a practical independence, he accustomed them by the sheer weight of his moral and spiritual authority to look to Rome for special guidance.

A delightful tale relates how Gregory first conceived the mission to the Angles and Saxons. While walking near the Roman slave market, he spotted some youthful Angles for sale and noted sadly that such bright-looking lads should be slaves of darkness. "When told they were Angli" he replied that they had the faces of *angeli* (angels) and should be coheirs with them in heaven. They were from Deira? Again he responded with a pun: They must be saved from *de ira Dei* (the wrath of God). Their King was named "Aelle?" "Alleluia," Gregory exclaimed, should be chanted in the land!

Later, as Pope, he personally commissioned a Roman monk named Augustine to convert the Angles and Saxons and was elated at the speedy conversion of King Aethelbert of Kent. The Pope maintained a close relationship with the new Church—a prototype of the relationship that for nearly a thousand years remained a marked characteristic of the English Church. Later, when missionaries such as the great Boniface (d. 754) went in their turn from England to convert inner Germany, they worked in a spirit of filial submission to Rome. In consequence, the whole of Western Europe was brought into a close relationship with Rome.

Gregory was also able to link the Spanish Church more closely with

Letter of St. Gregory. French, 1150–1200. Bibliothèque Nationale, Paris (ms. Lat. 2287, fol. lv). © *Giraudon/Art Resource, New York.*

Rome. Shortly before his accession to the papal throne, Recared, the Visigothic King, abjured Arianism after hearing a debate between the Arian and Catholic bishops and embraced the Catholic faith at a great synod at Toledo in 589. A letter announcing the historic event reached the new Pope shortly after his coronation, and Gregory sent Recared relics of the chains of St. Peter. Gregory also prepared the way for the eventual conversion of the Lombards by his diplomacy and his close friendship with Theodolinda, the Queen of two successive Lombard rulers, Authari and Agilulf.

So Gregory set the papacy and the Church on a path that was to make it the predominant force in shaping a new civilization out of the ruins of the old—a new political and cultural and social unity called Europe. In alliance with the Franks and aided by the monks, his successors would continue—with some notable interruptions—his effort in laying the groundwork for a distinctively Christian political and social order.

After the papacy, the most important spiritual force in the making of Catholic Europe were the monks. The role of the monks is directly related to the breakdown of city life that accompanied the dissolution of the Empire. Now an agrarian economy and rural society prevailed, providing a grave challenge to the Western Church since, unlike the Church in the Eastern Empire, it was still largely an urban religion, with little influence over the peasants in the countryside.

It was the monks who provided an ideal solution to the problem. Their monasteries, located in the countryside, proved to be very effective centers of the missionary activity among the heathen folk. This was the lesson provided by the life of Martin of Tours (d. 397), who was not only the founder of Gallic monasticism but also the greatest missionary to rural France.

The monastic movement had its biggest impact on the newly converted Celtic lands of the Far West, where it was introduced by St. Patrick (c. 461). The social unit here was the tribe and not the city, and so from the start the Church was organized along monastic rather than episcopal lines. Monasteries rather than episcopal cities became the normal centers of ecclesiastical life as well as great schools of learning. The leaders of Celtic Christianity were the famous abbots like St. Samson, St. Illtyd, St. Cadoc, St. Gildas, and St. David, or in some cases even abbesses.

These Irish monks were the leading missionaries of the age, and they carried their monastic ideal across the length and breadth of Europe in the sixth and seventh centuries: Luxeuil, founded by Columbanus around 590; Jumièges in France; Stavelot and Malmédy in Belgium; St. Gall in Switzerland; and Bobbio in Italy were all founded by Irish monks. They proved to be the indispensable means of Christianizing the peasants, whose life and work the monks shared. The monks cleared the forests and put back into cultivation much of the land desolated by the barbarians. But more important, the monks completely remolded the peasant culture in the spirit of the new religion. The sacred wells, sacred trees, and sacred stones were still reverenced, only now they were associated with Christian saints.

Up to this point the dominant kind of monasticism was the Irish type, as codified by Columbanus, which closely imitated its Egyptian prototype, with its emphasis on asceticism and the eremetical life. But its very success pointed up its defects: its lack of strong authority, its excessive rigor as to mortification, its failure to specify a balanced schedule. There was need for another type of rule more suited to the Western temperament. The man who provided it was St. Benedict, who founded the monastery of Monte Cassino around 520. His *Rule* reflects the Latin genius for organization. It quickly spread, be-

St. Patrick, Bishop of Ireland.
Giambattista Tiepolo
(1696–1770). Museo Civico,
Padua, Italy.   © *Cameraphoto/
Art Resource, New York.*

coming the universal form of Western monasticism. No single person, except
Gregory the Great, did more than Benedict to stabilize the barbarian peoples
and plant the Church solidly in their midst.

Benedictine monks brought Christianity to England (Augustine came
from Pope Gregory's Benedictine monastery, and the great English Benedictine abbeys—Ripon, Hexham, Wearmouth, and Jarrow—proved to be centers not only of missionary activity but also of a new vital Christian culture

St. Benedict. Hans Memling (1425/40–1494). Uffizi Gallery, Florence.   © *Scala/ Art Resource, New York.*

that arose in the years between 650 and 680. During the eighth century the Anglo-Saxon Benedictine monks were outstanding for their religion, scholarship, and literature amid the general state of decadence.

It was also Benedictine monks who proved to be the most powerful force for the papalization of the West. Intensely devoted to Rome and the papacy, they were the chief agents of the Popes in the ecclesiastical reforms of the eighth century. The most notable example was Winfrid (d. 754), later called St. Boniface, the "Apostle of Germany," founder of the medieval German Church. Sent by the Pope as his vicar and assisted by bands of Anglo-Saxon monks and nuns, he uprooted German heathenism and established abbeys and bishoprics.

Boniface was also instrumental in preparing the way for the alliance of the papacy and the Franks that was to be decisive for the future of Europe and the creation of Latin Christendom. The opportunity to do this was given him by the Frankish King, who invited him to reform the Frankish Church, which by this time had lapsed into a state of corruption. In a great series of councils between 742 and 747, Boniface led a successful effort to revive discipline and forge strong links between Rome and the Franks. This activity was consummated in 754, when the alliance of the papacy and the Frankish monarchs was sealed.

To understand how this happened, one must keep in mind the situation of the papacy since Gregory I. Gregory had become the actual ruler of Rome and the surrounding territory in a process that was duplicated in many cities in the barbarianized West. The bishop was often looked up to by the people as their natural leader, and he was able to devote the vast resources of the Church to the public welfare. This was especially true of Rome, whose supposed ruler was the distant exarch at Ravenna, the vicar of the Eastern Roman Emperor. But the actual ruler was the Pope, the exarch being only a shadowy, ineffectual figure compared to the bishop of Rome. By the time the Lombards occupied Ravenna in 751 and chased the exarch out, it really didn't matter, for the Pope had long since been recognized as the only effective ruler of non-Lombard Italy.

It was the Pope then who had to deal with the Lombard problem. Though converted to the Church, the Lombards still nurtured the ambition of making themselves masters of the whole Italian peninsula. This was something the Pope was determined not to allow. Since his own forces were obviously not adequate to stem the Lombard advance, the Pope turned to the Franks for help. This was a wise move for several reasons: First, Boniface's reform of the Frankish Church had greatly strengthened its bonds with Rome; second, the Franks lived at a distance and hence would not be, it was hoped, in a position to dominate the papacy; and finally, Pepin (d. 768), their ruler, had recently indebted himself to the Popes, having asked and received papal sanction for his seizure of the crown from the descendants of Clovis. The Pope's act strengthened the King's authority, and Pepin was grateful.

So with Rome at the mercy of the Lombards, Pope Stephen II, a Roman of noble blood, set out on a journey of unparalleled historical importance. He crossed the Alps in mid-October 753 and met the King at Ponthion, on Epiphany 754; the Frankish monarch dismounted and prostrated himself before the Pope and then took the bridle and led the papal horse forward. In the conference that followed, Pepin guaranteed the Pope's rule over a large portion of Italy, from Parma and Mantua to the borders of Apulia, including the former exarchate of Ravenna. In effect, he constitutionally established a dominion of the Pope that was recognized in public law and possessed of independent status. In turn the Pope anointed Pepin and his two sons, Charles and Carloman, and granted them the title "Patricians of the Romans."

"This was an epoch-making event, for it marked not only the foundation of the papal state which was to endure until 1870, but also the protectorate of the Carolingians in Italy and the beginning of their imperial mission as leaders and organizers of Western Christendom," historian Christopher Dawson has noted.[2] This donation of Pepin had to be ratified by force of arms when Aistulf, the Lombard leader, refused to recognize it. After subjugating Aistulf, Pepin took the keys to the liberated cities and placed them together with his written donation on the tomb of St. Peter.

On the eve of his death in 768, Pepin divided his realm between his two sons. When Carloman died in 771, Charles took over as sole ruler. As patrician or protector of the Romans he was soon called on to carry out his responsibilities. He had to march against Desiderius, the Lombard ruler who had attacked Rome. He crushed Desiderius and made himself King of the Lombards, though he never succeeded in completely mastering them. Their duchy of Benevento in the South was able to keep its independence. In that same year (773) he made a solemn entry into the Eternal City, embraced the Pope on the steps of St. Peter's, and renewed the donation of his father, confirming the Pope in his possession of the papal states. But Charles soon showed that he intended to act as the Pope's sovereign as well as his protector. He issued orders to the Pope and supervised the administration of the states.

His biographer, Einhard, described Charles as huge in stature, physically vigorous, a tender father, affable and popular with his subjects, a man of profound Christian conviction, and imbued with a strong sense of a God-given mission to unify the peoples of the West under the Christian banner.

With this in mind he engaged in countless military campaigns on all the frontiers of his empire, extending his rule over the larger part of Western Europe. In the Southwest he struck against the Arabs and fortified his frontier along the Pyrenees; in the Southeast he incorporated Bavaria into his kingdom, and by his defeat of the Avars he prepared the way for the Frankish colonization of present-day Austria and parts of Hungary. But his most important conquest was in the East. Here for thirty-two years he fought the heathen Saxon and, in spite of repeated setbacks, finally managed to subject them to the Christian faith and his own political authority. This meant that the

---

[2] *The Making of Europe* (London: Macmillan, 1932), p. 215.

Coronation of Charlemagne at St. Peter's in Rome by Pope Leo III. Miniature from *Grands Chroniques de France* (second half of fourteenth century). Musée Goya, Castres, France. © *Giraudon/Art Resource, New York.*

broad German plains as far as the Elbe were incorporated permanently into his realm. Then he rounded off these conquests with campaigns against the Slavs.

By the year 800 his realm stretched from the Atlantic to southern Italy, from the Pyrenees to the Elbe—virtually reconstituting the political unity of the Western Roman Empire. But his title was still "King of the Franks and Lombards and Patrician of the Romans." Would it not be fitting, some wondered, to call him "Emperor" also? The answer was given on the occasion of his visit to Rome in the year 800, where he had to investigate some grave accusations—adultery and perjury—leveled against the reigning Pope, Leo III (d. 816). While not subject to trial, the Pope was only able to clear himself by publicly swearing on the Gospels his innocence in the royal presence.

And so it happened that sometime later, on Christmas Day, Charles was present at Mass in St. Peter's when suddenly Leo set a crown on his head while the whole assembly roared out, "Hail to Charles the Augustus, crowned of God, the great and peace-bringing Emperor of the Romans."[3]

The wording of the acclamation should be noted: He was "crowned of God." The act was regarded as the will of God, who had acted through the

[3] Einhard, *The Life of Charlemagne* (Ann Arbor: University of Michigan Press, 1960), pp. 56–57.

Pope. This theocratic idea was to remain an essential mark of the new Empire, and it was therefore "Holy." Second, it referred to him as Emperor of the "Romans," showing that it was regarded as the continuation of the Roman Empire.

Charles himself, it seems, was taken by surprise and was even reluctant to accept the title at first. Perhaps he disliked the implication that the Pope could confer such a dignity; perhaps he feared trouble with the Eastern Emperor, who might see it as an act of rebellion. In any case, the deed was done. Charles was Emperor, and it was the Pope who had crowned him. The alliance of the Franks and papacy was gloriously consummated. Gregory, Benedict, and Boniface had not labored in vain. Christendom was now a reality. A new era began in the history of the West and of Rome.

Chapter 11

HILDEBRAND'S REVOLUTION
MAKES THE POPES SUPREME
IN CHRISTENDOM

The empire created by Charlemagne was thought of in an ideal way as a continuation of the Roman Empire, but it had neither Roman Law nor Roman legions, neither Rome as its capital nor the Senate. It was a shapeless and unorganized conglomeration, with no urban centers and little trade. Its officials were neither civic magistrates nor trained civil servants; it boasted only territorial magnates and tribal chieftains. But nevertheless, it embodied in its own way a great idea: the concept of Europe as a commonwealth of Christian peoples, a single society embracing a wide variety of peoples, organized in numerous states but bound together in a framework of mutual rights and duties and united in a common faith and a common moral and intellectual culture. To that commonwealth all Europeans felt they belonged even after the breakdown of Charlemagne's experiment and the rise of feudalism, and it was the same idea that inspired the formation of the new order that arose in the West in the eleventh century.[1]

This union of temporal and spiritual in one commonwealth meant in practice that this unique body had two heads. But who was the final authority—Pope or Emperor? Church or state? It was a question that would trouble minds and cause rivers of blood to flow when the great Pope Gregory VII,

[1] Description in Christopher Dawson, *The Making of Europe* (London: Macmillan, 1932), p. 203.

known as Hildebrand, in the mid-eleventh century revived the long-dormant claim that final authority rested with the Pope.

AS LONG AS Charlemagne ruled, there was no problem. No one dared to challenge his supremacy. He concerned himself with everything that affected the government of the Christian body—not excluding matters involving the life of the Church. It was not quite what the Popes had bargained for when they sealed the alliance with his father, Pepin.

Charlemagne's exercise of authority over the Church was, indeed, in opposition to the long-standing papal theory about the relation of the temporal to the spiritual authority. As formulated by Pope Gelasius (d. 496), this theory gave the Pope the right to direct and orientate the Christian commonwealth toward its final goal: eternal salvation. The Emperor's function was merely to promote the temporal welfare of its members and to protect their corporate union. This was symbolized in the coronation ceremony when the Pope placed a sword in the hands of the Emperor.

In line with this theory, the Popes after Charlemagne tried to assert their supreme authority over Christendom—and with some success—during the ninth century. Pope Stephen crowned Louis the Pious, Charlemagne's son and successor, in 816 at Rheims, and made it clear that the crown itself derived from the successor of Peter. Further strengthening of the papal position occurred in 823 when Louis's son Lothar I came to Rome to be crowned. Henceforth Rome was considered the only right and proper place for imperial coronations.

Succeeding Popes in the ninth century continued to assert this supremacy of the spiritual over the temporal power and maintained successfully—more or less—the right of the Church to intervene in the affairs of state. This theocratic view of the social order was made to prevail so that the state was no longer regarded as something distinct but was seen rather as an aspect of the Church.

The apex of this trend was reached with the pontificate of Nicholas I (858–67), who acted as the arbiter of Western Christendom. In crowning the Emperor and giving him the sword, he made clear the act's symbolic meaning: The Emperor's duty was to act as the protector of the Roman Church, the epitome of the whole Church. John VIII (d. 882) advanced the cause of papal supremacy by successfully asserting the right of the Popes not only to crown but also to choose the Emperor. This happened in 875, when he offered the crown to Charles the Bald. One indication of this general re-cognition of the Pope's supremacy over the temporal order is a change in ter-minology: His residence at the Lateran after 813 or so is no longer the "Patriarchate" but the "Sacred Palace of the Lateran."

But then the whole question of papal and imperial authority faded away as both Empire and papacy began to disintegrate. Constant division and quar-reling among the heirs of Charlemagne was a major factor in the breakdown of the Empire. Louis the Pious (d. 840), the weak and indecisive son of Charles, had four sons, who quarreled constantly among themselves and with their father over their respective shares of the Empire. Eventually the three surviving sons, Louis the German, Charles the Bald, and Lothar, divided the Empire into three separate parts, the Western (corresponding roughly to modern France) going to Charles, and the Eastern (corresponding roughly to modern Germany) going to Louis, with Lothar taking the elongated section in between.

For a brief moment the Empire was put back together again under Charles the Fat when both the East and the West Franks accepted his rule. But they rebelled and deposed him in 887. The Empire crumbled totally while Viking and Magyar invaders ran amok, ushering in a period of barbar-ian anarchy and carrying Europe into the age of feudalism.

It would be difficult, as Dawson says, to exaggerate the horror and con-fusion of the dark age that followed the breakdown of the Carolingian ex-periment. The Synod of Trosle recorded the despair of the bishops at the prospect of the complete ruin of Christian society:

> The cities are depopulated, the monasteries ruined and burned, the country reduced to solitude . . . as the first men lived without law or fear of God, abandoned to their passions, so now every man does what seems good in his own eyes, despising laws human and divine and the commands of the Church. The strong oppress the weak; the world is full of violence against the poor and of the plunder of eccle-siastical goods. . . . Men devour one another like the fishes in the sea.[2]

With the Empire in decay, its sister institution, the papacy, also slid slowly into the abyss. It became a slave to local Roman factions and the vic-

[2] Dawson, *Making of Europe,* pp. 266–67.

tim of political intrigue, losing all moral and spiritual authority. It reached the nadir in the pontificate of John XII (d. 964), who ascended the throne at the age of eighteen and recalled by his dissolute style of life the age of the Roman Emperor Nero.

With such Popes on the seat of Peter, complete oblivion covered the once-exalted claims of the papacy to supreme authority over Christendom. And when the Empire revived in the tenth century and Christendom with it, it was the Emperors who were in a better position to exercise the supreme authority—both temporal and spiritual.

This revival of the Empire occurred in the Kingdom of the East Franks (the German segment) under a new dynasty of Kings. Feudalism had not made as much progress here as elsewhere, thanks to the strong cohesive tribal consciousness of the four German peoples—the Saxons, Bavarians, Swabians, and Franconians. Here language, law, and tribe occupied relatively defined and solid areas. This new Empire was considered a continuation of Charlemagne's, though, in fact, it was much smaller, since it did not include any French or Spanish territory. It was indeed predominantly German, though reaching into Italy—the first of Germany's three Reichs.

The origin of this new version of the Empire can be traced to Henry the duke of Saxony, but it was his son Otto the Great (d. 973) who consciously revived the tradition of Charlemagne by seeking the crown from the Pope. Otto's coronation took place February 2, 962, in St. Peter's Basilica, with Pope John XII presiding.

In reviving the Empire, Otto made great use of the Church, which he found to be the most effective force in the struggle against disorder. He regarded the bishops as his most suitable collaborators by reason of their education and their lack of children. This last fact was especially important, since one of the chief threats to monarchy in a feudal society was the practice of families getting control of land and regarding it as their own independent domain and thus creating a rival dynasty to the King. Unmarried bishops could not pass duchies or counties on to their sons. This meant that at the death of the bishop, the King was once more free to choose the man he preferred for the job as duke or count instead of seeing the position automatically pass to the son of the deceased. So wherever he could, he placed bishops in charge. His own brother, Bruno, the archbishop of Cologne, he installed as duke of Lotharingia.

For such a system to succeed it was necessary to have the cooperation of the Pope, who in spite of the papacy's degraded state was still recognized as the head of the Church. This is why Otto sought his crown from the Pope, confirmed the donations of Pepin and Charlemagne, and guaranteed the independence of the papal states.

But understandably, the previous claims of the papacy to supremacy over the temporal power were set aside, if not forgotten, in this new Saxon Empire. The future relationship of the Saxon Emperors with the Popes was, in fact, foreshadowed in the way Otto treated John XII. Within a year of the coronation, Otto had John deposed on the charge of treason and had a layman elected in his place. Otto ruled that in the future no Pope was to be consecrated until he had first taken an oath of allegiance to the Emperor. In the new Ottonian Empire the Popes, like the bishops, were to be the nominees and the lieutenants of the temporal sovereign. There followed over the next century a succession of Ottos and Henrys who carried on Otto's intimate union of Church and state—employing bishops as officials of the crown, making and unmaking Popes as they saw fit, but often at the same time showing remarkable zeal for the reform of the Church.

Henry III (1039–56), the most powerful of the Emperors, was the preeminent example of this approach. A royal theocrat who often dressed in the robes of a biblical high priest, ornamented with apocalyptic and zodiacal emblems to symbolize his regal-sacerdotal role, he believed himself appointed by God to take care of all the interests of his people. He chose bishops and Popes, making sure in each case that the candidate was fit for the office. When Benedict IX (1032–45) was chased out of Rome by an anti-Pope who in turn was replaced by the virtuous archpriest, John Gratian, Henry intervened, and in synods held at Sutri and Rome deposed all three men. And characteristically, the Popes he subsequently installed—Clement II (d. 1047), Damasus II (1048), Leo IX (1054), and Victor II (d. 1057)—were men of the highest caliber.

This dominance over the Church by the lay power was true not only in Germany—everywhere in Europe the feudal potentates were applying more or less the same kind of system, using the Church as they saw fit. The old canon law that required that a bishop be elected by clergy and people was completely forgotten. Actual control over the appointment was seized by the King and his great vassals. A ceremony called lay investiture reflected this fact: The bishop-to-be knelt before the lord, rendered him homage and fealty, and received from him his staff and ring. The land and attached jurisdiction also conferred on him at the same time were regarded as a fief whose feudal obligations took precedence over ecclesiastical ones. The whole transaction was tainted with simony besides, since the new bishop ordinarily paid a heavy fee for his promotion. Moreover, this simony—commerce in spiritual goods— was rife throughout the whole Church. The parish priest too was subject to laymen by the proprietary system of ownership whereby laymen owned the Church property and hired the priests they pleased. This control by laymen was in obvious contradiction with the ancient canon law and tradition of the Church and seemed to many to be a violation of its intrinsic liberty and very nature.

So as spiritual energy began to flow through the Church again—as in the great monasteries reformed by Cluny, the influential Burgundian monastery founded in 910—it would be only a matter of time before Churchmen came forward who were unafraid of asking this portentous question: How can laymen hold supreme authority over the body that Christ had committed to his apostles and their successors, the bishops? The very reform of the papacy that Henry III ironically enough did so much to advance finally brought men to the fore who undermined his system by daring to ask this question. Outstanding among them was Cardinal Humbert (d. 1061), whose *Libri adversus simonaicos*—the first frontal attack on the whole position of laymen within the Church—denounced the proprietary Church system and lay investiture as twin manifestations of the same evil: perversion of proper order. The principle of right order in the Church, he argued, demanded that laymen be obedient to the clergy. Bishops must first be elected by the clergy, then acclaimed by the people; no longer should they be invested with the insignia of their office by laymen. Rather, after election, they should be examined and then consecrated by the metropolitan and the neighboring bishops.

But he went even further, reviving the ancient doctrine of Pope Gelasius in asserting not only that the laymen must obey the priest inside the Church, but that even outside, in the temporal order, they are subject to the spiritual authority of the hierarchy. This conclusion Humbert drew by rigorous logic from his basic premise: the unitary nature of society. Since Church and State actually form one body, Christendom—whose animating principle is the faith—it can be directed to its final goal, eternal salvation, only by the priesthood. Therefore, whenever the spiritual and temporal come into conflict—as often they must—the spiritual authority must have the final word.

It was a bold stroke indeed—nothing less than a claim for the Pope of total sovereignty over the world, and a program for revolutionizing the whole feudal social economic and political order as it had developed since Otto the Great.

But before anyone could even dream of carrying it out, the papacy itself had to be liberated from the iron grip of the Emperor. The chance occurred when Henry III died in 1056, leaving behind only his six-year-old son, Henry IV, while Pope Victor died the very next year. The reform party in the Curia seized this golden opportunity by electing one of their own, Stephen IX; when he soon died, they elected, in spite of the machinations of the Roman nobles, another reform-minded Churchman, Nicholas II (d. 1061). The way was now clear for the epoch-making decree of 1059, which formally excluded the Emperor and the riotous Roman nobles from a part in papal elections. Henceforth only the cardinals were to elect the Pope, although some type of confirmation was allowed to the Emperor. The decree was upheld in its crucial trial of strength in 1061 at the death of Nicholas. In the teeth of violent opposition from the Roman nobles, the cardinals elected another reformer, Anselm of Lucca—Alexander II—who in order to mount his throne had to overcome the combined forces of the Roman nobles, Lombard bishops, and imperial magnates.

But it was only with the election of Hildebrand, Gregory VII, in 1073 that a man arrived on the scene with willpower colossal enough to put Humbert's theory into practice and assert papal supremacy in a thorough fashion. Hildebrand's physical and mental qualities were unexceptional: Small in stature, weak in voice, he was only moderately learned, but he had the fiery temperament of an Old Testament prophet and drew men to him by the vigor of his imagination, the bright keenness of his eyes, and his tremendous passion for righteousness. As his famous *Dictatus papae* (1075) shows, he was committed to an unqualified view of papal authority: All souls must obey his definitions of right and wrong; he had an unlimited power of excommunication and absolution; God alone could be his judge. In accordance with Gelasian theory, he claimed the right to punish and even depose disobedient rulers, for the papacy was to the Empire as the sun to the moon.

As the new Pope assumed command, he found a somewhat encouraging situation; under the reinvigorated papacy, the reform movement had made progress. The papacy had vindicated the independence of its own elections, gained recognition of its authority over all archbishops and bishops, and was beginning to recover its rule over the papal states. But there were many problems. The clergy stoutly resisted the papal decrees against simony and clerical marriage, while the arrogant and ill-disciplined young Henry IV showed little sympathy with the idea of reform and was obviously bent on keeping royal control over episcopal nominations.

Things began well, however, in Gregory's relations with the Emperor. A deadlock over an episcopal appointment to Milan was broken when Henry yielded to the papal will. It seemed a good omen, and Gregory joyfully entertained a magnificent dream of a united Empire and papacy working together in harmony for the good of souls, with neither infringing on the other's proper sphere of power. But Henry's compliance was feigned, due only to pressure from internal troubles in Germany. He was waiting for these to clear up before he showed his real intention of subordinating the Pope.

The issue that forced a showdown was the system of lay investiture or lay control over episcopal appointments which, as we have seen, the reformers considered the root of evil in the Church. They wanted instead a return to free elections, which they believed would give the Church personnel equal to the tasks of reform. And a decree against lay investiture was passed by Gregory's synod in 1075. But Henry was not about to give up his control over his bishops. If he and other rulers of the time could not control the clerical landowners whose fiefs were scattered across their domains, their whole civil administration would be disrupted. And so in deliberate defiance of the decree, he invested his own choice for archbishop of Milan, a certain Tedald.

A momentous decision now had to be faced: Was the Pope really supreme on earth? Gregory was not the kind of man to sidestep. He sent Henry an ultimatum: Either respect the investiture decree or face excommunication and possible deposition. It reached the Emperor while he was still fresh from a victory over the rebellious Saxons and in no mood to submit. Gathering his puppet bishops around him in a Council at Worms, he pronounced scathing judgment upon "Hildebrand, at present not Pope but false monk," and denounced him for daring to threaten him with deposition, "as if the kingdom and the empire were in thine and not in God's hand!" And he cried out, "Descend and relinquish the apostolic chair which thou hast usurped. . . . Descend, descend, to be damned throughout the ages."[3]

This insolent decree was read by the Pope to a hastily assembled synod of

[3] *Readings in Church History,* ed. C. Barry, O.S.B. (Westminster, Md.: Newman Press, 1960), I, pp. 244–45.

bishops, who reacted with fury. Calling on St. Peter, Gregory then proceeded to excommunicate Henry and his accomplice bishops and declared Henry deposed.

Events then moved swiftly to a climax. The papal ban struck Henry with devastating effect. His supporters melted away, and his enemies used it to rally against him. A diet at Tribur on October 10, 1076, gave Henry until February 22, 1077, to obtain absolution and invited the Pope to preside at a German council to determine the Emperor's worthiness to reign. In desperation Henry acted with singular resolution. Taking only a few supporters, his wife, and his infant son, he braved the wintry snow and ice of the nearly impassable Alps, and in January 1077 reached the castle of Countess Mathilda at Canossa, where the Pope had stopped on his way to Germany. There, garbed in penitential rags, Henry stood barefoot in the snow-filled courtyard for three days begging absolution from the Pontiff. Gregory searched his soul in

Charles V at the attack on Tunis and Pope Gregory VII pardoning the Holy Roman Emperor Henry IV (1056–1106) at Canossa in the presence of Countess Mathilda and Abbot Hugh of Cluny on January 21, 1077. Sala Regia, Vatican Palace, Vatican.
© Scala/Art Resource, New York.

an effort to escape an awful dilemma. His political sense told him not to trust the fallen monarch, not to let the German princes down, and not to forfeit the best advantage he had; but his conscience as a priest prevailed, and reluctantly he gave Henry absolution.

Henry's enemies were not deterred; they deposed him anyway and elected Rudolf, duke of Swabia, as Emperor. Then both parties appealed to the Pope to decide between the contenders. But Henry was unwilling to submit to a papal decision, and so Gregory proceeded to excommunicate him again and depose him as contumacious at a Lenten synod in 1080. And imprudently he went out on a limb, prophesying that Henry would be defeated or dead within a few months.

The prophecy boomeranged when Henry triumphed over Rudolf. Public opinion in Germany turned against the Pope, who now appeared to be the aggressor—having exceeded his powers in trying to dethrone the temporal head of Western Christendom. Henry, in consequence, could count on more support, and so once more in concert with his bishops he pronounced sentence of deposition against Gregory and put an anti-Pope in his place. Then Henry marched on Rome and besieged Gregory. The Roman people were unequal to the rigors of a long siege and, led by a majority of the cardinals, weakened in their loyalty to Gregory's cause until finally Henry was able to bribe them into handing over Rome. The Pope barely managed to escape into the castle of Sant'Angelo.

The next move came from the papal vassal, the Norman ruler of southern Italy, Robert Guiscard, who came to Gregory's rescue and drove Henry out. But in doing so, he reduced Rome to cinders and ashes. The infuriated populace blamed the destruction on Gregory, who had to seek refuge with Robert in Salerno. There, overwhelmed by a deep sense of failure and with the anti-Pope once more ensconced in Rome, Gregory breathed his last on May 25, 1085, uttering the words, "I have loved justice and hated iniquity; therefore I die in exile."

Gregory was dead, but his cause remained very much alive. His immediate successor was something of a neutral nonentity, but with the election of Urban II, in 1088, Gregory's legate to Germany in the critical years 1084–85 and like himself a Cluniac monk, the right man was found to continue the work. Urban was dedicated like Gregory to the task of emancipating the Church from lay control, but unlike Gregory, he was essentially moderate and pragmatic.

While Henry IV floundered around in Italy trapped by his enemies, deserted by his wife and son, and fated to die amid the wreckage of all his hopes, the papacy under Urban moved from success to success. Urban held a synod at Clermont in 1095, where he called the knights of Christendom to a crusade against the Moslems. With overwhelming enthusiasm, the lords of Europe rallied around the papal banner. It was a striking demonstration of the power the Pope now exerted over the minds and hearts of men—a moral authority that no Emperor or King could hope to rival.

Nevertheless, the question of lay investiture with its many thorny aspects was not easily solved. But finally various forms of compromise were worked out in the different countries of Europe. Three main points were agreed on: The bishop would henceforth be elected by the clergy, with a certain minimal participation of the laity—and in the presence of the monarch and therefore to some extent under his influence. The new bishop would no longer be invested with the spiritual insignia of his office—his ring and staff—by the secular ruler. He would be invested, however, by the temporal ruler with the symbols of his temporal authority and offer homage to him; in Germany this homage was to take place before consecration. The German version of this settlement was embodied in the Concordat of Worms (1122).

This compromise meant that the Emperor could still exercise great influence over the choice of bishops. The final victory of the papacy was not due simply to the logic of Hildebrand but owed much, if not more, to a shift in dynasties. When Henry IV's son, Henry V, died in 1125, he was succeeded by Lothar II of the Welf family, which had traditionally supported the Popes in the struggle with Henry. This coupled with the fact that Lothar needed the Church's help in securing his position enabled the Popes to gain control over the German bishops.

So Hildebrand's dream finally materialized—with more than a little help from the accidents of history. But the fact remained: There was now a new papacy symbolized by the right of the Popes to wear the imperial insignia, including the tiara, a conical-shaped headdress with a crown surrounding it. (Later this was changed to two crowns by Innocent III and to three by Boniface VIII.) The Pope was now indeed a world ruler and would dominate the life of Europe—both spiritual and temporal—for centuries.

Chapter 12

THE PAPAL MONARCHY
AT ITS ZENITH

After tracing the successful struggle of the Popes to assert their supremacy over the Emperors we now turn to a closely connected theme: The parallel development by which the Popes vindicated their long-standing claim to absolute sovereignty over the Church. This development has peculiar significance, since the Popes today still make basically the same claim to sovereignty over the Church, while their struggle with the Emperors has only historical interest.

PAPAL CLAIMS TO sovereignty over the Church can be traced back to the fourth century; there is little evidence of any such claim before then. During the first three centuries the organization of the Church developed along the lines of the Roman imperial administration. The churches located in the provincial capitals acquired metropolitan status, which involved a certain amount of jurisdiction over their sister churches, while some acquired suprametropolitan or primatial status. This structure allowed for graduated levels of autonomy; it stressed the collegiality of the bishops and their need to meet often in council to exercise their joint responsibility over the life of the Church. It is still the concept of Church order found in St. Augustine, for instance, who with his fellow African bishops resisted the efforts of Rome to encroach on their independence.

However, a much more centralized idea of Church structure was developed in Rome and given definitive theoretical form by Pope Leo the Great. It saw the Church as a pyramid, with its sides converging upon Rome as its apex—a system quite at odds with the African and Eastern conciliar concept. Thanks to many factors, Rome was able to organize the Western Church in accordance with its pyramidal conception. The Popes were so successful in concentrating authority in themselves that the ancient concept of collegiality of bishops was lost, and with it the whole idea of unity in plurality. The entire Church was identified with the local church of Rome; its liturgical and disciplinary customs were made normative for the entire Western Church. It is still today, in spite of Vatican II's revival of collegiality, the ruling curial model of Church authority.

Numerous historical forces converged to establish the Pope in a position of absolute control over the Western Church. Byzantine power over Italy faded away. This left a political vacuum filled by the bishop of Rome, who became the chief political authority in Italy. The papal alliance with the Carolingian monarchy unified the West politically and spiritually around Rome.

The African Church—the only Latin Church with a tradition of resisting Roman encroachments—disappeared under the Moslem deluge. The Anglo-Saxon missions, which were carried out under Roman leadership, tied the English Church closely to the apostolic see. Subsequent Anglo-Saxon missionaries to the Continent brought with them the same concept of a papalist Church and so effectively subordinated these other churches to Rome.

An indication of the great strides made by the papalist idea of Church authority by the ninth century is the organization under Charlemagne: New ecclesiastical provinces were set up and old ones restored by sole authority of the Holy See. In the early Church such matters were the work of the episcopate in council. Another sign of this advance of papal power is the conferring of the pallium, a band of white wool worn around the shoulder. What was originally a mere honorary ornament now becomes a sign of the authority of Rome over the metropolitan, who received it from the Pope at the time his election was confirmed. The whole ceremony conveyed the idea that the new bishop was a deputy of the Pope.

Various legends also made their contribution to the cause. One of these—the cult of Peter as the gatekeeper of heaven—appeared at this time. Brought to the Anglo-Saxons by Roman missionaries, it exerted a powerful influence over them and over their German converts. Another one that had great currency in the early Middle Ages attributed the actual foundation of the principal Western churches to the Roman See.

But most influential of all was the *Pseudo-Isidorian Decretals,* which were drawn up around 850 in the chancery of a Frankish bishop. This collection contained a clever mixture of forged and authentic papal and conciliar documents. It falsified the history of papal relations with the other churches by tracing papal authority over them back to the earliest period; Popes about whom we actually know nothing were pictured as vigorously exercising authority over the other churches. On such a spurious basis the *Pseudo-Isidorian Decretals* asserted the absolute and universal supremacy of the successor of Peter: The Pope is sovereign lawgiver whose consent is necessary for the validity of all conciliar decrees. He is likewise supreme judge—no bishop may be deposed without his intervention, and his court is the court of last appeal for all major cases.

Nicholas I (d. 867) utilized the *Decretals* in his effort to raise the papacy to the position of absolute control over the Church. In unprecedented fashion, he proceeded against the archbishops who were the chief opponents of his program, deposing the archbishops of Cologne and Trier and forcing the most powerful one of all, Hincmar of Rheims (d. 882) to yield in a dispute over the right of one of his suffragans to appeal to Rome. But this movement toward an absolute papal monarchy over the Church was arrested when the papacy was caught in the general breakdown of civilization occurring in the latter part of the ninth century. With the dissolution of the Empire, the papacy fell under the control of the Roman nobility and then of the German Emperors, as we have seen. Nicholas's type of papal sovereignty remained hardly a memory.

But a revival of this idea occurred with the pontificate of Leo IX (1048–54), a Church reformer whose broad experience in pastoral and diplomatic work, wide travels, and deep reading made the ideal person to raise the papacy once more to a position of leadership over the Church. He made a tour of the churches of Christendom, holding numerous councils that decreed that bishops must be elected by clergy and people and that excoriated the prevailing abuses—simony and clerical marriage. In this way he dramatized the authority and jurisdiction of the papacy and thus conferred the stamp of authenticity on what was for centuries only a theory of canon law. He reorganized the chancery in line with the increased activity of the Popes and brought into the Curia men of talent who were animated with the best ideas of the day. Succeeding Popes carried on in the spirit of Leo, greatly assisted by the election decree of 1059 that gave control over papal elections to the cardinals and enabled them to keep the reforming spirit alive in Rome.

The stage was thus set for the appearance of the fearless Hildebrand, who took over in 1073 with his exalted idea of papal monarchy. We have already seen his titanic duel with Henry IV over lay investiture. But of much more lasting significance was Gregory's successful assertion of absolute papal power over the Church. Drawing on such sources as ancient canon law as well as the forged *Pseudo-Isidorian Decretals,* Gregory molded a theory of papal monarchy that he trenchantly expressed in his *Dictatus papae:*

> [T]he pope can be judged by no one; the Roman church has never erred and never will err till the end of time; the Roman church was founded by Christ alone; the pope alone can depose and restore bishops; he alone can make new laws, set up new bishoprics, and divide old ones; he alone can translate bishops; he alone can call general councils and authorize canon law; he alone can revise his judgments; his legates, even though in inferior orders, have precedence over all bishops; an appeal to the papal courts inhibits judgment by all inferior courts; a duly ordained pope is undoubtedly made a saint by the merits of St. Peter.[1]

This theory of papal power, joined as it was with a claim to supremacy over society as a whole, has been called "one of the grandest, most integrated, and best-developed systems that has ever been devised for the conduct of human life."[2]

It all required an elaborate machinery that was gradually developed over the next several centuries; the chief instruments used were councils, legates, papal letters, and the Roman tribunals. In each of these departments we see a constant and amazing growth of activity during the following centuries. The Popes became the busiest men in Europe; their interventions reached down into the lowest strata of society.

This centralization, no doubt, met the needs of a world that still rested

[1] R. W. Southern, trans. and ed., *Western Society and the Church in the Middle Ages* (Hammondsworth, England: Penguin Books, 1970), p. 102.
[2] Ibid., p. 105.

precariously on the brink of anarchy. Parish priests could find in the papal court protection against eviction and the guarantee of a minimum income that could not be plundered easily. Both laymen and priests were subject to a discipline that was clear-cut and not too onerous, providing rules for all the main occasions of Christian life—they dealt with baptism, confirmation, confession, communion, penance, alms, usury, last wills and testaments, burials, graveyards, and clerical dress.

In fact, we can safely say that the papal monarchy succeeded only to the extent that it was accepted by large numbers of influential people. The religious orders, for instance, found in papal authority their strongest safeguard against the tyranny of the local bishop or local lord, while the clergy in general reaped substantial benefits from its exercise, including security for their property and immunity from secular jurisdiction.

The Popes at first did not claim the power to appoint the bishops. In fact, they fought the mighty battle over lay investiture to restore the right of election to the clergy and people. Their effort was to some degree a success: By the middle of the twelfth century there was general recognition of the right of the clergy to elect the bishop. However, the elections were often disputed, forcing the Pope to step in as arbiter. This could and often did turn into a long, drawn-out quarrel, with the Pope trying every means to get the rival parties to agree on a candidate before settling the matter by simply appointing a bishop on his own. And by the fourteenth century the Popes solved the problem by simply reserving to themselves the right to make all episcopal appointments—a very imperfect solution, however, since it once more involved the secular ruler, whose co-operation was needed in order to secure compliance with papal appointments.

The imposing papal monarchs of the twelfth century carried on in the Gregorian spirit, devoting themselves with exceptional energy to the task of supervising the spiritual well-being of Christendom. When they clashed with the secular princes they usually managed to come out on top. This was true, for instance, in the celebrated affair that pitted the outstanding administrator and canonist, Pope Alexander III (d. 1181), against Frederick Barbarossa, the most memorable of Emperors since Charlemagne and one of history's most famous reactionaries. When the Pope opposed his plan to subjugate Italy and suppress the liberty of the Lombard League towns, Barbarossa took Rome by storm and enthroned his own anti-Pope. But Alexander, in alliance with the Lombard towns and backed by the major European powers, dealt a crushing

Thomas Becket being
murdered in the cathedral.
Playfair Book of Hours, fol.
176. Victoria and Albert
Museum, London.
© *Victoria and Albert Museum,
London/Art Resource, New York.*

blow to Frederick at the Battle of Legnano (1176). The final act of the drama
took place in St. Mark's Square, Venice, where the two protagonists met for a
settlement and where Frederick, overcome by sentiments of reverence, threw
off his imperial mantle and knelt before the aged Pontiff, who with tears in
his eyes raised him and embraced him.

At the same time, another impressive victory of the papacy over the temporal power occurred in connection with the tragic case of Thomas Becket,
former chancellor and intimate friend of English King Henry II. As archbishop of Canterbury, Thomas showed himself fully committed to the Gregorian conception of the Church's authority and refused to barter away what he
regarded as essential prerogatives of the Church. Papal authority over the
Church was one of the issues at stake, inasmuch as Henry's *Constitutions of
Clarendon* (1164) tried to restore Church-state relations to their pre-Gregorian
days by severely limiting papal control over the English Church.

Thomas escaped Henry's wrath by fleeing to France in 1164. When he came back in 1170 he was armed with full powers from the Pope to impose censure on the King if he attempted to revive the *Constitutions.* Thomas's brutal murder in his cathedral at Canterbury in the late afternoon of December 29, 1170, by four of Henry's enraged barons is one of the best-reported events of medieval history. Confronting the archbishop, vested in mitre and cope to celebrate vespers, the barons smashed his skull with their swords, scattering his brains on the stone floor. Before the final blow struck, Thomas was able to murmur, "I accept death for the name of Jesus and his Church." The news of the crime spread quickly and provoked a spontaneous cry of horror throughout Europe in a situation comparable to President Kennedy's assassination in our own day. Henry saved his crown only by submitting to the papal envoys and swearing obedience to Alexander III and promising to abrogate all his infringements on the authority of the Church and the Pope.

At the time Becket was murdered, Lothario di Segni, an Italian of noble family, was only ten years old. He was destined to become the most powerful of medieval Popes—Innocent III. As a young theological student in Paris, di Segni crossed the Channel to see the actual spot of Becket's martyrdom; like Becket he was absolutely devoted to the Gregorian view of papal supremacy. Elected Pope himself in 1198 at the age of thirty-seven, he raised the papacy to its highest medieval level of spiritual and temporal authority.

A man of small stature but enormous talent, admired rather than loved, Innocent had one of the finest legal minds of the age, as is shown by his thousands of letters. They reflect a wide-ranging grasp of the Church's situation and a tremendous concern for its welfare. He advanced the concept of papal sovereignty by claiming that the temporal power itself was derived from the Pope, and he used the comparison of sun to moon to describe the relations between the spiritual and temporal authority. He was the first Pope to take the title Vicar of Christ. By his interventions in the political affairs of Europe he made himself the arbiter of its destiny, and while probably one of the most powerful rulers in its history, he was certainly one of the most intellectual.

A pressing political problem faced him immediately on his taking office: a dispute between two contenders for the imperial crown, Philip and Otto. Innocent's choice fell on Otto, who in return pledged his assistance in maintaining the independence of the papal states. When war broke out, Otto proved the weaker and was forced to seek refuge in England. But with the help of an assassin who eliminated Philip, Otto finally acceded to the throne.

Pope Innocent III. Thirteenth-century mosaic. Museo di Roma, Rome. © *Giraudon/ Art Resource, New York.*

Once crowned, however, Otto reneged on his promises and invaded the papal domain.

The Pope resorted to his ultimate weapons—excommunication and deposition—and then looked around again for another Emperor. This time he chose a youth of sixteen, grandson of Barbarossa, and his own ward—Frederick II, ruler of Sicily. Frederick solemnly swore to keep Sicily separate from the Empire, and in the Golden Bull of Eger (1213) granted the Pope immense authority over the Church in Germany, including the right to decide disputed episcopal elections. But it required another war to settle the issue between Otto and Frederick—England siding with Otto, and France with Frederick. The epochal Battle of Bouvines (1214) decided the question in favor of the papal standard-bearer, Frederick, who would one day out-Otto Otto in treachery toward the papacy.

Probably the greatest triumph of Innocent's spiritual sword was his victory over King John (d. 1216) of England after a quarrel that proved to be a memorable event of the King's reign and of some importance for world history because of its relation to the signing of the Magna Carta. John was a bad man—unbalanced, cruel, cynical, happiest in the company of fellow scoundrels who enjoyed his rodomontades in mockery of everything serious and sacred. Greedy and indolent, he was to die appropriately from gorging himself with peaches and new cider.

His trouble with Innocent began when in defiance of Canon Law requiring free elections, John tried to impose his own nominee as archbishop of Canterbury. Upon appeal, Innocent decided against John and proposed Stephen Langton for the office. Stephen was duly elected by the clergy, but John refused to allow him entry into England. The Pope, who all along had strictly adhered to Canon Law, had no other alternative but to place England under interdict: No religious services except baptisms and funerals were permitted. The interdict dragged on for nearly six years, while the religious life of England virtually ceased: churches boarded up; bells silent; and priests idle, many of them in exile as John, in retaliation, struck back hard by terrorizing the clergy and confiscating their property.

But Innocent finally brought John to his knees in 1213 when in alliance with Philip Augustus of France, he threatened an invasion of England. It was too much for John; he felt unsure of support from his subjects, whose loyalty had been severely strained by the interdict. He submitted abjectly, performed an act of homage, and placed England under feudal vassalage to the Pope.

But then a paradoxical switch occurred, a second act in the drama, placing the Pope and John together on one side and Stephen Langton, the archbishop, and the barons on the other. The latter revolted against certain abusive demands and tyrannical acts of the King, and with the advice and support of Langton decided to force a written guarantee of their rights from the King. A duel of wits and arms ensued. John took the cross, pleading a crusader's immunity and claiming the right to papal arbitration. But the barons finally forced him to sign the Great Charter or Magna Carta at Runnymede on June 15, 1215. It consecrated the principle of government by law rather than arbitrary despotism and so represents the beginning of the English Constitution.

It was all only a game for John, however. As soon as he could, he appealed to the Pope as his overlord and was able to have the Charter quashed by Innocent. The Pope was unaware of the actual situation, being preoccupied at the time with his ecumenical council and seeing only the legal aspects of the matter. He thought the Charter invalid because it was obtained by force by barons acting as judges in their own case. He excommunicated John's enemies and suspended Langton from office. However, when John died suddenly, most of the nation rallied around the young King, Henry, and the archbishop—reconciled with the Pope during a visit to Rome—came back to act as mediator, resolving the quarrel.

Another King who was forced to recognize Innocent's superior authority was Philip Augustus of France (1180–1223). Some strange physical aversion caused him to separate from his beautiful wife Ingeborg of Denmark on the very morrow of their wedding in 1193. In spite of failure to obtain an annulment, he began living openly with his mistress while making life as miserable as he could for Ingeborg. She refused to accept her fate and importuned the Pope to grant her justice. His predecessor only temporized—but not Innocent. He resolved to show that Kings too were subject to the moral law, and though he had important political reasons for desiring Philip's friendship, Innocent decided in view of the King's stubbornness to lay an interdict on France. It was only lifted when Philip submitted and acknowledged Ingeborg as his Queen. He still refused to treat her as his wife, however, and the whole affair dragged on for many years, the Pope adamantly refusing to grant a divorce. Finally, after twenty years of struggle, the King suddenly capitulated and restored Ingeborg to all her rights as wife and Queen.

As the chief spiritual authority in Christendom, the great legislator Popes like Innocent were concerned with the whole gamut of human behavior and tried to regulate in detail the life and status of each member of the Church. Their decrees were embodied in the Canon Law, which was the most civilized law of the age and vitally influenced the quality of medieval civilization. These papal laws often took the form of answers to particular queries by the bishops and were—in theory at least—binding on the whole Church. As one of the greatest of the legal geniuses who occupied the throne of Peter, Innocent made a substantial contribution to the mass of papal decretals that eventually were incorporated into Gregory IX's collection of *Decretals* (1234)—the first to have the force of universal law.

The legislative career of the Pope reached its climax at the Fourth Council of the Lateran, which he assembled in 1215—the most imposing gathering of the Middle Ages, with its four hundred or more bishops, eight hundred abbots and priors, and numerous ambassadors from all the kingdoms. In accordance with Innocent's constant effort to raise the standards of lay and clerical life, the Council made obligatory annual confession of serious sin and annual reception of the Eucharist. It prescribed the conditions for valid election of bishops, the qualifications for admission to the clergy, and even regulated such details of clerical life as style of dress and types of permissible recreation. Innocent also reorganized the papal Curia to cope with the constantly increasing demands made on it. Three main sections were established: The Chancery, dealing with records and bulls; the Camera, dealing with finances; and the Judiciary.

One instrument of papal control over society that originated at this time and that was viewed with much repugnance in later times was the Inquisition. And it is one of Innocent's less glorious titles to fame that he was the first Pope to apply force on a considerable scale to suppress religious opinions. The New Testament certainly contains no basis for a theory of persecution, but after the conversion of Constantine, the Roman Emperors began the policy of using force against heretics—sometimes even the death penalty. This tactic met with little opposition from the Fathers of the Church. Augustine, in fact, elaborated a whole theology of persecution but, in general, the use of fierce tortures or the death penalty was opposed. But from the middle of the twelfth century we see legal thought, both secular and ecclesiastical, going beyond this—even to sanctioning death as a possible punishment for obstinate heretics. The first such prescription is found in an edict of Peter of Aragon (1197). The chief influences that brought about the change were texts of the Old Testament uncritically and unhistorically interpreted; the great revival of Roman Law, which prescribed the death penalty for heresy, although it was rarely if ever used in Roman times; the fact that with the emergence of Christendom the Church had become an all-inclusive society comparable to the state and in its totality scarcely distinguishable from it, so that heretics were viewed as a menace to the social order.

Innocent first found force necessary in dealing with the Cathari, an antisocial sect whose members preached that the material universe was the creation and tool of Satan; hence they condemned the use of all things material, prohibited marriage, encouraged suicide, and in general stood for a morality that strangely combined asceticism and immorality. The movement found a favorable climate in southern France, and in many places even won over the majority of the populace. But until Innocent's time the Popes were too distracted by their conflicts with the Emperors to give it much attention. With his customary energy and decisiveness, Innocent on taking office immediately took action to stem the tide. His first plan was to use persuasion, and he sent the dynamic preacher Dominic (d. 1221) to France, but ten years of peaceful effort brought little improvement. Then in 1207 Innocent's legate Peter of Castelnau was brutally murdered at the instigation, it seems, of a suspected Catharist, Count Raymond of Toulouse. A need for different tactics seemed imperative. A crusade was proclaimed against these Albigenses, as they were sometimes called: Two big armies under Simon de Montfort converged on southwestern France, stormed the cities of Beziers and Carcassonne, and massacred their inhabitants. Finally, at the Battle of Muret, they decisively crushed the heretics.

It was in connection with this crusade that the papal system of Inquisition originated—a special tribunal appointed by the Popes and charged with ferreting out heretics. Until then the responsibility devolved on the local bishops. However, Innocent found it necessary in coping with the Albigensian threat to send out delegates who were entrusted with special powers that made them independent of the episcopal authority. In 1233 Gregory IX organized this *ad hoc* body into a system of permanent inquisitors, who were usually chosen from among the mendicant friars, Dominicans and Franciscans, men who were often marked by a high degree of courage, integrity, prudence, and zeal.

Though few of its members were the fanatics and sadists found in lurid anticlerical accounts of the Inquisition, still the system itself offers a disconcerting commentary on medieval standards of justice. Its victims were accused on the basis of anonymous denunciations; they were not allowed witnesses in their favor nor given counsel; the innocent as well as the guilty were often forced to confess by the use of brutal torture, which was definitively prescribed in the bull of Innocent IV of 1252, *Ad extirpanda.*

There were indeed questionable aspects. But we may say in general that the universal papal monarchy—which dated from Gregory VII and reached its zenith with Innocent III—was in many ways a remarkable success. In all the disorder of the times it represented a stable element and stood for ideas of order and righteousness. By its proclamation of the Truce of God and its ban on tournaments, it worked against feudal lawlessness, "while the example which it presented of a spiritual monarchy uniting the nations under its dominion was the very opposite of that anarchy which unrestrained feudalism produced in temporal affairs."[3] By their pre-eminent interest in the formulation and enforcement of law, these lawyer Popes contributed much to the fundamental order of medieval society and put the modern world very much in their debt.

[3] *The Cambridge Medieval History,* vol. 6 (New York: Cambridge University Press, 1936), p. 643.

Chapter 13

THE EASTERN SCHISM

From the time of the Council of Chalcedon (451) when Rome rejected its Canon 28, which granted great jurisdictional powers to Constantinople, relations between the two sees were marked by occasional episodes of high tension. Many diverse forces—political, social, cultural, and religious—were pulling the two sees apart. A complete rupture even occurred when the Patriarch accepted Emperor Zeno's *Henoticon* (482), which seemed to disavow the Chalcedonian definition regarding Christ; relations were only restored when Constantinople abandoned its position. The subsequent Monothelete controversy—over the question of Christ's unity of will—ended with the Roman view triumphant over Constantinople, but the papacy did not emerge from the affair completely unscathed: Pope Honorius was anathematized at the Third Council of Constantinople (680) as a heretic along with four Byzantine patriarchs. Then the Moslem seizure of the three patriarchates of Alexandria, Antioch, and Jerusalem and their isolation left the patriarch of Constantinople the unquestioned head of Eastern Christendom.

The Eastern Emperors' attempt to enforce a policy of iconoclasm (the abolition of all religious images) in the eighth century again brought conflict with the Popes. Moreover, the Emperor's refusal to send military assistance in 753 after an urgent appeal led Pope Stephen to turn instead to the Franks, inaugurating the policy that was to lead to Charlemagne's imperial coronation. Another schism did not occur, however, until the advent of Patriarch Photius (d. 895). It proved to be only temporary. But trouble broke out again at the time of Patriarch Cerularius (d. 1058), and this time schism permanently separated East from West.

THE PHOTIAN SCHISM can be traced to the year 858, when the Patriarch of Constantinople, Ignatius, was deposed by Emperor Michael III and replaced by Photius, much to the dismay of Pope Nicholas I (d. 867), who in spite of difficulties with Ignatius was still horrified at the apparent irregularities of his deposition. Nicholas sent legates to Constantinople who decided in favor of Photius. But when Photius indicated that he did not accept the Pope's supremacy, the Pope in turn refused to recognize him as Patriarch. The trouble was aggravated by the situation in the Balkans, where the Roman missionary Bishop Formosus collided with Byzantine emissaries over his attacks on Byzantine traditions regarding marriage of the clergy, the Lenten fast, and the Western addition of *Filioque* to the Creed. Photius took up his pen to denounce the enormities of the Romans to the other Eastern Patriarchs.

At this juncture Basil the Macedonian usurped the throne in 867, removed Photius, and restored Ignatius. A new Pope, Hadrian, sought a reconciliation, sending delegates to attend a council at Constantinople in 869. But the climate at the council did not favor a restoration of good relations. The members refused to endorse a statement brought by the legates declaring that the faith was kept inviolate by the Holy See, and they assigned the Church of Bulgaria to Constantinople in spite of Rome's claim over it.

Then Ignatius died and Basil reappointed Photius, who now proved eager to repair relations with Rome. Another council was held at Constantinople in 879 which annulled the acts of 869 and recognized the perfect orthodoxy of Rome. Even Bulgaria was handed back to Rome, although its King, Boris, refused to go along with this. So the episode ended with a complete reconciliation between the patriarchate and the papacy. Friends of Ignatius, however, hurried to Rome and spread false rumors, which developed into a legend of another excommunication of Photius.

The tenth century was one of relative peace between the two sees—a peace favored by the friendly political relations of the Popes who ruled Rome from 904 to 962 with the Byzantines, who once more had established their control over southern Italy. But the old issues had not been resolved; they merely were dormant. The revival of the Western Empire once more stirred them up. When Otto the Saxon in 962 revived the Empire, he assured the pre-eminence of German influence over Rome for the next century and therefore of the principles of reform that had orignated in the North. This also meant the permanent addition of *Filioque* to the Creed. This Latin term, interpolated into the early Creed, expressed the idea that the Holy Spirit proceeded from both the Father and the Son. This usage first occurred in Spain, probably at the Third Council of Toledo (589), and made its way to the Carolingian court, whence it was brought by German ecclesiastics to Rome. After some hesitation it was finally sung in Rome around 1000 and adopted as part of the official doctrine.

Its adoption was extremely offensive to the East. For the Westerners it was merely a refinement of an idea already contained in the Creed; but for the Easterners, whose history made them more sensitive to Trinitarian terminology, its addition upset the delicate balance of properties within the Trinity. Their understanding of the Trinity emphasized the omnipresent and pervasive nature of the Holy Spirit and would only allow them to say that the Holy Spirit descended *through* the Son, not *from* the Son.

Involved in the dispute was an even more basic issue, however: the nature of ecclesiastical and papal authority. The attitude of the Easterners toward papal authority and primacy was undefined and ambiguous. For them ecumenical councils were the one inspired doctrinal authority; to add to a creed issued by a council was to question the council's authority. Only another ecumenical council could amplify or explain the definition of a previous council. A term they might tolerate on purely speculative grounds meant a lapse into heresy if it were added unilaterally to the Creed by the Western churches. Nor could the pronouncement of a Pope change this.

But this did not yet mean an actual schism. In fact, the peoples of Christendom were in closer touch with each other at the beginning of the eleventh century than at any period since the coming of the barbarians. Pilgrims in large numbers headed East to Jerusalem, while the Moslems showed a friendly attitude. And as communications improved, there was some attempt to define more clearly the relations between the two sees. In 1024 Patriarch Eustathius, with the backing of Emperor Basil II, proposed a formula that allowed for the primacy of Rome but left Constantinople self-sufficient and autonomous. At first, it seems, the Pope agreed, but the Cluniac monks objected to this parceling out of the one, indivisible domain of St. Peter, and so the Pope withdrew his agreement. So Pope and Patriarch remained estranged. Political events were soon to considerably exacerbate matters.

The return of the Byzantines to power in southern Italy met with considerable resistance and periodic revolts. One of these took place in 1020 when an Apulian leader by the name of Melo took up arms against the Greek oppressors and sought help from some Norman knights who happened to be passing through on pilgrimage. The revolt failed, but the Normans stayed on and under the family of the Hauteville began a systematic conquest of the South. At first the Popes looked on with little regret at the Norman victories over the Byzantines, for though these conquerors were freebooters, they were Latin Catholics. But when the Normans began to threaten his own frontiers, Pope Leo (d. 1054) decided the time had come to form an alliance with the Byzantine Emperor to suppress them. However, a problem soon arose in regard to the territories that the Normans had already brought under Latin domination. The Pope had no intention of allowing them to revert to Byzantine rule nor to allow Greek ecclesiastical usages to be restored. The whole trend in Rome at this time of the reformed papacy was toward conformity and strict discipline.

At the time the Patriarch in Constantinople was Michael Cerularius, who had ascended the throne in 1043. He was a former civil servant with all the limitations that implied, possessing very little of the subtlety and wit or theological culture of a Photius, arrogant, ambitious, and immensely popular with the people. He also had a rather low opinion of the papacy, not being aware of the changes brought about in Rome by recent reforms. Taking his cue from the Pope's insistence on conformity to Latin usages in Norman-occupied territory in Italy, he, in turn, ordered the Latin churches in Constantinople to adopt Greek usages. Upon their refusal, he closed them and ordered Leo, archbishop and head of the Bulgarian Church, to write to the bishop of Trani in Apulia in southern Italy and denounce such Latin customs as the use of unleavened bread in the Eucharist. This letter was to be passed on to the Pope.

This aggressive broadside reached Pope Leo at an unfortunate moment: He had just been defeated by the Normans and was being held in honorable captivity at Benevento. His cardinal secretary, Humbert of Moyen-Moutier, translated it for him and probably—with his little knowledge of Greek—exaggerated its offensive tone. The Pope, who had expected friendly co-operation from the Byzantines, was outraged and was about to dispatch a reply when a courier arrived from Constantinople with two conciliatory letters from Emperor and Patriarch advocating closer unity. Most regrettably, however, Cerularius addressed the Pope as "Brother" instead of the customary "Father" and signed himself "Ecumenical Patriarch," which the Romans misconstrued as a claim to headship over the whole Church. (The Byzantine use of *Oikoumene* actually only meant "the Empire.")

The next lamentable episode must to some extent be blamed on the hot-tempered and truculent Humbert, who had no love for the Greeks. He decided that legates must be sent to the Byzantine capital, and he drafted two letters for them to carry—one for the patriarch and one for the Emperor. The one to the Patriarch condemned his assumption of the title "Ecumenical," took umbrage at his criticism of Latin usages, and prayed that the legates would find him repentant.

On their arrival the legates, one of them Humbert himself, were so offended by the protocol of their reception that they merely thrust the letter into the hands of Cerularius without a greeting. Cerularius was dumbfounded. Having heard much about Pope Leo's gentility and courtesy, he simply could not believe that such a man who, he knew, moreover, was a prisoner and hence likely in no position to dispatch legates, would authorize such boorish legates or such a letter. He refused to accredit the legates' authority or have any dealings with them.

The Emperor, on the other hand, received them well—which encouraged Humbert to publish certain documents in defense of Latin usages. In turn a Byzantine monk came out with a rebuttal that was very critical of Latin celibacy and other practices. Humbert then lost his temper and blasted the monk with a venomous screed and heatedly raised the provocative question of *Filioque.* Cerularius continued to ignore their presence. So finally, with his patience exhausted, Humbert and his colleagues strode into the Church of Santa Sophia on Saturday, July 16, 1054, right before the chanting of the afternoon liturgy and laid on the altar a bull excommunicating Cerularius, Emperor Michael Constantine, and all their followers, and then departed, ceremonially shaking the dust off their feet.

Few ecclesiastical documents of such great moment contain, as historian Stephen Runciman says, so much humbug.[1] Besides refusing the title of Patriarch to Cerularius both personally and as bishop of Constantinople, the bull accused the Greeks of simony (the major vice of the Western Church at the time, as Humbert knew better than anyone), of rebaptizing Latins (untrue), of allowing priests to marry (incorrect), of baptizing women in labor, of jettisoning the Mosaic Law, of refusing communion to men who had shaven their beards (untrue), and finally, of omitting a clause in the Creed(!).

The populace, which was already angry with the Emperor for the favor

[1] Francis Dvornik, *The Eastern Schism* (Oxford: Oxford University Press, 1955), p. 48.

he had shown to the Latins, rioted. Only by ordering the bull to be publicly and solemnly burned did the Emperor succeed in calming the city. A synod condemned the actions of the legates and solemnly anathematized Humbert and his companions while carefully avoiding mention of the papacy.

This left the door open for the Pope to resume friendly negotiations—and, in fact, since Pope Leo died before the legates' arrival in Constantinople, the legates had been acting without actual authority, so it would have been easy for a subsequent Pope to repudiate their action without any loss of prestige. The whole episode could have been glossed over as a mere unfortunate lapse. And at first, it was viewed this way in the East. But in the West, it was different. With Humbert's star continuing to rise in the Curia, his version of the affair—which sounded like a hymn of triumph—was accepted as the right one. Subsequent Popes followed his line. Pope Gregory VII was Humbert's closest friend and would not have dreamed of repudiating his action. Humbert, they believed, did the right thing in excommunicating an unrepentant and contumacious bishop; since the Patriarch's successors also refused to seek absolution, they too were regarded as partaking in the schism. By continuing to elect and support schismatic bishops, the whole patriarchate of Constantinople was eventually included in the excommunication.

Then, to complicate matters further, Gregory VII's policies led him into

Meeting of Countess Mathilda with Pope Gregory VII. Giovanni Francesco Romanelli (c. 1610–62). Vatican Museums, Vatican. © *Scala/Art Resource, New York.*

a close alliance with the Normans, while the Eastern Emperor found it useful to cultivate the friendship of Henry IV, Gregory's archenemy. Finally, Gregory excommunicated the Byzantine Emperor Alexius in 1081. By the year of Gregory's death in 1085, relations between Eastern and Western Christendom were extremely cold. Still there was as yet no actual schism.

A thaw seemed possible with the election of Urban II, who was a states-man to the marrow, a strong man of good will who shunned strife and con-troversy. He opened negotiations with the Byzantine court and lifted the ban of excommunication against Emperor Alexius. In response, Alexius held a synod at Constantinople, which found that the Pope's name had been "inad-vertently" omitted from the diptychs, which in Byzantium as in Rome listed bishops and others who were worthy of the prayers of the faithful. (Through-out the controversy both Rome and Byzantium had been removing the names of their opponents from their respective diptychs.) Alexius proposed the restoration of the Pope's name if the Pope would make a conciliatory gesture, but the gesture never came, and the Pope's name was never put back in the diptychs. Nevertheless, good relations between the two sees were resumed.

And so when Urban called for a crusade at Clermont in 1095, one of his motives was to bring help to the beleaguered Eastern Christians. It would help to dissipate past ill feelings and lead them to recognize the Pope as the leader of all Christendom.

But instead, the effect of the crusades was just the opposite. They proved disastrous to the cause of Christian unity. The Emperor and the crusaders quarreled over the reconquered city of Antioch. The average Eastern Chris-tian Byzantine soon learned to hate the rude, rapacious Western knights, who returned the compliment with interest. When the crusaders seized Antioch in 1098, their leader committed the unpardonable error of driving the Greek Pa-triarch into exile and installing a Latin Patriarch in his place. This schism at Antioch was really the beginning of the schism between the Eastern and West-ern Churches, for until then the other patriarchates were better disposed toward Rome than Constantinople, and if compelled to recognize any eccle-siastical superior would have preferred distant Rome to Constantinople.

Though it is impossible to give an exact date for the beginning of the schism, it was the Fourth Crusade (1202–04) that finally ended all hopes of reunification. The crusaders whom Innocent III directed toward the Holy Land were diverted instead by a young Byzantine prince pretender, who of-fered them great rewards if they would place him on the throne of Constantinople. Without consulting the Pope, the crusaders acquiesced. But the young prince proved inadequate as a ruler, and in the midst of terrible turmoil and confusion the crusaders in 1203 sacked the splendid city of Constantinople, not even sparing the churches. The outrage was stamped indelibly in the Byzantine memory and caused the definitive schism between the Greek and Latin Churches.

There were two later attempts to heal the breach with the Church of Constantinople, at the Council of Lyons in 1274 and at Florence in 1439, but they were only nominal; in both cases the motives were political. Though in each case Emperor and Patriarch subscribed to the reunion, they never affected the general life of the Churches. It is only in our own day in connection with the Second Vatican Council that significant steps have been taken that offer the hope of eventual reunion.

Chapter 14

CHURCH AND SOCIETY IN
WESTERN CHRISTENDOM

Medieval Christendom's boundaries continued to grow until the fourteenth century. The conversion of Franks, Lombards, Angles, Saxons, and Visigoths in the sixth and seventh centuries was followed by the conversion of Frisians and Hessian Germans in the seventh and eighth centuries. The forcible conversion of the Saxons by Charlemagne occurred at the end of the eighth century. The conversion of northern Germans and western Slavs took place during the ninth, tenth, and eleventh centuries. And finally the Baltic peoples were incorporated into Christendom in the thirteenth and fourteenth centuries.

The Scandinavian Kings were very instrumental in the Christianization of Denmark, Norway, and Sweden. Danish King Sven (d. 1014) and his son Canute (d. 1035) brought missionaries into Denmark, while two Norwegian Kings, both named Olaf, did the same for Norway in the eleventh century. Paganism held out longest in Sweden, but with the conversion of its neighbors Denmark, Norway, and Poland, pressures mounted, and by the end of the eleventh century most of the resistance was overcome. In 1164 the Pope made Uppsala a metropolitan see for all Sweden.

During the great migrations the Slavs spread across central Europe and occupied the wide stretch of land from the Dnieper to the Elbe and Saale rivers, including Bohemia. Cyril (d. 869) and Methodius (d. 885) had some success as missionaries to the Slavs in Moravia in the ninth century, and Cyril invented the Slavonic alphabet by combining Greek letters with some new ones in order to provide the Slavs with a liturgical language.

But it was not until the tenth century that Christianity made real progress among the Slavic peoples. The Bohemian princes looked to Germany for protection against the fierce Magyar invaders and were therefore influenced toward Christianity; in 973 a bishopric for Bohemia was erected at Prague. Thence it spread among the Poles, whose renowned Prince Mieszko (d. 990) firmly established the Polish Kingdom and presented his realm to St. Peter and the Pope. A papal charter of the year 1000 gave Poland its own ecclesiastical organization under a metropolitan at Gnesen. In this way Poland was brought into the Western orbit. The conversion of the Hungarians was likewise carried out during the tenth and eleventh centuries.

For a time it looked as if Russia might follow Poland and Hungary into the papal orbit. Founded as the Kievan state in the ninth century by Viking traders who gradually integrated with their Slavic subjects, Russia received missionaries from both East and West as early as the ninth century. But it was only under Vladimir (d. 1015) that Christianity was officially adopted. After conversing with emissaries of the Pope and Patriarch as well as with Moslems and Jews, the Russian prince weighed the pros and cons and finally decided to accept baptism in the Byzantine Church—a decision of vast import for the religious future of Russia. As a derivative Church of the Byzantine, Russia followed Constantinople into schism from Rome in the next century. The last Eastern Europeans to accept Christianity were the Baltic people of Livonia, Prussia, and Lithuania in the thirteenth and fourteenth centuries.

HOW DID THE Church go about ministering to the spiritual as well as temporal needs of its vast conglomeration of members—estimated at the time of Innocent III to number some seventy million? The ecclesiastical organization that embraced them all (except for a tiny minority of Jews) was divided into some four hundred dioceses, each ruled by a bishop or archbishop who was canonically subject to the Pope, although often he was more an agent of the King. Besides being a great landowner and feudal overlord, the bishop or archbishop was judge and legislator, head of the local ecclesiastical hierarchy. He was often related to the most powerful families in his region and nominated to the office as a reward for his administrative talents or outstanding service in secular government, for Kings as a rule depended on the clergy to staff their civil service, since lay education was rare throughout the Middle Ages. These clerical civil servants were often in minor orders and were only ordained as priests upon being appointed to a bishopric. A typical example would be a fourteenth-century English bishop, William of Wykeham. He built an outstanding career in the royal service as head clerk of the office of works—a post he practically created. He was so busy as privy councilor that the chronicler Froissart applied to him the biblical verse, "Everything was done through him and without him nothing was done."[1] When elected bishop of Winchester in 1367 William was immediately made chancellor of the realm as well.

The tasks of the bishop were many and varied: administrative, judicial, and spiritual. One of his chief duties was to conduct visitations of the religious institutions in his diocese. He usually held the visitation in the local church and would summon the clergy of the area and several laymen to attend. After verifying the credentials of the clergy, the bishop would interrogate the laymen about the behavior of the clergy—whether they performed their duties properly, whether they wore the clerical dress, whether they frequented taverns or played dice. And the laity too had to answer for their conduct. Finally, the bishop would inspect the physical state of the church and the condition of its appurtenances. The bishop also held synods of his clergy, at which time he laid down the law on the great variety of matters subject to his jurisdiction. His greatest power, and one that was often a cause of lay resentment, was his law court, where he exercised jurisdiction on a wide assortment of matters, including moral behavior, marriage, and last testaments.

One of his most important spiritual duties was ordaining men to the priesthood. Since there were no seminaries for the training of candidates (these were only prescribed by the Council of Trent), those who wished ordination simply presented themselves three days before the ceremony and took a three-day oral exam. If they could show that they had a firm grasp of the Catholic faith and could express it in simple language, they were admitted to ordination, provided they were of canonical age (twenty-four years for the priesthood) and were not disqualified by reason of servile birth, illegitimacy, or bodily defects.

Each diocese was subdivided into parishes, which were usually staffed by the so-called secular priests. The priest shared in the bishop's sacred powers of consecrating and administering the sacraments. Unlike the bishop, he was usually drawn from the lower classes. Once appointed to the parish by the

[1] Quoted in M. Deansley, *A History of the Medieval Church* (London: Methuen, 1954), p. 194.

bishop or lay patron or, as sometimes happened, elected by the congregation, he had duties much the same as today: saying Mass for the faithful, especially on Sundays, baptizing, hearing confessions, attending to the sick, and burying the dead. It was his special duty also to exhort his parishioners to care for the poor. He might also act as chaplain to a parish guild, which might be partly fraternal and partly devotional in character.

The local priest was often hardly distinguishable from his parishioners, even though in theory and theology there was supposed to be a sharp separation. According to the Gregorian concept the priests were to form a disciplined army moving completely in step under the Pope, set off from all profane occupations, with their special uniform, the long cassock (a relic of the Roman toga), and ruling over an obedient and receptive laity composed of kings, lords, and peasants alike. And one of the main objectives of the Gregorian reformers was to restore the rule of celibacy, which by the eleventh century had fallen into decay. Their zeal against clerical marriage was prompted in part by their realization of how marriage tended to assimilate the clergy to their lay surroundings. They had considerable success in restoring celibacy and bringing greater clarity and precision to Church legislation in the matter. At the Second Lateran Council (1139) they finally managed to have all clerical marriages declared null and void.

But just how effective these laws were is open to question. Clerical concubinage apparently remained widespread during the Middle Ages, and there always seemed to be a plentiful supply of bastard children of priests. One author found that on one day (July 22, 1342)—chosen at random—the Curia issued 614 dispensations for marital impediments, 484 of which had to do with the bastards of priests.[2] Nevertheless, infractions of the law by bishops seemed to have been comparatively rare.

It was at the Mass that the separation of clergy from people was made dramatically evident. While the Mass had retained its basic meal structure, even in the early centuries it began to move away from its original character as an action of the whole community. This tendency was intensified during the early Middle Ages. The people were gradually excluded from all participation, and the Mass became exclusively the priest's business, with the people reduced to the role of spectators. In the medieval Mass the priest no longer wore his ordinary street clothes, as he once did, but glided into the sanctuary

[2] *Histoire de l'Église,* ed. A. Fliche and V. Martin (Paris: Bloud & Gay, 1959), p. 161.

draped in a heavily embroidered chasuble and began to whisper the prayers in a language no longer understood by the people. They stood at a distance, separated from him by a heavy railing, which emphasized the sacredness of the sanctuary. No longer were they allowed to bring up their ordinary bread for consecration; the priest consecrated unleavened bread already prepared in coinlike form. Nor were they allowed to take the wafer in their hands, standing as they once did; now they had to kneel and receive it on the tongue, while the chalice was withheld from them.

The transcendental, awesome, and mysterious nature of the Mass was allowed to blot out almost completely the original spirit of community participation. It was something that happened at the altar, it was the "epiphany of God." It was something you watched. The various actions of the priest were no longer intelligible in this context, so they were given mystical and allegorical significance. The Mass became a kind of pageant representing the life, death, and sufferings of Christ. The "Gloria" was sung to remind one of the angels announcing the birth of Christ. Then came the reading of the gospel— the tale of his public life and preaching. This was followed by silent prayers of the priest, who signified Christ praying in the garden of Gethsemane. When he stretched out his arms, he represented Christ suffering on the cross. Five times he made the sign of the cross over the chalice and host in order to signify the five wounds. When he knelt it was to signify Christ's death, and when he stood up again, it was to signify his resurrection.

Only monks, nuns, and priests received communion frequently. The main object of the layman in coming to Mass was to see the consecrated wafer, and for many the climax came when the priest elevated it after the Consecration. A warning bell was rung beforehand to alert the faithful, many of whom would wander around town going from church to church just to be present at the elevation. Sometimes they would pay the priest a special stipend just to hold the host up higher and for a longer time, and some even engaged in lawsuits in order to get the best place for viewing the host. This attitude gave rise to various devotions that focused on the host. The entire town would come out on such feasts as Corpus Christi in June, when the priest would carry the host through the town encased in a glittering gold monstrance.

Besides the secular clergy, whose main responsibility was the care of the parishes, there were (and still are) a large body of priests, monks, brothers, and nuns who lived in monasteries and religious houses and were called regular as distinct from secular. The term derived from the Latin word *regula*, or rule, and was used because these religious followed a common rule of life based on the observance of the three vows of poverty, chastity, and obedience.

The regulars were further subdivided into monks and friars, each group having female counterparts. The friars made their appearance in history much later than the monks.

In spite of a brief reform led by Benedict, abbot of Aniane (d. 821), the monasteries fell prey to the same evils and disorders that afflicted secular society during the breakdown of the Carolingian Empire. Many of them fell into complete decadence and in some cases were hardly more than strongholds of brigands. But a powerful movement of reform began at the monastery of Cluny in Burgundy, where a series of strong abbots—Odo (d. 941), Mayeul (d. 994), and Odilo (d. 1048)—restored the strict observance of the Rule of St. Benedict and provided a model of reform that spread to numerous other monasteries in the Netherlands, Italy, Spain, England, and Germany.

Until the Cluny reform there was no such thing as a monastic "order." Each monastery was an independent, self-governing unit immediately subject to the Pope or local bishop. But the Cluniacs introduced a new concept: The various monasteries were grouped together in a religious "order" under the centralized authority of the abbot of Cluny, to whom they owed absolute obedience. At the same time they enjoyed complete exemption from the authority of the local bishop. The Cluny Order by the year 1100 embraced some two thousand abbeys, priories, and cells.

The Cluny reform made an important contribution to the progress of spirituality in the medieval Church. It was also an outstanding champion of the papal monarchy and was no doubt the chief spiritual power behind the Gregorian reform and its struggle for the liberation of the Church from control by the laity. It is no coincidence that Gregory VII himself, as well as his dynamic successors Urban II and Paschal II, was a Cluniac.

The success of the Cluny reform was due to the consistency with which its leaders insisted upon strict observance of the Rule of St. Benedict, with its moderate asceticism: silence in church and cloister, exclusion of meat from the diet, and elimination of private property. As time passed, however, the monks acquired extensive tracts of land, which they ornamented with magnificent architecture.

A certain spiritual mediocrity began to manifest itself, and a new group of reformers arose within the order who were unhappy with the growing luxury. Under Robert, the abbot of Molesmes, they migrated in 1098 to Cîteaux, a desolate spot in the diocese of Châlons in France. This move marked the beginning of a new monastic order, the Cistercians, whose third abbot and true founder was an English saint and mystic, Stephen Harding (d. 1134), a monk who combined exceptional administrative gifts with a passionate love of poverty. But the decisive event in its history was the arrival at Cîteaux in 1113 of Bernard, a brilliant nobleman of twenty-two who brought with him a band of thirty disciples, including his own brothers. Three years later he himself founded the daughter abbey of Clairvaux and remained its abbot until his death in 1153. Henceforth as preacher, author, and guide of souls, he was the chief force behind the spiritual revival of the twelfth century as well as being one of the most illustrious statesmen of the time.

Under the influence of such leaders, the white-and-black-robed Cistercians soon reached a position of unrivaled influence in the Church at large. By 1120 they moved into Italy, by 1123 to Germany, by 1128 to England, by 1132 to Spain, and by 1142 to Ireland, Poland, and Hungary. In time, over six hundred monasteries professed allegiance to Cîteaux.

Their constitution, drawn up by Stephen Harding, insisted on a puritanical simplicity and extreme poverty, while it struck a balance between the extreme centralization of Cluny and the local autonomy of the traditional Benedictines. Each monastery with its abbot was under the immediate supervision of its parent or founding monastery, while it in turn exercised the same jurisdiction over the monasteries it founded. A certain democratic character was provided by the yearly chapters or assemblies, which gathered the abbots and representatives of all the houses; they had the right to depose the abbot of Cîteaux and thus were able to keep in check any autocratic tendency on the part of the head abbot.

The Cistercian experiment also influenced a movement of reform among the parish clergy in the twelfth century. Most notable of these movements was that of the Premonstratensians, founded by St. Norbert (d. 1134), a friend of Bernard. Borrowing liberally from the Cistercian system while basing themselves on St. Augustine's rule, they soon spread to almost every country in Europe.

The monastic and ascetic impulse found another type of manifestation in the orders of hermit monks who, departing from the standard Benedictine Rule, chose to live in seclusion, with only a minimal amount of community life. St. Romuald (d. 1027), for instance, took up his abode on a desolate mountain at Camaldoli in Italy with a few brethren and spent the time in silent prayer and meditation while living in extreme poverty. This developed into the Camaldolese order, which received papal approval in 1072. The same ideal of complete isolation from the world and absolute poverty was embraced by the founder of the Carthusians, Bruno, a native of Cologne who in 1084 settled in the rugged mountain wilderness of La Chartreuse near Grenoble, France. The Carthusians pushed austerity to the very limits of human endurance, with long fasts and a diet almost restricted to vegetables. Their growth was accordingly slow, but by the fifteenth century they numbered some 150 monasteries. Down to our times they have persevered in fidelity to their original ideal without ever needing a reform, a unique case in the history of religious orders.

The ideal of the monastic orders was complete withdrawal from the world. A new type of religious order, however, arose in the thirteenth century whose aim was to pursue the monastic ideals of renunciation, poverty, and self-sacrifice while staying in the world in order to convert it by example and preaching. These were called friars, from the Latin word *fratres,* meaning brothers. They were also called the mendicant orders because of their practice of begging alms to support themselves. They were represented mainly by the Franciscans, Dominicans, Carmelites, and Augustinians. They were, in part, an instinctive response to new social conditions caused by the rise of towns, the revival of commerce, and the growth of population. The shift of population from the countryside to the towns posed a big problem for the Church, whose venerable structures were geared to the old rural, feudal society. It stood in danger of losing touch with the masses who had moved away from the rural parishes and who now lived in the slums that clustered outside the walls of the medieval towns. The mendicant orders proved a godsend in the new urban apostolate.

Their origin may be traced to Francis of Assisi, born in 1181 or 1182, the son of a rich cloth merchant; he was a generous, poetic, high-spirited youth who dreamed of performing daring deeds of chivalry. But after a brief disillusioning career as a soldier, he found himself irresistibly drawn to the Gospel of Jesus Christ and decided to surrender completely to the Lord. He took the words of Jesus literally, and stripping himself of all his possessions, set out barefoot and penniless to preach repentance and a simple message of trust in God and joy in the sheer wonder of God's goodness. The crowds who listened to Francis grew, and a circle of disciples formed around him. He drew up a simple rule for these "brothers" and took it to Pope Innocent III, who reluc-

Confirmation of the Rule of St. Francis. Fresco from *The Life of St. Francis.* Giotto di Bondone (1266–1336). San Francesco, Assisi, Italy. © *Scala/Art Resource, New York.*

tantly gave it verbal sanction. The new order of Friars Minor, as they were now called, continued to multiply and soon spread across Europe.

The simple rule drawn up by Francis contained hardly more than a few of his favorite quotations from the Gospel about love and poverty. Sober spirits, however, realized that a more down-to-earth, businesslike constitution was needed if the order were to survive. Pope Honorius (d. 1227) concurred, and Cardinal Ugolino—who realized the great potential of the movement—helped to draw up a rule that provided a more realistic and orderly government for the thousands of men now involved. But Francis looked on with increasing anguish at what he saw as a harsh and legalistic metamorphosis of his life's dream. In his *Testament,* written shortly before his death in 1226, he uttered a wistful protest and tried to call the order back to his lovely Lady Poverty. But after his death the *Testament* was invalidated and the friars were enabled by legal fictions to possess land and goods. However, a permanent group of dissenters—the Spirituals—persevered in demanding a return to the ideals of Francis and engaged in intense and often ugly controversy with the Conventuals—the party who believed in adjusting the ideal to new conditions.

The other great order of friars, the Dominicans, was founded by Dominic de Guzman (d. 1221), the son of a Castilian noble, in connection with his efforts to convert the Albigensian heretics. Through his friendship with Cardinal Ugolino, he was able to meet Francis and was much impressed by his commitment to poverty. He introduced the idea into the rule for his new order, which he had based mainly on the old Rule of St. Augustine. Unlike Francis, however, Dominic stressed the need for intellectual training to ensure the success of his monks' preaching. And to this day both orders still retain something of their founders' spirit: The Dominicans tend to be scholarly, orthodox preachers and writers, while Franciscans will more likely be activists, perhaps even radicals, with a touch of Francis's merriment.

Together with the less numerous Carmelites and Augustinians, also stemming from this period, these mendicant orders were directly subject to the Pope and proved to be his most effective auxiliaries in tackling the new urban apostolate of the thirteenth century. They supplied most of the Church's leaders of thought and learning in the Middle Ages; they were its most effective preachers; they excelled as confessors and were the ones chiefly responsible for

The Story of San Domenico di Guzman: The Burning of the Books. Pedro Berruguete (1450–1504). Museo del Prado, Madrid.   © *Scala/Art Resource, New York.*

making the confessional an important part of Catholic piety; they were as well the outstanding missionaries to foreign lands.

Bishops, priests, monks, friars, nuns, they were by and large the most educated, the most cultivated, and the most respected members of medieval society during the period of the Church's ascendancy, and they constituted a much larger percentage of the population than they do today. Their large number enabled the Church to dedicate itself to a wide range of social services, constituting a kind of Department of Health, Education, and Welfare. The Church's care for the unfortunates was concentrated in its hospitals, which at that time were not restricted to care for the sick but ministered to all kinds of needy persons. As such it was the descendant of the *hospitium* of the fifth-century bishop, who was required by Canon Law to spend a certain portion of diocesan revenue on the poor—a stipulation he carried out largely by endowing a *hospitium* or home for the poor. The medieval bishop carried on this tradition. At his consecration he was asked whether he would show kindness to the poor, to strangers, and to all in need. This duty he fulfilled by founding and supporting hospitals—not only near his cathedral but also in other towns throughout his diocese. In the fourteenth century, records show that there were eight hospitals in Canterbury, seventeen in London, and eighteen in York, offering food and lodging for the poor. Some hospitals specialized: They might be dedicated, for instance, to the relief of Jews who after their conversion could no longer earn a living by usury; or they took care of the insane (these date only from the fourteenth century) or lepers. It was only with the beginning of the Black Death (c. 1350) that the ordinary hospital out of necessity began to devote itself mainly to the sick.

In harmony with the Church's actual ascendancy over society, its theologians and philosophers developed a social theory that envisaged the whole social order as an organic hierarchy whereby all of man's secular activities were ordained to his religious and supernatural goals as means to ends. Each person was assigned by mysterious destiny to a higher or lower place, and each class contributed to the functioning of the whole body. This theory left little room for ideas of change or social reform; the social condition was simply a given. The task of each person was to live up to the calling that God had given him and to remain in the station in life to which he had been born. Social well-being depended on each class performing the functions and enjoying the rights proportioned to it. All the ugly and discordant features of social relationships—the violence, inequities, war, poverty, serfdom, and misery—were regarded as the result of sin and hence a permanent part of man's pilgrimage here on earth. The only thing the Christian could do about them was alleviate as best he could the suffering of the individuals.

Within this limited framework the Church's great theologians worked out an ethical system to provide answers for every conceivable moral question. In so doing they based themselves on the Scriptures, on Natural Law (defined as the dictates of human reason insofar as it prescribes actions appropriate to the purpose of each human power or faculty), and on the divine authority of the Church, especially as reflected in the dictates of the Pope.

The medieval theologians even dared to assert that man's economic activities were subject to moral law. In fact, in the medieval view, the businessman was presumed guilty until proven innocent, since his pursuit of profit for profit's sake was regarded with great suspicion by Churchmen, who saw it as simple avarice—the most dangerous of all sins. Hence the Church strove valiantly to subject even the economic appetite to its laws. Its ban on usury (defined as taking interest merely for the act of lending) was constantly reiterated, with great emphasis. The Council of Lyons (1274) supplemented the basic prohibition by rules that virtually made the moneylender an outlaw. The Council of Vienne (1312) went even further, by ordering the repeal of all civil law that sanctioned usury. But as Richard Tawney has pointed out, the main point and the one that intrigues many today who are distressed by the economic egotism fostered by capitalism was "the insistence of medieval thinkers that society is a spiritual organism, not an economic machine, and that economic activity, which is one subordinate element within a vast and complex unity, requires to be controlled and repressed by reference to the moral ends for which it supplies the material means."[3]

The Church claimed marriage, the family, and all that pertained to it as its very special province. It upheld the unity and indissolubility of marriage and tried to bring some order into the realm of sex. It continued to condemn abortion and infanticide as heinous crimes and severely punished those guilty. It insisted on the human rights and dignity of women, although unfortunately its celibate clergy often lapsed into an almost hysterical disdain for everything feminine.

A Church that aspires to completely dominate a whole culture must know how to compromise with the radical demands of the Gospel. Perhaps

---

[3] Richard Tawney, *Religion and the Rise of Capitalism* (London: John Murray, 1926), p. 61.

nowhere is this more evident than in the question of war. In comparison with the Eastern Christians, whose stand against war was generally consistent, Western Christendom appears much less enlightened. The barbarian invasions and the conditions of feudal society made war a constant fact of life; ecclesiastics tried to channel this bellicose energy for the Church's own purposes. Holy war in the service of the Church was regarded as permissible and even desirable. Popes even led armies into battle and ranked the victims of a holy war as martyrs.

However, a peace movement did begin in France in the tenth century at the Council of Charroux in 989, where the bishops of Aquitaine proposed the Peace of God, outlawing war against the clergy, women, the poor, and the defenseless. A series of Church councils followed in France, which prescribed oaths to be taken by the nobility to limit their war-making propensities. Then Leagues of Peace were organized—the first one by the archbishop of Bourges in 1038—committing the members to take up arms if necessary to suppress those who made war. Supposedly seven hundred clerics alone perished in one such war for peace. A more practical measure was the Truce of God in the eleventh century, a movement inspired by the Church. It prohibited all warfare on holy days and during Lent and Advent and other special feasts. Violation brought with it automatic excommunication.

The Church still taught as late as the eleventh century that it was a grave sin to kill a man in a battle waged for only secular purposes. And even though the Battle of Hastings in 1066 was blessed with papal approval, the victors were given severe penalties for the deaths they had caused. Somewhat later the theologians revived Augustine's theory of the "just war," which allowed secular rulers the benefit of the doubt unless they were acting against papal interests. And so actually it became very difficult for Churchmen to declare that any properly authorized war was unjust.

It is in this context that we must try to understand the Crusades, which were such a remarkable expression of the medieval mind. Pope Urban II set them in motion in 1095, and throughout their long history they remained a largely papal enterprise. Urban addressed the Christian knights present at the Council of Clermont that year and summoned them to turn their fighting spirit to a more fruitful purpose by rescuing the Holy Land from the infidel Moslems. Under the hypnotic spell of the Pope's brilliant oratory and his promise of an eternal reward to those who died in the cause, the knights thundered in reply: "God wills it"; they sewed red crosses on their tunics and immediately laid plans for the expedition.

As with most major movements in history, a complex of motives and circumstances played a part in the genesis of the Crusades. The Normans, Italians, and French had already assumed the offensive against the Moslems and wrested control of the western Mediterranean from them; they were now ready to turn to the East. The reform of the papacy under Hildebrand meant that people now looked to the Pope as head of Christendom and were ready to follow his lead. Stories were also circulating about the harsh treatment of Christian pilgrims to Jerusalem at the hands of the infidel, inflaming Western opinion. The Eastern Emperor, Alexius, appealed to Urban for help in recovering Byzantine territory in Asia Minor from the Turks, while Urban saw a chance to reunite Eastern and Western Christendom under papal headship. Not the least of the factors was the dynamic personality of Urban himself, whose extraordinary energy and organizing ability did much to assure the initial success of the movement.

A medley of motives inspired the rugged knights: love of adventure, devotion to Christ, and lust for land. Under such leaders as Hugh of Vermandois, Raymond of Toulouse, Godfrey of Bouillon, Robert of Flanders, Stephen of Blois, Bohemond of Taranto, and the papal legate, Adhemar of Puy, the crusading armies were assembled in Constantinople by May 1097; they swore an oath of fealty to Emperor Alexius and then captured the Moslem capital of Nicaea. One of the great epics of military history then occurred as the mailed knights and sturdy foot soldiers trekked across Asia Minor fending off attacks by Turkish horsemen though tormented by lack of food and water and the extreme heat. After four months they reached Antioch and laid it under siege. There on June 28, 1098, they won the decisive victory that determined the successful outcome of the First Crusade.

On June 7, 1099, their army of twelve thousand—about half of those who began the march across Asia Minor—arrived at the strongly fortified walls of Jerusalem. At the second attack it fell, and on July 1 the victors poured out their feelings in the Church of the Holy Sepulcher and then poured out indiscriminately the blood of the inhabitants—Moslem and Jewish, men, women, and children.

In spite of their oath to Alexius the crusaders formed only a loose confederation, unified only by their undefined allegiance to the Pope and his legate, Adhemar, but torn by personal animosities and rivalries. A heavy blow to even this frail unity occurred when the lovable and tactful Adhemar perished in an epidemic after the victory at Antioch. Disunity continued to characterize the history of the Latin kingdom of Jerusalem and its theoretically subject fiefs in Syria—the county of Tripolis, the county of Edessa, and the principality of Antioch. Another serious misfortune was the crusaders' failure to capture the important cities of Damascus, Emesa, Hamah, and Aleppo. When the Moslems finally united they began a piecemeal reconquest that even the Second Crusade (1147) failed to arrest. The smashing victory of Saladin at Hattin in 1187 and his capture of Jerusalem climaxed the reconquest. Nor could the Third Crusade (1189–92) and all the succeeding ones restore Latin supremacy over the Near East.

There is no doubt, however, that the Crusades contributed much to the developments of the time: the rise of commerce and towns, the growing sense of nationality, the expansion of intellectual horizons, and the increase in the prestige of the papacy. But in none of these instances was the influence decisive. The taste for Eastern spices, silk, and metalware, for instance, was already stimulated by a trade that was growing independently of the Crusades; the

Portrait of Saladin (1138–1193), sultan of Egypt. Anonymous. Uffizi Gallery, Florence.   © *SEF/Art Resource, New York.*

crusaders' effect on the rise of commerce was not as crucial as is sometimes supported. Probably their most important effect was to retard the Turkish advance into the Balkans for three hundred years.

As we can see from this brief survey, the Church's impact on medieval society was profound. In every department of life one found the Church present. Under the leadership of the Popes, the priests, monks, friars, and nuns who were the spiritual elite of medieval society labored steadily to instill faith in the illiterate masses, to give them at least a glimpse of truth and goodness beyond the grim facts of their narrowly circumscribed lives. But how successful were they? Did the Gospel penetrate beyond the surface of medieval life? Was it distorted in its transmission to the masses? These are questions that nearly transcend the boundaries of historical science. But perhaps some judgment can be made. There is no doubt that the Church made great compromises in adapting the message of its founder to the exigencies of a feudal society. Its barbaric holy wars, its crude anti-Semitism, its sanguinary Inquisitions, and its chase after witches, are enough to show how far compromise could go. But at the same time, the urge to reform was never absent either. There was always a prophetic current critical of the establishment and anxious to lead Church and society to greater fidelity to the demands of the Gospel as they were then understood. One has only to think of such movements as Cluny, the Cistercians, and the Franciscans to appreciate this fact. And one can agree with the conclusion of a recent study by Francis Oakley, ". . . for whatever its barbarisms, its corruptions, its malformations, whatever its evasions and dishonesties, in the medieval church men and women still contrived, it would seem, to encounter the Gospel."[4]

---

[4] Francis Oakley, *The Medieval Experience* (New York: Charles Scribner's Sons, 1974), p. 71.

Chapter 15

THE ARISTOTELIAN
INVASION

We have seen how with the fall of the Roman Empire the torch of learning in the West flickered and nearly died out. Intellectual life—of the most rudimentary kind indeed—was practically confined to the monasteries during the seventh and eighth centuries. Then Charlemagne made a magnificent effort to revive learning. His capitularies decreed that every bishop should set up a school at his cathedral. He gathered scholars around his own palace, and a small number of learned monks—Alcuin being the most illustrious—shed some light amid the surrounding darkness. But the breakdown of the Carolingian Empire once more disrupted the orderly life necessary for education, and schooling again became the virtual monopoly of the monasteries in the ninth and tenth centuries, the most famous being Fulda in Germany. Only a few luminaries stand out in this general eclipse of culture: Walafrid Strabo, Hrabanus Maurus, Einhard, Alfred the Great—none of them, with the exception of Irishman John Scotus Erigena (d. c. 875), really original thinkers.

But in the eleventh century an intellectual awakening began that transformed the cultural life of Europe. It was associated at first mainly with the monasteries but soon also manifested itself in the cathedral schools of northern Europe and the urban schools of Italy. It found its most characteristic expression, however, in the newly founded universities, which around 1170 began to replace the cathedral schools as the most vital centers of learning. It was mainly at the universities that theologians of genius worked to harmonize the data of human experience with the data of faith. The most successful in this enterprise was Thomas Aquinas, whose synthesis of Aristotle and the

Gospel in his *Summa* represents the summit of Christendom's intellectual achievement.

THE RISE OF the universities was only one of the most noteworthy features of the great upsurge of town life that began in western Europe in the eleventh century. While in Italy a skeletal form of town life had survived the barbarian invasions, in northern Europe town life and commerce virtually ceased. But in the eleventh century, improvements in methods of agriculture brought a higher yield of crops, population increased, commerce revived, and wagons loaded with cargoes of grain, lumber, spices, fine cloth, wines, and salt began to move again across the old trade routes. Ancient towns came back to life, and new ones sprang up as centers of trading activity. The surplus population gravitated from the countryside to the towns—providing manual labor for the industries and a market for the commerce. Only a few of these towns numbered populations in the tens of thousands, and they never comprised more than 10 per cent of the total population, but they furnished the vital centers of medieval life. The prosperous burghers who inhabited them provided the economic resources for the intellectual and artistic achievements of that age—notably the universities and the cathedrals.

The founding of the universities cannot be precisely dated, since they evolved almost imperceptibly out of the cathedral or urban schools. Several of them—Paris and Bologna in particular—began to overshadow the others and drew great crowds of students from all over Europe. As their numbers grew, the members began to feel the need to organize to protect their mutual interests. They found a model close at hand in the existing guilds of merchants and craftsmen, which regulated the relations of those working in a particular business or craft and protected the rights of the members. And so the university—organizationally speaking—was nothing more in its origin than another guild, in this case a union of scholars, which like other guilds regulated the conditions for reception of the various degrees. At first both students and masters were almost all members of the clergy (the term "layman" being synonymous with illiterate) and as such enjoyed special privileges—often including subsidies from the Church. Sometimes this took the form of board and room provided in well-endowed colleges. They could also count usually on help from the Pope in their frequent conflicts with the town, for the universities provided one of the great instruments used by the papacy in dominating the Church. Pope Gregory IX issued a bull in 1231—the Magna Carta of the University of Paris—that clearly defined its essential rights, including the right to boycott. In appreciation for this help, the University of Paris became the favorite of the papacy.

Favored by the Popes and even by secular rulers, universities multiplied, adopting as models the organization of Paris or Bologna. They included Salerno (c. 1200), Oxford (c. 1200), Cambridge (1209), Naples (1224), Padua (1222), Pisa (1303), Salamanca (1220), Toulouse (1230), Prague (1348), Heidelberg (1385), and Louvain (1425) Paris, however, remained preeminent and served a student population reckoned at around five thousand.

Only three branches of knowledge were regarded as worthy of advanced study: medicine, law, and theology. These, together with the preparatory liberal arts, formed the four faculties. Law meant both Canon Law and civil law. The monk Gratian made Bologna the Canon Law capital of Europe. In his immortal *Decretum* (c. 1140) he assembled a vast number of canons or sacred laws decreed at innumerable Church councils, put them in order, and clarified their meaning with a brilliant commentary. The study of civil law began with the rediscovery of the Emperor Justinian's *Code* in the eleventh century. Bologna also led the way here, and produced the finest civil lawyers in Europe.

Medicine for a long time was hardly more than a science of folklore practiced by herbalists, witches, and bonesetters. Leeching was a favorite remedy, and most monasteries deputed someone for this task. The scientific study of medicine began with the introduction of Greek and Arabic texts, such as Galen and Avicenna, during the eleventh century. The first faculty of medicine was established at Salerno, and it seems to have been remarkably progressive. Others followed at Bologna and elsewhere. They were handicapped by a servile attitude toward their Greek and Arabic sources, but still they made some real advances—especially in surgery, hospitalization, and the use of quarantine. A public health board flourished at Venice as early as 1377.

The scientific study of nature was retarded by the low level of mathematical knowledge, but there was still some progress in the experimental and physical sciences—notably at Paris and Oxford. Robert Grosseteste (d. 1253), bishop of Lincoln, wrote on astronomy, mathematics, physics, and optics, and proposed the theory that light energy is the basis of physical phenomena. Franciscan Roger Bacon (d. 1292) was an irascible genius who delighted in challenging the conventional ideas of his age. He was deeply committed to experimentation, invented a rudimentary telescope and thermometer, and anticipated other developments by his prophecies of mechanical transport on land, water, and in the air. But modern scholars tend to rate his actual achievements as less significant than Grosseteste's.

But the real queen of the medieval sciences was theology. The best minds of the Middle Ages devoted themselves to its study, and it was in this field that medieval scholars made their most significant contributions.

The traditional method used in its pursuit was the so-called *lectio* or reading, which was merely a critical reading or exegesis of sacred Scripture. In addition, the writings of the holy fathers of the Church were utilized to elucidate individual scriptural passages. Their opinions were catalogued and compared with one another. In the best example of this method—the famous *Sentences* of Peter Lombard (d. 1160)—there was some attempt to organize the material and arrange it according to topics such as the Trinity, Creation, Incarnation, and Sacraments to face new problems and offer new opinions. But still the whole emphasis was on the acceptance of tradition and authority, rational speculation being kept to a minimum.

A new approach began in the twelfth century under the influence of the renewed study of Aristotle, the great master of rational speculation. Until then only his *Categories* and *Interpretation* had been known in the West and studied in Latin translation. They contained the essential techniques of ancient reasoning, and as interest in things intellectual revived, their study became the focus of the revival.

It was the fascinating, stormy, and tragic Abelard (d. 1142) who did the most to popularize these logical studies at Paris; he pioneered in using Aristotelian categories of thought in order to reach a deeper understanding of the Christian dogmas. He took a carefully reasoned approach to theological questions, not denying the role of authority but making every allowance for rational objections and natural human feelings. In other words, he was the first theologian to view theology as a whole and attempt a grand synthesis of the data of reason with the data of faith. In so doing he provided us with a new understanding of what theology was all about.

But he was limited by the small number of Aristotle's works that were available, and he died on the threshold of the momentous revolution in medieval thought that was caused by the rediscovery of Aristotle's complete works. Over a period of roughly a hundred years (1150–1250), all of Aristotle's writings were translated and introduced into the West, accompanied by a

Abelard and Héloïse. British Library, London (miniature from the Royal MS. 16 F2, fol. 137).   © *Art Resource, New York.*

formidable number of Arabic commentaries as well as by other scientific and philosophical works, Jewish and Arabic. This amounted to a vast new library. The work of assimilating and mastering it occupied the best minds of Christendom and profoundly altered the spiritual and intellectual life of the West.

Its effects on theology were earthshaking. The translation and dissemination of the complete works of Aristotle confronted Christian thinkers for the first time with a completely rationalistic interpretation of human experience and indeed of the whole of knowable reality. Aristotle was an encyclopedic writer whose thought covered the whole spectrum of Greek science and philosophy: botany, zoology, astronomy, physics, logic, metaphysics, epistemology, ethics, and political science, not to mention various minor inquiries. He classified, organized, and systematized all the available knowledge of his day and always from an utterly rationalistic point of view. He saw the world as one vast, self-contained, self-explanatory organism.

This invasion of Aristotle, accompanied by the work of such masterful Arabic commentators as Avicenna (d. 1037) and Averroës (d. 1198)—who emphasized the unspiritual and nonreligious character of the philosopher's thought—precipitated a grave crisis for the intellectual leaders of the West. It offered a totally rationalistic and this-world solution to all the major problems facing humanity. Assimilating and harmonizing all of it with the Christian faith constituted a tremendous task. The effort to do so profoundly altered the spiritual and intellectual climate of Christendom. It inaugurated a period of unparalleled intellectual activity and ferment that reached its climax in the thirteenth century, especially at Paris and Oxford, and in the schools of the newly founded mendicant friars.

Ecclesiastical authority reacted at first with predictable caution and prudence. Bishops gathered at a council at Paris in 1210 forbade the Parisian masters to lecture on the natural philosophy of Aristotle—a ban reiterated by the papal legate, Robert de Curzon, at Paris in 1215. However, this interdiction was gradually lifted when it proved impossible to enforce, the curiosity of the hungry minds at Paris being too powerful to control. Moreover, the ban was never applied at Oxford, and so the schoolmen at Paris resented the discrimination. So by the middle of the thirteenth century the study of Aristotle was in full swing. It is at this point that we see emerging several great systematic works of Christian thought that endeavored to incorporate into one harmonious Christian theology everything deemed true in Greek and Arabic scientific thought. Three men stand out head and shoulders above the rest: a Franciscan, Bonaventure (d. 1274), and two Dominicans, Albert the Great (d. 1280) and Thomas Aquinas (d. 1274).

Bonaventure was the first to construct a cohesive theological system with all of its parts interrelated and based on a clearly defined conception of the relative role of reason and faith. His native bent, however, was mystical, and he tended unduly to subordinate the natural human urge toward reason to the authority of tradition and faith.

Albert the Great, on the other hand, was determined to uphold the value of natural rational knowledge and to defend its autonomy within its own sphere. And since he saw Aristotle as the supreme exemplar of this attitude— the principal guide and repository of human reason—he made it his principal mission in life to make the whole corpus of Aristotle known in the West, supplemented by whatever human science had discovered since. Albert's intrepid faith convinced him that nothing uncovered by research could prove detrimental to the Christian revelation, and he felt that the cause of the faith would ultimately be served better by honest recognition of difficulties than by fearful condemnations. His project was encyclopedic in scope. Thirty-eight huge tomes remain as a monument to his intellectual audacity.

Albert's universal genius embraced the whole scientific realm of his day, and his works served as the starting point for most of the intellectual currents of his time. However, he never succeeded in his main objective: a total reinterpretation of Aristotle in harmony with the Christian faith. Fortunately, however, he inspired his brilliant student, Thomas Aquinas, with the same vision. Like Albert, Thomas was confident that faith and reason were ultimately compatible, and like him he recognized the complete autonomy of secular knowledge as a domain of human experience subject to its own proper laws. He mastered all the thought of his time, and his massive collection of works include every type of theological and philosophical work. His ambition was to do for Christian civilization what Aristotle had accomplished for the pagan.

He completely assimilated Aristotle and expropriated his fundamental intuitions—but did not uncritically accept the whole Aristotelian doctrine. Drawing on the entire Western philosophical tradition—Platonists and Neo-Platonists, Arabs as well as Christians—he was able to construct a new, original philosophy: Thomism, the first original metaphysics since Aristotle. By an ingenious synthesis of Aristotelian, Platonic, and Christian insights, he developed as his central idea a rational understanding of God as the creator and

Portrait of St. Thomas Aquinas. Joos van Ghent (1460–80). Louvre, Paris. © *Giraudon/Art Resource, New York.*

source of all being, goodness, and truth, present in all beings by his power and essence, the uncaused cause, in whom alone essence and existence are one.

With this philosophy as his basis and making use of all available sources of knowledge, he then wrote his masterpiece, the *Summa Theologica* (1266–74)—the summit of his life's work and one of the finest hours of human genius. Every important question of theology is treated from every angle conceivable in his day. The solutions he gives reveal his astonishing versatility, and while they are often unsatisfactory in the light of the present explosion of knowledge, they are still worthy of consideration because of Thomas's incredible learning, philosophical profundity, and unrivaled clarity of thought and expression.

Because of Thomas's unique ascendancy, until recently, over modern Catholic thought, one sometimes imagines that he reigned serenely over his own times as well. But historians pursuing their research into the multifaceted Aristotelian revolution sketch a much different picture. They have uncovered a most controversial Thomas, the target of furious hostility from important Churchmen of his day, a liberal caught in the eye of an ecclesiastical hurricane during his last years of teaching at Paris—a situation that curiously enough left no echoes in the placid, limpid syllogisms of the *Summa* he was writing at the time.

We now know that already by the year 1267 several bitterly opposed factions had formed in the Church over the issue of Aristotelianism and its relation to the faith. There were the radical Aristotelians (we might call them the modernists) led by Siger of Brabant, whose overzealous devotion to the pagan philosopher led them into heresy. Opposed were the conservatives—many of them Franciscans, like their leader, John Pecham (d. 1292), a renowned professor at Paris and later archbishop of Canterbury. They were no doubt supported by Bonaventure himself, whom they claimed together with Augustine as their masters. They lumped Thomas and the radical Aristotelian Siger together, considering Thomism equally dangerous to the faith. Unable or unwilling to grasp the profundity of its masterful synthesis, they saw in Thomism only a pernicious rationalism whose heretical tendency appeared in Thomas's numerous innovations, mainly in his views on the unity of intelligence in all men, the eternity of the world, the freedom of the will, and the knowledge and providence of God.

But the most dangerous of Thomas's newfangled ideas in their eyes was his assertion of the unity of "form" in man. To understand Thomas here we must keep in mind that this basic concept of form and matter was Aristotelian; it involved his idea of reality as explainable in terms of two principles: *matter,* meaning the potential of something to become real or actual; and *form,* that which actualizes this potential and hence makes a thing what it is.

Now, for Aquinas the soul as a spiritual substance (and therefore completely simple, unmixed with matter) was related to the body as its "form" and superseded all other forms, such as the form of vegetativeness or the form of bodiliness. This opinion corresponded with Aristotle's teaching that the soul was the first "entelechy" or perfection of the body.

The rival Augustinian conception held that the soul was a complete entity acting upon the body—an idea incompatible with the Aristotelian conception of a single substantial form for every being. The Augustinians also failed to posit a clear distinction between substantial and accidental forms and between an objective and factual plurality of forms and a merely mental and logical plurality, and so the way was left open for them to assert an actual plurality of forms of equal metaphysical significance.

Thus the conservatives regarded the human being as a composite of many separate entities, each having its own matter and form: the human soul, the body, the vegetative principle, the sensitive principle. As to how all of these were united to form a unity in one person, there were various theories. Some held that they were united under the one life form of the intellective soul; others, that they possessed an autonomous existence of their own and were only joined extrinsically to the soul; still others saw them as forming a hierarchy over which the soul exercised a directive function.

"In opposition to all these theories," historian Dom David Knowles has written, "Thomas set his thesis, which developed and clarified that of Aristotle, that the soul, as pure form, actualizes the body as its matter and that the intellective soul contains in itself in an eminent degree all the perfections of the sensitive and vegetative souls, which it supplants in the embryo of the human being at the moment of its creation."[1]

Pecham erroneously contended that Aquinas had invented this doctrine. The truth of the matter is that Thomas's true originality consisted in the way he considered the question from a metaphysical angle, while previous thought focused on the psychological aspects. This was in accordance with his insis-

---

[1] David Knowles, *The Evolution of Medieval Thought* (New York: Random House, 1964), p. 295.

tence on substantial unity as a metaphysical reality. "Nothing is purely and simply a unity," he said, "unless it has a single form that determines its essence for a thing derives its being and its unity from a single source."[2]

The question, as Dom Knowles remarks, was not merely academic. The old idea of the soul as an entity or substance in its own right entailed a view of the soul as having a vital power possessing a rich life of faculties, virtues, and superior potentialities—the concrete, immortal, personal core of a human being. But the soul in Aristotle's theory is hardly more than a metaphysical abstraction, a logical necessity; he was not interested in the question of its immortality and left the matter unresolved. So in subscribing to Aristotle's theory, Aquinas left himself open to some difficult objections from the conservatives.

In 1277 the archbishop of Paris, Stephen Tempier, upheld the conservatives in a decree that condemned 219 errors; it was primarily aimed at the radical Aristotelians, but it also stigmatized some of the basic Thomist ideas as heretical. It was the most solemn condemnation of the Middle Ages and was repeated in England by the archbishop of Canterbury, Robert Kilwardby, and again by the man who succeeded him shortly thereafter, John Pecham.

The consequences of this confusion of Thomas's orthodox thought with heretical Aristotelianism were grave and far-reaching. Theologians henceforth divided into sharply opposed schools, and their bitter and sterile polemics cast discredit on their common enterprise, retarding for many centuries recognition by the Church of the unique value of the Thomist synthesis.

The Neo-Augustinianism of Pecham and his conservative coterie was unable to hold its own for more than twenty years or so. A much more powerful alternative to Thomism, however, was worked out by John Duns Scotus (d. 1308), perennially celebrated for the extreme subtlety of his thought, a theologian who seems to have deliberately chosen an adversary relationship to Thomism. He denied Thomas's distinction between essence and existence, arguing in favor of a plurality of substantial forms in man. He held against Thomas that the will rather than the intellect was the determining factor in human decisions and denied the Thomistic thesis that we can reach natural certainty about immortality. As the mainstay of the Franciscan school he commanded a larger following than Thomas in the late medieval period.

In spite of their many differences, Thomists and Scotists at least agreed

---

[2] Ibid.

Portrait of John Duns Scotus.
Joos van Ghent (1460–80).
Galleria Nazionale delle
Marche, Urbino, Italy.
© *Scala/Art Resource, New York.*

on one crucial point: the knowability and intelligibility of things. They both held that we can know the essences of things through the intellect's power of abstracting what is universal from the singular and concrete data of our experience. It was on this point that the last great medieval Scholastic, William of Ockham (d. 1349/50) broke decisively with both schools and shattered the already shaky structure of Christian Aristotelianism. He denied the very existence of a mental process of abstraction and excluded all knowledge of the extramental world except the intuitive knowledge of individual things. Universals or essences, for Ockham, were purely intramental phenomena, mental artifacts.

The effects were devastating indeed: Metaphysics was rendered practically impossible, while theology, deprived of its metaphysical foundations, became increasingly a mere arid controversy over words. Ockham taught that God was purely unknowable on the natural rational level of thought; his moral decrees, for instance, were not in evident correspondence with the nature of things (which he held we also could not know) and therefore could only be understood as arbitrary. God might just as well have commanded us to do the opposite; he could have commanded us to hate him above all things.

Ockham's star rose quickly, for his nominalism suited the temper of his age; it henceforth dominated the universities and philosophical and theological speculation of the last medieval centuries. It reflected the breakdown of unity in all departments of the life and thought of Christendom during the later centuries of the Middle Ages—a phenomenon already perceptible by the year 1300.

Part   Three

THE UNMAKING OF
CHRISTENDOM

A.D. 1300–1650

Chapter 16

THE DECLINE OF
THE PAPAL MONARCHY

The Popes who followed Hildebrand succeeded to a remarkable degree in establishing their supremacy over Christendom. Under these imposing papal monarchs Christendom enjoyed its golden age in the thirteenth century—the era of its most splendid achievements, intellectual, artistic, and spiritual. But the onward sweep of history could not be held back, and the rise of national monarchies in the thirteenth century presaged the decline of both the imperial and papal authority and the end of papal Christendom.

The decline of papal authority became evident—ironically—in the very aftermath of their complete victory over the Hohenstaufen Emperors. The means used by the Popes to crush the Emperors were, in fact, so political in nature as to obscure the spiritual cause the Popes were trying to uphold. The outcome was a grave loss of their spiritual prestige—a situation that was quickly exploited by the ambitious national monarchs. Philip the Fair of France led the onslaught of the nation states on the papal monarchy when he literally kidnaped Pope Boniface VIII and then constrained Boniface's successor to remain in France. The subsequent Avignon period of the papacy (1305–78) saw a further weakening of papal authority as it became identified in the popular mind—rightly or wrongly—with French interests.

THE CONFLICT WITH the Hohenstaufen Emperors in the thirteenth century was merely another chapter—the most consequential, it is true—in the struggle between the papacy and German Empire that began with Hildebrand. To understand this struggle it is important to keep in mind that the Popes did not claim authority over the temporal order as such but only insofar as it involved moral decisions. But as is still true today, the precise boundaries between the purely temporal and the spiritual, or as we would say today, between Church and state, were nearly impossible to define, and peculiarly so at that juncture of human history when there was no thought of trying to separate them. The Popes consistently upheld the Gelasian theory according to which they had the right and the duty to oblige princes to rule according to the principles of divine justice. While admitting this in theory, perhaps, the Emperors, on the other hand, were reluctant to accept papal dictates that interfered with their actual exercise of power. Another potent issue bearing on the struggle was the conflicting claims of Emperor and Pope to control the ancient capital of Rome. The Popes could not relinquish their rule over Rome and the Papal States without jeopardizing their necessary independence, while the Emperors wanted to possess Rome in order to secure their power in the Italian peninsula as compensation for their inability to control the rebellious German feudal nobility.

The struggle of the papacy with the Hohenstaufens can be traced to the pontificate of Innocent III, who successfully deposed Emperor Otto and personally selected the young prince who was to replace him—his own ward and the grandson of Barbarossa, Frederick Hohenstaufen, the King of Sicily. Ironically, Frederick, whose reign stretched from 1211 to 1250, proved to be the most dangerous of all the adversaries of the papacy, and the conflict between himself and the Popes ultimately proved disastrous for both institutions.

Relations with Frederick began on a good note. In return for Innocent's help in securing the imperial crown, he issued, as we have said, the Golden Bull of Eger (1213), which recognized and guaranteed the integrity of the Papal States, including its recent acquisitions, and emancipated the German Church from imperial control by guaranteeing free episcopal elections and conceding to the papacy the right to decide disputed elections. The satisfaction of both Frederick and the Pope was manifest in Frederick's coronation ceremony at Rome in 1220. Frederick was solemnly escorted through the town by a colorful retinue; he knelt before Innocent's successor, Pope Honorius, kissed his feet, and was then anointed by the Pope on the arm and between the shoulder blades. Then, clad in the imperial vestments, Frederick entered St. Peter's through the silver gate. The Pope there crowned him with miter and crown and handed him the sword, which he lustily brandished three times to show that he was the protector of St. Peter, after which he received the scepter and imperial orb. At the High Mass that followed, he received communion at the Pope's hands and the kiss of peace. Finally all moved in procession outside, where the Emperor held the stirrup of the Pope's horse and led him a few paces forward before mounting his own white horse to return to his camp.

But Frederick soon aroused suspicion when he began to make aggressive moves against the Lombard towns—which the Curia naturally saw as a prelude to an attack on the Papal States. Pope Honorius, mild and conciliatory, temporized, but his successor, Gregory IX (d. 1241), a marvelous, energetic seventy years old, decided to meet the issue squarely. In 1227 he excommunicated Frederick—ostensibly for procrastinating in the fulfillment of his vow to go on crusade—and declared a holy war against him. It was a battle of titans: Frederick—short and stout with red hair, physically unprepossessing, a genius of sorts—was deceitful, cruel, sensual, and bizarre in his tastes. His allies regarded him with suspicion; his enemies saw him as anti-Christ. But no one denied his extraordinary talent for governing men.

In material strength the Pope was definitely at a disadvantage: He had no army of his own except for some small levies off the papal estates, and while

Frederick II crowned by Honorius III, Vincent de Beauvais. From a fifteenth-century manuscript, *Le Miroir Historial.* Musée Condé, Chantilly, France.   © *Giraudon/Art Resource, New York.*

he could call on help from his allies in the Lombard cities, they were too often busy fighting among themselves. As Pope he was head of a vast, well-organized institution, it is true, but he could not always depend on the obedience of the bishops, while his own turbulent city of Rome was unpredictable in its loyalties. This was true even of the College of Cardinals. But Frederick too had handicaps. His German followers showed only weak loyalty, and he was never able to put more than fifteen thousand men on the field at any one time. Even the small Italian cities could withstand him for months.

After some indefinite skirmishes, peace was patched up for a time. But after Frederick's victory over the Lombard town of Cortenuova in 1238, Gregory again excommunicated him. At every High Mass in every church throughout the world, to the accompaniment of bell and burning candle, the priest was to proclaim Frederick's expulsion from the community of believers. And Gregory shot a frenzied encyclical at him that began with the words: "Out of the sea rises up the Beast, full of the names of blasphemy who raging with the claws of the bear and the mouth of the lion and the limbs and likeness of the leopard, opens its mouth to blaspheme the Holy Name and ceases not to hurl its spears against the tabernacle of God and against the saints who dwell in heaven. . . ." Frederick was, the encyclical continued, "a scorpion spewing passion from the sting of his tail . . . a dragon . . . a hammer of the world. . . ."[1]

To deal with the situation, Gregory summoned a council to meet in Rome, but Frederick waylaid the cardinals attending it and fettered them in golden chains. Three months later, in August 1241, Gregory lay dead.

After an incredible conclave lasting almost two years, a successor was chosen—but he died before being consecrated. Then a Genoese was elected, Fieschi, who had previously shown signs of friendliness to Frederick. The Emperor breathed a sigh of relief and waited for the new Pope Innocent IV to lift his excommunication. But Frederick miscalculated. Innocent realized that it would have to be a fight to the finish, since Frederick would exploit any compromise in order to reduce the Church to servility. Innocent pretended therefore to negotiate, while stalling for time. When his plans were laid, Innocent escaped to Lyons, in France, called a general council of the Church, and in 1245 once more solemnly excommunicated and deposed Frederick as a sacrilegious, notorious, heretical blasphemer and oppressor of the Church.

[1] E. Kantorowicz, *Frederick the Second* (New York: Frederick Ungar, 1957), p. 498.

Frederick's wrath knew no bounds. "I have been anvil long enough," he cried, "now I shall play the hammer."[2] The war that ensued covered all of Italy, spread to Germany, and shook Christendom to its foundations—proving, in fact, disastrous for both Empire and papacy. Scenes of horror were enacted in towns and cities all over Europe, as partisans of Pope and Emperor, opposing parties called Guelf and Ghibelline, fought for control. Frederick saw papal assassins and conspirators in every shadow and treated hapless suspects with the utmost barbarism: He had them blinded with red-hot irons, dragged to death by horses over stony ground, sewn up in leather sacks with poisonous snakes, and tossed into the sea. The Pope for his part mobilized every resource of the Church and effectively deployed his spiritual artillery: indulgences for fighting the holy war against Frederick, excommunication, interdict. With magnificent concentration, he strained every fiber of the Church in order to crush one of the most lethal enemies it ever faced.

Frederick seemed on the point of victory when he suffered a terrible defeat in 1248 at Parma, which he had had under siege for several years. Taking advantage of his absence, while he was out hunting, the besieged Parmans burst from behind their walls and burned down his camp, an entirely new city called Vittoria. He was able to recover, however, and again seemed near victory when he was struck down by illness and succumbed in 1250; he died clothed in Cistercian robes after receiving the last sacraments from his chief counselor, Archbishop Berard. Frederick's body was carried to the cathedral of Palermo and buried in a majestic sarcophagus of dark-red porphyry. With him were buried the Hohenstaufen dreams of world empire.

Henceforth the Popes were determined to keep Sicily and the Empire separate. Their first problem therefore was to find a ruler for Sicily who would have no claim to the Empire. This obviously ruled out the Hohenstaufen descendants of Frederick: his sons, Manfred and Conrad, and his grandson, Conradin. The Curia finally found what they were looking for in Charles of Anjou, the brother of the King of France, Louis IX, who later was canonized. Charles solemnly agreed to keep Sicily and the Empire separate. The success of the papal policy was consummated when the other crown—the Empire's— was after a long interregnum finally conferred on Rudolf of Hapsburg, a pious and worthy candidate who promised to be docile and who was elected Emperor in 1273.

---

[2] Ibid., p. 599.

In the meantime, Charles of Anjou managed to secure his hold over Sicily by two great victories: Manfred was slain in battle, and the last Hohenstaufen heir, Conradin, a youth of sixteen, was captured and beheaded in a square at Naples in 1268. His tragic fate secured the papal victory over the Hohenstaufens, but the Popes paid a high price for it. Their use of spiritual weapons in what seemed to many a mere political struggle greatly lowered papal prestige and authority in the public estimation.

Charles, the conqueror of Sicily, found his work all cut out for him. The Sicilians were a haughty people who fiercely resented the French occupation and hated the French soldiers. Notoriously adept at intrigue and conspiracy, the Sicilians began to plot the regime's overthrow. A few French soldiers provided the spark when they recklessly made advances to some pretty maidens during Easter festivities in a crowded church piazza at Palermo on Easter Monday in 1282. A brawl turned into a riot; the cry "Death to the French" echoed quickly across the island, and there was a wholesale slaughter of the French garrison. These "Sicilian Vespers" marked the end of Charles Anjou's rule in Sicily.

The revolution wrote a glamorous chapter in the Sicilian struggle for liberty, but it proved to be an absolute catastrophe for the spiritual authority and prestige of the Holy See—turning into a kind of Vietnam for the papal monarchy. It involved the Popes in a disastrous crusade against the rebels that in the end was unsuccessful. Charles was unable to restore French rule over the island. The humiliation for the papacy was crushing: As with Frederick, the papacy had thrown everything into the struggle—men, money, and spiritual weapons, and all to no avail. The previous affair with the Hohenstaufens was bad enough; but the sight of the Vicar of Christ using spiritual weapons in order to subjugate a freedom-loving people was too much. The conscience of Europe was dismayed. How far respect for papal authority was eroded was soon to be revealed.

The Sicilian war dragged on, and the next papal election found the College of Cardinals bitterly divided over the succession in Sicily and grouped around two powerful Roman families: the Orsini, who favored the French descendants of Charles of Anjou; and the Colonna, favoring the Spanish House of Aragon. The deadlock was finally broken by one of the strangest occurrences in the history of papal elections: Someone shouted the name of Peter Morrone, a barely educated hermit famed for holiness; all present felt inspired by the Holy Spirit, and suddenly and enthusiastically responded to the weird suggestion. The startled monk was brought from his mountain retreat and crowned Pope Celestine V.

He proved totally unequal to the demands of the office, disgusting the cardinals with his eccentricities, ineptitude, and subservience to Charles of Naples, who practically held him in captivity. Fortunately Celestine had the good sense to realize what harm he was doing to the Church, and stepped down in 1294 after less than a year—the last Pope to resign the august office voluntarily. The cardinals, with a sigh of relief, immediately elected Benedict Gaetani, a tall, bald, clean-shaven diplomat with prominent ears and strongly marked features who had made a brilliant curial career, tarnished only by his blunt incisiveness and fearful outbursts of temper. As Boniface VIII (1294–1303), he began a reign that was to mark a watershed in European and Church history.

Few Popes had a more exalted sense of papal authority, and few were as energetic in its exercise. Boniface promulgated his own revision of Canon Law—the Sext; he proclaimed the first papal jubilee, in 1300, which drew a million pilgrims to Rome; he intervened constantly in the affairs of individual dioceses. In Italy he tenaciously pursued the papal policy of guaranteeing the independence of the Papal States by a system of direct conquest and alliances. He was determined, like his predecessors, to impose a papal vassal on Sicily, but like them he failed and finally settled for a compromise peace.

On the international stage, where the defeat of the Hohenstaufen left no serious rival to papal authority, Boniface acted as the unchallenged arbiter of European affairs. But this situation was not destined to last very long. A new political force was beginning to gain momentum: nationalism. It would replace the idea of Christendom with the theory that the largest autonomous unit should be the territorial or national state. It was espoused by various monarchs who gradually built up their power over their people in hopes of shaking off the papal yoke as soon as they were strong enough.

Such a monarch was Philip the Fair, who reached the throne of France in 1285. He was an extremely amoral and cunning tyrant whose only aim in life was the creation of a strong French nation. It was fateful for the future of the papacy that precisely at that juncture a profoundly conservative and intransigent man should occupy the seat of Peter, a Pope unable even to imagine what a new world of nation states might mean for the Church.

The conflict between Boniface and Philip began over the issue of clerical taxation. Like other Kings of Europe, busy consolidating their realms, Philip needed money and found the wealth of the Church a temptation too great to resist. When he imposed some extremely heavy taxes on the clergy, Boniface responded with his maladroit bull *Clericis Laicos* (1296), which levied excommunication on anyone taxing clerical property without authorization from the Holy See. Philip retaliated by forbidding the export of any monies from France, cutting off a major source of papal revenue. But a final confrontation was postponed when both sides accepted a compromise solution.

Philip remained fixed, however, in his resolve to break the Church and make it a useful servant, only biding his time until he enjoyed more favorable political conditions. Apparently he felt the time was ripe in 1301, when he intervened in the case of the maverick bishop of Pamiers, who was arrested and accused of a variety of crimes. In violation of clerical immunity, Philip subjected him to a trial that was a caricature of justice and that Philip no doubt regarded as a kind of trial balloon—if he could get away with it, he would know what to do next. For Boniface it was the climax of the perfidious King's outrages against the Church, and he would not let it pass. His bull *Ausculta Fili* was outspoken: It reminded Philip of his subordination to the Pope (*ratione peccati*—when there was a question of sin involved), it listed Philip's crimes, and it summoned the French bishops to a council to be held at Rome.

And now Philip made his appeal to the new historical force, national sentiment, which was invulnerable to the spiritual weapons of the Pope. Launching a new and powerful weapon—public opinion—he mobilized an unscrupulous smear campaign against Boniface. A falsified bull was circulated representing the Pope as claiming direct temporal power over the King. When the public showed itself properly outraged at this supposed example of papal arrogance, Philip convoked the three estates to register public support—a concerted defiance of Rome that marked a new advance in the history of the French Government. By trickery and duress he won over at least half of the clergy.

It was amid these depressing circumstances—with only half of the French bishops present at the council the Pope had called to Rome—that Boniface promulgated the bull *Unam Sanctam,* the most famous statement of papal prerogatives. It set forth no new doctrines; it spent little time on argument or proof, but merely reiterated in resounding trumpet blasts of Latin the traditional claim of the papacy to ultimate sovereignty over the Christian European social order. This, it says, is a power given by Christ to St. Peter, an ordinance established by God that must be obeyed. The Pope can be judged by no man but by God alone; no earthly power can claim independence of the Pope, and insofar as any act has moral implications, it is subject to his judgment. The temporal power is therefore subordinate to the spiritual power, and every human creature must be subject to the Roman Pontiff.

Philip called a meeting of his council that included a good representation of the higher clergy. This assembly then issued a call for a general council of the Church and drew up a tremendous indictment of Boniface. An ingenious mixture of truth and fantasy, it seized on trivial incidents and magnified angry casual utterances of the Pope as though they were doctrinal declarations. The Pope was accused of being an open materialist, with no faith in the immortality of the soul; of not believing in transubstantiation, of neglecting to fast, of forcing priests to reveal the secrets of the confessional; of practicing nearly every form of sexual misconduct; of keeping a private demon and consulting sorcerers; of being an outrageous simonist; of setting up silver images of himself in the churches; and of desiring the ruin of France. There was no attempt here to face the real issue as defined by *Unam Sanctam*. Philip's document concentrated on Boniface the man, and in its very excess of vituperation showed up the very real weakness of Philip's case.

Boniface had not yet taken the final step: excommunication. But now he acted. At his residence in Anagni, his native city, situated on a rocky crag above the broad valley of the Sacco River south of Rome, he prepared the bull that would excommunicate Philip and release his subjects from their obedience. But a daring plan had already been concocted by the King: His henchman Nogaret was ready to capture the Pope and bring him to France, where he would be forced to summon a council that would then depose him. Nogaret was already in Italy when he heard of the impending bull. He acted swiftly. On September 3, 1303, with three hundred horsemen and a thousand foot soldiers, he entered the town under cover of early-morning darkness through a gate left open by traitors and forced his way up the narrow streets to storm the papal palace. After a day of desperate fighting, his troops battered down the doors and found the aged Pope dressed in full regalia and, according to some accounts, seated on his throne with the cross in his hands.

Nogaret was unable to carry away his prisoner, however. The mercurial townspeople suffered a change of heart, rallied, and rescued the Pontiff. But the eighty-five-year-old man could not long survive such a trauma and died within a month.

As the drama at Canossa ushered in the period of papal greatness, so the tragedy at Anagni signalized its decline. The events of the next decade showed how surely Philip had gained the upper hand over the Popes. The next Pope died almost immediately after election. His successor—elected after a long deadlock—was a Frenchman, Bertrand de Got, archbishop of Bordeaux, who was still in France at the time of his election and was crowned Clement V in Lyons. Amiable, vacillating, and sickly, he was no match for the King. Philip was able to detain him in France by blackmailing him with the threat of staging a posthumous trial of Boniface. Using the same threat, he wrenched from Clement a condemnation of the Knights Templars at the Council of Vienne in 1312 to serve his own political purposes; it was one of the most scandalous defeats ever suffered by the papacy.

IN 1305 CLEMENT transferred the papal court to Avignon in southern France, thus beginning the Avignon period of the papacy—the time when the Popes ruled the Church from this town. Their stay here lasted until 1378, embracing the pontificates of seven Popes, and marked a further stage in the decline of the papal monarchy.

Avignon was an ideal location for the peaceful refuge, since its neighboring *comstat*, Venaissin, already belonged to the Holy See; it was strongly fortified and close to Italy. Clement thought of it only as a temporary residence while he cleared up the vexing problems raised by the French King. But once the Popes were established there, many factors prolonged their stay: the constant turbulence in Italy, incessantly at war; the intrigues of the French Kings, who hoped to use the papacy for their interests; the preponderance of French cardinals in the Curia; the illness of several Popes, and finally, their renewed, anticlimactic struggle with the Holy Roman Emperors, which increased the Popes' dependence on the good will of the French King.

At the accession of John XXII, Clement's successor, in 1316, it was quite obvious that the papacy had fallen on hard times. The Curia was disorganized by a long vacancy, the apostolic treasury exhausted by Clement's extravagances and its independence compromised by the intrigues of Philip. The Papal States were engulfed in war. A massive effort was obviously called for if the papacy was to survive as the chief spiritual power in Christendom.

To the credit of the Avignon Popes, it can be said that at least they tried. Without exception worthy and religious men, even austere in some cases, they consistently pursued the goal of reorganizing the administration of the

Church, refurbishing its finances, combating heresy, reforming abuses, proclaiming new Crusades, and propagating the Gospel. They labored tirelessly and effectively to revitalize their authority and make its influence felt in every corner of Christendom. They strengthened their control over appointments, even at the parish level. They encouraged the practice of appeals to papal tribunals. They strove with great energy for reform and did their utmost to restore to the cloisters the practice of poverty, work, and study.

Much of their work for reform was undone by forces beyond their control. One such force was the terrible Black Death, a quickly fatal disease spread by the black rat. The Black Death decimated the population of Europe, periodically flaring up every ten years or so after its initial outbreak in 1348. It depopulated the convents, depleted the ranks of the clergy, and profoundly disrupted monastic life. Besides, there were the continual wars waged by freebooters who roamed the countryside and found monasteries and convents particularly good targets to sack; they laid waste their fields, driving out the monks and violating the nuns. Amid all the disorder, many monasteries virtually expired, and the number of wandering monks increased, many of them swelling the bands of flagellants and fanatics—a dangerous rabble who seized Church property, defied all authority, and preached revolution.

In their efforts to govern the Church effectively in a time of extreme disorder, the Avignon Popes were hard pressed for money. As the first rulers in Europe to institute a regular system of taxation, the Popes had over the centuries developed a mighty fiscal machine that the Avignon Popes under the stress of new necessities now raised to a degree of efficiency unrivaled by any secular government. A vast array of ingenious taxes and fees were levied on bishops, abbots, and pastors. Some were payable directly to the Curia, some were collected by papal collectors who often had to resort to harsh measures to squeeze payment out of recalcitrants. Thus on July 5, 1328, in a single papal audience, no fewer than one patriarch, five archbishops, thirty bishops, and forty-six abbots were excommunicated for default on their taxes. Naturally, all of this provoked lively criticism at times and sometimes even rebellion. Contemporary chronicles tell of papal tax collectors being hunted down, thrown into dark prisons, mutilated, and even strangled by irate debtors.

These Avignon Popes—rightly or wrongly—put great faith in the efficacy of external pomp. In an age of increasing wealth, they felt it necessary to display a magnificence on a scale equal to their claims. A massive palace was built whose forbidding parapets still dazzle the eye of the tourist. A crowd of courtiers—knights, squires, and chamberlains, their ranks swelled by an army of hungry benefice seekers—filled the spacious rooms. The palace's luxurious furnishings were the talk of Europe. Avignon outshone all other courts by the extravagance of its style and the brilliance of its feasts. It was soon reckoned the most civilized court in Europe—a magnet for artists and scholars.

It was unfortunate that the Popes built up their administration and power without giving much attention to the remarkable revival of mystical devotion produced by the disasters of the fourteenth century or to the rise of an educated laity. And it seemed most questionable whether they could transform the hierarchy into a more spiritual-minded body of men living in closer conformity to the Gospel.

It was their constant intention to return to Italy as soon as they could pacify their rebellious states. A talented general was found in the person of Gil Albornoz, who was commissioned in 1352 to reimpose papal rule over the states. This was a heroic task, since they were in a state of near disintegration. The general's resources were meager at a time when warfare was becoming very expensive, with the advent of gunpowder; rude cannons now could fire five-pound iron balls, and soldiers had to be equipped with muskets and guns. But thanks to indomitable courage and skill, Albornoz was able to subdue the rebellious towns; he deserves the title Second Founder of the Papal States.

Escorted by two thousand men-at-arms, Pope Urban V entered Rome on October 16, 1367. The rejoicing of Christendom was premature, however, for Urban soon felt the ground moving beneath him as discord broke out in Rome. Longing for the sweetness and peace of his native land, he returned to Avignon. But his successor, Gregory XI (1370–77), realized that papal authority over the states might be fatally jeopardized if the Pope did not return soon and permanently to govern his Italian subjects—and urged on by St. Catherine of Siena, he once more returned to Rome. But hardly had he time to size up the situation before death carried him off on March 27, 1378. As the cardinals gathered in Rome to elect the next Pope, it was evident that the papal monarchy was at a turning point. The big question was: Could its decline be arrested?

THE PAPACY SURVIVES THE GREAT SCHISM AND PUTS DOWN CONCILIARISM

The scandal of the papacy's seventy-year absence from Rome was followed by the incredible disaster of the forty-year Great Schism, when two and eventually three Popes fought each other for control of the Church. To solve this crisis, an antipapalist theology of Church government—conciliarism—was brought forth. It asserted the supremacy of a council over a Pope and provided the Council of Constance with a way out of the schism. But in the circumstances the conciliar system of Church order proved unworkable, and the Popes were able to re-establish their supremacy over councils. But they were unable to regain their moral and spiritual authority.

A MAJOR FACTOR in the origin of the Great Schism was the part played by the people of Rome. Throughout the city's papal history, the Romans' behavior followed a curious pattern: They were extremely fickle, unpredictable, addicted to petty squabbles, showing little faith or piety, unruly, and in view of Rome's position as the center of the universal Church, strangely narrowminded. The Popes could never count on their loyalty for long; they would revolt on the slightest pretext and drive their ruler out, only to repent on the morrow and beg him to return. Few scenes were more characteristic or paradoxical in the history of the Middle Ages than the spectacle of the worldruling Pontiff in headlong flight from his capital with a blaspheming rabble at his heels, a rabble that soon afterward would piously entreat him to return; for in his absence they would quickly realize that they had lost their major source of revenue, the chief tourist attraction for the mass of pilgrims who streamed into the Eternal City, filling its coffers with their coins.

So one can imagine the intense dismay felt by the Roman populace at the death of Gregory XI: It meant once more a very good chance of their losing the Pope. In view of French predominance in the College of Cardinals, a French Pope might well be elected who would once more move the papacy back to Avignon. Dismay soon gave way to panic as the sixteen cardinals assembled on April 7, 1378. Some of them were assaulted in the street and warned by bullies to elect an Italian. A riotous crowd kept up a great uproar while the cardinals tried to deliberate in conclave. The guard of the conclave told them, "You risk being torn to pieces if you don't hasten to elect an Italian or a Roman."

The cardinals quickly elected an Italian, the archbishop of Bari, Bartholomew Prignano, who was not even one of their number. In the meantime, a mob in ugly mood had seized the papal wine cellars and invaded the Vatican; while waiting for Prignano to arrive, the cardinals dressed up one of their colleagues—Tebaldeschi—who was old and feeble, and they presented him in papal robes to pacify the crowd.

Whether the cardinals were really overpowered by fear and hence unfree when they elected Prignano—as they later alleged—will, it seems, remain forever one of the tantalizing but insoluble questions of Church history. Nevertheless, it should be noted that at first they offered the new Pope their homage and submission and in their correspondence at the time spoke of having "freely and unanimously" elected him Pope.

As vice chancellor of the Curia, Prignano was well known to the cardinals and highly regarded for his dependable character. Hence they were stupefied, to put it mildly, when the new Pope Urban VI suddenly showed himself a tyrant of the worst sort. Seizing any and every occasion, he upbraided them publicly and privately—often in paroxysms of rage—for their vices, their treachery, their luxury, their simony. The personality change was so radical that contemporaries as well as later historians feel that Urban may have been mentally unhinged by his sudden and unexpected election or perhaps by illness. His behavior brought on a terrible catastrophe for the Church—the Great Schism—justly named because of its exceptional duration and scope. Coming on the heels of previous misfortunes afflicting the papacy, it brought the papal office to the utter depths of degradation and did more than any other event to discredit its authority.

The schism began when the cardinals—whose original misgivings were greatly exacerbated by Urban's behavior—decided they had had enough. Abandoning Rome, they took refuge at Fondi, and then—thirteen in all— elaborated an encyclical in which they declared Prignano's election invalid and denounced him as anti-Christ, demon, apostate, and tyrant. The first secular ruler to join them was Queen Joan of Naples. Their number was also enlarged by the three Italian cardinals who soon joined them. On September 20, the dissidents unanimously elected a new Pope, Robert of Geneva, who took the name Clement VII.

Politics, as one might expect, played a big role. Both Popes received support from civil governments—splitting Western Christendom into two camps. The Holy Roman Emperor, England, the Netherlands, Castille, Hungary, Poland, and Portugal stood behind Urban, while France rallied to Clement VII, who returned to Avignon in 1379 and was soon joined by Scotland, Luxembourg, and Austria. Others, like Aragon, claimed neutrality, at least for a time, while Italy itself was too confused for either side to count on. At first both sides appealed to a decision of arms: Urban proclaimed a crusade against Clement and hired the sanguinary Charles of Durazzo to oust the renegade Queen Joan from Naples. The English invaded France in order to break its allegiance to Clement.

Both Popes found military operations very expensive, and the papal tax collectors were forced to use ever harsher methods to squeeze every penny out of their constituents—bringing papal popularity to a new low. Urban turned more violent and savage. Suspecting his own cardinals of plotting against him, he put them to torture, and five of them died shortly afterward, probably thrown overboard from the Pope's warship. After traversing Italy with his army, Pope Urban VI returned to Rome, where he died in 1389. His fourteen cardinals immediately elected a successor, who took the name Boniface IX. He proclaimed a jubilee year in 1390, and crowds flowed in to gain the plenary indulgence.

This rupture of the Church's unity was a terrible trial for believing Catholics—and all pious souls who loved the Church were shaken to the roots in seeing the papacy made an object of derision. Saints, intellectuals, and bishops on both sides, realizing that recourse to arms was a false avenue, offered several alternatives: arbitration, a general council, or resignation of both Popes.

This last idea was the solution favored at the University of Paris, where ten thousand responses were obtained in a poll of general student opinion.

For a time resignation seemed to offer the best chance of ending the schism. Hopes were stirred when the Avignon Pope, Clement VII, died in 1394, and each of the candidates to succeed him swore an oath that if elected he would resign his office. But the one elected, Benedict XIII, a formidable prelate of incredible tenacity and guile, soon showed that he had no intention of honoring his pre-election oath. In disgust, France finally withdrew its obedience officially in 1398, and a long duel began between the Pope at Avignon and the rest of France. The King, cardinals, and bishops tried every means to change Benedict's mind—they even laid siege to his palace—but all in vain. Their indomitable and wily adversary held out behind his battlements at Avignon—even refusing to shave his beard as long as the siege lasted—and after five years he tasted the sweets of victory: France totally capitulated and returned to his obedience.

Hopes were again renewed in 1406 with the election of a new Roman Pope, Gregory XII, a pious and austere churchman who seemed dedicated to restoring the unity of the Church and had sworn to resign if his rival at Avignon would do the same. Benedict for his part was faced with another move by his clergy to withdraw obedience and realized that he could no longer appear less anxious for reunion than his rival.

So finally realistic negotiations seemed about to begin: Both Popes agreed to meet to discuss their joint resignations. But then the insincerity of both men surfaced. Gregory trumped up some feeble excuses for not being able to go to the town chosen for the meeting place: Savona, west of Genoa, near the border of France and Italy. Benedict in the meantime secretly prepared a military expedition against Rome. Then Benedict agreed to go as far east as Porto Venere, while Gregory moved from Siena to Lucca—only a day's walk from a rendezvous acceptable to Benedict. But still the two would come no closer to each other.

Finally, in despair of seeing either Pope resign, the cardinals on both sides decided that a council would be the only solution. This idea of a conciliar solution to the schism was first enunciated in 1380 and had since been taken up by such eminent Parisian theologians as d'Ailly and Gerson. The general theory it involved was called conciliarism, and its basic principle was that in case of dire necessity a council could be called without the Pope's consent or even against his will, and its decrees would be valid without the Pope's consent. This doctrine of conciliar supremacy, which was to agitate the Church for the next thirty years, was revolutionary; papal supremacy over a council had the huge weight of tradition behind it. But the best minds of Europe agreed that it was the only answer—even if the Canon Law on papal prerogatives had to be sacrificed.

So at the behest of the cardinals of both allegiances, an imposing assembly of churchmen gathered at Pisa on March 25, 1409, including most of the dignitaries of the Church. Several officials even appeared on the cathedral steps and acted out a ceremony of summoning the absent Popes to present themselves. After a brief pause, the Popes were then declared contumacious and schismatical, notorious heretics, guilty of scandalizing the universal Church and therefore deposed. The townspeople reacted with wild joy and burned the old Popes in effigy. A new Pope was elected: Peter Philargi, cardinal of Milan, a seventy-year-old Venetian with an excellent reputation as a theologian, canonist, and diplomat. He took the name of Alexander V.

The miracle was premature. By their haste in electing a Pope the cardinals only aggravated the sickness, for the other Popes still commanded the allegiances of large parts of the Church. Moreover, the Council of Pisa did nothing for the reform of the Church except draw up a list of grievances that excoriated the prevalent abuses: the frequent moving of bishops from see to see, the extravagances of the papal taxation system, and the tendency of the papal court to infringe on lower jurisdictions.

The new Pope, Alexander V, did not even manage to reach his see of Rome before dying at Bologna on May 3, 1410. His successor, who took the name John XXIII, was an odd choice: Baldassare Cossa, who had made his reputation as a kind of ecclesiastical conquistador during the wars of the Great Schism and who had taken the lead in calling the Council of Pisa but who, according to many, perhaps libelous reports of the time, was a moral and spiritual cipher. In any case, John entered Rome behind an army on April 12, 1411, and as one of his first acts summoned a council to meet at Rome. According to a chronicle of the time, a screech owl settled on John's head at the opening of the council as he intoned the invocation "Come, Holy Spirit," and he was supposed to have muttered, "a strange shape for the Holy Spirit!" In any case, the council had to be suspended for lack of participants. Moreover, John's unscrupulous financial expedients and brazen nepotism alienated many of his supporters. It was soon rather obvious that if Christendom was to be restored to unity, John was not the man to do it.

But then a new personality entered the picture: Sigismund of Luxembourg, recently elected Holy Roman Emperor and dedicated heart and soul to the unity of both the Church and of Europe. After some arm twisting he secured John's agreement to his decree calling for a universal council of the Church to be held November 1, 1414, at Constance—an imperial city chosen for its location and salubrious climate.

And so, on October 28, 1414, John XXIII—with fatalistic forbodings—entered the town of Constance on a white horse clad in the vestments of the liturgy under a golden canopy followed by his cardinals amid the hosannas of a jubilant fanfare. A huge crowd of ecclesiastics from all over Europe filled the streets, and some thirty-six thousand beds, according to one chronicle, had to be found for the visitors, with two to a bed. Once again, as at Pisa, virtually the whole of Western Christendom was represented, including five patriarchs, twenty-nine cardinals, thirty-three archbishops, more than five hundred bishops, a hundred abbots, three hundred doctors of sacred science, and eighteen thousand other clerics.

In his opening address, John defined the objectives of the council as union and reform. But it was only with the arrival of Sigismund on December 24 that serious work could begin. The assembly was divided into conservative and liberal wings. The latter was made up of liberal reformers led by Gerson and d'Ailly, who were highly regarded for their writings in favor of conciliarism.

The first question facing the fathers was the momentous one presented by John himself. The liberals agreed that he must first be put down if unity was to be restored. All three Popes would then be persuaded, and if necessary forced, to resign. But the objective could hardly be attained by the traditional method of voting, which allowed one vote to each bishop. John had deliberately stacked the episcopate with his supporters, and he controlled a large bloc of votes, mainly Italian. A radical change in voting method was therefore imperative. The idea of voting by nations was proposed, with men like Cardinal d'Ailly, Philastre, and Robert Hallam leading the discussion. With the support of Sigismund, it was decided that the council should be organized into nations and vote accordingly. In addition, in the general wave of democratic enthusiasm, the right to vote was extended to doctors of theology and law and even to some laymen. Matters would therefore first be treated and voted on in the individual assemblies of each nation (eventually five were recognized: Italy, France, Germany, England, and Spain), and then after agreement was reached in the assemblies, each nation, acting as a unit, would cast its one vote.

John saw that he had been outmaneuvered, and at first, it seems, he decided to accept the inevitable. On March 1, 1415, he personally read before the council his solemn promise to abdicate whenever the other two Popes did so. Since it was felt they would soon follow suit, John's act was greeted with jubilation; Sigismund knelt and kissed the Pope's feet, while the church bells of Constance echoed the universal joy. But once again, bitter deception lay in store. On March 20, under cover of night, John, disguised as a groom, escaped from Constance, followed by a considerable number of council dignitaries from his entourage, and found refuge with his protector, the Duke of Austria. A great commotion broke out in the city when the news broke; a mob pillaged the papal palace, and the whole Council might have dispersed at that point had it not been for the presence of mind of Sigismund, who rode through the streets urging all to remain and to keep the peace.

Feelings were still running high, however, when Cardinal Zabarella addressed the full assembly on March 26. It was resolved that the departure of Pope John changed nothing. The Council decided to stay in session until the schism was healed and the Church reformed in head and members. Nor were the fathers dissuaded by conciliatory messages from John. They went ahead in a violent mood, and with Gerson and the University of Paris doctors leading the debate, passed a number of sweeping decrees, climaxed by the famous *Sacrosancta* of April 6, 1415—the most revolutionary of all conciliar decrees. It asserted the superiority of the council over the Pope declaring that it had "its power directly from Christ and that all persons of whatever rank or dignity, even Pope, are bound to obey it in matters relating to faith and the end of the Schism and the general reformation of the Church of God in head and members . . . and that any person . . . even a Pope who contumaciously refuses to obey . . . regulations enacted . . . by this holy synod, or by other general council lawfully assembled . . . shall . . . be subject to condign penalty. . . ."[1]

Great indeed now was the humiliation of the papacy in all three of its claimants. But most wretched was John, who soon found himself deserted by his protector and forced to surrender his papal seal and throw himself on the mercy of the council. He was taken back to Constance, tried by the council,

[1] *Filastre's Diary*, ed. L. Loomis (New York: Columbia University Press, 1961), p. 229.

found guilty of numerous crimes, and deposed. The Pope of the Roman line, Gregory XII, chose a more dignified end: He voluntarily resigned after officially convoking the council in order to formalize its legitimacy. The last member of the trio, the Avignon Pope, resisted the most heroic efforts of Sigismund, however, and remained adamant in his refusal to resign. Tried in absentia by the council and deposed, he took refuge in the impregnable fortress of Peñiscola on the coast of Spain, and there his line came to an end years later after an ignominious charade, when his last surviving cardinal elected himself Pope.

In the midst of all the furor over John, another event of immense significance took place: John Hus, the Prague reformer, was burned at the stake on July 6, 1415.

The next question facing the council was whether to elect the Pope immediately or to postpone this election until it first accomplished its other great objective: the reform of the Church. Many, including Emperor Sigismund, feared reform might be jeopardized if a Pope were elected first, since he would be able to block it. Finally a compromise was reached: The churchmen would first proceed with election of the Pope, but in order to guarantee that any Pope elected would carry out the reform, the decree *Frequens* was first passed on October 9, 1417, obliging all future Popes to call regular councils at stipulated intervals.

A new method of electing the Pope also reflected the radical spirit of the council: Six delegates of each nation—thirty in all—joined with the cardinals to choose the new Pope. On November 11, 1417, while a huge procession of clergy and laity chanted hymns outside—so sweetly and devoutly, one observer said, that it stirred many of the electors to tears—they chose Oddo Colonna, a prelate honored by all for his piety, moderation, and wisdom. Around this Pope, Martin V, Christendom was once again reunited. The Great Schism was over.

Successful as it was in attaining the first of its two major objectives—unity—the council failed tragically in regard to the second—reform. And yet everyone was conscious of the evil state of affairs caused by the Great Schism: the degradation of the papacy; the exorbitant demands of the rival papal tax collectors; the breakdown of the Church courts; the absenteeism of bishops; the ignorance and immorality of the clergy, and the simony everywhere—most blatantly in the Roman Curia, whose excessive dispensations and indulgences were the scandal of Europe.

Recognizing these abuses was one thing; getting the various interest groups to agree on their eradication was another. As it turned out, each interest group wanted to reform its rival but was reluctant to begin by reforming itself. Moreover and paradoxically, the very system of organizing the council into nations, which had enabled the council to repair the schism, was the cause of the failure to complete its other task—the reform of the Church; for this system pitted nation against nation, and their conflicting interests prevented them from agreeing on specific reform measures. As a result, the reform decree finally passed on March 21, 1418, was of the most vague and general kind: It limited papal powers, condemned simony, and called for regularity in clerical conduct. Other reforms were left for the Pope to carry out by means of concordats with the individual nations, the German Concordat of May 2, 1418, serving as a model. But this strategy proved woefully inadequate.

The liberals, however, still had hopes of carrying out a thorough-going reform of the Church by means of future councils as prescribed by *Frequens*. But for this to happen, Pope and council would have to work together harmoniously in the new relationship set up by Constance. But what if this failed to happen? What if, as some pessimists predicted, conflict and rivalry between Pope and council were to render the work of reform impossible? As happens too often, history vindicated the gloomy forebodings of the pessimists.

The newly elected Pope wisely decided to return to Rome, but it took two years before he could enter the capital of the world, which had fallen into a wretched, desolate condition—its inhabitants a prey to the wolves that roamed its streets. Martin proved himself a true Roman by the dauntless energy he showed in restoring and repairing the city's crumbling bridges, walls, and churches. And he once more secured papal rule over the states of the Church by the traditional system of family alliances. But unfortunately, preoccupation with this Italian game of war and intrigue forced him, as well as his successors before the Reformation, to subordinate the interests of the universal Church to the necessities of peninsular politics.

So while successful on the Italian political stage, Martin failed to lead the Church to the complete reformation that was so sorely needed. Had he been able to do so, the bitter conflict of Pope and council during the next pontificate might have been averted, as well as its long-term consequence: the Protestant Reformation.

Some historians put most of the blame on Martin, whom they accuse of sabotaging the council of Pavia-Siena after dutifully convoking it in 1423, as he was obliged to do by *Frequens*. Two things should be kept in mind, however: First, Martin wanted to restore papal monarchy within the framework of a moderate conciliarism; second, his lack of enthusiasm for the council might be justified by the contentious spirit it manifested and which seemed to be a carry-over from the bad days of Constance. In any case, the council was dissolved by his legates in 1424, with no accomplishments.

It was up to his successor, Eugenius IV, a tall, dignified Venetian, pious, austere, and learned—but lacking in tact and gentleness—to make the next attempt. Possibly from the beginning, he was opposed to the conciliarism that would turn the absolutely sovereign papacy into a limited monarchy. In any case, he soon found reasons to dislike the new council at Basel, whose convocation he had ratified and which had opened on July 23, 1431. Within a few months he and the council were at dagger's point. Shortly after the council opened, Eugenius began to receive tendentious reports about its character and circumstances. There were few prelates in attendance, it was asserted; there was disorder in the neighborhood of Basel; pro-Hussite sympathies were manifesting themselves. The Pope's poor state of health and the fighting going on around Rome lessened his interest in what was happening beyond the Alps. Moreover, the Greeks had showed some interest in a council of union, and Eugenius didn't want to have two councils running at the same time. So he decided to dissolve the council at Basel, and he gave orders to that effect in a bull to his legate, Cesarini.

It was a mistake, for, as Cesarini explained to him in a strong letter, the bishops at Basel were determined to deal with the tragic situation in Germany, where the low standard of the clergy cried out for immediate reform before new heresies could erupt. The members of the council therefore would not even entertain the idea of dissolution and would certainly defy the Pope, even if it meant a schism. But the Pope remained adamant and rejected Cesarini's plea. As Cesarini predicted, the council refused to accept the Pope's bull. While carrying on with considerable success its negotiations with the followers of John Hus, it advanced from a simple refusal to obey the Pope to a flat assertion of its conciliarist position: It declared itself superior to the Pope and insisted that it could not be adjourned or transferred, even by the Pope. Two months later it even ordered Eugenius to appear before it.

This was the culmination of a struggle against papal absolutism that began with Pisa's deposition of the two reigning Popes. But in proclaiming their authority over a legitimate and universally recognized Pope, the bishops at Basel carried their conciliarism to the point of absolute revolution.

But would they succeed? At first, it seemed likely. Fifteen out of twenty-one of the cardinals stood with the bishops at Basel. The number of bishops present continued to grow, and the greater part of Christendom's rulers rallied to their side. Eugenius himself was hard pressed by his enemies in Italy; he was even forced to escape in disguise in a boat down the Tiber. With much interior repugnance he finally capitulated, and in the bull *Dudum Sacrum* of December 1433, he retracted his previous acts against the council and recognized its rights without any reservation.

Basel then took up the great challenge of reform of the Church. Once again, as at Constance, insuperable difficulties began to crop up. Each interest group, it seemed, was expert in what was wrong with everyone else—as interminable discourses indicated—but each was loath to admit its own faults. One thing all could agree on, however: the papacy's need of reform. And the council went to work with a vengeance on the fiscal abuses prevalent in the Curia. But the bishops went too far when they swept away completely the Pope's right to tax the clergy, to collect the annates, and to promulgate indulgences. This was to make him a penniless figurehead and reduce him and the Curia to complete financial dependence on the council. They could hardly expect any Pope to agree to such a radical turnabout.

These measures completely alienated the Pope, and he only waited his chance to regain the upper hand. His opportunity came with the matter of reunion with the Greeks. After centuries of abortive efforts, the time seemed ripe for reunion of the Eastern Church and the Western Church. The Eastern Emperor, besieged by the advancing Turks, was anxious to have Western support, and he opened negotiations with both the Pope and the council.

The choice of the place to meet with the Greeks took on a decisive significance: The Pope wanted an Italian location; the council wanted a non-Italian location, lest a move to Italy be interpreted as a victory for the Pope. A three-cornered discussion then began among Greeks, Basel, and papacy, which lasted two years. Finally the Greeks accepted the Pope's suggestion and decided on an Italian city.

The decision produced a grave crisis for the council at Basel, where a split into factions occurred when a majority voted against moving to Italy, while a minority favored the papal plan. The vote on the question took place at the twenty-fifth session, on May 7, 1437, amid wild scenes of disorder as the leaders of both groups fought hand to hand to seize the rostrum, while their followers during the Mass faced each other like two armies. To confound the confusion, the decrees of both groups were read aloud at the same time. Many wept at the sight of the ugly commotion, and as one participant, Aeneas Sylvius Piccolomini, later Pope Pius II, remarked, one would not have deserved the name Christian if he did not grieve at such a spectacle.

It marked the beginning of the end for the council at Basel. Many bishops left in disgust and joined the Pope, who now being in a much stronger position transferred the council to Ferrara, Italy. By 1439 only a remnant still stood its ground at Basel; Cesarini deserted it on June 25, 1439. In defiance, the bishops at Basel deposed Eugenius, and on November 5, 1439, they elected their own pope, Felix V, history's last anti-Pope.

But by this time the triumph of Eugenius was assured. While the rump at Basel carried on its verbose wrangling, the Pope at Florence, surrounded by the majority of bishops, solemnly concluded the reunion of the Eastern Church and the Western Church on July 5, 1439, and was recognized by the Greeks as the true Vicar of Christ and head of the universal Church. It was hailed throughout Europe as a tremendous feat (although it was soon nullified by the refusal of the Eastern Church to ratify it), and it consummated the victory of the Pope over the conciliarists.

The council at Basel, however, stubbornly lingered on, though the great powers one by one deserted it; France, after passing the pro-Gallican Pragmatic Sanction of Bourges (1438), first declared itself neutral but soon declared in favor of Eugenius; Aragon and Scotland did likewise in 1443. Finally the Concordat of Vienna, signed in 1448 by the Holy See with Emperor Frederick and the German princes, gave the death blow to the Basel assembly. Its members were ordered by the Emperor to quit Basel. Felix resigned in 1449, and the council dissolved.

The papacy had triumphed over conciliarism, but it failed to re-establish its moral and spiritual leadership over Christendom. In many ways the real victor of the crisis was the modern state, which exploited the quarrel between Pope and council in order to expand its authority over the Church. In England, France, and Spain, at least, national churches were rapidly arising.

Chapter 18

THE CHURCH FAILS TO
REFORM ITSELF IN TIME

In the summer of 1454 one of the best-informed men in Europe, Aeneas Sylvius Piccolomini (later Pope Pius II), was traveling in Germany as papal legate a year after Constantinople had fallen to the Ottoman Turks. In a long letter he described his fears for the future of the Latin Christian world:

> I prefer to be silent and I could wish that my opinion may prove entirely wrong and that I may be called a liar rather than a true prophet. . . . For I have no hope that what I should like to see will be realized; I cannot persuade myself that there is anything good in prospect. . . . Christianity has no head whom all will obey. Neither the pope nor the emperor is accorded his rights. There is no reverence and no obedience; we look on pope and emperor as figureheads and empty titles. Every city state has its king and there are as many princes as there are households.[1]

One could indeed draw a pessimistic picture of the European Christian community at the time. The Great Schism was a thing of the past, but its spiritual effects were still prevalent. The conciliar movement was put down, but papal authority could not easily recover from those disastrous forty years when Christians witnessed three men wearing the papal tiara anathematizing each other.

[1] *Pius II: Opera omnia* (Basel, 1571), p. 656, quoted in M. P. Gilmore, *The World of Humanism, 1453–1517* (New York: Harper & Row, 1952), p. 1.

Pius II arriving at Ancona and calling forth the Crusade, *Scenes from the Life of Aeneas Sylvius Piccolomini.* Bernardino Pinturicchio (1454–1513). Liberia Piccolomini, Duomo, Siena, Italy.   © *Scala/Art Resource, New York.*

But it was not only the papacy that was in trouble; the condition of the Christian Church as a whole gave cause for alarm. At every level of Church life there were signs of grave disorganization and decay.

Let us begin at the top of the pyramid, with the Roman Curia. The reformers at Basel castigated it as the major scandal in the Church; but they were not alone: The Curia's wickedness was a constant theme of reform literature of the fifteenth century. All the evils of the Church were attributed to it: "The members were sick because the head was sick," it was said. And the cause of the sickness, they alleged, was simony.

Simony was at the heart of the curial system as it functioned before Luther. The Popes had gained control of a large number of ecclesiastical appointments, and their sale was a lucrative and even necessary source of papal income. By the time of Leo X (d. 1521), it is estimated that there were some two thousand marketable Church jobs, which were literally sold over the counter at the Vatican; even a cardinal's hat might go to the highest bidder.

Besides, there were an immense variety of taxes levied by the Curia on the newly conferred benefices. In order to ascend his throne as archbishop of Mainz, for instance, Albrecht of Brandenburg had to pay a tax of ten thousand ducats, and the indulgence that he promoted in order to secure the necessary funds involved him in an unsavory deal with the Curia. Luther's protest stamped this deal with everlasting notoriety—but actually it was quite typical of a deeply rooted curial practice.

Another curial practice odious to many of reforming temper was pluralism—the practice of conferring more than one ecclesiastical benefice or office on one man. This was simply a financial expedient—a means of supplementing the income of churchmen who were hard-pressed by the steeply rising inflation of the fifteenth century. It became increasingly difficult for princes of the Church to maintain the regal standard of living that was expected of them. And so a bishop might take charge of several dioceses in order to have sufficient income. Albrecht of Brandenburg again offers an example: Besides being archbishop of Mainz he held two other bishoprics and a large number of rich abbeys.

The practice by its very nature entailed absenteeism; indeed, some of these bishops never laid eyes on their dioceses. Obviously the morale of the Church suffered greatly; abuses of all sorts multiplied, since there was no authority on hand to check them. The literature of the period offers numerous examples of the cleric who after obtaining some benefice by using his influence in the Curia neglected its administration. "In Germany the percentage of resident pastors was fearfully small—as little as 7 per cent . . . ," it has been pointed out.[2]

Another ominous development was the monopoly acquired by the nobility over the high offices of the Church—which they often exploited for personal and worldly reasons. It was quite common for a prince to have his younger sons appointed to bishoprics as the only way of securing a style of living appropriate to their station. Lortz gives the example of Geneva, where between 1450 and 1520 no fewer than five ducal princes were bishops, and two of them were only eight years old at the time of their nomination![3] These men were often preoccupied with pleasure and material interests, and when the Reformation broke they were unable or unwilling to provide spiritual leader-

---

[2] J. Lortz, *The Reformation in Germany* (New York: Herder & Herder, 1968), p. 87.
[3] Ibid., p. 95.

ship. In fact, when Luther appeared many of them were among the first Catholics to turn their backs on the old Church in order to gain political or economic advantage from the new movement.

The lower clergy were in no better shape. As with the Curia and the higher clergy, we find every grade of decay: neglect of pastoral residence, accumulation of benefices, and utter worldliness. Besides, a whole clerical proletariat existed, the so-called Mass priests, who constituted in many cities as much as 10 per cent of the population; their only function was to say daily Mass. Preaching seems to have been on a very low level. Little attempt was made to instruct the young, and often the clergy themselves were as ignorant and superstitious as the rest. Concubinage was commonplace. The clergy's training was poor; only a small percentage had any university experience.

The picture presented by the religious orders is at least as dismal. Conditions, of course, varied much from country to country and order to order. The disasters of the Hundred Years' War (1337–1453) and the Black Death and the consequent prevalence of anarchy undermined monastic discipline and

Death strangling a victim of the plague. From the Stiny Codex, Czechoslovakia, fourteenth century. University Library, Prague.   © *Werner Forman/Art Resource, New York.*

left many monasteries incapable of recovery. In Italy and Germany also the strife between party factions, between Pope and Emperor, followed by the Great Schism in the Church brought monasticism to a low ebb. The Benedictine rule was a dead letter, while many monasteries were directed by non-resident, secular abbots. Nor were monasteries any longer the home of secular learning. The Benedictines were mere feudal relics, having lost all touch with the new social and cultural conditions. The Cistercians were not as clearly decadent—their twenty-four new foundations in the fifteenth century show that some vitality was left. However, in most monasteries community life had become only a memory; regular prayer in common was discontinued, and common property gave way to private property. Many monks obtained permission from Rome to live outside their monasteries, while those still residing within the cloister often held their own cells as personal property.

The mendicant orders too were in a sad state—a fact with alarming applications, since so much of the pastoral ministry depended on them. Monks and friars were favored targets of satirists; according to a popular proverb of the day, one would do better meeting a robber than a begging friar. A famous anonymous satire, *The Letters of Obscure Men,* and the writings of Erasmus show that many people regarded the sons of Francis and Dominic as a pack of indolent ignoramuses. Nor was such an opinion merely the stock in trade of the perennially cantankerous and disaffected intelligentsia; the same views are found among the most loyal Catholics—people like Ignatius Loyola and Thomas More.

It is obvious that there was great need for reform of the Church and, as the councils at Constance and Basel show most Catholic leaders were acutely aware of it. But the problem was how to achieve it.

The most popular and persistently recommended method was reform by a council of the Church and, in spite of the failure of Constance and Basel to accomplish it, the hope persisted. Many voices were raised in the latter half of the fifteenth century calling for a council—the voices of men deeply concerned with the welfare of the Church. After Basel's failure, however, it was obvious that such a council could only be carried out successfully under the leadership of the Popes.

Why did such a papal reform council fail to materialize in spite of the tremendous pressures in its favor? One important reason was the character of the papacy itself. This was the period of the so-called Renaissance papacy—a time when the Popes were more concerned with Italian politics than with the

Thought to be Sir Thomas
More (1478–1535). Hans
Holbein the Younger
(1497–1543). Uffizi Gallery,
Florence.   © *Scala/Art
Resource, New York.*

interests of the universal Church. Externally, it was a time of papal grandeur
as the Popes made Rome a foremost center of the Renaissance and inspired
imperishable works of art that to this day adorn the Vatican. But morally and
spiritually it was a time of terrible decline. In fact, under such Popes as Sixtus
IV (d. 1484), Innocent VIII (d. 1492), and Alexander VI (d. 1503), the papacy wallowed in corruption unparalleled since the tenth century. These men
virtually bought the tiara and used it mainly for the furtherance of personal
and dynastic interests—filling the College of Cardinals with relatives and unworthy candidates. They completely subordinated the religious functions of
their office to unworthy temporal aims. Politically they were great successes.
Julius II (d. 1513), a man of titanic character, made the Papal States a leading
power in European politics. But it was all achieved at a tremendous cost to
the integrity of the Popes' spiritual mission. The evil fruits would be abun-
dantly reaped with Leo X.

Absorption in politics and worldliness were not the only reasons for the
Renaissance Popes' failure to call a reform council. There was also the confusion over the relative authority of Pope and council. One must recall how the
previous councils of Constance and Basel had asserted their supremacy over

Pope Leo X with Cardinals Giulio de Medici and Luigi de Rossi (c. 1517). Raphael (1483–1520). Uffizi Gallery, Florence.   © *Scala/Art Resource, New York.*

the Pope; though Eugenius IV (d. 1447) defeated the rebellious council at Basel, it was mainly through political tactics that did not scotch the conciliar theory itself. Pope Pius II (d. 1464)—a conciliarist himself until 1445—tried to eradicate this idea of the council's supremacy over the Pope by his bull *Execrabilis* (1460), which condemned any appeal from the Pope to a council. But this by no means spelled the end of conciliarism. In France and Germany the bull met with vigorous opposition, and in fact outside Rome it was not generally accepted. Right down to Luther himself, secular princes and various ecclesiastical bodies, supported by a number of leading canonists and universities, favored the conciliar theory and continued to use the appeal to a council over the head of a Pope as a legitimate canonical device.

In the minds of the Popes, therefore, the call for a council was often tantamount to a cry of revolt. When faced with the demand for a council they stressed the practical difficulties involved in convening one and resorted to other evasions or made counterproposals. An added reason for papal caution was the way the conciliar idea was abused by secular princes. This occurred several times before the time of Luther, the most notable example being the council at Pisa, called by Louis XII of France in 1511 as a purely political maneuver. Hence even Popes concerned about reform preferred to think in terms of direct papal action, through legislative acts such as papal bulls and decrees, or through the work of papal legates.

This was the method adopted by Pius II, who was sincerely committed to reform; he drew up a bull, *Pastor Aeternus*, which drew its inspiration in part from Nicholas of Cusa's reform program. It bound the Pope himself to certain procedures in the government of the Church, but unfortunately Pius died before it could be issued. A long hiatus ensued in papal reform efforts, interrupted only when Alexander VI showed some interest in reform. A bull that he drew up but never published contained the most comprehensive reform program of the whole period between Basel and the Fifth Lateran Council (1512–17). It condemned such things as the political preoccupations of the cardinals and insisted on the duty of bishops to reside in their dioceses. But unfortunately, Alexander was soon distracted from the whole matter; he lost interest in the bull and never published it.

The last attempt at papal reform before the breakup of Christian unity was undertaken at the Lateran Council, originally summoned by Julius II, and concluded in 1517 under Leo X. Two Camaldolese monks, Giustiniani and Quirini, drew up and presented a reform program that ruthlessly criticized the ignorance of the clergy, papal absorption in politics, and bureaucratic centralization. It called for a whole range of constructive solutions: adequate training for the clergy, revision of Canon Law, and convoking of general councils every five years. It prefigured in a remarkable way the actual reforms of Trent; but its vision was too lofty and spiritual for the man on the throne of Peter at the time. Leo X (d. 1521) had no awareness of the volcano under his feet and little sense of responsibility for the salvation of souls. And so nothing was actually accomplished.

Reform of the Church by council and Pope was not the only possibility envisaged by reformers. Some favored another method: They saw reform beginning at the grass roots, on a small scale, with devout souls who by their personal sanctification, works of charity, and apostolic activity would move their own religious order or parish to undertake reform. It was a quiet, unspectacular way, slow and wearisome, demanding a great amount of patience and self-sacrifice in the face of inevitable misunderstanding and conflict. In religious communities it invariably meant returning to the original ideals of the order and a renewal of the common life, common prayer, and common table. When such a reform party imbued with such ideals appeared and gathered strength, it inevitably tried to secure religious superiors of like mind.

A number of such reform movements can be traced in the records of the fifteenth century: the Franciscan Observantines, led by the great saints and preachers Bernardine of Siena (d. 1444) and John Capistrano (d. 1456), the Benedictines of the Bursfeld and Melk congregations, the Dominican Lombard congregation, and Luther's own Augustinian monastery were examples of strict observance. But the melancholy fact is that not a single order was completely reformed. The work of reformers was constantly frustrated by the failure of Church leaders to support them.

An outstanding contribution to the work of such personal reformation was made by Geert Groote (d. 1384) of the Lowlands, who preached and lived a spirituality that called for a return to Christian inwardness. The *Imitation of Christ* captures its peculiar flavor. Two important fifteenth century congregations—the Canons of St. Augustine of Windesheim and the Brethren of the Common Life—owed their beginnings to Groote's inspiration. One order in the Church that never required reform was the Carthusians, who were able to exert considerable influence in favor of renewal during the fifteenth century. Their charterhouse at Cologne, for instance, acted as a spiritual center for the entire lower Rhine region.

There were also reforms associated with the secular clergy—the bishops and the pastors of parishes. These efforts were by their nature less likely to catch the eye than the reform of existing orders or the foundation of new ones. Undoubtedly we will know more about these movements as history continues its inquiry into diocesan archives and uncovers more information about bishops and pastors who ministered industriously to their flocks, held synods, and tried to engender a renewal of the Church. One of the outstanding experts in the period, Hubert Jedin, gives a whole list of such reforming German bishops of the fifteenth century and opines that more reforming activity was carried on in Germany than anywhere else, so that if the ecclesiastical revolution began in Germany, it was not in his view because conditions there were worse than elsewhere but because the spiritual awakening there made abuses all the more intolerable.[4]

There were also reform movements that began with the laity. The Ora-

---

[4] H. Jedin, *A History of the Council of Trent*, vol. 1 (London: Thomas Nelson & Sons, 1957), pp. 150–51.

tory of Divine Love, founded in Genoa shortly before the year 1500, was the most famous of these. The main idea of the members was to achieve personal sanctity by means of good works on behalf of others.

Another type of reform was attempted by secular princes: German territorial princes like the Saxon Dukes, who in 1485 were authorized by the Pope to reform the monasteries in their land, or the French Kings who used the great power they had over the Church to further reform. But actually only the Spanish Kings made any real progress in this task. Spain was peculiarly suited for this kind of reform, possessing a number of gifted monastic reformers and prudent and energetic bishops, most notably Ximenes de Cisneros, the experienced and ascetic archbishop of Toledo who for some forty years until his death in 1517 carried out an impressive reform of the Spanish Church. His new University of Alcalá he made a seminary of bishops and a center of humanistic studies that fused the new learning and the old theology in an original synthesis. Under men like Ximenes the King and clergy learned how to collaborate without detriment to the authority of either in a program that combined reform with respect for tradition. It is no accident that Spain provided the leaders of the extraordinary Catholic Reformation that swept the whole Church after the Council of Trent.

One more type of reform effort deserves mention here in this sketch of pre-Lutheran reformations. This was the kind urged by the Christian humanists. Humanism was an intellectual and artistic movement beginning with Petrarch (d. 1374) that gave a whole new direction to European thought. Unlike the Aristotelian-Scholastic mentality, its point of view was historical and above all critical. It was critical of longstanding Scholastic assumptions in philosophy and theology and in regard to the institutional Church, critical not only of patent abuses but also of venerable traditions. Its favorite weapons were ridicule and irony, which humanists like Erasmus (d. 1536) used relentlessly against Church customs and practices until they incurred—and perhaps justifiably in some cases—the charge of skepticism.

The humanists were dedicated to the idea of reforming the Church by example and education—on the assumption that learning, sacred or profane, would increase piety and that knowledge would make a man better. Such a belief about the nature of man was much too optimistic, as subsequent European history has only too forcefully demonstrated. Moreover, humanism itself contained too many ambivalences. Its rejection of Scholasticism was too sweeping and endangered the continuity of Catholic tradition. Its emphasis on nature rather than grace and its enthusiasm for secular values led in some cases to outright paganism. Though the leading humanists remained loyal to the old Church—Thomas More even to martyrdom—their reckless criticism of its most sacred institutions undoubtedly prepared the minds of many for Luther's all-out attack.

Nevertheless, humanism did make a positive contribution to the work of reform in influencing the renewal of theology that was to form an important feature of the Tridentine Catholic Reformation. The leading Catholic theologians of this period—Cano (d. 1560) and Vitoria (d. 1546)—would have been inconceivable without the achievements of humanism. Humanism's chief merit in this regard was its insistence on the historical character of Christianity and the need for theologians to nourish their thought constantly by the study of the sources—the Bible and the Fathers of the Church especially. This required an up-to-date study of the ancient languages and the use of methods of historical criticism that humanists like Valla (d. 1457) had developed. The prince of Christian humanists, Erasmus (d. 1536), devoted his life to laying the groundwork for this new biblical, critical, and historical theology. His Greek New Testament (1516) was the first of its kind in Western Europe, and his monumental editions of the Fathers—the fruit of his incredible capacity for work—provided scholars with access to the wealth of patristic thought.

To sum up, then, the general picture of reform activity before Luther shows a number of bright spots. Individual Christians—laymen and priests—anxiously pursued reform in many and various ways. The general state of the Church was one of pervasive corruption, nevertheless. Unimpeachable Catholic authorities at the time were the first to admit this. This is the substance of what Pope Adrian VI said in his message to the Diet of Nuremberg (1522); it is likewise the gist of the report of the commission of cardinals (1538) who were appointed by Pope Paul III to draw up proposals for reform.

A general reform of the Church could only have succeeded if it had reached the top and seized hold of the papacy itself. Unfortunately, this did not happen until after the Council of Trent. So as the historian Jedin says, "The Protestant Reformation owed its success to the fact that the attempts at reform which sprouted from the soil of the Church did not come to maturity."[5]

---

[5] Ibid., p. 165.

Chapter 19

LUTHER SPLITS
CHRISTENDOM

In spite of its many shortcomings, the Catholic Church in the year 1517 was still the mightiest institution in Christendom, supereminent in its influence on both public and private life. The Christian faith—as interpreted by the Roman Popes—was the foundation of public and private behavior. The leadership of the clergy was still generally respected in most domains of thought and life, in philosophy, science, the administration of justice, and charitable activity. Even the very life of the state seemed conceivable only on the basis of the Christian philosophy.

And yet within the short space of a few years this whole edifice came crashing down in one of the most awesome of historical cataclysms. As Lortz puts it, "one day the great patrician families of Nuremberg were calmly donating new, wonderful, costly altars and numerous splendid statues in honor of the saints; next day they were dragging out of the cloister the child whom they had dedicated to the life of perfection as a nun under the seal of the three-fold vows of the Church—rescuing her from the net of godless human ordinances, from the sacrilege of papistical idolatry."[1] The catalyst and to some extent the cause of it all was an Augustinian monk.

This monk, Martin Luther, was born in 1483 in Eisleben, Germany, the son of Hans and Margarete Ludher, who were of Thuringian peasant stock. Brought up in an atmosphere of traditional religious practice, he was given

[1] J. Lortz, *The Reformation in Germany* (New York: Herder & Herder, 1968), p. 20.

Portrait of the young Martin
Luther. Lucas Cranach the
Elder (1472–1553).
Germanisches
Nationalmuseum, Nuremberg.
© Scala/Art Resource, New York.

schooling of the kind customary at that time. He was intensively drilled in
Latin—giving him a strong linguistic foundation on which he built his later
acquaintance with Hebrew and Greek. Enrolling at Erfurt, the largest German university of the day, where Aristotle still reigned supreme, he was
awarded the master of arts degree in 1505.

His decision to enter a monastery a few months later was not inconsis-
tent with his deeply introspective and melancholy disposition, but the circumstances suggest that it may have been less than wholehearted. It was a
decision made in a moment of panic during a terrible thunderstorm after he
was thrown to the ground by a bolt of lightning. The monastery he chose was
the strictest religious house at Erfurt, and upon his entry in 1505 the young
novice monk found himself bound to a severe daily regimen of prayer, meditation, study, frequent fasting, and silence. All this no doubt reinforced his innate tendency toward introspection and brooding. There is little doubt that

he performed his duties with extreme seriousness, for he found favor with his superiors, and after only nineteen months he was ordained a priest, on April 4, 1507. He was then chosen to continue his theological studies.

Up to this point Luther seems to have enjoyed a good measure of spiritual peace—that sense of closeness to God that a religious novice often feels in the first years of his new way of life. But as he continued with his study of theology, he fell prey to moods of general depression; he suffered terrible trials and anguish of spirit, with sudden spasms of terror and despair gripping his heart, a torment so shattering, he said, that had it lasted even the tenth part of an hour, his bones would have crumbled into ashes. Deeply conscious of his sinfulness and guilt, he felt that at any moment he might be struck down by the living God and cast into hell. Craving certainty, he confessed frequently, even daily, fasted, and prayed; but he found little relief. And then in the extremes of his agony he even cried out his hatred of God, which in turn exacerbated his feelings of guilt. "For I hoped I might find peace of conscience with fasts, prayer, vigils, with which I miserably afflicted my body, but the more I sweated it out like this, the less peace and tranquility I knew," he wrote.[2]

His own later interpretation of his trials was that they were caused by the defective nominalist theology he was trained in. According to this theology he was supposed to merit salvation by his good works, whereas his own experience told him that he was completely impotent to do good. His so-called good works, he felt, were tainted by an all-pervading egotism. Above all, he could not find it in his power to rise to the love of God. How could one love a God who punishes sinners, who stood before him as an avenging God as the phrase "the justice of God" (Rm. 1:17) often reminded him?

While suffering intermittently these agonies of the spirit, Luther continued his theological career. He was assigned to lecture on Aristotle at the newly founded University of Wittenberg. Then in 1509 he began lectures in Erfurt on the *Sentences* of Peter Lombard. It was at this point that Luther began to read Augustine, who together with the Bible henceforth exerted a predominant influence on the formation of his very personal theology.

He was transferred to Wittenberg again in 1511, after a trip to Rome, which at the time seemed to have little influence on the development of his anti-Roman views. He took his doctorate in theology at Wittenberg, and then

---

[2] Quoted in G. Rupp, *The Righteousness of God* (London: Hodder & Stoughton, 1953), p. 104.

in 1513 he took over the chair of biblical theology as professor of exegesis—a post he was to hold for the rest of his life. And it was on the podium at Wittenberg before an audience of students that he delivered the remarkable commentaries on Psalms, Romans, Galatians, and Hebrews that contained the substance of his theology.

It was at the beginning of these lectures in 1513 that his spiritual crisis was resolved by an interior revolution that brought him to a new religious outlook. In essence his spiritual crisis was caused by an intense craving for certitude about his salvation. He tried to achieve this certitude by living so devoutly he could imagine himself appearing before God and saying: "Here you have holiness." But he found that the harder he tried the farther away he seemed from his goal.

The crisis was resolved when a kind of mystical illumination occurred which, as he said, opened the "saving Gospel" to him: the true meaning of Paul's phrase "the justice of God." Under the spell of his Nominalist mentors he had construed this to mean the justice by which God rightly punishes sinners. But now he realized that it meant the very opposite: It is the justice of God by which he justifies us through faith—a sense that became obvious to Luther when he juxtaposed the phrase "justice of God" with the phrase that follows in the same verse (Rm. 1:17), "the just man shall live by faith." In other words, it is not through our merits that we are saved but through the unfathomable mercy and boundless generosity of God, who justifies us in spite of our sins. Our part in the whole process is not active but passive.

With this doctrine of justification by faith, the young Augustinian now found a blessed confidence in place of despair, since he saw that the basis of his justification was not his own holiness but the mercy of God. Now he could have complete assurance of his salvation; true faith henceforth included the unshakable certainty of his own salvation. And it was only when he became convinced during the indulgence controversy that the Roman Catholic Church held a diametrically opposed theology—basing justification on the works of man, on self-sanctification, and therefore leaving the individual in a state of doubt and despair—that he felt obliged to oppose the Church. For Luther, true faith is present only when an individual is absolutely and personally certain about his salvation.

Luther arrived at this "new" understanding of the Gospel as early as 1514 while working on his commentary on the Psalms perhaps on Psalm 70 or 71. It was the starting point and remained the key to his distinctive theology and as such the basis of all subsequent Reformation theology. It is clear that in essentials this theology was completed before the beginning of his great struggle in 1517, and, as we have said, it was developed mainly in his early lectures—the commentaries of the years 1514 to 1517. One of the most significant achievements of Luther scholarship in the past forty years has been the discovery and publication of the original manuscripts of these lectures, which have revolutionized our understanding of Luther's spiritual development.

How compatible Luther's theology was with Catholic tradition is a question that has been debated ever since. There is no doubt that there was something new and original in Luther's theology; it was highly personal and charged with emotion—in sharp contrast with the cold, dry, Scholastic treatises of the day. Unlike too many presentations at that time, it was also profoundly biblical. It was also a practical and relevant theology, which focused on the actual issues of the day, and this contributed to its cachet of novelty. But none of these characteristics tell against it being accepted as basically Catholic, and, in fact, a recent Catholic scholar has affirmed that the real paradox of the Reformation is that until the Council of Trent, Martin Luther was one of the few theologians in Germany who uncompromisingly defended the biblical and Catholic teaching of man's bondage to sin.[3] And another Catholic has recently written a book indicating that Luther and Aquinas were in basic agreement on the question of the believer possessing certitude of salvation.[4]

Luther begins with the idea of God's justice—meaning God's saving righteousness, by which he extends to us in Christ the gracious gift of salvation. Human merit plays no role at this stage. Man, in fact, is totally corrupt, as is evident from concupiscence—the fermenting, restless egotism that vitiates our decisions at every level. Thus there is no free will; the human will is in itself totally enslaved to sin and totally rebellious to God. It is only through faith that we appropriate the salvation that God has effected for us in Christ, for God does not impute this sinfulness once we confess it by faith and hate it and seek to be healed of it.

Luther's conception of this process of salvation is a dynamic one: The righteousness of Christ becomes our righteousness. To avoid traditional Catholic caricatures of Luther's thought we must realize that the righteousness

[3] H. McSorley, *Luther: Right or Wrong?* (New York: Newman Press, 1969).
[4] S. Pfürtner, *Luther and Aquinas on Salvation* (New York: Sheed & Ward, 1964).

of Christ in Luther's mind was not something merely legal or forensically external but the personal presence and work of Christ and the Holy Spirit in the believer through faith. Hence there is no basis for the charge that his theory encouraged people to sin while cloaked under the external merits of Christ. His conception of the Christian life was anything but static; there was progress and the constant struggle against the passions. But while Luther's theology encompasses growth into righteousness, we must remember that for Luther this righteousness in no way could be called one's own. It was but a constant entering more deeply into Christ's righteousness. All of this was conceived from an eschatological point of view: One's righteousness was only the anticipation of God's final verdict, which he has already given in the saving intervention of Jesus Christ.

What then about good works? Does Luther make these superfluous if faith in Christ and his righteousness has already justified us? Luther himself answers: "The faith of none is so great that it cannot be, nor ought to be increased. Thus for its increase good works are to be done, and bad ones avoided.[5] But Luther stresses the divine initiative and action in our works; we are the instruments of God, the craftsman. "For grace and faith are infused apart from our work, and when they are infused, then the works follow."[6] As Luther taught, we do not obtain righteousness, but we stretch out toward it and always seek and ask that we may be justified so that the saints are at the same time sinners, sinners in fact, saints in hope.[7]

Luther's theology stirred up controversy; his opinions, such as those on the enslaved will and the utter gratuitousness of grace, boldly challenged the prevailing nominalism of the German universities and involved him in numerous disputes with his colleagues at Wittenberg and Erfurt. But such academic skirmishes had little interest for the public at large. It was only when he attacked the Church's system of indulgences—which touched the life of almost everyone—that the whole world began to listen in.

Like all enlightened men of the age, Luther was fully aware of the terrible state of affairs in the Church; his sermons before 1517 are sufficient indication of this. Like others he complained of the avarice, simony, and ecclesiastical jobbery connected with appointment to high and low office in the Church. But there is no indication that he felt these abuses warranted rev-

[5] Rupp, *Righteousness of God,* p. 198, quoting *Luther's Works.*
[6] Ibid., pp. 221, 390.
[7] Ibid., p. 225.

olutionary action—until he became convinced that the Gospel itself was at stake, that the Church was betraying the Gospel of Jesus Christ by teaching people that heaven could be purchased by good works.

For a theologian who held that the heart of religion was personal response, a man whose own religious experience and spiritual evolution was so bound up with the idea of the Gospel as offering God's free gift of salvation, Church practice of the day must indeed have been a sore trial; for in a thousand different ways the Church seemed to teach just the opposite or at least put excessive emphasis on the role of man in the work of salvation. There was, in fact, as Lortz says, an externalism run riot: pilgrimages of all kinds, a superstitious cult of relics of the saints, a semimagical and materialistic view of the efficacy of the mass—all giving the impression that heaven was something you could buy, like anything else.[8]

The most blatant example, however, was undoubtedly the cult of indulgences. In 1343 Pope Clement VI officially sanctioned the view that Christ and the saints had left a treasury of merits that other members of the Church could draw on for the remission of the temporal punishment due to their sins. One obtained a share in the merits by means of a Church indulgence—usually granted by the Pope in exchange for some good work, often a donation of money, performed by the recipients. Official doctrine always insisted on the need for an accompanying interior repentance on the part of the recipient too.

Eventually it became official doctrine that indulgences could be applied to the souls in purgatory on the supposition that as equal members of the Mystical Body of Christ they too could participate in the merits of their saintly fellow members. However justifiable such a teaching might have been in theory, in practice it was a dangerous development since it involved considerable ambiguity. Its actual efficacy was described in technical Latin as *per modum suffragii*—meaning "insofar as God hears the prayers of the Church." It also minimized, of course, the aspect of personal repentance that up to this time was always an important part of receiving an indulgence. A door was thus opened to the unscrupulous to present an indulgence as a quasi-automatic and easy means of salvation. And we know that this is what happened in the case of the particular indulgence that aroused the wrath of Luther and triggered his revolt against the Church.

[8] Lortz, *Reformation in Germany,* pp. 110–41.

It was a scandalous indulgence in several respects. First, it was ostensibly preached in order to rebuild St. Peter's, but it was actually concocted as a deal among the Fugger banking firm, the Roman Curia, and the twenty-three-year-old archbishop of Mainz, who agreed to split the proceeds. Albert, the archbishop, thus hoped to pay the immense tax of ten thousand ducats levied on him by the Curia for the dispensation he needed in order to hold three dioceses—Mainz, and Madgeburg (both archbishoprics), in addition to Halberstadt. Second, it was preached by Johann Tetzel, a Dominican whose sermons were sub-Christian: Drop a few coins in the box, he shouted to the gaping crowds, you can rescue the souls of your friends or relatives from the flames of purgatory!

The diocese of Mainz was neighbor to Luther's own, and the young professor, who was also parish priest of the village church, soon got wind of the sensational Tetzel through penitents in the confessional who had heard Tetzel preach the indulgence and thought they had some kind of license to sin. It was too much. The picturesque episode of Luther posting his ninety-five theses in Latin on the door of the castle church at Wittenberg is probably only a legend; what we do know for certain is that on October 31, 1517, he sent the theses to his bishop and to the bishop who had licensed Tetzel; and only when they failed to respond did he make his theses public—challenging his academic colleagues to a debate on the subject of indulgences. His aim was to challenge such interpretations as Tetzel put on indulgences—not to condemn them altogether. Luther wanted to put them in proper perspective and to voice his pastoral concern about the spiritual dangers they involved. As the parish priest of the town he found them an obstacle to the preaching of true repentance and interior conversion. After all, he insisted, they were merely remission of canonical penalties having to do with the terrestrial discipline of the Church. He denied that the Pope had any power over the souls in purgatory or that the Pope could control the merits of Christ and the saints. Finally, Luther denounced the indulgence preachers for their huckstering methods and for giving people a false sense of security by leading them to believe that a payment of money could appease the wrath of God.

Luther at first spoke out as a loyal Catholic, and when the controversy about his ideas erupted he was ready at first to submit them to the ultimate judgment of the Church. He did not see his theses as a revolutionary manifesto or as a call to the German nation. But he did strike a strong anti-Roman note, and there was a certain demagogic appeal in some of his caustic statements. Thesis 50, for instance, reads: "Christians are to be taught that if the pope knew the exactions of the indulgence preachers, he would rather that the basilica of St. Peter's were burned to ashes than built up with the skin, flesh, and bones of his sheep." Or No. 82: "Why does not the pope empty purgatory for the sake of holy love and the dire need of souls that are there if he redeems an infinite number of souls for the sake of miserable money with which to build a church?"[9]

Although no one showed up for the debate, within a few weeks the theses were translated into German and circulated widely. They became the talk of Germany. Sides formed quickly, and—almost against his will—Luther was pushed into the public arena as the champion of all those who for a multitude of reasons were itching to strike a blow at the ecclesiastical establishment.

One of the tragedies of the affair was that from the beginning Luther's opponents refused to meet him on theological and scriptural grounds. The archbishop of Mainz, who first reported him to Rome, showed concern only about the loss of income from the indulgence. Tetzel scorned Luther's invitation to debate, while Tetzel's brother Dominicans narrowed down the whole issue immediately to one of authority and in effect told Luther to accept the whole system of indulgences without cavil or be burned as a heretic. The only occasion for calm debate was furnished by Luther's fellow Augustinians at their chapter in Heidelberg, on April 26, 1518, where Luther won over the majority to his views.

Worst of all, Pope Leo X, who was preoccupied with Italian affairs and had no interest in theology anyway, regarded the situation at first as just another monks' squabble and showed little inclination to real dialogue. When he finally was made aware of the seriousness of the affair, he turned a deaf ear to Luther's humble appeal of May 30, 1518, and on the basis in part of spurious information summoned Luther to appear in Rome within sixty days to answer to the charge of heresy. The official document accompanying the summons was written by Prierias, his private theologian. It contained not even the barest recognition of the undeniable abuses connected with the indulgence system but instead indulged in an incredible tirade: Luther was "a leper and loathsome fellow . . . a dog and the son of a bitch, born to bite and snap at

---

[9] *Luther's Works*, eds. H. Lehmann and H. Grimm, vol. 31 (Philadelphia: Muhlenberg Press, 1957), pp. 206, 247.

the sky with his doggish mouth," having "a brain of brass and a nose of iron."[10]

However, a switch occurred thanks to a political factor, and Rome took a more conciliatory stand. Luther enjoyed the protection and support of his own ruler, Frederick, the elector of Saxony, who seems to have been impressed by the logic of Luther's position. The Curia, on the other hand, needed the assistance of Frederick in order to keep the Habsburg claimant, Charles, from the Empire's throne. So Cardinal Cajetan was instructed to meet with the monk at Augsburg to secure his recantation.

It was a fateful meeting. The two got entangled in the subtle problem of the relation of faith to sacrament, Cajetan upholding the primacy of the sacrament and Luther the primacy of faith. It ended in a deadlock, and Luther slipped away in the night of October 20, 1518, but not before dropping an ominous remark questioning papal authority. A few months later he issued an appeal for a general council.

Rome was still preoccupied with political matters, however, and the whole process against Luther was allowed to rest. An interim of slightly more than two years followed—years during which Luther threw himself into a great public debate, riding the crest of a deep wave of public interest and support, hammering out in sermons, pamphlets, and debates with incredible energy a powerful alternative to the Roman ecclesiastical and sacramental system—an alternative that made an enormous appeal to the German populace.

It involved a radically new conception of the visible Church which—against fifteen hundred years of Christian tradition—was declared to be not a divinely founded institution but simply a number of communities whose origin was human and historical. In this perspective the divine authority of the papacy and hierarchy simply collapsed, and with it the distinction between the laity and the priesthood. All of this was made clear in Luther's sensational debate at Leipzig in July 1519 with the leading German Catholic theologian John Eck, who cleverly got Luther to admit publicly that he no longer believed in the divine origin of papal primacy or the infallibility of general councils. For Luther "Scripture alone" was the supreme authority in religion—and henceforth this phrase became the rallying cry of all Protestants.

[10] J. Todd, *Martin Luther* (Glen Rock, N.J.: Paulist Press, 1964), p. 147.

Rome now at last took full cognizance of the crisis, and the Pope nominated a commission to study Luther's writings. After the report of several commissions the Pope finally issued the bull, *Exsurge Domine* on June 15, 1520. While stopping short of excommunication, this bull condemned forty-one propositions drawn from Luther's writings as "heretical, scandalous, or offensive to pious ears," but without saying which were which. Incredibly, this fatefully imprecise document was to remain the only papal statement about Luther's teaching until the Council of Trent a quarter of a century later. Eck brought the bull to Germany and found the populace ready to revolt if any attempt was made to squelch Luther.

In the meantime, Luther discovered that the Pope was anti-Christ—a charge that struck the popular imagination—and his attacks on the Pope became increasingly coarse and frenetic. Showing his almost demonic talent as a propagandist, Luther exploited to the full the potential of the newly invented printing press, through which his voice could be heard in even the smallest German hamlet, and he now addressed himself to the whole German nation in three revolutionary manifestos. *To the Christian Nobility of the German Nation, On the Babylonian Captivity of the Church,* and *On the Freedom of the Christian Man* represent his most important utterances as a reformer and were of the greatest importance in setting Germany ablaze.

To the Nobility called for a total reorganization of the Church after rehearsing many long-standing German grievances against the Curia. It called for an end to celibacy, Masses for the dead, and other traditional practices. A reform, Luther insisted, could only be carried through if the Pope's powers were severely limited; his temporal power must therefore be abolished and his function reduced to a kind of spiritual overseer of Christendom. Each local Christian community should take charge of its own affairs and elect its own ministers and bishops.

The *Babylonian Captivity* definitively abandoned traditional Catholicism and outlined a new theory about the nature of the Church and its sacramental system. Rejecting the Catholic idea of apostolic succession, it proposed as a first principle the common priesthood of all believers, which they share in virtue of their baptism. No sacrament has efficacy apart from the faith of the recipient, and Luther recognized only two sacraments: baptism and the Eucharist. Ordination, for example, was merely a means of providing order for the assembly.

In this way the Lutheran proclamation gradually took shape. Its potent popular appeal lay in its simplicity, which appeared so obvious when compared with the sophisticated and complex Catholic system. The Gospel, the Lutherans said, was simple; it had nothing to do with pomp and ritual; it spoke of no difference between clergy and laity.

The new Lutheran liturgy reflected this belief in simplicity. It stripped the Catholic Mass down to its bare essentials, made it understandable by translating it into the language of the people, and emphasized participation by the whole congregation, who were taught to sing stirring new hymns, many of them composed by Luther himself. The sermon was now made the central feature of the service, as enthusiastic preachers ascended the pulpit and thrilled the hushed congregations, who felt they were hearing the word of God for the first time in their lives. They were now invited to receive the wine as well as the bread of the Eucharist and to take them into their own hands.

On December 10, 1520, Luther, accompanied by his students and well-wishers, burned the Pope's bull *Exsurge* as well as a copy of the Canon Law. No action could have symbolized more appropriately Luther's irrevocable break with the papacy and the end of medieval Christendom.

It was now the Emperor's turn to act. One of the most stirring moments in the history of the Church and the world occurred when Luther, called before the estates of the realm at the Diet of Worms, April 18, 1521, before the Emperor and all the dignitaries of Germany, refused to recant because "his conscience was held captive to the Word of God."[11]

This could have meant the burning of Luther as a heretic, like his forerunner Hus a century before at Constance. The recently elected Emperor, Charles V, had vowed to stake his life for the extirpation of the heresy. But Charles found the estates reluctant to concur and had to temporize. When he was finally able to take action in May, Luther was safely hidden away in a castle at Wartburg—where he devoted his time to one of his most lasting achievements, the translation of the entire Bible into German.

In spite of Charles's ban, Luther's movement continued to spread like wildfire. The free cities of Germany were the first to officially declare for the new religion; they were followed by the electors. Obviously the motives of the individuals who chose one side or the other were mixed, and no historian can hope to determine the relative importance of the purely religious factor in-

[11] *Documents Illustrative of the Continental Reformation*, ed. B. J. Kidd (Oxford: Oxford University Press, 1967), p. 85.

Pope Clement VII with Charles V. Giorgio Vasari (1511–74) and assistants. Palazzo Vecchio, Florence.   © *Scala/Art Resource, New York.*

volved as against the nonreligious ones: greed for the wealth of the Church and desire to control all affairs in a given commonwealth without interference by the Pope. But it is interesting to note that at first the most active agents in the spread of Lutheranism were ex-priests and ex-monks.

It is well to remember too that for a long time the lines were not drawn as sharply as we sometimes imagine. There was much confusion over the exact issues, and the multitude of alternatives was bewildering. Some felt that all could be settled if only certain ecclesiastical abuses were straightened out. Others pointed to the theological disagreements as crucial but could not agree on their relative importance. The papal bull *Exsurge* seemed to assert that Luther's main errors concerned penance and indulgences, but Erasmus considered free will the main issue. The humanist scholar Melancthon was persuaded at Augsburg in 1520 that unity could be restored if only priests were allowed to marry and the chalice given back to the laity. Luther himself maintained that it was all about the proper understanding of Christ. And where did justification by faith alone fit in? Many who accepted Luther's understanding of the Gospel didn't feel it necessary to reject the old Church. Papal primacy, for instance, was still highly controversial within the Roman Church itself. Moreover, though Luther translated the Mass into German, he was conservative about introducing other changes. The prince bishops of Germany could give little leadership toward clarifying matters. Only a general council could have done this, and the Curia was still radically opposed to this.

As late as 1530 there was still general optimism about the possibility of reconciliation. Charles scheduled a diet for Augsburg for that year, and Melancthon, Luther's closest associate, who still considered himself a Catholic, drew up a confession, still the official basis of Lutheranism, which indicated only accidental differences with traditional Catholicism. But the exigencies of practical life soon proved decisive—whatever individual reformers may have thought about the exact relation of the movement to the old faith. Lutheranizing priests began to marry. Decisions had to be made about ecclesiastical practices and structures, ministers had to be trained and new congregations organized, since many felt that the ethical and religious principles of Luther could be preserved and put into practice only by creating new ecclesiastical structures. And so slowly, haphazardly, new Protestant congregations were set up that stood in opposition to the old parishes. Inevitably the leadership devolved on the ministers, who in spite of Luther's theory of the priesthood of all believers, acted as a distinct clergy and soon clericalized his Church along the same lines as the old.

Of great importance for the success of Protestant consolidation was the absence of Charles V during these years—1521 to 1530—for Charles was heavily involved in Spanish political affairs. So Germany was left like a pilotless ship at one of the most critical points of her history—until the religious schism developed to a stage beyond repair.

The fatal step was taken when both sides began to organize militarily. Chief among the factors was the Peasants' Revolt (1524–26). Many of the princes saw this revolt as an expression of Lutheran principles, and hence their suppression of the peasants could be interpreted as aimed at the suppression of Lutheranism as well. Recourse to arms to settle the issue was thus introduced into the struggle. The Protestant princes organized into the military Schmalkald League in 1531, and political and military factors began to dominate the great debate.

In his *Interim of Nuremberg* (1532) Charles V officially recognized the Schmalkald League. This Emperor, whose life spanned the whole period of the German Reformation, was the most devoted of all the servants of the Roman Church and—once awakened to the full gravity of the crisis—the most determined to save it. Beyond all Catholics of the time, including the Popes, he spent himself without measure in the effort to restore the medieval, universal, and unified Christendom.

For twenty years after the *Interim of Nuremberg* he alternated between the use of force and the use of theological conferences to this end. The high-water mark of dialogue was reached at Regensburg in 1541, when Protestants and Catholics came very close to agreement. The Protestants would have been satisfied with four main concessions: marriage of the clergy, communion in both forms, freedom to teach the Real Presence without defining its manner as transubstantiation, and freedom from papal jurisdiction as distinct from recognition of papal primacy. But Rome would not yield. Political reasons also played their part in Regensburg's failure. French interests opposed an agreement; so did the two Bavarian dukes, and the Pope himself was in part motivated by fear of any increase of imperial power. The complete failure of Charles's policy was registered in the Peace of Augsburg (1555), which sealed the schism and legally recognized in Germany both the Lutheran confession and the Catholic faith.

Luther's ideas winged their way to the four corners of Europe and found a receptive audience everywhere. They were soon taken up by enthusiasts who added their own innovations and then became the agents of ecclesiastical revolution in their own backyard. The success or failure of their effort depended very much on the attitude taken by their government. In fact, nowhere in Europe did a settlement in favor of Protestantism occur where the monarch was hostile to the new Gospel.

The outstanding example of this decisive influence of the monarch on the course of the Reformation was in England. Henry VIII (d. 1547) was himself a stanch advocate of Catholicism, and in spite of his schism with the Pope over his divorce, he wanted England to remain Catholic. But under his son Edward VI (d. 1553), Protestantism gained ground, with Parliament's imposition of the *Book of Common Prayer* and *The Forty-Two Articles*—later reduced to *The Thirty-nine Articles*—that form the basis of the faith of the Church of England. Mary Tudor's rule (1553–58) was too short for her to succeed in her aim of completely restoring Catholicism. Her stepsister Elizabeth (d. 1603), who followed her, was motivated more by political than religious considerations and devised a settlement that re-established a moderate Protestantism; it was couched in terminology of studied ambiguity that retained much from the Catholic past, including episcopal organization of the Church, for example.

Henry VIII. Hans Holbein the Younger (1497–1543). Galleria Nazionale d'Arte Antica, Palazzo Barberini, Rome.   © *Scala/Art Resource, New York.*

The first important division in the ranks of the Protestants occurred over the interpretation of Holy Communion. Zwingli (d. 1531), the priest who brought the Reformation to Switzerland, found himself at odds with Luther over the words of Scripture, "This is my body." In spite of his rejection of transubstantiation, Luther still retained the traditional interpretation that said that Jesus was really present in the bread and wine by a bodily and objective presence—not dependent upon subjective feelings and considerations. Zwingli, on the other hand, asserted a mere memorial presence of Jesus in the sharing of the bread and wine. A colloquy between the two leaders at Marburg in October 1529 failed to bring agreement and confirmed the disquieting fact that the principle—Scripture alone—might not be sufficient to maintain a consensus. Theologically Protestantism had to admit that it was a house divided, and so it was to remain during the succeeding centuries.

The divisions, however, have often been exaggerated. Actually, only three or four main types emerged: the Lutheran; the sectarians or radicals, which would include the Anabaptists, Quakers, and Baptists; the anti-Trinitarian and rational pietists who emphasized critical inquiry as well as mystical faith; and finally the Calvinists.

It was Calvinism that was to become the dominant international form of

Protestantism; only Germany and Scandinavia preferred Lutheranism. Most of the other countries that turned Protestant accepted Calvinism or something close to it. Its founder, John Calvin, ranks with Luther as one of the other giants of the Reformation. Calvin's life work, the *Institutes of the Christian Religion,* provided Protestants with a systematic theological exposition of their faith. Its clarity, logical cogency, and comprehensiveness secured for it incomparable authority among Protestants and contributed greatly to the extraordinary dynamism that enabled Calvinism to conquer a large portion of Christendom.

Chapter 20

CALVIN MAKES
PROTESTANTISM AN
INTERNATIONAL MOVEMENT

John Calvin, the architect of international Protestantism, was born at Novon, France, July 10, 1509, the son of a notary, Gérard Cauvin (Calvin is the Latinized form), and his wife, Jeanne Lefranc. With the help of Church benefices, John studied theology in Paris in preparation for the priesthood and then switched to law and classical languages, which he pursued under some of the most famous professors of the day at Orléans and Bourges. Calvin was always quite reticent about the details of his personal history and never spoke much about the spiritual development that led to his conversion to the Protestant cause in 1533 or 1534. However, his *Reply to Cardinal Sadoleto* (1539) sheds some light on this matter, especially in the passage where he relates the story of a hypothetical conversion to the Protestant faith which is very likely drawn from his own experience. The convert in question attributes his change of religious allegiance to a number of reasons: his failure to find peace of conscience through the medieval system of satisfactions and his soul's terror in this condition; the comfort brought by the new and very different doctrine of the sufficiency of Christ's work of satisfaction; the conviction that the aim of the reformers to correct the abuses in the Church was not schismatic in intention; and finally his belief that the papacy was not warranted by Scripture but was a tyranny based on empty claims.[1]

[1] John T. McNeill, *The History and Character of Calvinism* (New York: Oxford University Press, 1967), p. 117.

The Protestant reformer John Calvin (1509–64) as a young man. Flemish School. Bibliothèque Publique et Universitaire, Geneva. *© Erich Lessing/Art Resource, New York.*

At any rate Calvin eagerly devoted himself to his new religion and was soon in the forefront of the Protestant movement in France. To espouse Lutheran ideas at that time under the Catholic King, Francis I, was to invite trouble and it was not long in coming. Calvin found his situation in France untenable, especially after the Affair of the Placards, an episode which occurred in October 1534 when some Protestant enthusiasts papered Paris with posters denouncing the Mass. The authorities took stringent measures against the heretics and the Protestant martyrology began to grow. Unwilling to add his name to the list, Calvin took refuge in Basel.

It was here in 1536 that he published in Latin the first edition of his *Institutes of the Christian Religion,* a lucid handbook of Protestant doctrine that immediately lifted him to a position of eminence among the leaders of the reform movement. It was a book that continued to grow in size over the years as Calvin translated it into French and repeatedly revised and enlarged it. It is a book that has few rivals in the enormity of its impact on Western history and ecclesiastical and political theory.

Soon afterward, Calvin set out to visit Ferrara, where the seeds of an Italian reform movement were beginning to sprout. After a brief return trip to Paris he set out for Strassburg in June 1536 intending to lead a quiet life of scholarship and writing on behalf of the Protestant cause. But a detour he took by chance through Geneva set his life on an entirely different course. While stopping at Geneva he was induced by the Protestant reformer Guillaume Farel to remain and take part in the struggle to transform Geneva into a vital Protestant community. Farel and his companions had already gained the upper hand by their spirited preaching and their ability to vanquish their Catholic opponents in public debate. The Catholic bishop had been driven out, the Mass suspended, and a set of regulations adopted which imposed the reform on the citizenry. But opposition was still strong and Farel saw in Calvin the man of the hour and begged him to remain and complete the work.

After some hesitation Calvin accepted Farel's offer and set about the task of creating in his words a "well ordered and regulated" Church.[2] He drew up a confession of faith to be signed by each citizen to show whether one belonged to the kingdom of the Pope or the kingdom of Jesus Christ. Rules were drawn up for the proper and frequent celebration of the Lord's Supper and a system of discipline enacted that governed the behavior of the Genevans down to rather slight details. However, when Calvin and his colleagues demanded the right of the Church to enforce its discipline by the penalty of excommunication, the magistrates demurred, seeing in this a move to make the Church an independent power. Other issues caused tension, and opposition to the reformers reached a high pitch when a dispute arose over certain liturgical practices (such as use of the baptismal font) which the Genevans had resumed under pressure from neighboring Bern. Calvin saw this intervention by Bern as a violation of the autonomy of the Genevan Church and stoutly resisted the move. In consequence, Calvin, Farel, and their associates were banished from the town.

From 1538 to 1541 Calvin resided in Strassburg, which he visited at the invitation of Martin Bucer, an ex-Dominican Lutheran preacher who had considerable influence on Calvin's subsequent theological development. It was under Bucer's influence that Calvin shaped the form of public worship that was to become the standard for Calvinist churches. Opposed as he was to the heavy emphasis on ceremonies in the Roman communion, Calvin devised an extremely plain and simple rite that still preserved, however, the outline of the Roman Mass. While in Strassburg he also revised and published a new edi-

[2] Ibid, p. 138.

tion of his *Institutes,* began his outstanding series of Biblical Commentaries which eventually included all the writings of the New and most of those in the Old Testament. He also attended the colloquies at Worms in 1540 and Regensburg in 1541, convened by the Emperor Charles V, in an effort to heal the religious schism, although Calvin himself didn't think they had much chance of success. In 1540 he married Idelette of Buren, the widow of one of his converts. Their only child, a boy, died soon after birth.

In the meantime Geneva remained in turmoil, still divided over the issues that had forced Calvin out. His supporters finally gained the ascendancy and the city decided to invite Calvin to return. With great misgivings, but moved by a sense of divine vocation, Calvin re-entered the troubled city on September 13, 1541. He immediately set to work to turn the town of thirteen thousand inhabitants into a truly reformed Church and properly disciplined community. The blueprint for such a project being already firmly worked out in his mind, he was able within a few months to present his *Ecclesiastical Ordinances* to the General Council of Geneva which they officially adopted on Sunday, November 20, with modifications to safeguard their own civil jurisdiction. Together with the *Institutes* this design for an ideal Christian community was Calvin's lasting contribution to Christianity, for his constitution became the organizational basis for all the Churches that accepted Calvinist doctrine. In drawing it up, Calvin aimed to reproduce as far as possible the organization of the Church which he found in the New Testament. Four offices were established: pastors, teachers, elders, and deacons. Strict discipline was the key to success in Calvin's mind and he entrusted the task of disciplining the community to a body called the Consistory made up of the ministers and elders. They were charged with closely supervising the behavior of their fellow citizens, who, if necessary, could be excommunicated by the civil authorities.

Legislation closely regulating private behavior was not an unusual feature of medieval town life. What made Geneva unique at this point in time was the consistency and severity with which the laws were enforced. The records of the Consistory show that people were haled before the elders and magistrates for even trivial offenses: laughing during a sermon, singing songs defamatory of Calvin, dancing, or frequenting a fortuneteller. Geneva's public life gradually began to change under this strict regimen. Prostitution, a notorious feature of pre-Calvin Geneva, was stamped out, the theater was closed, and the death penalty was prescribed for adultery and was actually imposed in several cases.

Calvin is sometimes accused of ruling Geneva as a dictator. A misnomer, indeed, for Calvin held no political office and used no other means than sheer moral power to impose his idea of the good life on Geneva. Moreover, he was often in danger of losing his sway over the city, as he had numerous enemies who hated his unbending regime or disagreed with his interpretation of the Word of God. Calvin never shrank from conflict and, in spite of the shifting tides of public opinion that sometimes ran strongly against him, he always managed to defeat his foes and restore his dominance. Crossing swords with the pope of Geneva was a dangerous pastime and the vanquished often paid for it dearly. Jacques Gruet, for example, was one of the so-called Libertines who bitterly resented the life style imposed by Calvin. Gruet was arrested, tortured in the manner of his age, and, when evidence was found convicting him of blasphemy, beheaded. But Calvin's most celebrated victim was Michael Servetus, the Spanish physician and anti-Trinitarian who, while in flight from the Catholic Inquisition, mistakenly stopped at Geneva, where at the behest of Calvin he was arrested and after trial burned at the stake for heresy.

The crowning achievement of Calvin was the establishment in 1559 of the Geneva Academy, designed primarily to give a complete education to candidates for the ministry. It became a powerful center for the spread of Calvinism, as its students came from many lands to learn the theology of the Reformed Church at its source. Calvin suffered much from illness in his last years but remained at his post until the end came in 1564. His corpse, as one eyewitness recalled, was "followed by almost the whole city, not without many tears."[3]

As the supreme theological genius of Protestantism, Calvin laid the groundwork for subsequent theological developments within most Protestant non-Lutheran Churches. Calvin thought of himself as the successor of Luther and indeed stood in complete agreement with Luther on the basic principles of Protestantism: Scripture alone as the sole source of saving truth, salvation by faith alone, the priesthood of all believers. Indeed, it can be said that "the central teaching of Luther on justification of faith and regeneration by faith was preserved more faithfully and expressed more forcefully by Calvin than

---

[3] Ibid., p. 93.

by any other dogmatician of the Reform."[4] Nevertheless, as his thought matured he found cause to differ sharply with Luther on a number of important points—having to do with the Lord's Supper, the Canon of Scripture, predestination, the doctrine of the Church, Christology, and the sacraments.

Calvin is sometimes thought of as a rigorously systematic thinker who carried logical consistency to extremes in elaborating his synthesis of Christian doctrine. In fact, Calvin considered himself, and should be considered, as primarily a masterful expositor of the Scriptures, a biblical theologian who strove to transmit accurately and completely the whole message he found in Scripture and who laid great stress indeed on the point that Scripture contained all that was necessary for salvation. He organized his material around the grand themes that give unity to the Scriptures without trying to resolve the paradoxes and logical tensions to be found there.

Although one cannot single out any one doctrine as the foundation of his thought, a good starting point is his insistence on the absolute sovereignty of God. One of the most serious charges he leveled at the Roman Church was that it domesticated God. The God of the Roman Church in Calvin's eyes was "a God who could be summoned at clerical command, localized and dismissed by the chemistry of stomach acids."[5] In protest Calvin often insisted on God's absolute transcendence and total otherness, on his mysterious, incomprehensible essence, his unfathomable purpose, and his inscrutable decrees. He was a hidden God. Saving knowledge of him could only be found in Scripture and this only on condition that we read it with reverence, faith, and love. God reveals himself to us in Scripture only through Jesus Christ, who is the core and the whole content of its meaning.

How do we know that Scripture is true? For Calvin, it is only through the interior witness of the Holy Spirit that we can recognize in Scripture the Word of God speaking to us. Scripture in turn testifies to the all-embracing sovereignty of God and reveals Him as the Ruler who governs all things by his providence. It is in this context that Calvin formulated his much attacked doctrine of predestination according to which by God's eternal decree some are ordained infallibly to eternal life and others infallibly to eternal punishment. This was the Achilles' heel of his theology and the target of all his op-

---

[4] F. Wendel, *Calvin. The Origins and Development of His Religious Thought* (New York: Harper & Row, 1963), p. 133.
[5] Kilian McDonnell, O.S.B., *John Calvin, the Church and the Eucharist* (Princeton, N.J.: Princeton University Press, 1967), p. 163.

ponents. While it is true that Calvin here goes beyond the plain demands of Scripture, we must remember that he felt obliged to assert predestination in order to safeguard one of his main concerns, namely, the absolute gratuitousness of God's saving grace—in no way dependent on our merits or works.

In his doctrine of original sin, as often elsewhere, Calvin follows Augustine closely. Calvin teaches that through original sin man became utterly depraved and in his relation to God capable only of sinning. Man is saved from this plight by faith in Christ the sole mediator. But man does not initiate this movement of faith; rather, it is the principal work of the Holy Spirit. Faith, he says in his *Institutes,* "is a firm and sure knowledge of the divine favor toward us, founded on the truth of a free promise in Christ, and revealed to our minds, and sealed on our hearts by the Holy Spirit."[6] Faith unites us with Christ in a personal relationship of faith. But this faith in itself does not have any worth. It is only the instrument whereby we obtain freely the righteousness of Christ—which remains Christ's righteousness and is only imputed to us.

Unlike Luther, Calvin emphasized not only justification but also our sanctification. This does not mean that we grow intrinsically in righteousness but only that we become more and more aware of our own impotence and sinfulness as we are more deeply grafted into Christ, who accomplishes for us what we should have done ourselves. Even after our justification, our works are still contaminated by sin, but God nevertheless holds them acceptable. He not only justifies the sinner; he also justifies the justified in a process referred to as double justification. In this context also, Calvin explains regeneration. While remaining sinners, we nevertheless advance in holiness insofar as we are united with Christ. This grace that Christ gives us is irresistible and manifests itself especially in our readiness to deny ourselves and live in view of the life to come.

In his understanding of Christ, Calvin follows tradition very closely, affirming the dogmas of the ancient councils as to Christ's consubstantiality with the Father and the Holy Spirit and the personal unity of Christ's two natures.

When we come to Calvin's doctrine of the Church we find that Calvin stressed the importance of the Church as a divinely willed institution, as the

---

[6] John Calvin, *Institutes of the Christian Religion* (Grand Rapids, Mich.: Wm. B. Eerdmans, 1957), III, 2, 7.

means intended by God to help weak and infirm man along the path to salvation. The supreme Church for Calvin is the invisible one made up of the totality of the elect, but there was also the visible Church formed by the gathering of believers into one parish. For Calvin, who here follows Luther closely, the marks of a true Church are simple and evident: the Church exists wherever the Word of God is preached and the sacraments administered according to Christ's institution. Rejected was the Roman view that the Church existed only where bishop succeeded bishop. For him that was much too organizational a concept, too mechanistic, too concerned with structural continuity and not concerned enough with continuity and purity of doctrine. It is Jesus, Calvin holds, who calls the Church into being by his Word and his sacraments. And for Calvin there were only two sacraments attested to in Scripture: Baptism and the Eucharist.

One of the abuses Calvin saw rampant in the Roman Church was a quasi-magical and mechanistic use of the sacraments which he blamed on the official Roman doctrine that the sacraments conferred grace of themselves (ex opere operato). He therefore laid stress on the importance of the faith of the recipient and on the role of the sacraments as part of a personal dialogue between the believer and God. And he held that the administration of the sacrament must always be accompanied by a preaching and proclaiming of the Word. "Nothing . . . can be more preposterous than to convert the Supper into a dumb action. This is done under the tyranny of the Pope."[7]

In his doctrine of the Eucharist, Calvin followed closely the theology of his friend Martin Bucer, who tried to mediate the dispute between Zwingli and Luther mentioned above.[8] Luther, as we explained, insisted on the objective real presence of Christ's body in the bread and wine, while Zwingli upheld only a memorial presence. Bucer on the one hand agreed with Zwingli in saying that the divine gift was not given *in* or *under* the forms of bread and wine, but on the other hand Bucer agreed with Luther as to a true communication of the Lord's humanity in the sacrament. To harmonize the two views Bucer favored the statement that the divine gift was given not *in* or *under* but *with* the bread and wine: When the bread was eaten the divine gift passed into the faithful soul. Bucer's doctrine gradually established itself as the classical formulary of non-Lutheran Protestantism. Calvin took it up and stamped it with

[7] Ibid., IV, 7, 39.
[8] Ibid., pp. 218–19.

his own characteristic clarity and cogency. According to Calvin the bread and wine are as instruments by which Our Lord Jesus Christ Himself distributes to us his body and blood. The Eucharist was not a mere psychological aid to grasping spiritual reality but the means by which God accomplishes his promise. The presence of Christ in the Eucharist was an objectively real presence.

CALVINISM CENTERED IN Geneva became the great engine of Protestant expansion in Europe. Only Germany and Scandinavia preferred Lutheranism. Most of the other countries that turned Protestant accepted Calvinism or something close to it. Its progress in Switzerland was greatly helped by the formula of faith signed by Calvin and Zwingli's successor, Heinrich Bullinger, in 1549. Very influential also was the *Second Helvetic Confession,* a very Calvinistic document, which was signed by all the Swiss cantons except Basel and Neuchâtel and enjoyed wide popularity.

While no German city became Calvinist during Calvin's lifetime, the doctrines of the Genevan reformer found a favorable climate in the Palatinate under the Elector Frederick III (1515–76). This sincere and intelligent religious prince invited two outstanding Calvinist scholars, Zacharias Ursinus and Caspar Olevianus, to his University of Heidelberg and they collaborated in producing the *Heidelberg Catechism* (1563), which became the creed of the Reformed churches in Germany as well as those in Poland, Bohemia, Hungary, and Moravia. In addition to the Palatinate, the most important of the other German states which accepted Calvinist doctrine were Bremen, Anhalt, the main part of Hesse, and finally Brandenburg, a unique example where the Calvinist sympathies of the Electors secured for Calvinists a legal position although Lutherans remained in the majority.

In Huguenot France, in Holland, and in Scotland the Protestant movement assumed the form of Calvinism between 1559 and 1567. France became a veritable battleground for a series of wars between Calvinist Huguenots and Catholics that devastated the country. The Huguenots suffered a calamitous blow in the St. Bartholomew's Day Massacre when at the command of the Queen Mother, Catherine de Medici, thousands of them were caught by surprise and butchered. But the survivors managed to regroup and, under their leader, Henry of Navarre, continued the struggle. Henry, however, turned Catholic in order to unify the country under his rule, but his Edict of Nantes (1598) guaranteed liberty of conscience for the Huguenots.

At the time of the death of Calvin in 1564 Calvinism had already made significant progress in the seventeen provinces of the Netherlands (today mainly Holland, Belgium, and Luxembourg). They were ruled by the Spanish monarch Philip II who alienated the populace by his arbitrary taxation, his use of Spanish troops, and his repressive ecclesiastical policies. When war with the Spanish broke out, the courage and boldness of the Calvinists contributed greatly to the dynamism of the anti-Spanish movement and the leader of the rebels, William, the Prince of Orange, himself became a Calvinist. William was assassinated in 1584 but the victory of his son Maurice, who drove out the Spaniards, led to the establishment of the Calvinist Dutch Republic in the northern Netherlands, which became one of the most vibrant and flourishing centers of Calvinism.

Nowhere did Calvinism succeed as completely as it did in Scotland. Its implantation there was due mainly to John Knox, who learned his Calvinism from the lips of the master himself at Geneva. Knox was a Scottish priest who went over to the cause of the Reformation early in his career. He joined a group of rebels who had occupied the castle of St. Andrews after assassinating

The St. Bartholomew's Day Massacre. Sixteenth-century German woodcut. Bibliothèque de l'Histoire du Protestantisme, Paris.   © *Giraudon/Art Resource, New York.*

Cardinal Beaton, the primate of Scotland. Unable to withstand a battery of French cannon, the rebels were taken prisoner and Knox spent nineteen months in the French galleys. After other vicissitudes he ended up in Geneva with Calvin. Mary Tudor's death in 1559 enabled Knox and the other Calvinist refugees to return home. The withdrawal of both English and French troops by the treaty of Edinburgh, July 6, 1560, and the death of the regent, Mary of Guise, allowed Knox and his band of reformers to steer Parliament toward reformation ideas. The *First Scottish Confession,* a faithful reproduction of the basic doctrines of Calvin, was read in Parliament and passed without delay August 17, 1560. It remained the confessional standard until superseded by the *Westminster Confession* in 1647. A Calvinist form of the liturgy was adopted in 1564. When the Catholic Queen Mary Stuart ascended the throne of Scotland in 1561, she found the new religion already entrenched. She was undone by her marriage to the Earl of Bothwell after the murder of her husband Lord Darnley. With Mary imprisoned in an English castle, Knox could die in 1572 with the comfort of knowing that the reformed church was now deeply rooted in the life of the people. After his death the Scottish Church remained doggedly attached to its presbyterian form of Calvinism in spite of the energetic attempts of its Stuart Kings to make the Kirk episcopal.

The Calvinists also played an important, if belated, role in the English Reformation, but they never succeeded in dominating the English Church the way they did the Scottish and Dutch Churches. We must keep in mind that whereas in Holland and Scotland the Reformation began as a religious movement led by Calvinists, the Reformation in England began as a political affair engineered by the King himself, Henry VIII. Henry, in fact, stoutly opposed the Reformation ideas and even wrote a treatise against Luther, *The Defense of the Seven Sacraments,* which won for him from Pope Leo X on October 11, 1521, the title of "Defender of the Faith."

But Henry's relations with the papacy deteriorated rapidly when the issue of his divorce surfaced in 1527. He wanted the Pope to annul his marriage to Catherine of Aragon so that he could marry the current object of his passion, Anne Boleyn, who he hoped might also provide him with the male heir that he so desperately wanted. The Pope, Clement VII, found himself in a terrible predicament. On the one hand, Henry threatened to withdraw England from its papal allegiance if not satisfied, and on the other, Catherine produced good evidence to show that her marriage with Henry was valid. Moreover, the Pope was under considerable pressure to refuse the divorce from Catherine's uncle, the powerful Holy Roman Emperor, Charles V. Clement vacillated and finally revoked the case to Rome in July 1529.

Henry immediately summoned Parliament and his clever lieutenant Thomas Cromwell steered it through a series of Acts that gradually detached England from the Pope's jurisdiction and subjected the English Church to the King, who in 1534 was declared to be the supreme head of the Church of England. Among the few men of prominence, clergy or lay, who refused to swear to the royal supremacy were John Fisher, the bishop of Rochester, and Thomas More, the ex-Chancellor, both of whom were beheaded in 1535.

Henry meanwhile obtained his divorce from the new archbishop of Canterbury, Thomas Cranmer, who crowned Anne with great pomp in the abbey church at Westminster on June 1, 1533.

Next to his rejection of papal jurisdiction, the most revolutionary act of Henry was his dissolution of the monasteries from 1535 to 1540. Some nine thousand monks and nuns were turned out—some willingly—and an enormous amount of wealth changed hands. While no longer the powerful spiritual force and centers of learning they were in the early Middle Ages, the monasteries were an important part of traditional church life and their destruction was an important factor in the gradual triumph of reformation ideas in England. The spread of these ideas occurred in spite of Henry, who though defiant of the Pope remained deeply devoted to traditional Catholicism and was determined to maintain its substance. It is true that under the pressure of political necessity Henry allowed the publication of the ambiguous *Ten Articles* (1536) and he also approved of the Act that set up the English Bible in all the churches. But his *Six Articles* (1539) reaffirmed Catholic doctrine and imposed savage penalties for denial of transubstantiation, private Masses, private confession, or the need for clerical celibacy.

It was only with the death of Henry in 1547 and the advent of young Edward VI that the Protestant party in England took charge and Calvinist influence began to make itself felt. The leader of the Protestants was Thomas Cranmer, who in spite of his Protestant tendencies had managed to escape Henry's wrath. The revision of the English Church's liturgy through *The Book of Common Prayer* (1549) was largely his work and it is justly celebrated as a liturgical masterpiece. It follows the basic outline of the medieval Mass but at crucial points inculcates Protestant doctrines. However, Cranmer himself soon found it too conservative, influenced as he now was by his personal contacts with Martin Bucer, whom he had invited to England. He helped to secure its revision and the *Second Book of Common Prayer* (1552) reflects his efforts to simplify the English liturgy along Calvinist lines and move its Eucharistic formulas closer to the doctrine of the Swiss reformers.

The work of the Protestant Reformers in England was interrupted by Mary Tudor, who succeeded Edward in 1553 and was absolutely devoted to restoring papal authority in England. To that end she engaged in a full-scale persecution of dissenting Protestants and sent Cranmer himself to the stake. She only succeeded, however, in moving the English people closer to a genuine acceptance of Protestantism.

With the arrival of Anne Boleyn's daughter, Elizabeth, as Queen in 1558, the Calvinists strove in earnest to take over the English Reformation and shape it along their lines. Nicknamed "Puritans" they sought to cleanse the English Church of everything they considered superstitious, idolatrous, and popish. *The Book of Common Prayer,* revised again in 1559, especially bothered them for though it called the altar a table and no longer referred to the Lord's Supper as a sacrifice, it still retained much they thought unwarranted by Scripture, such as vestments, the sign of the cross, kneeling at communion and formal prayer. Their other main target was the office of bishop, which

Queen Elizabeth I of England, the Sième portrait, c. 1575. Federico Zuccaro (1543–1609). Pinacoteca Nazionale, Siena.   © *Scala/Art Resource, New York.*

they wanted to replace with a presbyterian form of church government such as prevailed in Scotland. Elizabeth turned a deaf ear to them, however, for she was committed to a policy of expediency in religious matters and wanted a national religion that would blend the Catholic, Lutheran, and Calvinist elements in a way that would unify all Englishmen in one Church. Although the Puritans had considerable influence on the formulation of the *Thirty-Nine Articles* (1563) they never succeeded in establishing a Calvinist system in England but remained under Elizabeth an important wing of the English Church fiercely hostile to their adversaries the Episcopalians, who still believed in bishops.

Under the Stuart Kings of England in the seventeenth century the struggle between Puritans and Episcopalians became extremely bitter. Both James I (1603–25) and Charles I (1625–49) steadily discouraged the Puritan and encouraged the anti-Puritan party within the Church of England. During Charles's reign the archbishop of Canterbury, William Laud (d. 1645), undertook an aggressive campaign for a full revival of the Catholic tradition in the Church and tried to force the Puritans to conform by the use of severe penalties. This led to the great Puritan migration to the New World. Some twenty thousand Puritans left England in the 1630s to join others already in New England in founding holy commonwealths based on Calvinist doctrine. Under the leadership of the Massachusetts Bay Colony, Calvinism flourished and greatly influenced the shaping of the new nation.

CALVINISM HAS NOT been immune to the shocks that all systems suffer as they pass through the crucible of history. Its adherents eventually split into a host of separate churches that often bickered with each other over trivial issues. Some of its key doctrines had to be abandoned as knowledge advanced and no one today accepts it as a complete system. But few would deny that Calvin's contribution to Christian life and thought has been of the highest order. And we can still meditate with profit on what he has to tell us about the transcendence and sovereignty of God, the depths of man's depravity, the absolute freedom of grace, and our call to a deep interior response of faith.

Chapter 21

THE CATHOLIC CHURCH
RECOVERS ITS SPIRITUAL ÉLAN

The Catholic Church's history from the very beginning has been punctuated with terrible crises: the persecutions by the Roman Empire, the rise of Arianism, the barbarian invasions, the struggle over lay investiture, the Schism of the East, the Great Schism. But it would hardly be an exaggeration to say that Luther's revolt was the most devastating of them all. Never before was there so widespread and sudden a desertion of its altars, and never before had so many priests and nuns abandoned their cloisters, almost overnight. When it was all over, half of Europe was lost to the Roman obedience, and the unity of Christendom was but a fading memory.

However, there is for Catholics a brighter side. An interior and spiritual renewal occurred within the Catholic Church during the sixteenth century that made it once more a vital and sturdy spiritual household—worthy of a Gregory VII or an Innocent III. There is much evidence, as we have seen, that this spiritual and interior reform antedated Luther and hence cannot be explained as a mere defensive reaction or Counter Reformation. On the other hand, there is no doubt that the Lutheran Reformation intensified the feeling of urgency—carrying forward the Catholic effort toward a deepened spirituality.

THE ORIGINS OF this renewal can be traced to certain initiatives taken in Italy and Spain. We have already mentioned the Spanish reform centered around Ximenes de Cisneros. The usually accepted starting point in Italy was the founding of the Oratory of Divine Love in Genoa in 1497; it was dedicated to personal spiritual renewal through the practice of regular religious devotions and the works of mercy. Its membership was half lay and half clerical. Similar groups soon spread throughout Italy, and around 1514 one even took root in the Roman Curia. Although it was predominantly a lay affair, it included in its membership some of the outstanding prelates of the day and numbered among its leaders a Venetian, Gaspar Contarini, who has been called "the heart and soul" of the reform movement in the Curia.[1]

A direct offspring of the Oratory was a new type of religious order, the Theatines, founded by members of the Roman branch of the Oratory, Gaetano de Thiene (d. 1547) and Gian Carafa (d. 1559), later Pope Paul IV. They were convinced that reform had to begin with the parish clergy, and so their object was to organize secular priests into communities based on the common observance of poverty, chastity, and obedience and to raise the level of clerical spirituality. The order became a seminary of bishops, a byword for austerity, and a continual force for the reform of the Italian clergy.

The idea caught on, and a number of similar orders sprang up—the Somaschi, founded in 1532 by Jerome Aemiliani and centered in Venice; the Barnabites in 1530; and the most successful of all, the Jesuits, who began as a small band of men personally recruited by Ignatius Loyola in Paris in 1534. They moved shortly afterward to Italy and Rome, where they received papal approbation in 1540. Another sign of the forces of renewal working in the Church in Italy were the Capuchins, founded in 1528 as an offshoot of the Franciscans; they wanted to restore the Franciscan Order to its primitive ideals. They multiplied rapidly and soon became a familiar sight in their coarse garment with its large square hood. They rivaled the Jesuits in numbers and in their influence on the course of the Catholic Reformation.

Another great influence on the spiritual revival of the Italian Church was Gian Matteo Giberti, a member of the Oratory of Divine Love and bishop of Verona from 1524 to 1543. The terrible sack of Rome in 1527 by invading German troops appeared as a divine warning to him, and he plunged into the work of pastoral reform in his diocese of Verona, which up to this point he had neglected. In an age when absentee bishops proliferated, Giberti showed the difference an energetic resident bishop could make for the life of the

[1] H. Jedin, *A History of the Council of Trent* (London: Thomas Nelson & Sons, 1957), p. 178.

Church. Carrying on a ceaseless round of searching visitations, he left no aspect of Church life untouched: Liturgy, parochial work, preaching, monastic communities, the social apostolate—all were the object of his wise reform decrees. Many of them were later incorporated verbatim into the general legislation of the Council of Trent. Even more important than Giberti's legislation was the example he gave—which showed the bishops of his day what could be accomplished by a full-time bishop resident in his diocese and wholly intent on reform.

But the problems facing the Church—doctrinal confusion, fiscal abuses, widespread ignorance, and organizational breakdown—were on too grand a scale to be tackled merely at the local level. And it is one of the great tragedies of Reformation history that it took so long to call a general council of the Church. It required no less than twenty-eight years after Luther first raised his cry! Numerous obstacles stood in the way: papal fears of a revival of conciliarism, opposition from antireform members of the Curia, the hostility of the German princes, and the political rivalry of France and Spain. It is to the enormous credit of Pope Paul III (d. 1549) that he was able to surmount them

Pope Paul III Farnese (1534–49). Titian (1488–1576). Museo Nazionale de Capodimonte, Naples. © *Scala/Art Resource, New York.*

all by his dogged perseverance and finally convoke the council that opened on December 13, 1545, in the northern Italian city of Trent, with some thirty bishops in attendance.

It took eighteen years for the council to complete its work, from 1545 to 1563, although it was in actual session for only a little more than three of these years. The first session came to an end in 1547, when Charles V returned to his policy of seeking reunion by dialogue between Catholics and Protestants in the hopes of finding an acceptable compromise. The long interlude of ten years between the second session (1551–52) and the third (1562–63) was due to a variety of causes: A new generation of political leaders appeared who were less concerned about religious problems, while Pope Paul IV, a vigorous, reform-minded Pope who reigned from 1555 to 1559, preferred direct papal action to a council. But his successor, Pius IV (d. 1565), reverted to the previous papal policy, and by dint of much diplomacy and tenacity finally succeeded in reassembling the Council for its third and last session.

The Council addressed itself to the problems of doctrinal confusion and organizational breakdown. In a series of important decrees—answering Luther's resounding denials with ringing affirmations—it drew a sharp line of demarcation between the Catholic and the Protestant teaching. Scripture and tradition were both declared necessary in determining the faith of the Church. On the issue of justification, which Luther considered the key to the whole dispute, Trent refused any compromise. The bishops denied man's total corruption by original sin and asserted that our justification was not actualized by faith alone but also by hope and charity as well. Moreover, charity had to be expressed in good works carried out by the co-operation of the human will with God's grace. Against Luther they also asserted the dogmas of the divine validity of the seven sacraments, the hierarchical nature of the Church, the divine institution of the priesthood, the traditional teaching on transubstantiation, and the sacrificial character of the Mass.

The doctrinal definitions they laid down were quite narrow. Not all Catholics agreed with them, but there was no longer any question about the limits of orthodoxy on important issues. The trend as a whole at the council was extremely conservative; the liberals were not given much of a hearing. Thus in requiring seminaries for the future training of priests, the bishops made sure that the training given would be highly traditional, and they paid little heed to the progress in biblical studies made by the humanists.

Council of Trent (1545–63). Anonymous, Italian School, sixteenth century. Louvre, Paris.   © *Réunion des Musées Nationaux/Art Resource, New York.*

In the same way they reaffirmed tradition as regards the structure of the Church. Their most important measure, no doubt, was acknowledging papal supremacy and so laying to rest the ghost of Constance. And by submitting its decrees to the Pope for confirmation and entrusting to him the task of carrying out its incomplete work, they further strengthened the hold of the Pope over the Church. Under the papal autocrat they placed episcopal autocrats by giving the bishop absolute control over his diocese. And they left no room for participation by the laity in the administration of the Church. In sum, they bequeathed to modern Catholics a highly authoritarian, centralized structure that was still basically medieval.

For the everyday life of the Church, probably nothing Trent did was more important than its reform of the Mass. The need for reform was obvious. The medieval Mass had become a theatrical-type spectacle, the faithful having lost the sense of participation that was at the heart of the ancient liturgy. Moreover, owing to the copying of liturgical books by hand and other factors, a great variety of local variations had crept in, some of them bizarre, disedifying ceremonies; and besides, there were celebrants who indulged their own eccentricities to the amusement and sometimes the scandal of the faithful. "A tangled jungle" is the way Jesuit scholar Joseph Jungmann describes the state of the Mass at the end of the Middle Ages. There was also a good amount of simony (priests hawking Masses) and superstition (Masses that had to be celebrated with twelve candles or seven candles or whatever in order to guarantee the promised benefits). The Protestants had been most vehement in denouncing such abuses.

The commission that Trent set up to reform the Mass did their work rather quickly, and in 1570 it issued the *Missale Romanum,* which was made binding on the universal Church and which remained virtually unchanged until the 1960s. Its introduction marked a new era in the history of the Mass: In place of the allegorical Mass there would now be the rubrical Mass—the priest being obligated under penalty of mortal sin to adhere to its most minute prescriptions. Here again it is the extreme conservatism of the council that strikes the eye. It is at least conceivable that they might have taken a creative approach. They might, for instance, have introduced the vernacular, which the Protestants had done so successfully. But instead they acted defensively and protectively. One reason for this was that in the polemical climate of the times they could not afford to admit that the Protestants could be right about anything. This would impugn the claim of the Roman Church to divine authority. Another reason was the still rudimentary state of historical knowledge. Scholars had not yet uncovered the complex history of liturgical evolution and the slow formation of the main liturgical families. Common opinion at the time believed that St. Peter had instituted the Catholic way of saying Mass.

The Tridentine Mass was tremendously effective in securing a uniform religious expression for Catholics throughout the world. And as a pedagogical tool for instilling the Catholic sense of tradition and emphasizing the clarity, stability, and universality of Catholic doctrine, it was superb. But on the negative side it helped engender the myth of the unchangeable Mass, the sign and proof of the unchangeableness of the Roman Church (a myth whose overthrow has lately caused such confusion). And above all it failed radically to restore to the people a sense of participation—forcing them to run after a multitude of extraliturgical devotions in order to satisfy their need to feel involved in the worship of the Church.

In spite of its notable limitations, the Council of Trent was certainly the pivotal event of the Catholic Reformation. It dramatically mirrored the vital spiritual energy once more pulsating through the Church; it defined the key doctrines of the Church; and it set the whole Church on the path of reform.

All of this we can now see in retrospect. But at the time, any pessimist familiar with the history of the previous reform councils might well have wondered whether all those decrees might simply remain dead letters.

But the pessimists were wrong for a change. One of the main reasons for this was the Roman Popes, who fortunately for the future of the Church were sincerely dedicated to carrying out the reforms dictated by Trent. Without their dynamic leadership the cause of reform would certainly have remained a mere vain aspiration.

The first and greatest of these reform Popes was Pius V (d. 1572), previously renowned as a relentless inquisitor; he set such a high standard of papal morality that it has never again suffered any serious relapse. An ascetic, mortified man who loved nothing more than prayer, he transformed the Vatican—by rigorous measures and example—into a kind of monastery. Throwing himself into the work of reform with indefatigable energy, he published the *Catechism* of the Council of Trent, a clear, concise summary of Catholic beliefs and practices, and also the previously mentioned *Missale Romanum,* or *Revised Roman Missal,* which imposed a uniform liturgy on the whole Catholic world. But probably his most important contribution was cleaning out the long-entrenched curial bureaucracy, with its notorious policy of selling office to the highest bidder. Only a man of his tough fiber would have dared to tackle such a job, and he succeeded only by dint of heroic determination.

His successors kept steadily at the work of reform. Gregory XIII (d. 1585), who won a lasting niche in history by his reform of the calendar (1582), was not an ascetic like Pius. But assisted by Charles Borromeo, Gregory kept his administration fixed on the goals of reform. To guarantee the most rigorous execution of Trent's decrees, he appointed a committee of four of the most zealous reforming cardinals. His successor, Sixtus V (d. 1590), was energy personified. Elected at sixty-five, he was an unhandsome man whose countenance was dominated by a large and heavy nose hanging over a dark chestnut beard tinged with gray; his arched and extraordinarily thick eyebrows framed small eyes whose glance was so piercing that one look from him sufficed to secure compliance. The towering obelisk he erected in St. Peter's Square still reminds us of the imaginative and grandiose urban renewal programs he initiated. He was a man of big ideas, though some of them—like his plans to conquer Egypt—were too ambitious to carry out. He showed the sternness of his nature by the ruthless measures he took against the bandits

St. Charles Borromeo. Orazio Borgianni (1578–1616). San Carlo alle Quattro Fontane, Rome. © *Scala/Art Resource, New York.*

who infested the Papal States. A report from Rome in 1585 stated that there were more bandits' heads exposed on the bridge of St. Angelo than melons sold in the markets. On the other hand, he was less severe in his treatment of crimes against the faith. Only five persons were executed for this reason under Sixtus, three of them priests who were burned at the stake in one auto-da-fé in 1587. Although he lapsed into some of the inappropriate fiscal policies of bygone days, he did continue the work of reform—appointing only men of sterling qualities to the cardinalate. He left behind a permanent mark on the Church's administration by his reorganization of the Curia, which gave it the basic centralized and uniform structure it has retained throughout modern history.

At the death of Sixtus it was evident that the Popes once more had a firm hand on the helm of the Church. Though their domain was no longer the whole of Western Europe, as in the Middle Ages, they once again wielded an influence over the Church that they had not exercised since the Great Schism.

One of the most potent instruments used by these Popes of the Catholic reconquest was the Inquisition. A creation of the medieval papacy, it had fallen into virtual disuse—outside of Spain—until it was reconstituted by Pope Paul III in 1542. This Roman Inquisition, supplemented by the Congregation of the Index (established in 1571 and which periodically issued a list of condemned books), proved very effective in suppressing heresy in Italy and Spain. No one, however high in office, was beyond its fearful reach. The primate of Toledo, Archbishop Carranza (d. 1576), was himself arrested and kept for seventeen years in its prisons on the mere suspicion of heresy. Intolerance and repression, we might add, were not confined to the Catholics; Protestants also used similar coercive methods against dissenters.

BESIDES THE REGENERATED papacy, another institution proved of singular importance in the success of the Catholic reform: the Jesuit order. In fact, no single Catholic did more than its founder, Ignatius Loyola, to offset the devastation inflicted by Luther. Of course, the bantam-sized ex-soldier could not foresee this when he gathered a small band of men around him in

St. Ignatius Loyola receives the papal bull from Pope Paul III ordaining the Jesuit order. Juan de Valdés Leal (1622–90). Museo de Bellas Artes, Seville.   © *Scala/Art Resource, New York.*

Paris and induced them to join him in a little church on the hill of Mont-martre in 1534 to take vows of chastity, obedience, poverty, and a pilgrimage to Jerusalem. Loyola created a force that would help transform the Catholic Church and shape much of its history for the next four centuries. He was a God-intoxicated soul, a mystic with a unique genius for communicating his own love of God. His *Spiritual Exercises*—the fruit of his religious experi-ence—became the chief instrument in molding the spirituality of his order and proved many times over their remarkable power of changing men. The effectiveness of this amazing little book was due to the extraordinary fashion with which Ignatius combined—by an uncanny instinct—the accumulated spiritual wisdom of the past with the immediate lessons he drew from his own unusual experiences. It deeply influenced the whole Catholic Reform move-ment by its insistence on the necessity of a profound interior life of prayer as the source of the apostolate and of all effective action in the Church. And as used by the Jesuits, especially in their retreats, it proved capable of being ap-plied to men at all levels of spiritual need.

The Jesuits were committed to serve God by serving the Pope and the Church in whatever capacity they were needed. They were flexible and even rev-olutionary in the way they changed and even discarded traditional religious practices. Daily prayers in common according to a fixed schedule were dropped, for instance—a move that shocked contemporaries. They re-examined everything traditional, in fact, only retaining what promoted their pastoral aims and main tasks: preaching, giving retreats, teaching, and administering the sacraments.

The progress of the order was astounding. At the time of Ignatius' death in 1556 it numbered some 936 members and had sunk its roots into most of the Catholic countries of Europe. Its members distinguished themselves in every form of the Church's apostolate and won renown as preachers, builders, teachers, writers, founders of colleges, pastors of souls, and confessors. Many of them carried the Gospel overseas as missionaries. All in all, they engaged in a range of activity unparalleled by any of the other orders. The results were es-pecially dramatic in German-speaking lands and in central Europe, where whole regions—including Poland in its entirety—were brought back to the Roman obedience.

Next to Ignatius himself, no Jesuit was more influential than Peter Cani-sius (d. 1597)—called the second apostle of Germany—a priest who engaged in a multifarious range of religious activities with singular success. Though the volume and manifold nature of his work had an almost chaotic effect on his daily life, he was able to remain essentially a man of prayer. He was a remarkably effective preacher, organizer, and confessor, but his greatest gift to the Catholic Reform movement in Germany was his *Catechism*—a compendium of Catholic doctrine that he published in varying forms to match different levels of age and education. It enjoyed over 130 editions and was so popular that, as Lortz says, Catholicism in Germany was henceforth inconceivable apart from it.[2] We might add that from our standpoint today it compares unfavorably in some ways with the *Roman Catechism* of Pius V, which was more positive in its approach and more ecumenical: Pius' work aimed mainly at the renewal of the inner life of the Church and presented the Christian message in more positive and comprehensive terms. Canisius' catechism, on the other hand, shows how this earlier spirit of ecumenism was blighted by an increasing emphasis on controversy.

Canisius was also largely responsible for the foundation of colleges at Augsburg, Munich, and Innsbruck. This educational work was, in fact, one of the principal means used by the fathers in their efforts to promote the Catholic renewal. Here again they had a major influence on something quite new in the history of the Church—the founding of religious orders organized solely to carry on teaching as a Christian work of charity.

Besides the papacy and the Jesuits, the other major agency in the success of the Catholic Reformation was the bishops. The Council of Trent viewed the reform of the bishops as the key to the reform of the rest of the Church. They were ordered to reside in their dioceses and not leave without permission; they were to preach regularly, visit their parishes, hold annual synods, build seminaries, ordain as priests only candidates who were rigorously tested, root out concubinage among priests, keep an eye on the discipline of convents and religious houses, and give good example in their own dress, charity, and modesty. Their authority was strengthened to enable them to deal effectively with abuses.

It was a high ideal but not an impossible one, and soon there were many bishops who measured up to the standards set at Trent. The severely ascetic Charles Borromeo of Milan was undoubtedly the most important example of this reformed episcopate. From 1565 to 1584 he ruled the diocese of Milan, embracing more than a half million souls, where he followed the prescriptions

---

[2] J. Lortz, *The Reformation in Germany* (New York: Herder & Herder, 1968), II, p. 169.

of Trent to the letter. The reform legislation, which he promulgated in numerous synods, was copied by bishops around the Catholic world. Through his influence and that of other men, like St. Thomas of Villanuova (d. 1555), the spirit of Trent gradually penetrated the entire Catholic episcopate and stamped the entire Church with a characteristic physiognomy. A Catholic diocese would henceforth be run in military fashion. Trent's strengthening of episcopal authority enabled the bishop to stamp out quickly any challenge to orthodoxy or uniformity.

IN CONJUNCTION WITH the Tridentine Reformation a new type of Catholic spirituality appeared that was to remain the standard for the following centuries. The Tridentine decree on justification stressed the importance of good works—exerting a decisive influence on the direction taken by this spirituality in the modern era. It meant that Catholics would conceive spiritual perfection as involving a high degree of personal activity—combining an active striving after self-control, the acquisition of virtue, and a zeal for the good works of mercy and charity. At the same time the decree also encouraged a meditative form of mental prayer, which was already highly cultivated in the fifteenth century. Under the influence of such masters as Loyola, Scupoli, Francis de Sales, Vincent de Paul, and de Bérulle, this developed into the very quintessential act of Catholic reform spirituality. A science of meditation originated, which became one of the most important tools used by Church leaders in the reform of clergy and laity.

To balance this emphasis on one's own activity, there was an equal insistence on the priority of God's grace; in a sense it is God who does all. And so there was also great emphasis placed on those visible channels of God's grace—the sacraments. A eucharistic piety was fashioned that became the distinguishing feature of modern Catholicism: Devout Catholic laymen now began to receive Communion once a week and confessed their sins frequently rather than once yearly, as in the medieval Church. Many priests and bishops now began the daily celebration of Mass. This eucharistic piety was extended to include a wealth of nonliturgical practices, such as the adoration of the host in such services as benediction and forty hours.

Tridentine spirituality was then sacramental, centered on the Eucharist. It was exacting, making stiff demands on its practitioners: self-discipline, self-control, and regularity in prayer. It was practical in the way it closely associated good works with self-improvement. And finally, in accordance with the dominant cultural trend of the times, it was humanistic—at least in its assumption that each person had it in his power, to some degree, to determine his own fate.

This spirituality found its finest expression in a considerable number of vigorous, colorful men and women whose impact was strong enough to create distinct schools (Oratorian, Carmelite, Salesian, etc.) modeled after their example. One of the most influential of these saints was no doubt Philip Neri (d. 1595), founder of the Oratorians. A man who combined whimsical cheerfulness and zest for life with a deep interior spirituality, Neri exerted extraordinary influence over people of every walk of life in Rome during the latter part of the sixteenth century, and as confessor of Popes and cardinals he assisted in the transformation of the Roman Curia itself. His school of spirituality—called Oratorian from the community of priests he founded by that name—included another outstanding exponent in the French author de Bérulle (d. 1629), a cardinal and leading statesman.

The leaders of the Spanish Carmelite school, Teresa of Ávila (d. 1582) and her friend and disciple, John of the Cross (d. 1591), were both reformers of their respective Carmelite orders in the face of savage opposition. Both were endowed with great mystical powers and both were gifted with unrivaled literary skill in depicting the various stages of mysticism. Teresa was the first to give a scientific description of the entire life of prayer—from meditation to the mystical marriage. Her finest mystical work is *Las moradas* or *El castillo interior* (1583). John's best loved poems include *Noche oscura del alma, Llama de amor viva* and *La subida al Monte Carmelo.*

The Salesian school was founded by Francis de Sales (d. 1622), who as bishop of Geneva successfully accomplished the difficult and dangerous mission of winning the people of the Chablais district back to the Catholic faith. His writings are not only highly regarded guides to the spiritual life but also are considered among the classics of French literature.

Other notable examples of Catholic spirituality during this period were Jane de Chantal (d. 1641), the protégé of Francis de Sales who founded the Congregation of the Visitation Sisters, and Vincent de Paul (d. 1660), whose Congregation of the Mission (1625) did much to raise the standards of the French clergy. With Louise de Marillac he founded the Sisters of Charity in 1633, the first Catholic female religious society without enclosure. The sisters were dedicated to work among the poor and sick. Vincent's life span coincided

St. Teresa. 1827. François
Gérard (1770–1837). Maison
Marie-Thérèse, Paris.
© *Erich Lessing/Art Resource,
New York.*

with a remarkable renaissance of mysticism in the French Church, when many
saints of lesser fame also flourished.

ANOTHER MANIFESTATION OF the revitalized spirituality of the post-
Trent Church was the imposing theological and intellectual revival associated
with the leading Catholic universities: Salamanca, Rome, Paris, and Louvain.
Central to the whole enterprise was the renaissance of interest in Thomas
Aquinas, whose works, thanks to the Jesuits, won nearly universal acceptance
as basic texts.

Robert Bellarmine (d. 1621), professor of theology at Gregorian University in Rome, was the most illustrious defender of the traditional faith in the
polemics with the Protestants. His *Disputationes de Controversiis Christianae
Fidei* (1568–93) was a massive, systematic presentation of the Catholic position. Its defense of papal prerogatives exerted enormous influence on the de-

velopment of the doctrine of papal infallibility. His concept of the Church appears extremely juridical today, but it remained the standard Catholic one until Vatican II. His fellow Jesuit luminary, Francis Suarez (d. 1617), wrote commentaries on Aquinas marked by a definite originality. Suarez's systematic approach and careful attention to historical data gathered from patristic and conciliar documents set a high standard for modern Catholic theology. Although his thought occasionally soared to the pinnacles of Trinitarian speculation, his most substantial contributions occurred in speculations about the nature of grace and in the field of international law.

Another sign of the spiritual energy stirring the Church to renew itself is found in the work of the missionaries who crossed the oceans in constantly increasing numbers during the sixteenth century. At the dawn of the age of discovery, Catholic priests would invariably accompany the explorers and, as they opened up a whole new era in Europe's relations with the rest of the world, this missionary effort remained an important part of the whole enterprise. Prince Henry the Navigator's pioneering explorations of the African coast led to the establishment of Catholic missions there. Then Columbus carried missionaries to America, where three episcopal sees were organized as early as 1511. These missions flourished and were the basis for the conversion of all of Central and South America.

Some attempts had been made during the Middle Ages to bring the Gospel to the Far East; the Franciscan John of Montecorvino went to Peking as archbishop in 1307. But the promise was cut short by the rise of the hostile Ming dynasty in China and the coming of the Black Death to Europe. The modern missionary movement to the Far East goes back to 1498, when the Portuguese reached India and made Goa the center of missionary work. But the really significant date is 1542, the year Francis Xavier, S.J., landed in Goa after a thirteen-month voyage from Lisbon and began to preach, baptize, and convert multitudes. After numerous trips to the cities and ports of India and Indonesia, he landed at Kagoshima in southern Japan. Two years later he set out for China but died on a desolate offshore island in 1552. The mission he left in Japan at first made progress, but a terrible persecution broke out in 1638 that took the lives of thirty-five thousand Christians and left behind only a remnant, who were forced to practice their religion underground until missionaries arrived again in the middle of the nineteenth century.

The Chinese mission dated from 1581, when a number of Jesuits led by Matteo Ricci arrived. Ricci won prestige among the Chinese by his scientific knowledge, his clocks, and his maps. He converted many Chinese by skillfully adjusting the message of Christ to accommodate Chinese ideas. But his toleration of the continuation of semireligious rites by Chinese converts later occasioned much controversy among missionaries and was only finally settled by Pope Clement XI (d. 1721), who decided against Ricci's methods. This decision meant that potential converts were made to feel that accepting Christianity meant repudiating their whole culture. The tragic consequences of the Pope's act coupled with the decline of Portuguese power in the East greatly crippled the missionary effort in China. As with Japan, the whole work had to be started over again in the nineteenth century.

A work somewhat similar to Ricci's was begun in India by Robert de Nobili, S.J. (d. 1656), who adopted the lifestyle of the Brahmins. An eminent linguist, he wrote more than twenty books in Sanskrit, Tamil, and Telugu, including hymnals and catechisms. The most successful Catholic missionary effort in Asia took place in the Philippines, where a bishopric was set up in 1581. By 1595 a college was opened in Manila. Today there are some twenty million Catholics in the country, about 80 per cent of the population.

Until the end of the eighteenth century, missionary work was carried on almost exclusively by Catholics; but in the Far East, as we have seen, it had only marginal effect. In part this was a result of the advanced state of culture and religion among the natives, who were inclined to eye the foreigners with a certain disdain; it was also related to the missionaries' close connection with European colonialism. A most important act for the future of the Catholic missionary effort was the establishment in 1622 of the papal Congregatio de Propaganda Fide (Congregation for the Propagation of the Faith) whereby the Pope centralized all mission activity under his authority. It struck at the system of royal patronage, which enabled Catholic governments to control and often exploit the Catholic missionary movement for political purposes.

BY THE END of the Council of Trent in 1563 Protestantism had already established its sway over half of Europe. This trend was reversed, however, during the remainder of the century. With the publication of Trent's decrees and with the upsurge of new vitality in the Church—manifest especially in the Jesuits and the regenerated papacy—the Catholic Church began to recover large blocs of territory. Poland turned back to Catholicism; large parts of Germany, France, and the southern Netherlands were likewise restored to communion with the Holy See, while the Protestants made no significant gains after 1563. And overseas Catholic mission gains compensated for the losses suffered in Europe.

One must not underestimate the part played by political forces in fixing the religious map of Europe in the sixteenth century. We cannot forget that there were inescapable political consequences involved in the decision to accept or repudiate Rome. It meant for each government having greater or lesser power over ecclesiastical affairs or the power to seize ecclesiastical property.

The most powerful late sixteenth-century monarch, Philip of Spain, was a zealous champion of the Roman Church and did all he could to restore Europe to obedience to the Pope. He launched his mighty armada in 1588 against England partly with this purpose in mind. Its defeat was a big setback for the political Counter Reformation. Elizabeth, Queen of England, for her part used political methods to fasten Protestantism on her kingdom. France was the theater of a seesaw struggle between Catholics and Huguenots that lasted forty years and only came to an end when the victorious Protestant King Henry IV embraced Catholicism and in his Edict of Nantes (1598) decreed freedom of conscience for all of his subjects. Sweden narrowly missed being forced back to the Roman obedience by its Catholic King Sigismund. He was defeated by his Protestant Uncle Charles at the Battle of Stangebro in 1598 and driven out of the country together with his Jesuit allies.

The last of these religious wars took place in Germany—the Thirty Years' War (1618–48). It signalized the breakdown of the Peace of Augsburg (1555) and the increase of Catholic power in Germany thanks to the dynamism of the Tridentine reform. The Catholic Habsburg Emperor Ferdinand of Austria was victorious in the first phases of the war and was on the verge of establishing the political ascendance of Catholicism over Germany. But at this point King Gustavus of Sweden intervened—ostensibly to save the Protestant cause. But his alliance with a cardinal, Richelieu of France, against Catholic Austria in 1631 showed how political considerations had already begun to overshadow religious ones in the grand game of European politics. The Treaty of Westphalia (1648) brought the Thirty Years' War to an end. Catholics, Lutherans, and Calvinists were accorded equality before the law in Germany.

It was certainly clear at this point that the unity of medieval Christendom was gone forever. The demarcation of territory between the Catholic Church and other forms of Christianity was settled for the next three hundred years. It was significant that the most populous countries and (except France) the most powerful ones—the ones that were in the next century to dominate diplomacy and politics—England, Sweden, and Prussia—had all turned Protestant.

The post-Trent Church obviously could not hope to dominate Europe as the medieval Church had. But thanks to the Council of Trent and the tremendous movement of reform it engendered, the Catholic Church in the seventeenth century was once more a strong, self-confident, spiritually revitalized organization. Faced with a phalanx of innovators who seemed bent on jettisoning the entire medieval heritage, the bishops at Trent had reaffirmed almost every jot and tittle of the tradition. It was a rigoristic and authoritarian institution they set up, but it was also a dynamic spiritual force capable of meeting once more the religious needs of a large portion of the human race. Thanks to Trent, the Pope was once again in complete command of the Church. Under him and with the help of the regenerated old orders and enthusiastic new orders and aided by the better-trained diocesan priests, the bishops were able to carry out a vast reformation. On every front—spiritual, intellectual, cultural, and missionary—they scored great victories. The spiritual élan of this Tridentine Church was marvelously captured in stone by the twin masters of the baroque, Bernini and Borromini. Under papal patronage, they filled Rome with fountains, statues, and churches in the new style to celebrate the resurrection of the Church of Rome. Two of them are of incomparable power: Bernini's immense elliptical colonnade that frames the piazza of St. Peter's, and his towering, twisting bronze baldachino over St. Peter's tomb. Contemplating them today one can still feel the excitement and the drama of this amazing chapter in the history of the Church.

Part Four

THE CHURCH IN A
STATE OF SIEGE

A.D. 1650–1891

Chapter 22

THE CHALLENGE OF THE
NEW THOUGHT

By the middle of the seventeenth century it was evident that the vigor of the Catholic Reformation was spent. Protestants and Catholics had settled for an uneasy truce. The most vital impulse in European thought would no longer originate from within the Christian churches. Europe was ready to follow a different course. A host of European minds, some of them quite alienated from the Church, were busy sketching a new world view that would come to dominate Western civilization and orient Western man in entirely new directions. The thinkers who participated in this movement, known as the Enlightenment, covered the whole field of knowledge that was heretofore considered the exclusive province of the Church and offered a different view of the cosmos, the nature of man, of society, of history, of morals, and of religion. The world picture they created meant a loosening of state and society from ecclesiastical controls and gave rise to a largely secular culture. Their principles were no longer drawn from the Bible or Church authority but were arrived at independently by reason and social experience.

The Catholic Church's reaction to the rise of modernity was largely defensive and negative. It was often unable to meet the free thinkers on their own grounds and frequently resorted simply to condemnation of their ideas and forceful repression. The result was a divorce of secular culture from the Church and the state of siege mentality that characterized modern Catholicism down to our day.

THE ENLIGHTENMENT HAD its origin in the new cosmology, which originated with Copernicus. Rejecting the idea of the earth as the center of the universe—a position held by all medieval thinkers, who took it from the Greeks,
Ptolemy, and Aristotle—Copernicus favored a sun-centered universe, a theory
that postulated the fantastic notion that our seemingly static earth was actually
spinning around the sun at an incredible rate. A succession of brilliant
minds—Kepler, Galileo, and Newton the most noteworthy—gradually revolutionized our understanding of the physical universe along Copernican lines.

This new cosmology was terribly threatening to the Church. Its ideological and theological substructure, Scholasticism, was based on Aristotle's philosophy which, thanks to Aquinas, was made to dovetail nicely with the
sacred Scriptures. The new cosmology seemed to entail a thoroughgoing rejection of the entire philosophy of Aristotle and hence would shatter the doctrinal framework of the Church. Galileo, it is true, offered the Church a
method of reconciling Scripture with the new science he was in the process of
founding. In his letter to Castelli he said:

> The authority of the Sacred Scriptures has as its sole aim to convince
> men of those truths which are necessary for their salvation. . . . But
> that the same God who has endowed us with senses, reason and un-

Galileo Galilei Before the Inquisition. Joseph Nicolas Robert-Fleury (1797–1890).
Louvre, Paris.   © *Erich Lessing/Art Resource, New York.*

derstanding should not wish us to use them and should desire to impart to us by another means knowledge which we have it in our power to acquire by their use—this is a thing which I do not think I am bound to believe.[1]

But his words went unheeded, and the Church condemned his view that the earth moved around the sun. In the thirteenth century, Aquinas had taken a creative approach to Aristotelianism when it was regarded as a threat to the foundations of the Church's doctrine. But the Church of the Counter Reformation refused to recognize in Galileo another Aquinas, suffered a failure of nerve, and henceforth resorted increasingly to condemnations as a means of dealing with intellectual challenges.

Another movement of the Enlightenment that provoked the Church's urge to condemn was critical rationalism. Its founder, René Descartes (d. 1650), applied to philosophy the mathematical method already proven so effective in science. He based his whole enterprise on a method of radical doubt that supposedly enabled him to reach a number of absolutely certain truths. It was essentially the same procedure used by seventeenth-century physicists who accepted nothing as true until it was established beyond all possible doubt. Descartes broke radically with all past philosophy and questioned all authorities. He attacked the Aristotelians for their blind reliance on Aristotle. Although he himself did not extend his methodic doubt to truths of the Catholic faith, his principle of doubting everything was soon extended to every aspect of the Christian tradition and even to the very idea of tradition itself. Traditions were regarded as the epitome of inherited prejudices, and critical historical science was to take the place of tradition. As the main stronghold of tradition, the Christian Church was a primary target for the rationalists, the leader of whom was Pierre Bayle (d. 1706), who focused his acute critical faculty on matters touching religion and its historical foundations.

One of the founders of biblical criticism, French Oratorian priest Richard Simon, tried to show the Church that criticism did not have to be destructive. In his *Critical History of the Old Testament* (1678), he insisted that the Bible must be studied critically, like any other historical document; he questioned many of the traditional assumptions regarding the authorship and

---

[1] Quoted in *Science and Religion,* ed. Ian Barbour (New York: Harper & Row, 1968), p. 31.

René Descartes (1596–1650).
Frans Hals (1580–1666).
Louvre, Paris.   © *Réunion des
Musées Nationaux/Art Resource,
New York.*

historical character of the Bible, but he wrote as a champion of the Catholic
faith hoping to demonstrate the validity of the Catholic understanding of tradition. His work alarmed Church authorities, however; Bossuet took one look
at its Table of Contents and called for the police to suppress it. Another great
opportunity was missed to adapt the Church's doctrine to the new ideas. As
with Galileo, the problem lay with the rigid understanding of tradition as formulated by Trent. Trent had laid down that Scripture must be interpreted according to tradition, which it defined as the way Scripture was understood by
the Fathers of the Church. In practice, this meant that Catholic thought
would not be allowed to move beyond the patristic parameters and hence
would have increasing difficulty in dealing with the advance of secular
thought.

Another major source of conflict between the Enlightenment and the
Church was the issue of religious freedom. The medieval idea of the need for
unity of religion as the basis of the social order was still strong in both the
Catholic and Protestant world. Every country had its established Church.
Bodin's idea that religious unity was not necessarily the supreme social good
had not yet won acceptance. The individual was not free to worship God as
he saw fit. Even in countries where a measure of toleration was granted, there

was a strong tendency to revoke such privileges, as in England in 1660 and France in 1685.

The philosophers of the Enlightenment found this state of affairs atrocious and devoted their best energies to the fight for religious freedom. One of their main arguments was based on the very personal nature of a religious commitment since, as they said, religious truths, unlike scientific truths, are not susceptible to objective proof. Therefore coercion is intrinsically evil, since it destroys personal choice, which is the essence of a religious commitment.

As Diderot put it:

> The mind can only acquiesce in what it accepts as true. The heart can only love what seems good to it. Violence will turn a man into a hypocrite if he is weak and into a martyr if he is strong. . . . Teaching, persuasion and prayer, these are the only legitimate means of spreading the faith.[2]

Closely connected with their devotion to religious freedom was their belief in personal autonomy. This meant that a person should accept as true only what seemed true to him on the basis of intrinsic rational evidence—never on the basis of authority alone, whether of Scripture, the Church, or some other external agency.

The Churches, needless to say, showed little sympathy with these ideas of religious freedom and autonomy. With notable exceptions the churchmen could not shake off habits of mind ingrained in Church discipline and policy for a thousand years. Because of its high degree of centralization and efficiency, the Church of Rome proved to be more successful than the other churches in detecting and suppressing heresy, and therefore it was looked on more than the others as a bastion of bigotry and intolerance.

The Christian doctrine of original sin was also the subject of bitter disagreement between the Churches and the philosophers. Original sin was the Christian answer to the age-old problem of human evil and wickedness—why violence, wars, murders, crimes of every sort? Christians traced moral evil back to the primeval apostasy in the garden of Eden—a theory that the en-

[2] Quoted in J. Livingston, *Modern Christian Thought* (New York: Macmillan, 1971), p. 8.

lightened philosophers found most repugnant to common sense and to reason. In their view, man was born naturally good and endowed with powers of reason that—if properly used—would assure him of an adequate measure of natural happiness.

Closely connected with this issue was the question of progress: Are men getting better and happier all the time, and are they heading for a golden age? The "enlightened" said "Yes"; the Christians, "No." The attitude of the enlightened was definitely a change; all previous thinkers located the Golden Age in some idyllic period of the past when man was supposed to have been completely happy and at his best.

One reason for the optimism that was such a characteristic trait of the enlightened was the real material progress registered by the development of scientific technology; roads were obviously better in the eighteenth century than they were in the seventeenth; coaches were more comfortable; there was greater accumulation of wealth. There was also—thanks to Newton—a new confidence in the power of human reason, and the feeling that the evils of superstition, fanaticism, dogmatism, and unreason would be conquered; a growing belief shared by few Christians that by improving education and applying rational principles to social life men would quickly gain the happiness so far denied them by archaic institutions and the conspiracy of vested interests.

The Marquis de Condorcet was one of the most fervent apostles of the new religion of humanity and progress. In his sketch of universal history he painted a vision of worldly redemption, of an earthly paradise equivalent to the heaven of the Christians. He called it the tenth epoch, a time when superstition would be overcome, crime would cease, and war would be banished from society, for all of these evils were due to ignorance and would be cured by the progress of science. With England, France, and the United States in the vanguard, all humanity would ascend to higher and higher planes of physical, intellectual, and moral achievement.[3]

The preachers of the new secular faith raised basic issues and questioned many of the most sacred tenets of the Christian Church regarding the nature of man, the source of evil, the rights of the individual conscience, and the purpose of life. It remained for the Deists to strike at the very heart of the Christian religion by denying the very idea of revelation. Dismissing revela-

---

[3] *The Enlightenment*, ed. F. Manuel (Englewood Cliffs, N.J.: Prentice-Hall, 1965), p. 14.

tion as superfluous, they advocated a reasonable, "natural" religion—one that was supposed to be simple and sufficient for human needs. The very existence of an orderly universe was for them sufficient demonstration of the existence of a God who planned, built, and set in motion the world machine. Their religion was basically a rational theism, which they combined with a radical criticism of the Bible. The obviously spurious character of its prophecies and miracles proved to their satisfaction that it was unworthy of being considered the vehicle of a special revelation.

Deism began in England with Lord Herbert of Cherbury, who thought natural religion would bring an end to religious strife. A number of English pamphleteers took up the cause, men like John Toland, author of *Christianity Not Mysterious,* and Anthony Collins and Matthew Tindal, whose *Christianity as Old as the Creation* was regarded as the Bible of Deism. The books stirred up considerable furor. Deist tendencies found their way into some of the churches in the form of Unitarianism and definitely colored the language of the pulpit. Preachers laid great stress on the reasonableness of Christianity and searched diligently for arguments to prove the credibility of prophecies and miracles. The debate was closed by Anglican bishop Joseph Butler, whose *Analogy of Religion* laid bare the simplistic reasoning of the Deists and concluded rather paradoxically that Christianity was just more probable than Deism.

The struggle between the new and the old faith lasted longer and was more bitter in France. The Deist Voltaire (d. 1778), in the name of the Enlightenment, declared war on the Church, on its dogmas, its ethics, its traditions, and its clergy. Nothing escaped his savage attacks: the Trinity, the chastity of the Virgin Mary, the presence of the body and blood of Christ in the Mass. The morality of the "Chosen People" he found abhorrent, and the history of the Church nothing but a sanguinary compilation of idiotic wrangling leading to war and mass murder. Voltaire was never dull, and he was often witty. His *Dictionnaire Philosophique* (1764) was his anti-Christian summa; it was burned in Geneva, the Netherlands, France, and the Holy See. Its pervasive irony is caught in the following passage:

> While the style of Kings and Chronicles is divine, still, the actions reported in these histories are perhaps not so divine. David assassinates Uriah; Ishbosheth and Mephibosheth are assassinated; Absalom assassinates Amnon; Joab assassinates Absalom; Solomon assassinates

Voltaire (1694–1778). Catherine Lusurier (c. 1763–81). Châteaux de Versailles et de Trianon, Versailles.   © *Réunion des Musées Nationaux/Art Resource, New York.*

Adonijah, his brother; Baasha assassinates Hadab; Zimri assassinates Elah; Omri assassinates Zimri; Ahab assassinates Naboth; Jehu assassinates Ahab and Joram. . . . I pass over many other assassinations. It must be admitted that if the Holy Spirit wrote this history, he didn't choose a very edifying subject.[4]

The debate between Voltaireans and Christians in France, between Catholics and unbelievers, covered much ground and raised many issues. It is noteworthy that the French Catholics never produced apologists equal in brilliance to Voltaire, Diderot, Rousseau, and their company. No Bishop Butler appeared to rout their enemies. Nevertheless, they found some worthy spokesmen. The Jesuit monthly *Journal de Trévoux,* for instance, was among the most erudite and objective periodicals of the day. And it was a great calamity for the Church when the Jesuits were suppressed in 1763, since they offered the best hope of leading the Church to a more positive relationship with the Enlightenment.

The inroads made by skeptical thought into the Church in France were suddenly revealed in the Prades affair, which erupted in France in 1752. The

[4] Quoted in P. Gay, *The Enlightenment* (New York: Alfred A. Knopf, 1967), p. 394.

Abbé de Prades presented a thesis for a degree in theology at the Sorbonne that was supposed to be a summary of arguments in defense of the Christian revelation. Further examination, however, showed that it bore remarkable resemblance to the ideas of Diderot, editor of the suspect *Encyclopédie;* in the guise of an apology it amounted to nothing less than a full-scale attack on fundamental dogmas of the Church. When the news broke that the Sorbonne itself was contaminated by rationalism, a public uproar exploded. The crisis helped to divide France into two camps—more clearly defined than before as it became more and more evident that the Enlightenment was irreconcilably opposed to Christianity.

In the next few decades before the French Revolution, the skeptics made constant progress in spite of the Church's attempt to suppress them. The Encyclopedists found ways of evading the official censors—who in turn often helped by relaxing their vigilance. We must not forget either that the new breed had an easier position to uphold: They were missionaries of a new faith whose dogmas of progress, liberty, reason, and nature seemed more in harmony with the political, social, and cultural trends of the age than traditional Christianity; they also had the advantage that novelty always enjoys, while

Denis Diderot, encyclopedist (1713–84). Jean Honoré Fragonard (1706–32). Louvre, Paris.   © *Réunion des Musées Nationaux/Art Resource, New York.*

Catholic apologists by comparison only seemed to be repeating what people had always heard.

Nevertheless, on the eve of the French Revolution, it was still not clear that the Church had lost the battle for the mind and heart of Europe. The violent and systematic anticlericalism of Voltaire, for all its brilliance and the enthusiasm it aroused among the educated, still reflected the thought of only a restricted sector of the general public.

Chapter 23

THE CHURCH TORN BY
INTERNAL STRIFE:
JANSENISM AND GALLICANISM

While the Church continued to lose ground in its struggle with critical rationalism and liberalism during the seventeenth and eighteenth centuries, it was also weakened interiorly by several violent controversies—over Jansenism and Gallicanism—which divided it and hindered it from adequately responding to the free thinkers.

Jansenism originated with the bishop of Ypres, Cornelius Jansen (d. 1638), a professor at Louvain University, whose book *Augustinus* was only published after his death. Jansen appealed to the authority of St. Augustine in expounding theories on the nature of original sin, human freedom, and the nature and efficacy of God's grace. At the root of his system was a belief in the radical corruption of human nature, which to the authorities smacked suspiciously of Calvinism. After a decade of violent debate in France his whole theology was examined by a papal commission at the request of the French bishops, reduced to five succinct propositions, and condemned by Pope Innocent X in the bull *Cum Occasione* of 1653.

But this did not put an end to the affair. Jansen's followers, led by Antoine Arnauld (d. 1694), and with unofficial headquarters among the nuns of the convent of Port Royal, refused to capitulate. They trumped up a clever distinction between "fact" and "law" to salvage their orthodoxy: The five

Cornelius Jansen, bishop of Ypres (1585–1638), signed Louis Dutielt and dated 1659. Châteaux de Versailles et de Trianon, Versailles. © *Réunion des Musées Nationaux/Art Resource, New York.*

propositions condemned by the Pope were indeed heretical, they maintained, but they did not accurately reflect the true doctrine of Jansen's *Augustinus.* Moreover, the identity of the five propositions with the authentic teaching of Jansen, they asserted, was a question of fact and as such did not fall under the purview of the Church's infallibility. The French Assembly of the Clergy, however, in 1654 affirmed—to the contrary—that the doctrine condemned by the Pope was indeed identical with Jansenism.

But the Jansenists were able to hold their own; their convent of nuns at Port Royal was famous for its austerity, its intense contemplative life, its studious atmosphere, and the many novices it attracted; it served at the same time as a center for an intellectual and spiritual elite of Paris who included some of the most influential members of Parisian society. Their most valuable convert was the brilliant mathematician and inventor Blaise Pascal, who after joining their ranks penned in their defense his masterpiece of satire, the *Provincial Letters* (1656–57)—a devastating attack on their chief enemies, the Jesuits.

The Jesuit and the Jansenist theologies proceeded from a different view of the nature and effects of original sin—coming to different conclusions on a number of crucial points. According to the Jansenists, original sin completely vitiated human nature, subjecting man to concupiscence, unruly passions, all imaginable physical and psychic ills, ignorance, and finally death. The Jesuits, on the other hand (following their favorite authority, Luis Molina [d. 1600]), did not subscribe to so pessimistic a view of the effects of original sin; they held that it merely deprived man of the supernatural gifts bestowed on him—leaving him in the condition of nature, in possession of the powers and subject to the debilities he would have had if he had never been raised to the supernatural state.

Both views had important implications for morality. Because of their optimistic view of human nature, the Jesuits stood for a morality that in many ways resembled the purely naturalist morality of the enlightened Deists and rationalists. Like them they preached the dignity of human nature, and like them they made "nature" the norm of morality, although they did not understand nature in exactly the same way. The Jesuits affirmed that even without grace a person could observe moral rectitude at a natural level and by his own free will perform acts that were morally good.

The pessimistic theology of the Jansenists was reflected in their moral rigorism; since they held that without the constant help of grace man remained totally depraved, all his actions were wicked and even his pretended virtues were vices. Grace was only given to the predestined; others were inexorably doomed to eternal punishment for their sins through no fault of their own, since they simply did not receive the necessary grace.

From the start the Church leaned toward the Jesuit theology and eventually decided in its favor. It was definitely more suitable for a Church that aimed to embrace all men and that traditionally offered a saving grace in its sacraments that was available to all, and that always taught that human effort counted for something in the work of salvation.

But for a time Blaise Pascal and the Jansenists were able to put the whole Jesuit system of morality in a bad light. They accused the Jesuits of preaching an easygoing morality in order to gain power and influence over the masses. By an ingenious use of quotations from Jesuit authors in his *Provincial Letters,* Pascal won over a considerable number of readers. Fortified by the support of public opinion and led by the indomitable Arnauld—an incredibly prolific writer—the Jansenists continued to defend their position and won over some of the clergy and even some of the bishops.

Finally, the Jansenists were ordered by the King, Louis XIV, and the Pope, Alexander VII, to sign a statement renouncing their errors. Under extreme pressure they resorted to another stratagem—the position of "respectful silence"—meaning that while refusing to accept papal infallibility as to questions of fact, they promised to maintain a respectful silence regarding the accuracy of the papal bull. At this point a new Pope, Clement IX (1667–69), was elected, and as a desire for peace was manifest on both sides, a truce was

Blaise Pascal. Philippe de Champaigne (1602–74). Private collection, Paris. © *Giraudon/Art Resource, New York.*

arranged whereby the Jansenist bishops signed the formulary with certain reservations of their own.

An uneasy peace ensued during which the Jansenists, led by Arnauld, fortified their position. Pope Innocent XI (d. 1689) himself seemed to lean in their direction by his condemnation of 65 propositions drawn from Jesuit moral authors; the Jansenists also had the satisfaction of seeing one of their sympathizers, De Noailles, consecrated archbishop of Paris. However, a new offensive was mounted against them at the turn of the century when the Jesuits attacked Quesnel, Arnauld's successor, whose book *Réflexions Morales* (1693) reaffirmed all the substantive tenets of Jansenism. The recently elected Clement XI (d. 1721) was also unfavorably disposed, and in his bull *Vineam Domini* (1705) he condemned their tactic of "respectful silence." The King drove the nuns out of Port Royal and leveled it to the ground. Finally, Clement launched his bull *Unigenitus,* which condemned 101 propositions drawn from Quesnel's book. The reaction revealed a deep division in the French Church; sixteen or so bishops, led by the cardinal archbishop of Paris, and a large number of the clergy refused to submit, claiming that a papal bull was infallible only if it obtained the assent of the universal Church, and they appealed over the head of the Pope to a future general council.

But the Jansenists were unable to maintain their position. Cardinal de Noailles submitted in 1728, the Sorbonne in 1730; by 1760 only half a dozen bishops showed any Jansenist leanings, and their support was mainly confined to the lower clergy and laity. They became a small, hunted, and persecuted sect, but with the exception of the Dutch Jansenists, who nominated for themselves a schismatic bishop of Utrecht, they never formally broke with the Catholic Church.

Gallicanism was another movement that greatly agitated the Church during the seventeenth and eighteenth centuries. Gallicans were opposed to Roman papal centralization and wanted to restrict the scope of papal interventions in the affairs of the national Churches. They also insisted on the dignity and independence of the bishops and severely limited papal authority over temporal rulers. On the theological level, they denied the personal and separate infallibility of the Pope, since they held that infallibility belonged only to the whole Church and therefore could be expressed either through general councils or through papal decisions if these were ratified by the assent of the universal episcopate.

Though Gallicanism received its name from the French Church (in

Latin, *ecclesia gallicana*) it was not a phenomenon restricted to the French Church. In part it reflects a general trend of European governments to subordinate the Church and make it a department of the state. Whether we take the Church of England, the Lutheran Churches in Germany and Scandinavia, or the Catholic Churches in the Habsburg or Bourbon dominions, the picture is basically the same: a tight union of Church and state, with the Church reduced to the junior partner.

The Catholic Church, with its independent head located outside the country, was in a better position to resist the trend. But even in Catholic countries the monarchs managed to obtain a large amount of control over their Churches. By concordats, for instance, the Bourbons and Habsburgs acquired the right to nominate bishops and to prohibit the publication of papal decrees.

In the latter part of the seventeenth century, Louis XIV nearly led the French Church into schism in his efforts to dominate the Church.

Louis was the greatest monarch of the time and carried France with him

Louis XIV of France (1638–1715), painted in 1701. Hyacinthe Rigaud (1659–1743). Louvre, Paris. © *Réunion des Musées Nationaux/Art Resource, New York.*

to the pinnacle of European power. After finally stripping his nobles of their power, he brought them to Versailles to ornament his grandiose palace. With the aid of ministers of genius such as Colbert and Louvois, he succeeded in greatly strengthening the national economy, establishing sugar refineries, iron works, glass factories, and textile industries to enrich his nation of twenty million people. The army organized by Le Tellier and Louvois reflected the strong centralization Louis imposed on France; no longer were its commanders to run things on their own—from top to bottom, its four hundred thousand men were subjected to elaborate discipline. In his foreign policy, Louis was intent on extending the frontiers, with the ultimate aim, it seems, of restoring the Holy Roman Empire, with himself wearing the imperial crown.

In his policies toward the Church, Louis was governed by the prevailing Gallicanism and constantly encroached on the spiritual power. He unilaterally extended the royal right of *regale,* a traditional prerogative that allowed the King to administer and appropriate the revenue of a diocese and make appointments on the death of a bishop and during the interim before the election of a new bishop. In flagrant contempt for Canon Law, Louis extended this right to cover the new territories conquered by his army.

The Pope at the time, Innocent XI (d. 1689), austere, scholarly, unworldly, beloved for his piety and generosity, would not be intimidated by the awesome power of the "Sun King." He dispatched a brief condemning the King's action and entreating him to forgo the right of *regale.* At first the King tried to evade the issue. But when the Pope insisted and even threatened Louis with spiritual sanctions, Louis finally resorted to a time-honored custom: He rallied the clergy to his side and hurled his defiance.

The Assembly of the Clergy, which he convoked, lasted from October 30, 1681, to May 9, 1682. Under the leadership of bishops like Bossuet, whose sermon "On Unity" urged the prelates to moderation, it formulated its Gallican standpoint in the notorious *Four Articles.* While acknowledging the primacy of the Popes as successors of Peter, the articles denied their authority over temporal affairs; reasserted the validity of the decrees of the Council of Constance, which affirmed the superiority of general councils over a Pope; made the authority of papal decrees conditional on their acceptance by the Church; and rejected the separate infallibility of the Pope.

The King ordered these articles to be taught in all universities and seminaries as official doctrine. Rome was outraged; in its eyes the Assembly had overstepped the bounds of its authority by treating of matters that properly belonged only to a general council. Moreover, the declaration itself was seen as opposed to the constant teaching of theologians and hence were at least suspect of heresy.

A veritable war broke out between France and the papacy, which lasted until the death of Innocent in 1689. But both sides refrained from pushing the matter to its logical conclusion: schism. The Pope refused to canonically install the King's episcopal nominees—which soon left many dioceses without bishops. The King threatened Italy with invasion and seized the papal province of Avignon, but as a recent convert to a devout practice of the Catholic faith he resisted the temptation to take the fatal course of Henry VIII.

The intransigent stand of Innocent proved wise in the long run. After his death a compromise was arranged: The King agreed not to require the teaching of the *Four Articles,* while the Pope yielded on the matter of the *regale.* The issue of papal infallibility was side-stepped, since it was not yet considered ready for definition. Gallicanism, therefore, as a theological position—covered by the authority of the incomparable Bossuet—continued to be taught in the universities and seminaries, and in its parliamentary form it dominated Church-state relations during the eighteenth century. But by his firm handling of the crisis, Innocent prepared the way for the papacy's eventual victory over Gallicanism two centuries later at the First Vatican Council.

Gallicanism was also sprouting in German soil, and in the eighteenth century it took a form named Febronianism, after its leading spirit, Nicholas von Hontheim (d. 1790), who wrote his tracts under the pseudonym of Febronius. Like Gallicanism, it espoused the superiority of a general council over a Pope, the right of appeal to a general council against a papal decision, the denial of the separate infallibility of the Pope, and affirmation of the divine right of bishops. Moreover, the Pope was allowed no direct jurisdiction over the affairs of the individual Churches. It was also ecumenically oriented in its program of reform, aiming at a restoration of the Church to the primitive purity of its original constitution in the hope of rendering possible a complete reunion of all the Christian Churches. A major source of its inspiration was extensive historical research into the history of the early Church.

Febronius's ideas found a ready acceptance among the German prince bishops who chafed at the controls exerted over them by the papal nuncio and Curia—controls that were doubly odious since they were much tighter in Germany than in other countries, where royal absolutism generally kept the

Curia at bay. Sixteen of the twenty-six German bishops refused to publish Rome's condemnation of Febronius; his own superior, the archbishop-elector of Trier, would not take action against him. Hontheim, himself, however, finally submitted and wrote a somewhat ambiguous retraction. But his ideas continued to ferment, and in 1786 the archbishops of Cologne, Trier, Mainz, and Salzburg met at Bad Ems and issued a kind of declaration of episcopal independence from Rome that closely adhered to Febronius's program. It failed to rally the other German bishops, however, who in the crunch preferred Rome's yoke to that of the archbishops. But Febronian episcopalianism was only definitively stamped out, like Gallicanism, at Vatican I.

All told, the eighteenth century was not a great era for the papacy. Challenged in its spiritual authority by Jansenists, Gallicans, and Febronians, it also suffered from the constant encroachments of the secular governments on its traditional rights and prerogatives.

The big rival Catholic powers—the Bourbons and Habsburgs, rulers of France, Spain, and Austria—exerted heavy influence on the papal elections, and by their power of veto were able to block any candidate regarded as unfriendly to their interests. This meant that the men elected were invariably compromise candidates. As a consequence, the eight Popes who ruled from 1700 to 1800 were, with the exception of Benedict XIV (1740–58), mediocre personalities—several of them very old when elected, one being nearly blind—and unable to reverse the constant decline in the Church's fortunes and influence.

Moreover, their spiritual authority was gravely compromised by their status as temporal rulers of the Papal States—still as in the Middle Ages a narrow strip of land, economically poor and with the reputation of being one of the most weakly administered and backward countries of Europe. Theoretically the Papal States were supposed to guarantee the spiritual independence of the Holy See, but actually they often forced it into the game of shifting alliances and power politics at the expense of its spiritual mission. The atmosphere of the Curia struck many observers as unreal; its official communiqués, couched in pretentiously grandiloquent terms, were in glaring contrast with its actual prestige. And as the century wore on, much of the intelligentsia of Europe came to regard the Roman Church as a venerable anachronism more and more identified with political and social structures doomed to collapse as the world moved toward a profound transformation.

This weakness of the papacy was clearly revealed in the suppression of the

Jesuits. The most successful of the orders founded during the Catholic Revival of the sixteenth century, the Jesuits consistently held their membership near the thirty thousand mark and maintained leadership in many fields of the Church's apostolate—theology, teaching, the missions. They even succeeded in stamping the whole Church with their characteristic form of spirituality, with its emphasis on the practical and its exuberance in external devotions. Of course, their very success soon gained them an abundant supply of enemies and critics: Jansenists, who accused them of dispensing cheap grace and encouraging laxity in their moral direction; Gallicans, who resented their zealous loyalty to the Pope; resentful politicians, who envied their influence as confessors of Kings and princes. Nevertheless, they seemed stronger than ever at the beginning of the eighteenth century. But then a swift decline began, which finally ended in their suppression by Pope Clement XIV in 1773.

Why? Some point to the Jesuits' reputed arrogance and to an exaggerated esprit de corps that alienated the sympathies of many would-be friends. But more important, it seems, was their failure to adapt intellectually to the demands of the age; they were the most respected and progressive educators in the seventeenth century, but they failed to keep up with the progress of the exact and experimental sciences. The Jesuits were also too conservative in theology and philosophy and so lost their pre-eminent position in these domains also.

In addition, a series of mishaps occurred in the eighteenth century that exposed them to the vengeance of their numerous enemies. First, there was the papal condemnation of their mission strategy in China, which embraced a policy of accommodating the Christian faith to Chinese Confucianism and ancestor worship. Their opponents, the Franciscan and Dominican missionaries, accused them of making dangerous concessions to paganism. Finally, Pope Clement XI condemned the Jesuit practice in his constitution *Ex Illo Die* (1715), reiterated by Benedict XIV in 1742.

Another severe blow to their prestige struck when they came into conflict with the Portuguese and Spanish governments over a communal system they had developed in Paraguay to protect the Indians from exploitation by colonial traders. The Jesuits were accused of fomenting revolution among the Indians and were chased out in 1750. The whole affair aroused the enmity of the two governments against the Jesuits.

The final blow fell with the financial collapse of the order in France, caused by an enterprising wizard, Father Lavalette, who ran a maritime business that practically monopolized commerce with the island of Martinique. When his company went bankrupt, the whole Jesuit order in France was made to bear the responsibility. All of its property in France was confiscated, and the order itself was completely suppressed in France in 1764. They were also driven out of Spain and Portugal at the same time.

It only remained for a Pope to be elected who would succumb to the mounting pressure from all sides for the complete suppression of the order. This happened in 1769 with the election of Clement XIV (Ganganelli), a man of rather weak character, whose promise to suppress the Jesuits undoubtedly figured as a prime factor in his election. The suppression was an ugly affair. The Pope showed less than candor in his letter of suppression, which made no mention of the political pressures involved. The Jesuit general was thrown into prison, where he died in misery. It meant the destruction of some six hundred religious houses, the closing of hundreds of schools, and the uprooting of over twenty thousand priests and brothers. It was indeed a fitting prelude to the terrible disasters about to afflict the whole Church.

During the eighteenth century the Church reached a nadir of its prestige and influence. The scholastic and sterile controversy over the nature of grace, the decline of the papacy's vigor, the suppression of the Jesuits, the failure to come to terms with the new insights of the philosophers and scientists—these are only some of the manifestations of a general spiritual and intellectual debility. There were also others we have not discussed, such as the languishing of missionary effort and the decadence of the religious orders. No doubt a major cause of this dismal state of affairs was the alliance of throne and altar that had come to mean in practice the subjection of the Church to the state. But extricating the Church from a system that had lasted since Constantine could hardly occur without a tremendous social and political upheaval.

Chapter 24

THE FRENCH REVOLUTION
SHATTERS THE CHURCH OF
THE OLD ORDER

In spite of the many signs of interior decay, the Catholic and Protestant Churches of Europe in 1789 were outwardly prosperous and powerful—if anything, too much an integral part of the social order. They were established as official religions, and their hierarchies held privileged positions and enjoyed all the prerogatives and trappings of the aristocracy. This union of Church and state was a system that had lasted more than a thousand years and seemed destined to go on for yet a long time. But the storm of revolution suddenly burst across France and then Europe as a whole, and struck the Churches everywhere with a hurricanelike force. The first to feel its full impact was the French Church, which was so gravely shattered by the blow that it could never permanently recover its traditional dominant position. Catholic Churches elsewhere in many cases soon met a similar fate. The Protestant Churches were not as severely affected at first, but the forces set in motion by the revolution—liberalism and democracy—eventually had a similar disrupting effect on all the Churches.

IN MANY WAYS the French Revolution was the climax of the Enlightenment. The French Revolution began as a nonviolent experiment in reforming the French Government: Twelve hundred selected deputies came to Versailles from every corner of France at the bidding of the King to solve a grave financial crisis in the spring of 1789. Once gathered there, the six hundred commoners or Third Estate decided that France needed a much more radical and comprehensive reform than any envisaged by the King. They wanted to replace the *ancien régime* by a society based on the political and economic ideas of the Enlightenment, the experience of the British with representative government, and the social and economic realities of late-eighteenth-century France. This meant doing away with all privileges due to birth, giving the middle class political power, and putting an end to arbitrary government. They also stood for complete economic freedom and abolition of all controls—allowing each the unrestricted enjoyment of his private property. Feeling themselves the vanguard of a European crusade, they hoped to build a society that would be more efficient, more humane, and more orderly than the old order was.

The first step they took was to declare that Louis XVI would no longer be allowed to rule as a monarch by divine right but would have to share his power with the elected representatives of the nation. At first, the King and the nobles resisted this startling proposal. But in their oath taken on the Tennis Court (June 20, 1789), the Third Estate manifested its unflinching determination, and when the King ordered them to desist, they defied him. Unwilling or unable at the moment to use force, Louis capitulated and allowed them to meet as the National Assembly.

The Revolution turned bloody when Louis brought in mercenary troops to re-establish his absolute power. The people of Paris stormed the Bastille and formed their own army, the National Guard, while a general uprising throughout the country put power in the hands of the revolutionaries. No longer master of events, the King was left with no option but submission. His only chance of retaining some measure of authority depended on how skillfully he would deal with the National Assembly. As it turned out, he gradually alienated public opinion by engaging in treacherous plots against the Revolution, and so brought on his own execution and the establishment of the Republic.

As an integral part of the old order, the Catholic Church was bound to be intimately affected by its overthrow. But few at the outset seemed to have any presentiment of the tremendous upheaval in store for an institution that in 1789 held a privileged position as the only form of public Christian worship allowed by the state; whose hundred thousand or so clergy—the First Estate—formed virtually a state within the state and controlled all education and public relief; whose parish priests were the sole registrars of births, marriages, and deaths; and whose officials had power of censorship over publications deemed harmful to faith and morals.

There were, it is true, signs of a widespread impatience with the organization of the Church, as indicated in the *cahiers*—petitions for reforms drawn up by the voters. The *cahiers* called for sale of Church lands, end of payments to Rome, and the reduction or dissolution of the monastic orders. Again, Voltairean skepticism had made some inroads, especially among the aristocrats and upper levels of the middle class. But the Church still had a strong hold on the majority of Frenchmen.

At first there was no conflict between the Revolution and the Church. The clergy, in fact, acted as saviors of the Revolution when they voted with the Third Estate against the nobility and the King in favor of constituting a National Assembly. And the clergy continued to co-operate by willingly surrendering their privileges; they even accepted the confiscation of the Church's extensive property (with its consequence the suppression of the religious orders)—a measure taken to deal with the country's bankruptcy.

On their part, the laymen of the National Assembly showed at first no animus toward the Church. They agreed to recognize the Catholic Church as the official form of worship, even though—against clerical wishes—they accorded civil rights to Protestants and Jews. But the leaders soon blundered into a quarrel with the Church—provoking a schism between the Church and the Revolution that retarded for over a century the reconciliation of the Church and liberalism.

The conflict with the Church began when the Assembly took up the reform of the Church—embodied in the Civil Constitution of the Clergy. As with all areas of French life, such a reform was long overdue, as the clergy themselves were ready to admit. Nor was there repugnance at the idea of the state undertaking such a reform—it seemed a logical corollary of the union of Church and state. Moreover, many of the reforms proposed were obvious and well thought out: The parasitic chapters attached to cathedrals were swept away; pastors were at last to be given a decent income; and new and logical parochial and diocesan boundaries were drawn up.

But the decrees went beyond the reform of abuses and aimed at a revolution of the Church's structure: They democratized the French Church, eliminating all control of the Pope over its internal affairs, providing for election of bishops and priests like other civil servants. Then they took the fatal step—

the capital error that was to split France and the Revolution right down the middle: They tried to force the clergy to accept this radical reform of the Church by imposing on all Church office-holders an oath of compliance that they could not refuse without forfeiting their office. It was formulated with deliberate ambiguity; it obliged them to "maintain . . . the Constitution decreed by the National Assembly and accepted by the King," so that those who refused could be accused of being disloyal to the Revolution.

A compromise might conceivably have been worked out. One thinks of how Napoleon and the Pope later on were able to reconcile differences over the reorganization of the French Church through long and patient negotiations. But the National Assembly showed little disposition toward compromise. They remembered how cavalierly Joseph II had reformed his Austrian Church, how Catherine II of Russia had reorganized the Polish dioceses. Perhaps they genuinely believed their reforms only embraced temporal matters. Perhaps they did not believe bishops and priests heroic enough to sacrifice their revenues and their livelihood over a matter of principle or that priests would desert the Revolution that the priests themselves had helped create.

In any event, there were two ways that approval of the Civil Constitution of the Clergy might have been secured: either through a national council of the bishops or by appeal to the Pope. The first method was ruled out by the National Assembly for fear that such a council might become a forum for counterrevolutionary propaganda. So the clergy were left with only one alternative: to appeal to the Pope to authorize them to accept. Pius VI, an absolute monarch himself and already very cold to the French Revolution, took eight months to come to a decision: On March 10, 1791, he issued a condemnation and forbade the clergy to take the oath.

But by this time the French clergy had already been forced to declare themselves. The previous January they were presented with the oath and made to decide. All but seven of the bishops and about half of the clergy rejected the oath. While many of the bishops as members of the nobility may have been motivated by plain hatred of the Revolution, this would not account for the lower clergy, many of whom were profoundly committed to the Revolution and its promise of social regeneration. Moreover, by refusing they exposed themselves to privation, exile, and even death. But their primary allegiance was to the Church, whose spiritual sovereignty they felt was at stake in the matter. It seemed clear to them that the representatives of the nation had violated this sovereignty by legislating in matters ecclesiastical on their own authority and in high-handed fashion demanding adherence to their decrees before the Church itself had spoken.

On the other hand, those who took the oath could invoke honorable arguments for their stand. They believed that in taking the oath to the "Constitution" they were merely giving a broad general assent to the new order in France, not necessarily approving of its specific religious stipulations. After all, they could reassure themselves, the King had himself accepted it, and they could assume that the Pope—whose delay in the meantime was most perplexing—would likewise yield. They could also appeal to Gallican precedents. Unfortunately, their bishops were of little help in the quandary, with their tradition of aloofness from the lower clergy and their obvious identity of interest with the old regime.

In this state of confusion and ambiguity, it was only natural for the priests in any one area to stick together for mutual support. This would explain the pattern we find. In some parts, 80 per cent or more of the clergy refused the oath, while in others a similar percentage accepted it. The Civil Constitution was almost totally accepted in the center, the Ile de France, and the southeast, and almost totally repudiated in Flanders, Artois, Alsace, and Brittany.

Henceforth two Catholic communities faced each other in almost every town and village of France: the Constitutional Church, led by the bishop and clergy who took the oath and who were installed in their posts after election by the people; and the nonconstitutional or nonjuring Church, whose clergy remained loyal to Rome. Farce and tragedy often intermingled when a constitutional priest came to take possession of a parish where sentiment ran high in favor of the incumbent nonjuring priest. In one town someone put a cat in the tabernacle, which jumped out and clawed the face of the new priest who unsuspectingly opened it during Mass. One poor constitutional priest made the mistake of accepting a dinner invitation from a dissident parishioner, who split his skull with a hatchet as he crossed the threshold.

At first, the nonconstitutional priests were only subject to ouster from their rectories and churches. However, the mere fact of refusing the oath to the Civil Constitution was enough to render them suspect of disloyalty to the Revolution itself in the eyes of many. They were lumped with the aristocrats who were openly or secretly scheming to overthrow the Revolution.

The logic of events soon fortified these suspicions and made the position of the nonconstitutional clergy very precarious. Nor were they helped by the papal legate to Germany, who preached counterrevolutionary sermons to

French aristocrat refugees. The flight of the King also affected their situation adversely, since he openly displayed his sympathy with the nonjuring clergy, and his treason seemed to implicate them. Finally, when Austrian and Prussian troops invaded France to put down the Revolution, a persecution began of all those looked on as potential traitors. A savage decree was passed on May 26, 1792: Every nonjuring priest who was denounced by twenty "active" citizens was to be deported. Some thirty thousand to forty thousand priests were thereupon driven out of their native towns and hounded into hiding or exile. Later (on March 18, 1793) the death penalty was imposed on those deportees who dared to return. But even at the height of the Reign of Terror a good number of nonjurors heroically remained and exercised their ministry in cellars and garrets, offering Mass for a handful of faithful or giving absolution surreptitiously to upcoming victims of the guillotine.

The first slaughter of priests occurred as the Duke of Brunswick approached Paris with his hussars. With the city in the grip of hysteria and panic, a mob rushed to the prisons, whose inmates were considered the chief source of conspiracies against the Revolution. It so happened that the first victims taken and lynched were 20 priests awaiting deportation, and in the bloodbath that followed from the second to the fifth of September, 3 bishops and 220 priests lost their lives.

But for the loyal constitutional clergy, things went well at first. They intoned the traditional "Te Deum" to celebrate the victories of the revolutionary armies and proclaimed new laws from their parish pulpits. But these happy relations did not last long. After the overthrow of the monarchy, friction developed between the constitutional Church and the state, and relations became increasingly abrasive. Political factors may have had something to do with this: The clergy as a rule were still royalist and opposed the execution of the King; many of them were linked with the Federalist movement, which flared into open rebellion in Bordeaux in May of 1793.

But actually more fundamental reasons were responsible: The Revolution began to take on the character of a religion in itself. Some of its patriotic ceremonies featured sacred oaths and sacred trees, and some of the localities substituted patriotic names for the religious names of its streets. Compiègne replaced the names of the saints with revolutionary heroes, as did many others. Infants were given "un-Christian" baptismal names. Church bells and chalices were seized and melted. The resulting tension between the values of the Revolution and those of Christianity was exacerbated by the anticlericals, who attacked the clergy for being different: Why shouldn't they get married like everyone else and increase the number of patriots?

It was only one step from this to the effort to uproot Christianity from France altogether. The first move in the dechristianization was the adoption of the Republican calendar on October 7, 1793. It was designed to remove all vestiges of Christianity: The Gregorian calendar was discarded; the Christian Sunday and the seven-day week were suppressed, and a ten-day week was put in its place; all religious holidays were canceled, and all reference to the birth of Christ was dropped by establishing a new era dating from the start of the French Republic, September 22, 1792. The new calendar was supposed to epitomize the cult of "reason" and reverence for an idealized "nature."

The second move to dechristianize France began in the provinces under the aegis of the agents of the National Convention—men sent out with virtually unlimited powers to deal with the emergency situation created by the invasion of France and the counterrevolution within the country itself. One of these, a fanatical, bloodthirsty ex-priest named Fouché, opened up a dechristianizing campaign in the Church of Saint-Cyr at Nevers on September 22, 1793, by unveiling a bust of Brutus, a saint to revolutionaries, and denouncing "religious sophistry" from the pulpit. Thenceforth, wherever he traveled he turned the churches into "Temples of Reason" and presided over ceremonies that caricatured the Catholic liturgy; he pressured the clergy to resign and to marry, he ransacked the churches and ordered the burial of all citizens in a common cemetery whose gates he marked with a sign: "Death is an eternal sleep." A host of imitators soon undertook the same kind of tactics throughout France.

Paris had to show that it was not to be outdone by the provinces. Its churches were all closed by order of the Commune. Its constitutional bishop, Gobel—poor man—was startled out of his sleep and ordered to resign by a band of *sansculottes* (the proletariat have-nots). He obliged them and went back to bed. The new cult of Reason was celebrated with great éclat in Notre Dame, where an actress was enthroned on the high altar as Reason's goddess.

One of the most formidable voices in the anti-Christian chorus was Hébert, hero of the Parisian underdogs; his journal, *Père Duchesne,* specialized in scathing denunciations of rich and corrupt politicians. But he reserved his juiciest four-letter words for the priests—power-mad hypocrites, he called them, who betrayed Jesus, *"le bon sans-culotte"*—the best Jacobin who ever lived.

Regional studies, while not complete, show that by the spring of 1794 the dechristianizers had achieved a wide measure of success. The cathedrals and parish churches of most towns and villages were turned into "Temples of Reason." But in rural France, where the majority clung to the old religion, the operation could only be carried out by armed force.

Many priests and even bishops abandoned their ministry—some of them taking wives as a proof of their break with orthodox Catholicism. At Beauvais about fifteen priests, including the bishop, married, and by 1803, a total of 50 of the 480 priests in the Department of the Oise had done so. All told, about 4,000 priests married during the Revolution. The motivations, as one would suspect, were mixed. Many were only temporizing until better times and simply married their housekeepers pro forma. Others used dechristianization as an excuse for doing something they had always wanted to do. Some justified themselves by pointing out that celibacy was merely an ecclesiastical law.

A number of renegades willingly defrocked themselves and even took a lead in the dechristianization, and like Fouché and Lebon, figured prominently in the chronicle of sacrilege. Some of them embraced the social egalitarian ideas of the extreme left; others succumbed to the fashionable sexual romanticism spawned by writers like Rousseau. But most of those who abdicated did so under pressure and in desperate and feverish circumstances.

The total number of priests who put aside the cloth would, it seems, number around 20,000—most of them constitutionals who were an easier target for the dechristianizers than the nonjurors, most of whom had already been forced to emigrate or go into hiding. But though acting under compulsion, their "apostasy" had the effect of wrecking and discrediting the constitutional Church.

In attempts to destroy Catholicism, the dechristianizers did not intend to leave a religious vacuum, for they still shared the *ancien régime*'s principle that no state could survive without a public religion. The new French religion, they decided, would be philanthropic Deism. In devising its liturgy, they followed at first the example of Paris, whose festival of Reason featured, as we have seen, the enthronement of a young girl as goddess of Reason. So innumerable young girls decked out as Reason or Liberty or Nature led processions through innumerable towns to altars erected to the new religion.

However, Robespierre found the worship of reason too close to atheism for comfort and preferred something a little closer to Christianity: his cult of

Maximilien de Robespierre
(1758–94). Anonymous,
eighteenth century. Musée de
la Ville de Paris, Musée
Carnavalet, Paris.
© *Giraudon/Art Resource,
New York.*

the Supreme Being. And he succeeded in carrying a motion in the Convention, on May 7, 1793, which dedicated France to this cult. He envisaged it as
a religion that would be all-embracing and would gather Catholics and
Protestants around the same altar. It would have only one dogma (the immortality of the soul) and only one precept (do your duty as a man).

His new liturgy was inaugurated on a beautiful day in June 1794, with
himself as high priest: Dressed in a sky-blue coat, his hair carefully powdered,
he led a procession from the Tuileries bearing a bouquet of berries, grain, and
flowers. The people sang republican hymns, and after a sermon, Robespierre
ignited an artfully made cardboard figure labeled Atheism; it crumpled, and
then out of its ashes stepped another figure representing Wisdom.

Robespierre himself crumpled shortly afterward, and with him his cult of
the Supreme Being. For a time a number of revolutionary and Deistic cults
vied with each other for public favor, one of the most successful called
Theophilanthropy and influenced by the ideas of Rousseau. But none of them
lasted. In spite of curious imitations of Catholic practice, such as the altar to
Marat, the republican sign of the cross, or feasts in honor of revolutionary
events, they were all too vague and abstract to catch the imagination of a

largely illiterate populace. A momentary delight might be taken in a "Republican Lord's Prayer" with its petition: "Give us this day our daily bread, in spite of the vain attempts of Pitt, the Cobourgs, and all the tyrants of the Coalition to starve us out," but the novelty soon wore off and the homilies of the local politicians proved a stifling bore. The new religions were never abolished; they just faded away.

Dechristianization itself had spent its force by 1794, and with the decree of February 21, 1795, which guaranteed the free exercise of any religion, there was a rush to open the Churches again.

At the very moment that the Catholic Church in France seemed on the point of revival, the Revolution struck at the person of the Pope himself. This was brought on by Napoleon's startling Italian campaign of 1796, when he occupied Milan and set up a number of republics in northern Italy on the French model. At first he spared Rome. In the Treaty of Tolentino he recognized the sovereignty of the Pope over the Papal States and only demanded some moderate spoils of victory. But when on December 28, 1797, a corporal of the pontifical guard assassinated a French general, French troops were sent into Rome, and Pius VI was taken prisoner. General Berthier was then ordered by the Directory to remove the Pope to France—away from the Austrians, who might try to rescue him. The rigors of the journey were too much for the eighty-one-year-old Pontiff, and he expired at Valence.

The conclave for the election of the next Pope opened on November 30, 1799, at Venice, under the protection of the Emperor of Austria because of the great political instability at Rome. A compromise candidate, the Benedictine bishop of Imola, Chiaramonti, was chosen after a long and wearisome conclave. It proved to be a happy choice, for the new Pope, Pius VII, proved to have just the right combination of qualities to meet the crisis in the Church.

While the conclave was in progress, Napoleon had again moved his troops into Italy, and a few months later, on June 14, 1800, he decisively defeated the Austrians at Marengo and made himself master of Italy.

The future of the Church in a worldly sense now seemed to hinge on the intentions of this strange genius who had vaulted into power over France—a country whose continuing revolutionary élan made her the most powerful state in Europe. He liked to think of himself as the heir of all that was "reasonable, legitimate, and European in the revolutionary movement," in

Pope Pius VII (1742–1823) in 1800. Jacques-Louis David (1748–1825). Châteaux de Versailles et de Trianon, Versailles.   © *Réunion des Musées Nationaux/Art Resource, New York.*

Goethe's phrase—and in fact, Napoleon's Code did embody the essential elements of the Revolutionary program by its affirmation of the equality of all citizens before the law, the right of the individual to choose his profession, the supremacy of the lay state, and a regime of tolerance for all religious beliefs. On the other hand, by his willingness to curtail individual liberty in the interests of government and by his own autocratic policies, he foreshadowed the reactionary attitude that was to dominate European courts after 1815.

In regard to the Church, Napoleon showed his wonted genius for grasping the complexities of an intricate situation. Religious peace being his goal, he realized that it could not be obtained without recognizing the great power that the Catholic Church still held over the souls of Frenchmen. The bankruptcy of dechristianization was obvious to him, if not to wishful-thinking liberals. But how to heal the now deeply rooted and bitter division between constitutional and nonjuring clergy? This he again realized could only be accomplished by winning over the nonjurors, who were much more numerous and influential than the constitutionals, to accept a settlement along the lines of the earlier Civil Constitution—a maneuver he knew would be impossible without the aid of the Pope. So he told Cardinal Martiniana: "Go to Rome and tell the Holy Father that the First Consul wishes to make him a gift of thirty million Frenchmen."[1]

The agreement between Napoleon and the Pope was contained in the Concordat of 1801—the prototype of subsequent nineteenth-century concordats. Its signing was celebrated with fitting pomp at Notre Dame Cathedral on Easter 1802. The First Consul was met at the great west door—like any Bourbon King—by the archbishop, and at the elevation the troops presented for the thirty-two-year-old Corsican general: The Church was recognized "as the religion of the great majority of Frenchmen," the agonizing schism between the constitutional and nonjuring clergy was ended, and Napoleon had solved one of the most vexing problems he inherited from the Revolution.

The chief points of the Concordat were five: All bishops, both constitutional and nonjuring, had to hand in their resignation to the Pope; the First Consul had the right to name the bishops, and the Pope had the right to institute them canonically; the Church would not seek to recover its alienated property; the clergy would derive their income from salaries paid by the state; and the practice of the Catholic religion would be subject to whatever police regulations were required for the public order.

This last article was in Napoleon's mind the heart of the Concordat and the means by which he intended to minimize papal control over the French Church and to make it actually as Gallican as in the old regime. He unilaterally attached seventy-seven organic articles to it, which severely limited communications between Rome and the French bishops. He also made the teaching of the Gallican articles of 1682 obligatory in all seminaries.

Subsequent relations of Napoleon with the Pope were stormy. He induced Pius to attend his coronation as Emperor—to dramatize for all Europe the fact that the papacy, which condemned the Revolution, bestowed its blessing on its firstborn successor, the Empire. But he soon learned that the Pope would not be a puppet when Pius refused to compromise the neutrality of the Papal States by joining in a blockade against England, as Napoleon demanded. When the Emperor seized the Papal States, Pius excommunicated him. Napoleon had him arrested (1808) and carried off to France—his captors not even allowing him the time to change his clothes. For nearly six years the Supreme Pontiff had to endure a humiliating captivity. Often he was de-

---

[1] J. McManners, *The French Revolution and the Church* (London: S.P.C.K., 1969), p. 143.

The consecration of Emperor Napoleon I and the coronation of Empress Josephine in the cathedral of Notre Dame, December 2, 1804. Jacques Louis-David (1748–1825). Louvre, Paris.   © *Erich Lessing/Art Resource, New York.*

prived for long periods of time of counselors and even cut off from all communication with the outside. But he passed his days serenely—like a monk—reading and praying and remaining steadfast in his determination not to yield in matters of principle. He also made good use of his only weapon by refusing to institute any new bishops canonically. By 1814 there were many vacant French dioceses. After Napoleon's defeats in Russia, with his enemies encircling him, he finally made a virtue of necessity and ordered the Pope restored to Rome. On May 24, 1814, the Holy Father once more entered his city, surrounded by children carrying palms and a wildly applauding crowd.

The Congress of Vienna (1814–15) brought a general peace to Europe after nearly thirty years of war—a peace that lasted a hundred years. It disavowed the Revolution, restored the old order, put the Bourbons back on the throne of France, and perched Napoleon on a rock two thousand watery miles away. It also restored the Pope as the absolute monarch of the Papal States. But it could not undo the work of the Revolution—the magnitude of social and political transformation was too extensive. France and the rest of Europe could never return permanently to a hierarchical society—held together by an alliance of throne and altar, where status was determined by birth and where monarchs ruled by divine right.

The bitterness, hatred, and enmity aroused by the Revolution would poison the life of France for a long time and create such a fundamental cleavage in French politics that no regime until 1870 was able to maintain itself for more than two decades. Moreover, the schism between a considerable body of Frenchmen and the Church was final; dechristianization as a program failed, but anticlericalism remained as its permanent vestige. The Church lost in large measure its control over the daily life of the people. The process of secularization introduced by the laws of 1794 opened a new chapter, and the secular spirit continued to spread. Civil divorce, civil marriage, and the secular school system were its most visible expressions.

Elsewhere the Catholic Church was also profoundly transformed by the Revolution, and nowhere more dramatically than in Germany. Here the Catholic prince bishops lost their feudal princedoms. And when the reorganization of the Church was carried out at the demise of Napoleon, a large proportion of Catholics were put under Protestant rulers. Church property was taken over and monasteries dismantled. The Church was reduced to an agency of the state; its schools and clergy were supported by the state.

But though the Church suffered grave damage, the effect of the Revolution on the papacy was beneficial—in fact, it helped to create the more powerful papacy of the nineteenth century. The fact that Napoleon and the Pope alone settled the fate of the French Church foreshadowed things to come. And Pius VII greatly enhanced the papal image by his heroic stand against the tyrant. But more fundamental reasons were ultimately responsible. In shattering the ancient monarchies, the Revolution liberated the Church from the servitude to Gallican monarchs and the so-called enlightened despots who placed their creatures on the throne of Peter, co-opted the Catholic missionaries for their colonial aims, and installed puppet bishops in their kingdoms. With the end of the old order the Popes could now make Rome once more the vital center of Catholicism and guide the Church back to its true spiritual mission. Gallicanism was not yet completely dead—many bishops still embodied its spirit—but the clergy would become more and more ultramontane, looking to Rome for leadership, while the overseas missions were to revive under Roman command.

Chapter 25

PIUS IX SAYS NO TO THE
LIBERAL CATHOLICS

The liberal Catholics were a group of brilliant thinkers and writers who contributed much to the remarkable Catholic revival of the early nineteenth century. Unlike many of their confreres, they were optimistic about the direction of the post-revolutionary world. They wanted the Church to abandon its state of siege mentality and get down to the task of finding a more positive relationship with the liberal secular culture. Above all, they wanted the Church to get behind the liberals in their efforts to create parliamentary regimes based on constitutionally guaranteed freedoms, including freedom of religion. Their first setback occurred when their ideas were condemned by Pope Gregory XVI and their leader, Lamennais, deserted them. The advent of his successor, the reputedly liberal Pius IX, revitalized the liberal Catholic movement. But Pius lacked any sympathy with liberalism and proved unable to find a modus vivendi with their doctrines. All hopes of finding one were dashed when he got locked in combat with the Italian liberals who wanted to liberate his own Papal States. Unable to withstand their superior military strength, he turned his spiritual weapons on them and condemned the whole ideology of liberalism in his *Syllabus of Errors* (1864). It effectively squelched the liberal Catholics and hardened the Church in its long-standing state of siege mentality in regard to modern liberal secular culture.

THE ERA THAT began with the downfall of Napoleon witnessed a full-scale revival of the Catholic Church, a spiritual and intellectual renaissance that made it once more a vital institution and a powerful force in public affairs. It was an amazing reversal. The revolutionary period saw the Church stripped of its privileges, its Pope imprisoned, its property confiscated, its monasteries emptied, its priests and nuns slaughtered and driven into exile, its very existence called into question. And even though it was propped up again by Napoleon, it was treated by the Corsican adventurer as his handmaid: He humiliated the papacy, considered the bishops his creatures, even rewrote the Church's catechism and dictated the discipline it was to follow.

But after Waterloo the Church returned to health and vigor. The heroic refusal of Pius VII to bend the knee to Napoleon won the admiration of Europe, and the papacy's renewed moral authority helped Consalvi to win back the Papal States at the Congress of Vienna. An astonishing sign of the Church's vitality was the re-establishment of the Jesuit Order in 1814. It soon numbered recruits in the thousands and extended its organization into most of the Catholic countries of Europe. Many new religious orders sprang up, such as the Marianists and the Society of the Sacred Heart; empty seminaries started to fill up, and the churches were crowded. The Society of the Foreign Missions was re-established in 1815, and together with the Jesuits it helped to rekindle missionary zeal. This spiritual awakening brought many Catholics back to lives of prayer and sacrifice, and the Christian virtues were practiced to a heroic degree by souls like John Vianney, the Curé of Ars, who revitalized the French clergy by his example and drew huge numbers of penitents to his confessional. Likewise St. Clement Maria Hofbauer, the Redemptorist, inspired a revival of Church life in southern Germany.

There was also an intellectual side to the Catholic revival. Many European thinkers turned away from the skepticism and rationalism of the eighteenth-century Enlightenment: They regarded its view of human nature as superficial, and they could no longer accept its mechanistic view of the universe and its idea of the mind as something like a calculating machine. After the savage wars and irrational fury of the French Revolution, which culminated in the futile bloodbaths of Napoleon, they were skeptical about the dogma of progress and the simple goodness of human nature. They found Diderot's and Voltaire's system of values simplistic and searched for a view of life that made greater allowance for such needs as faith, reverence, mystery, and respect for tradition. Some of them had already found it in the Vicomte de Chateaubriand's *The Genius of Christianity* (1802)—a hymn to the aesthetic glories of the Catholic Church—and many followed him back to the

Church. A good number of renowned intellectuals around Europe took the same path and converted to romanticism, political reaction, and the Catholic faith. The outstanding thinker of this group was Friedrich von Schlegel, who saw "tradition as the expression of a slow evolution ripened in the womb of time, a work not of arbitrarily deciding reason, but of mysteriously working life."[1] He idealized the Holy Roman Empire and dreamed of a European confederation under the Pope. Of equal importance was Joseph von Görres, who put his exceptional journalistic talents to the service of the papacy and the German Catholic Church.

It was during this period of its extraordinary revival that the Catholic Church was first confronted squarely with the momentous question of how it was going to relate to liberalism—the new political movement that espoused the ideals of the Enlightenment and the French Revolution. It was a question that would agitate Christians and especially Catholics for nearly a century and divide the Church into two sharply opposed blocs.

Liberalism drew its supporters largely from the rising middle and professional classes. They wanted a parliamentary system of government based on a written constitution that would guarantee personal rights, including freedom of religion. Rationalists and secularists in regard to religion, they opposed the Church's control over such matters as marriage and education—an approach not calculated to win them many friends among churchmen.

The period after Waterloo (1815–30) was a time of trial for the liberals. The monarchs restored by the Congress of Vienna dusted off their thrones and sat tight. They surrounded themselves with conservative statesmen like Metternich, the Austrian minister, who lent his name to the era, a man whose main concern was to keep the ghost of the French Revolution from rising again. He saw Jacobins and liberals under every bed and radical students in every disturbance. To squelch revolutionary ideas he used a secret police, censorship of books, and watchdogs at the universities.

With men like Metternich firmly in control everywhere, the liberal cause seemed hopeless. The autocratic Habsburgs controlled the destinies of Middle Europe from the Baltic to Sicily. The Prussian King, it is true, toyed, at first, with the idea of granting a constitution to his subjects, but when Karl Sand, a young theological student, assassinated an agent of the Russian Czar,

---

[1] Quoted in F. Artz, *Reaction and Revolution* (New York: Harper & Row, 1963), p. 59.

he and the other German rulers were persuaded by Metternich to issue the Carlsbad Decrees, which greatly tightened the control of the secret police over the universities. Liberals everywhere were forced into hiding.

The conservative backlash struck very hard in Spain, where Ferdinand VII arrested all prominent liberals, re-established the Inquisition, and ordered the restitution of all ecclesiastical and feudal property confiscated under Napoleon. In France, the restored Bourbon King Louis XVIII showed surprising talent at first in steering a course between the right and the left; but the profound cleavage between the two finally made moderation impossible, and he and his successor, Charles X, gradually veered to the right. Even in England reaction held sway. Parliament in 1819 passed the Six Acts—the most repressive laws enacted in that country for generations. The thought behind them was expressed by the Duke of Wellington: "Our example will render some good in France as well as in Germany, and we must hope that the whole world will escape the universal revolution which seems to menace us all."[2]

Nurturing no love for the liberals, the Christian Churches allied themselves solidly with the monarchs and the nobles in their efforts to restore the old order. The word "revolution" held no charms for the clergy. In England the Methodists did yeoman service in drawing the lower classes away from revolutionary ideas. The Catholic clergy, who for the most part had good reason to hate the Revolution, preached the gospel of obedience to the established order in season and out, although in a few countries—Ireland, Poland, and Belgium—the clergy played an important role in stirring up discontent. In France, the clergy showed special zeal in the cause of reaction. In concluding religious missions they would sometimes burn the works of Voltaire and administer an oath to all present to maintain religion and legitimate government. In the Papal States, the reactionaries took over after the death of the moderate Pius VII in 1823 and the retirement of his Secretary of State, Consalvi. The Curia abolished all the innovations introduced by the French and Napoleon—from law courts to vaccination. Priests were once more put into all the important offices in the Papal States, and the Jews were returned to their ghettos.

The Church gained much from its alliance with the conservatives. Regarded by the monarchs and nobles as the bulwark of the social order, it was

[2] Ibid., p. 126.

restored in many countries to its position of privilege and supported by grants from the government. In France, the restored Bourbon regime once more put education largely under the control of the clergy—at least on the primary and secondary levels. Encouraged by the Comte d'Artois (after 1824 Charles X), the clergy had high hopes of recovering its lands, of abolishing the Napoleonic University, with its state monopoly of education; and of removing the obligation of civil marriage, as required by the Code Napoleon.

However, a movement began to woo the Catholic clergy away from their alliance with the conservatives. Its beginning is associated with a French priest of Breton origin, Felicité de Lamennais (d. 1854), a frail, commonplace-looking genius whose temperament inclined him to a prophetic, visionary role; his writings contain predictions that show an astonishingly accurate insight into the future shape of European and Catholic history. After a youthful enthrallment with the free thought of the Enlightenment, Lamennais was won over to the service of the Church and eventual ordination by his brother, a pious priest, Felicité de Lamennais's enormously successful writings helped to spur the Catholic revival. Conscious of the profound social and psychological transformation wrought by the French Revolution, he developed an extremely radical view of the new role of the Church in a postrevolutionary society and so became the founder of liberal Catholicism.

The experience of the Church during the Bourbon restoration as well as the example of other countries like Ireland convinced him that the Church must be completely separated from the state. It must sunder the golden chains that fettered it to the monarchy; only in this way could it obtain the freedom necessary for its inner renewal and so become more faithful to the Gospel and more relevant to the society of its day. Moreover, he felt that the reactionary monarchy was doomed, and he wanted the Church to have no share in its ruin. Instead, he argued, the Church should seek its strength in a strong papacy—an idea that made him also one of the founders of nineteenth-century ultramontanism.

Once you accept the liberal idea of separation of Church and state, Lamennais argued, then you must necessarily accept the rest of the liberal program: freedom of education—because without it true religious freedom and freedom of thought could not be safe-guarded; freedom of the press—since a Christian must believe in the power of truth rather than trusting in censorship, which never succeeded anyway in stamping out error. Finally, Lamennais moved a half century ahead of his times—even beyond most liberals—by espousing complete democracy, demanding universal suffrage as the only way of achieving these freedoms. This was in accord with his doctrine of the universal consensus of mankind as the basis of religious certainty. Casting off its age-old reliance on the monarchies, it must now trust in the people.

By 1831 Lamennais had built up a following in France among the younger clergy and educated laymen. Some of the most talented Catholics of the day gathered around him, including Count Montalembert and Father Lacordaire. With their help he began a daily newspaper, *L'Avenir* (The Future), with the slogan "God and Freedom." Its aim was to sow the seeds of liberal Catholicism. "Let us not tremble before liberalism," he told his readers, "let us catholicize it."[3]

But the bishops preferred to tremble. The archbishop of Paris fulminated against him for trying to subvert the order Jesus Christ established on earth. Separation of Church and state, he argued, would mean abject poverty for the Church. Lamennais agreed—but welcomed that prospect, for he saw the combination of freedom and poverty as essential. Only by suffering physical wretchedness and poverty freely could the priest really feel solidarity with the whole of humanity and especially the poor and the weak, those tortured like Christ on the cross.

Lamennais could not convert the bishops to his dream. They felt that his ideas of democracy and separation would mean the ruination of the Church. They banned *L'Avenir* from the doors of the churches. Its circulation figures—never very high—began to slide, and its finances slipped into the red. Its readership was by its nature limited, since liberal Catholicism was an entirely new idea, and even secular liberals were not sympathetic to its democratic spirit. A sensational idea then occurred to Lamennais: Why not appeal to the Holy Father? "But what if we are condemned?" Montalembert exclaimed. "It is impossible, Charles," Lamennais answered. "We cannot be condemned."[4]

It was a fatal mistake. As the foremost ultramontane champion in France of Rome's authority, Lamennais may have felt that gratitude would move the Pope to some gesture of support. But he should have known better than to

[3] Quoted in A. Vidler, *Prophecy and Papacy* (New York: Charles Scribner's Sons, 1954), p. 194.
[4] Ibid.

expect the Pope to jump on the liberal bandwagon at this juncture of affairs. Gregory XVI (d. 1846) was a former Camaldolese monk; as ruler of the Papal States he was utterly cold to the spirit of liberalism and revolution, and, in fact, he was engaged at the very time—with help of Metternich's troops— in trying to put down the revolutionary Carbonari, who were terrorizing the countryside and assassinating papal officials.

Lamennais, Lacordaire, and Montalembert—"the pilgrims of God and of liberty," in their words—reached Rome on December 30, 1831. To their dismay, one of the first sights that greeted them was the papal police conducting a group of poor wretches chained together crying piteously for alms. Lamennais, Lacordaire, and Montalembert drew up a long memorandum, which they submitted to the Pope through the good offices of Cardinal Pacca, the dean of the Sacred College. It surveyed the relations of Church and state during the restoration of the Bourbon monarchy and argued that after the revolution of July 1830, which overthrew the Bourbons again, complete separation was the only feasible solution. It also told the story of their journal and the opposition it encountered and concluded by urging the Pope to make a pronouncement.

Then an agonizing wait began. As the weeks wore on, Lamennais became depressed by the spiritual and political atmosphere and began to sense the futility of his mission. In one letter he spoke bitterly of Rome as a great tomb containing nothing but worms and bones. The Pope, he said, was pious but profoundly ignorant of the state of society, a hapless captive of corrupt rulers.

The Pope's reply did not come until August 30, 1832, after the disappointed pilgrims had already left Rome. His encyclical *Mirari Vos* was a scathing denunciation of the doctrines of liberal Catholicism, although a personal letter from Pacca to Lamennais tried to soften the blow. The encyclical rejected the separation of Church and state, denounced liberty of conscience as sheer madness, and referred to liberty of the press as abominable and detestable. The Pope demanded unqualified submission to the encyclical, and Lamennais spent more than a year in correspondence with the Holy See trying to salvage both his conscience and his loyalty to the Church. At first he submitted by resorting to a distinction between the Pope's authority in spiritual matters as opposed to temporal matters. But the Pope still demanded an unqualified submission. Then news came of how Gregory had denounced the Polish rebellion and lent his moral support to the schismatic Russian Czar, who brutally suppressed the uprising. It was too much for the abbé. He decided the issue was clear: The hierarchy had "divorced [itself] from Christ, the Savior of the human race, in order to fornicate with all his torturers."[5]

In view of the Church's sorry experience with the liberals of the French Revolution, in view of the tumults in the Papal States aroused by liberals of the same ilk, and above all in view of the close association of liberalism with the skeptical philosophy of the Enlightenment, it does seem that Lamennais was naïve in trying to push the Church to declare officially that liberalism was a system superior to the one under which it had lived and prospered for a millennium. It would obviously take more time and experience for the Church to make the distinction between the philosophy of liberalism and the political and social techniques it made use of.

And it is well to note that while political pressure no doubt weighed on the Pope's decision, the standpoint of his encyclical was primarily doctrinal and theological. Rome saw in liberalism two main errors: a rejection of all supernatural revelation, and religious indifferentism. The liberal doctrine of popular sovereignty and the demand for freedom of the press and freedom of worship were vitiated in the eyes of the Pope since they were derived from such obviously false assumptions.

When all this is said, it still seems unfortunate that Gregory embraced the other extreme and virtually canonized the existing social order as having permanent and even divine validity—an attempt to bind the Church and Europe to forms of government and society that had seen their day. The open schism between liberalism and the Church that began with Pius VI's condemnation of the French Revolution was hardened by this action of the Pope. Nevertheless, while the cause of liberal Catholicism suffered a grave setback in the Lamennais affair, it won a victory at the same time in Belgium, where liberals and Catholics shared a common hatred of the Dutch rule that had been imposed on them by the Congress of Vienna. They ousted the Dutch King in the revolution of 1830 and—liberals and Catholics together—drew up the very liberal Belgian constitution (1831), which was based on the very liberties condemned by the Pope in *Mirari Vos*. In the meantime, the secular liberals achieved remarkable success elsewhere as the forces of revolution made headway against the spirit of Metternich. Men like Bolívar and O'Higgins carried the revolution to triumph in South America; by the year of Bolívar's death in

[5] L. Le Guillou, *Les Discussions critiques. Journal de la crise mennaisienne* (Paris: A. Colin, 1967), fragment 3. Cited by M. J. Le Guillou in *Concilium* 7, no. 3 (September 1967), p. 59.

1830, many of the Latin American countries had adopted liberal republican constitutions. Revolutions were put down in some of the Italian states and in Poland, but the Greeks liberated themselves from the Ottoman Empire. In 1830 the liberals in France installed a liberal monarch, Louis Philippe. In Great Britain the liberals won a big victory in the Reform Act of 1832, which enabled them to share power with the conservatives. In central and eastern Europe, however, reactionary conservatism remained in control.

In spite of Lamennais's defection, the liberal Catholics did not abandon ship; Montalembert took over at the helm. Without abandoning their commitment to modern liberties, they adopted a pragmatic stance and sought to avoid confrontation with the papacy on the level of theory. Montalembert formed a Catholic political party—the first in Europe—dedicated to securing liberty for the Church in education. Lacordaire devoted his marvelous rhetorical talent to the pulpit of Notre Dame, where he exerted considerable influence over the intelligentsia. Frédéric Ozanam, another devout liberal Catholic, founded the Society of St. Vincent de Paul in order to aid the poor.

The year 1848 was an important one for the liberals. Moved by the success of their fellows in western Europe, those in central and southern Europe showed increasing boldness and demanded constitutions guaranteeing individual liberties. After violent conflict they were able to drive the monarchs out of many capitals and forced Metternich himself to flee from Vienna. Though setbacks occurred when the Austrian armies reoccupied Vienna and put down revolutions in Bohemia, Italy, and Hungary, and the Prussian King recaptured Berlin, the fact remained that the liberals had demonstrated their considerable strength even in areas thought safe for autocracy. The liberal Catholics were more than ever convinced that the Church had to find a more positive relationship to liberalism than that expressed in *Mirari Vos* or risk losing all influence over the culture of the day.

It is well to keep in mind the diversities of liberalism presented by its history. The first stage of liberalism—which found expression in the French Revolution—was predominantly a political liberalism concerned with establishing constitutional guarantees for the rights of the individual: freedom from arbitrary taxation and imprisonment, freedom of speech and association. Under the influence of romanticism, political liberalism was extended to include opposition to the domination of one nation by another. Liberals demanded liberation for "oppressed" and "enslaved" people and joined forces with nationalists.

With the advance of industrialization, another form of liberalism came to the fore: economic liberalism. These liberals dreamed of a coming materialistic millennium, which could be realized if only the businessman and industrialist was given complete freedom of operation. Their ideal was a free market unencumbered by any combinations, whether of employers or workers. They were against all customs, duties, and tariffs—protective measures of any kind—and were particularly hostile to trade unions. So effective was the opposition to labor unions that it was not until 1871 that unions obtained legal recognition in England and not until 1906 that they could securely conduct even peaceful strikes there.

Other liberals, however, saw the danger in economic liberalism—perceiving how, in a time of huge corporations and trusts, tyrannical power could be concentrated in the hands of a few and annihilate the freedom of the less fortunate. They pointed to the workingman, who was now merely grist for the economic mill, mere chattel to be sold on the market under the sway of the law of competition. And so economic liberalism began its terrible adversaries, socialism and even anarchism.

By the mid-nineteenth century, liberalism manifested a multiform character. As Carlton H. Hayes says, "There was a political, an economic, an intellectual liberalism. There was a radical, an atheistic, a moderate, a conservative, a Christian liberalism. Wherefore such diverse groups as English Tories and French Radical Republicans, Italian followers of Mazzini or of Cavour, German admirers of Bismarck and German disciples of Karl Marx were all somewhere in the liberal tradition."[6]

In time, however, the economic liberals acquired a virtual monopoly over the term; they were the sectarian Liberals (with a capital letter), the ones mainly responsible for giving liberalism an ugly connotation in the minds of many: the Liberal industrialists, big businessmen, bankers, railroad builders, traders.

The liberal Catholics had little sympathy with economic liberalism; they favored adapting the Church only to what was best in liberalism. They felt that greater freedom for the individual would mean real progress for humanity. Moreover, they felt instinctively that the future was on the side of the Liberals. It was inevitable, they argued, that some mistakes would be made in trying to realize a more just society, one more comfortable to the dignity of

[6] *A Generation of Materialism* (New York: Harper & Row, 1963), p. 48.

the individual. It would take time and patience. They wanted the Church to welcome the new order with the same youthful energy with which it had adapted to other great historic and cultural mutations instead of foolishly binding herself to a decayed and dying system.

Their opponents, the integralist Catholics, on the other hand, wanted the Church to declare all-out war on the principles of the French Revolution, which they saw as the work of Satan. They saw nothing good in liberalism, which had opened up, they thought, an unbridgeable chasm between the modern world and the Church. Faithful to the spirit of Gregory XVI, they wanted the Church to seek wherever possible a close alliance with any regime that would closely unite Church and state. These Catholics were authoritarian and intransigent in temperament; their chief spokesmen were Louis Veuillot, editor of the *L'Univers;* a Spaniard, Donoso-Cortés; and the Italian Jesuits who edited *La Civiltà Cattolica.* By 1850 the Church everywhere in Europe was divided along these lines, each group looking on the other with a certain amount of suspicion—the integralists detecting heresy in liberal Catholicism, while the liberal Catholics suspected the integralists of constantly reporting them to Rome.

The opposition between the two parties was peculiarly sharp in France where Veuillot, a journalist with a genius for sarcasm and invective, hammered away daily at the fallacies of liberalism in his *L'Univers.* He won over a large part of the clergy and succeeded in reinforcing their authoritarian and doctrinaire tendencies. At his side stood imposing authorities in the French Church. One of these was Cardinal Pie (1815–80), who, though admittedly untypical, illustrates the absurd lengths to which an integralist could go in identifying the Church with crusading royalism: He surrounded himself with legitimist bigots, helped raise a regiment of papal volunteers to defend the lost cause of the Papal States and, on the side, endorsed the effort to recover Christ's Sacred Prepuce, "the only part of Christ's body left behind when He ascended into heaven." Another integralist was Dom Guéranger, the narrow-minded abbot of Solesmes and one of Pope Pius IX's favorites. To counter their influence Montalembert took over a monthly, *Le Correspondant,* with several collaborators. They were soon joined by one of the leaders of the French hierarchy, Monseigneur Dupanloup, outstanding preacher and bishop of Orleans since 1849, the *enfant terrible* of the episcopate, who often barely managed to keep his fiery temperament under control. He too was most anx-

ious to find a way out of the impasse between the Church and the revolutionary modern world.

Elsewhere in the Catholic world the same type of polarization occurred.
But although the basic issue remained the same in each instance—how the
Church should relate to the movement for greater freedom—the terms of the
debate changed with each country. The German liberal Catholics, for example, never regarded separation of Church and state as an ideal; but their leaders, like Bishop Ketteler of Mainz, only thought that in certain circumstances
it might be the lesser of evils. In general, as we shall see in the next chapter,
the German liberal Catholics were more concerned with the issue of freedom
within the Church. Their leader, Professor Doellinger, called for greater freedom for theologians. His disciple, John Acton, took the same line in England,
and in his liberal Catholic *Rambler*—which he took over from Newman
in 1858—preached the doctrine of intellectual freedom. The Belgian liberal Catholics, after the encyclical *Mirari Vos,* under their leader, Archbishop
Sterckx, espoused a pragmatic attitude and defended the liberal orientation of
the Belgian Church as the only feasible policy in their circumstances. However, in the 1850s a group of liberal Catholics emerged there who took a more
positive view of liberalism; even on the ideological level, they proposed it as
more consonant with the Gospel than the old order.

The election in 1846 of Pius IX (Pio Nono in Italian) first was good news
for the liberal Catholics and a cause of alarm for Metternich, since the new
Pope was reputed to be something of a liberal. At first Pius lived up to the reputation: He issued a general amnesty for political prisoners, made provision
for sharing the government of the Papal States with laymen, and finally
granted his subjects a constitution that set up a bicameral form of government
whose lower house, the Council of Deputies, was elected by indirect suffrage.
And although the constitution left the Pope an absolute veto, it still represented a real division of power, since any civil administrative or political law,
including the imposition of taxes, had to be voted by the councils. It also included a form of habeas corpus and abolished political press censorship.

The Pope's reforms were hailed with enthusiasm by liberals around the
world. But in no way did they actually represent a conversion to liberal
Catholicism; Pio had no intention of implementing liberal ideas on freedom
of religion and, in fact, still refused to accord civil and political equality to
Jews in the Papal States. To a great extent the Pope was only yielding to the

political pressures of the moment. But at least it seemed a promising beginning.

The whole experiment soon broke down, however. The Pope's parliament declared war on Austria in an attempt to ally the Papal States with the Risorgimento—the great Italian movement of liberation and unification. But Pius, although very sympathetic to the cause of Italian unity, could not see himself involved in a war against Catholic Austria, and he imposed his veto. It was an extremely unpopular step and caused fury to run wild in the streets of Rome. Demonstrations were staged, riots broke out, and the democratic extremists exploited the widespread discontent. An assassin stabbed and mortally wounded the Pope's Prime Minister on the steps of the Council Chamber and a revolution erupted. A mob of citizens and soldiers surrounded the papal palace, trained a field gun on it, and made the Pope a virtual prisoner. But by a clever ruse the Pope, garbed as an ordinary priest, managed to escape to Gaeta in the south, where he had to take lodgings at first in a second-class hotel. The leader of the Italian liberation movement, Giuseppe Garibaldi, entered Rome with his ragged followers and helped set up a democratic republic. A little later Giuseppe Mazzini arrived and inaugurated his new religion of humanity and progress, although he refrained from indulging in anything like Robespierre's fantasy of inventing a new liturgy.

The poorly organized democrats, however, were soon chased out by French bayonets, and the Pope rode back through the Lateran gate on April 12, 1850—escorted by French troops and resolved to show no more leniency toward liberalism. The happenings at Rome had proven for him beyond the shadow of a doubt that liberalism meant only anarchy and persecution of the Church. He would continue to carry out reforms but would allow no more talk about constitutions if he could help it. Nor did his subsequent experience in any way disabuse him of this attitude.

Liberals, in the meantime, had taken over the northern Italian state of Piedmont, and under Camillo Cavour, the Prime Minister, carried through a number of laws offensive to the Church. They abolished most of the religious orders and stripped the Church of control over education. But worse was in store. Cavour conceived the audacious idea of uniting the whole of Italy under the Piedmont liberal monarchy. His first objective was to seize the Papal States, leaving only the city of Rome for the Pope. He was able to engineer a series of uprisings in the Pope's domain, and then under pretext of restoring order move his army in and occupy the land. The Pope made a valiant effort to resist the aggressors; his tiny army of Swiss Guards was enlarged by volunteers recruited from Catholic countries around the world. But they were no match in numbers or training for the Piedmontese and were cut to pieces at Castelfidardo in 1860. This left the Pope holding only the city of Rome and its environs.

At this point one may well wonder why the Pope did not bow to the inevitable and accept the settlement offered by Cavour. In exchange for his renunciation of the Papal States, it would have guaranteed complete independence and liberty for the Pope; entire and exclusive jurisdiction of the Pope and bishops over the clergy; complete freedom of religious education; ownership of the palaces, galleries, and monuments traditionally belonging to the papacy; and a regular agreed-upon income for the papal court, for the Sacred College, and for the episcopate and clergy as a whole. It would have given the Church complete freedom in the sphere of preaching, teaching, the press, and association. In other words, it was a settlement not too dissimilar to the one actually negotiated seventy years later in the Lateran Treaty.

Such a settlement would also have secured the same civil liberties for the subjects of the Papal States as were already enjoyed in Piedmont and would have relieved the Pope of the terrible burden of his little kingdom—an increasingly glaring anachronism in a world of big powers. One could hardly argue any longer that the Papal States were necessary to secure the independence of the Pope's spiritual authority, since in order to retain them he was increasingly dependent on France and Austria.

For some time the matter hung in the balance. Reactionaries and those of liberal tendency in the Curia pulled the Pope one way, then the other. Cardinal Antonelli (d. 1876), Secretary of State and chief of the reactionaries, was in many ways the evil genius of Pio Nono. Cardinal Antonelli's mentality is revealed in his constant assertion that the laws of the Church, being eternal, cannot be subject to political necessity and that before Pio could hand over even a jot of his rights as Vicar of Christ on earth, it would be his duty to seek, as did some of his predecessors, some other Avignon in a neutral section of Europe.

Various reasons determined Pius' final policy. There was the resentment at Sardinia's past Machiavellian maneuvers and aggressions. There was also his strong feeling of personal obligation to maintain unimpaired the heritage of the Church, as all his predecessors had done since the time of Pepin. "If the Lord wants me to lose the Papal States," he would say, "then let him take them away. I cannot hand them over." There was also his realization that a takeover by Piedmont would mean the installation of a liberal secular regime over the whole of Italy, with the concomitant spread of heretical doctrines. An insight into his feelings in this regard are found in a conversation he held at the time with the British attaché, Odo Russell, about the possibility of an Italian confederation as the best answer to the problem. The Pope remarked that he could never accept British representation in such a confederation, since Britain would probably advocate freedom of the press, an institution he could not consider consistent with the laws of the Church, which was obligated to guide public opinion and inculcate morality on the minds and the behavior of the people. Never, the Pope insisted, could he allow the press to be free in the states of the Church, since morality forbade it.[7]

So the Pope finally decided on a policy of intransigence. He decided to spare no effort to recapture his territories, and he declared war on the secular liberal concept of the state now embodied in the government of Piedmont. His final "No" to the liberals and the liberal Catholics was his *Syllabus of Errors*. But before recounting that episode, something must be said about another aspect of the liberal Catholic movement—their quest for greater intellectual freedom in the Church.

---

[7] N. Blakiston, *The Roman Question* (London: Chapman & Hall, 1962), p. 248.

Chapter 26

THE SYLLABUS OF ERRORS
SQUELCHES THE LIBERAL
CATHOLICS

Another important issue in the debate between liberals and conservatives in the nineteenth-century Church had to do with the question of intellectual freedom. Unlike the advocacy of political liberalism, which found its strongest leaders in France in the circle around Montalembert, this issue was explored most vigorously and intelligently by the German Catholics. This was in keeping with the obvious superiority of their theological and historical scholarship. As the only Catholic community in the world with theological schools located in the secular universities, they were forced to keep in touch with scientific developments and so were more acutely aware of the need of the Church to face realistically the problems raised by modern culture. They saw that the Church could only deal effectively with the arguments raised by the rationalists by emulating their spirit of scientific impartiality. And so the German Catholic scholars broke away from the obsolete Scholastic texts and developed new scientific methods to defend the faith, with intellectual freedom presupposed as a sine qua non.

The German liberal Catholics were more than confident in their ability as Church apologists to hold their own in the intellectual free market. They could point to a number of important scholars who showed that the German Catholic Church possessed genuine intellectual vitality. Catholic theologians of the Tübingen school beginning with Johann A. Möhler (d. 1838), lay converts of genius such as Friedrich von Schlegel (d. 1829) and Joseph von

Görres (d. 1848) were leaders in the Catholic revival. By 1850, Ignaz von Doellinger (d. 1890) was unquestionably the leader of the German liberal Catholics. A Church historian primarily and professor at Munich since 1826, Doellinger had gained an enviable reputation by a series of remarkable studies, including a four-volume *Church History* (1833–38) and the *Reformation* (1848). In addition, he was deeply involved in journalism and political activity. Although originally ultramontane and conservative in Church matters, he was gradually led by his historical studies to adopt a liberal attitude in regard to Church authority.

The issue of intellectual freedom was also vigorously debated among English Catholics, thanks to the influence of Doellinger's young protégé, John Acton, scion of an old Shropshire family. Acton's family tree spread great branches throughout Europe, and Acton was nothing if not cosmopolitan, having mastered six languages in his youth. The great formative influence on his mind was his four-year sojourn at Munich, where he lived with Doellinger as his friend and student. On Acton's arrival back in England in 1854 he felt it his mission in life to introduce into the Catholic body the German historical method and its spirit of free inquiry. And he found in the Catholic monthly the *Rambler* a perfect organ for the dissemination of liberal Catholic ideas.

To his great joy he was able to enlist in the cause an Oratorian priest, John Henry Newman. As the leader of the Oxford movement, Newman occupied the center of the English ecclesiastical stage during the 1830s and 1840s. By his sermons at St. Mary's, Oxford, his writings and personal example, and in close association with his friends John Keble, Hurrell Froude, and Edward Pusey, Newman had stirred the Anglican Church to a deep theological and spiritual renewal. But eventually he felt compelled by the inner logic of the movement to submit to Rome, and after an agony of mind and heart, he left his maternal Church and became a Roman Catholic priest.

While never fully subscribing to Acton's brand of liberal Catholicism, Newman was sympathetic to its basic goal of reconciling faith with modern culture insofar as that was possible. So while contributing several articles to the *Rambler,* he also tried to influence its tone, which he found needlessly flippant at times and calculated to antagonize the already alarmed bishops. Newman, it may be added, had little sympathy with the free thinkers of the day and considered their brand of liberalism the bane of society. He looked back wistfully to the Christian liberty of thought of the Middle Ages and regretted the tight discipline increasingly exercised by Rome.

The struggle of the liberal Catholics for greater intellectual freedom in the Church was severely hampered by the deteriorated state of the Catholic intellect itself. Outside of Germany intellectual life in the Church was at a very low ebb. The disruption of French Catholicism during the Revolution gravely retarded intellectual pursuits and lowered the quality of teaching in the French seminaries; the French clergy weren't able to pursue higher studies on the university level until late in the nineteenth century. The resurrection of the University of Louvain augured well for the future of theology in Belgium, but there were few signs elsewhere of revival. Austria, Poland, and Spain, with a few unexciting exceptions, produced no Catholic intellects of any significance. And one could hardly expect to find original thinkers in Rome itself, where in 1820 a book espousing Newton's theory of gravitation was put on the *Index* and where the salvaging of the Papal States was the chief preoccupation. The "safe" sciences—Canon Law, liturgy, and archaeology—it is true, were cultivated with some degree of expertise under Pio Nono; De Rossi's work on the catacombs excited considerable interest, and the Jesuits Passaglia, Schrader, and Franzelin at Gregorian University made respectable contributions to positive theology.

Nor did the liberal Catholics expect much from the neo-Scholastic renaissance that was gaining momentum and was soon to become the dominant intellectual force in Catholic seminaries and theological faculties. Its leaders tended to be conservative and authoritarian. To place this neo-Scholastic renaissance in proper perspective, we must recall that during the Counter Reformation medieval Scholasticism was revived but then again fell into complete obscurity during the Enlightenment. And by the year 1800 the theologian who quoted Thomas, Scotus, or Suarez was rare. Cartesianism and Newtonianism had given the coup de grâce to Aristotle, and Scholasticism, with its heavy debt to the Greek philosopher, suffered accordingly. But around 1800 a movement began to revive the medieval system. As in the sixteenth century, the revival was decidedly Thomist in emphasis and was again the work of Jesuits, many of them associated with *La Civiltà Cattolica,* their monthly founded in 1850. Outstanding among the leaders of the Thomist renaissance were such priests as d'Azeglio, Curci, Sordi, Liberatore, and Vincenzo Pecci, archbishop of Perugia and later Pope Leo XIII.

Outside Italy the revival of medieval Scholasticism was most successful in Germany, where the diocese of Mainz played a leading role and where Bishop von Ketteler's seminary housed many of its leaders. A team of professors there edited the journal *Der Katholik,* which pursued an aggressive line of propaganda in favor of restoring medieval Scholasticism to honor in the Church. The idea was taken up enthusiastically by scores of influential bishops and priests like Archbishop Reisach of Munich, Cardinal Rauscher of Vienna, the Jesuit professors at Innsbruck, and most notably a German Jesuit, Kleutgen, considered the most original and profound of the nineteenth century's neo-Thomists and chief defender of the Scholastic citadel.

By 1850, as neo-Scholasticism gathered strength, two rather well-defined schools of thought formed in Germany and to some extent elsewhere over the issue of the Church's proper relationship vis-à-vis modern culture: the Ultramontanes, led by the neo-Scholastics of Mainz, vs. the liberal Catholics, led by Doellinger and his Munich school. In the mind of the former, modern culture was hopelessly rationalist and secular and inimical to the Church; they therefore favored a state-of-siege strategy and authoritarian methods. They wanted the Catholic faithful protected from contamination by secularism and rationalism and welded into a disciplined army led by zealous and pious priests trained in seminaries isolated from the pernicious influences of secular culture. To achieve this aim, they favored strengthening Rome's authority over the Church. Catholic theologians, in particular, were to be subjected to a tight censorship and be compelled to give assent not only to the dogmas of the Church but even to the ordinary teaching as laid down by the Roman congregations. In effect, this meant a monolithic conformity to the Scholastic tradition, which had succeeded in gaining predominance over the minds of the Curia.

On the other hand, the Munich school, led by Doellinger, was more optimistic about modern culture; it was an optimism based on a profound confidence in Catholicism's perennial vitality and its ability in the past to assimilate the good in any culture while escaping its excesses. Rather than tighter control by Rome over scholars and theologians, they wanted them to have more independence. As Lord Acton put it:

> [The Catholic scholar] must meet his adversaries on grounds which
> they understand and acknowledge . . . [he must discuss] each topic
> on its intrinsic merits—answering the critic by a severer criticism,

the metaphysician by closer reasoning, the historian by deeper learning, the politician by sounder politics and indifference itself by a purer impartiality. In all these subjects . . . [he] discovers a point pre-eminently Catholic, but also pre-eminently intellectual and true.[1]

With Rome itself at the time literally under siege by Garibaldi and in a state of theological and intellectual disarray, it is not surprising that the conservative Scholastics of Mainz soon got the upper hand. They carried on an aggressive campaign against the "liberals" and were aided in this by the nuncio at Munich. Though they counted within their ranks men of real talent and breadth of view, too many of them unfortunately were anti-intellectual bigots completely ignorant of the positive results of historical research and readily inclined to identify their own opinions with orthodoxy itself. Rather than wrestle with the knotty problems raised by historical and biblical research, they preferred the easier recourse to an instant authority and systematically denounced to Rome all those who did not share their narrow theological views. Many of their attacks were totally unjustified and were inspired more by personal rivalry than by love of truth. Their first great success came with the condemnation of Austrian philosopher Anton Günther, a theologian of genius, whose wide circle of followers included the archbishop of Vienna, Cardinal Schwarzenberg.

The conflict between the two parties became increasingly bitter as Doellinger reacted to the tactics of the "Romans" by loading sarcasm and invective on the Scholastics and pointing with scorn to the low level of learning at Rome. Nevertheless, it was Doellinger who tried to bring about a reconciliation between the two schools. He and some colleagues sent invitations to most of the leading German scholars to attend a congress in Munich scheduled for September of 1863. The attendance surpassed all expectations; most of those invited showed up—with the exception of the Tübingen faculty and the Jesuits. Doellinger delivered the keynote address, "The Past and Future of Theology," in which he sketched a program for revitalizing Catholic theology. This classical statement of intellectual liberal Catholicism began with a brief history showing how successively Greeks, Italians, Spaniards, French, and English theologians had exerted the dominant influence and concluded that it was now the turn of the German Catholics to take up the torch, since they

[1] *Essays on Church and State* (London: Hollis & Carter, 1952), p. 84.

were the ones best trained in history and modern philosophy, the two sciences that henceforth would shape the content of theology, since the Scholastic approach was now obsolete.

He then finally addressed himself to the crucial issue—the intellectual freedom of the Catholic scholar—and made a forceful plea for his right to work untrammeled by authority, arguing that intervention by Church authority was needed only in the rare cases, where his conclusions were in obvious contradiction with the dogmas of the Church. Otherwise he demanded a great amount of freedom for the individual theologian; his errors would not be fatal, since it was the very mark of a healthy theology to be able to correct its own mistakes. The only effective weapons against error, he asserted, were the weapons of science, not ecclesiastical censure.

Acton, in the pages of his *Home and Foreign Review,* hailed the speech as the dawn of a new era in theology and argued that Doellinger had safeguarded the legitimate rights of authority in the Church by professing his complete submission to defined dogma. Pio Nono, however, was deeply disturbed by the liberal *pronunciamento* of Doellinger, and in a brief to the archbishop of Munich emphatically laid down the hard line: The Catholic scholar must be subject to the ordinary magisterium (the Church's teaching function), as well as to the decrees of the Roman congregations; and he deplored Doellinger's negative attitude toward Scholasticism.

A month before the Munich congress another impressive assembly of Catholics was held at Malines; the leader of the French liberal Catholics, Montalembert, before an immense audience of cardinals, bishops, priests, and laymen, called on the Church to embrace the modern liberties and get in step with the rest of the world. He held Catholic and liberal Belgium up to the eyes of the world as proof that the Church could flourish in the climate of liberty. The old regime of intolerance, Inquisitions, and unions of thrones and altars was in the last stage of decrepitude and could never be revived, and Catholics should be among the first rather than the last to applaud the fact. Thunderous applause greeted his words, and he received the personal congratulations of the cardinal archbishop of Malines.

Both events—the Munich congress and the assembly at Malines—joined with other signs, convinced the Pope that the liberal virus was spreading with fearful rapidity through the Church, and he finally decided to take a step he had been contemplating for some time: the issuance of a general condemnation of modern errors, including those associated with liberalism. It would be a summary of the condemnations he had issued over the past fifteen years.

And so his famous *Syllabus of Errors* appeared on December 8, 1864, accompanied by an encyclical, *Quanta Cura.* The *Syllabus of Errors* listed eighty errors, including rationalism, naturalism, a socialism that would subject the family totally to the state, and liberal capitalism that had no other end than material gain. For most people, however, the most startling thing was the condemnation of freedom of religion, progress, and liberalism found in Error No. 77: "It is no longer expedient that the Catholic religion should be treated as the only religion of the state, all other worships whatsoever being excluded," and No. 80: "The Roman Pontiff can and ought to reconcile and harmonize himself with progress, with liberalism, and with modern civilization."

The public commotion that resulted was without parallel in the modern history of the Church until our own day. Unlike *Mirari Vos,* issued when majority sentiment in Europe was still conservative and reactionary, the *Syllabus* struck against the broad mainstream of public opinion. Even the average Catholic was shocked to hear the Pope condemning progress and modern civilization. Moreover, the formulations of the *Syllabus* lent themselves readily to misinterpretations, since they consisted largely of verbatim extracts lifted out of their context in previous papal documents and that could only be properly understood if put back in that context. Error No. 80, for instance, was taken from an allocution of the Pope's protesting against Piedmont's spoliation of convents and harassing of priests and that had concluded: The Roman Pontiff does not have to reconcile himself with progress and modern civilization "if by the word 'civilization' must be understood a system invented on purpose to weaken, and perhaps to overthrow, the Church. . . ."

But the average reader did not realize when he read the encyclical that this is what the Pope meant by "civilization," and might easily conclude that the Pope had declared war on the modern world.

To forestall such a disaster, a French bishop, Félix Dupanloup, came to the rescue. Working day and night, he was able quickly to publish a skillful commentary that placed the propositions of the *Syllabus* in their original context. And by means of a subtle distinction between thesis and hypothesis was able to show that Rome did not mean to condemn or repudiate the liberal constitutions actually in force in such countries as Belgium, England, Latin America, and the United States. Put on sale on January 26, it sold out in two hours, and within three weeks one hundred thousand copies were distributed, not counting numerous translations.

The liberal Catholic movement was not completely destroyed by the *Syllabus,* but it was certainly checked. Most liberal Catholics remained in their former opinions, and thanks to Dupanloup they could not simply be condemned as heretics, but they were in disgrace and on the defensive, especially since Pius himself favored those who swallowed the encyclical whole hog. And so they had to be extremely prudent in order not to draw down more lightning. But some were less prudent than others: The liberal archbishop of Paris, Darboy, for example, said in an appeal to the Pope: "You have just . . . condemned the principal errors of our time. Now turn your eyes toward its honorable and good features and give them your support. . . . For it is your duty to . . . reconcile liberty with authority."[2]

[2] R. Aubert, *Le Pontificat de Pie IX* (Paris: Bloud & Gay, 1963), p. 261.

Chapter 27

PIO NONO CARRIES ULTRAMONTANISM TO A GRAND TRIUMPH AT VATICAN I

One of the most remarkable trends in nineteenth-century Catholicism was the tremendous increase in the power and influence of the papacy. This resurgence of ultramontanism was closely associated with the Catholic revival of the early nineteenth century. The Ultramontanes were Rome-centered Catholics who in contrast with the Gallicans, their adversaries, saw a strong papacy as the only salvation of the Church in an age of godless, anti-Christian, and anticlerical liberals. No one was more fervently ultramontane than Pius IX himself, and his long reign (1846–78), coupled with numerous other religious, social, and political factors, enabled him to steer the movement to its climax—the definition of papal infallibility at Vatican I. This increase of spiritual authority more than compensated for his loss of temporal authority. It also set the Church's stamp of approval on his condemnation of liberalism and hardened the Church in the state-of-siege mentality that Pius himself did so much to foster.

NUMEROUS REASONS CAN be found for the strong ultramontane upsurge in the early nineteenth century. First, political conservatives saw in the papacy a strong bulwark against the revolutionary ideas. Second, Pius VII's heroic defiance of the autocratic Napoleon enhanced the prestige of the papacy. Third, the clergy, who had been stripped by the Revolution of their property and privileges, found Rome their only defense against the whims of the lay state, which wanted to make them mere civil servants. Fourth, many priests who suffered persecution for their obedience to Rome came out of their experience strengthened in their loyalty. Fifth, the Concordat of 1801, requiring that the whole French episcopate tender their resignation to the Pope, struck a heavy blow at Gallicanism by providing an unprecedented and awesome demonstration of the Pope's power over the bishops. Sixth, the same concordat, by giving the bishops almost unlimited authority over their priests, drove the latter into the arms of the Pope as their only safeguard against episcopal arbitrariness.

On the literary front two important French writers, Lamennais and de Maistre, greatly advanced the cause of ultramontanism. The latter's book *Du Pape* (1819)—a best seller in its day—argued in favor of an infallible authoritarian papacy as indispensable to a conservative European political order. Lamennais for his part won over a large section of the younger clergy to his vision of a cohesive Church closely linked with the Pope and ready to struggle with the new and godless liberal order. So it took only twenty years in France to gain wide popular acceptance of the ultramontane Church order—stressing the personal infallibility of the Pope and close control by the Roman Curia over the internal affairs of the Church.

Conditions in Germany also favored a grass-roots ultramontane movement. During the Revolution numerous sees remained vacant for a long period; in the interim the German Catholics got accustomed to depending on Rome for dispensations and other necessities. Moreover, thanks to the gerrymandering of the Congress of Vienna, Catholics found themselves everywhere in a minority. In dealing with the Protestant governments, they learned to appreciate Rome's help and support. On the other hand, these Protestant governments also found it to their advantage to deal with Rome rather than with the local churches, since they didn't want to do anything that would encourage the rise of a strong national German Catholic Church.

However, Gallicanism still remained strong for some time, especially the moderate kind found in Bailly's *Theology*, a standard seminary textbook. And the struggle between the two viewpoints divided the Church; it often involved a conflict of generations, with the older priests clinging to the Gallican traditions imbibed in their training. It also involved a conflict of styles of religious life, as the Gallicans objected to the centralizing and authoritarian characteristics of the new system. Others disliked the externalism of its new style of piety, emphasizing frequent reception of the sacraments and numerous devotions.

A critical turning point in the struggle between Gallicans and Ultramontanes in France occurred in 1852 when the Gallican bishops, led by the archbishop of Paris, issued a long memorandum, the *Mémoire sur le droit coutumier,* which insisted on the rights of each diocese to regulate its own affairs. Rome, which up to this point had more or less observed a prudent neutrality, now seized this as an occasion for stepping in on the side of the Ultramontanes. Pius issued *Inter Multiplices*—a stinging rebuke to the Gallican signatories of the memorandum—and from this time on used a definite strategy in order to further the cause of ultramontanism. Bishops were prohibited from holding national councils, regarded as possibly dangerous forums for Gallican ideas. Books of Gallican tendency were regularly put on the *Index,* including a treatise on Canon Law written by the vicar general of Paris, and the clergy and faithful were encouraged to have constant recourse to Rome—over the heads of their bishops if necessary.

In this way Pio Nono was gradually able to tighten his control over the bishops. Thanks to the extraordinary length of his reign—the longest in history—he was able to shape the character of the episcopate by choosing wherever possible men of strong ultramontane tendency and also by keeping in close contact with them. He used the apostolic nuncios as watchdogs to keep the bishops in line; recalcitrants were sometimes invited to a personal audience, which could be stormy. He also spared no pains in winning over the lower clergy to ultramontanism. One measure that proved most effective was the establishment of national seminaries in Rome, where young seminarians brought to Rome could imbibe the Roman spirit at its source. The American College, started in 1859, was only one of many such foundations.

The proclamation of the dogma of the Immaculate Conception on December 8, 1854, represented a distinct triumph for the Ultramontanes, as the whole affair was deliberately staged to dramatize the authority of the Holy Father, who read the decree with the bishops looking on as simple spectators.

Most effective among the allies of the Pope in this great ultramontane campaign were the religious orders, many of them already headquartered in Rome and therefore ideally suited to be his agents in spreading the ultramontane spirit and doctrines to their far-flung outreaches. The Jesuits in particular were well fitted for this purpose, and they had immense influence on the Pontiff, who tended to adopt their viewpoint in many matters of ecclesiastical politics, theology, and spirituality. Their journal *La Civiltà Cattolica* was thought of as the mouthpiece of the Holy See.

The Pope tended to bypass the College of Cardinals in dealing with day-to-day problems and depended most on a number of personal friends and counselors such as Antonelli, who remained Secretary of State from 1849 to 1876; Cardinals Bedini, Patrizi, and Barnabo, who exerted a lot of influence over certain departments; and several non-Italian priests—an Englishman, Talbot, and a Belgian, de Merode. Unfortunately, however, none of these men—in the opinion of historians such as Professor Roger Aubert—were endowed with the qualities of historical sense and political sagacity demanded by the extremely complicated situation of the Church.

But historians agree that what counted most in the triumph of ultramontanism was Pio Nono himself—one of the most remarkable men to occupy the chair of Peter, a man of profound religious faith and total confidence in God, a man absolutely devoted to the interests of the Church. Not gifted with great intelligence and rather superficially trained in theology, he nevertheless had a shrewd sense of affairs, radiated strength of character, and was able to captivate almost everyone who met him by his handsome presence, musical voice, and subtle combination of dignity and informality. He quickly broke with the venerable tradition that kept the Pope isolated from the people. He loved to walk around Rome chatting and joking with the people, making little gestures that soon became legends—like the time he stopped the tears of a little girl who dropped a bottle of wine she was carrying home when he bought another one and handed it to the surprised child. His most effective way of reaching the people, however, was through audiences; he was the first modern Pope to use them on a grand scale. These often took up his whole day, but they were invaluable for the ultramontane cause since they brought many average Catholics from around the world into personal touch with their Holy Father. A decidedly new feature of modern Catholicism developed from this: personal devotion to the Pope.

The success of Rome's strategy was clear by 1860; thanks to the causes mentioned, the ultramontanist current deeply penetrated the Catholic clergy and masses in astoundingly rapid fashion. Cardinals Rauscher at Vienna, Reisach at Munich, Manning at Westminster, and Cullen at Armagh presided over churches strongly committed to the Roman theology of the Church, which emphasized centralization and the personal infallibility of the Pope. By

1863, for instance, only eleven dioceses still clung to their non-Roman liturgies; even the Sulpicians, stalwart Gallicans since their beginning, were converts to ultramontanism.

At times this ultramontane enthusiasm for things Roman and the Pope got out of hand—"idolatry to the papacy," the archbishop of Rheims called it, referring to exaggerations such as that reported of one bishop who claimed that God was incarnate in the Pope or the general tendency of these neo-Ultramontanes, as the extremists were called, to attribute infallibility to every papal statement.

Strong opposition to this ultramontane movement was rather limited. Most of it was found in the universities of Germany and among the French bishops. Doellinger was the leader of the German intellectuals who opposed it as an antihistorical conception of Church order alien to the modern concepts of liberty and, in fact, nothing but a medieval creation based on notorious forgeries. The French Gallicans were led by Maret, one of the few theologians of real value on the episcopal bench, and by Darboy, archbishop of Paris. Behind them stood a coalition of bishops who regarded the *Syllabus of Errors* as a disaster and ultramontanism as a leap in the wrong direction. Nor could even the offer of a cardinal's hat turn Darboy around, as Pio Nono found out. Also among the opponents were the liberal Catholics who repented of their original ultramontane faith; they now feared a centralization of Church government that would confide the destiny of the Church to men who—as the *Syllabus of Errors* proved—were profoundly ignorant of the needs and aspirations of the modern world.

The first official public announcement of the Pope's intention to call a general council occurred in 1867, when the bishops gathered to celebrate the eighteenth centenary of the martyrdom of Sts. Peter and Paul. The impression was given that the purpose of the council would be to rally the Church against the rationalism of the nineteenth century, as the Council of Trent had done against Protestantism in the sixteenth. The two parties—Ultramontanes and Integralists together on one side, Gallicans and Liberals on the other—girded themselves for a crucial test of strength. The big question in their minds was whether or not the council, the first Vatican Council, would confirm the growing ultramontane trend and ratify Pius' anti-liberal, state of siege position as defined in his *Syllabus of Errors*.

An article published in *La Civiltà* on February 6, 1869, stirred up the wrath of the Liberals by attempting to cut off all debate:

Everyone knows that Catholics in France are unfortunately divided
into two parties: those who are simply Catholics, and others who call
themselves Liberal Catholics. . . . The Catholics . . . hope that the
council . . . will proclaim the doctrines of the *Syllabus* . . . and will
accept with joy the proclamation of the dogmatic infallibility of the
sovereign Pontiff . . . [and] will define it by acclamation.[1]

The liberal Catholics reacted with vigor to this trumpet blast. Doellinger
published *The Pope and the Council,* an erudite study presenting the history
of the papacy as a history of usurpation of power over the Church. Following
his lead, many German intellectuals as well as the German bishops themselves
declared against the opportuneness of defining papal infallibility. In France,
Bishop Maret published a more moderate reply, *On the General Council and
Religious Peace,* based on the Gallican thesis that papal statements need the
consent of the episcopate in order to enjoy infallibility. Bishop Dupanloup
also produced a pamphlet that declared the definition of papal infallibility
inopportune. This preconciliar debate served at least one useful purpose: It
brought the issue of infallibility to the fore, so that when the seven hundred
or so bishops assembled on December 8, 1869, they had a pretty good idea
of the terms of the debate. And it was soon evident that they were divided
into two groups: an overwhelming majority who favored a strong statement
defining papal infallibility and reaffirming the *Syllabus,* and a minority who
opposed any such moves.

In spite of its numerical inferiority—never more than 20 per cent of the
Council—the liberal minority was nevertheless an imposing body by reason
of the important sees represented: nearly the whole Austro-Hungarian episcopate, most of the German bishops, a good third of the French, and numerous American bishops from large dioceses. The minority came to the Council
with considerable fear of finding everything prearranged and the Curia prepared to use the bishops merely as rubber stamps to ratify what had been determined in advance. The minority feared in particular that the Curia would
engineer a move to have papal infallibility accepted by simple acclamation instead of by vote.

Their fears and misgivings were confirmed during the first weeks. Several

[1] R. Aubert, *Le Pontificat de Pie IX* (Paris: Bloud & Gay, 1963), p. 316. I am much indebted to
Professor Aubert for the material in this chapter.

grave errors of judgment were committed that further alienated them and helped to harden them in an attitude of systematic opposition. First, they were very annoyed to find on their arrival that the Pope himself, contrary to the procedure at Trent, had drawn up the ground rules in advance and greatly restricted their freedom of initiative. Only the Pope, for instance, was allowed to propose questions to the council. The choice of St. Peter's basilica as their assembly hall was another grievance; its acoustics were very poor and unsuited for real debate, and the minority suspected that it was deliberately chosen on this account. But what caused the greatest consternation was the high-handed maneuver by which Cardinal Manning deprived them of any representation on the key committee—*De Fide*—that would be responsible for drafting any statement on infallibility. So it was in a climate of suspicion and discontent that the bishops began to work on the first draft document submitted to them: a statement on the errors of modern rationalism.

Then two more maneuvers by the majority aroused more bitterness. A modification of the rules was made that allowed for a motion of cloture at the request of only ten bishops. And it was also determined that any motion could be carried by a mere majority. This abandonment of the traditional principal of moral unanimity made many of the minority think seriously about leaving Rome and challenging the legitimacy of the council.

At the request of 380 bishops, an extremist definition of papal infallibility was appended to the schema on the Church, which previously contained only a general statement about papal primacy. Delivered to the bishops on March 6, it brought the issue out into the open. An intense agitation began as partisans on both sides strove to win over the undecided through personal contact as well as by hastily printed leaflets. The Liberals and Gallicans stressed the danger of emphasizing the authoritarian character of the Church in an age so enamored of liberty, while the other side argued that unlimited freedom of thought was the greatest menace to the Church. The minority were more sensitive to the complex nature of the Church's constitution and afraid of disturbing the delicate balance of power between Pope and bishops, while the majority were more concerned about extirpating the remnants of Gallicanism.

The Catholic press around the world took sides, and attempts were made to stir up Catholics to put pressure on the bishops in favor of one side or the other. A remark by Newman referring to the leaders of the majority as an "insolent and aggressive faction" was published and caused a certain sensation, as

did a letter Montalembert published shortly before he died in which he castigated the attempt to "sacrifice justice, truth, reason, and history as a holocaust
to the idol they have erected in the Vatican."[2] But the most damaging attack
on the credibility of the council was Doellinger's tendentious chronicle that
he published under the pseudonym *Quirinus* and that he based on correspondence with eyewitnesses; it put the machinations of the majority in the
darkest light and helped permanently to discredit the council among large
sectors of public opinion, especially in Germany.

But though the majority had succeeded in getting the question of infallibility on the agenda, things were still moving so slowly that they estimated
it would take a whole year before they could begin debate on this topic. So
once again they made a special appeal to the Pope in a petition signed by
around a hundred bishops asking that Chapter 11, dealing with infallibility,
be taken out of its order and be considered first. Exasperated by this attempt
to invert the order of discussion, the minority remonstrated with the Holy Father about the dangers of treating the Pope's prerogatives before dealing with
the Church as a whole. But Pius once again sided with the majority. Chapter
11 was therefore recast into a separate, brief constitution of four chapters entitled *De Summo Pontifice* and immediately passed out to the bishops for examination.

The debate on this schema lasted from the middle of May until the middle of July 1870, during which time the minority made a futile effort to ward
off the inevitable. A brilliant phalanx led by Hefele, Rauscher, Maret, Ketteler,
Strossmayer, and Darboy presented the minority point of view, questioning
the expediency of defining infallibility, pointing out the historical and theological problems it raised. But the majority were not going to be dissuaded by
argument from a course they had long before decided on. Ill prepared for the
most part to cope with their more learned adversaries on intellectual grounds,
they merely waited with impatience until they could decently move to close
debate.

However, the effort of the minority was not completely wasted. This is
indicated by the concessions made to their point of view in the speech by a
Dominican, Cardinal Guidi, the most distinguished theologian of the majority. He proposed a formula that would speak of the infallibility of the Pope's
doctrinal definitions rather than of the "infallibility of the Pope"—a phrase

[2] Ibid., p. 345.

that connoted an idea of his personal infallibility. And Guidi suggested including a clause obliging the Pope to make a serious examination of tradition—which, Guidi said, would normally include consultation with the bishops. Although Guidi's conciliatory proposals found favor with both sides, he later received a stinging rebuke from Pio Nono, who shouted at him, *"Tradizione! La tradizione son' io!"* ("Tradition! I am Tradition!")

Still another gesture of conciliation was made by the official secretary of the Committee on Faith, Gasser, who in his authorized commentary stressed the numerous conditions needed for a papal decree to qualify as infallible: It must be *ex cathedra*—that is, the Pope must act as supreme pastor; it must deal with a doctrine of faith and morals; and the divine assistance (not inspiration) that protects him from error is due to the gift of infallibility not granted exclusively to the Pope but to the Church itself. Gasser affirmed the exact "coincidence of papal infallibility with the infallibility of the Church."[3]

Many entertained hopes of finding a formula that would somehow reconcile both points of view: the insistence of the minority that the bishops be associated with the Pope in any exercise of infallibility, and the determination of the majority to repudiate the Gallican thesis requiring consent of the bishops to make a papal definition irreformable. But the task proved insurmountable. Darboy, at the head of an imposing delegation, personally pleaded with the Pope to have some words inserted in the final formulation that would imply participation by the bishops in the papal exercise of infallibility. But in the end Manning and his group prevailed; the final formula definitely excluded the need of any such participation. Definitions of the Roman Pontiffs, it stated, were of themselves irreformable.

It might be noted that most of the bishops were moderates and were anxious to find some compromise formula rather than to crush their opponents. This was particularly true of the Italians, who made up a third of the assembly and had no part in the original politics of putting infallibility on the agenda. And according to some recent studies, it seems that the majority would have finally rallied to a compromise formula had it not been for Pius IX, who upheld the intransigents.

Some sixty bishops of the minority, unable in conscience to subscribe to the definition and unwilling to expose their dissent to the public eye by voting in the negative, quietly packed up their bags and left Rome. The remain-

---

[3] Ibid., p. 356.

ing 535 bishops registered their approval of the final text in the midst of a frightful storm on July 18, 1870.

They were dismissed immediately afterward until November. But Italian history barged in and prevented the continuance of their work. Caught in a war with Prussia, France pulled her troops out of Rome and left the way open for the troops of united Italy to occupy Rome. This happened on September 20. The Pope in protest declared himself a prisoner in the Vatican and prorogued the Council *sine die.*

Those bishops who deserted Rome without voting had in some cases a severe struggle of conscience before submitting to the Vatican decrees. One of the most reluctant was Bishop Hefele of Rottenburg, who blamed the Jesuits for making a caricature of the Catholic Church. But eventually all of the minority bishops submitted and accepted the decree—consoling themselves that they had at least stymied the extremists. The only large-scale resistance to the decree occurred in German university circles, where many professors, under the influence of Doellinger, rejected the definition of infallibility.

The decree on infallibility completed the rout of the liberal Catholics. A few like Newman took comfort in the idea that future councils would rectify whatever was exaggerated in the decree, but others, like Acton, abandoned any hope of liberalizing the Catholic Church.

Liberal Catholics, like liberals in general, considered the dogma a blow to progress and freedom. A little more historical hindsight, however, helps us see the dogma as the Church's way of defending itself against the liberal state— which in practice tended to be less liberal than it was supposed to be, especially in regard to the Church.[4] The liberal state could easily assume an infallibility of its own and infringe on the proper freedom of the Church. Under the old regime the clergy was able to protect its interests by means of various privileges and the financial independence secured by its large landed estates. But the clergy of the new order, as the Concordat of 1801 shows, was becoming a salaried bureaucracy and hence more easily controlled by the government. In these circumstances the Church could easily lose its international character. It was these political conditions that necessitated the dogma of papal infallibility for the same reason that the political conditions of the eleventh century necessitated the papal decree on lay investiture: The liberty of the Church was at stake.

[4] R. Binkley, *Realism and Nationalism* (New York: Harper & Row, 1963), pp. 60–61.

FORTIFIED BY THE acts of the First Vatican Council, Pius continued his policy of intransigence toward modern secular liberal culture and showed clearly that he was unable to adapt the Church to the profound social and political transformations going on around him. At his death in 1878 the Church was left in a virtual state of war with the rest of society—a *Kulturkampf* by no means limited to Bismarck's Germany.

Pius IX's real success was with the interior renewal of the Church, and he deserves credit for the magnificent leadership he gave in deepening its sense of piety and spirituality. Under his guidance many of the old religious orders were revitalized and many new ones founded. The Jesuits nearly doubled their membership during his reign and once more exerted a mighty influence in all fields of the apostolate. The Dominicans and Franciscans likewise made considerable progress, as did the order of Saint Sulpice, the Brothers of the Christian Schools, the Passionists, and the Redemptorists. The same was true of the venerable monastic orders—the Benedictines, Cistercians, Trappists, and Carthusians—which filled their new monasteries with enthusiastic recruits.

Many new orders of women and men were founded—too numerous even to list here. Some of the most successful were the Fathers of the Blessed Sacrament, Maria Reparatrix, and Don Bosco's Salesians. New missionary societies also sprang up, as, for instance, the White Fathers and the Society of the Divine Word.

The ultramontane movement fostered by Pius IX also favored a new style of piety—one that encouraged frequent reception of the sacraments, emphasized devotion to Mary, and engendered many sentimental devotions, such as to the Sacred Heart. In spite of certain excesses, this ultramontane spirituality represented an authentic renewal of the Catholic tradition by its rediscovery of the sacramental character of Catholic life, the reality of the supernatural, and above all the centrality of Christ—true God and true man. It succeeded in removing from the Catholic consciousness the vestiges of the cold, rationalistic, and Deistic tendencies so prevalent among Christians during the eighteenth century.

Part Five

THE STATE OF SIEGE
IS SLOWLY LIFTED

A.D. 1891–

Chapter 28

SOCIAL CATHOLICISM AND CHRISTIAN DEMOCRACY

Pius IX's successor, Leo XIII (1878–1903), was not a liberal Catholic but a widely traveled diplomat and deeply sensitive scholar who knew that it was absolutely imperative for the Church to meet the real needs of the age and break out of the state-of-siege mentality so much a part of its history since the Enlightenment. In contrast with Pius IX's reign, his pontificate was one long and somewhat successful effort to place the Church on a new footing in regard to modern secular culture. He tried to wean the French Catholics away from their alliance with the moribund monarchists. He restored good relations with Germany after the *Kulturkampf* (Bismarck's effort to destroy the Church's political and social influence). Leo tried to update the Church intellectually in line with the progress of biblical and historical research—instituting a biblical commission and opening the Vatican archives to historians. But his most enduring claim to the Church's gratitude was the leadership he gave in regard to the new problems created by the Industrial Revolution. His encyclical *Rerum Novarum* (1891) was the Magna Carta of social Catholicism, the movement that more than any other within the Church gradually forced Catholics out of their medievalism and state of siege mentality and inspired them to grapple realistically with the problems of the twentieth century.

Social Catholicism was the response of the Church to new conditions of society caused by the Industrial Revolution and the advent of the mass society. The latter part of the nineteenth century witnessed a remarkable leap forward in the self-awareness and political and social consciousness of the

Pope Leo XIII (reigned 1878–1903). Anonymous. Museo del Risorgimento, Milan.   © *Scala/Art Resource, New York.*

masses, who previously had taken little part in the decision making that shaped their lives.

The most important factor in bringing the masses to power, no doubt, was industrialization—the progressive mechanization and concentration of production methods, which began first in Great Britain in the textile factories at the end of the eighteenth century. It quickly transformed the British way of life. Modes of travel and communication were revolutionized after 1825 by the railway and electric telegraph. The European continent followed suit, though it lagged behind a full generation, remaining predominantly agrarian during the first half of the nineteenth century. Nevertheless, by 1851 many of the major European cities were linked to each other by railroads.

The age of Leo XIII saw the real debut of mass society and culture. It was the age of industrial barons—the Rockefellers, Carnegies, Krupps, and Nobels—whose steel and coal factories set the pace. The extent can be gauged by the fantastic spread of railroads, which in the United States leaped from 70,000 miles in 1873 to 193,000 by 1900. Europe by comparison reached 172,000 by 1900, while the world total amounted to 600,000 miles. This industrialization brought great numbers of people off the land and herded them into congested areas of smoky factories and dingy streets in a way that made the average person peculiarly susceptible to mass suggestion and mass action.

The emergence of the masses was also due to several other factors. One was the unprecedented growth in population, which set in about 1760 and continued throughout the nineteenth century. Europe's population rose from 140 million in 1740 to 188 million in 1800 to 266 million in 1850, increasing again by 130 million during the next fifty years, not counting the great numbers who emigrated abroad. Another factor was the rise of popular education and the growth of literacy. As late as the 1860s the vast majority of Europeans were still illiterate. But by 1900 illiteracy was virtually wiped out in northern and western Europe; by that date around 95 per cent of the population could read and write. Less success was registered in south-central Europe, where half of the Italians, for example, were still unable to read, and there was hardly any success as yet in eastern Europe. In close relationship with the growth of mass literacy, there arose popular journalism; the daily newspaper fed the appetites of the millions for excitement and sensation and was molded by and helped mold their opinions, prejudices, and tastes. Finally, the advent of democracy gave political power to the masses when the vote was extended to all adult males in most countries of Europe during the latter part of the century, although with certain qualifications.

Leaders of the Church realized that if it was to survive in this new situation and have any effective influence over the masses, it would have to make important adaptations. In particular, it would have to accept the liberal techniques: freedom of the press, democratic constitutions, separation of Church and state, and civil liberties, including freedom of religion and trade unions. Therefore, although his predecessor resisted accommodation to the modern world and condemned these things as the expression of liberalism, the flexible and clear-sighted Leo XIII made distinctions that made it possible for Catholics to accept the techniques of liberalism without subscribing to its philosophy. As he said in his encyclical *Libertas* in 1888, it was a vain and baseless calumny to accuse the Church of looking unfavorably on most modern political systems and of rejecting all the discoveries of contemporary genius.[1] In this spirit Leo began the work of reconciling the Church with the modern world and led the Church in taking a firm grip on the problems of modern mass society.

[1] *The Great Encyclical Letters of Pope Leo XIII* (New York: Benzinger Bros., 1903), p. 135.

The most crucial problem generated by the new industrialized mass society was the social question: the problem of the exploited and oppressed factory worker. As Thomas Carlyle said in 1843, "I venture to believe that in no time since the beginnings of society, was the lot of those same dumb millions of toilers so entirely unbearable as it is even in the days now passing over us."[2] Poverty and misery were, of course, not something new; but as Carlyle realized, the ancient poverty and misery was actually worsened by the coming of machinery. Statistics show that whereas in the sixteenth century the lowest class, the "poor" who lived on the brink of starvation, numbered one fifth of the population, in the nineteenth century they had increased to a third or more. Moreover, there is good evidence that the average worker—a millhand, for example—could barely earn enough to support a family with three children, even when he was fully employed.[3]

Conditions in the new factories and slums were abominable. Men as well as women and children (boys and girls under eighteen regularly made up half of the labor force) were forced to work twelve to fifteen hours a day at wages kept to a minimum. They could be laid off at any time without warning. They were obliged to spend 60 to 80 per cent of their income on their diet, which consisted of only bread and potatoes and an occasional cabbage. Their bare subsistence wages allowed them no margin for savings, and when they were laid off they would be in immediate danger of starving. They lived with their whole family in a single room in a dirty tenement and were lucky if they didn't have to share it with other families. The squalid streets around them were littered with garbage, and being without adequate sewers, they reeked with the smell of excrement.

It was only slowly that Catholics began to take cognizance of the "social question" and to begin the combination of reflection and action that gave rise to social Catholicism. Here as elsewhere, Lamennais anticipated later developments in the Church by his perceptive analysis of the worker problems and his attempt to stir up Catholic interest in the social question. In order for social Catholicism to emerge, two conditions were necessary. First, Catholics had to take cognizance of the exceptional gravity of the social problems and the need to talk no longer of the *poor* but of *poverty* and to undertake collective action for reform rather than trusting to individual charity. Secondly,

[2] Quoted in W. L. Langer, *Political and Social Upheaval 1832–1852* (New York: Harper & Row, 1969), p. 181.
[3] Ibid., p. 185.

there had to be a sufficiently optimistic attitude toward the future that would encourage the formulation of theoretical solutions and practical proposals.

The outstanding initiatives were taken in Germany, Belgium, Italy, and France, with the German Catholics leading the way. A German bishop, Wilhelm Ketteler (1811–77), as early as 1848 faced squarely the problem of the factory worker in sermons and books. He sketched out a Catholic solution that he marked off from both socialism and sectarian liberalism, pointing out the dangers in both the unlimited competition of liberal capitalism and the exaggerated state control of the socialists. He defended the right of state intervention against the liberal capitalists and the right of private property against the totalitarian tendencies of the socialists. Above all, he insisted on the right of workers to form their own associations, and he called for a whole series of reforms, including profit sharing, reasonable working hours, sufficient rest days, factory inspection, and the regulation of female and child labor. In 1869 he told the German bishops at Fulda that the social question was more acute and serious than any other, and he gave a powerful exposition of what had to be done to deal with it effectively.

Other Catholic leaders appeared who tried to organize the workers and to alleviate their miseries. But their ideas failed to penetrate the mass of their fellow Catholics, while they themselves were handicapped by antiquated ideas and attitudes. They remained essentially precapitalist and predemocratic, and they nostalgically longed for a return to the medieval guild system.

The socialists, therefore, seemed to many workers to offer the only hope, and there was a rapid proliferation of socialist parties generally committed to the Marxian historical dialectic. One appeared in Germany by 1875, in Austria and Switzerland by 1888, in Sweden and Holland by 1889, and in Italy, Poland, and Finland by 1892.

By 1880, in fact, it was pretty clear that the working class in France was already lost to the Church. Various reasons may be cited for this: the generally reactionary character of Church leadership at the time; and the reluctance of Catholics to adopt new democratic procedures, their refusal to accept the idea of class conflict, and their paternalistic desire to protect the workers or to use them against socialism.

But in the 1880s a new spirit began to appear. A number of Catholics began to take a more realistic approach—one that recognized the right of the worker to control his own destiny; it was, no doubt, in part inspired by fear of losing the whole working class to the socialists. One of the chief men responsible for this change was Henry Edward Cardinal Manning (d. 1892), a convert from Anglicanism who successfully identified the English Roman Catholic Church with the cause of labor. As early as December 1872, Manning appeared at a meeting held to promote the cause of farm workers. It was a courageous act, since it was the first time in England that a Roman Catholic prelate had so openly taken the side of labor. He followed this up with a letter to the Prime Minister, Gladstone, urging the passage of laws prohibiting the labor of children under a certain age and regulating housing. In 1874 he delivered a lecture "The Rights and Dignity of Labour" in which he forcefully defended the right of the worker to organize, called for laws to regulate the hours of work, and made a plea for people to look into the horrible abuses associated with child labor. He also agreed to serve on a royal commission on housing and advocated a radical approach to town planning that was far in advance of general thought.

In 1889 the London dock strike occurred—a big turning point in the history of labor in England—and though Manning was already eighty-two years of age, he took the lead in forming an arbitration committee. Though officially a mediator, his sympathies were with the dockers. He played a most important role in bringing about a settlement satisfactory to the workers, and they later showed their gratitude by organizing a huge cortege at his funeral.

He himself reflected after the strike, "I have been turning over the strike matters, and the more I think, the more I am on the side of Labour."[4] To win a reputation as a friend of labor at that time was quite courageous since, as he knew so well, the new social Catholicism was the most hateful of doctrines to those of the English faithful who looked upon the Church as the guardian of their interests, and religion as the best protection of their property.

Another of his most important acts as a friend of labor was the help he gave Cardinal Gibbons of Baltimore in saving the Knights of Labor from condemnation by Rome. The Knights were the most powerful American labor union of the time, with two thirds of their members Catholic, including their president, Terence Powderly. A move to have them condemned by Rome was mounted by some conservative American and Canadian bishops. Like Cardinal Gibbons, Manning thought that such an act would be disastrous and might permanently alienate the working classes from the Church. So he exerted all the influence he could on the Curia, and in private correspondence

---

[4] V. McClelland, *Cardinal Manning* (London: Oxford University Press, 1962), p. 147.

and public utterance he made it apparent where he stood. When Gibbons went to Rome in 1886 to defend the Knights, Manning provided him with information about curial politics, whose opinion was worth gaining, who should be consulted, and so on. Gibbons himself later on gave credit to Manning for Rome's final verdict favorable to the Knights.

Another important influence on the development of social Catholicism was the so-called Fribourg Union, which consisted of social Catholic leaders who met annually for a week from 1884 to 1891. Under the presidency of Mgr. Gaspar Mermillod (d. 1892), who became a cardinal in 1890, the participants pooled their ideas and experiences showing definite signs of the new spirit among Catholics in regard to the social question. They agreed on the need for state intervention, and the need for workers to have separate unions in opposition to the standard Catholic position which advocated joint unions of employer and worker; they also affirmed every person's right to work and to a living wage and called for insurance against sickness, accidents, and unemployment.

As Alec Vidler says, there emerged in the eighties what is no exaggeration to call a profound Catholic sociology, one that offered a powerful alternative to the other major ideologies of the day—economic liberalism or socialism.[5] It was this progressive Catholic social thought which Pope Leo XIII summarized and presented in his encyclical *Rerum Novarum* which he issued in 1891.

Against the socialists the encyclical insists on private property as a natural right and asserted that the family is the primary social unit, prior to the state, and also rejects class warfare as an inevitable necessity. Against the liberal capitalists it upheld the need of some state intervention to safeguard the spiritual and material interests of the worker. It asserted the right of the worker to a living wage, refusing to allow the right to be subordinated to the necessities of so-called economic laws. It defended the right of the worker to organize to protect his interests. Finally it emphasized the importance of religion in fostering relations of justice and charity among men.

The encyclical *Rerum Novarum* has been rightly called the Magna Carta of social Catholicism, since it summarized the best Catholic thought on the social question, brought the main issues into focus, and laid down the main lines that Catholic social thought would henceforth follow. It also challenged

---

[5] A. Vidler, *Social Catholicism* (London: S.P.C.K., 1964), p. 146.

Catholics to get involved in the struggle for social justice and reform of the social order.

Of course, the encyclical went unheeded by many Catholics. It did not stop the spread of Marxian socialism among the workers, but it did meet with considerable response. And it had significant influence on two of the most powerful manifestations of social Catholicism: the Christian trade unions and the Christian democratic parties.

These Christian trade unions were at first merely clubs for workers—often run by priests in paternalistic fashion and designed to provide certain basic services for the downtrodden workers. But in the 1880s numerous Christian trade unions arose that were run by the workers themselves. This was true of the German *Workers' Welfare Association* (1879) and the *Belgian Anti-Socialist League* (1878), and above all the *Belgian Democratic League* (1891), which was the immediate ancestor of the Christian Workers' movement and which quickly numbered eighty thousand members. In Holland the first congress of the Catholic Workers' movement held in 1895 drew together forty-nine representatives of Catholic local unions. Similar movements took place in Italy and in France.

A special movement for young workers was begun by a Flemish priest, Father Cardijn (later a cardinal), who founded the Young Christian Workers, or JOC, in 1912 in order to organize the working-class youth in the neighborhood of his parish in Brussels. It involved the members not only in purely trade union business but also in a comprehensive range of activities, including a high degree of religious practice. In spite of the great demands it made on the time and energies of its members, it proved very successful, and by 1925 it reached a membership of some twenty thousand. Since then it has dominated the Belgian Christian Youth movement and also became the model for a similar organization of French working youth. The JOC has shown a remarkable capacity for understanding the problems, adopting the language, and reaching the mind of the working class, and its militants have provided a vital link between the Church and the workers' world in the countries where it has taken root. A rally in July of 1974 drew forty thousand members to Versailles, where they reaffirmed their allegiance to Christ and to the struggle of the working class.

In spite of bitter opposition from the socialists, the leaders of the Christian trade unions refused to get bogged down in mere antisocialism. But while agreeing with the socialists that important changes were necessary in the capitalist order, they developed a positive program, which differed from that of the socialists on three main points: They emphasized the need for decentralization as opposed to socialist belief in state control. They favored what might be described as "collaboration through conflict—employer-worker collaboration was possible and indeed necessary, though it could become effective only if each party was ready and able to stand up for its own views and interests."[6] And finally, they insisted on the cultivation of individual personality as the goal, rather than the socialist tendency to subordinate the individual to the mass.

In the beginning the Christian trade unions were dependent on Church personnel and Church inspiration; in many cases their first organizers were priests. And even when they came of age, it was difficult for them to sever their links with the Church. The issue of their relation to the Church was finally hammered out in a grand debate centered in Holland and Germany, which led to a general agreement that Christian trade unions might be denominational, interdenominational, or even neutral, as in the United States, but that no Christian should join a union whose policies did not reflect the Christian point of view. In general a dual pattern emerged: In Belgium, Switzerland, and Holland, the link between churches and trade unions remain much closer than in Germany, France, and Italy.

The formation of the International Federation of Christian Trade Unions in 1920, with 3.5 million members, showed that the movement had reached considerable maturity. They still lagged far behind the socialists and communists, however. But after World War II the Christian trade unions began to increase rapidly. Now in Holland and Flanders they are larger than the other two major unions—the Communists and Social Democrats—while in France and Italy they outnumber the Social Democrats and have made considerable gains at the expense of the Communists. In the German-speaking countries, where the Social Democrats are strongest, the Christian trade unions rank ahead of the Communists.

The Christian Democratic parties developed in close connection with the Christian trade union movement. When these parties suddenly emerged in 1945 as the most powerful political force in Western Europe, many people were startled. But it was no surprise to those familiar with the history we have

---

[6] M. Fogarty, *Christian Democracy in Western Europe 1820–1953* (London: Routledge & Kegan Paul, 1957), p. 191.

been sketching here. The time had simply come for an idea that could be traced back to the rise of modern social Catholicism in the nineteenth century.

The Christian Democrat founding fathers were a number of bold and perspicacious Catholics in the 1890s who gave a new direction to Catholic social action by rejecting the traditional Catholic social medieval philosophy, which favored a hierarchical society, inequality of classes, and patronage of workers by the upper classes. Instead they wanted the workers to get more involved in the political and social decision-making process. They strove to organize the workers politically and obtain the vote for them so worker representatives could get elected to parliament to fight for legislation that would guarantee the right to bargain collectively and to obtain a living family wage and decent conditions of work.

The Belgian Catholics, here as in so many areas, led the way. Leaders of Christian Democratic persuasion were able to work within the established Catholic party—which dated back to 1869 and was strongly conservative—and gradually swing it over to its progressive views in spite of powerful opposition from the reactionaries. A whole series of progressive social reforms were carried out in Belgium, with the Catholic party playing a pivotal role: universal suffrage, housing policies, old-age pensions, eight-hour day, and protection for a union's right to organize.

It meant a lot for the future of the Church in Belgium that the Christian Democrats were thus able to identify the Church with the promotion of social justice and to give Catholicism a new image as a progressive social force. After the disruption of World War II, the Christian Democrats—now called the Social Christian party—has consistently shared control over the country with the Socialists.

The German Catholic Center party (1871) during the 1870s and 1880s acted defensively in accepting monarchism. Fear of the anticlericalism present in a potentially democratic state led it to concentrate on defending the rights of Catholics within the existing structure of the German Empire. It was not till the end of the century that the Christian trade unions and the Catholic workers' leagues could make their weight felt. By the 1920s the Center party could take considerable credit for the fact that in such matters as social insurance, factory regulations, and trade union protection, Germany was a world leader. After the Nazi interim, the Center was resurrected as the Christian Democratic Union under Konrad Adenauer's baton and with a heavy increment of Protestant membership. Like the other Christian Democratic parties in Europe it has been a major force in political life, and under Adenauer, Chancellor of West Germany (1949–63), it played a large role in integrating the Federal Republic into the Western European community of nations.

In some countries, notably Germany, Holland, and Belgium, the pioneer Christian Democrats at the turn of the century faced the problem of inserting a social and democratic element into a pre-existing Christian party. But in others, notably Italy and France, the strategy demanded attracting support from outside for a movement that started as Christian Democratic.

The Italian Christian Democratic party was only formally launched in 1919, when Pope Benedict XV agreed to relax ecclesiastical control over the whole complex of Catholic social organizations—trade unions, co-operatives, and friendly societies that had taken shape during the last decades of the nineteenth century. Under prompting by a Sicilian priest, Don Luigi Sturzo, who had long called for a socially progressive party of Christian inspiration, their leaders agreed to combine their forces into a new political party. Its first electoral test came in 1919, when it won 100 seats in parliament, securing 1 million votes as against 1.5 million for the Socialists. Like the German Catholic Center party, it hoped to be the pivot for all the democratic forces of society, but it was unable to stop Mussolini and his Fascists from gaining power. Much of the responsibility for their failure was due to Pius XI, who feared the Socialists more than the Fascists and who was too easily beguiled by Mussolini, who promised to resolve the conflicting papal and Italian claims to the city of Rome. Pius pulled the rug out from under Sturzo and his Christian Democrats when he denounced any possibility of a Catholic understanding with the Socialists. Vatican maneuvers subsequently brought about Sturzo's exile.

The Church at first compromised itself with the Fascist regime—but not fatally. Pius XI himself became increasingly hostile to Mussolini, and when the Fascist regime began to crumble, many of the leaders of the anti-German resistance turned out to be Catholics. It was these men who reconstituted the Christian Democratic party in 1945—this time with full backing from the Church. Since then the Italian Christian Democratic party has been the most powerful of Italy's political parties, regularly polling from 35 per cent to 40 per cent of the vote. Under Christian Democratic rule, postwar Italy developed into a world industrial power, and living standards and educational levels rose accordingly. But the elections of June 1976 showed that a sizable number of Italians no longer look to the Christian Democrats for further progress and are turning to the Communists. But the Christian Democrats still are in control of the government.

The last formed and least powerful of the Christian Democratic parties in Europe was the French Popular Democratic party, which first appeared on the scene in 1924. Its role during the resistance against Germany in World War II strengthened its appeal, and in 1944 it was reborn as the Popular Republican movement. In 1946 it polled 25 per cent of the popular vote—almost as much as the Communists—but when the youthful wing of the party showed itself really serious about reform in accordance with progressive social Catholic thought, the conservatives transferred their vote to De Gaulle.

By 1950 Christian Democratic parties held majorities or near majorities in the parliaments of Holland, Belgium, Luxembourg, Germany, Austria, and Italy and were substantially represented in those of France, Switzerland, and Norway. While still mainly a European movement it has also spread into underdeveloped Latin America. There it has manifested a leftward tendency, which has found its most able spokesman in Archbishop Helder Camara of Recife, Brazil. In Chile, the Falange Nacional, a party founded in 1938 on Neo-Thomist principles, evolved by 1957 into a Christian Democratic party, and under former President Eduardo Frei Montalva favored a policy of land reform, education, and other development programs for the masses. But the recent military takeover has indicated the difficulty that faces any Christian Democratic party tied to the middle class if it tries to espouse any radical social change.

The Popes have continued to issue encyclicals on social problems; these encyclicals reflect the evolving Catholic consensus and the trends and pressures of various interest groups within the Church. In the midst of the terrible worldwide Depression and to commemorate the fortieth anniversary of *Rerum Novarum*, Pius XI issued his encyclical *Quadragesimo Anno* in 1931. Together with his other pronouncements on social issues, it indicated how social Catholicism since Leo XIII had developed into a coherent social philosophy more than able to hold its own against its chief rivals, materialistic Marxism and materialistic liberal capitalism.

Various points touched on by Leo XIII were defined more precisely by Pius. He still recognized private property as a natural right but hedged it about with further limitations, condemning its arbitrary use and all superfluous accumulation. He also developed the concept of a salary not governed simply by economic laws but what he called a "living wage"—one that enabled a man to support his family in some comfort and also to put away savings.

In the light of the laissez-faire mentality dominant in his times, Leo felt it necessary to call for more state intervention. But Pius in an age of growing totalitarianism proposed, as a safeguard against tyranny, the principle of subsidiarity—meaning that the state or higher authority should leave to the lesser and subordinate organizations whatever they could competently handle. The state should see its main role as coordinating, planning, urging, and restraining the work of the lower bodies.

Pius took a comprehensive view of the whole social order, which he saw must be reconstructed in order to reflect the Gospel. The new social order he called for would be one pervaded by the spirit of justice and charity, one in which each person's rights would be recognized and safeguarded by institutions and structures built on "social justice"—a term he introduced into the Catholic vocabulary and made a key term of social Catholicism.

The Popes have continued to add to the social doctrine of the Church, and a vast corpus of papal statements on the social question now exist that have served to keep Catholic thought in touch with the accelerated developments of a revolutionary world. Pope John XXIII celebrated the seventieth anniversary of *Rerum Novarum* by issuing his *Mater et Magistra* (1961), which noted the important developments in Catholic social thought since the days of Leo. In *Pacem in Terris* (1963) he outlined the requisite conditions for peace among the nations. His successor, Paul VI, also made notable pronouncements on social matters. His *Populorum Progressio* focused attention on the problems of the underdeveloped countries and reminded the wealthier countries of their responsibilities in alleviating their poverty.

These papal announcements have been noteworthy for their increasingly acerbic criticism of capitalism, their increasing tendency to limit the right of private property in the light of its social function, their concern with the causes of poverty, their awareness of the oppressive social structures that perpetuate exploitation, their insistence on the right of the worker to bargain collectively, and their recognition of the need for government intervention. They have consistently reminded Catholics of their duty to engage in social action, and more recently have stressed the need for Catholics to enter into dialogue with all men in order to participate in building a more just social order. Likewise they have urged Catholics to give their support to international agencies that are working for a just world community, and they have called on all men to devote their best efforts to bring about total disarmament and to work for the immediate banning of nuclear weapons. They have also pointed out the necessity of putting limits on national sovereignty.

These documents show a gradual recognition of democracy as the form of government most in harmony with the innate dignity of man and the best guarantee of basic human rights. Their conceptual framework has been the basic moral norms and principles of the Catholic tradition: God as the foundation of the moral law and of all human authority, the obligation of authority to serve the common good, the family as the basic unity of society, the dignity of the human person, and the importance of truth, justice, and love as the basic norms of all human and social endeavor. The Second Vatican Council summed up the best fruits of social Catholicism in its statements, most notably in its constitution on the *Church in the Modern World,* where we find certain new emphases and advances in thought.

Chapter 29

THE MODERNIST DEBACLE

The Modernist crisis erupted in the Church with great suddenness. Like the debate over liberal Catholicism, the main issue was the quest for a new modus vivendi with the secular liberal culture. But the Modernists took a much more radical line and were even ready to call into question the very meaning of dogma and the traditional understanding of the Church's authority.

To understand the violence of the polemics and the bitterness aroused as well as the extreme measures taken against the Modernist dissenters by the authorities, it is well to keep in mind the general state of intellectual affairs in the Church at the end of the nineteenth century. As we have seen, Pius IX succeeded in putting down the liberal Catholic movement, and the First Vatican Council ratified his general policy of hostility to modern culture. At his death in 1878 the Church resembled a well-organized fortress prepared for a fight to the finish with the main cultural and political movements of the day.

During the pontificate of his successor, Leo XIII (1878–1903), it became evident how formidable were the intellectual challenges confronting Christian doctrine by reason of nineteenth-century scientific developments, in particular, those dealing with the historical study of the Bible and the origins of Christianity and the evolutionary view of man's origins associated with Darwin. Moreover, a philosophy of materialism—powerfully reinforced by Marxism and Darwinism—was also spreading and striking deep roots in men's minds. And although a large majority of Europeans still professed some form of Christianity, a significant minority repudiated it, and a large number were drifting away.

Pope Leo, who was a well-traveled curial diplomat before being made bishop of Perugia, was conscious of the crisis, and unlike the reactionary Pius

IX was anxious to reconcile the Church with modern life and culture as far as possible.

But Leo was definitely not a liberal Catholic. His views on religious liberty and the restoration of the Papal States were much closer to those of Pius IX than to those of the liberal Catholics. He was conservative and medieval in his outlook toward purely intellectual and theological issues. With his help the Neo-Scholastic movement triumphed completely, and he issued an encyclical, *Aeterni Patris,* which exalted St. Thomas and proposed his teachings as the very touchstone of Catholic orthodoxy. Thomism interpreted in the most narrow and unhistorical way took possession of all the chairs and schools of Rome and from there conquered the rest of Catholic academia.

But as Leo's pontificate wore on, a small but growing number of Catholic scholars began to feel that the restoration of medieval Scholasticism was not the answer; the Neo-Thomist synthesis, as marvelous as it was for its own times, was simply not broad enough to deal with the manifold problems raised for the Catholic faith by the developments of modern culture. They were especially concerned with the general ignorance of historical method manifested by the leading Neo-Thomists. Following in the footsteps of Doellinger and Acton, they broke out of the narrow mold of Scholasticism and searched for ways of expressing their Catholic faith that would make sense to the modern mind. They professed fidelity to the spirit of Thomas rather than the letter. They were all later to be lumped under the pejorative epithet "Modernist," but they were actually never anything but a loose coalition of scholars linked together only by their somewhat vague aspiration of narrowing the gap between Catholicism and modern culture.

In spite of Leo's own narrow Thomism, they were encouraged by the general impression he gave of openness to modern culture and by a number of moves he made: making Newman a cardinal, opening the Vatican archives to historians, issuing progressive encyclicals on social reform, and calling on French Catholics to accept the republic.

Their leaders were a relatively small group of brilliant scholars active in many fields: the French priests Duchesne, Loisy, and Laberthonnière in Church history, biblical exegesis, and philosophy, respectively; the Italian priests Genocchi, Minocchi, and Semeria in biblical exegesis; the English Jesuit Tyrrell and the French layman Blondel, both in philosophy; the Italian novelist Fogazzaro; and the English layman Von Hugel—who was a kind of jack of all trades. The only two members of the hierarchy prominently identified with them were Archbishop Mignot of Albi and Bishop Lacroix of Tarentaise.

In spite of their wide diversity of interests and occupations, they all shared certain things in common: a deep commitment to historical and critical methods, which they felt could rejuvenate theology and contribute to a general renewal of religious life in the Church; an aversion to Scholasticism and Thomism; an extreme sensitivity to authoritarianism, especially the papal brand and to any infringement on the freedom and independence of their respective sciences. On the negative side, they were no doubt excessively influenced by the prevailing positivism and were inclined to ascribe certitude too hastily to the untested conclusions of research. Nor did they reckon realistically enough with the profound conservatism of their fellow Catholics as regards traditional religious forms.

The mentality of their opponents offered a striking contrast. They were Scholastics—generally ignorant of the historical and critical methods of research, medievalists who put no faith in the conclusions of modern science, seeing in them only the work of a destructive and skeptical rationalism. The idea of a personal conquest of the truth—so dear to the Modernists—was to them mere pride and folly. One's only salvation, they held, lay in absolute obedience to the Church. Even some of their best representatives, such as the outstanding professors Louis Billot, Orazio Mazzella, and Salvatore Talamo, were hindered by grave limitations in their methods, by arid formalism, abuse of the argument from authority, an inadequate knowledge of modern philosophy, and almost complete lack of historical sense.

It was the conflict of these two viewpoints that provoked the Modernist crisis.

Though the issues ranged far and wide, the real focus of the controversy was in the field of biblical studies. It was there that the discrepancy between Catholic dogma and modern science seemed most critical from the Modernist standpoint. To understand this we must realize what tremendous strides were made by the critico-historical study of the Bible during the second half of the nineteenth century, where, as in other fields of historical research, German scholars led the way. One of the most notable was Julius Wellhausen, who definitively proved that Moses did not write the Pentateuch, as tradition claimed. Studies like his brought into focus the human and relative side of the

Scriptures, showing the discrepancies between biblical assertions and proven historical and scientific fact—thus challenging the traditional Christian concept of biblical infallibility.

This challenge was keenly felt by a number of Catholic biblical scholars, including even the octogenarian Newman. Anxious to reconcile the idea of error in the Bible with the dogma of its divine inspiration, they came up with a number of novel hypotheses. The most daring appeared to be those of a French priest, Alfred Loisy (1857–1940), whose lectures at the newly founded Institut Catholique in Paris were profoundly disturbing to tradition-minded Catholics. As he said in a summary of his ideas at the time:

> The Pentateuch, in its present form cannot be the work of Moses. The first chapters of Genesis do not contain an exact and reliable account of the beginnings of mankind. . . . All the historical books of the Bible, including those of the New Testament were composed in a looser manner than modern historical writing, and a certain freedom of interpretation follows. . . . We have to concede a real development in the religious doctrine contained in Scripture.[1]

The Pope was himself gravely disturbed by what he saw as a dangerous penchant for novelties among Catholic scholars, and he decided to call a halt. This came in his encyclical *Providentissimus Deus* (1893)—a sore blow to the progressives, for they felt it reflected little understanding of the really crucial problems facing Catholic scholarship. It ruled out any possibility of error in the Bible and urged Catholic scholars to take as their unerring guides the ancient Fathers, the Scholastic theologians, and above all St. Thomas.

Nevertheless, Leo did not close all doors. His Secretary of State, Cardinal Rampolla, was liberal in tendency and was able to maintain a certain spirit of tolerance in the Curia toward critical scholarship. So when Leo announced the creation of a pontifical biblical commission in 1902, the Modernists regarded it as a good omen. But their hopes were dashed when its membership was revealed: The forty names included an overwhelming preponderance of Scholastic, noncritical scholars. "A victory for the other side," Von Hugel groaned.

---

[1] Alfred Loisy, *My Duel with the Vatican* (New York: E. P. Dutton, 1924), pp. 148–49.

Nevertheless, Loisy went ahead with his studies, and in 1903 he published his *L'Évangile et l'Église* (The Gospel and the Church), a book that quickly achieved fame or infamy as the chief manifesto of Modernism. It was composed during the leisure imposed on him by Church authorities, who removed him from his post at the Institut Catholique. It was ostensibly a refutation of the German historian Adolf Harnack (d. 1930), whose book *The Essence of Christianity* presented Jesus as a kind of nineteenth-century liberal reformer preaching a nondogmatic religion based on the brotherhood of man and the fatherhood of God. But in fact, Loisy's actual intention was to use Harnack merely as a springboard to present a full-scale reinterpretation of the Catholic faith—one that involved major modifications of its traditional dogmas.

Loisy argued that critical historical science demanded that the Chalcedonian Christ who was God and man must be discarded and replaced by a Jesus who was only a prophet with a unique consciousness of being God's Messiah to announce the imminent end of the world; the founder of the Church and its sacraments would have to be replaced by a historical figure who died with no thought of a Church succeeding him and certainly with no intention of providing it with sacraments. The Church itself therefore only originated when the kingdom predicted by Jesus failed to arrive; its hierarchical structure centered on the Roman primacy did not come from Jesus but was invented under the pressure of historical circumstance. In sum, its dogmas must be regarded not as fixed, unchangeable truths but as attempts to summarize its experience.

As to how such enormous changes could be reconciled with the need for continuity so essential to the Catholic self-understanding, Loisy offered only some rather vague and confusing answers. From the very beginning, he argued, the Church did not preach an unchanging absolute doctrine but a message of hope embodied first in the symbol of God's kingdom and subsequently in the visible society, the Church. Moreover, he insisted that the identity of the religious object or fact is unchanging and so provides a principle of continuity; nor will the historical facts, once accurately established, be modified. Another of his favorite concepts was "vitality": The necessities of life dictated the true forms of true religion, and so the developments of Catholicism were true, since they were caused by these vital necessities. He also made use of concepts like "the Christian conscience" as a means of affirming "continuity between Roman structures and dogmas and their shadowy antecedents in Jesus and the gospels."[2] Much to Loisy's surprise, the book stirred up a tremendous storm, especially in France, where it was condemned by the archbishop of Paris and, together with several other of his works, was put on the *Index*.

At the same time, other Catholic scholars of Modernist bent were busy postulating novel theories in other fields, which at first view seemed at variance with Catholic tradition. There was, for example, the French philosopher Maurice Blondel (d. 1949), who was busy trying to find an audience for his non-Scholastic philosophy of immanence, which took as its starting point not the objective supernatural revealed order but the subjective religious needs of man in order hopefully to lead the modern unbeliever to recognize that his very nature required the supernatural. His friend Lucien Laberthonnière (d. 1932), an Oratorian priest, elaborated a novel view of dogmas, which he saw not as mysterious enigmatic formulas devised by God to humble man but rather as truths whose validity was proven by their value for the moral life. He regarded Thomas Aquinas as almost a total disaster for the Church and was almost fanatically hostile to the whole Aristotelian-Thomistic tradition. In his view its attempt to combine Greek idealism and Christian thought was foredoomed—the two being absolutely incompatible, since Greek idealism was abstract, static, impersonal, and individualistic, while Christian realism was concrete, dynamic, personal, and social.[3]

Another French priest, Louis Duchesne (d. 1922), a Church historian, was busy renovating his field by a peculiarly sharp and critical attitude toward ecclesiastical legends. Other lesser lights were also engaged in the same enterprise of intellectual renewal in the Church, particularly in England, France, and Italy.

Outstanding for various reasons was the English Jesuit George Tyrrell (d. 1909), journalist, preacher, spiritual director, and scintillating stylist. Converted to the Church in his early youth, he entered the Society of Jesus and was eventually appointed to teach Scholastic philosophy at Stonyhurst. But a study of Newman and a friendship with Blondel caused him to break with Scholastic categories of thought, which he felt had turned Catholicism into an abstract, dry intellectual system.

For Tyrrell revelation could not be identified with a series of propositions

---

[2] W. J. Wernz, "Loisy's 'Modernist' Writings," *Downside Review* (January 1974), p. 32.
[3] A. Vidler, *A Variety of Catholic Modernists* (Cambridge, England: Cambridge University Press, 1970), p. 85.

but was primarily an experience of the divine grounded in the absolute imperatives of the conscience. The God whom men experience in this way had his supreme manifestation in Jesus Christ. The dogmatic formulas of the Church were merely attempts to conceptualize and formulate the actual revealed truth in the thought patterns of the time. Hence a dogmatic formula of one age might even contradict the dogmatic formula of another time—at least verbally.

Like many Modernists, Tyrrell saw the authoritarian methods of Pius X as a terrible abuse of Church authority; he wanted a democratic Church whose officials were to be only the spokesmen of the evolving community consensus. His idea of infallibility anticipated the one held currently by many liberal Catholics: "It really means that the Church is infallibly moving through tortuous paths to the right end, even when her back is turned to the goal."[4] Tyrrell's daring speculations touching the very nerve center of Catholic dogma were bound to alarm authorities, and he soon found his position as a Jesuit untenable.

In time the hierarchy reacted with increasing vigor. To understand their predicament, one has to keep in mind the importance and number of the problems being raised; the haste, lack of wisdom, and imprudence of many Modernists; the mere urge to destroy on the part of some; and the fear the bishops felt of the impact of all of this, especially on the more impressionable younger clergy. After the condemnation of Loisy, other condemnations followed. Laberthomière, Fogazzaro, and Tyrrell all felt the sting of the lash. A decree of the biblical commission of 1906 affirmed that Catholics must hold that Moses was the author of the entire Pentateuch—a decision that Von Hugel interpreted as another victory for the "neo-Scholastic utterly unhistorical, uncritical minds" in Rome.[5]

Finally, by the spring of 1907, observers felt it would be only a matter of time before Rome issued a general condemnation of the new ideas. This happened when the decree *Lamentabili* of the Holy Office appeared on July 3, 1907, condemning a list of sixty-five errors—at least half of them drawn from Loisy's writings and the others from a wide assortment of Catholic theologians, Tyrrell in particular. It was followed shortly afterward, on September 8, 1907, by the encyclical *Pascendi.*

[4] L. Barmann, *Baron Friedrich von Hügel and the Modernist Crisis in England* (Cambridge, England: Cambridge University Press, 1972), p. 148.
[5] Ibid., p. 132.

Among the errors condemned in *Lamentabili* were: that the Jesus of history was much inferior to the Christ of faith; that his knowledge was limited; that he did not always have consciousness of his Messianic dignity; that he could have been in error; that he did not institute the Church and the sacraments; that his resurrection was not a fact of the historical order; and that the Roman primacy was not of divine origin. Perhaps the heart of the whole decree was the last error, No. 65: that modern Catholicism cannot be reconciled with true science unless it is transformed into some kind of non-dogmatic Christianity. It was the main reason for Rome's objection to the whole movement.

Pascendi represents a debatable attempt to systematize the inherently unsystematic thought of the Modernists. It found their unity in certain false philosophical premises that they supposedly held in common: immanentism—which asserts that man's religious experience begins with awareness of an interior religious need; agnosticism—or the denial that we can know anything beyond changing phenomena; symbolism—whereby dogmas and sacraments of the Church are true only insofar as they spring from, foster, and nourish one's religious sense, or, in other words, insofar as they are merely an objectification of the individual's subjective religious needs; evolutionism—denoted as "practically their principal doctrine" and defined to mean that everything—dogma, Church, worship, sacred books, even faith itself—is liable to substantial change.

The composite picture given here of Modernism is no doubt artificial, but even Loisy and Tyrrell grudgingly admitted that it did spotlight their main ideas. But much about the circumstances of the encyclical and its wording does seem regrettable. It presumes bad faith and imputes evil motives to zealous Catholic scholars who were at least asking the right questions, and it presents a sad spectacle of the highest authority in the Church resorting to sarcasm and invective in what was supposed to be a magisterial judgment; it abounds in such harsh phrases as "poisonous doctrines . . . most pernicious of all the adversaries of the Church . . . the root of their folly and error . . . boundless effrontery . . ."

To extirpate Modernism, the Pope called for measures that smacked of the worst features of the medieval Inquisition. Vigilance committees were to be set up in every diocese to detect any sign of Modernist doctrines. In addition, each diocese was to have a body of censors who were to watch over all literature in any way connected with the Church. These agencies were to observe strict secrecy in all their proceedings. Seminarians were to be indoctrinated in the Scholastic system—in its Thomist form—as the basis of all sacred studies. And finally, all priests and teachers were required to take an oath against Modernism.

A coin struck on June 29, 1908, to commemorate the fifth anniversary of Pius X's pontificate bore a fitting emblem—it showed him in the act of slaying the Modernist dragon. And slay it he did. Under pressure of the measures he applied, the Modernist movement simply collapsed. A few sporadic efforts were made to rally its spokesmen to lead a resistance movement within the Church, but their number was not significant, nor could it be—since those attached to Modernist ideas never formed more than a small minority. Tyrrell denounced *Pascendi* in the columns of the London *Times* and was excommunicated; he died the following year without formal reconciliation. Loisy suffered a similar fate, but unlike Tyrrell regarded it as a blessing and died peacefully thirty years later outside the Church. A few of the other leaders left the Church to the accompaniment of crashing cymbals and flashing fireworks, but the rest submitted with more or less grace.

The thrust of the encyclical was so vague and broad that almost anyone could be accused of Modernism except authors of Scholastic textbooks. This, coupled with its violent tone and the extreme measures of repression it called for, brought on a veritable reign of terror in the Church by self-appointed inquisitors. Most notorious of these integralists—as they called themselves—was Monsignor Umberto Benigni, a prelate working under Cardinal Merry del Val in the Secretariat of State. With the latter's aid and support and with the blessing of Pius X himself, he set up a society (the *Sodalitum Pianum*). It eventually included a network of spies who had important connections in leading Catholic dioceses and who kept their activities covert by the use of a fantastic secret code. They regularly engaged in personal attacks, via the columns of Catholic journals, on suspect Modernists whose names, in consequence, were often placed on blacklists drawn up by their enemies and sent to Rome. Any Catholic who showed lukewarmness toward Scholasticism or favored such initiatives as Christian democracy or ecumenism might suddenly find himself the target of their venom. No one, however high his rank in the Church, was safe if he aroused their suspicions.

Cardinal Mercier himself was on their blacklist. And many personal tragedies occurred when their victims were driven from their offices and teaching posts and even from the priesthood itself. The excesses of Benigni and his ilk were only brought to an end when Benedict XV became Pope in 1914.

Modernism was indeed successfully stamped out, but at a tremendous price; the Catholic intelligence was inoculated against error, but the dosage was almost fatal. The liberal Catholic movement suffered another grave setback, and social Catholicism lost a decade of valuable time. Many of the Church's most brilliant thinkers were silenced or driven out of theology and into a kind of spiritual schizophrenia. Catholic seminaries remained medieval ghettos until the middle of the twentieth century, and future priests were taught a biblical fundamentalism embroidered with theories like the one that proved that Jonah could have lived inside the whale, since a French scholar had found toads that lived inside stones for thousands of years.

As one familiar with history knows, a crisis not resolved is a crisis postponed and destined to erupt again with greater violence. One wonders if a less hysterical and more historical approach to Modernist errors might not have proven wiser in the long run. What was of value in liberal thought might then have been sifted out in leisurely fashion and assimilated, and the Church spared the trauma it now suffers with the sudden reappearance of the questions first raised by the Modernists.

On the other hand, one might justify the severity of the hierarchy by admitting that their primary responsibility was not to history but to millions of souls who knew nothing about Wellhausen and whose faith would have been gravely disturbed if the speculations of a Tyrrell or a Loisy became common currency in its pulpits. And, it must be added, some of the Modernists engaged in systematic deceit by using pseudonyms and ambiguous formulas to cloak their radical rejection of the traditional faith in order to stay in the Church and subvert it from within.

But whoever deserves the most blame, the Modernist crisis was a catastrophe for the Church. It led to an intellectual sterility that still weighs heavily on its life and caused a cultural lag that was most apparent in Italy itself, where the long arm of the Curia made the repression most severe. The Italian clergy were completely isolated from university life in their country, and even at Rome, ecclesiastical standards of scholarship fell very low.

Chapter 30

THE CHURCH MOVES OUT TO
THE WHOLE WORLD

After the great missionary expansion of the period of Catholic renewal of the sixteenth and seventeenth centuries, there followed a great decline in the eighteenth; the general spiritual debility of the Church during the Age of Reason was clearly reflected in the mission fields, where the work of the great pioneers Xavier, Ricci, and others in Asia was almost completely undone and where for the most part it was necessary to begin all over again.

The spiritual revival of the Catholic Church during the nineteenth century found an important outlet in missionary zeal, and a whole new period of the missions began. Historians generally give Pope Gregory XVI (1831–46) the credit for inaugurating this new epoch. Of great importance here was the remarkable revival of religious orders of men and of women—many of them dedicated to missionary work. They included the rejuvenated old orders such as Jesuits, Franciscans, and Dominicans as well as new ones like the Scheut Fathers (1862), the White Fathers (1868), and the Mill Hill Fathers.

A comparable awakening of missionary zeal also stirred among the Protestants. From 1792 numerous Protestant missionary societies were founded, the London Missionary Society (1795) being one of the most important.

Gregory XVI looked on India as one of the most promising mission fields, which though fallen on hard times still remained intact—unlike Japan and China—and where Goa still remained a flourishing Catholic community. He nominated four vicars apostolic to supervise the new missionary effort. The work continued to thrive under Pio Nono, who was also an outstanding missionary Pope and who was able to establish Catholic missionaries in al-most every part of the world. Under Leo XIII's pontificate there were twenty bishops in India. The Jesuits founded numerous colleges and began the prepa-ration of an intellectual elite.

Since then the Church has been able to make substantial progress in this vast subcontinent, which since 1947 has been divided into predominantly Hindu India and predominantly Moslem Pakistan (and with the addition of Bangladesh in 1971). By 1958 a large percentage of the clergy and religious (about 75 per cent) were native Indians, including forty-five of seventy-seven bishops. By 1962 Catholics numbered some six million, with the large ma-jority of them concentrated south of an imaginary line drawn between Goa and Madras. An impressive network of institutions—colleges, schools, hospi-tals, and homes for the aged, made it possible for the Church to reach out beyond its own confines and to influence considerably the general life of India. Mother Teresa, founder of the Missionaries of Charity, won worldwide renown for her work in the slums of Calcutta.

China, the most populous of all the countries in the world and the cen-ter of a civilization that at one time rivaled the Roman in wealth, culture, and size, exerted a special fascination on missioners. Ricci and others, as we have seen, made considerable headway in the seventeenth century, but most of the gains were lost during the eighteenth. But a revival of missionary activity—both Protestant and Catholic—began toward the middle of the nineteenth century, and by 1890 some 500,000 baptized Catholics could be counted, in-cluding 369 Chinese priests.

A period of great turmoil began with the invasion of China by the colo-nial powers, who opened it to their merchants and soldiers and divided it into their respective spheres. There followed China's humiliating defeat by the Japanese in the 1890s, the Boxer Rebellion, and China's division into spheres of influence by the Western powers. The fabric of the old Chinese culture and tradition was torn apart, and the Confucian monarchy, which had ruled China for centuries, was replaced by a Western-style republican form of gov-ernment. China was brutally kicked into the twentieth century.

All of this was accompanied, as might be expected, by a great weakening of the traditional religions: Confucianism, Buddhism, Taoism, and polythe-ism. A unique opportunity seemed at hand for Christianity as many of the spiritually uprooted seemed willing to listen to the message of the Gospel. And rapid advances were made by both the Roman Catholics and the Protestants. The Roman Catholics numbered nearly two million by 1922 and showed a significant increase in native clergy.

But after 1922 a strong anti-Christian movement began to take hold; Christianity was denounced as a tool of imperialism, and religion itself was depicted as obsolete by the militant Communists, who under Mao Tse-tung were fashioning a powerful, disciplined party.

Nevertheless, until the Japanese invasion of 1937, the Church continued to grow and had reached nearly three million members. There was a growing awareness of the need to develop a native clergy, thanks in particular to the efforts of Père Lebbe (d. 1940), a Belgian missionary who made it his aim in life to bring about a radical change in missionary methods. Coming to China in the spring of 1901, right after the Boxer Rebellion, he was shocked by the attitudes of the missionaries. European and Chinese priests ate at separate tables; few of his colleagues knew Chinese well, and some could not even read it. The Chinese seminarians were given inferior courses to keep them humble. The faithful had to kneel when greeting a missionary and were not permitted to sit in his presence. Prospective converts were enticed to instructions by gifts of food or money.

Lebbe campaigned strenuously to change such practices and also insisted that missionaries dissociate themselves from all foreign governments. In 1919 he had the satisfaction of seeing most of his ideas incorporated into Benedict XV's revolutionary missionary encyclical *Maximum Illud,* which laid down three fundamental principles: promotion of a native clergy, renunciation of all nationalistic attitudes, and respect for the civilization of the mission country. Lebbe also had the happiness of seeing Pius XI consecrate six Chinese bishops in 1926.

At the end of World War II the Church looked forward to a promising era of opportunity. The number of priests had more than doubled, and the hierarchy now embraced twenty archdioceses and seventy-nine dioceses and included a newly made cardinal, Thomas Tien, the archbishop of Peking. Catholics operated several universities and numerous colleges, lower-level schools, orphanages, and homes for the aged. Though Christians, both Protestant and Catholic, still did not constitute even 1 per cent of the population, Christianity was beginning to exert a significant influence.

The Communist conquest of China, however, which was completed by 1950, brought on a tremendous trial for all Christians. They were accused of being tools of Western imperialism, a charge unfortunately justified to some extent by the history of the Christian missions. All foreign missionaries were either expelled or imprisoned—often after cruel and farcical "public trials."

The Communist strategy was to completely detach the Chinese Catholics from any foreign ties. A Catholic Patriotic Church, completely independent from Rome, was set up, and its hierarchy was initiated with the consecration of two Chinese priests in 1958 by four legitimate Roman Catholic bishops. With the almost complete blackout of information, it is difficult at present to judge the success of this effort, though it is estimated that by 1962 some forty-two bishops were illicitly consecrated, and recent Vatican reports say that the Roman Catholic Church in China has been virtually wiped out.

Next we turn to Japan, where the history of the missions has been an amazing saga of heroism since the first Christian gospel preached by Francis Xavier in 1549. For nearly a century the Church made great progress through

Francis Xavier. Anthony van Dyck (1599–1641). Pinacoteca, Vatican Museums, Vatican.   © *Scala/Art Resource, New York.*

the work of the Franciscans and Jesuits in spite of sporadic persecutions. But in 1638 the Shogun Hideyoshi decided to exterminate Christianity. When the Christians of Shimbara revolted, some thirty-five thousand of them were massacred. Some of the victims were subjected to the intolerable torture of the pit: hung upside down suspended in a hole in the ground and kept in agony for days by torturers who bled them slowly from their temples. There were many martyrs and many apostates, until finally all signs of Christianity were obliterated. Japan was sealed off from all foreign contacts for two centuries.

It was the United States that opened up a new era of the missions when Commodore Perry appeared with a naval squadron in Edo Bay in 1853 and signed a treaty of commerce and friendship with the Shogun in 1854. A year later, Catholic missionaries from Paris entered Japan and began evangelizing anew. Then an amazing thing happened: A small band of Japanese visited the little mission chapel at Nagasaki and caught the eye of Father, later Bishop, Petitjean, by their unusually pious demeanor. Conversing with them, he was dumbfounded to learn that they were believing Christians who had secretly managed to hold onto the essentials of the Christian faith for two centuries, although without priests and totally isolated from the outside world. Other groups of these crypto-Christians were gradually discovered scattered in the islands and mountains around Nagasaki—numbering in all some ten thousand. Their organization was almost everywhere the same: Usually there were two male leaders who conducted the prayers every Sunday, baptized, and ministered consolation to the dying.

When news of this reached the ears of the Japanese authorities, they reacted with fury, for Christianity was still a proscribed religion. They meted out cruel punishment to these heroic believers, some of whom died, while others went into exile.

World opinion stirred up by press reports, however, finally brought an end to the persecution, and in 1889, complete freedom of worship was granted in the new constitution. Missionaries were able to proceed with the slow work of individual conversion, and by 1891, when Leo XIII set up a Japanese hierarchy with the metropolis at Tokyo, there were some 45,000 Catholics.

Progress during the twentieth century for both Protestants and Catholics was slow but steady. The first native bishop was consecrated by Pius XI in 1927 and placed over the diocese of Nagasaki. By 1936 Catholics totaled some 108,000. A Japanese was appointed archbishop of Tokyo in 1937. The

Jesuit college, Sophia, became a full-fledged university. In 1940 the entire episcopate was handed over to native Japanese, and at the outbreak of World War II, Catholic membership stood at 121,000.

World War II brought many difficulties. All foreign missionaries were interned. Many churches were laid waste by the air raids, and in Nagasaki alone about 8,500 Catholics—the nucleus of the oldest Catholic community—perished in the nuclear holocaust.

The end of the war left Japan in a state of complete economic and moral collapse. The official state religion, Shinto, was abolished, and many disillusioned Japanese seemed ready to turn to the Christian religion. Some observers predicted a great wave of conversions. While these hopes proved unrealistic when reconstruction took priority and the Japanese became obsessed with their economic miracle, still the pace of conversions was accelerated. An estimate in 1973 counted some 359,000 Catholics and almost twice that number of Protestants. The number of Japanese priests (almost four hundred) had more than doubled since 1949. There was also a good increase in the number of schools, hospitals, and charitable institutions run by Catholic sisters and lay brothers, the majority of whom were Japanese.

Elsewhere in Asia, missionaries have planted flourishing Christian communities.

In Korea, Christianity experienced a phenomenal growth in the decade immediately following the war (1950–53) as foreign missionaries from Europe, the United States, and Mexico poured in. A number of the native Koreans who studied abroad—including quite a few priests—returned with advanced ideas on social reform, to become a thorn in the side of the authoritarian Park regime. One of the most prominent Catholic spokesmen for social justice has been the bishop of Won Ju, Tji Hak Soun, who was recently arrested in connection with a demonstration of dissent. His conviction and sentencing to fifteen years' imprisonment has created grave tension between the government and the 800,000 Catholics.

Remarkable success has also attended missionary efforts in Indonesia, especially since the overthrow of the Sukarno government by General Suharto in 1966. A recent figure has 7 million Protestants and 5 million Catholics—nearly 10 per cent of the country's total population. The Catholic Church has considerable strength among the intellectual and economic elite, and the largest daily newspaper is run by Catholics.

There are also communities of at least 100,000 Catholics in Pakistan,

Taiwan, Hong Kong, Ceylon, Malaysia, Burma, and Thailand. In Vietnam Catholics constitute 1.5 million out of 42.6 million.

All told, Catholics number over 48 million in Asia, but 32 million of these are found in the Philippines. In sum, the Church is hardly more than a presence and constitutes only 2.5 per cent of the total Asian population.

Finally, we take up the mission story of Africa, which is one of incredible success during the past century.

Christian missionary action in Africa practically ceased during the Age of Enlightenment. A few attempts were made at the end of the Napoleonic Age to set up missions along the coast, but with little reward. Then came the penetration of the interior of Africa in 1849 by the Protestant missionary David Livingstone (d. 1873), who proved that a white man could survive there. His experience aroused the interest of both Protestants and Catholics in the possibilities for Christianity in the vast area south of the Sahara.

The most important mover and shaker on the Catholic side was the fiery Lavigerie (d. 1892), former bishop of Nancy, who as archbishop of Algiers hoped to make it the base for the conversion of the entire continent. With this grandiose scheme in mind he founded the Society of Missionaries of

David Livingstone (1813–1873), English explorer and missionary in Africa. Anonymous.   © *Art Resource, New York.*

Africa, or White Fathers, in 1868. Unable to make any headway in the face of Moslem fanaticism, he turned gladly to the new vistas opened up by Livingstone and sent his men in 1879 into equatorial Uganda, where Protestant missionaries had already begun work. The hardships and dangers they had to face were atrocious: sudden death in the bush, savage men and savage animals, unbearable heat, treacherous guides and porters, and frequent sickness.

The King of Uganda, Mutesa, a handsome, proud monarch whose only concern was to keep the foreigners at bay, played Protestants, Catholics, and Moslems against each other in a subtle game of intrigue. His successor, Mwanga, at first showed favor to Catholic missionaries but soon proved to be a bloodthirsty tyrant and burned alive twenty-two Catholics and eleven Protestants for refusing to indulge his homosexual lust. The Uganda martyrs were recently canonized.

But the missionaries made real progress and found the ordinary African quite receptive to the Gospel. The Baganda or Ugandans were a simple, happy people, loquacious, fond of tall stories, interminably social, and vastly interested in everything. They would crowd into the missionary's hut and stay until he finally had to chase them away. By the time of World War I the White Fathers and their Mill Hill colleagues could count nearly 150,000 converts.

As marvelous as the success of the mission effort in Uganda, it is eclipsed by the achievement in the former Belgian Congo, now Zaïre, which by reason of its size (the largest political unit south of the Sahara) and its mineral wealth will undoubtedly play a big role in the future of Africa. It was allotted to the Belgians when Africa was carved up by the European powers in the 1880s. Catholic missionaries, who enjoyed the special favor of the Belgian Government, made much progress—the White Fathers leading the way here, as in Uganda. By 1959 Catholics numbered about 36 per cent of the population and, with Protestants added, constituted a Christian portion that represented about half of the population. Native Congolese priests totaled about 400.

Situated on the eastern border of the Congo, Rwanda and Burundi (formerly Rwanda-Yrundi, a single political unit) provide another example of spectacular gains. They too were opened up for Catholicism by the White Fathers. About half of their populations are now Christian, the overwhelming majority Roman Catholic.

Phenomenal gains have been made in the East African countries of Kenya, Malawi, Tanzania, Uganda, and the South African country of Zambia, according to a recent report of their bishops. Between 1949 and 1974 the number of Catholics in the five countries, whose total population now stands at 45 million, rose from just above 2.5 million to 9.93 million—a 290 per cent increase. African vocations have likewise made spectacular progress. Thus the number of priests rose from 280 to 1,159; bishops, from 1 to 45; nuns, from 1,396 to 4,844; and brothers, from 0 to 405.

East and west of Zambia lie Mozambique and Angola. With help from Portugal, the Catholic missions made good strides in Angola, so that Christians, including the much smaller body of Protestants, constitute around a fourth of the country's population, though in Mozambique the advance has been much slower.

South Africa, under the dominance of Boers and Britons, has not been a promising mission field for the Catholic Church, and it has remained a small minority. However, in Lesotho (formerly Basutoland) it has penetrated very deeply into the tribes there, so that by 1960 it claimed 41 per cent of the population.

The final area outside of the Moslem belt is West Africa, where over 62 million Nigerians make up the largest population bloc in Africa, by nation, south of the Sahara. Here the Christian community is sizable, and the missions, both Protestant and Catholic, for a long time provided nearly all the education available; as late as 1961, the large majority of the children received their elementary education in Church or mission school, while almost all who moved to higher education in Nigeria itself studied in Christian schools and universities. As a result, most of the Nigerian political leaders who have lately come to the fore are at least nominal Christians.

According to some calculations, black Africa will be 57 per cent Christian by the year 2000, and in Africa as a whole, Christians (175 million Catholics, 176 million Protestants) will surpass the 326 million Moslems. But while conversions continue at a good pace and Africa seems well on the way to becoming a Christian continent, there is no excuse for complacency. The Church in Africa faces some severe problems. Islam remains a persistent adversary, and its adherents are on the increase. Another threat to African Christianity stems from the failure of the missionaries to accord sufficient importance to African culture and traditions. Christianity was preached in an exclusively Western form and identified with European culture. This caused the alienation of many Africans who have concocted their own hybrid forms of Christianity in a wild array of sects. The Second Vatican Council at least took cognizance of this situation, and in its document on the missions, *Ad Gentes,* it called for a complete rooting out of all vestiges of Christian cultural imperialism. Finally, there is also danger from the considerable increase in materialism and skepticism, the almost inevitable concomitants, as experience elsewhere suggests, of industrialization and urbanization.

Chapter 31

THE AMERICAN CHURCH

No missionary territory in the nineteenth century registered more sensational gains than the Catholic Church in the United States. Thanks to a massive influx of Catholic immigrants—Irish, German, Italians, Poles, and others—the growth of the Catholic Church far outstripped the nation's growth. The American bishops were able to successfully integrate these heterogeneous, polyglot newcomers into the Church structure and provide a huge network of schools, hospitals, and other institutions for them that were soon the envy of the Catholic world.

THOSE WHO FIRST planted the Catholic Church in North America—outside the original thirteen colonies but within the present boundaries of the United States—were bands of Jesuit, Franciscan, Capuchin, Recollet, and other missionaries. Moved by tremendous zeal to save the souls of the Native Americans, they suffered every form of hardship, even torture and death, to build their little churches and gather around them the nucleus of a Catholic parish. The Franciscan Junípero Serra and the Jesuit Father Eusebio Kino are the most famous of the hundreds of priests who evangelized the Native Americans in the vast Spanish territory stretching from Florida to California. They taught them the arts of civilization as well, and left souvenirs of their labors in names like San Francisco, San Antonio, and Los Angeles.

Northward lay the huge French area, which also drew many Catholic missionaries, Jesuit, Capuchin, Recollet, and others. The Jesuit Père Jacques Marquette, discoverer of the Mississippi, and the Jesuit martyrs Isaac Jogues, Jean de Brébeuf, and their companions were among the many who ministered to the spiritual and temporal needs of the Hurons and other Indian tribes. The missionaries also helped establish French Catholic outposts on the Great Lakes and down through the Ohio and Mississippi valleys, a chapter in Catholic history that is recalled by names like Detroit, St. Louis, Vincennes, Louisville, and Marietta.

Within the thirteen English colonies, Catholics faced a different type of situation. Like the Puritans and Quakers, the English Catholics had come to America to escape persecution. The opportunity to do so was afforded them by their coreligionists, George Calvert, the first Baron of Baltimore, and his brother Leonard, who founded Maryland as a haven for persecuted Christians. At first the colony hewed to the Calverts' ideal, and Catholics and Protestants lived peacefully side by side in a spirit of mutual toleration that was embodied in the famous Act of Toleration of 1649. But when political predominance passed to the Protestants in Maryland, Catholics were subjected to severe restrictions on their religious liberty. The only other colony where Catholics were found in any significant number before the Revolution was Pennsylvania, where the liberal policy of the Quakers encouraged Catholics to settle.

The American Revolution brought about a big change in the fortunes of American Catholics. The legal disabilities under which they labored were gradually lifted, beginning with Maryland's and Pennsylvania's adoption of religious liberty in 1776.

Until the Revolution, Catholics in the colonies were under the rule of a vicar apostolic resident in London. But with the advent of American independence and the more favorable climate for Catholics in the United States, Rome felt it was time for them to have a bishop of their own. The man chosen was John Carroll.

The American Church was singularly fortunate in this man chosen to guide its destiny and to lay the groundwork for its future expansion. As head of the American Catholic missions, John Carroll had already proven to be a wise and humane superior, and his priests showed their feelings about him when in 1789 they elected him the first American bishop by a nearly unanimous vote (twenty-four to two). He came from an old and distinguished Maryland family. One of his cousins, Charles, signed the Declaration of Independence, while his brother Daniel was a delegate to the Constitutional Convention. A Jesuit until the order's suppression in 1773, John Carroll was

John Carroll (1735–1815),
first Roman Catholic bishop
in the United States, in 1812.
Engraving by William
Satchwell Leney (1769–1831)
and Benjamin Tanner
(1775–1848). Smithsonian
Institution, Washington, D.C.
© *National Portrait Gallery,*
Smithsonian Institution/Art
Resource, New York.

a highly educated scholar and a man of broad vision and genuine spirituality,
totally dedicated to the arduous task that lay before him.

In building the institutions necessary for the growth of the Church he received much assistance from the various religious communities of men and women who began entering the States during his tenure. The first to arrive were four cloistered Carmelite nuns, who opened a contemplative convent in 1790. A few years later three Poor Clare nuns founded a school for girls at Georgetown, which shortly afterward was taken over by the first group of Visitation nuns who came to the United States. The first native sisterhood, the Sisters of Charity of St. Joseph, was founded by Elizabeth Seton (canonized in 1975) at Emmitsburg, Maryland, in 1809, and they opened Catholic elementary and secondary schools in a number of communities.

Male religious orders also played an important role in laying the foundations of Catholic institutional life in the United States. Four French Sulpicians came in 1791 and opened the first seminary, St. Mary's, in Baltimore. And when the Jesuit order was re-established in the United States in 1806, members of this order took over Georgetown College. The first Augustinian, Matthew Carr, arrived in 1795, while the Dominicans began their history here when Edward Fenwick, later first bishop of Cincinnati, and several companions inaugurated the first American Dominican house at St. Rose Priory near Springfield, Kentucky, in 1805. Many other religious communities eventually settled in the United States, and together with various native ones played an immense role in building the Church in the United States.

A problem that was to haunt the American bishops for many decades surfaced during Carroll's administration: the attempt by laymen to get control of the property of the Church and to arrogate to themselves the right to choose their own pastors and dominate Church affairs. Carroll had only limited success in dealing with this problem, but in other respects he was more fortunate. He saw his little flock, which at his consecration in 1790 numbered some 35,000 (out of 4 million Americans), grow to nearly 200,000 by his death in 1815. His diocese was subdivided in 1808, when four other dioceses were added: Boston, Philadelphia, New York, and Bardstown (later Louisville).

While thoroughly loyal to Rome, Carroll was also thoroughly American, enthusiastically and profoundly committed to its basic principle of separation of Church and state. He stamped this positive attitude toward the American system indelibly on the mentality of American Catholics, who in this sense at least remained consistently in the liberal Catholic camp.

The Age of Carroll was followed by the Age of John England, first bishop of Charleston and for over twenty years the most powerful voice in the American hierarchy. John England was very much alive to the possibilities for the Catholic Church in the new land, and he earned an early grave for himself by his unremitting toil in behalf of the Church. No American bishop was more anxious than John England to break down the walls of prejudice that kept his fellow Americans from a true understanding of the Catholic Church. He jumped at any chance to speak before non-Catholic audiences, and his reputation as a speaker put him somewhere in the galaxy of Webster and Calhoun. His two-hour address before the United States Congress was undoubtedly the greatest triumph of his career. Extremely conscious of the need to adapt the Catholic Church to the American spirit, he set up a system of ecclesiastical government that enabled the clergy and laity to participate in formulating diocesan policy. As an exercise in democracy it was unfortunately too far ahead of its time to survive when England died in 1842.

Not the least of John England's contributions to the American Church was his insistence that the archbishop of Baltimore gather the American bishops together in council. England's advice finally prevailed, and the subsequent councils held at Baltimore from 1829 to 1884 (seven provincial and three plenary councils) represented the most persistent and successful exercise in collegiality carried on by any group of Catholic bishops during the nineteenth century. Led by a number of remarkable prelates—besides England himself, men like the scholarly Francis Patrick Kenrick, bishop of Philadelphia; Martin Spalding, archbishop of Baltimore; John Hughes, archbishop of New York; John Purcell, archbishop of Cincinnati, and frontier bishops like Simon Bruté and Benedict Flaget—the bishops steered the burgeoning young American Church through crisis after crisis.

Under their able leadership, new dioceses proliferated as the Catholic Church kept pace with the rapid westward movement of the American frontier. By the time of the fourth provincial council in 1840, the archiepiscopal see of Baltimore presided over fifteen suffragan sees: Boston (1808), New York (1808), Philadelphia (1808), Bardstown (1808), Charleston (1820), Richmond (1820), Cincinnati (1821), St. Louis (1826), New Orleans (1826), Mobile (1829), Detroit (1833), Vincennes, (1834), Dubuque (1837), Nashville (1837), and Natchez (1837). Nowhere in the Catholic world was the spread of the Church so impressive, as each council at Baltimore marked another step forward in organizational expansion. When we come to the first Plenary Council of Baltimore in 1852, we find six provinces now organized: Baltimore, Oregon City, St. Louis, New York, Cincinnati, and New Orleans, each with an archbishop, and under these provinces were ranged twenty-six suffragan sees. By the time of the third plenary council in 1884, the number of archiepiscopal sees had increased to eleven, Boston, Milwaukee, Philadelphia, Santa Fe, and Chicago having been added, while the number of dioceses had increased to fifty-four.

In their work at the councils in Baltimore, the bishops were obliged to adhere to the norms laid down by the Council of Trent (1545–63), and they were concerned with applying Trent's decrees to the particular circumstances of the American Church. In doing so they ranged over a multitude of concerns. They prescribed the proper rites for the administration of the sacraments, determined the age of confirmation, laid down rules for the reverent giving of Holy Eucharist to the sick, determined qualifications for Catholic burial, discountenanced funeral orations, fixed the amount of the stipend offering for Mass, ordered confessionals to be erected, and laid down the conditions for conferring plenary indulgences. Recognizing the importance of marriage, they commanded marriages to be celebrated in the parishes of one of the couples marrying, and they warned Catholics against mixed marriages while requiring a pledge from the non-Catholic party in a mixed marriage to allow the children to be brought up Catholic. They tried to regulate the daily life of the priest in minute detail, down to such particulars as his mode of dress (making the Roman collar obligatory in 1884), his type of recreation (forbidding him to attend theaters or horse races), and the furnishings of his rectory. They showed an increasing concern about the dangers to the faith of Catholic children attending public schools and gradually forged the policy that led to making parish schools mandatory in 1884.

The uniform system of discipline enacted by the bishops at Baltimore was a magnificent achievement and laid a solid foundation for the Catholic Church in the United States.

One of their most pressing concerns was the constant influx of immigrants, who persistently swelled their congregations. This flood began in the 1820s, with the first wave of Irish immigrants. Largely because of Irish immigrants, the number of Catholics jumped from about 500,000 (out of a U.S. population of 12 million) in 1830 to 3,103,000 in 1860 (out of a U.S. population of 31.5 million)—an increase of over 800 per cent—with the number of priests and the number of churches increasing proportionately. So large was this increase that by 1850 Roman Catholicism, which at the birth of the nation was nearly invisible in terms of numbers, had now become the country's largest religious denomination.

The next era, 1860 to 1890, was equally impressive, as the growth of the Church far outstripped the growth of the national population, the Church tripling in size while the nation was only doubling. By 1890 Catholics numbered 8,909,000 out of the nation's 62,947,000. German Catholics, who were previously far less in number, now began nearly to equal the number of Irish immigrants. The wave of immigration, lasting from 1890 to the immigration laws of the 1920s, brought a preponderance of Italians and eastern Europeans. Over a million Italians alone came during the two decades from 1890 to 1910.

The reaction of the ordinary American to this invasion of Catholics was understandably one of concern. He did not relish the prospect of being inundated by people whose habits, customs, and religious practices appeared foreign and threatening. Sometimes these vague fears were exploited by unscrupulous demagogues, and mobs would vent their wrath on the nearest Catholic institutions. One of the most conspicuous of such episodes occurred in 1834 after the appearance of a series of books and pamphlets vilifying the Church and depicting nuns and priests as hypocritical demons of lust and greed. The Reverend Lyman Beecher stirred up a mob that proceeded to burn down a convent and school conducted by Ursuline nuns at Charlestown, Massachusetts. In the ensuing years "No Popery" gangs burned some Catholic churches and lynched a number of Catholics. In the 1850s the Know Nothings succeeded the Nativists. The Civil War and its aftermath distracted the "No Popery" advocates, but the movement flared up again when the American Protective Association was organized in 1887. Its members swore never to vote for a Catholic and never to hire one or go on strike with one if at all possible. Anti-Catholic feeling was still strong enough as late as the 1920s to enable the Church's enemies to pass the Immigration Restriction Laws of the 1920s. Anti-Catholic sentiment also figured in the activities of the Anti-Saloon League of the 1920s and the campaign against Al Smith, the first Catholic of a major party to run for the presidency.

In order to survive in such hostile surroundings, the American Catholic Church naturally developed a defensive and aloof attitude, turning inward on itself and devoting its best energies to building up a little world of its own that would provide an alternative to the culture dominated by the Protestants. Central to this scheme of things was the parish school. To understand the origins of the Catholic parochial school system we must remember that the first big wave of Catholic immigrants coincided with the spread of the public school system in this country. But when Catholics entered their children in these public schools they soon found the Protestant atmosphere of the public school a detriment to their children's Catholic faith. In the New York schools, for instance, the Protestant version of the Bible was the only one allowed, and when Bishop Hughes protested, he met with an angry rebuff. So the bishops at Baltimore gradually became more insistent on the need for Catholics to build and operate their own schools. As a model they turned to the type of school opened by Elizabeth Seton and her Sisters of Charity at Emmitsburg, Maryland, in 1810. By 1840 there were at least two hundred of these parochial schools in operation, half of them west of the Alleghenies. They formed the nucleus of what was to become the largest system of private schools in the world. The biggest turning point in their expansion occurred when the third plenary council at Baltimore in 1884 decreed that every parish should have a school.

Besides the parish school, the bishops found it necessary to establish many other types of institutions in order to protect their flock from the contaminating influences of a Protestant and secular society. What was to become a huge network of orphanages, hospitals, old-age homes, etc., began in October 1814, when three of Mother Seton's Sisters of Charity opened the first Catholic orphanage in Philadelphia. Fourteen years later the same order of nuns opened the first American Catholic hospital in the same city; it was the forerunner of some nine hundred such institutions that now exist in the United States. Another means found most effective in safeguarding the faith of the faithful and molding them into a loyal body was the Catholic press. Here as in other fields it was the imaginative John England who led the way in 1822, with his *United States Catholic Miscellany,* the first American weekly Catholic newspaper. The idea quickly caught on, and many other dioceses could soon boast of a weekly journal, though few of them could rival the intellectual content of England's paper.

The number of German Catholic immigrants began to increase rapidly during the 1840s and 1850s, and in the latter decades of the nineteenth century, surpassed the number of Irish Catholic immigrants. The Germans naturally wanted their own parishes where they could hear sermons in German, confess in German, and have their children instructed in German, a parish where they could also preserve their own religious customs. To meet these needs a German national parish, St. Nicholas, was organized in New York City in 1833. As the number of German immigrants grew, these German parishes multiplied especially in the Midwest, where a high concentration of German immigrants were found in the so-called German triangle formed by Milwaukee, Cincinnati, and St. Louis. The German parish exhibited a distinctive character as its members took a special pride in maintaining their Old World customs and were much devoted to pomp and ceremony and elaborate musical programs as a feature of their liturgy. They also often indulged their fondness for processions when their many different parish societies took part, each marching under their own banner to the strains of a military band.

Conflict between the German element in the American Church and the Irish, who dominated the American hierarchy, was an old story by the 1880s. Many parish chronicles told how the two groups often bickered over a host of issues. But in the 1880s and 1890s the antagonism between Irish and Germans was intensified for various reasons and turned into a crisis of major proportions for the burgeoning American Church.

The crisis began when a number of prelates of outstanding ability began calling for an end to the separatism and aloofness of American Catholics and urged them to move into the mainstream of American life. Foremost among those calling for a thoroughgoing Americanization of the Catholic Church in the United States were Archbishop John Ireland of St. Paul; Monsignor Denis O'Connell, rector of the American College in Rome; Bishop John Keane, first rector of Catholic University of America; and John Lancaster Spalding, ordinary of Peoria. Their aims were similar to the liberal Catholics in Europe insofar as they shared their desire to reconcile the Church with modern culture. Like the European liberal Catholics, they were optimistic about the direction taken by modern political and intellectual movements and wanted the Church to adjust its traditional positions in order to endorse political democracy, modern scientific methods of research, efforts at social reform, and ecumenism. The most powerful advocate of Americanization, Ireland was inspired by his experience on the American frontier to believe that the United States was ripe for conversion if the Church could only shake off its foreign image. With his friends in the hierarchy, backed by most of the Irish clergy in the Midwest and West and by his favorite religious congregation, the Paulists, as well as most of the faculty at the Catholic University of America, he orchestrated a campaign to demonstrate the profound agreement of Catholic aspirations with the aspirations of the American people. Endowed with tremendous vitality and enormous oratorical talent, Ireland stirred up a controversy that shook the American Church to its foundations.

His main adversaries were the German Catholics, who in these decades were pouring into America in great numbers. Attached as they were to their Old World traditions and language, they instinctively rejected Ireland's plea to Americanize. Moreover, they had long-standing positive grievances against the Irish-dominated hierarchy. They wanted more bishops of German extraction and more independent German parishes. Their attempts to sway Rome along these lines, however, were frustrated by Ireland's ability to outmaneuver them in the Curia. A furious storm broke when a German Catholic layman, Peter Paul Cahensly, backed by various European Catholic organizations, presented a memorial (the Lucerne Memorial) to Pope Leo XIII in 1891. It sketched a dark picture of the plight of German Catholics in the United States and called for remedies, including more bishops of German background in the United States hierarchy and more separate German parishes. The Americanist bishops were deeply disturbed by this intrusion of the outsider, Cahensly, into their affairs and succeeded in convincing Rome that Cahensly's

plan would divide the hierarchy into antagonistic nationalist blocs and fragment the American Church into separate ethnic ghettos. Ireland's victory,
however, only hardened the German Catholics all the more against his program of Americanization.

No words of Ireland's incensed the German Catholics more than his address to the National Education Association at St. Paul in 1890, when he delivered a glowing hymn of praise to the public school system, spoke of the
Catholic schools as an unfortunate necessity, and proposed a compromise that
would allow Catholic schools to be run as public schools during regular
school hours and only used after hours for religious instruction. (Rome eventually gave grudging approval to Ireland's alternative but at the same time encouraged the Catholic bishops to continue building a separate Catholic
school system.)

The school issue definitely crystallized the anti-Ireland forces into a large
coalition made up of the mass of German Catholics, the Jesuits, and some potent allies among the Irish Catholics, principally Archbishop Corrigan of New
York and his suffragan Bishop McQuaid of Rochester, who were generally un-
sympathetic to Ireland's liberal ideas and found his blustering personality offensive. The newly founded *American Ecclesiastical Review* acted as one of the
main organs of this faction, and it often aimed its fire at the Paulist *Catholic
World*. Another strong voice on the German side was Monsignor Joseph
Schroeder, professor of dogmatic theology at the University, an imported continental scholar who attacked the ideology of the liberals.

The differences between the two forces were compounded by other divisive issues. The progressives wanted Catholics to get involved in movements
for social reform and, when necessary, even to join with non-Catholics in various societies whose aim was social betterment. The conservatives opposed
Catholic participation in such societies, especially if they involved a secret,
oath-taking ceremony, as many of them did. The conservatives could point to
the Church's prohibition of Catholic participation in the Masons as an indication of the Church's general attitude toward secret societies, and for this reason the conservatives opposed Catholic participation in the Knights of Labor,
the largest labor organization of the day, and they wanted Rome to condemn
the Knights. But Cardinal Gibbons, who generally favored the progressive
point of view, succeeded with the help of Ireland and Keane in dissuading
Rome from such a move. But the progressives were not able to keep Rome

from condemning Catholic membership in other secret societies, such as the Odd Fellows and the Knights of Pythias.

Another focal point of controversy was Catholic University of America. As the brainchild of John Spalding, and with Keane as its first rector when it opened in 1889, it quickly became the stronghold of the progressives, who hoped it would provide a Louvain-style intellectual atmosphere in training leaders for the American Church. But the fledgling school drew constant fire from the conservatives and for a long time had great difficulty measuring up to its founders' expectations.

As the debate became increasingly acrimonious, Pope Leo became seriously worried lest the American Church tear itself apart. He decided to step in, and in October of 1892 he sent Archbishop Francesco Satolli to become his first apostolic delegate to the American Church with the hope that Satolli would be able to heal the breach between the two factions. This plan misfired, however, when Satolli was rebuffed by Corrigan and taken in tow by Ireland and Keane.

At this point the conservatives sharpened up their strategy—basically the old idea that the best defense is a good offense. Led by Monsignor Schroeder, they began to harp on the theme that the Americanizers were guilty of the false liberalism already condemned in the *Syllabus of Errors* as well as being tainted by doctrinal minimalism and antipapal tendencies. The progressives played into their hands by participating in the World Parliament of Religions held in Chicago in September 1893. Bishop Keane delivered a speech for Cardinal Gibbons, who was ill, and delivered several other papers.

Whether Satolli really believed the progressives guilty of false liberalism as charged, it is difficult to say, but the fact is that he did begin to distance himself from the progressives while showing evident signs of favor toward the conservatives. Several blows suffered by the liberals showed which way the wind was blowing. Monsignor O'Connell was removed from his post at North American College in 1895 and Keane from his at the University.

The din of the American controversy reached to Europe, and it was there that the final decisive battle was fought. Ireland had stirred up great interest in his ideas when he barnstormed France in 1892 and was warmly toasted as a symbol of American democracy. The French liberal Catholics hoped that he might have some influence on their royalist fellow Catholics and help to change their negative attitude toward democracy and social reform.

Ireland's visit stirred up some debate in the French Church, but the whole affair was pretty well forgotten until a book appeared, *Le Père Hecker Fondateur des "Paulistes" Américains, 1819–1888,* that celebrated the leading ideas of Ireland and the Americanizers. This was a French translation of an American biography of Father Isaac Hecker, edited with a preface by Abbé Klein, a French priest and stanch admirer of Ireland and containing an introduction by Ireland himself. Hecker was one of the most notable of the converts to the American Catholic Church in the nineteenth century. After entering the Church in 1844, he joined the Redemptorists and was ordained in 1849. After some difficulties with his superiors, he left the community and founded his own order, the Paulists. It was at this point that he began to develop his very personal ideas on how the Church must adapt to the American mentality if it wanted to make any real progress in converting Americans. Hecker had considerable influence on the American liberal Catholics. In his preface to the French edition of Hecker's life, Ireland extolled the convert priest as one predestined to teach the Catholic Church how to adjust to the modern spirit of freedom and democracy.

The book was widely acclaimed and aroused considerable interest. And a strong body of opinion hostile to the book was soon formed: Hecker's main ideas were labeled "Americanism" and denounced as the same heretical liberalism condemned by the *Syllabus of Errors.* The attack on Hecker broadened out to a general attack on the ideas of Ireland and the Americanizers. A whole stream of books and articles appeared in France accusing the Americanists of propagating erroneous opinions about the role of authority in the Church, of favoring the natural over the supernatural virtues, and of weakening the dogmas of the Church.

In time Pope Leo felt compelled to step in. When rumor spread that the Pope was about to condemn Americanism, Ireland rushed to Rome and Gibbons cabled a protest. But they were too late. The Pope's letter to Gibbons, *Testem Benevolentiae,* appeared in early February 1899. It took note of the view that some ideas and tendencies labeled "Americanism" were circulating in the Church: namely, false ideas about adapting the Church to modern ideas of freedom and authority, a tendency to esteem the so-called natural and active virtues over the passive and supernatural ones, and finally a rejection of external spiritual direction in favor of interior guidance by the Holy Spirit. If this is what people meant by Americanism, the Pope said, then Americanism was to be condemned. While the encyclical mentioned no names, it was obvious that the letter was aimed at the liberal Catholic camp. While he privately bemoaned the Pope's letter, Ireland publicly displayed a nonchalant attitude and denied that he or any of his friends ever held the ideas condemned by the Pope. The Pope's letter did usher in a period of relative peace in the American Church, as German and Irish calmed down. Nobody changed sides as a result of *Testem*. The Americanists continued to hope for changes that now seemed most remote, while their opponents continued to work against them. The Catholic Church in the United States remained authoritarian and entrenched in its ghetto.

One of the concerns of Ireland and his followers was to change the attitude of their fellow Catholics toward social reform, an attitude that was extremely conservative. Catholics were urged customarily to practice individual acts of charity and the traditional corporal works of mercy, and they were taught that spiritual reform, not social change, was what really mattered.

It was not until the mid-1880s that the progressive Catholics began to take an interest in such questions as trade unionism and justice for the poor, but these questions remained secondary in the Church during the decades of controversy over Americanism. While many Protestants tried to explore the social implications of the Gospel, Catholics expended their energies mainly in the quarrel between German and Irish Catholics. However, as an urban Church composed mainly of working people, the Catholic Church remained in close touch with the problems of labor at the grassroots level and veered naturally to the side of labor during the harsh industrial disturbances associated with such names as Homestead, Pullman, and the Haymarket. Pope Leo's encyclical *Rerum Novarum* helped to quicken American Catholic sympathies with the cause of labor, and gradually a number of leaders came forward to educate the Church on its responsibilities in bringing about social reform. Outstanding among them were two priests, Peter Dietz (d. 1947) and John A. Ryan (d. 1945). Dietz worked with Catholic members of the AFL and opened a social service school in Cincinnati. It inculcated in its hundreds of graduates the necessity of systematic, organized effort if the Church's impact on social reform was to be effective. The demise of his school in 1923 at the hands of Archbishop Moeller and some conservative Republicans of Cincinnati was a big setback for social Catholicism in the United States.

John A. Ryan came to national prominence and began his forty years of tireless efforts to arouse the Catholic social conscience with his book *A Living Wage* (1906). It was not, however, until the hierarchy began to move as a body that Catholic social action began to exert significant influence on the nation's life. This involvement of the hierarchy in social issues dates back to World War I, when the National Catholic War Council was founded to coordinate the Catholic contribution to the war effort. Out of the council came a permanent organization, the National Catholic Welfare Conference, a peacetime coordinating agency for Catholic affairs. Its eight departments included one devoted to social action, which under its director, John A. Ryan, turned its attention to the pressing social problems of the United States.

It immediately displayed the liberal thrust it has maintained over the years in its first major statement: a document drawn up by Ryan and issued as the bishops' pastoral for 1919. Popularly known as the *Bishops' Program,* it became more widely known than any of the other sixty or so postwar proposals for social reconstruction. It called for legislation to guarantee the right of workers to bargain collectively, a minimum-wage act, social security, and health and unemployment insurance. Though denounced in the New York State legislature as socialistic, it proved astonishingly on target: All but one of the proposals were later incorporated into the New Deal legislation of the thirties. In the meantime, however, Catholic social actionists had to pass through the discouraging twenties, when America retreated from its historic commitment to securing greater liberty and justice for all.

There were definite signs of an awakened Catholic social consciousness as the nation moved into the thirties. And most Catholics welcomed the New Deal as a consonant with their vision of social justice as most recently explicated in Pope Pius XI's encyclical *Quadragesimo Anno* of 1931. No Catholic was more enthusiastic about the New Deal than John A. Ryan, who was generally recognized by this time as the leading Catholic spokesman on social issues. For his multitude of admirers, Ryan's scholarly and measured words seemed to combine the best of social Catholicism with the best in the American progressive tradition. Ryan's was the most persistent Catholic voice among those calling for strong government action to promote a humane social order, and he exercised a tremendous influence in moving Catholics to a positive understanding of their social responsibilities.

In sharp contrast with Ryan's scholarly endeavors to educate American Catholics stood the performance of the sensational and demagogic Charles Coughlin, the radio priest of Royal Oak, Michigan. The immense size of the audience that listened in on his Sunday afternoon broadcasts testified to his uncanny talent for articulating the fears and suspicions of millions of Americans, both Catholics and otherwise, who felt victimized by the Depression. Coughlin drew on Scripture, the papal social encyclicals, and American populist and even radical literature in excoriating the legions of enemies he found responsible for the plight of the poor and wretched. At the peak of his power in 1936 he felt strong enough to challenge Roosevelt himself—a move that proved disastrous—and Coughlin's influence began to wane. He also alienated many of his former supporters by his hysterical anti-Semitic tirades, his fascistic tendencies, and his opposition to America's entry into the war until he was eventually silenced by Archbishop Mooney of Detroit. While no one did more than Coughlin to dramatize the fact that the Catholic Church was concerned with social justice, his contribution otherwise to American social Catholicism was small.

Consistently opposed to Coughlin were the members of the Catholic Worker Movement founded by Dorothy Day and Peter Maurin. Their aim

Dorothy Day, founder of the Catholic Worker Movement, in 1933. © *Bettmann/Corbis.*

was to identify as completely as possible with the poor and downtrodden. With this in mind, Dorothy opened a House of Hospitality in the New York Bowery in 1933, the first of many that spread around the country. They offered a warm welcome and a warm meal to the homeless, unemployed, and hungry. These houses drew together a large number of apostolic and socially conscious young Catholics who practiced voluntary poverty and acted as effective propagandists of the Church's social doctrine by applying papal social teaching in a wide variety of social action. Their paper, the *Catholic Worker*, was devoted to the cause of labor and soon reached a circulation of one hundred thousand. The Catholic Workers protested against the impersonal, mechanistic character of a technological society and stressed one's personal responsibility for injustice. They formed small communities of persons committed to living in solidarity with the afflicted and suffering while devoting themselves to prayer and frequent reception of the sacraments. Unlike most social Catholics, the Catholic Workers did not hesitate to point out the tremendous failures of the American system, its materialism, racism, and imperialism. As pacifists, they condemned America's entry into World War II and in consequence lost much of their support. But they played a prophetic role in the Church. By challenging the prevailing narrow Catholic mentality that equated morality with opposition to indecent movies and birth control, they helped many of their coreligionists to adopt a more profound view of social reconstruction.

The advent of mass unionism in the United States with the formation of the CIO in 1935 stirred interest among Catholics in the social encyclicals, and a sizable number of priests began to educate themselves in industrial problems. A new type of priest appeared, the labor priest, who picketed with the workers and set up schools in order to instruct labor organizers in the basics of Catholic social doctrine. Eventually there were more than a hundred of these labor schools, where priests acted as advisers to Catholic members of the big unions in their struggle against Communist infiltration, racketeering, and union bossism. But in spite of the work of the labor priest, and in spite of the high percentage of Catholics in the ranks of organized labor, Catholic thought, as the historian David O'Brien says, exerted little influence on labor's development.[1]

---

[1] David O'Brien, *American Catholics and Social Reform* (New York: Oxford University Press, 1968), p. 119.

One issue of social justice that remained largely ignored by the Church in the 1930s was racial prejudice. Until the end of World War II, Catholics conformed to the general practice of Americans in segregating their schools and churches. Few Catholic voices were raised in protest, although Father John LaFarge, S.J., and the Catholic Interracial Council, which he helped to found, worked heroically to change Catholic attitudes. It was only after the war, however, that a number of Catholic bishops, led by Archbishop Rummel of New Orleans, Cardinal Meyer of Chicago, Cardinal O'Boyle of Washington, Cardinal Ritter of St. Louis, Archbishop Lucey of San Antonio, and Bishop Waters of Raleigh, North Carolina, began to desegregate their schools and churches and urge their people to change their attitudes. Many of the clergy began in earnest to fight racial prejudice and discrimination, but it proved immensely difficult to arouse the conscience of the average Catholic, priest or layman, on this score.

The immigration restriction laws of the 1920s brought an end to the massive and constant increase of the Church's numbers. Henceforth its rate of growth followed basically the same curve as that of the Protestant Churches. In 1950, for instance, Protestants constituted 33.8 per cent of the population, and Catholics, 18.9 per cent. By 1958 the Protestant percentage had increased to 35.5 and the Catholic to 20.8. Organizationally the Church in the United States continued its remarkable progress: Metropolitan sees were erected at San Antonio (1926), Los Angeles (1936), Detroit, Louisville, and Newark (1937), Washington (1939), Denver (1941), Indianapolis (1944), Omaha (1945), Seattle (1951), and Kansas City, Kansas (1952), while a number of American bishops were made cardinals: Dennis Dougherty of Philadelphia (1921), George Mundelein of Chicago and Patrick Hayes of New York (1924), Samuel Stritch of Chicago, Francis Spellman of New York, Edward Mooney of Detroit, and John Glennon of St. Louis (1946), James McIntyre of Los Angeles (1953), John O'Hara of Philadelphia and Richard Cushing of Boston (1958), and Albert Meyer of Chicago and Aloisius Muench of Fargo (1959).

Catholics continued to pour their best energies and resources into the educational effort. By 1954 there were 9,279 elementary schools enrolling 3,235,251 pupils, 2,296 secondary schools with 623,751 students, 224 colleges with over 280,000 students, and 294 seminaries with 29,578 students.

One sign, perhaps, of growing spiritual maturity among American Catholics was the great increase in vocations in the contemplative life. After

World War II hundreds of young men began filling up the contemplative, mainly Trappist, monasteries scattered around the country. This influx was due in part to the widespread influence of a convert, Thomas Merton, whose autobiography, *The Seven Storey Mountain,* provided a fascinating account of the spiritual odyssey that led him into the Trappists.

By the 1950s it was quite obvious to most observers that the Catholic Church in the United States had become a thoroughly American institution. The era of Protestant dominance was over. The political significance of this fact was underscored when John F. Kennedy was elected the first Catholic President of the United States, an event that coupled with the reign of Pope John and the calling of his council definitely marked the beginning of a new era in the history of American Catholicism.

Chapter 32

THE POPES OF THE
TWENTIETH CENTURY

Giuseppe Sarto, or Pius X—the first Pope elected in the twentieth century (1903) and the first Pope to be canonized (1954) since the sixteenth century—was the son of poor peasants from Riese, an obscure village in northern Italy. After his ordination in 1858 he gained a rather wide experience as a parish priest, as spiritual director of a seminary, and as a chancery official, impressing everyone at the same time by his deep spirituality. In 1884 he was made bishop of Mantua, where he showed a marked zeal for reform. Finally, in 1893, he was transferred to Venice as patriarch and cardinal. In spite of his advance up the ranks of the hierarchy, he remained dedicated to the tasks of the parish priest and loved nothing more than catechizing children, saying Mass, and hearing confessions. Even as Pope he retained the heart of a simple parish priest and manifested a warmth, humor, affability, and gentleness that won the hearts of pilgrims from all corners of the world.

His most important acts as Pope were inspired by the same pastoral sense and solicitude. His love of the Mass and his desire to have it performed in the most dignified manner was embodied in his decree on the reform of sacred music (1903). Of similar inspiration was his decree urging all the faithful to frequent Communion and admitting children to this sacrament at the earliest possible age.

Of all his initiatives, however, the one that probably left the deepest stamp on the Church of our times was his project for a codification of Canon Law, which Cardinal Gasparri carried out at his behest but which was only promulgated in 1917, under Benedict XV. It reflected Pius X's own highly authoritarian and conservative concept of Church structure.

Unlike his predecessor, Leo XIII, Sarto was little concerned with reconciling the Church with the modern world; his general attitude toward the cultural and political trends of the day was, in fact, negative and in line with a general pessimism about temporal progress endemic in the postrevolutionary Church. He had, for instance, little love of the new trend toward democracy that was sweeping the world; he thought it violated the natural hierarchical order of society, and he did his best to cool whatever enthusiasm for democracy existed among Catholics. Christian democratic movements were either destroyed, as in the case of Marc Sangnier's *Sillon,* or forced to bide their time.

The same intransigence characterized Pius' handling of the Modernist crisis which, as we have seen, ended in an impasse for Catholic thought.

Pius, however, showed keen insight into one aspect of the Church's relation to the modern world. When France unilaterally abrogated the Concordat (originally signed by Napoleon and Pius VII) and then tried to reduce the Church to financial dependence on the state by getting it to accept a system of state subsidies, the Pope reacted with vigor. He felt that the French Church would be better off stripped of all its possessions and forced to rely only on its own inner riches, its traditions, its spirituality, and the devotion of its clergy and people. And so he ordered the French bishops to reject any financial ties with the state. The wisdom of his stand seems to have been vindicated by the subsequent history of the French Church, which though poverty-stricken played a leading role in the renewal that engendered Vatican II.

Pius died as Europe plunged into the inferno and was succeeded by Benedict XV (1914–22), the least physically impressive of twentieth-century Popes—a frail, stoop-shouldered little man who came from a Genoan patrician family, the Della Chiesa. After his ordination in 1878 and further studies in Rome he was snatched up by the Curia, where he worked under Cardinal Rampolla, eventually Leo XIII's Secretary of State. With the accession of Pius X, Rampolla was replaced by Merry del Val, and Della Chiesa found himself—through no fault of his own—something of an outsider. He was kicked upstairs to Bologna as archbishop and deprived for six years of the red hat traditionally conferred on Bolognese ordinaries as a matter of course. But whatever injustice he suffered from his enemies in the Curia was more than recompensed when the cardinals chose him as Sarto's successor.

They were looking for a peacemaker, and Benedict did not disappoint their hopes. Peace and conciliation were the objectives he unswervingly pursued from the first moment of his pontificate. Peace—first in the Church, which was bitterly divided by the anti-Modernist zealots who had been allowed to run riot during the previous administration. And one of his first acts was to call a halt to the witchhunt after "Modernists."

But seeking peace among the great powers engaged in the horrendous conflict was an altogether different matter and called for superhuman tact and diplomatic subtlety—qualities with which he was superbly endowed.

His opposition to the war was absolute; intellectually and morally he stood in the vanguard with those who found the war totally unjustifiable. For him it was the "darkest tragedy of human hatred and human madness."[1] And unlike the jingoist prelates who in the belligerent countries disgraced the Christian name, he utterly rejected any attempts to justify it by recourse to ancient theories about "just wars."

Neverthless, he refrained from openly condemning the war, since this would have posed a terrible dilemma for Catholics on both sides who were unfortunately not prepared theologically and emotionally to take up such a radical position. He contented himself, therefore, by general appeals to both sides to end the mad, useless carnage. And finally he issued his celebrated but futile "Note to the Heads of State at War" in August 1917. His proposals were realistic, calling for suspension of hostilities, systematic and regulated disarmament, and the establishment of arbitration, including international sanctions—ideas which, in fact, were quite close to President Wilson's subsequent "Fourteen Points."

Benedict's unequivocal condemnation of the war and his refusal to take sides were widely misinterpreted by both sides, who wanted him to condemn the other side as the aggressor. He was vilified in the press and even excluded from the Versailles Peace Conference. As time passes, however, there is growing recognition of the truly prophetic role he played.

Peace between Church and state was another imperative he fully appreciated, and he took major steps in this direction by his overtures to the French Government that led to the resumption of diplomatic relations in 1920. He also made the first official approaches to the Italian Government for the settlement of the Roman question, which had tragically divided Italians since the seizure of the Papal States in 1870.

[1] C. Falconi, *The Popes of the Twentieth Century* (Boston: Little, Brown, 1967), p. 117.

One of the most important initiatives of his pontificate was his epochal missionary encyclical *Maximum Illud,* called the charter of the Catholic missionary movement of this century.

On a more personal level, one of the most attractive features of the frail, reserved aristocrat was his boundless charity. He was never able to refuse a plea for help, and he literally emptied the Vatican treasury, so that at his death there was not even enough money to cover the expenses of the conclave.

His successor, Achille Ratti, Pius XI (1922–39), followed a most unlikely path to the papal throne. The son of a modestly prosperous textile manufacturer, he spent the first thirty years of his priestly life as a librarian—first at the Ambrosian library in Milan and then from 1911 to 1918 at the Vatican, where he gained international recognition for his research. It kept him quite removed from the bitter controversies swirling through the Church over the Modernist question. His first entry into the world of action occurred when he was sent to Poland in 1918 as apostolic visitor and then nuncio in order to assist in the reconstruction of the Polish Church after the devastation of the war—a most difficult assignment. After its long subjection to Austria, Germany, and Russia, Poland was given its independence in 1919. Ratti's task was to secure the rights of the Catholic Church in the new state and forge strong relations with Rome. His successful acquittal of the mission demonstrated his exceptional qualities of courage and decision, and upon his return in 1921 he was appointed archbishop of Milan and made a cardinal. Five months later, the death of Benedict XV brought him to Rome for the conclave that elevated him to the throne of Peter.

He immediately indicated a major objective of his pontificate—reconciliation with Italy—by appearing on the outer balcony of St. Peter's to give his first papal benediction—something no Pope had done since Pius IX in 1846. The moment was a critical one for Italy. The ebullient Mussolini and his rowdy Blackshirts were busy digging the grave of Italian democracy. Pius was inclined to think that Italy needed a strong man to establish order and saw in the blacksmith's son the one ordained by providence to settle the Roman question. Pius helped to smooth Mussolini's way to power by withdrawing Vatican support from the Catholic Popular Party and causing the resignation of its leader, the priest Don Sturzo.

The Pope reaped his reward when Mussolini signed the Lateran Concordat and Treaty with the Vatican in 1929. In return for the surrender of papal claims to Italian territory, the treaty granted the Pope a munificent sum of money and complete sovereignty over Vatican City—the forty-acre complex of buildings and gardens around St. Peter's Basilica in Rome. In addition, the Concordat accorded to the Catholic religion a privileged status in Italy and imposed Catholic teaching as the norm for religion courses in the state school system.

Pius' tenure coincided with the rise of dictators to power in many other European states, and as with Mussolini he did not hesitate to come to terms with them, even when it meant sacrificing Catholic political parties. In Germany the situation was complicated by the deviousness and mendacity of Adolf Hitler, whose National Socialist Party had been condemned by the German bishops more than two years before his seizure of power on January 30, 1933. On March 23, however, Hitler upset all calculations by declaring before the Reichstag that he regarded the churches, Catholic and Protestant, as "the most important factors in the preservation of our national heritage." Promising full respect for church rights, he demanded from the churches an immediate choice between cooperation for "the political and moral purification of our public life," and open conflict. Despite grave misgivings about the sincerity of this proferred cooperation, the Catholic Center Party decided it could not be rejected and gave Hitler the crucial votes he needed for emergency powers, hoping to obtain in return a moderating influence on Hitler's future actions. Within days the German bishops, likewise responding to Hitler's pledge of respect for church rights, withdrew their previous condemnations of his movement, though not of its underlying anti-Christian philosophy. By June, Hitler was achieving the demise of all other political parties but his own. The last to yield was the Center Party, which voted its dissolution on July 5. Three days later the Vatican gave its assent to a Concordat, by which Hitler pledged respect for church rights in Germany. Though the negotiations had been going on in Rome for weeks, the Vatican delayed acceptance of Hitler's terms until the demise of the Center Party, founded sixty years previously to protect the rights of German Catholics, and Hitler's use of his emergency powers to suspend the constitution made it evident that there was no way church rights in Germany could be defended save through a Concordat.

Altogether Pius negotiated eighteen concordats, whose main objectives were to secure freedom for Catholic Action, to obtain legal status for Church marriages, and to give the Holy See exclusive control over the appointment of bishops.

His pontificate registered impressive accomplishments: He established 128 residential sees, founded many new institutes and ecclesiastical colleges in Rome, and canonized thirty-three saints.

Pius was a pragmatist in his political views and had no ideological preference for Fascism. In fact, he condemned the Fascist ideology and did not bless the Italian campaign in Ethiopia—accusations to the contrary notwithstanding. Neither was the Vatican pro-Fascist in the Spanish imbroglio. By the end of 1935, in fact, the Vatican had reached a modus vivendi with the Republican government of Spain, realizing that monarchism was dead. Only two conditions were attached: that the Republicans maintain law and order and that they stop the antireligious excesses of the extremists. But they were able to do neither. The fanatics who destroyed the churches and convents and murdered the priests and nuns also destroyed the Spanish Republic. The Vatican at length went over to the side of Franco's nationalists.

That Pius was not pro-Fascist is also evident from his handling of the French Action Française. This was a movement originating with Charles Maurras, a gifted ideologue who was antirepublican, fanatically nationalist, and an agnostic who had seduced a large number of Catholics into his camp of reactionaries and Fascists. Pius saw through the fallacies of Maurras and issued a condemnation of the movement in a decree of the Holy Office of 1926. In so doing, he helped make the French Church safe for democrats.

Personally Ratti was reserved in manner and strongly self-disciplined; his record-breaking Alpine exploits also showed him to be a lover of adventure. On papal ceremonies he projected an aura of solemn majesty, inspiring awe even in those least susceptible to ecclesiastical pomp.

One of the first photos taken of him after his elevation showed him sitting on his throne with his right hand clenched in a fist. It was a good symbol of his style. Conscious of his absolute sovereignty, he ruled in the fashion of the great medieval Popes. Making himself conversant with every detail of affairs, he tried to keep in close touch and make all the decisions himself. He demanded and expected absolute compliance with his orders, and the first to tremble before an audience with him were often the cardinals themselves. He forced Cardinal Billot to hand over his red hat when Billot opposed him over the Action Française question and would have done the same to Cardinal Innitzer, archbishop of Vienna, when Innitzer blessed Hitler's takeover of Austria, had it not been for adverse repercussions on the Austrian Church. Pius made his sovereignty felt by studiously keeping his distance and cultivating an atmosphere of isolation. No less a figure than Hermann Goering, second in rank in the Nazi hierarchy, confessed that he felt overawed when ushered into his presence.

Definitely not the type to shrink from conflict, Pius saved the independence of Catholic Action in Italy by forcing Mussolini to back down after the dictator tried to suppress this key Catholic organization. And it remained during the Fascist regime the only nongovernmental organization not completely under the thumb of the government.

And when Hitler showed increasing belligerence toward the Church, Pius met the challenge with a decisiveness that astonished the world. His encyclical *Mit brennender Sorge* was the "first great official public document to dare to confront and criticize Nazism" and "one of the greatest such condemnations ever issued by the Vatican."[2] Smuggled into Germany, it was read from all the Catholic pulpits on Palm Sunday in March 1937. It exposed the fallacy and denounced the Nazi myth of blood and soil; it decried its neopaganism, its war of annihilation against the Church, and even described the Führer himself as a "mad prophet possessed of repulsive arrogance."[3] The Nazis were infuriated, and in retaliation closed and sealed all the presses that had printed it and took numerous vindictive measures against the Church, including staging a long series of immorality trials of the Catholic clergy. At Koblenz, 170 Franciscans were arrested and prosecuted for the corruption of youth and for turning their monastery into a "male brothel." A Hitler Youth film was circulated that showed priests dancing in a bordello.

Increasingly distressed by Hitler's and Mussolini's treatment of the Church and by their vicious racist policies, Pius was preparing an explosive encyclical denouncing Fascist crimes and racism when he was overtaken by death on February 10, 1939.

The sixty-five cardinals who gathered two weeks later to elect the 261st successor of St. Peter were hardly puzzled over their choice. All eyes were on Eugenio Pacelli, who had won universal renown by his brilliant career as Pius XI's Secretary of State and in his unprecedented global travels had impressed everyone by his aristocratic bearing, personal piety, and quiet affability. Moreover, with the world poised for war, the *purpurati* were in no mood to take chances; a man well schooled in the Vatican tradition of diplomatic finesse

[2] Ibid., p. 230.
[3] A. Rhodes, *The Vatican in the Age of the Dictators* (London: Hodder & Stoughton, 1973), p. 205.

Pope Pius XII.
© *Bettmann/Corbis.*

seemed an absolute necessity. And so when the crowd in the piazza outside saw the white smoke rise from the chimney only a few hours after the conclave opened, they knew it had to be Pacelli.

This tall, stately ascetic who two weeks later was crowned with the tiara as Pius XII was the only Pope of the twentieth century who did not hail from northern Italy. As his aquiline nose might suggest, he was a born Roman. Profiles of his half-sad countenance under a white skullcap, deep-set eyes, and long, bony fingers clasped in prayer were reproduced in countless forms and became the visible symbol to the world of the unity and spiritual strength of Catholicism as the world itself came apart at the seams.

Only two weeks after Pius' coronation, Hitler sent his tanks rumbling into Czechoslovakia—bringing the world only an inch away from global war. Pius made the most strenuous efforts to ward off the catastrophe—he even endangered his own personal safety by acting as an intermediary between the Allies and the underground German resistance movement, which in the spring of 1940 plotted to overthrow Hitler and seal peace with the Allies.

Italy's declaration of war placed the Vatican in a most delicate position—

a little island in the Axis sea. It had to use the utmost circumspection to avoid being attacked as an accomplice of the Allies.

The Pope made every effort to maintain an appearance of impartiality between the opposing blocs. Thus in spite of his almost pathological fear of Communism, he lent no support to Nazi attempts to portray their invasion of Russia as an anti-Communist, religious crusade; his hatred of Nazism, in fact, was only second to his hatred of Communism. But at the same time he had a special love of the German people and culture and strove for a peace that would ensure their legitimate rights and interests. And when the war took a dramatic turn in favor of the Allies, he was frightened by the prospect of a Communist victory and worked for a negotiated peace that would not give total victory to either the Soviet Union or Germany.

One question often arises in this connection: Did Pius carry neutrality too far in refusing to publicly denounce the Nazi atrocities against the Jews, the Poles, the Serbs, and others?

There is no doubt that the Pope was fully informed about the extent and the nature of these crimes, and yet he kept silent, except for some vague and generalized references to Nazi crimes.

No doubt a complex of reasons motivated him: fear of even more savage measures if he protested—as actually happened in Holland when the Dutch bishops spoke out against the Nazi deportation of Jews; an unwillingness to jeopardize his official neutrality; the threat of terrible reprisals against the Church; realization that nothing would deter the hysterical Hitler from his "final solution," joined to the hope of being able to do more for the victims behind the backs of the Nazis, as long as their wrath was not aroused by public denunciations—in Rome alone over five thousand Jews were given asylum in convents and monasteries belonging to the Vatican, while Pinchas Lapide, former Israeli consul in Italy, credited the Holy See and the Church with saving some four hundred thousand Jews from certain death. Anthony Rhodes, in his *The Vatican in the Age of the Dictators,* agrees that in private the Pope did much for the Jews.

Yet for many, these reasons seem specious, and in their eyes the whole affair has cast a long shadow over an otherwise brilliant pontificate. The only consideration, they maintain, for one claiming to be the Vicar of Christ should have been his duty to voice the abhorrence of the human conscience at such incalculably monstrous evil.

Whatever truth may lie in this opinion, it is at least certain that Pius was a man of the utmost personal rectitude of conscience and that his decision to remain silent caused him deep anguish. If indeed he erred, it was probably due to excessive preoccupation with diplomatic considerations.

Recent publications from the Vatican archives show that although Vatican relief efforts were very expensive and time-consuming, the results were rather insignificant and disappointing. As in so many other fields, the experience of World War I afforded little guidance. At that time the Vatican received co-operation from the Ottoman Empire and the Russian Empire, and the relatively primitive technology made it rather easy to distinguish between combatants and noncombatants, while there were few political or racial refugees. But in World War II, the Soviet Union and Germany refused to co-operate, while the improved methods of bombing victimized entire populations and racial and ideological fanaticism created enormous numbers of refugees. The Vatican's relief task took on huge dimensions and became nearly impossible to carry out. Nor did the moral authority of the Pope always function effectively enough to secure the results intended. Nevertheless, food, clothing, and medical supplies were dispatched on a large scale, while the Vatican radio sent out as many as twenty-seven thousand messages a month in order to find missing persons. The Holy See also exerted great efforts to save Rome from destruction.

As conditions in Italy deteriorated near the end of the war, the Vatican also joined in the efforts of the anti-Mussolini forces to get Italy out of the war and took part in the armistice negotiations. It involved considerable risk since, as the Pope very well realized, if Mussolini and the Germans found out, they would have inflicted severe reprisals on the Church. But he felt that he could not stand by while Italy sank into chaos and ruin. His role, however, was actually not decisive, and in the end the armistice was reached by other channels.

The end of the war saw the prestige of the papacy at an all-time high. Many nations had ambassadors accredited with the Vatican. The President of the United States sent his personal representative, while a constant stream of the world's celebrities moved through its portals. The Holy Year of 1950 brought millions of more humble pilgrims to the tomb of Peter. The Pope gave daily addresses on every conceivable subject and was widely quoted around the world. The number of Catholic dioceses increased during his reign from 1,696 to 2,048. The Vatican's economic power followed suit as its heavy investments in real estate and industry brought it a big share of the postwar

Italian boom, and its newly created bank—or, more properly, the Institute for the Works of Religion—did a brisk business.

Although Pius had striven to maintain impartiality during the war, the upsurge of antireligious Communism in the West after the war caused him to align the Church more and more with the Western democracies. Instead of trying to foster détente with the Iron Curtain countries, the Pope, in fact, helped to exacerbate relations by using every means to mobilize world opinion against the Communists. With Italy and Rome itself under grave danger of a Communist takeover, he issued a decree in 1949 by which all Catholics belonging to the Communist party were automatically excommunicated. He also tried to use his influence over the dominant Christian Democratic party to get a ban on the Communist party in Italy.

In internal Church affairs also, the Pope drove a hard line and stood firm against most attempts at innovation, perhaps feeling that the climate of opinion in the Church was not yet ready for the obviously needed modernizations. But he did give the College of Cardinals a majority of non-Italians—for the first time in modern history. However, he carried to new heights the almost mythical exaltation of the monarchical papacy and continued to centralize power in the Curia at the expense of the bishops—an extreme of papalism that would soon bring a reaction.

He was extremely cautious as regards theological and liturgical developments. Two of his major encyclicals, *Divino Afflante Spiritu* and *Mystici Corporis* both of 1943, were, however, certainly progressive documents, the one allowing Catholic biblical scholars to apply the methods of form criticism in their exegesis, and the other summing up recent theological developments that emphasized the unity of the Church in the Mystical Body of Christ.

But in general Pius evinced little sympathy or understanding toward the new currents in theology and tried to apply the brakes to certain fast-moving French and German theologians. Like his predecessors since Leo XIII, he equated theology with Thomist theology, and in his encyclical *Humani Generis* he warned Catholics against possible aberrations of the new historical theology.

When he died in 1958, the fifty-one cardinals (only seventeen of them Italians) who met to elect the next Pope were almost evenly divided between those who felt the need for a definite break with Pacelli's triumphalist Church and those in favor of continuing it. The one finally chosen after a three-day struggle supposedly reflected a compromise: Angelo Roncalli, the seventy-six-year-old patriarch of Venice, reputed to be moderate and conciliatory. Probably no one on either side had even an inkling of the revolutionary ideas percolating behind the old man's peasant face as they knelt to do him homage.

The first surprise came when he chose the name John—a name that hadn't been taken since the notorious anti-Pope John XXIII had been deposed at the Council of Constance. Roncalli soon showed that he would not be intimidated by Vatican protocol or inhibited by the memory of his august predecessor. As people soon realized, this priest, clad in a white cassock with his rotund frame, massive head, big nose, and powerful jaw was a totally new kind of Pope: a simple, spontaneous person who loved life and loved people and was not at all afraid to show it. Heedless of papal etiquette, he invited friends to his dinner table and wandered through the streets of Rome, speaking with all and sundry, visiting hospitals and prisons and making little gestures and telling jokes that soon were repeated around the world. One of the favorites was how, as he recounted, he often awoke during the night, thinking himself still a cardinal and worrying over a difficult decision he would have to make. He would then say to himself: "I'll talk it over with the Pope!" But then he would remember, *"I'm the Pope!"* "Well," he would conclude, "I'll talk it over with Our Lord!"

At first the world was astonished—people had almost forgotten that Popes were also human beings—but then they took him to their hearts and poured out their affection for him. Gradually every detail of his past was dug up and became familiar: his birth of a poor peasant family near Bergamo; his entrance into a seminary at the age of fourteen; his work as a young priest secretary as professor of Church history and as secretary to the man who so greatly influenced him, Bishop Radini-Tedeschi; and his long, humiliating nineteen-year exile as a papal envoy in the Near East, followed by his turn as nuncio in Paris and finally as patriarch of Venice.

Though his pontificate was destined to be one of the shortest in modern history (four years and seven months), it was undoubtedly one of the most important and, in fact, really amounted to a revolution that brought to an end the Tridentine Era of the Church and the whole fortress mentality characteristic of the Roman Catholic Church since Trent.

It could all be summed up in the word "dialogue"—the dialogue he opened up with the world. Thus he addressed his great encyclicals *Pacem in Terris* and *Mater et Magistra* to all men of good will and spoke in terms of values respected by all, and he appealed to all to work together to build a better world. He extended friendly arms to Christians of other communions and made their leaders feel welcome in the Vatican, where he received them as brother speaking with brother. He reversed dramatically the anti-Communist policy of Pius XII and went to the very limits of possibility in his quest for a more harmonious relation with the Communist world.

However, all of this might easily have perished at his death, and a still-conservative Curia might easily have interred his revolution with his bones, were it not for his convocation of the Second Vatican Council (1962–65), where the whole Church, assembled in its bishops, fulfilled his magnificent dream of a heart-to-heart conversation with the whole of humanity on the major spiritual issues of the day.

Chapter 33

THE RESURGENT LIBERAL CATHOLICS
RING DOWN THE CURTAIN
ON THE POST-TRENT CHURCH
AT THE SECOND VATICAN COUNCIL

John XXIII announced his intention of calling an ecumenical council at the ancient Roman basilica of St. Paul's Outside the Walls on January 25, 1959, which would have as its task to promote the unity of all Christian peoples.

John attributed his idea simply to an inspiration of the Holy Spirit. Another way of putting it would be that the council was John's solution to a problem that was beginning to preoccupy thoughtful Catholics everywhere: How could an ancient Church that prided itself on being unchangeable and antimodern survive in a world undergoing social, political, and cultural transformations of unprecedented magnitude?

By the year 1959, in fact, the world and Europe seemed on the threshold of an entirely new era. In the short space of fifty or so years, profound scientific, technological, cultural, and social developments had so changed the conditions of life that one felt separated from the previous four hundred years by a wide gap. A term had even been coined—"post-modern"—to describe this sense of living in a new historical period.

To single out any one factor responsible would seem quite arbitrary, but many historians would agree that scientific and technological developments should be listed first in the order of importance. Just to single out the most

Pope John XXIII gives the
benediction.   © *Bettmann/*
Corbis.

important in a continuing stream of inventions would consume too much
space here. Many of them, like electricity, the internal-combustion engine,
the telephone, telegraphy, the microphone, the camera, the record player, the
bicycle, and the typewriter had already made their appearance before 1900,
but it took more time for them to be fully exploited. And in most cases it
was only after World War I that their full impact was felt. Other epoch-
making inventions—alloy steels and aluminum, synthetic rubber, plastics,
and artificial fabrics like nylon—have radically changed the material basis of
society.

Technology also revolutionized modes of communication and trans-
portation: The automobile, the airplane, radio, movies in color and sound,
and television have ushered man into the era of the global village.

So it was to a world swept by hurricane winds of change that news came
of John's decision to call an ecumenical council of the Roman Catholic
Church. The announcement struck the Roman Curia like a thunderbolt. The
word "council" sounded too much like "revolution": Only the Lord could pre-
dict what three thousand bishops might do if they got out of hand. And so

they girded themselves for battle. Their strategy was clear. Evidence indicates they intended to secure control of the council and make sure they kept control. At first they succeeded. Curial officials monopolized the key positions on the preparatory commissions that drew up the proposals or schemata. After sifting through thousands of suggestions sent in by the bishops of the world, they drew up seventy proposals or schemata to be submitted to the council. These ranged over a bewildering variety of subjects—revelation, ecclesiastical benefices, spiritualism, reincarnation, etc.—and were larded with the traditional denunciations and anathemas. If all went as planned, the Curia expected the bishops simply to put their stamp of approval on them and return home. The council would then slip into the past and be remembered only as another glorious Roman pageant.

It was an open question in the minds of astute observers whether this Curial strategy would succeed when the council opened on October 11, 1962. The occasion was marked by ceremonies of dazzling brilliance, an endless procession of bishops vested in flowing white damask copes and miters moved majestically past the towering obelisk of the Bernini piazza and up the broad steps into St. Peter's basilica. As the Pope entered—borne aloft on his portable throne—he was greeted with a huge burst of sound as the organ boomed and applause roared from the assembly. Dismounting, he made his way between the tiers stacked with bishops stretching the entire length of the nave, and reaching his place at the twisted bronze canopy, he turned toward the bishops and intoned the opening liturgy.

At its conclusion five hours later, John mounted the rostrum and delivered one of the most remarkable papal addresses in the entire history of the Church. In subtle but unmistakable language he disassociated himself from the Curia's narrow, defensive view of the council and urged the bishops instead to undertake a great renewal or updating of the Church. Unlike the prophets of doom and gloom among his counselors, he said, he preferred to take an optimistic view of the course of modern history. And he emphasized the need for the bishops to take a pastoral approach: They must not engage in sterile academic controversies but must find meaningful, positive, and fresh ways of stating the Church's age-old doctrine—having no doubt in mind as he spoke the seventy ludicrously Scholastic and outdated proposals already prepared by the Curia as the basis for the bishops' discussions.

But it was obvious to his listeners that to succeed in carrying out John's wishes, they would first have to break the stranglehold the Curia already held over the council. The key to control over the council were the ten commissions (operating much like U.S. congressional committees), each of which had a more or less defined area of competence, such as theology, liturgy, missions, etc. Their task was to draft the documents that were submitted to the bishops for debate and then hammered out in the light of this debate and resubmitted for final approval by the bishops. In an unwieldy assembly of several thousand, the commissions exercised enormous discretionary power over what was finally to be included or excluded from the documents.

So the power struggle between the bishops and the Curia focused immediately on getting control of these commissions, each of which was to have sixteen elected and eight appointed members. The Curia had already hand-picked lists of candidates, which they submitted to the bishops on the very first day, hoping to get their nominees elected before most of the prelates really caught on to the game. However, the very first speaker, Cardinal Lienart, upset their applecart when he asked how the bishops could be expected to vote intelligently for total strangers, and he moved for more time so the bishops could draw up their own lists. His motion was adopted, and the bishops adjourned.

"Bishops in Revolt!" the headlines screamed. The result, in fact, was a startling defeat for the Curial party; the men elected were, in general, independents who reflected rather well the various tendencies among the world episcopate.

They soon found that sixty-nine of the seventy draft documents already drawn up were so outdated and textbookish as to be useless even as starting points for debate and had to be completely rewritten. Fortunately, however, for the morale of the assembly there was one schema (as these documents were called) that could be immediately debated—the one on the liturgy; it was also a forward-looking and balanced document and also an ideal starting point, since as events were to show, it was the reform of the liturgy that dramatized for the average Catholic the meaning of the council.

The subsequent debate on the liturgy revealed a growing progressive mood among the bishops, who showed themselves humble enough to call in the best theologians available to bring them up to date on the latest developments. Their whole performance confirmed Pope John's genial intuition that powerful if latent forces for change were running strong in the Church.

Voices of impressive authority spoke on both sides of the issues during the debate by the bishops. But it was soon obvious that those favoring sweeping changes were in the ascendancy. Archbishop Hallinan of Atlanta, Georgia, one of the champions of reform, noted how amusing it was at times to hear bishops speaking in elegant Ciceronian Latin while arguing for the use of the vernacular languages.

The division into liberals and conservatives or progressives and traditionalists appeared, which was soon to manifest itself time and again during the next four years: Cardinals Doepfner of Munich, Alfrink of Utrecht, Koenig of Vienna, Suenens of Belgium, Doi of Tokyo, Leger of Montreal, Ritter of St. Louis, Meyer of Chicago, and Maximos IV Saigh of Antioch, with the African bishops in a solid bloc, threw their weight regularly on the side of change, against a conservative minority. Led by Curialists, Ottaviani, Staffa, Bacci, the U.S. apostolic delegate, Vagnozzi, Irish Dominican Cardinal Browne, and U.S. Cardinals Spellman and McIntyre, the conservatives tried in vain to stem the tide. "Are these fathers planning a revolution?" Ottaviani exclaimed.

But the critical test of strength between the two mentalities came on Wednesday, November 14, 1962, when Ottaviani introduced the second draft document, *On the Sources of Revelation*. The first speaker, Lienart, criticized it harshly as an unsuitable statement of the Catholic position on this key issue; others noted its monolithic preference for one school of theology; its cold, Scholastic formulas; and its condemnatory and negative tone. Prestigious scholar cardinals like Alfrink and Bea echoed the same sentiments, and finally Bishop De Smedt of Bruges voiced an eloquent plea for a completely new document drafted in the spirit of dialogue with other Christians.

The fate of the council and the future of the Church really hung in the balance as the votes were gathered, for unlike the one on the liturgy, this document dealt with absolutely fundamental principles of theology and doctrine; its viewpoint was the one that had governed the Church's thinking since Luther, the one the bishops themselves had assimilated in their seminary training and had used all their lives as their spiritual compass. To reject it would take a real act of intellectual courage on their part, for it would mean nothing less than a rejection on the intellectual level of the whole state of siege mentality characteristic of modern Catholicism.

As it turned out, the vote to reject it failed by a tiny percentage to secure the necessary two-thirds majority. At this point, the Pope intervened to break the deadlock rather than have the bishops discuss a document which nearly two thirds of them already rejected in toto. He ordered it sent back to a special commission to be completely rewritten. This was a most decisive step, and if any one conciliar act signalized the end of the Tridentine era, it was surely this.

Nevertheless, the bishops were still floundering around, and a deep sense of frustration could be felt in the baroque aula of St. Peter's. After nearly two months of deliberations and interminable speeches, they still had no definite sense of direction. It was at this juncture that Cardinal Suenens, primate of Belgium, proposed a blueprint: Focus all debate around the idea of the Church, he urged, so that as Vatican I was remembered as the Council on the Pope, Vatican II might be remembered as the Council on the Church. Study the Church, he suggested, first in its inner mystery and constitution and then in its relation to the world. This would mean engaging in a triple dialogue: with the faithful themselves, with the separated brethren, and with the world outside. An immense outburst of applause (in violation of council rules) showed that he had hit a bull's-eye, as did the subsequent endorsement of the idea by such cardinals as Montini and Lercaro.

Having found their way at last, the fathers were happy to take their first recess, on December 8, 1962. Before they reconvened, Pope John was taken from the world he had so captivated, and the council faced a new crisis: Would the new Pope carry through John's bold adventure?

It was with a sigh of relief that the progressives learned of the election of John Baptist Montini as his successor, a progressive obviously committed to the Johannine revolution. Pope Paul VI was sixty-five years of age, a northern Italian of diminutive stature and solid middle-class family. His father was a journalist and member of the Italian parliament during the pre-Fascist era and very much involved in the defense of the Church against anticlericals and socialists. The bookish young Montini, whose frail health kept him from residing in the seminary during his priestly studies, was ordained in Brescia and then sent for further study to Rome, where he was invited by Monsignor Pizzardo in 1922 to join the Vatican diplomatic staff. After a brief spell in Warsaw he returned to the Eternal City, where for the next thirty years (1924–54) he served in the Secretariat of State while also acting as chaplain for a time to the Federation of Italian Catholic University Students—work that brought him into a few rowdy encounters with Mussolini's thugs. He also worked in close association with the then Cardinal Pacelli, (later Pius XII), and traveled widely, even to the New World, and made many contacts in many countries. In 1954 Vatican politics led to his ouster and exile to Milan, where as archbishop he plunged into a ceaseless round of pastoral activity—saying Mass in foundries and industrial plants, attending sport and festival activities, and showing a constant concern with the problems of the poor and the alienated workers. Pope John made him his first cardinal and dropped broad hints of his desire to have him as a successor.

The new Pope opened the second session of the council (September 29 to December 4, 1963) with a magnificent address that reiterated the goals enunciated by Suenens: renewal of the Church, unity of all Christians, and dialogue with the world.

The debates in the second session ranged over such topics as ecumenism, religious liberty, modern communications, and anti-Semitism. The first document to command their attention was *On the Church,* a lengthy treatise which, as finally approved *(Lumen Gentium),* is one of the most important statements of the council. Its most controversial chapter proved to be the second one, which dealt with the doctrine of collegiality or the right of the bishops to participate as a body in the full and supreme authority of the Pope over the Church. Although this idea was deeply rooted in tradition, it appeared heretical to the conservatives accustomed to Pacelli's type of absolute monarchy.

The sharp division of opinion over the issue precipitated another crisis. The theological commission, headed by Ottaviani and charged with making the necessary revision in the document, moved at a snail's pace, and, in fact, a significant number of its members were opposed to the idea of collegiality as a dangerous infringement on the Pope's authority; they filibustered while seeking a way of watering down the statement.

But the four moderators led by Suenens circumvented them by submitting five questions containing the substance of the chapter directly to the assembly. The answers, they figured, would clearly indicate the mind of the bishops on collegiality and hence would stop the filibuster and force the commission to incorporate the results of the vote in their document. But the other directing agencies of the council—the presidents, the coordinating commission, and the secretariat—questioned the moderators' right to submit such a vote to the assembly. A conflict raged behind the scenes; finally, a compromise was reached: The moderators would be allowed to submit their orientation votes this one time, but not again. The accord was reached, no doubt, with the help of Paul VI, who showed his attitude at a special Mass when he warmly embraced the cardinal of Malines, who had just delivered a sermon urging the bishops not to lose courage but to continue to respond to the Pope's invitation to travel the road of dialogue and openness.

The vote by the bishops showed a definite preponderance in favor of collegiality, resolving the issue and decisively confirming the progressive tendency of the council.

Another moment of drama occurred a little later, when Cardinal Frings of Cologne sharply criticized Ottaviani's Holy Office for its methods, such as condemning writers without even a hearing; Frings called them a scandal to the modern world. The object of the attack—the old, nearly blind son of a baker from the tough Roman Trastevere slums—rose to his feet and vehemently rejected the accusation as due to ignorance.

The third session (September 14 to November 21, 1964) opened with a liturgical demonstration of collegiality as the Pope and twenty-four bishops concelebrated a Mass. One of the most important debates of this session had to do with the previously mentioned schema, *On the Sources of Revelation,* now called simply *On Divine Revelation;* it was now completely rewritten and reflected progressive theological tendencies in its acceptance of the results of modern biblical and historical research.

Debate was also begun on Schema 13, *The Church in the Modern World (Gaudium et Spes),* undoubtedly the most ambitious project of the Council both in its length and scope as well as in its objective, which was to begin a realistic dialogue with the modern world. During the debate on this schema, Cardinals Leger, Suenens, and Alfrink created a great stir when they called for reappraisal of the official Catholic teaching on marital morality, especially in regard to the problem of artificial birth control.

Another delicate topic that required treatment in any dialogue with the modern world was the question of religious liberty. If the Church was to speak with any effectiveness to the world, it certainly had to update its stand on this matter. The classical Catholic position, as enunciated in the *Syllabus of Errors,* claimed preferential treatment of the Catholic Church by the state while according only tolerance to other religions. This was a terribly burdensome anachronism for progressives and, led by the Americans, they asked for a statement proclaiming the Church's total commitment to complete religious liberty. A draft statement was finally drawn up by Cardinal Bea's secretariat for Christian unity.

It was generally known that a powerful minority led by Ottaviani still held to the old principle that error has no rights and were trying to bottle up the document in the commissions. Many of the bishops therefore were very ill at ease and wanted the vote taken as soon as possible. So they reacted strongly when on November 19, Cardinal Tisserant suddenly announced that no vote would be taken at that session on the question of religious liberty. The words brought the bishops to their feet; they swarmed into the aisles and milled around, obviously dismayed and upset. Someone grabbed a piece of paper, and a petition was hastily drawn up on the spot, quickly signed by more than four hundred, and then presented immediately to the Pope by a delegation led by Cardinals Meyer and Ritter. Paul refused, however, to contravene Tisserant's decision, and the matter was left hanging in suspense until the fourth session.

The bishops were also annoyed by a number of unilateral papal interventions instigated, no doubt, by the conservatives: The Pope, in order to pacify the minority, made last-minute changes in several key documents. One such change, in the constitution *On the Church,* emphasized papal primacy and the independence of the Pope at the expense of collegiality; another rendered the decree *On Ecumenism* less conciliatory toward the Protestants. Since these insertions were made right before the final voting on the documents, the bishops were practically forced to accept them or otherwise risk losing the entire documents. Distasteful as they were to the majority, they were nevertheless the price of obtaining virtual unanimity in the final balloting.

In the interim between the third and the final session Paul journeyed on a pilgrimage to the Eucharistic Congress in Bombay, where his reception by millions of Indians surpassed all expectations. Even the Communist press admitted that the exuberant crowds, the cheers, and the excitement exceeded anything in recent memory. He returned in time to open the fourth session (September 14 to December 8, 1965) and received a thunderous *"Viva il Papa!"* when he announced that he would personally go before the United Nations General Assembly to make an appeal for peace.

Tops on the agenda was the statement on religious liberty, which after much revision appeared satisfactory to the progressives. It affirmed the right of persons not to be coerced in any way in their religious beliefs and practices, and it acknowledged that the Church had at times sinned against this principle. American cardinals Cushing, Spellman, and Ritter gave the draft statement ringing endorsements. Cardinal Heenan quoted Newman's famous toast to conscience first and then to the Pope. But the intransigent tradition-alist leaders Ruffini, Siri, and Carli, with the majority of the Spanish bishops, worked strenuously to delay voting. But this time the Pope stepped in and in-sisted on a vote being taken immediately. He did not dare to appear before the United Nations without a decisive vote of the council in favor of religious liberty. The balloting indicated an overwhelming majority in favor of the document's strong affirmation of freedom.

Paul's visit to the UN in October was synchronized ingeniously with the discussion in the Vatican Council of the fifth and final chapter of Schema 13, "The Community of Nations and the Building Up of Peace." The Pope's rat-ification of the UN as he spoke to the assembled nations in person was one of the great moments of the Vatican Council. A TWA Boeing 707 sped him afterward back to Rome, and forty-six minutes later he alighted from a black Mercedes at the portico of St. Peter's and again received a tremendous *"Viva il Papa!"* from the bishops.

They were kept extremely busy putting the final touches to a wide vari-ety of documents that were promulgated at that session: They dealt with the pastoral office of the bishop, priestly life and ministry (which skirted clear of the vexing problem of celibacy), a condemnation of anti-Semitism, the re-newal of the religious orders, seminary training, Christian education, the mis-sions, the lay apostolate, and non-Christian religions. Two documents in particular—the constitution *On Revelation* and the pastoral constitution *On the Church in the Modern World*—generated intense debate before they were finally approved and promulgated.

The final voting session was attended by 2,399 bishops, and then the closing was celebrated with a ceremony outside in the piazza witnessed by thousands of pilgrims and sightseers and carried to the world by television.

The Second Vatican Council, the twenty-first in the history of the Church, was undoubtedly the most important religious event of the twenti-eth century to date. It brought some 2,500 of the top leaders of the world's largest religious body together for four three-month sessions over four years and engaged them in debate on most of the vital religious issues facing mankind. It issued all told some sixteen documents (four constitutions, nine decrees, and three declarations), which won the virtually unanimous consen-sus of the participants and which when implemented would produce far-reaching changes in Catholic communities around the world. It was the first ecumenical council in history to assemble with hardly any interference from secular governments, and the first to have other Christians in attendance as official delegates of their respective Churches.

Only time would tell, of course, which of the documents issued by the Council would prove of lasting significance and which would be remembered only as a celebration of the *Zeitgeist*. But it seems that at least five of its major changes will have a lasting effect.

First, the changes brought about in the liturgy—principally in the Mass—were the most visible and startling to the average churchgoer. The decree on the liturgy provided for translating the Latin text into the modern languages, and urged all concerned to make the liturgy intelligible to the layman and to secure their participation in the fullest manner.

Second was the definite advance in the Church's self-understanding as reflected especially in *Lumen Gentium*. Since Luther's day at least, the Catholic doctrine of the nature of the Church—as formulated in the works of theologians like Bellarmine—put much emphasis on its institutional, juridical, and hierarchial character; a rigid separation was posited between the clergy and laity—the clergy ruled, the laity obeyed. Treatises on the Church made much ado about who had what power over whom. This kind of thinking reached its apogee at Vatican I, which conceived of the Church in a very authoritarian way.

Vatican II definitely moved away from such a legalistic view. *Lumen Gentium* shifts the emphasis from the Church as a pyramidal structure to the Church as the whole people of God, and it lays stress on the fundamental equality of all as regards basic vocation, dignity, and commitment; it dwells on the common priesthood of the faithful. Office in the Church is seen as primarily one of service to the community. Authority is seen as the means of promoting the intimate fellowship of the Church, a fellowship that finds its principle of unity indeed in the collegial fellowship of Pope and bishops as successor to the apostolic college but that widens out to embrace all the members in a sweet fraternity of love and mutual service. The affirmation of the collegial relationship of Pope and bishops was, no doubt, the most important single contribution of *Lumen Gentium,* since it corrected the tendency to see the Pope as somehow isolated and set over the Church. The practical import of all this created a veritable revolution in the machinery of the Church as a greatly increased number of persons were drawn into the decision-making process on every level.

Third was the change in attitude and practice as regards other Christians. Rome held aloof from the ecumenical movement among Protestants until Pope John's arrival on the scene. Then the council slowly caught on to the spirit of his new approach to Christian unity. Its document on ecumenism *(Unitatis Redintegratio)* put the whole matter of Protestant-Catholic relations in an entirely new perspective. The ultimate goal of ecumenism was no longer viewed as the return of individual Protestants to the Catholic Church; the objective now was rather the reunion of all the separated brethren, whose status as true ecclesial communities was recognized. To hasten the day of reunion, Catholics were encouraged to enter into dialogue with other Christians, to engage in common prayer with them, and as far as possible to work in concert with them on social problems. Doctrinal difficulties were not minimized, nor did the council renounce the Catholic Church's claim to unique ecclesial status as containing the fullness of the means of salvation, but attention was drawn to the vital elements of the Christian tradition that were already held in common with most other Christians. Finally, the Catholic Church publicly confessed its own share of guilt in causing and perpetuating Christian disunity and committed itself solemnly to a continual self-reformation—which would involve correcting its own deficiencies, even extending to its past formulations of doctrine.

Fourth, the Council showed a much greater regard for the historical dimension in the Church's faith and life. In place of the nonhistorical Scholastic theology, with its emphasis on immutable ideas and essences, which since the days of Thomas Aquinas characterized Catholic thought, Vatican II manifested an openness to the totality of Christian and human history and fully recognized the historical conditioning that has affected every aspect of its tradition; even its sacred books, which previously were regarded as the work of a few human authors whom God had inspired to reveal his message, were now viewed as intimately involved in human history. "Liturgical forms and customs, dogmatic formulations thought to have arisen with the apostles now appeared as products of complicated processes of growth within the womb of history."[1] The use of the historical-critical methods of research was countenanced by the fathers, who finally faced squarely this portentous issue first raised by the Modernists.

[1] J. Ratzinger, *Theological Highlights of Vatican II* (Paramus, N.J.: Paulist/Newman Press, 1966), p. 99.

Finally was the council's call for dialogue with the modern secular world. This is especially the theme of its pastoral constitution, *On the Church in the Modern World*—a statement that marks a new departure in ecclesiastical literature in many respects, but especially in its language—so free of all archaic terminology—and in the utter realism with which it faces the Church's situation; it seems to embody more clearly than any other documents of the council the big heart of Pope John himself, pervaded as the document is with the spirit of love and concern for the whole human family. For the first time in modern history, the Church accepts the progressive cultural and social movements of modern history, which it previously regarded with much skepticism if not outright condemnation. It notes without regret the passing of old forms of thought and feeling and social relations, and while not indulging in naïve optimism, it sees the possibilities for human liberation that all of this entails. Abandoning its Constantinian and Tridentine triumphalistic manner, it places itself humbly at the service of humanity and points out how both Church and world can find common ground in their mutual recognition of the dignity of the human person and the nobility of his vocation to build the human community.

Chapter 34

THE SOUND AND FURY
OF RENEWAL

A tidal wave of change was set in motion by the Second Vatican Council. The decade after its closing in 1965 appears as the most tumultuous in the whole modern history of the Church. So many spiritual and religious landmarks were suddenly swept away that the average Catholic was left in a state of complete bewilderment. No doubt much of this sense of uprootedness is simply one manifestation of a general feeling common to everyone today and so well described by Alvin Toffler in his *Future Shock* and attributed to the constant acceleration of change affecting every aspect of our lives—not only religion, Toffler says, but all the old roots, family, nation, community, and profession are now "shaking under the hurricane impact of the accelerative thrust."[1]

For the average Catholic the first wave of the deluge struck when the new liturgy was introduced shortly after the council. Having been taught to think of the Mass as a mysterious unchangeable set of ceremonies originating with Christ himself, the average Catholic was not intellectually, spiritually, or emotionally prepared for what happened. The altar was brought forward, and the priest now faced the congregation; instead of whispering the prayers in Latin, he now read them aloud in the language of the people. Many of the old rites and ceremonies were discarded. Previously the faithful were taught to keep a prayerful demeanor and attitude, hardly noticing their neighbor, but now they were asked to turn and greet him with a "sign of peace."

As might be expected, once the myth of the Mass as a transhistorical, un-

---

[1] *Future Shock* (New York: Random House, Inc., 1971), p. 35.

changeable rite was exploded, all sorts of things began to happen. Some were angered and felt betrayed and stopped going to church. Others took the changes as a signal to improvise on their own; instead of attending the regular parish Mass, they gathered in small groups—often including a "liberated" priest—and discussed inspirational readings, sometimes chosen from the Scriptures, and then with little ceremony simply passed around ordinary bread and wine after reciting Christ's eucharistic words.

At the other extreme stood those who regarded the changes with abhorrence and tried to maintain the Latin Tridentine Mass. With the help of sympathetic priests they found ways of carrying on the old liturgy.

Most Catholics, however, accepted the changes more or less gracefully but with little enthusiasm and have learned to take in stride the continuing series of changes that have modified not only the Mass but the other sacraments as well.

The excitement over liturgical change, however, soon appeared mild in comparison with the uproar generated by more crucial issues. The bishops soon found that the debate over modernization could not be confined to the relatively placid precincts of episcopal assemblies. Priests and laymen soon jumped into the act, and the din of controversy exceeded anything in memory. Thanks to the omnipresent media, it was immediately reported around the world when priest or nun squared off against bishop, or even bishop against cardinal or cardinal against Pope.

The central issue was that of authority. Until the arrival of Pope John and the Second Vatican Council, the typical Catholic took the authoritarian structure of the Church as a dictate of divine revelation. They thought of the Pope as a kind of superhuman potentate whose every word was a command invested with supernatural authority; they even regarded the bishop with awe. In this state of affairs, few Catholics questioned the autocratic procedures customary in the Church, though to outsiders they often appeared medieval. The bishop, for instance, was seldom challenged in his claim to rule his diocese as a personal fief, and the same held good for the pastor in running his parish.

But the seeds of a democratic revolution were sown at Vatican II, particularly in such acts as its emphasis on the Church as being primarily the whole people of God, its call for dialogue between all members of the Church, its assertion of the collegiality of Pope and bishops, and its call for the erection of priests' senates and of pastoral councils that would include the laity.

The problem for the liberals, however, was that in spite of all these fine words, in practice little was changed. The basic structure still remained pyramidal, with power flowing downward from the Pope, its infallible head. And the Second Vatican Council took pains to safeguard his absolute authority; its concept of collegiality merely gave the bishops a consultative position, leaving the Pope free to use them or not in his governing of the Church and granting him broad discretionary powers as to the calling of synods and as to the topics to be discussed. The same was true of other reforms endorsed by the council; the bishop, for instance, still remained juridically absolute in his power over his diocese.

In the light of the new understanding of the Church projected by the Council, however, many Catholics found these authoritarian structures intolerable and scandalous and began to agitate for democratic reforms. They dissented, demonstrated, engaged in Church sit-ins, and made use of the press. They also received support from such prestigious bodies as the Canon Law Society of America, which in 1966 said that the Church should strive for maximum feasible participation by all in the deliberative and decision-making processes.

In most countries the bishops showed great reluctance to move down this road. But in Holland bold initiatives were taken in an effort to reform the decision-making process. The bishops set up the National Pastoral Council, based on very democratic and representative principles. Its delegates were elected by the people and charged with voting on proposals that often originated at the lowest level.

The debate over the manner in which authority is exercised in the Church reached a state of extreme tension when Pope Paul issued his encyclical *Humanae Vitae,* condemning the use of artificial methods of contraception, including the pill. He put his authority on the line—making his decision against the overwhelming majority of his birth control commission. The whole affair precipitated the most serious crisis for papal authority since Luther. Leading theologians, priests, a good section of the Catholic press, and even various national episcopates took stands somewhat at variance with the papal declaration.

Gradually there formed a strong body of opinion critical of the Pope for not acting collegially with the bishops in issuing his encyclical. The outstanding spokesman for this point of view was Cardinal Suenens, archbishop of Malines, Belgium, since 1962 and one of the architects of Vatican II. In speeches, press conferences, and writings, Suenens called for an end to the

Pope Paul VI.
© *David Lees/Corbis.*

Hildebrandine papacy and never tired of reiterating his theme: The Pope should no longer act as though he were outside the Church or above the Church. In elaborating major decisions he should be manifestly in union with the college of bishops. And he outlined a platform for progressives in the Church based on "coresponsibility"—a term he preferred to democracy. "The leader," he said, "is no longer the man who has all the answers but the man who succeeds in creating the environment in which dialogue, research, and constructive criticism are possible and in which the answers emerge by the gradual process of consent. I think that is the future direction of the Church—all parts moving together through, with and under authority."[2]

The root of the current problem of authority in the Church, as Suenens saw it, was a conflict between two theologies: One sees the Church as above all a fellowship of spiritual communities held together in essentials by their recognition of papal primacy; the other, the traditional one, still sees the

[2] *National Catholic Reporter,* September 3, 1969, p. 8.

Church on the Hildebrandine model—a superstate governed by an absolute monarch whose aim is to impose the maximum amount of conformity.

One of Suenens' major concrete suggestions was to terminate the old role of the papal nuncios as watchdogs of the Vatican whose job was to keep the bishops of any particular country in line. He wanted them transformed into mere ambassadors or mediators whose main task would be to keep Rome in touch with the national episcopates as well as with the individual governments. The national episcopates in turn would send similar representatives to Rome for the same purpose. Another proposal he made was to have the Pope elected by the bishops. If the laity took part in the election of bishops—which he also proposed—then they too would have some influence on the selection of the Pope.

This was the background of the Second Synod of Bishops, held in October 1969. Observers expected a confrontation between the Suenens-type progressives and the traditional papalists. But it never materialized as the Suenens forces failed to rally any appreciable support. The bishops merely agreed that it would take more time to work out the full implications of collegiality. And in a key proposition they reaffirmed full freedom for the Pope to act on his own, both in governing and in exercising his teaching authority. They also timidly expressed the hope that he would willingly accept their collaboration, just as they promised to seek his collaboration in their own declarations and decrees. This latter proposition passed with only 4 dissenting votes out of 143.

Since then it seems obvious that the Vatican is determined to keep the bishops in line. It has won a notable victory in Holland, where over the protests of the Dutch episcopate it elevated two stanch conservatives to the episcopate. And it forbade the continuance of the democratically elected Dutch National Pastoral Consultation, which was supposed to be a permanent body replacing the National Pastoral Council.

The whole controversy over the exercise of authority in the Church, painful and disturbing as it is for the faithful, has certainly aroused the ordinary member of the Church to a much greater awareness of his own personal responsibility. It has made him realize that the hierarchy does not have all the answers, and it has forced him to think about the role of the individual's conscience.

In the pre-Vatican II Tridentine Church the independence of the individual conscience was kept to a minimum. In fact, the task of the layman was simply to obey the directives of the bishops and priests, and when perplexed to consult a confessor who, skilled in casuistry, could usually come up with a concrete solution. The mood of questioning engendered by the events of the past decade wrought an enormous change in all of this. Many Catholics suddenly found themselves no longer willing to give blind obedience to Church authority. And in a few years the climate in the Church changed so drastically that few bishops dared to espouse a hard line on Pope Paul's birth control encyclical. Most of them have followed a generally permissive policy. Father Bernard Häring, one of the chief opponents of the papal position, retained his post as professor of moral theology at the Redemptorist seminary right in Rome itself.

An important reason for this weakening of the Church's absolute authority in the realm of morality is a deepened sense of history. Catholics are now more aware of the relative nature of past decisions by ecclesiastical authority in the realm of morality. They are also very conscious of the failure of Church authorities in recent times to give strong leadership on moral issues—war, race, peace.

Numerous prominent Catholic moral theologians have accepted this trend toward greater recognition of personal responsibility and have lent it their support, with theoretical arguments along personalist lines. As one Catholic moralist, Fr. J. H. Walgrave, O.P., recently put it, all morality involves encounter with the other person; in measuring the morality of our acts, recourse to absolute standards—whether derived from a revealed code or natural law—is often impossible. It is often a matter of choosing among competing values, sacrificing some to realize another. And Father Häring, in a recent address to two hundred Italian moral theologians, declared, "Whoever requires automatic conformity of all believers to a formulation of natural law made without any regard for the concrete facts sins not only against the respect due to conscience but also against that due to the Church's teaching authority itself."[3]

One of the most important spokesmen of this new approach to morality is J. Fuchs, professor for many years at the Jesuit Gregorian University in Rome. In several recent addresses he has sketched the outlines of a dynamic and evolutionary Christian approach to morality, as opposed to the static one

[3] *The New York Times* (April 6, 1970), p. 3.

so long prevalent in the Church. Its fundamental principle is human dignity: Whatever promotes human dignity, whatever contributes to humanization is moral. Lying and adultery are excluded, for instance, not because we are Christians but because we are human. Morality therefore will develop in tandem with our understanding of the nature of humanity. New data from the human sciences can lead to changes in morality. Many of our moral rules are only provisional. The Christian Gospel does not give us any additional concrete rules of morality; it does, however, point us in a certain direction by equipping us with deeper insights into such basic moral options as love and forgiveness.

Moreover, as Christians we are obliged to do out thinking about morality in dialogue with a community that has been nourished by a certain moral tradition. This moral tradition is summed up in the official teaching of the Church and shows that in certain situations Christians have always acted concretely in the same way. Such consistency itself provides a presumption that a particular way of acting is the right way, willed by God. Nevertheless, this official teaching is not infallible, even though the Church is guided by the Holy Spirit.

The difficulty of harmonizing this personalist approach to morality with the traditional, norm-centered school was underscored by the "Declaration on Certain Questions Concerning Sexual Ethics" *(Persona humana),* issued by the Vatican on January 15, 1976. In preparing the document, an attempt was made to utilize the insights of both the personalist and the traditional schools, but the task proved impossible, and the final text, it seems, simply reproduced in large part a recent work of Cardinal Palazzini, a practitioner of the old methodology and one of the authors of the statement.[4] Principles are laid down and conclusions drawn without much reference to the complexities of individual persons. One of the many Catholic theologians who took a very negative view of the document was Father Charles E. Curran, a professor at Washington's Catholic University and one of the outstanding champions of the personalist school. He characterized the document as "theologically inaccurate, psychologically harmful, and pedagogically counterproductive."[5] Curran objected most strenuously to the document's teaching that masturbation

---

[4] Richard McCormick, "Notes on Moral Theology," *Theological Studies* 38 (March 1977), pp. 112–13.
[5] Ibid., p. 110.

was an intrinsically and seriously disordered act. While not denying that masturbatory acts constitute a withdrawal from the full meaning of sexual behavior, he insisted that when they are viewed in the context of the person and the meaning of human sexuality, they "do not constitute such important matter . . . providing the individual is truly growing in sexual maturity and integration."[6]

One of the most difficult moral precepts in the Church's moral tradition has been its absolute prohibition of divorce. According to this law, no truly sacramental marriage between baptized Catholics can be dissolved—even by the Pope. In cases where the partners no longer can live peacefully together, they might be granted ecclesiastical permission to separate but without the right to remarry as long as either partner remains alive. In spite of the tremendous hardships this policy created for those involved in broken marriages, few dared to challenge the law until Vatican II.

But once the façade of immutability and infallibility began to crack under the pressure of postconciliar events, a number of priests and theologians began to question the wisdom and scriptural validity of the rigid divorce law. They want the Church to continue preaching the sacredness of marriage as a sacrament and as a divinely willed lifelong commitment. But they call for a more flexible pastoral approach in dealing with couples whose marriage has failed. Some even want the Church to give up its marriage tribunals altogether and leave the whole business of marriage legislation to the civil courts. Some pastors regularly circumvent the tribunals by giving their pastoral blessing to Catholics whose second marriages cannot be regularized by Church authorities. As with the birth control controversy, the debate promises to be long and painful but probably not so traumatic, since many Catholics are learning to live with diversity of opinion, even on important issues.

It is not only traditional moral precepts that have been called into question; some prominent theologians have even subjected traditional dogmas to critical scrutiny. Many of these theologians were first given notoriety at the Second Vatican Council when their ideas won the approval of the progressive bishops and were incorporated into the decrees. Since these theologians were regarded with suspicion before the council, their sudden rehabilitation had the earmarks of a Horatio Alger success story, and as the powers behind the scenes they were elevated to almost rock-star celebrity. The Rahners, Schille-

---

[6] Ibid., pp. 109–10.

beeckxs, Congars, and Küngs were suddenly in great demand on the lecture circuit, and their opinions were featured in the headlines of the world press.

Bold theories and reinterpretations of dogmas that formerly slumbered in the pages of obscure theological monthlies now became front-page news, and Catholics were regaled almost weekly with the latest Dutch speculations about the Eucharist, original sin, or papal infallibility.

The impetus for all of this was no doubt given by Pope John in his opening address to the Council when he called for a study and exposition of doctrine that would employ the literary forms of modern thought, since he said: "The substance of the ancient doctrine is one thing and the way in which it is presented is another." In this phrase John seemed clearly to endorse the concept of historicity—the idea that Church doctrinal formulas are not immutable in themselves but historically conditioned answers given by the Church at a particular moment to questions raised by the thought currents of a particular time. Until Vatican II the general feeling in the Church was that its dogmatic formulas were unchangeable—concepts like transubstantiation, infallibility, original sin, and sanctifying grace were regarded as perfect expressions of the truths contained in the Scriptures and definitive formulations that would be valid as such until the end of time. And Pius XII in his encyclical *Humani Generis* decried attempts by some theologians to update the Church formulas and "to weaken the significance of the dogmas . . . by seeking to free them from concepts and formulations long held by the Church and to return instead to the language of the Bible and the Fathers. . . ."

John, however, gave a clear signal in favor of the new school that subscribed to historicity. And his initiative was followed up in many of the conciliar decrees—notably in its decree *On Divine Revelation,* which made full allowance for the historical dimension of Christian doctrine.

The guiding principles of this historical view of dogma were first worked out by a number of French theologians in the 1940s. These were mainly priests associated with the Dominican school of Le Saulchoir in Étiolles, and the Jesuit school of Fourvières at Lyons under such leaders as Yves Congar (b. 1904), M. D. Chenu (b. 1895), Henri de Lubac (b. 1896), Jean (later Cardinal) Daniélou (d. 1974), and to some extent Teilhard de Chardin (d. 1955)—men who were concerned with the problem of relation of faith and doctrine to the changing context of cultures and civilizations. Or as one of the younger members of the school, E. Schillebeeckx (b. 1914), puts it: "The problem of the language of faith . . . presents us with a conflict between the historical ambiguity of Jesus' life, work and death on the one hand, and on the other, the religious and social expectations, aspirations and ideologies [derived] from [what] was expressed in Jesus himself. . . ."[7]

The guiding principles of this new historical theology were: 1. the inadequacy of every era to define truth for future eras; 2. the traditional Neo-Scholastic view of revelation as the transmission of definite fixed concepts was replaced by the idea of revelation as a personal self-disclosure by which God encounters the total person and communicates with him in a historical dialogue; 3. no formula of faith can therefore exhaust the truth; it can be exchanged for another formula more meaningful to the contemporary mind; 4. every formulation of a divine mystery is only the beginning, never the terminus; 5. a theory of the development of dogma that has many links with Cardinal Newman's seminal "Essay on Development," which emphasized the social, historical, and nonconceptual forces impinging on this process.

One of the first attempts after the council to reformulate Catholic doctrine in accordance with this "new theology" was the Dutch *New Catechism,* which appeared in October 1966 under the general responsibility of the Dutch hierarchy. Its fresh, novel approach captured attention, and it was soon translated into many languages and became an international best seller.

But it was too novel for many, and complaints soon brought the Holy See into the affair. A commission of cardinals was appointed by the Pope to examine it, and they issued a report on October 15, 1968, that listed a number of doctrines that the cardinals found inadequately treated, including the explanation of original sin, the nature of the eucharistic sacrifice, the virginal conception of Mary, infallibility, and the source of authority in the Church. And they asked that it be rewritten with the modifications needed. After lengthy negotiations between the Holy See and the Dutch bishops, a compromise was reached: The amendments recommended by the Holy See were included in an appendix.

Some churchmen were alarmed at the unprecedented wave of theological speculation, and an attempt was made by Cardinal Ottaviani at the First Synod in 1967 to persuade the bishops to issue an updated *Syllabus of Errors.* But in spite of their own concern, the bishops refused to retreat back into the fortress; they renewed their commitment to dialogue and freedom. They

---

[7] *The Crisis in Religious Language,* eds. Johan Baptist Metz and Jean-Pierre Jossua (New York: Concilium, 1973), p. 33.

agreed, nevertheless, that the theologians were going too far and too fast for the man in the pew. Their solution to the problem was to set up an international commission of theologians to aid the Holy See in dealing with the doctrinal confusion. Thirty well-known scholars drawn from a wide spectrum of theological thought and geographical areas were appointed. It included such progressives as Rahner, Congar, and De Lubac, although it omitted some other notables like Schillebeeckx, Bishop Butler, and Küng.

Hans Küng is a Tübingen theologian who has pushed the concept of historicity to its ultimate limits by calling on the Church to admit that its dogmas might not only be historically conditioned, open to extension, and replaceable, but even downright false. In his book *Infallible? An Inquiry*,[8] for example, he called for a revision of the dogma of papal infallibility, which he said should not simply be reinterpreted but actually discarded, since it was disproved by historical and biblical research and was no longer operative.

In obvious reaction to Küng's ideas, the Sacred Congregation for the Doctrine of Faith issued on June 24, 1973, a "Declaration Against Certain Errors of the Present Day," in which it repeats the Catholic teaching on the infallibility of the Church and the Pope, which, it says, is a charism that guarantees immunity from error to Pope and bishops when they define doctrine. However, it does admit the factor of the "historical condition that affects the expression of Revelation"[9] and that can be found in the language used, the incompleteness of formulation of the doctrine, and other circumstances that might affect the expressions used. It therefore admits the possibility of finding later formulas that would improve the way of formulating the dogma. But it excludes as untenable by Catholics all dogmatic relativism, which would hold that dogmas are only a series of approximations, always falling short of the truth.

In addition, the Roman authorities instituted a process to examine officially the orthodoxy of Küng's views and repeatedly requested him to come to Rome for discussions, which he persistently avoided, claiming that he would not receive a fair trial. He demanded the right to see the full dossier on his case before submitting to any inquiry and also wanted to choose his own defense counsel.

Many theologians regard the Küng affair as the acid test of how liberally

[8] Hans Küng, *Infallible? An Inquiry* (Garden City, N.Y.: Doubleday, 1970).

[9] "Declaration in Defense of the Catholic Doctrine" (Washington, D.C.: U.S. Catholic Welfare Conference, 1973), p. 7.

the Church will interpret its Vatican II declarations favoring freedom of inquiry. Although the *Index of Forbidden Books* was abolished in 1965 by Pope Paul, many theologians claim that an inquisitorial mentality still holds sway in Rome, and they cite the Küng affair as a case in point. In 1968 some 1,360 theologians signed a statement calling for due process for theologians in cases where the Roman authorities object to their teaching.

But amid all the upheaval, no postconciliar trend has been so disturbing to the bishops as the spectacular decline in vocations and the exodus of large numbers of priests, brothers, and nuns. From 1962 to 1974 the total number of seminarians in the United States alone decreased by 31.4 per cent, the number of religious brothers by 20 per cent, and the number of sisters by 18 per cent. The number of American priests who left the public ministry between 1966 and 1972 stands at around 8,000, or thirty times what it was in any corresponding period before the council. Moreover, figures released in 1974 show that while the Catholic population around the world increased since 1960 from 530 million to 659 million, the number of priests has remained virtually static.

No doubt the desire to get married has been a major influence on the decision of many to leave the priesthood, and polls taken worldwide indicate that a majority of priests favor changing the law of celibacy. But there is much more to the crisis than that, and it is doubtful whether a mere change in the law of celibacy would halt the leakage from the priestly ministry.

The root cause of the crisis, it appears, is the question of the priest's identity: What does being a priest really mean today?

Before the council the answer was easy. Most Catholic priests would have readily accepted Cardinal Suhard's famous definition given in his book *Priests Among Men:* "He is not a lay person vested with a temporal function but a man set apart from the faithful, endowed by God with transcendent powers and marked with a consecrating character which sets him apart, makes him at once a pontiff and head in the community of the baptized."

The changes of the past ten years, however, have called into question all three basic points of this definition: the sacred character of the priest, his apartness, and his unique powers.

First, the sacredness attached to the very person of the priest is now seen as a historical development that is unsupported by the data of the New Testament, and even an actual hindrance to the exercise of the ministry in a world that no longer thinks in terms of the sacred and the profane as two distinct realms.

Second, by emphasizing the nature of the Church as the whole faith community, it set in motion a democratic trend that makes the old caste system of priesthood seem medieval. Moreover, for various reasons the Church is becoming the affair of the personally committed rather than the born Catholic type. And hence there is no longer as much need for the priest to bear practically the whole burden of the Church's mission—which takes away one of the main historical reasons for his being set apart.

Finally, his strictly cultic tasks—presiding at the Eucharist, administering the sacraments—have lost some of their capacity to make him feel set apart in view of Vatican II's affirmation that all the faithful participate in the priesthood of Christ and in view of the proposals to restructure the ministry to allow a greater variety. Moreover, on his own terrain of theology, in this age of specialization the priest often finds himself challenged by laypersons who may be better informed on particular topics than he is. Finally, laymen are beginning to take over much of his job of administration.

It is no wonder then that many priests suffer from a sense of confusion about their role.

With regard to the problems facing the priest, the Dutch Church once again showed its willingness to grapple publicly and imaginatively with key issues of renewal. At the Dutch Pastoral Council held at Noordwijkerhout in January 1970, an overwhelming majority voted that the compulsory link between celibacy and ministry be abolished. The Dutch bishops agreed to work in consultation with the universal Church for changes whereby married priests could be admitted to service in the Latin Church and priests who had married could be reinstated in the ministry under certain conditions.

But this door opened to change by the Dutch was quickly slammed shut by their brother bishops in the Synod of 1971, when they reaffirmed the Church's determination to maintain its law of celibacy for priests.

Like the secular priests, the nuns and priests of the religious orders have also entered a period of severe crisis. In fact, probably no sector of the Church has been so polarized as these communities of men and women bound to God, to each other, and to the Church by their vows of poverty and chastity and their obedience to a rule of life derived from some saintly founder. The battle between advocates of radical change and upholders of the status quo has torn apart many of these communities, some of whom have lost more than half of their membership. Until the council these orders were often rigidly, even grotesquely, traditional, with their outlandish dress and huge, fortresslike convents and monasteries. So in their case, especially, the council's call for change and updating was bound to be extremely disruptive.

One of the most evident signs of Christian renewal since the council has been the progress toward greater Christian unity. This has been true both on the local level, where Roman Catholics and other Christians have worked—often with great success—to remove age-old barriers between them, and also on the upper levels, where a series of important doctrinal agreements have been reached by theologians.

Until the Second Vatican Council, the twentieth-century ecumenical movement was principally the work of Protestants, beginning at the World Missionary Conference of Edinburgh in 1910. Numerous world assemblies followed, including the Edinburgh Conference of 1937, which approved the proposal for a World Council of Churches, which was formally organized at Amsterdam in 1948. Its member churches officially proclaimed their faith in Our Lord Jesus Christ, God and Savior, and committed itself to "help the Church penetrate the churches and make them one."

In spite of fruitful contacts between some groups of Catholics and Protestants, the Catholic Church officially held aloof from the movement until the Second Vatican Council, when it laid down a whole new approach to the problem of Christian unity. Above all, by loosening up the simple identification of the Church of Christ with the Roman Catholic Church, it gave an entirely new focus to the dialogue between these two divisions of Christendom.

Since then many things have happened. Symbolic of the changed situation was Pope Paul's visit to the headquarters of the World Council of Churches at Geneva in 1971, where he recited the Lord's Prayer with its leaders.

Without attempting to describe even in general terms the revolutionary changes that have affected Protestant-Catholic relationships on all levels, we will just limit ourselves to listing the main doctrinal agreements that have been reached by officially commissioned groups of theologians—keeping in mind that these conclusions do not imply official status but are aimed at consensus building and eventual official approval.

Historically, the main theological differences have involved the relation of Scripture to tradition, the role of Mary in man's salvation, the true meaning of the Lord's Supper, the nature of the ordained ministry, and papal primacy and infallibility. On all these points there have been significant advances, as theologians in dialogue have been able to reach a consensus that was previously considered impossible.

Considering the historic centrality of the Eucharist in Christian faith and worship, it was fitting that it be given the greatest amount of attention. Progress here has been substantial through such dialogues as the Lutheran-Catholic Consultation on *The Eucharist as Sacrifice* (1968) and *Eucharist and Ministry* (1970), the *Anglican/Roman Catholic Windsor Statement* on the Eucharist (1971), and the report of the Groupe des Dombes, composed of French and Swiss, Lutheran, Reformed, and Catholic theologians. There was general agreement that Christ is present body and blood in the eucharistic mystery and that the sacrament makes present his sacrifice.

This growing consensus has affected the question of intercommunion as Protestants and Catholics have wondered whether they should not at least occasionally share the bread and wine together at their services. The *Vatican Ecumenical Directory* of 1967 allowed Protestants to receive at a Catholic Eucharist in case of grave spiritual need, but it made no provision for reciprocity. Some Catholic bishops, however, have allowed their faithful to take the Protestant Eucharist under limited conditions, including basic agreement on faith in Jesus' Real Presence.

The closely related issue of valid ministry has also been much discussed and explored by teams of Catholic and Protestant experts. Up to this point the Roman Catholic Church has always insisted that for a valid ministry one must be ordained by a bishop who was himself linked by imposition of hands with the historic episcopacy, supposedly stretching back to the Apostles.

But the tendency among the dialogic groups has been to situate valid ministry in a broader context. Apostolic succession is not simply identified with the historical chain of bishops but depends also on fidelity to the Gospel and conformity of life and word to the teaching of the Apostles. Insofar as a Church is apostolic in this sense they consider its ministry valid.

But most Catholics still hold that due to the rupture of the sixteenth century the Protestants lost contact with the historic chain of bishops, thus losing the fullness of the sign of apostolic succession, and hence these Catholics argue that episcopal ordination is something that all Christian communities should strive for.

Notice we say "most Catholics"; a *Memorandum* issued by some very prominent Catholic and Protestant theologians in Germany refused to place such a high value on episcopal ordination. This controversial document, issued by the University Ecumenical Institutes, maintains that the unbroken sequence of imposed hands was only a help in safeguarding the apostolic tradition and merely a good sign of the continuity and unity of the Church. Ordination itself, they hold, is only the customary way of being commissioned for service to the Church. It is merely the recognition of a call already given by the community or the Holy Spirit and gives one a participation in the mystery of Christ. For this reason, therefore, the document called for mutual recognition of ministries by Protestant and Catholic Churches, since the differences are no longer of such weight as to require separation.

Most observers, however, would probably agree with theologian Avery Dulles that the authors of the *Memorandum* have gone too far too fast. Serious doctrinal differences over ordination, episcopacy, and papacy preclude still, it seems, any full mutual recognition of ministries. And so at this moment both sides have a serious question to ask themselves: Protestants, whether the episcopacy of apostolic succession is not still the surest safeguard and clearest sign of pastoral authority and of the unity and authority of the Church. Catholics, whether their episcopal office as presently structured reflects historical conditioning rather than New Testament imperatives and is therefore in need of radical change if it is to serve as a unifying office for the whole Christian community.

The thorniest question of all is that of papal primacy—the chief issue that split the Christian Church in both the Eastern Schism and the Protestant Reformation.

Even on this question there has been some progress, although no such breakthrough as in the case of the Eucharist. Sentiments expressed by certain Christian leaders outside the Roman communion show a willingness to grant the bishop of Rome a pastoral sort of primacy. This idea has been voiced before his recent retirement by no less a figure than the Archbishop of Canterbury, Michael Ramsey.

The two most significant dialogues on this issue, however, have been the one involving American Lutheran and Roman Catholic theologians, completed in 1974, and the one involving Anglican and Roman Catholic theologians, completed in 1975. In the Lutheran-Catholic dialogue both sides agreed that a trajectory of images in the New Testament indicates that Peter exercised a ministry that involved responsibility for the unity of the whole

Church. They also agreed that for many centuries the bishop of Rome validly succeeded to this Petrine office and in so doing made notable contributions to the cause of Christian unity. Finally, they agreed that history since the Reformation shows that Christians still have need of such a Petrine office and that the papacy in spite of its notable failures still has the best claim to such an office. But before the Lutherans would accept any kind of papal primacy over the Church, it would have to be extensively restructured so as to eliminate its autocratic and bureaucratic features.

The participants in the Anglican-Roman Catholic dialogue reached conclusions quite similar to those just mentioned. Like the Lutherans, the Anglicans recognized the value of an office of universal primacy such as the bishop of Rome alone has exercised and alone still does exercise. And they agreed that in any future union the bishop of Rome would be the appropriate one to hold such an office. Like the Lutherans, however, the Anglicans still recognized some difficulties that remained, not insuperable they believed, but ones that would require further study before they could accept papal primacy. These included their fears of abuse of papal power and reservations they entertained about two infallibly defined Marian dogmas, the Immaculate Conception and the Assumption.

On the hypersensitive issue of Mary's role in man's salvation, there has not yet been a great amount of dialogue. In fact, a recent listing of conferences held between U.S. Catholic and Protestant theologians over the last ten years does not mention a single one devoted to Mary.[10] This is a somewhat surprising fact when we recall that the Second Vatican Council laid down the groundwork for a new approach that does much to meet traditional Protestant objections to the Catholic position on Mary.

This new Catholic approach to Mary can be summarized in several points. First, after much debate the bishops decided not to issue a separate treatise on Mary but to include its statement on Mary as simply one chapter in its general Dogmatic Constitution on the Church, *Lumen Gentium*. The implications of this decision were significant. It indicated that the bishops wanted to emphasize the fact that in spite of her unique prerogatives Mary was still to be regarded as a fellow member of the Church and not as some kind of semi-divine being exalted above the Church, all impressions to the contrary caused by misguided piety notwithstanding. Second, there was a dis-

---

[10] *1976 Catholic Almanac* (Huntington, Ind.: Our Sunday Visitor, 1975), pp. 337–41.

tinct biblical emphasis in the Council's text on Mary, an emphasis duly acclaimed by Protestant observers at the Council. This effort to stay close to Scripture helped the bishops to produce a very sober treatise free of the excesses that have often characterized even official documents on Mary. The Council, in brief, stated that Mary was deserving of special honor and reverence as Mother of God and Mother of the Redeemer. She was also to be honored as Mother of the Church insofar as she co-operated out of love and embraced God's saving will with a full heart so that in Augustine's words, "there might be borne in the Church the faithful, who are members of Christ their Head." Moreover, she was to be hailed, venerated, and invoked "as a preeminent and altogether singular member . . . model and excellent exemplar (of the Church) in faith and charity," free from all stain of sin and a model of holy virginity and motherhood.[11] And while admonishing the faithful to persevere in the various forms of piety that devotion to Mary has produced, the bishops at the same time cautioned them against exaggeration and vain credulity.

Third, the bishops took another step that could further the cause of greater agreement about Mary. They laid down what might be called the principle of doctrinal relativity. This idea is contained in two important points that they make in their document on Ecumenism: First, that even past doctrinal formulations of the Church may be in need of reform; and second, that the truths of faith do not all occupy the same level of importance but form a hierarchy. These admissions have profound ecumenical implications. They allow much more flexibility for Catholics in discussion with Protestants since they would seem to permit disagreement on secondary issues if unity can be reached on more important ones. Theologian Avery Dulles, S.J., for instance, recently invoked the principle of a hierarchy of truths when he called for Rome to lift the anathemas directed against those who deny the definitions of the Immaculate Conception and the Assumption.[12]

While Protestant and Catholic theologians have moved slowly in exploring the ramifications of the Council's new approach to Mary, the impact of the Council on Marian devotion and theology within the Catholic Church has been enormous. As in so many other areas, it opened up an entirely new chapter. There has been a great decline in traditional forms of piety toward

[11] *The Documents of Vatican II* (New York: America Press, 1966), p. 86.
[12] *Origins* (Washington, D.C.: National Catholic Documentary Service, December 26, 1974), pp. 417–21.

Mary: rosaries and medals have been tossed away, statues of Mary have been removed, hymns to Mary have faded out of memory, and May Day celebrations have disappeared.

Marian theology too has been much affected by the critical attitude engendered by the Council. A recent survey of studies on Mary from 1966 to 1975 notes that since the Council comprehensive studies of Marian doctrine have all but ceased.[13] Much attention, on the other hand, is being devoted to the Scriptural and historical foundations of Mariology. Moreover, while little work is being done on topics like the Immaculate Conception, Mary as Mediatrix or Co-Redemptrix—topics formerly favored—questions like the virginity of Mary and the relation of the Church to Mary are intensely debated and studied.

The issue of Mary's virginity came to the fore when the Dutch Catechism appeared in 1966 and critics pointed out that it had side-stepped the question of the virgin birth. A commission of cardinals appointed by the Pope ordered the Dutch bishops to issue a revised edition of the Catechism clearly teaching the virginal conception of Jesus, but the Dutch bishops refused. A compromise was finally reached when the latter agreed to add an appendix containing the Vatican's instruction reiterating the traditional doctrine on the virgin birth.

Since then there has been considerable debate among Catholic theologians as to whether Catholic faith demands belief in Mary's virginity as a biological fact or whether one could regard the assertion of the virgin birth as a symbolic concept. To put it in even more precise technical terms: "Whether the virginal conception of Jesus in the Matthean and Lucan infancy narratives might simply be regarded as a theologoumenon, i.e., a theological assertion that does not directly express a matter of faith or an official teaching of the Church, and hence is in itself not normative, but that expresses in language that may prescind from factuality a notion which supports, enhances or is related to a matter of faith."[14]

Considering the emotionally charged nature of the issue and the fact that it concerns a point that no Catholic would have dreamed of debating a few years ago, the controversy has been carried on with a relative serenity and objectivity that speaks well for the sophistication and maturity of the Catholic

[13] J. Fitzmeyer, S.J. "The Virginal Conception of Jesus in the New Testament," *Theological Studies* 37 (June 1976), pp. 253–89.
[14] Ibid.

community of scholars. If we are to believe Father René Laurentin, one of the outstanding defenders of the traditional position, the school of opinion favoring a merely symbolic interpretation of the virgin birth is now the dominant one among continental European Catholic theologians. In fact, he maintains that the pendulum has swung so sharply that one even has difficulty getting a hearing for the traditional view. He is hopeful, however, that once Catholics have learned to cope with the new and intoxicating atmosphere of freedom in the Church and have learned to take the constantly shifting theories of exegetes and historians in stride, they will recognize the scriptural necessity of the virgin birth and the importance of affirming it in the physical real sense in order to maintain the integrity of the Catholic faith.[15]

THE DECADE AFTER the Second Vatican Council has been one of exceptional turmoil not only in the Church but in civil society as well. As the American historian Sydney Ahlstrom says in regard to the United States, it has been a time when "the old foundations of confidence, patriotic idealism, moral traditionalism and even of historic Judaeo-Christian theism, were awash. Presuppositions that had held firm for centuries—even millennia— were being widely questioned."[16] For Catholics, it amounted to a major revolution or, as some have called it, a Copernican shift in consciousness. Thanks to the Second Vatican Council, Catholics have been forced to re-examine many of their most cherished practices and traditions. Such a process was bound to be disruptive, but the sheer magnitude of the crisis it provoked astonished everyone.

---

[15] *Revue des Sciences philosophiques et théologiques* 60 (1976), pp. 451–500.
[16] Sydney E. Ahlstrom, *A Religious History of the American People,* vol. 2 (New Haven: Yale University Press, 1974), p. 600.

Chapter 35

THE BARK OF PETER IN
STORMY SEAS (1976–1989)

Many storms have crashed around the Church in its long history and threatened to overwhelm and destroy it. The latest one began with the Second Vatican Council as it unleashed galelike winds of change that since then have continued to blow across the Church. Momentous changes indeed; changes that have affected "the entire very coherent, doctrinal-moral-liturgical arrangement . . . inaugurated by the Council of Trent," as Father Frans Van Beeck, S.J., says.[1]

No doubt one of the most difficult changes for the average Catholic to digest was the call of the council for openness and dialogue with other churches and religions. It struck very hard at the Catholic sense of identity. Before, the Council Catholics knew who they were, since they knew who they weren't. They defined themselves over against the non-Catholics—the Protestants, members of other religions, secular humanists, etc. Individually Protestants and other non-Catholics, they believed, might be saved by reason of their invincible ignorance, but no power to save could be ascribed to their institutions as such.

But the Council did a 180-degree turn. It recognized the merits and salvation potential of the other churches and even other religions. In doing so it broke down the boundaries defining the Catholic faith experience and opted for a strategy of openness and dialogue. It thereby confronted Catholics with a difficult challenge. Instead of defining themselves by their separateness and

---

[1] *Catholic Identity After Vatican II* (Chicago: Loyola University Press, 1985), p. 19.

exclusiveness, Catholics would have to forge a new form of identity. They would have to learn how to be open to other faiths while maintaining their own specific identity.

As Father Van Beeck says, preserving identity while remaining open is a process that will continue to entail much pain and confusion. "It is a process . . . likely to be carried along on the tide of risk taking and withdrawal, expansion and contraction, exhilaration and disappointment, consolation and desolation, integration and disintegration . . ."[2]

Moreover, as an astute observer points out, "Two of the great supports of Catholic identity have been rocked. The first is Catholic schools, which are fewer in number, and serve fewer Catholics. The second is the dramatic increase between 1960 and 1985 of mixed marriages. Religious socialization is very different in a mixed marriage than it is in a marriage between two Catholics. That is a problem that nobody in the institution wants to tackle but it has, as the Orthodox Jewish community has found, profound implications for a continuing identity. It is possible that in the next century Catholics will be ten per cent rather than a quarter of the population."[3]

The leakage is already apparent. Polls indeed show that the Church is losing many of its adherents who are alienated and drifting away. A recent *New York Times*/CBS poll in fact showed that about one person out of five brought up as a Roman Catholic no longer considers himself or herself an adherent of the faith, and "the loss through such defections is about three times as large as the Church's gain through conversions."[4]

Nonetheless Catholics who remain are strongly attached to their Church. According to an extended poll by Castelli and Gallup, American Catholics who have stayed are in the midst of a religious revival; the Vatican Council has actually been a raving success if measured by the attachment of the Catholic laity to their Church—indeed, by "their sense of ownership of the Church," which is remarkable; they have more "confidence in the Church than in any other institution," with 85 per cent saying that their lifetime experience of the Church has been "overall positive."[5] But this, of course, does

[2] Ibid., p. 19.
[3] Dr. William McCready in Eugene Kennedy, *Tomorrow's Catholics, Yesterday's Church* (New York: Harper & Row, 1988), p. 41.
[4] *The New York Times*, September 10, 1987, p. 10.
[5] George Gallup, Jr., and Jim Castelli, *The American Catholic People* (Garden City, N.Y.: Doubleday, 1987), p. 43.

not reflect the much more negative feelings of the 24 per cent (16.5 million) who consider themselves "unchurched" (attending Mass only for weddings or funerals, if at all).[6]

But what about the priests? Being involved with the Church on a daily basis, they were bound to feel the impact of the changes more acutely. Their "identity crisis," in fact, has been more severe as is evident in the precipitous decline in their numbers. Vatican statistics show that of 368,000 parishes in the world, 157,000 have no resident priest; in the United States about one in ten parishes is already without a resident priest.

A Dutch study showed that on an index where 100 would represent complete replacement by ordinations for every 100 losses due to death or resignation, the Netherlands registered 8, Belgium 15, Germany 34, France 17, Italy 50, Ireland 45, Spain 35, and Portugal 10. The same is more or less true of seminarians, who in almost every country in Europe and North America have decreased by half over the past decade.[7]

In the diocese of Chicago almost half of those ordained since 1976 have resigned and married.[8] Researchers indicate that the Catholic Church in the United States will have 50 per cent fewer active clergymen by the end of the century than it had in 1966, while in many other countries the prognosis is even worse.

As a result, a change in our understanding of ministry is emerging. Under the pressure of the shortage of priests, there has been a tremendous growth of new, nonordained ministries, such as catechists in Africa and leaders of base communities in Latin America. History, it seems, is forcing the Church to break away from the clerical caste mentality, with its stranglehold on ministry, in favor of a theology that looks to the natural leaders of a community to take up forms of ministry previously reserved to the ordained, celibate, male clergy. It seems likely that this process will continue until these leaders who have come to the fore—whether married or not, whether male or female—will be installed by the community as their priests, perhaps with the prior permission of the authorities, perhaps only in an ex post facto way. The alternative is to believe that hundreds of thousands of Catholic communities around the world will accept being permanently deprived of the Sunday Eucharist.

[6] *Ibid.,* pp. 162–64.
[7] "The Future of Ministry," *America,* March 28, 1981, p. 244.
[8] *The Tablet,* November 12, 1988, p. 1301.

Of course there is another possibility—that the authorities themselves will take the initiative and end the shortage by doing away with the requirement of celibacy and also by ordaining women.

As to enforced celibacy, the arguments in its favor no longer seem persuasive to a great number of Catholics. The concept of ritual purity (sex defiled the priest) on which it was originally based now seems bizarre, while the main argument now used to justify it—that celibacy allows the priest to be totally at the disposal of his people—seems a somewhat idealized version of the facts.

As to ordination of women, while that door has been slammed shut, we might note that the Church has slammed other doors shut just as hard only to open them later under the pressure of circumstances. Moreover, if we look at the actual statement of Paul VI in rejecting the ordination of women, one can see he did not preclude the possibility of an eventual change in the policy.

THE POLISH POPE

The man who is presently Pope, however, is dead set against such changes. As supreme pastor of a flock still in disarray from the shock waves of Vatican II and the birth-control crisis, Karol Wojtyla, it seems, has dedicated himself to a strategy of "restoration"—a concerted effort to recuperate those parts of the great Catholic tradition which he and his colleagues feel have been neglected and almost lost in the aftermath of the Council.

When he was elected Pope on October 16, 1978, his choice of a name that embodied the names of his three predecessors seemed to indicate an intention to continue their liberalizing policies. He was considered a theological moderate and a liberal on social issues and had been an active participant in the Second Vatican Council.

Born at Wadowice, a village near Krakow, Poland, on May 18, 1920, into a worker's family, Wojtyla at an early age experienced his share of the horrors of our century. His youth was spent under the shadow of the swastika when the Nazis invaded his homeland in 1939 and reportedly sent him into forced labor. Then the Russians took over at the end of the war and subjected his homeland to Stalinist terror.

Ordained in 1946, he spent several years pursuing theological studies in

Pope John Paul II on a visit to
Kimasi.   © *SIPA PRESS/Art
Resource, New York.*

Rome, where he did a doctoral dissertation on Max Scheler, one of the leaders
of the school of phenomenology. However, he seems to have been much more
influenced by the scholastic modes of thought characteristic of his Roman professors. This is indicated by his penchant for abstractions and deductive logic.

People found his background rather intriguing for a Pope. A factory
worker who wrote plays and dated before deciding for the priesthood, he was
considered something of an intellectual, being the author of three books and
numerous scholarly articles. Also his working-class background seemed to
make him a providential leader of the Church in competing for the loyalty of
the masses in Communist-ruled countries.

An important part of his strategy of "restoration" is to strengthen loyalty
to papal authority by projecting the image of an energetic leader fully in
charge, determined to lead. To this end the Pope has become an extremely visible head of the Church. Indeed no Pope has been more visible on the world
stage than the ubiquitous Wojtyla.

A TRAVELER IN ALL SEASONS

By the time he reached the twelfth year of his pontificate in October 1989, he had made some forty-two foreign trips. Thanks to television there are few who have not seen the Pope kneeling to kiss the tarmac of an airport as crowds waited to welcome him. The pattern of his visits has become ritualistic and routine: his waving to enormous crowds from the "popemobile," his papal Mass with hundreds of thousands of communicants, his visits to the various institutions of the host church and the formal, carefully worded addresses on major issues facing the Church, as well as his care to meet with leaders and members of other churches and faiths in ecumenical settings.

The extent of his travels is truly extraordinary. He began these "pilgrimages of faith" only a few months after his enthronement when he landed in Santo Domingo on the island of Hispaniola, the site of the first Mass said in the new world. After that he traveled to Puebla in Mexico and then a few months later to Poland where he was greeted by a million co-religionists. A few months later he came to New York to address the United Nations in General Assembly where he championed the primacy of spiritual values and applauded the Universal Declaration of Human Rights. At Yankee Stadium he called for Americans to share their wealth with the poor of the Third World.

The only interruption of any length in his travels was due to the attempt on his life on May 13, 1981, by Mehmet Ali Agça, a young Turkish hired assassin who shot him at point-blank range as he rode slowly around St. Peter's Square, greeting the faithful.

The wound was severe and required him to be hospitalized for three months. But by February of the following year he was ready to fly again, making seven trips abroad during 1982. One of the most notable was his pilgrimage to Great Britain where he celebrated an ecumenical service with Anglican Archbishop Robert Runcie in Canterbury Cathedral.

And so, year after year, he has continued leapfrogging by jet over the wide world, carrying his message to teeming urban centers as well as the backwaters of civilization, flying over 400,000 miles in a heroic effort to unify his restless flock of 900 million and keep them attached to traditional teaching. However, many would agree with Eugene Kennedy that these "papal visits belong to a bygone era of spectacles, of world fairs and centenary exhibitions, of nineteenth-century circuses, Teddy Roosevelt's great white fleet sailing majestically into the great harbors of the world to show the flag."[9]

One of the memorable episodes during all this barnstorming occurred at the airport in Nicaragua in 1983 where in full view of world television he shook his finger at a kneeling priest, Fr. Cardenal, who had refused to obey orders to resign his post in the Nicaraguan government. And later at his Mass in Managua, he engaged in a shouting match with the unruly *campesinos* who took offense at his apparent coolness toward their revolution.

In May of 1985, beginning a trip to the Benelux countries, the Pope arrived in the Netherlands to face a deeply divided Church with a large element actively hostile to his position on some key issues. There were rowdy demonstrations and some troublemakers even burned him in effigy. Even the loyal Catholics seemed unenthusiastic. He got an earful of harsh criticism, which he seemed to accept with serenity. Some young people voiced their inability to accept his hard-line teachings on sexuality, and even some of the bishops voiced their concern at the pain of those finding it difficult to remain in the Church.

Nothing could be more in contrast with this than his experience in Poland where, it is widely believed, the mood of sheer exultation caused by his election and his visit there in 1979 energized the Solidarity labor movement and helped to make it a constructive force for the renovation of Polish society. His third visit there, June 8, 1987, coincided with the National Eucharistic Congress, when a million people gathered in procession in Warsaw. It was a moment when people were predicting the imminent demise of Solidarity, and the government made it clear they wanted him to steer clear of the whole question. But instead the Pope took every opportunity to sing the praises of Solidarity. In fact, his stouthearted faith in Solidarity and his discussions with Lech Walesa and General Jaruzelski no doubt helped to turn the tide and prepare the way for the legalization of Solidarity—a pivotal event and a forecast of the remarkable changes that swept through the Communist world in 1989.

His visits to the major Marian shrines at Fatima and Lourdes have underscored his very strong devotion to the Blessed Mother. At Fatima in 1982 he reconsecrated the whole world to the Virgin and prayed for its deliverance

[9] *Tomorrow's Catholics, Yesterday's Church*, p. 47.

from hunger, sins against life, injustices, and nuclear war. His encyclical *Mater Redemptoris* (March 25, 1987) offered "a comprehensive scriptural, conciliar, and theological meditation on the Mother of God to all Christians," calling on them to accept her as the source of unity because she is their "common mother." Prominent voices from the Lutheran and Anglican communities noted that while they could not agree with all the essential doctrines of the encyclical, they welcomed the message.

Some of Wojtyla's ecumenical overtures have been especially noteworthy, such as his visit to the Lutheran church in Rome (1983) as well as his second visit to Germany in 1987, when he acknowledged the salutary effect of the Reformation in renewing the Church and even the papacy. Here one should also place the previously mentioned joint celebration with Archbishop Robert Runcie in Canterbury Cathedral in 1982, his visit to the headquarters of the World Council of Churches in Geneva (1984), and his visit to the United States in the fall of 1987, which saw him engage in interfaith and intra-Christian ecumenical meetings that were truly pathbreaking. In a university stadium in Columbia, South Carolina, he greeted by name the twenty-four denominations gathered to worship and spoke warmly of the common scriptural bonds they shared with Catholics.

Nor has he limited his encounters to those with members of the Christian faith. He has made a special effort to engage in dialogue and prayers with non-Christians. He prayed with the chief rabbi of Rome in the Jewish synagogue there (1985), gave an address to a stadium full of young Muslims in Morocco (1985), and recited prayers with a group of animists in Togo (1985). In India in 1986 at the Indira Gandhi Stadium in New Delhi, he addressed by name Hindus, Muslims, Sikhs, Buddhists, Jains, and Parsees. But undoubtedly his most significant interfaith encounter so far was the gathering at Assisi in October of 1986, where at his invitation some 150 representatives of a dozen world religions joined him and other Christian leaders (including the metropolitan of Kiev) in a world day of prayer for peace.

Not least among the talents that have stood him in such good stead as missionary to the world has been his remarkable linguistic ability. People have come to expect a virtuoso performance in a plethora of tongues when he addresses the crowds gathered in St. Peter's Square.

After thirty-seven pilgrimages the Pope issued a kind of state-of-the-world address in his seventh encyclical *Sollicitudo rei socialis* (December 30, 1987), focusing especially on the Fourth World (*sic*) bedeviled, as he noted, by extreme poverty, homelessness, and joblessness traceable in part to the breakdown of systems.

Whatever the ultimate verdict of history may be as to the enduring value of the Pope's initiatives, there is little doubt that John Paul II has kept the papacy squarely in the forefront of the Catholic consciousness while winning the respect and to a large extent even the admiration of the world. He has, in fact, managed to project two rather different images: the kind-hearted, accessible pastor of his people, surrounded by his adoring flock as he lifts up a little child, and the savvy player on the chessboard of world politics.

He has indeed greatly magnified the diplomatic clout of the Vatican. The huge, enthusiastic crowds that turn out for a papal visit far surpass the reception accorded other dignitaries—a fact certainly not ignored by the politicians. Moreover, the Pope has enhanced his personal influence by his innumerable audiences with heads of state and other world leaders as well as by the trouble he he takes on his journeys to meet with these leaders in their own countries. Add to this his unceasing exhortations addressed to the world, as well as some notable diplomatic coups, such as the Vatican's successful mediation between Chile and Argentina (the Beagle Channel Accord), and above all the crucial part he has played in the formation and success of Solidarity in Poland.

THE POPE VS. THE THEOLOGIANS

As to the internal life of the Church, his strategy, as we've said, seems to be clearly a policy of "restoration," which involves emphasizing papal authority and putting the clamps on dissent. Many think, however, that the liberalization of Catholics has gone too far for them to automatically obey any longer the dictates of an authoritarian Pope. *Humanae Vitae*, it seems, marked the end of this kind of rule. The chances of reviving it successfully seem remote.

We must remember that there were many rumblings before the volcano erupted on the day Paul VI issued his anti-pill edict. At Vatican II the bishops seemed to speak out of both sides of their mouth when they called for "a lawful freedom of inquiry" on the one hand while reiterating the traditional doctrine of the need to give a "religious submission of mind and will to the ordinary magisterium" on the other.

In the immediate aftermath of the Council there were already some prominent voices that called for more democracy in the Church. One of these was no other than Leon Cardinal Suenens of Belgium in his book *Co-responsibility in the Church*.[10] Many other articles and symposia in this vein prepared the ground for the liberalization of the Catholic mind.

However, the present Pope is totally out of sympathy with any such liberalization and has spared no efforts "to get the horses back in the barn." Seizing every occasion, he has made his mind very clear. He has castigated the so-called smorgasbord approach of some Catholics who would pick and choose among the teachings of the Church. He expects Catholics to hew the line and give full assent to the teaching of the "ordinary magisterium" of the bishops, i.e., those teachings on faith and morals that—although not considered dogmatic and infallible—are commonly proposed by the bishops in their day-to-day ministry and are also contained in the various letters and decrees of the Vatican congregations as well as the various encyclicals and letters of the Pope. This would obviously include such teachings as the Vatican's prohibition of artificial contraception, its ban on homosexual acts, and certainly its absolute condemnation of abortion.

If the polls are any indication, however, the dissenting but mostly mute laity go on their way blithely undaunted by the papal fulminations. Polls conducted by the *National Catholic Reporter, The New York Times, The New York Times Magazine,* and *Time* support polls taken by Castelli and Gallup, which, for instance, show that 73 per cent of American Catholics favor a change in the birth control teaching, 69 per cent a change in the Church's attitude toward divorce and remarriage. On abortion a large number feel it should be a matter of individual conscience. As to ordination of women and the discipline of celibacy, here again a large number favor change.[11]

While dissenting laity remain generally untouched, a number of dissenting theologians have felt the sting of the papal whip. They have been accused of sowing confusion among the faithful and of using the media to set up a countermagisterium.

The Vatican first bit the bullet on this whole matter when in December 1979 it censured Hans Küng after a lengthy investigation. The widely read Swiss theologian was disqualified from teaching theology in the name of the Church. Always in the front trenches of the battle for a more liberal church,

---

[10] New York: Herder & Herder, 1968.
[11] George Gallup, Jr., and Jim Castelli, *The American Catholic People* (Garden City, N.Y.: Doubleday, 1987), pp. 50, 101, 182.

Küng had caused special consternation when he questioned the dogma of papal infallibility.

Since then a number of other liberal theologians have been disciplined by the Vatican. In the United States Charles Curran has been singled out for his stands on various issues of sexual and marital morality that are definitely at odds with the official teaching of the Church summed up in the "Declaration on Sexual Ethics" (1975). Curran holds that contraception is permissible in some circumstances, that homosexual acts in the context of a loving relationship striving for permanency are objectively good, that the Church should change its absolute prohibition of remarriage in the case of a divorced person, that it should also at least tolerate more liberal views on other issues such as sterilization, masturbation, abortion, and premarital sexual relations.

The basic issue in the dispute is really the right to dissent publicly from official Church teaching. The Vatican refuses to recognize any such right on the basis of Canon 752, which states that the faithful Catholic must render religious submission to doctrines on faith and morals proclaimed by the Pope and bishops in the exercise of their authentic teaching office (magisterium).

The rigorous interpretation given this canon, however, seems open to question, for history tells how often dissent has played a creative role in deepening the Church's understanding of its doctrines. Much of the progress achieved at Vatican II, in fact, was due to the work of dissenting theologians whose views labeled "heresies" before the Council were adopted as official teaching at the Council.

The Louvain professor of moral theology Father Louis Janssens, in a recent article entitled "The Non-infallible Magisterium and the Theologians," recounts the sad stories of numerous Catholic theologians of the twentieth century who were "bloodless martyrs."[12] Striving to be loyal both to the Catholic faith and the demands of scholarship, they dared to dissent from certain official teachings that in conscience they could not subscribe to.

A number of them came under fire for using the tools of the critical-historical method (a method later endorsed at Vatican II), including the great biblical scholar Father M. J. Lagrange, O.P.; the dean of French historians Monsignor Louis Duchesne; Fr. M. D. Chenu, O.P.; and Yves M. J. Congar, O.P. Some of their groundbreaking books were put on the *Index* and they suf-

---

[12] The phrase is from Monsignor Pietro Parente, a definitor of the Holy Office and one of their persecutors who later acknowledged his mistake. Cf. Louis Janssens in *Louvain Studies* 14 (1989), pp. 209–10.

fered various penalties. Conservative Catholics, the so-called integralists, ha-
rassed Lagrange, Duchesne, and other scholars active during the Modernist
crisis with charges of heresy. The "integralist" leader Monsignor Umberto Benigni set up an international network of spies and informers to blacken their
reputations by innuendos and rumors. Benigni's work was blessed and fi-
nanced by Pope Pius X, who kept in touch daily with Benigni.[13]

Another example closer to home is provided by the case of Fr. Henry
Poels, a professor at the Catholic University of America, who questioned a terribly conservative decree of the Biblical Commission of 1906 that stated that
Moses was substantially the author of the Pentateuch. Poels was ordered to
swear that he "believed in conscience that Moses was the author of the Pentateuch," something his scholarly conscience could not allow him to do. And
he was fired.

But the most dramatic example is the story of John Courtney Murray, the
American Jesuit who in the late 1940s began a series of articles in *Theological
Studies* reexamining the official and classic Catholic teaching—moldy, medieval, and much at odds with the American Constitution and the spirit of
the country—namely, that in an ideal order, the Catholic Church alone
among religious bodies should enjoy the support of the State and alone have
the full freedom to propagate its teachings. The corollary was that when and
if Catholics achieved a political majority in the United States, they would be
obliged to clamp restrictions on the liberty of other churches—a situation actually prevailing at the time in such Catholic countries as Spain and held up
as a model of Church-State relations by no other than the head of the Holy
Office, Cardinal Ottaviani.

Murray fully realized, as did most historically conscious American
Catholics, how outdated this teaching was and how harmful to the Catholic
cause. And he believed that the historical method was the key to changing it.
The historical method he felt could enable Catholics to distinguish between
the permanently valid principles contained in the doctrine (such as the right
of the Church to freedom and independence from the State) and what was
merely time-conditioned and changeable (such as the idea of union of Church
and State). The latter could undergo change or development.

But the historical method was still looked askance at by the Roman authorities. And Murray was incautious enough to take issue publicly with Car-

---

[13] See fuller description in chapter 29, "The Modernist Debacle."

dinal Ottaviani's position, reiterated in a recent lecture, that "error has no rights." The fat was in the fire. Murray was told by his Jesuit superior to lay off Church-State relations.

The whole climate, however, changed when the Second Vatican Council opened. It soon became clear that Murray's type of historical method would prevail over Ottaviani's type of thinking. After being disinvited to the first session, Murray was invited to the second where, in close collaboration with the American bishops, he played an important role in the framing of the Council's *Declaration on Religious Freedom*. The concept "Error has no rights"—a mainstay of the Vatican's argument justifying intolerance—was buried forever.

Besides historical difficulties, another problem with the Vatican's disallowance of public dissent has to do with the sheer mass of teachings put forth by the Pope and the bishops. Which of these are binding? Does the Vatican really mean that public disagreement with any of these teachings is verboten? For instance, the American bishops call for a 3 to 4 per cent rate of unemployment in their pastoral on the economy.

In actual practice, what it often seems to boil down to is you're safe as long as you don't take issue with the Church's stand on sexual morality and medical ethics.

A group of prominent American theologians took up this point in several questions they addressed to Ratzinger's Congregation: "(1) Which noninfallible teachings are serious enough to provoke such a result [the disciplining of Father Curran] and how are those teachings determined? (2) How many noninfallible teachings would one have to disagree with before this result would follow, and how is that number determined? (3) If disagreement with any noninfallible teaching is sufficient to provoke this result, on what theological, doctrinal, or historical basis is that principle deduced?"[14]

Curran also tried to get the Vatican to spell out its reasons for prohibiting public dissent but failed. Cardinal Ratzinger and the Congregation for the Doctrine of the Faith would provide only hints of a rationale with their references to the danger of scandalizing the faithful or fomenting disrespect for the teaching office of the Church.

The reaction of informed American Catholics to the disciplining of Curran was as diverse as one might expect, ranging from conservative author

[14] Richard McCormick, "L'Affaire Curran," *America*, April 5, 1986, p. 266.

Michael Novak's support of the action to dismay voiced by the liberal Catholic press. Both *America* and *Commonweal* lamented the damage it would cause to the morale of the Church in the United States. While liberal theologians saw the issue as basically about the claims of truth, others like Archbishop Pilarczyk of Cincinnati no doubt spoke for many hierarchs in seeing the issue as basically a matter of public order. Those who openly oppose a noninfallibly proposed Church teaching, he says, are disruptive of public order in the Church and "do so at their own risk," for there is definitely a limit to how much dissent authorities will tolerate.[15]

Pilarczyk's view of the issue as basically one of public order is interesting. Historians point out how this tendency of the hierarchy to reduce doctrinal questions to questions of public order can be traced back to the period of the Restoration after the French Revolution. As Rome lost temporal power it was able to compensate by greatly increasing its power over the control of doctrine. Or, as Guiseppe Alberigo puts it in a recent article, "The axis of Church government was transferred to the doctrinal domain by using the delicate and highly sensitive authority to determine conformity to the doctrinal content of the Gospel as an everyday instrument of regulating the life of the ecclesial community."[16]

In the process a once balanced and pluralistic ecclesiology that included a complementary role for the faithful and theologians was lost. The monolithic ecclesiology that replaced it insisted on a clear-cut distinction between the *teaching* Church (the magisterium) and the *learning* Church—the rest of the faithful, including the theologians, who were consigned to a purely passive and receptive role.

It was this distinction that was called into question by the facts of the Council. In changing such doctrines as the Church's teaching on religious freedom, the bishops appealed to the principle of development of doctrine. But this development would not have occurred if theologians like John Courtney Murray had not dared to question the teaching of the magisterium. In fact numerous theologians played an active role in the various developments of doctrine that occurred at the Second Vatican Council. The "learning Church" in fact frequently taught the "teaching Church" insofar as many of the bishops' interventions at the Council were drawn up by the theologians.

[15] "Dissent in the Church," *Origins* 16 (July 31, 1986), no. 9, pp. 175–84.
[16] "Authority in the Documents of Vatican I and Vatican II," *Journal of Ecumenical Studies* 19 (Spring 1982), pp. 119–45.

Another way the Council undermined the sharp distinction between the teaching and the learning Church was by its emphasis on how the gifts of the Spirit are distributed to all the members of the Church so that the faithful can assist the hierarchy "in interpreting the many voices of our age,"[17] thus assisting the hierarchy in penetrating and better understanding revealed truth in which they enjoy competence.

Several other statements helped to break down the rigid distinction between the learning and the teaching Church. The Council called for dialogue not only with the world but within the Church itself between the pastors and the faithful. It also stated that "all the faithful, clerical and lay, possess a lawful freedom of inquiry and of thought, and the freedom to express their minds humbly and courageously about those matters in which they enjoy competence."[18]

To sum up the doctrine of the Council: All the faithful share in the dialogic teaching and learning process by which the Church develops its doctrine.

It is interesting that in June 1989 the American bishops embodied this doctrine in their paper "Doctrinal Responsibilities," which contained a long-stalled set of guidelines dealing with disputes between bishops and theologians.[19] Overwhelmingly approved, it sets forth the "distinct but complementary" responsibilities of bishops and theologians in upholding Catholic teaching. Bishops are "authoritative teachers" charged with preserving the integrity of doctrine, while theologians have the task of improving understanding of faith by scholarship and "critical inquiry." It insists on the right of theologians to "freedom of inquiry and expression of scholarly opinion" and sets up guidelines for dialogue between bishop and theologians when a dispute arises. One especially noteworthy point is its declaration that the teaching of bishops should meet with a religious reception "proportionate to the degree of authority with which it is presented."

However, in November 1989 at the behest of the Vatican, they shelved these new procedures which they had worked on for six years.

The dismay of many theologians at Vatican policies finally found an outlet in July 1989, when hundreds of them from at least eight countries signed a statement challenging the Pope's conservative leadership. They found at the root of their distress a "new Roman centralism" that "is limiting local

---

[17] *Gaudium et Spes,* 44.
[18] Ibid., 62, 92.
[19] Meeting at Seton Hall University, Orange, N.J., in June 1989.

churches and theological freedom as well as pluralism and the ethos of believers." They condemned the Pope's consistent practice of neglecting consultation with the local churches and ignoring their wishes while imposing on them his handpicked ultra-conservative bishops. Finally they accused the Pope of trying to smother debate on moral issues by equating certain traditional Church norms of morality with divine revelation itself.

One way of looking at the current crisis of authority is to see it as the travails of a Church still trying to make the transition from a classicist to a historically conscious world view. The classicist mentality viewed the Church as moving through history but more or less unaffected by history. The historically conscious point of view, however, acknowledges how much institutions, governing precepts, and basic ideas about religion and morality are shaped by history and therefore how relative they are. This historical consciousness became a dominant feature of European culture in the nineteenth century. Catholic officials, however, saw the historical method as a lethal threat to the Church's whole system of supposedly immutable doctrines and they fought desperately to shield the faithful from the dangers of history. They fell back especially on Scholastic philosophy with its façade of immutability. The battle with the Modernists largely revolved around this issue.

It was only many years later at Vatican II that the Church began to employ gingerly the perspective of historical consciousness, especially in the documents *Gaudium et Spes* and *Dignitatis Humanae* with their recognition that the claims of human dignity are conditioned by the evolving human consciousness and cannot be defined fully apart from cultural situations.

Probably no area of Catholic thought has been more affected by historicism than moral theology. One may even speak of a . . .

REVOLUTION IN MORAL THEOLOGY

It's hardly an exaggeration to use this term for one of the most far-reaching developments in the post-Vatican II period and one that underlies a great deal of the tension in the Church. The face of moral theology, in fact, has been so radically altered it is hard to realize that only a few decades ago world-famous theologians were debating such topics as whether chewing gum broke the Eucharistic fast or whether a person should be allowed so many ounces of food for breakfast during the Lenten fast.

In an article, Richard McCormick lists what he thinks were the main factors in the "revolution." In addition to the acceptance of the historical dimension, there have been profound shifts of emphasis in the realm of Catholic ecclesiology (our understanding of the Church). The Council taught us to look on the Church not only as a hierarchical institution but also as Sacrament, as People of God, and as Servant. Each of these insights opened up new perspectives on a variety of moral issues. Moreover the assertion of the collegial nature of Church authority encouraged a new way of looking at the use and limits of authority in moral questions as well as the rights of the individual conscience.

Another important shift was the Council's adoption of an ecumenical point of view. No longer could Catholic moral theologians ignore the experience, reflection, and wisdom of the other Christian churches.

There was also the profound influence of Karl Rahner's anthropology, especially his concept of the fundamental option. It holds that one exercises full freedom only at one's deepest spiritual level or core, the area of total self-disposition, of radical conversion. It is only at these depths of freedom that one can speak of mortal sin. "Actuations of this intensity of freedom may be called 'fundamental options' precisely because of their depth, stability, and permanence."[20]

The implications of accepting this point of view for the future of Catholic moral theology were enormous. It greatly affected the treatment of such questions as the nature of sin, conversion, virtue, confession, temptation, and laws of the Church.

The Council also emphasized the nature of the Church as an eschatological, very imperfect, and unfinished reality. Thus certain moral doctrines previously regarded as immutable might now legitimately be re-examined.

Another very important, even revolutionary, shift was the acceptance of proportionalism—a new way of looking at actions causing a double effect, one good and one bad. According to this theory, one did not sin in causing the bad effect if there was a proportionate reason, since one's intention was aimed at the good effect and not at the bad. In this view very few actions could be labeled as intrinsically evil.

The issuance of *Humanae Vitae* was certainly another factor in the revo-

---

[20] Richard McCormick, "Moral Theology 1940–1989," *Theological Studies* 50 (March 1989), p. 8.

lution. By appointing a commission to study the Church's condemnation of artificial contraception, the Pope gave the impression that he needed more than the inspiration of the Holy Spirit to make the right decision. The whole affair communicated a more relative view of papal authority than had previously held sway. Thus when Paul rejected the conclusion of his Commission, many Catholics were no longer ready to give blind obedience to his decree. Moral theologians in particular were forced to entertain previously unasked questions such as how conscience is to be formed, the response due to the ordinary magisterium, and the meaning of the guidance of the Holy Spirit. Richard McCormick says he could think of no moral issue or event in this century that impacted so profoundly on the discipline of moral theology.

Finally the Curran affair too has played a part. The Vatican Congregation for the Doctrine of the Faith censured Father Curran for writings that questioned official teaching on contraception, homosexuality, and other sexual and medical issues. Archbishop James Hickey of Washington, chancellor of Catholic University, then withdrew Curran's canonical mission to teach and suspended him from his post. These actions by the hierarchy gave special prominence to the issue of the right to publicly dissent from some authoritative but noninfallible teaching. McCormick thinks the implications of Rome's treatment of Curran are very grave for the future of Catholic moral theology.

Other movements and developments that McCormick lists as contributing to the revolution in moral theology were the emergence of *feminism,* which encouraged many women to enter the field of Catholic moral theology; the *maturation of bioethics,* which by its complexity forced the professional to lay aside the myth of the omnicompetent moral theologian—those seeking to attain any degree of authority in the field would have to specialize; *liberation theology,* which greatly heightened awareness of our excessive emphasis on individual (especially sexual) morality to the neglect of the social dimension while it also reminded us of our duty to participate in constructing a just social order. Finally there was Vatican II's adoption of the *personalist standard* so that the criterion of moral rightness must be "the person integrally and adequately considered."[21] A morality centered on analyzing the nature of the act was giving way gradually to one that judged actions good or bad insofar as they promoted or did not the overall well-being of the persons involved.

[21] Ibid., p. 16.

THE HUNTHAUSEN CASE

One of the most startling—and for many U.S. Catholics disturbing—developments of the eighties occurred in September of 1986 when the news broke that Archbishop Raymond Hunthausen of Seattle had been stripped of much of his authority by the Vatican. A conservative bishop was appointed to share his ministry and to take charge of a number of crucial areas of diocesan life.

Hunthausen was cited for a lack of firmness in governing his diocese—in particular for permitting a number of abuses such as sterilizations in Catholic hospitals, misuse of marriage annulments, and affiliations with homosexual groups. He was already regarded as one of the most controversial Catholic prelates in the U.S. In 1982, for instance, he began to withhold half his federal income tax to protest the stockpiling of nuclear weapons. In fact, many suspected it was this activism in the anti-nuclear weapons movement that made him the target of the conservatives whose complaints were no doubt a factor in Rome's action.

For his part Hunthausen insisted on his total loyalty to the teaching of the Church; others, moreover, wondered why he was singled out, since the practices condemned were so widespread in the U.S.

A resolution of the affair was finally announced by the Vatican in April 1989 after it accepted the report of a commission that recommended that Hunthausen's authority be restored and a Coadjutor Archbishop be appointed. Hunthausen stoutly maintains that his archdiocese has remained fundamentally the same and was never in violation of Vatican doctrine; nor has he had to alter the general direction of his ministry or compromise his liberal beliefs.

The whole affair reveals the tensions existing between some of the three hundred American bishops and the Vatican, which is trying to pressure them into greater allegiance to orthodox Catholic teaching. Observers believe that the American penchant for debate and dissent is regarded with peculiar anxiety by the Vatican because of the size and influence of this country.

One of the fundamental causes of the tension is the difficulty of defining the proper balance of power between the Vatican and the various national bishops' conferences. These conferences have played an increasingly important role in the Catholic Church since the Vatican Council in the mid-1960s emphasized collegiality—the idea that the bishops have a collective responsibility in the governance of the Church.

However, conservatives, including Cardinal Ratzinger himself, were unhappy with the growing role of these national conferences, which they do not regard as genuine expressions of collegiality. In the conservative view, the conferences are merely convenient administrative structures with little real authority. A working paper articulating this point of view was drawn up at the Vatican in late 1987.

But a very strongly worded critique of the document was issued in November 1988 by a panel of prominent American bishops. It scored the Vatican paper's defensive and negative tone, its confusing use of terms, its distortion of passages from the Second Vatican Council, and its slighting of precedents from the ancient Church. They urged that an entirely new working paper be drawn up. Their critique was later accepted by the National Conference of Bishops, which rejected the document and its thesis that the bishops should be mere conveyors of Vatican teachings to the flock. Rejection of the Vatican document came after a lively debate during which one prelate called it a "used car that could not be fixed, regardless of how much money you pour into it."[22]

SCHISM

The bishop who has given the Vatican the biggest headache is Archbishop Marcel Lefebvre. This French prelate brought about the first major schism in the Church for more than a century when on June 20, 1988, he ordained four bishops and was thereupon excommunicated by the Pope.

Lefebvre's schism originated in his refusal to accept the changes ordained by the Second Vatican Council. The scion of a French industrialist with monarchist views who instilled in him a gloom-and-doom view of modern history, Lefebvre had his conservative upbringing reinforced by his training in a Roman seminary whose Rector was a disciple of Maurras, an infamous French reactionary and friend of the Nazis. As a participant in the Second Vatican Council, Lefebvre lobbied against the liberals and tried in vain to persuade Pope Paul VI to reject some of the Council's major decrees. Three in particular infuriated him: religious liberty or rejection of a privileged position for the Church; ecumenism or the recognition of the truth claims of other

[22] *The New York Times*, November 17, 1988.

churches and religions; and collegiality of bishops with the Pope. The passage of these decrees convinced Lefebvre that the Council had fallen into heresy and was not the work of the Holy Spirit but the work of the devil.

To propagate this negative view of the Council, Lefebvre in 1970 set up the ultraconservative St. Pius X fraternity with headquarters in Econe in southern Switzerland. The movement soon spread around the world, although attracting large numbers, it seems, only in France. Estimates vary but Vatican officials figured the total membership to be around 100,000 before the excommunication. The touchstone and symbol of their rejection of Vatican II is their devotion to the Mass said in Latin according to the rite decreed by the Council of Trent—the Mass of St. Pius V.

THE ECUMENICAL MOVEMENT

The Second Vatican Council urged Catholics to work and pray for greater unity among the churches. It especially recommended dialogue with other Christians as a way of achieving unity. Since then the sheer number of ecumenical dialogues has been amazing, but in spite of agreement on certain issues, the committees have found that the major divisions between Protestants, Catholics, and Orthodox show no signs of disappearing. Important doctrinal differences still remain involving such questions as papal primacy, the Marian dogmas (the Immaculate Conception and Assumption), and apostolic succession.

The difficulty of reaching agreement is seen even in the paper *Baptism, Eucharist, and Ministry* hailed as a monumental ecumenical achievement. Accepted in 1983 by the World Council of Churches after being drafted by its Faith and Order Commission at Lima the year before, it was notable for several reasons. First, it represented the work of some 120 theologians and Church leaders from all parts of the world, including Roman Catholics and Orthodox as well as Protestants. Second, it provided a very fine synthesis of many previous dialogues.

However, the Vatican response so far has been very discouraging and creates what appears to be "an ecumenical logjam."[23] In fact the paper does

[23] George Vandervelde, "BEM and the 'Hierarchy of Truths'; A Vatican Contribution to the Reception Process," *Journal of Ecumenical Studies* 25 (Winter 1988), no. 1, p. 82.

contain some notable ambiguities, covering over significant doctrinal differences.

How can the present impasse be resolved? Certainly not by simply bypassing the controverted dogmas and uniting on a purely pragmatic basis, as some have suggested. Catholics in particular could never so minimize the importance of the dogmas that constitute the very substance and core of the Church's spiritual life.

One recent proposal—by Karl Rahner, attempting to steer between Scylla and Charybdis—aroused much interest and also much consternation in certain quarters. He claimed that so much agreement has already been reached that the separated churches should simply now unite. The only proviso being that they agree not to condemn the disputed dogmas of the other as contrary to the Gospel.[24]

But his opponents argued that this would undermine the teaching authority of the Church and inculcate a skeptical attitude in Catholics themselves toward the dogmas in question, thus sowing seeds of confusion in the Church.

Avery Dulles also finds Rahner's solution too facile and does not look for any quick resolution of the doctrinal impasse. He believes three steps need to be taken before the doctrinal basis for full communion can be reached.[25]

First, most of the churches could already take the step of jointly declaring their allegiance to the teaching of Scripture and the creeds and ecumenical councils of the early centuries.

Further progress could be made by taking a more historical and culturally pluralistic approach to the dogmas that still separate us. He quotes the view of prestigious French Catholic ecumenist Yves Congar that "Doctrines that were too narrowly stated in terms of a given social and intellectual framework often need to be reappropriated in terms of a larger context and a fuller reflection on the testimony of Scripture and tradition." Experience, in fact, shows that such terms as "transubstantiation" and "infallibility" can be reinterpreted in ways that render them intelligible, tolerable, or even acceptable to communities that previously rejected them.

Moreover, as Dulles says, the historical approach might also enable us to

---

[24] *Unity of the Churches: An Actual Possibility* (Philadelphia: Fortress Press, 1985).
[25] "Paths to Doctrinal Agreement: Ten Theses," *Theological Studies* 47 (1986), pp. 32–47.

reach substantive agreement on certain truths without imposing identical doctrinal formulations on each.

Also we must keep in mind Vatican II's assertion that a hierarchy of importance exists among Catholic doctrines.

With dialogues undertaken along these lines there is no reason, Dulles argues, why the churches might not advance to the second step of declaring that some or all of the doctrinal positions of the other churches are not contrary to the Gospel and therefore not condemnable.

The third and final step would occur when the churches progressed "to the point of positively accepting one another's binding doctrinal formulations, with whatever added interpretations or explanations are needed to guard against possible deviations."

But a discouraging fact important to keep in mind is that even if doctrinal differences could be resolved, a mighty *if,* there would still remain a major obstacle to reunion—the differences between the Protestant and Catholic churches over ethics.

In fact the social and ethical issues may loom even larger than the doctrinal issues as divisive factors. There are vast differences between the churches over abortion, the death penalty and euthanasia, active homosexuality and premarital sex, women's rights, birth control and new reproductive technologies, economic and peace issues. That virtually no dialogue has occurred on such issues may itself be an implicit recognition of how difficult any reconciliation is deemed to be.

Moreover the cold, stern face of authority that Rome now projects has slowed down much of the ecumenical thrust. The disciplining of Curran and Hunthausen, the silencing of Leonardo Boff,[26] the treatment of the liberals in the Dutch Church, the inquisitorial tactics of the Congregation for the Doctrine of the Faith, etc., have had a very depressing effect on ecumenists in the Protestant ranks. In their view Rome seems to have gone out of its way to show its disdain for values that Protestants (especially in North America) regard as an important part of their heritage: pluralism, a large amount of freedom for theological inquiry, and a high regard for democratic decision making.

As James A. Nash, executive director of the Massachusetts Council of Churches, said recently: "In the absence of structural changes, what kind of

[26] See page 455.

unity, if any, is possible for relatively democratic and pluralistic churches with a church that stresses hierarchy and homogeneity?"[27]

Into this deadlock stepped Oscar Cullmann, one of the giants of the ecumenical movement, who offered a solution that aroused considerable interest and even won the praise of Cardinal Ratzinger himself.[28] It is unrealistic, Cullmann says, to look for any unification of the churches that would mean fusing them together in one Church. In fact, we must go back to the first centuries of the Church's history, the age when the communion of the churches was still rather informal, to get some light on how to reconcile unity with diversity. For history shows how the peculiar charism of each local church (e.g., Judaeo-Christians or Hellenists) was respected by the others and enriched their total communion. It was only when a charism was sinfully pushed to excess that schism occurred.

Likewise, in succeeding centuries we can see how various ecclesiastical charisms found fullest expression in particular Christian confessions. The specific charisms of the Protestant churches, for instance, Cullmann sees as their concentration on the Scriptures and their great devotion to Christian liberty; both, however, can fall into excess: Biblicism can degenerate into intolerance and liberty into anarchy. Catholicism, on the other hand, is blessed by the gift of universality and organization. But the first can lead to syncretism and the second to totalitarianism.

Cullmann sees the formation of separate Protestant churches as necessary in order to preserve their distinct charisms in their full vigor. However, now God seems to be calling the churches to a closer communion but a communion that must still allow for each church to retain its autonomy in order to preserve its distinctive charism. Cullmann would characterize this communion as "pacific coexistence." Some form of structure, it's true, would be necessary to strengthen this communion, i.e., some kind of representative assembly along the lines of the various national councils of churches—but with only moral authority over the member churches.

Until unity is reached, however, Cullmann frowns on any practice of general intercommunion since he thinks the essential shared faith basis is lacking. But as a step on the way he suggests reviving the ancient Christian love feast

---

[27] "Vatican Disciplining an Ecumenical Stumbling Block," *National Catholic Reporter* 23 (May 1, 1987), pp. 15–16.

[28] Oscar Cullmann, *Unity Through Diversity* (Philadelphia: Fortress Press, 1988).

or agape meals. In the context of a worship service Catholics and Protestants could have a festive meal together celebrating the unity they already share.

Whatever we may think of Cullmann's proposal, it does seem only realistic to recognize with Avery Dulles that: "We have no antecedent certainty that we shall reach the ultimate goal of our ecumenical pilgrimage before the end of historical time."[29]

But our efforts are not wasted for every step toward agreement deepens the communion among Christians and enriches each of them with a more balanced grasp of the revelation to which they bear witness.

LIBERATION THEOLOGY

The appearance of liberation theology is certainly one of the most significant developments of the last several decades. According to its practitioners it represents a "new way of doing theology,"[30] for while classical theology aimed at a deeper understanding of faith *(fides quaerens intellectum),* liberation theology aims to transform the world—echoing in this respect at least Karl Marx's famous dictum: The task of philosophy is not to understand but to change the world.

Moreover, classical theology seemed removed from day-to-day experience—especially experience of the sufferings of the poor. Liberation theology, however, has grown out of the experience of certain Catholics with the harsh reality of the miserable poor.

Finally while classical theology interpreted Jesus' message of the kingdom mainly as a guide to personal morality, liberation theology sees it as above all a call to struggle against the social forces of oppression. Advances in social justice and love they see as partial realizations of the kingdom, steps toward its final consummation.

A crucial event for the rise of liberation theology was the meeting of the Latin American bishops at Medellín in 1968. It was in their documents collected under the title *Justice and Peace* that several of the major themes of liberation theology were first given prominence: the injustices visited on the

---

[29] "Paths to Doctrinal Agreement," *Theological Studies* 47 (1986), p. 47.
[30] Alfred Hennelly, *Theologies in Conflict* (Maryknoll, N.Y.: Orbis Books, 1979), pp. 26–29.

people of Latin America by neocolonialism and imperialism, reinterpretation of salvation to include liberation from every form of servitude, and the kingdom of God as beginning in this world.

The leaders included: Helder Camara (Brazil); Juan Luis Segundo, S.J. (Uruguay); Gustavo Gutierrez (Peru); Enrique Dussel (Mexico); Segundo Galilea (Argentina); G. Arroyo, S.J. (Chile); José Miguez Bonino (Argentina); Jon Sobrino, S.J. (El Salvador); and Leonardo Boff (Brazil).

Gutierrez and his colleagues have definitely put a new spin on a number of classical themes of theology: God, creation, Israel, Jesus Christ, the Church—reinterpreted in the light of their experience of the poor. They take a profoundly historical approach to God, whose self-revelation and the human response to it they see as an ongoing historical process. The God revealed in Jesus Christ is not a Greek "unmoved mover" but a God whose very essence consists of love.

They prefer the term liberation to salvation in order to get away from unworldly ideas of salvation and to stress the need of Christians to struggle for a just society. Therefore they redefine the task of evangelization to include transforming social action (praxis) as well as helping the poor become aware of the causes of their distress (conscientization). They stress the mission of the Church to take part in building the kingdom by being a visible sign of the presence of the Lord within the struggle. Therefore they insist the Church must again become poor in solidarity with the poor if it is to be an authentic sign.

Boff, one of the leaders, notes five emphases that distinguish liberation theology from traditional theology: (1) the primacy of the anthropological element over the ecclesiological, since their focus is primarily on the person who is to be helped and humanized rather than on the Church; (2) the utopian perspective is placed over the factual—the future over the past, since they see the social process as permanently open to transformation—a possibility opened up by Jesus; (3) the critical over the dogmatic, to counteract the tendency of institutions to fossilize; (4) the social over the personal, in view of the increasing misery of the masses; (5) orthopraxis over orthodoxy—Christ didn't come to give us a set of intellectual concepts to master but a new way of acting and living in the world.[31]

Liberation theologians see one of their main tasks as discernment, i.e.,

[31] Ibid., p. 32.

discovering what criteria the Church should use in formulating its response to the changing social and political environment in Latin America.

How influenced are they by Marxism? No one accuses them of subscribing to Marx's atheistic dialectical materialism, but they have been charged with using Marxist analysis as a tool—exclusively, according to Father Arrupe, the Jesuit General in a famous letter of 1980. But Gutierrez denies the charge. Of course, he says, insofar as Marxist concepts have entered into the social sciences they naturally make use of them as they make use of Max Weber's and whoever has made a contribution.[32]

Closely connected with liberation theology is the grass-roots movement called base communities—loosely organized small groups of Catholics drawn largely from the poor urban and peasant masses who come together to pray, to worship, and to apply the Gospel to their situation of poverty and oppression. One means of doing this is through dialogue-type sermons at Mass.

In spite of furious opposition from conservative Catholics and the hostility of right-wing regimes, the proponents of liberation theology felt they were on the right track and fully in line with the direction taken by the bishops of the world since Vatican II. After all, they would argue, in their Synod of 1971 the bishops declared that "action on behalf of justice and the transformation of the world fully appear to us as a constitutive dimension of the preaching of the Gospel, or . . . of the Church's mission for the redemption of the human race and its liberation from every oppressive situation," an idea they repeated at the 1974 synod. And the document from the Latin American bishops meeting at Puebla in 1979 reflected liberation theology in its statement that the Church should have a "preferential option for the poor."

But winds in Rome were shifting, and as the clouds continued to darken, the man who drew down the lightning was a gentle Franciscan padre from Brazil named Leonardo Boff, who was born in 1938 and was at one time a student of his nemesis Joseph Cardinal Ratzinger. Apparently Boff was singled out by Ratzinger for having the temerity to apply liberation theology to the Church itself.

The book that stunk in the nostrils of the Cardinal overseer of orthodoxy was Boff's *Church: Charism and Power* wherein he summoned the Church to a conversion, to forsake the path of power and return to the kind of Church Jesus had in mind, one that would embrace "poverty, rejection of false secu-

---

[32] "Liberation Theology," *Theology Digest,* Spring 1988, p. 34.

rity, acceptance of the inability to control the future . . ."[33] Boff wanted to restore respect for the many gifts or charisms promised by Jesus to all the members of the Church.

Boff, however, had not become a Quaker. He recognized the need for some form of authority to stave off the anarchy possible when charisms are given free reign. But he finds the Church's present way of exercising power and control abusive and a cancer in its body—most evident in the inquisitorial spirit that, he claims, still dominates the Vatican.

Boff's remedy for what ails the Church is exactly the opposite of the Cardinal's. Boff wants a decentralized Church, Ratzinger an even more centralized one. The Church today, in fact, Ratzinger says, is like a construction site where the blueprint has been lost and each worker is doing his own thing.

Boff was invited to have a "colloquy" with Ratzinger in Rome, but Boff wanted it in Brazil instead. However, he finally agreed to meet with Ratzinger in Rome in September of 1984. Before the two met, the Vatican on September 3 fired a warning shot across Boff's bow with its "Instruction on Certain Aspects of the 'Theology of Liberation,'" which charged the liberationists with an "uncritical use of Marxist modes of analysis"—an accusation Boff saw as a canard. He was, in fact, dismayed by the straw man set up by people with obviously little awareness of the Brazilian situation.

An interesting aspect of the episode was the intervention in support of Boff by Paulo Evaristo Cardinal Arns, Boff's friend and former teacher and archbishop of São Paulo. Together with Aloisio Cardinal Lorscheider and Bishop José Ivo Lorscheiter (president of the Brazilian Bishops' Conference), Arns insisted on being present at the colloquy. After being at first rebuffed, the three prelates finally accepted a compromise whereby Ratzinger and Boff would first confer alone and then Arns and his colleagues would be allowed to sit in on a second colloquy between the two.

Arns's intervention highlighted the fact that this whole affair was not an exercise in abstruse theological semantics but a debate over the future of the Church in Brazil. Arns and Boff were leaders of the "new" Church being forged in the bloody turmoil of revolution and counterrevolution in Latin America, a Church no longer bridesmaid to dictators but a friend of the poor, a Church whose priests and religious live and work in slums and the villages

---

[33] Quoted in Harvey Cox, *The Silencing of Leonardo Boff* (Oak Park, Ill.: Meyer-Stone Books, 1988), p. 54.

with the people's own organizations and speak much less about Fatima and devotion to the Sacred Heart of Jesus and much more about the Jesus who showed special love for the poor. It is a Church slowly gaining ground, it seems, against its enemies the great landowners, business moguls, and wielders of power who can still count on a large segment of the clergy and hierarchy as their allies.

After studying Boff's responses, Ratzinger and his staff finally concluded that their reservations about his book "had not been substantially overcome" and so a formal notification was issued to this effect and Boff was ordered to be silent for an indefinite period. Boff humbly accepted the reprimand and said that he preferred "to walk with the Church rather than to walk alone with my theology."[34]

But events soon took a happier turn for the friar and his friends. A meeting of the senior bishops of Brazil with the Pope revealed that the Pope was much better disposed toward the new theology than people thought. At the same time, Boff was released from the silencing order. And finally a more positive critique of liberation theology was issued by the Vatican on April 5, 1986—the "Instruction on Christian Freedom and Liberation."

The Instruction makes two main points: First, it rejects Marxism with its systematic recourse to violence and its doctrine of class warfare; second, it does not reject the basic ideas of liberation theology but seeks to correct what it regards as certain exaggerations.

At the outset the Instruction notes that real progress has been made in the cause of human liberation: slavery has been abolished, some strides toward greater equality have been taken, the evil of racism has been made evident. But as industrialization spread, a new form of slavery appeared—the misery of the factory workers who became mere pawns in the hands of the industrial tycoons. Movements arose to liberate them, but espousing collectivist ideas, they often ended in creating forms of totalitarian tyranny as oppressive as the poverty they were intended to overcome.

While not mentioning Marxism by name, it warned against all collectivist solutions to poverty. But it also scored individualistic ideologies and recommended instead the concept of human solidarity as a basic principle of social theory. Solidarity, it declares, is necessary if the grave socio-economic problems of our times are to be solved: solidarity of the poor among them-

[34] Ibid., p. 105.

selves, of workers with other workers, of rich with poor. If this spirit were to take hold, we could fashion a more human world, a world in which each individual can give and receive, and where the progress of some will no longer be an obstacle to the development of others.

However, the supreme principle of the Church's social doctrine, the Instruction says, is Jesus' great commandment of love, which in application may take various forms in accord with the changing circumstances of history. As compassionate disciples of the Lord, the Church exercises a special option for the poor and shows them a loving preference. However, it does not want this special option to be a source of partisan conflict. It reminds the advocates of liberation, therefore, that poverty takes many forms, and the Church's compassion and love must extend toward the poor of whatever kind—the infant in danger of being aborted, the elderly, the abandoned, the lonely.

It also takes issue with liberation theology's insistence on sin as primarily social. The concept of sin, it says, primarily refers to the individual who is free to violate the moral law. Only secondarily and derivatively can "sin" be applied to social structures in the sense of "social sin." In virtue of the primacy of the person, it insists on the need for individual conversion as well as structural reform.

It emphasizes "work" as in a sense the "key to the whole social question" and affirms the priority of work over capital—again in virtue of the primacy of the person. A sound system of labor relations must be put in place by the cooperation of employers and workers with the essential support of the public powers. Only then will a profound and peaceful revolution be possible.

It condemns systematic recourse to violence, which, it says, only leads to greater servitude. It rejects the theory of class warfare, namely, that such warfare is a law of history and necessary at each stage of history when the time comes for the oppressor class to be overthrown. Rather, the Christian will always prefer the path of dialogue and joint action. But it also condemns the various forms of violence, especially covert forms, used by the rich, the police, and governments against the poor. Recourse to armed struggle it would admit only as a last resort to put an end to an obvious and prolonged tyranny. Moreover the continuing refinements of technology available to tyrants makes nonviolence more and more a preferable option.

Finally it insists on the need for the clergy to stay clear of direct involvement in the political process, which it believes should be the duty of the laity.

To summarize, the Vatican Instruction proposes as an alternative to Marxist collectivism and individualistic capitalism a system based on the recognition and acceptance of several essential values: the priority of work over capital; access for everyone to the goods needed for a human, personal, and family life worthy of the name; the right of every person to work; the primary social task as the creation of jobs; provision of wages that allow for a truly human standard of living; the right of private property subordinated to the common good; worker participation in the decision-making level of an enterprise.

The document was welcomed in Brazil by Arns and most of the bishops. Boff applauded the Vatican for giving a "newly universal dimension" to "values that were initially only those of the Third World." The most surprising development was a papal letter to the Brazilian bishops at their annual assembly in April 1986 that endorsed their work, referred to their "dear base communities" and spoke of the chance the bishops had "to renovate all of Catholic theology."

But renovating Catholic theology has always been a perilous enterprise, and Boff was reminded of this once more with the publication of his book *E a Igrega se fez povo (And the Church Became People)* written during his "silence." The book carried the argument of *Charism and Power* further by arguing that historically the Church didn't start with the hierarchy but with the grass roots, i.e., poor and humble people. The hierarchy only came later. This is a clue to what is needed today if the Church is to be, as well as claim to be, "the people of God." For the masses of the poor are again taking initiative as in the early days of the Church and are creating true communities—the base communities. Those who would lead them must respect their hegemony and work with them as part of the community and not over them.

The alarm bells went off again in Rome, and once more Ratzinger set up a commission to study Boff's latest writings.

While Boff and Ratzinger engaged in what was mainly an academic exercise, the debate was carried on with bombs and guns in Central America.

ROMERO AND EL SALVADOR

A major testing ground for liberation theology was El Salvador. The revolution there has not been as in Nicaragua an uprising against a corrupt dictator who had alienated even the upper classes and the United States. It was a struggle against an oligarchy and military strongly supported by the United States.

The ruling oligarchy's fortune rested on coffee and land. Their brutal exploitation of the peasants caused an eruption of violent revolution in 1932, the *Matanza,* which was savagely repressed with the slaughter of 10,000 people. Efforts toward land reform were again made in the 1960s but were adamantly rejected by the oligarchy. While the military strengthened its hold over the country in the ensuing decades, some efforts were made to organize the workers and the peasants. A union movement began to take shape with the help of the American Institute for Free Labor Development sponsored by the AFL-CIO and backed by the United States government and business. There were strikes, which were met by repression.

The Christian Democratic party was formed in El Salvador in 1960 with anti-communism and reform high on its agenda. Together with the United States government and the Catholic Church, they pinned their hopes on economic development as the key to solving El Salvador's poverty. However, by the early seventies it was clear to many reform-minded people that "development" was not the answer but was part of the problem, that further "development" in fact would only make things worse for the impoverished.

A number of radical groups sprang up—the FPL (Popular Liberation Forces), the ERP (People's Revolutionary Army)—devoted to the overthrow of the system. In response a right-wing paramilitary group ORDEN (Democratic Nationalist Organization) was set up by government authorities.

The Church too had originally bought the concept of "development" as the best way to social progress. But a shift occurred when the Latin American bishops opted instead for the concept of "liberation" at Medellín. As a follow up to Medellín some two hundred Salvadoran bishops, priests, sisters, and laypeople met in June 1970 for a Pastoral Week that provided a platform for new directions in their pastoral ministries. It admitted that the Church had failed to advance liberation, and yet "people still look to the Church as the force that can liberate them." It was resolved to form base communities, to end clericalism, to form leaders dedicated to the integral development of the human person and the formation of communities, to work for conscientization of the people, to struggle against obstacles to peasant unionization.

No one seemed to realize what murderous passions the Pastoral would unleash against the Church.

The first to feel their impact was Father Rutilio Grande and a team of Jesuits who applied the new pastoral approach to ministry in the town of Aguilares and the surrounding area where tens of thousands of peasants worked in the sugarcane fields to supplement the meager living they scratched from their own small plots of land.

Their condition was extremely miserable. "By the Salvadoran government's own estimate, a minimum diet (corn, beans, rice, less than two pounds of meat a month) cost a family of six around $533 a year. A simple minimum diet was beyond the reach of the vast majority."[35] To aggravate the situation, the number of landless had continued to increase from 11.8 per cent in 1961 to 40.9 per cent in 1975. Doomed to a slow death from malnutrition, many of them felt that "it was better to die of a bullet than die of hunger."

Using the techniques based on the experience of the base communities, the Jesuits organized a number of communities of Christians committed to the struggle for justice and peace.

A number of popular organizations were also formed, the largest being the Revolutionary People's Bloc (BPR). The landowners, however, were determined to strike back and formed FARO (Agricultural Front of the Eastern Region). They unleashed a newspaper campaign vilifying the popular organizations and directed some of their wrath against the Jesuits.

On February 23, 1977, Oscar Romero was installed as the Archbishop of San Salvador. He was regarded as a conservative indisposed to confrontation tactics, but his transformation into a fearless champion of the underdogs was amazingly swift. A few days after his installation a fraudulent election gave the presidency to General Romero (no relation), the choice of the landholding oligarchy. Thousands gathered on the plaza in a vigil to protest; they were set on by government forces and massacred.

It was only a few weeks later that Father Rutilio was ambushed and killed while driving through the canefields on his way to say Mass. Romero, the nuncio, four bishops, two hundred priests, and a large crowd attended the funeral. One of the priests present, Father Alfonso Navarro, was himself gunned down a few months later in his parish house by terrorists who called themselves the White Warriors Union. They gave as a pretext several assassinations

---

[35] Philip Berryman, *The Religious Roots of Rebellion* (Maryknoll, N.Y.: Orbis Books, 1981), p. 112.

Archbishop Oscar Romero of
San Salvador.
© Leif Skoogfors/Corbis.

attributed to left-wing guerrillas. In the meantime handbills appeared with
the message "Be a Patriot. Kill a Priest!" The White Warriors Union warned
all Jesuits to leave the country within thirty days or be eliminated.

The toll on the clergy at this point was dreadful: In the five-month period after Romero's installation, eight priests had been expelled from the
country, seven refused reentry, two jailed, one beaten, two tortured, four
threatened with death, and two killed.

The government, with the aid of right-wing assassins, stepped up its repression while the popular organizations retaliated in kind. Then on the the
morning of October 15, 1979, less than three months after the Sandinista victory over Somoza in Nicaragua, some four hundred officers of the Salvadoran
army pulled off a coup without firing a single shot. The victors formed a junta
composed of both hardliners and reform-minded young officers and civilians.

But this "last chance" for El Salvador failed when the hardliners in the
junta squeezed out the reformers. When the leftists staged a huge march of

some 200,000 people to celebrate their recent unification, security and plain-clothes forces sniped at them from buildings and killed some twenty-one people. Major Robert D'Aubuisson gained increasing prominence as the leader of the far right.

Romero spoke out with increasing boldness and revealed his basic sympathy with the aims of the popular organizations. He praised the Revolutionary Coordinating Body of Mass Organizations (a union of popular organizations) while calling the Christian Democrats in the government to take action against those responsible for the repression or be regarded as accomplices themselves. In fact, as Berryman says, at this point "the majority of the Christian Democrat leaders most respected for their intelligence and honesty left the party; the ones who remained were considered 'politicians' in the pejorative sense."[36]

On March 23, 1980, Romero in his customary hour and a half radio sermon saw the basic question as how to take the least violent way out of the country's crisis. He concluded by urging the soldiers to stop firing on their own unarmed brothers and sisters, for no soldier, he said, is obliged to obey an order against God's law. And "In the Name of God," he told the government, "stop the repression."

The next day as he was celebrating Mass, he prayed that the Eucharist would "feed us so that we may give our body and our blood to suffering and pain, as Christ did, not for himself but to give ideas of justice and peace to our people." At that moment a sharpshooter in the aisle at the rear raised his rifle and put a bullet through Romero's heart. He died shortly afterward.

Thousands of mourners led by four bishops and 400 priests accompanied his body in silence to the Central Plaza where 30,000 gathered for the funeral held on the cathedral steps. Then while the ceremony was in progress, the sound of gunfire and explosions suddenly stunned the crowd. Before they could reach cover, twenty-six persons were killed and 200 injured.

Not quite a year later, on December 4, the bodies of four American women working with the poor were uncovered in a crude grave near San Salvador: Dorothy Kazel, an Ursuline nun from Cleveland; Jean Donovan, a volunteer layworker from the same city; and two Maryknoll sisters, Ita Ford and Maura Clarke. They had been seized two days before while driving from the San Salvador airport and had been raped and murdered.

[36] Ibid., p. 149.

The list of martyrs continued to grow with the names of other Salvadoran priests, nuns, and catechists added during the rest of the decade, victims of the violence that took over 70,000 people during that period—many of whom died at the hands of right-wing death squads acting in collusion with the military.

One of the most brutal episodes occurred in the early morning of November 16, 1989, when six Jesuits working at Central American University in San Salvador were dragged from their beds by thirty armed men in uniform and machine-gunned to death. Their cook and her daughter were also slaughtered. The feeling of horror and revulsion around the world was enormous, and the government, though under the control of the right-wing Arena party, could no longer afford the appearance of a cover-up. The ensuing investigation and trial resulted in two high-ranking members of the military being found guilty and sentenced to a term of thirty years in prison, though they were amnestied in 1993.

THE CHURCH'S PURSUIT of its social justice agenda elsewhere has not been as dramatic as in Latin America. In the United States since Vatican II, the bishops have made many pronouncements on a wide range of issues involving social justice. Their most comprehensive one was their 1986 pastoral "Economic Justice for All: Catholic Social Teaching and the U.S. Economy." Its hard-hitting critique of America's cultural and economic values and its indictment of the system's bias against the poor aroused the ire of conservatives who accused them of economic ignorance.

In their document the bishops called for a new "commitment to economic justice" and urged vast changes in economic policy—most of them in sharp conflict with the reigning Reaganomic philosophy. Among measures called for are the reduction of unemployment to 3 to 4 per cent, a reform of the welfare system establishing a national minimum benefit to meet basic needs, and a revamping of the tax system. They also pointed out how the distribution of income and wealth in the United States is so inequitable that it violates minimum standards of distributive justice. They upheld the right of workers to organize while denouncing the union-busting tactics that have been increasingly employed of late. Another target they aimed at was the massive sums devoted to defense spending, which they said drains financial resources that should be directed to meeting human needs.

While the bishops wrestled with the country's economic and social issues, they themselves were hard put to deal with one of the most volatile issues facing the Church: its refusal to allow the ordination of women. While the Church has made some progress in overcoming its historic sexism (in many dioceses, for instance, women are increasingly found in important administrative positions), committed feminists say this is only window dressing. Dire predictions have been made about the consequences if the Church continues its present exclusion of women from the ranks of its real decision makers. A "staggering" exodus of women will occur, according to Margaret Ellen Traxler, founder of NCAN (National Coalition of American Nuns), unless there is a change.

As advocates of the ordination of women, the nuns in NCAN and other feminists in the Church point out that many of the major documents of Church tradition are shot through with anti-female prejudice. How such prejudice developed in the Church in spite of the radical openness of Jesus himself to women is an intriguing question that they have explored in a growing number of studies. They see Jesus himself as revolutionary in his acceptance of women as equals and his rejection of any use of God to perpetuate patriarchal or hierarchical relationships. However, as they see it, the regression to these forms of relationships occurred already with Paul. Theologically, they say, Paul's heart was in the right place insofar as he saw that the coming of Christ had abolished all inequality, including that between men and women. But socially he was conservative and unwilling to challenge the existing order. Unfortunately, his radical theological vision was forgotten while his practical dictates as to the subordination of women became normative, although Paul saw them only as a concession to the social order of his day.

Taking up the next stage in the development of anti-female prejudice in the Church, the critics of Christian tradition view the Fathers of the Church as reinforcing the fallacy of intrinsic female inferiority. The Fathers did this by finding many arguments, specious as they were, in Scripture and philosophy to justify the actual social inferiority of women. Their tendentious interpretation of such scriptural passages as those relating Eve's creation from Adam's rib and Eve's part in Adam's fall was most important in this regard. Fathers like St. Augustine also held a dualistic view of the body as antagonistic to the spirit, seeing woman as dominated by bodiliness in comparison with man, who stood for the predominance of the spirit. So they saw the defects of the woman as the defects of bodiliness: sensuality, pettiness, maliciousness. For

Augustine "this definition of femaleness as body decrees a natural subordination of female to male as flesh must be subject to spirit in the right ordering of nature."[37] And since femininity was so closely associated with the debasing carnality that drags man down from his spiritual heights, woman's perfection would consist in transcending whatever was peculiar to the female body. Ascetics like St. Jerome seem obsessed at times with details of dress, adornment, and physical appearance: the virgin must blot out whatever was specifically female in her visual image by eschewing all adornment, veiling her face and limbs, and wearing unshapely dress.

The reluctance of the Fathers to recognize women as fully human is also found in the thought of the scholastic theologians. For Thomas Aquinas the inferior and subordinate status of women was not only one of the most obvious facts of existence, it was also a divinely ordained condition whose origins were fully explained in Scripture, and he interpreted Genesis and the Pauline epistles in this sense. Moreover, he found a confirming explanation in Aristotle, who defined woman as a misbegotten male. In this view the male seed carried in its potency the total genetic structure of the offspring and therefore should reproduce by nature the image of its origin, that is, another male, unless some accident happened to the male sperm, in which case a female was begotten, or more properly "misbegotten."[38]

In the Incarnation, God had to assume the male form because only in the male is the image of God, that is, intellectuality, seen in its fullness. For the same reason, women were to be excluded from the priesthood since being in a state of subjection they could not congruously exercise the functions of leadership involved in the work of the priest.

The roots of anti-female prejudice in the Church do indeed go very deep, a prejudice which the feminists see as the main obstacle to ordination of women. But a different point of view was taken by the Vatican in its Declaration of October 15, 1976, which reiterated Church opposition to ordaining women. According to the Declaration, the Church refuses to ordain women not because of anti-female prejudice but because it wants to remain faithful to the example of Jesus Christ himself who did not choose to bring women into the ranks of his twelve apostles in spite of the fact that he showed a singular lack of prejudice toward them. And in fact, the Vatican document says,

[37] Quoted in *Religion and Sexism*, Rosemary Radford Ruether, ed. (New York: Simon & Schuster, 1974), p. 157.
[38] *Summa Theologiae, Pars Prima*, q. XCII, art. I.

the symbolism inherent in the sacramental role of the priest demands that only males be ordained. For when he consecrates the bread and wine at the altar, the priest takes the part of Christ himself—he is a sign of Christ. And since Christ was a male, the priest must be a male since the maleness of Christ was not accidental but essential to the profoundly symbolic nuptial language of Scripture that describes God's people as the spouse of God, the divine bridegroom. So only a male priest can fittingly symbolize Christ as the bridegroom comes to possess in spiritual communion his bride, the Church.

Needless to say, the Vatican's arguments failed to convince advocates of women's ordination and the debate goes on.

John Paul II, however, was determined to hold the line. His encyclical *On the Dignity of Women* held little comfort for Catholic feminists. Women, he preached, should find their identity in motherhood or virginity, and he paid little attention to other possible ways women might find fulfilment. Meanwhile the number of Catholics favoring the ordination of women continue to increase.

Chapter 36

ON THE THRESHOLD OF THE
THIRD MILLENNIUM

A POLARIZED CHURCH

In August 1996, before his untimely death, Cardinal Joseph Bernardin of Chicago announced a project he called "Common Ground." Concerned about a mean-spiritedness he noted among Catholics, he hoped to bring Catholics of differing opinions together for the kind of dialogue that would bring healing.

The initiative reflected the concern of many bishops around the world about the polarized state of the Catholic Church. This was mentioned in the previous chapter as a growing problem during the 1970s and '80s, and since then there has been no letup. The history of the Church shows that the phenomenon is not unusual. But it did seem new for those who grew up in the lock-step mode of the pre–Vatican II Church with its defensive mentality and naïve understanding of papal infallibility. The huge turnaround with Vatican II occurred as the Church began to shed its siege mentality and open itself to what was best in the modern world. But conflicting interpretations of Vatican II have caused increasingly sharp polarization between liberals and conservatives. During the nineties this polarization revolved especially around such issues as abortion, clerical celibacy, sexuality, the ordination of women, contraception, and the application of the Church's doctrine on social justice, and liturgical reforms.

Pope John Paul II himself continued to hew to a hard line on these hot-button issues, but his broad global popularity remained unshaken and perhaps was even enhanced by the sense of certainty and confidence he projects in an age riven with anxiety. Typical was the reaction of one woman during his visit to Rio de Janeiro when he reiterated his hard line on contraception: "I admire the Pope and agree with his teachings. I just can't follow them." One of the funniest incidents occurred in Santagio de Chile, where the Pope questioned thousands of Chilean youngsters. "Do you give up the idol of wealth?" he cried. "Yes," shouted the kids. "Do you give up the idol of power?" "Yes." "Do you give up the idol of sex?" "Nooo," they roared.[1]

In view of the stern "papa knows best" image Pope John Paul II projects, many are surprised at the enthusiastic response he draws from young people, who flock in huge numbers to the Masses he celebrates in the open air. At times he tempers the wind to the shorn lamb. Addressing 400,000 youths at Cherry Creek State Park in Denver, Colorado, at World Youth Day in August 1993, he departed from his text. Instead of his usual exhortations concerning the nation's moral decline, he spoke in positive tones as a pastor to his flock. The young Catholics, many of whom openly disagree with the Pope's strict stand on sexual morality, responded joyfully to his positive message of hope and belief.

Undeterred by increasingly noticeable symptoms of Parkinson's disease, John Paul continues on his way, still the traveler in all seasons as speculation grows about his possible resignation. At the same time, he continues to fulfill his duties as bishop of Rome. On December 16, 2001, for his 300th pastoral visit, he came to the Rome parish of Santa Maria Josepha del Cuore di Jesu, where he was greeted by a brass band and a large crowd of well-wishers. In fact, he has visited far more parishes than any previous Pope and still hopes to visit the remaining thirty-four parishes in Rome.

No one knows what verdict history will render about his pontificate, one of the longest on record, but a recent writer who called him the pivotal personage of this century may not be far off. Firmly and stubbornly, he has guided the Church through the current crisis, which he sees as a struggle against moral relativism and secularistic hedonism. Undaunted by the sheer magnitude of the forces arrayed against religion, he continues to witness to the meaningfulness of faith. And as the Church shakes and trembles under the Siberian blasts from the desert of modern skepticism, his singular

---

[1] Carl Bernstein and Marco Politi, *His Holiness: John Paul II and the Hidden History of Our Time* (New York: Doubleday, 1996), p. 409.

charisma has proved to be a most formidable tool for keeping the Church together.

Moreover, as the *New York Times* editorialized on the occasion of his fourth visit to the United States, in October 1995, the Pope has made himself a central figure in twentieth-century affairs. As a constant voice for peace and human rights in a violent world, he has transcended national and theological boundaries. At the United Nations he delivered a plea for an end to ethnic conflict, the acceptance of diversity, and commitment to morality in the family of nations. On the same visit he preached to a soggy but jubilant crowd of 83,000 people at Giants Stadium and urged the United States to preserve its openness to immigrants as a "welcoming culture" and to defend the "unborn child" in the name of American civil rights. Later, at another Mass before 125,000 people in the rain-soaked playing fields of Central Park on October 8, he exhorted his hearers to care for the poor, the hungry, the homeless, and people with AIDS.

The Pope often speaks out for the economically and socially marginalized whose plight is often visible to him in his travels. He is reminded of the scandal revealed by a recent *U.N. Human Development Report:* Twenty percent of people living in high-income countries consume 86 percent of the world's resources, goods, and services, while the poorest 20 percent consume just 1.3 percent.

On his visit to Mexico January 2000, he was clearly dismayed by the poverty and warned that an unbridled free-market system threatened the human race with subtle forms of slavery. Yet paradoxically he has struck hard at "liberation theologians" and practically dismantled progressive dioceses in Latin America, silencing some of the most eloquent voices who speak for the dispossessed. And as he continued to reshape the Latin American hierarchy, he reminded the bishops that although they should take better care of the poor, they should also minister to the rich. The bishops of Latin America remain divided: on one side are those who continue to urge change in the Latin American Church and the conservatives, who are allied with the Vatican officials.

At the synod of Bishops in October 2001, Archbishop Telesphore Toppo of Ranchi, India, created a sudden and dramatic silence when he said forcefully that the synod was "the beginning of a silent revolution." Speaking of the events of September 11, he said, "God speaks through signs and events, but who is listening?" He then prophesied that the Church was entering a new phase, one that demands that "bishops and the Church become the Church of the poor," specifically citing Pope John Paul's words at the beginning of the synod.

COLLAPSE OF COMMUNISM

The Pope played an important role in the collapse of Communism. His visits to Poland energized the Catholic populace for spiritual resistance and provided the inspiration needed for the workers to organize Solidarity, the union that eventually was able to topple the Communist regime.[2] Gorbachev himself stated, "One can say that everything that has happened in Eastern Europe in recent years would have been impossible without the Pope's efforts and the enormous role, including the political role, he has played in the world arena."[3]

When praised for his role in bringing down the Soviet colossus, the Pope urged people not to oversimplify the matter, saying in an interview, "It would be simplistic to say that Divine Providence caused the fall of Communism. It fell by itself as a consequence of its own mistakes and abuses. It fell by itself because of its own inherent weakness. . . . It had revealed itself to be an unattainable utopia because some essential aspects of the human person were neglected and negated: Man's irrepressible longing for freedom and truth and his incapacity to feel happy when the transcendent relationship with God is excluded."[4]

But after the fall of Communism, the Church in Poland has been a disappointment for the Pope. In a subsequent visit to his homeland he noted the same materialism that he believes has undermined Christian faith and caused a huge decline in Church congregations in Europe. A poll taken in 1995 by the Italian Bishops Conference found that only 23 percent of Italians regu-

---

[2] Carl Bernstein and Marco Politi in their biography of the Pope even claim that the Vatican worked out a deal with President Reagan whereby the United States would assist Solidarity and Solidarity and the Pope would help the United States pull Poland out of the Soviet orbit. Supposedly, the Pope also promised to lean heavily on the liberation theologians in Latin America and favor the bloc of center-to-right-wing forces there. Bernstein and Politic argue that the Pope was willing to make such a deal because he believed in Reagan's sincere desire for peace and his hope of removing nuclear weapons from the planet. The Pope also seemed reassured by Reagan's expressed conviction that the basic issue between the two power blocs was spiritual. Christianity versus atheistic Bolshevism. He was also impressed by Reagan's belief in the mission of the United States to promote the "indispensable conditions of justice and freedom, of truth and love that are the foundations for lasting peace." Other authoritative observers like George Weigel dismiss the story as unsubstantiated.

[3] Ibid., pp. 12–13.

[4] Ibid., pp. 482–83.

larly attend Mass, and 60 percent never go to confession. In Africa and Asia, however, the Church is growing rapidly.

INTERFAITH RELATIONS

One of the Pope's top priorities has been the cultivation of better interfaith relations. The latest effort was the assembly of world religions he convened at Assisi, Italy, on January 24, 2002. It drew together 250 leaders from a dozen religions that included Muslims, Jews, and Christians, as well as native African religions, Buddhism, Hinduism, and Zoroastrians. In his opening address he insisted on his belief that "whoever uses religion to foment violence contradicts religion's deepest and truest inspiration." The attack on the World Trade Center in New York on September 11, 2001, was clearly uppermost in the Pope's mind as he quoted from the third-century bishop St. Cyprian: "Let us pray to the heavenly father. Let us implore him as befits those who weep over the ruins, and who fear for what remains standing."

The remarkable numbers attending the Assisi event showed how much goodwill the Pope had garnered by his unceasing efforts at interfaith healing and mutual understanding in his visits to Israel and major Muslim countries. Despite continuing violence in the Middle East, a dozen Jewish leaders and thirty Muslim religious leaders came to Assisi from Iran, Iraq, Saudi Arabia, Pakistan, and Egypt. Sheik Al-Azhar Muhammed Sayid Tantawy, the grand sheik of the Al-Azhar mosque and Islamic Center in Cairo, thanked the Vatican for its "honorable support of the Palestinian people." The Orthodox hierarchy was represented by the vicar of the patriarch of Moscow. No doubt Bartholomew I, the patriarch of Constantinople and leader of the Greek Orthodox Church, expressed the hope of those attending when he noted the need to "rediscover the real essence of religion, beyond prejudices and national or ethnic differences. There is a momentum for that after what we saw last September."

One of the memorable images of the Pope in his pursuit of better relations between the religions was captured during his visit to the Wailing Wall in Jerusalem, when he slipped his written prayers into a crevice of the stones. This visit to the Holy Land was certainly one of the outstanding events of his pontificate.

Still, his most cherished ecumenical goal remained, reunion with the Orthodox churches, whom he calls the "other lung" of the Church. In this quest, he has made numerous visits, the most memorable being to Athens in 2001 when he apologized for the sacking of Constantinople by the Crusaders.

An important step forward in the ecumenical movement was the recent publication of the *Joint Declaration on the Doctrine of Justification by Faith*, written by Lutheran and Roman Catholic theologians, in 1998. Disagreement between Luther and the Catholic Church about this issue was a major cause of the Reformation in the sixteenth century. So how was it possible to reconcile these two seemingly opposed views that have divided the two churches for centuries? No doubt the work of the Second Vatican Council paved the way by its willingness to take a new look at old problems, as well as the work of a number of Catholic theologians, including especially Karl Rahner's theology, centered on Christ and grace, whereby even one justified remained a "sinner" insofar as the effects of sin still influenced the will.

The agreement actually sums up the conclusions of dialogues held between Lutherans and Catholics over the preceding twenty years. It doesn't resolve all differences on the issue between the two churches but explains them in terms of different use of language and "theological elaboration and emphasis," which do not negate the consensus regarding basic truths.

To further the cause of Christian unity, the Pope has broken with precedent in truly remarkable ways. As the world approached the third millennium, the Pope literally begged other Christians to join him in the search for unity. In his plea he noted how Christians have disfigured the image of Christ by their betrayals, their weaknesses, their bickering and dividedness. They even rejoice in their alienation from each other. He knows only too well his own Church's responsibility for the shattered kingdom of Christ and he gives credit to the "churches of the reformation" for beginning the ecumenical movement. For his part, he promised to take the path of humble repentance and not cease asking forgiveness for his own Church's sins of commission and omission, for its intolerance, its deceitfulness, and triumphalism.

Most important, he admits that it is his own office in the succession of Peter that has sometimes been a great obstacle to the task of reconciliation. He looks for a new way to exercise his Petrine ministry so that it might truly take up Peter's task of confirming his brethren. But he cannot achieve this alone, he says, and he calls on the bishops and theologians of other churches to help in a re-examination of the role of Peter. "I want this to be done in the light of Christ's word, his wish and prayer for unity." Many aspects," he says, "need to be examined: doctrinal, disciplinary, social, historical, and political considerations."

Whether such a an amazing request has any precedent in the history of the Roman Church is an interesting question. It would be hard to find one. Were it not for the cacophony of the media with its constant daily deluge of facts overwhelming people's attention, more people might be aware of this fascinating spiritual quest of the Holy Father.

This is quite a paradox—a Pope pleading for a new way of exercising the primacy—a Pope with such an autocratic image, one who has achieved a centralization of papal power hardly matched in previous history.

One prelate who responded to the Pope's call was Cardinal Koenig, of Austria, who said at the time that there certainly is need for a new model of exercising papal authority. The world, he said, is increasingly adverse to the present patriarchal, authoritarian, and ethnocentric one. König calls for a model of the church as a communion of communions.

THE ISSUE OF RELIGIOUS PLURALISM

By his efforts on behalf of interfaith relations, the Pope has helped bring the issue of religious pluralism to the fore in the Catholic Church and has sharpened a debate that has been going on for some years. The debate came to a head in a recent exchange between Cardinal Ratzinger, head of the Vatican Congregation for the Doctrine of the Faith, and a seventy-seven-year-old Jesuit professor in Rome, Jacques Dupuis. During thirty years spent in India, Dupuis had found much to think about as to the role of the other religions and he has developed a theology of religious pluralism that tries to move Catholic theology beyond the limits set by Vatican II.

The longstanding exclusivist approach whereby there was no salvation outside the Church (in Latin: *extra ecclesiam nulla salus)* was modified at Vatican II and a more inclusivist theology was adopted that reflected the German Jesuit Karl Rahner's idea of the anonymous Christian, who is saved by Christ though not aware of it. But this has not proved to be a realistic basis for dialogue with other religions. Lately, therefore, some Catholics have proposed a third, or pluralistic, approach, according to which God works through many incarnations: via Christ, via Krishna, via Muhammad. But this relativistic approach seemed incompatible with the Catholic tradition.

Here is where Father Dupuis enters the picture with a subtle theology he has worked out that is pluralistic without being relativistic—or so he claims.

Dupuis holds that the spirit of God is universally present and active, before and after the event of Jesus Christ—in his life, ministry, death, and resurrection. In other words, he asks whether, after the Christ event, the Spirit of God is present and operative only through the glorified humanity of Jesus Christ. No, he says, if you take into account all the biblical data that distinguish between the "Spirit of God and the Spirit of Christ." This biblical data show that there has been a saving action of the Holy Spirit that extends beyond the risen humanity of Jesus.

After all, it is a teaching of the Second Vatican Council that the Holy Spirit was already present and working in the world before the Christ event. So why would one say that no action of the Spirit as such is conceivable after the event of the Incarnation, though it is related to that event? Although there is one plan of salvation, there are complementary aspects in this one plan. "Elements of truth and grace are present in human cultures and religions, due to the combined action of God's Word and his Spirit." Hence, one can recognize a mediatory function of those religions in communicating God's offer of grace and salvation.

In short, Dupuis likens God to a potter working with two hands. With one hand He saves through the risen Christ, and with the other, through the Spirit. The two ways are distinct but complementary and together they constitute one plan of salvation. Thus one can speak of a religious pluralism in view of the actual history of how God has reached out to mankind by leading them through various "paths" or "ways" of salvation. From this perspective one can speak of the other ways as divinely willed.[5]

But the Vatican Congregation for the Doctrine of the Faith, in a notification, took issue with Dupuis on five important doctrinal points, which it said must be clarified in order to prevent error. Basically, the Vatican insists that Jesus is the sole and universal mediator of salvation and his Church is the sign and instrument of a salvation for all for all humanity. Nor are the different religions of the world to be thought of as complementary ways of salvation, though the Holy Spirit does accomplish salvation through the elements of truth and goodness they contain.

Father Dupuis called the Vatican's notification "not very pleasant." The whole process took two and a half years, during which he was obligated to silence. After submitting more than two hundred pages in response to a ques-

[5] *The Tablet,* March 3, 2001.

tionnaire, he was informed that his answers were not satisfactory and on September 4, 2000, he was asked to sign a fifteen-page draft of a notification that found "grave errors" in his work. But Father Dupuis did not sign the notification, stating, "The text contained false accusations against my book, to which I could not subscribe."[6]

On September 6, Cardinal Ratzinger issued a document named "Dominus Deus" which was obviously aimed at Dupuis and which, in line with traditional Catholic theology, described other denominations as "deficient." It raised an ecumenical storm and was criticized by several cardinals for its tone and timing. The next day Dupuis received a new draft of the notification in which the charges of "grave errors" were toned down to "ambiguities." This Father Dupuis signed, but soon there were more ambiguities: The Vatican said signing obliged him to "abide" by the notification, whereas Dupuis argued that signing only obliged him to "take into account" the notification.[7]

THE CANONIZING POPE

Among noteworthy aspects of John Paul's pontificate has been the large number of canonizations John Paul has made—more than any other Pope. As of February 2002, the number of new saints was 455, and 1,277 beatified. No doubt, the Pope's aim is to point up the spiritual fecundity of the Church, "like a father proudly showing off his children." The saints are symbols of a flourishing religious life, "role models . . . and a stimulus to overcoming sagging priestly vocations."[8]

The process leading to the canonization of the celebrated Mother Teresa was begun by Archbishop Henry D'Souza of Calcutta in July 1999, after the

---

[6] Ibid.

[7] (1) The notification affirms that Jesus is the sole and universal mediator of salvation for all humanity. Hence one must not posit any separation between the Word and Jesus. Furthermore there is a salvific activity of the Word as such in the divinity, independent of the humanity of the Incarnate Word. (2) It affirms the unicity and completeness of Christ's revelation, which offers all that is necessary for salvation. The elements of salvation in other religions are ultimately derived from the source-mediation of Jesus Christ. (3) The universal salvific action of the Holy Spirit does not extend beyond the one universal salvific economy of the Incarnate Word. (4) All are called to become part of the Church, which is the sign and instrument of salvation for all people. It is wrong to consider the different religions of the world as ways of salvation complementary to the Church. (5) Although it is legitimate to maintain that the Holy Spirit accomplishes salvation through the elements of truth and goodness present in the various religions, Catholic theology does not consider these religions, as such, to be ways of salvation. Nor are their sacred texts to be regarded as complementary to the Old Testament.

[8] Bernstein and Politi, *His Holiness,* p. 393.

Pope waived the five-year waiting period after death. Mother Teresa died in September 1997, at the age of eighty-seven, of cardiac arrest in Calcutta, India, where she worked with the destitute for five decades. Her Missionaries of Charity now number over four thousand nuns and four hundred brothers who run homes, clinics, and schools in over a hundred countries.

Many of the saints John Paul canonized—such as Anuarite Negapeta, an African nun killed by a Simba soldier in Zaire while defending her vow of virginity, and Father Maximilian Kolbe and Edith Stein, both of whom died at Auschwitz—were chosen as examples of Christian courage.[9]

The canonization of Edith Stein, known as Sister Benedicta, in October 1998 focused attention on a fascinating personality and caused some bitter controversy. Sister Benedicta was a key figure in a central drama of the twentieth century. A Jewish intellectual who became a Carmelite and was killed in the gas chamber at Auschwitz, she confronted in her person the incomprehensible evil of Hitler and the Holocaust. Her canonization provoked a heated Jewish response. Jews argued that she was sent to the gas chambers because she was a Jew, not because she was a nun. Though the press highlighted the dismay of Jewish leaders, over a hundred of Edith Stein's relatives attended the canonization, in recognition of the profound Jewish roots of her Christ-centered destiny. But many within the German Jewish community, including her own mother, had not been able to accept her conversion to a faith they held responsible for the long history of ignominy and persecution they had suffered.

Born on Yom Kippur, October 12, 1891, Edith was the youngest of the family's seven living children. She had no memory of her father, who died when she was only two. However, her mother took over the father's business and ran it successfully while raising a family. From her earliest days, Edith showed the brilliant intelligence and steely determination that would lead her to excel in philosophy. At the University of Göttingen, she came under the lasting influence of Edmund Husserl, the father of phenomenology, a philosophy that emphasizes looking at reality objectively and concretely while appreciating the role of one's subjective intentions in directing one's attention.

In the course of her studies she happened upon the autobiography of St. Teresa of Ávila and devoured it in one night. "This is the truth," she exclaimed. St. Teresa's life confirmed Edith's growing sense of the reality of

[9] Ibid.

Christ's power over evil and the light he shed on the mystery of the Cross. This mystery she found illuminated by the teachings of John of the Cross and she devoted her efforts to developing a philosophy of the person based on John's teachings on the Cross. Her "Science of the Cross," however, remained unfinished while Hitler, whom she called the Antichrist, filled Germany with his raucous, bloodthirsty message. His followers, she said, "desecrate the images of the cross and make every effort to tear the cross out of the hearts of Christians. . . . The world is in flames, the battle between Christ and the Antichrist has broken into the open. If you decide for Christ, it could cost you your life." Edith Stein and her sister Rosa, a Third Order Carmelite, were seized from the Carmelite convent in Echt, Holland, in late July or early August 1942. They were murdered at Auschwitz with their Jewish brothers and sisters.

Another controversial canonization was that of the founder of the organization Opus Dei, Josemaría Escrivá, which took place on October 6, 2002. Founded by Father Escrivá nearly three quarters of a century ago, Opus Dei has for many decades hovered on the fringes of Church life. It was regarded with some reservation because of the atmosphere of secrecy that surrounds it and such practices as the commitment of its members to celibacy and the exercise of self-flagellation. Since Escrivá's death in 1975, however, it has gathered increasing strength, as is indicated by the canonization of the founder. It is making good headway in the United States, where its three thousand members follow its policy of finding influential posts in the professions and the business world. The overall intent is to achieve holiness in the world through prayer and the adherence to Catholic teachings on all issues, including birth control, abortion, and homosexuality. In view of the controversial nature of Escrivá and of the organization he founded (now with some 85,000 members), some thought it strange to allow a speeding up of the process. Opus Dei (the name means "God's Work") has often been criticized for secrecy, authoritarianism, and methods that induce a fear-inspired attitude. Some former members have called their experience "brainwashing." One ex-member said, "When I left, I found I could love God out of love, not out of fear." Another ex-member, Fr. Felzmann, now a priest of the Westminster archdiocese, thinks that members of Opus Dei are essentially "antiworld" and are out to be an "elite." He is completely against the canonization of Escrivá, whom he knew as a personal friend. A Benedictine oblate and former member, Ruth Walker of New Zealand, was given instruction by an Opus Dei chaplain at the time of her conversion and found the society's members "nostalgic for a rigidly hierarchical, safe environment . . . where the Gospel can't spring any surprises on them."[10]

However, there are signs that the organization is loosening up. Some recent ex-members, such as Christopher Howse, an editor of the *London Daily Telegraph* who left Opus Dei in 1998, calls his experience quite positive. Howse thinks the organization's ascetic principles have real merit in their emphasis on the need to struggle against one's natural cravings. The author of a recent investigation of Opus Dei, Annabel Miller, found the organization's members open and friendly, though she found their spirituality too intense and not "sensual" enough. Not her cup of tea. But she concluded: "All in all a helpful way to be a better Christian."[11]

HITLER AND PIUS XII

The biggest storm has been raised by the possible canonization of Pius XII. The news triggered a spate of books dealing with Pius XII's response to the Holocaust, by both his accusers and his defenders. The accusers maintain that Pius XII failed to speak out forcefully against the Nazi massacre of the Jews, thereby revealing the hypocrisy of the Vatican's claim to moral authority. It is interesting that some of the accusers are lapsed or angry Catholics who are driving a liberal intra-Church agenda calling for big changes in the Church's positions on, especially, sexual issues. The controversy is also being fueled by an opposition to Pope John Paul II that borders on the extreme.[12] As one might expect, the books vilifying the wartime Pope have gained the most attention, so much so that the "silence of the Pope" has become the accepted judgment of his stance in the public forum.

A recent article by an American rabbi, David G. Dalin, challenges this judgment.[13] He calls making Pius XII a target of moral outrage a failure of historical understanding, and he thinks Jews should reject any "attempt to usurp the Holocaust" for the partisan purposes at work in this debate. Dalin sur-

---

[10] *The Tablet,* November 17, 2001.
[11] Ibid.
[12] See these critical works: John Cornwell's *Hitler's Pope,* Garry Wills's *Papal Sin,* Michael Phayer's *The Catholic Church and the Holocaust, 1930–1965,* Susan Zuccotti's *Under His Very Window,* James Carroll's *Constantine's Sword.* The defenders: Pierre Blet's *Pius XII and the Second World War,* Margherita Marchione's *Pope Pius XII,* Ronald J. Rychlak's *Hitler, the War and the Pope,* Ralph McInerny's *The Defamation of Pius XII.*
[13] *The Weekly Standard,* February 26, 2001.

mises that well-known Jews such as Albert Einstein, Golda Meir, Moshe Sharett, and Rabbi Isaac Herzog would likely have been shocked at these attacks on Pope Pius. Einstein, for instance, in an article in *Time*, paid tribute to Pius and noted that the Church alone "stood squarely across the path of Hitler's campaign." Dalin points out that "Rabbi Herzog, the chief rabbi of Israel, sent a message in February 1944 declaring 'the people of Israel will never forget what His Holiness . . . [is] doing for our unfortunate brothers and sisters in the most tragic hour of our history.' " Dalin cites these tributes as recognition of the work of the Holy See in saving hundreds of thousands of Jews.[14]

It is true, Dalin says, that Pius has had Jewish detractors such as Günter Lewy and Saul Friedländer, who he thinks were wrong in their view that an overheated anti-Communism led Pius to support Hitler as a bulwark against the Russians. And he names some Jewish defenders of Pius, from Pinchas Lapide (*Three Popes and the Jews,* 1967) to the Jewish historian Sir Martin Gilbert, who recently remarked that Pius deserves not blame but thanks.

Dalin describes a basic technique used by the accusers of the Pope: "It requires only that favorable evidence be read in the worst light and treated to the strictest test, while unfavorable evidence is read in the best light and treated to no test." Actually, as Dalin shows, "The best historical evidence now confirms that Pius XII was not silent and that almost no one at the time thought him so." The numerous testimonies to Pius's interventions against Nazi atrocities include several editorials in the *New York Times,* including one in January 1940 that praised the Pope for speaking out about the dreadful cruelties inflicted on the Jewish and Catholic Poles, as well as a report in March 1940 that spoke of the Pope's defense of the Jews. In the following year, an editorial called Pius XII "a lonely voice in the silence and darkness enveloping Europe . . . calling for a 'real new order' based on 'liberty, justice, and love.' " Also, a report of a plea by the Pope for the Jews in France appeared in the issue of August 6, 1942.

Dalin notes how Marcus Melchior, the chief rabbi of Denmark, argued that "if the pope had spoken out, Hitler would probably have massacred more than six million Jews and perhaps ten times ten million Catholics." The disaster for Holland's Jews that occurred when the Dutch bishops spoke out is proof enough of this point.

[14] Ibid., p. 6.

Dalin's conclusion is the opposite to that of the author John Cornwell in his book *Hitler's Pope.* Far from being "Hitler's Pope," Pius was the closest Jews had come to having a papal supporter—and at the moment when it mattered most."[15]

Strong advocates on both sides have become deadlocked. The accusers of Pius, such as John Cornwell and Zuccotti, maintain that the Pope was a cowardly pro-Nazi who put the Church's interests ahead of the call of conscience. His defenders, such scholars as Ronald Rychlak and Ralph McInerny—with equally impressive documentation, argue that the Pope spoke out as forcefully as he could in the circumstances, for he realized that more emphatic interventions would only have made things worse for the victims. A good piece of advice was recently voiced in *Le Monde,* which called for a release of the complete archival material relating to Pius's reign. Only then, with complete transparency achieved, will it be possible to fully resolve the issue. In any case, the Israeli ambassador to the Vatican, Aharon Lopez, has urged the Church to wait fifty years before moving ahead with plans to canonize Pius XII.

PIUS XII AND THE GERMAN BISHOPS

More light is shed on the subject by the correspondence between Pius XII and the German bishops (published in 1966), which shows how he agonized throughout the war over how best to proceed. To understand the material, one must keep in mind that the Church's opposition to racial doctrines was never in question. In 1928 the Holy Office in Rome issued an explicit condemnation of anti-Semitism. And from 1930 on, the German bishops repeatedly declared Nazi racial views to be incompatible with Catholic teaching.

When Italy and Germany established close ties after 1936, Pius XI (Pope from 1922 to 1939) acted to keep the Italian people from having close dealings with the Nazis. He demonstrably left Rome on the eve of Hitler's visit to that city.

In 1937 he issued a denunciation of Hitler (though not by name) in the encyclical *Mit brennender Sorge (With Burning Concern),* the first great official public document to dare to confront and criticize Nazism."[16] It had been drafted by Pacelli (later, Pius XII) and a small group of German bishops and it repeated earlier condemnations of racism.

---

[15] Ibid.
[16] Carlo Falconi, *The Silence of Pius XII* (London: Faber, 1970) p. 117.

And in his first encyclical, *Summi Pontificatus,* issued in October 1939, Pius XII used material from an encyclical drafted for Pius XI (never issued because of the latter's death) to condemn what the *New York Times* called in a front-page headline DICTATORS, TREATY VIOLATORS, RACISM. Under his direction the Vatican radio station broadcast numerous reports of Nazi atrocities in Poland.

On April 30, 1943, Pius XII wrote to Bishop von Preysing of Berlin about his concern that public papal protests could provoke reprisals, thus worsening the sufferings of the Nazis' victims. Therefore, he told von Preysing, he would basically leave it to the bishops on the spot to decide how and in what form to protest.

Bishop von Preysing favored a straightforward strategy giving maximum publicity to the condemnation of Nazi crimes, but he was opposed by Bishop Bertram, president of the German bishops' conference, who favored a more cautious approach. The two men had been at odds over the issue since Hitler's assumption of power in March 1933.

Until then, the German bishops had insisted that anyone who subscribed to the Nazi philosophy was unworthy of receiving the sacraments. And in the elections of 1932 and 1933, they forbade Catholics from voting for Hitler. But when Hitler took power, Bertram, as president of the bishops' conference, was able to persuade the bishops to modify their previous warnings. He argued that as the legitimate head of the German nation, Hitler deserved obedience; moreover, he had made a solemn promise to respect Church teaching. Also, Hitler had declared before the Reichstag in March 1933 that he would make the two confessions, Catholic and Protestant, the "cornerstone of the work of national renewal."

Von Preysing was heartsick at the acquiescence of the German bishops. He tried but failed to get his colleagues to issue a statement alerting Catholics to the contradiction between the Christian faith and the deceptive rhetoric of the Nazis. But Bertram urged the clergy to be more "circumspect" in their behavior. This was at the very time unimaginable things were happening in Germany and priests and laymen were being thrown into concentration camps. Apparently, the eighty-year-old Bertram was haunted by memories of Bismarck's *Kulturkampf,* which had involved the persecution of German Catholics, the horrors of which Bertram had experienced as a young man. He believed that open opposition to rulers devoid of moral principles would be counterproductive. Henceforth Bertram responded to Nazi persecution of the Church with a host of meticulously formulated private protests, which the authorities either rejected or more often simply ignored.

Many historians believe the more aggressive strategy favored by von Preysing and those who stood with him would have had greater success in mobilizing German Catholics to resist Hitler. The journalist and historian Donald Nicholls believes that it was in fact tragic that Bertram should have been at the head of the German episcopate rather than the more clear-sighted von Preysing, because of Bertram's inadequate view of the spiritual resistance power of the German Catholics. After all, during Hitler's rise to power, 4 million to 5 million Catholics (some 40 percent) stood solidly behind the Center party, the only party besides the Social Democratic party that never wavered in its loyalty to the Weimar Republic. As Nicholls notes,[17] certain Catholic districts are recorded to have resisted the lure of National Socialism far better than the Protestant ones, and certain heavily Catholic areas, such as that of Cologne-Aachen, proved real bulwarks of the faith, against which Hitler proved impotent. But after the monster's takeover, and in spite of signs that the German Catholics were willing to take the path of resistance, no resistance materialized.

How to explain this? Catholics uttered a moving cry to the bishops in 1935, listing all the sufferings of the German people under the new regime, and asked them what they should do. The bishops replied with a letter full of solicitude and warm feelings but offered nothing to guide them in an unprecedented situation. It left them to endure "martyrdom without mandate." From then on the German Catholics were in retreat. Nicholl concludes that the German bishops did not lack courage, but they were hampered by a tradition within German Catholicism that encouraged suffering in silence, which is especially clear in the case of von Preysing, who realized the need to break out from it and take public action but was hamstrung by the tradition.[18]

---

[17] *The Tablet,* July 30, 1994.

[18] A recent study shows that nearly one hundred Jesuits were detained in Dachau, drawn from every country under Nazi occupation. A host of other Jesuits managed to avoid discovery and capture. On the eve of the attack against the Soviet Union, Hitler ordered the dismissal of all Jesuits from the army because their influence was considered subversive. See Vincent Lapomarda, S.J. *The Jesuits and the Third Reich* (Lewiston, N.Y.: Edwin Mellen Press, 1989). The experience of members of other religious communities was probably not much different.

A CALL FOR REPENTANCE

Pope John Paul II has not been loath to admit the Church's failings as a human institution and has urged the Church to atone for its transgressions, including its acquiescence in human rights abuses under totalitarian governments of the twentieth century. He calls it a "purification of memory" that would prepare the Church for the new millennium. A list of his apologies could be compiled. Before a visit to the Czech Republic in December 1999 he apologized for the "cruel" execution of Jan Hus, who was burned at the stake in 1415. He has been especially insistent on acknowledging the Church's being guilty of anti-Semitism and notes often that the Second Vatican Council condemned anti-Semitism and called for brotherly dialogue between Catholics and Jews on biblical and theological issues.

The papal letter "We Remember: A Reflection on the Shoah," urged Catholics to repent for what they did to help cause the Holocaust and to become more aware of their own faith's Hebrew roots. The Pope has continued to make extraordinary efforts toward reconciliation with the Jewish community. In Holy Week of April of 1993 he welcomed the chief Rabbi of Rome to a concert at the Vatican auditorium commemorating the Holocaust. In an interview at the time, he affirmed the right of Jews to return to a homeland in Israel. And as mentioned above, the most impressive of the Pope's gestures was his visit to the Wailing Wall in Jerusalem.

PAPAL LOQUACITY?

The Pope speaks eight languages, has visited 115 countries, and has written enough addresses, papers, briefs, bulls, encyclicals, and letters to fill 150 books. His book *Crossing the Threshold of Hope* became a number-one best-seller in the United States.[19]

His encyclical *Fides et Ratio (Faith and Reason)* of October 1998 was anticipated with special interest. After all, he was supposed to be an existentialist and a phenomenologist as well as a personalist in his mode of philosophizing. Therefore, many thought such an intellectual Pope might have a new approach to the centuries-old conflict between faith and reason. Philosophers of the Enlightenment as well as men like Hegel and Kierkegaard had tried and

---

[19] *The New York Times,* October 26, 1994.

failed to reconcile the two, but it was thought that this unusual Pope might inject a new dynamic into the search for a solution.

The disappointment was sharp. Actually, the Pope proved that he was just a Thomist in a new suit. His stance was still the classical Catholic one: Philosophy must be subordinate to faith. But many were consoled that at least he didn't impose Thomism as the official guide in Catholic theological studies, as Pope Leo XIII had in the previous century.

It would take a gigantic leap of faith to believe, as the Pope seems to, that after Descartes, Kant, and Heidegger, philosophers would discard their "methodic doubt," relinquish their hard-fought struggle for autonomy, and settle down again as the *ancillae theologiae* (handmaidens of theology). While some applauded his insistence on the role of reason in avoiding sentimentalist superstition, in fact he failed to point the way to reconciling philosophy with the Church and only seemed to prove that the classical Catholic philosophy was no longer relevant to the problems of modernity. He showed that the Church's system of thought, based on classical philosophy, was suspended in the air without a substructure grounded in modern reality. The Dominican scholar Joseph Moingt says that the only solution appears to be to move beyond the old faith and reason problematic and reinvigorate the Church's witness by an evangelical renewal. The Pope's contention in the document that the flight of intellectuals from the Church was due to a faulty modern philosophy leaves out more obvious reasons, such as the face the Church has presented too often since the French Revolution. Surely by the time of Pius XII, the air had gotten very musty in the corridors of the Vatican, although one should not oversimplify the situation, for no one really had the answers as to how the Church could or should adjust to the new democratic, postmodernist society. But the fact remains that for many, especially intellectuals, Vatican II came too late.

Moingt thinks that the future of the Church depends on how well it is able to rearticulate the relations of faith and reason in a way that would correspond to modern realities: The faith reinvigorated by returning to its evangelical mission and reason not in the classical sense of *ancilla theologiae* but rather understood as an ongoing search for answers to the questions of meaning in order to give new life to the Christian tradition.

DISSENTERS BEWARE

One indication of the breakdown of the Church's Greek-Latin patrimony and its faith-reason dialectic is the relatively new phenomenon of Catholic dissent. The crackdown on theologian dissenters was noted in the previous chapter, and they were castigated in John Paul's encyclical *Fides et Ratio,* where he criticized them for their rejection of the philosophic tradition of the Church and their recourse instead to modern human sciences.

One initiative taken by the Vatican to reinforce orthodoxy was the issuance in May 1994 of the new *Catechism of the Catholic Church,* the first comprehensive statement of Catholic doctrine in four hundred years. By August of 1994, it had sold most of the 2.1 million copies in print in the United States and booksellers were clamoring for more. The catechism came down solidly for the traditional morality of the Church on abortion, euthanasia, divorce, and artificial birth control. But it also listed a whole range of social sins, including tax evasion, drug abuse, mistreatment of immigrants, financial speculation, paying unjust salaries, environmental abuse, artificial insemination, genetic engineering. MAD (Mothers Against Drunk Drivers) was no doubt happy to see drunken driving condemned, but not the ordination of women. While condemning homosexuality, it calls for compassion for homosexuals, who do not choose their orientation, while insisting they should remain chaste nevertheless.

Criticisms of the text include complaints that it ignores recent developments in theology and uses the Bible inaccurately, fails to distinguish clearly between central Catholic beliefs and less important ones, and elevates debatable theological positions to the level of orthodoxy.

The moral strictures of the catechism by all accounts found little resonance with Catholic youth, who seem increasingly to look elsewhere for moral guidance.[20]

---

[20] It is an acute dilemma for the Church and one that must be addressed realistically, according to Jack Dominian, an English Catholic psychiatrist and marriage counselor. First of all, he insists, the Church must recognize that the sexual revolution is here to stay. As he says, much of it has trivialized sex, but much has enhanced it. If the Church is to recover some credibility in this area it must develop a theology based on love and understanding of sexual intercourse as a prime life-giving force of love. The Church must offer a theology of marriage that will invite the young to embrace a sexual morality that is biblically based, one that can persuade them to shape their behavior by the principle of love. Sadly, the young are being left to do it on their own. But as we note below, the Pope's "Theology of the Body" could do much to redress this situation if it gains wide acceptance.

One of the most divisive issues in the Church is the question of women's ordination as priests. The issue arose in the Church in the 1970s under the influence of the feminist movement, theological speculation on the nature of the priesthood, and the Anglican Communion's allowing women priests. *Inter Insigniores (Among the Characteristics)* was issued in October 1976 by the Congregation for the Doctrine of the Faith (CDF), which barred ordination of women (see previous chapter). But instead of closing off the debate, it only intensified it.

In December 1990, more than four hundred American and Canadian theologians had endorsed a statement by a committee of the Catholic Theological Society of America, that accused the Vatican of obstructing change in the Roman Catholic Church, inhibiting freedom of expression, and wrongly restricting the role of women. They also accused the Vatican of trying to diminish the role of its bishops and churches in favor of more centralized control. In an op-ed in the *New York Times,* Archbishop Rembert Weakland said that old Roman Catholic assumptions of the inferiority of women were reinforced by their exclusion from the priesthood and suggested that the door should be opened to further discussion and dialogue, even if it were painful.[21]

By 1994, the Pope decided that a papal statement was needed to settle the issue. In a papal letter, *"Ordinatio Sacerdotalis,"* he briefly summarized the position of the Church and said that "the Church had no authority whatsoever to confer priestly ordination on women" and that "this judgment is to be definitively held by all the Church's faithful." But when a bishop asked whether "definitively" mean that the teaching was part of the deposit of the faith, the fat was in the fire. The CDF had no qualms about responding that it was indeed.

But theologians immediately went to work on the CDF's response questioning how two admittedly noninfallible documents—a papal letter and a statement of the CDF—could *infallibly* identify a teaching as part of the deposit of the faith?

To show the difficulty of appealing to the sources used by the CDF to justify the ban on ordination of women, a recent writer in the *The Tablet* noted how the same sources had been used by the Church to sanction slavery. As recently as June 20, 1866, the Holy Office had upheld the slave trade as

---

[21] *The New York Times,* December 6, 1992.

moral.[22] The justification was based both on philosophy (natural law) and on revelation (divine law). Various quotations from Scripture were cited in support of this position (Leviticus 25:39–55; 1 Peter 2:18; Luke 17:7–10; 3:11–22; 1 Timothy 16:1–10). The Fathers of the Church and local church councils laws, Popes, and theologians were cited in the attempt to show that the approval of slavery was part of an unbroken, universal tradition.

But by 1866 most countries had already abolished slavery and the tide of public opinion had moved decidedly against any toleration of it. In effect, the Holy Office, claiming to be the guardian of truth, was defending a practice that was both humanly degrading and theologically wrong. "But at the same time a whole succession of theologians had already denounced it, anticipating the true Catholic teaching and tradition as now enshrined in the second Vatican council," wrote John Wijngaards in *The Tablet.* He cited other instances where the magisterium fell behind the times: charging interest, authorship of Scripture, democracy, trade unions, and ecumenism. What does this say about its present hard line on contraceptives, optional celibacy, and ordination of women, he asks.[23]

A week after the issuance of *Ordinatio Sacerdotalis,* a petition signed by 1.5 million churchgoing German Catholics called for sweeping reforms of church, including ordination of women priests. It indicated the mounting evidence worldwide that large numbers of Catholics simply ignore much of what the Pope says. For their part theologians continued to argue for the right of dissent from official Roman Catholic teaching as part of the process of doctrinal development.[24]

Interestingly, at the fiftieth annual meeting of the Catholic Theological Society in June 1995, one third of the members attending were women. The meeting revealed how the Church's theology, which was once a very model of timelessness, is said to have changed more in the last fifty years than in any half century since the Middle Ages.[25] Not surprisingly, in June 1997, after a yearlong study, the Society overwhelmingly urged the Roman Catholic Church to continue discussing the possibility of ordaining women as priests.

[22] The statement signed by Pope Pius IX declared that "it is not contrary to the natural or divine law for a slave to be sold, bought, exchanged, or given, provided in the sale purchase, exchange or gift, the due conditions are strictly observed which the approved authors describe and explain."

[23] *The Tablet,* December 12, 1998.

[24] *The New York Times,* June 19, 1999.

[25] Ibid., June 20, 1995.

In face of the brouhaha, many bishops, and certainly the Pope, have come to feel that the freedom ushered in by Vatican II has been abused by theologians in the Catholic colleges and universities. At stake is the sense of Catholic identity in these institutions. Rome's remedy emerged in the document called *Ex Corde ecclesiae,* which the American bishops formally endorsed in November 1999. It authorizes the local bishop to issue a *mandatum* (Latin for "commissioned") to theologians certifying that their teaching is "authentic Catholic doctrine." How mandatory the *mandatum* is supposed to be for a theologian teaching in Catholic colleges and universities seems to be left up to the local bishop.

While dissenters among the laity go on their way, the theologians are the ones at risk. The Pope has continued to bring the papal crozier down on the heads of theologians as he did with Küng, Curran, and others, who disregard his policy. A document approved by Pope John Paul states that theologians who find themselves unable to accept certain teachings should raise their objections only in private and not turn to the mass media.[26]

On January 4, 1997, a seventy-two-year-old Asian theologian, Tissa Ballisuriya, a Sri Lankan, was accused of deviating "from the integrity and truth of the Catholic faith" and was excommunicated. He was accused of questioning such basic Roman Catholic beliefs as original sin and the Immaculate Conception and of advocating religious relativism. However, the ban was lifted when an understanding was reached with Ballisuriya. The rising tide of relativism is seen by the Pope as the gravest threat to dogmatic faith since Marxism.[27]

CONGAR

Paradoxically, though, while leaning hard on dissenters generally, in 1994 John Paul made a legendary dissenter, Yves Congar, a cardinal. Congar died in June 1995, a year after receiving the honor. A herald of Vatican II, his life and work epitomize the huge transition the Catholic Church underwent during the twentieth century. In fact, if one were to choose a single Catholic theologian to illustrate the progress of Catholic theology in the twentieth century, one could hardly make a better choice.

Congar experienced the evils of both wars, for his hometown, Sedan, was

[26] Ibid.. June 27, 1990.
[27] Ibid., March 5, 1998.

occupied by the Germans during World War I. During World War II he was taken prisoner and interned in the infamous Colditz prison camp for "dangerous officers."

A Dominican theologian, he had focused very early in his career on the problem of the division among Christians and launched a famous theological collection, *Unam Sanctam,* which paved the way for Catholic ecumenists.

He was considered a dangerous dissenter and near heretic during the freeze on Catholic theology imposed by Pope Pius XII. In fact, Pius's encyclical *Humani Generis* (1950) was inspired by a concern with theologians like Congar. But he lived to see his views of ecumenism endorsed by the bishops at Vatican II. No man did more than Congar to break the stranglehold scholastic theology had on the mind of the Church. Instead of endlessly repeating the formulas of Aquinas, like his fellow Dominicans, he sought inspiration in the history of the Church. His mastery of church history, in fact, led to his first important work, *Vraie et fausse réforme dans l'église (True and False Reform in the Church).*

But like all dissenters he paid a heavy price. Exiled from his teaching post at the famous Le Saulchoir house of studies and tightly restricted from speaking and publishing, he barely managed to hang on with the help of his friends. In his diary he describes the torment he suffered from the Curial inquisitors, who sought every way to entrap him. He speaks of being "crushed, excommunicated by a pitiless system." But this veteran of World War II knew how to fight. And it was a grim battle indeed against a centralized hierarchical institution "addicted to papalotry," for a lone soldier like himself, fighting for his understanding of the Church as the "people of God." In his diary he says, "There is a pope who thinks of everything, who says everything, to whom true Catholics owe blind obedience." His vindication at Vatican II is a remarkable chapter in the history of the Church and a great lesson for those fighting for change in the Church not to despair. How paradoxical was his elevation to the cardinalate by a Pope so uncomfortable with dissent.

SEX AND THE POPE'S THEOLOGY OF THE BODY

The area of sexual morality is the flashpoint in the struggle over dissent from the traditional teaching of the Church. Traditional Catholic sexual morality was partly based on so-called natural law, according to which a human organ was inscribed with a purpose that should not be frustrated. The Pope departs from this tradition and sets forth a biblical view, a theology of the body that has gotten a wide hearing and, according to many, holds great promise for re-newing Catholic doctrine on this crucial issue.

As a phenomenologist reflecting on sexuality, John Paul goes back to the story of Adam, which he accepts as myth, to recapture the wonder of things at the beginning. The book of Genesis, he says, teaches us fundamental truth about the human condition and the meaning of our sexuality. In Genesis man's creation in the image of God is linked to the human capacity to pro-create, to be co-creator with god. This image of God is also reflected in the human power of making moral choices. In fact, the Creation accounts testify to the dignity of being human in which sexuality, procreation, and moral choosing are intimately linked.

The second point Genesis brings out is Adam's original solitude. It is in this "being alone" that he discovers that he is neither an animal nor God, in other words that he is a "person." Moreover, he is an "embodied" person, for there is no human choosing or acting without a body. The body through which we express who we are and act out the decisions we make is not acci-dental to who we are.

The third point is that men and women are images of God, not only through intellect and free will but above all through the communion of per-sons that man and woman form right from the beginning. Thus man becomes the image of God in the moment of communion, in a radical self-giving and receiving of another that reaches its fullness in the act of procreation. Adam symbolically affirms the yearning for this radical giving of self and receiving of another when he recognizes Eve as "flesh of my flesh." This yearning is at the foundation of our humanity. This self-giving in procreation shows forth the image of God, for procreation reproduces the mystery of creation. This act of co-creation shows the purpose of sexuality.

If sexuality is built into us from the beginning, then why, the Pope asks, were Adam and Eve ashamed of their nakedness? They were not ashamed as long as they were united in mutual self-giving, he argues. Shame occurred when the other was turned into an object and the self-giving expressed in the original communion of male and female was undone by lust. Instead of self-giving, lust involves satisfying one's own needs rather than seeing sex as a gift of oneself motivated by love. Even in marriage this adultery of the heart oc-curs when by lustful looks a husband turns his wife into an object and shat-ters the communion of persons. This statement created a furor in the press, but not with those who accepted the Pope's argument that sexual love within marriage is an icon for the interior life of God in expressing the communion of persons.

The Pope then descended into the most controversial part of his theology of the body when he took up the issue of contraception. He contended that chemical means to limit births are dehumanizing, for they belong to the domination of nature but not to the realm of sexual love. Use of the natural rhythms of the body is a more humanistic method of exercising procreative responsibility and living marital love chastely. It is also more in tune with the sacramental character of marriage, for it gives bodily expression to the truth that married couples are the minister of the design that God has built into procreation. He claims that certain things are not to be done that demean our humanity and damage the communion of persons which sexual love is intended to foster.

As George Weigel says in his *Witness to Hope*[28], the Pope's frank and forthright discussion of sexuality and emphasis on our intrinsic embodiedness as male and female is virtually without precedent in the Church. He believes that it could do much to exorcise the demon of Manichaeism that has plagued the Church's doctrine on sexuality. Whether it will do much to alter the apparently fixed outlook of Catholics on the topic is another question.

Meanwhile, the revolution in moral theology we noted in the previous chapter shows no signs of letting up. In fact, it is quite apparent that many Catholic moral theologians have embraced the revisionist point of view.[29] But the Pope emphatically rejected the revisionist theology in his encyclical *Veritatis Splendor.*[30]

---

[28] George Weigel, *Witness to Hope* (New York, HarperCollins, 1999), p. 342.

[29] See chapter 35. The big problem with revisionist moral theology is the difficulty of finding in experience the analogies that natural law ethics has itself always sought. For revisionists the path ahead seems to lie in an inductive search for the enduring essence or kernel of truth in the diversity of experience. It would be a search for ways of decision making that are not modeled on natural law but that accord with the command "Love in all you do." Within this method of morality there would be no concrete norms but directions in which to look for analogies of behaviors. By an inductive process we find out not what we should do but how we should proceed. "What human beings share is, then, not a constitution but a dynamism, a 'radar beam' searching for the good, a historical process—not absolute rules. Obviously, the type of discussion involved in such a dialogic moral search would allow for dissent in defining the concrete norms for the here and now."

[30] A number of revisionist theologians claim that the Pope has misrepresented their position. See M. Allsopp and John O'Keefe, eds., *Veritatis Splendor: American Responses* (Kansas City, Mo.: Sheed & Ward, 1995).

Although many bishops, priests, theologians, and laypeople have questioned the wisdom or relevance of some of the Church's moral teachings, John Paul II has repeatedly firmly rejected every deviation from traditional doctrines. There was to be no change in the Church's ban on Communion for Catholics who had divorced and remarried, on the use of contraceptives, on artificial insemination, or on the use of condoms in a world horrified by the spread of AIDS and threatened by overpopulation. He also vigorously reasserted the Church's condemnation of homosexuality.

One commentator said: "The headlong flight back to doctrinal conformity and away from the relative tolerance and flexibility that had marked much of the pontificate of Pope Paul VI was most emphatic in the area of sexual morality."

The Vatican's uncompromising stand on sexual morality has elicited the most severe criticism in poverty-stricken underdeveloped countries. The typical Vatican position is found in the latest document, "The Reproductive Health of Refugees," which takes issue with a 1999 interagency field manual, *Reproductive Health in Refugee Situations.* The Vatican document reproves the U.N. for urging those working with refugees to take a "non-judgmental approach" to extramarital sex, homosexual relations, and sexual education for young people. It especially denounces a neutral moral approach on sexual education for young refugees. "Rather than being educated for real love within the prospect of marriage and a future family, the Vatican says, these boys and girls are introduced into the world of individualistic and irresponsible sexual pleasure, which increases the risk of extending the HIV-AIDS epidemic."[31]

One of the topics on which Pope John Paul has been most emphatic is what he claims are contemporary threats to the dignity of human life. Summing these up in the phrase "the culture of death," he has spoken out on the inviolability of human life and the idea of life as a divine gift. His encyclical *Evangelium Vitae,* signed on March 25, 1995, takes up this theme again in magisterial fashion. It was praised by the religion editor of *Newsweek* as "the clearest, most impassioned and most commanding encyclical" of the pontificate. It reiterates in solemn form the condemnation of direct and voluntary killing of the innocent in abortion and euthanasia. And in a striking departure from the Church's tradition he added a section on capital punishment,

[31] *The Tablet,* November 17, 2001, p. 1650.

which he rules out except in cases of "absolute necessity." He declares that "to-day . . . as a result of steady improvements in the organization of the penal system, such cases are very rare, if not practically non-existent."

He voiced his opposition to the death penalty in an address to 100,000 people in a sports arena in St. Louis, Missouri, in January 1999 when he called on American Catholics to oppose capital punishment. Led by the Pope, Catholic authorities are lining up more and more against the death penalty. The now-deceased John Cardinal O'Connor, archbishop of New York, expressed his deep personal opposition to capital punishment, warning that it tends to single out certain racial groups and offers a deceptively simple approach to wider problems. O'Connor showed his typical chutzpah by presenting his view at a special annual Mass at St. Patrick's Cathedral attended by hundreds of police officers.

THE POLARIZED CHURCH

A sign of the widespread intra-Church dissent from the official Catholic teaching on sex is the recent call by the Austrian Catholic Men's Association for a Church ceremony blessing homosexual union. It was rejected by the Austrian bishops.[32] The Association insisted that homosexuality was probably a genetic variant that one did not choose. But the bishops declared that such a step was contrary to the authoritative teaching of the Church and was opposed by all the Catholic bishops' conferences. They did, however, reiterate the teaching of the Catholic Catechism, which forbids all discrimination against homosexuals.

There were even some episcopal dissenters. No doubt the most colorful one is the French bishop Jacques Gaillot, who was removed from his diocese with no prior warning because he had insisted on speaking out in favor of married priests, the use of condoms by people with HIV, and respect for committed homosexual relationships. Unruffled, Gaillot merely constituted

---

[32] An interesting question is how Catholics who disagree with the Pope's unyielding stands on sexual issues manage to negotiate their continuing membership in the Church. Michelle Dillon studies this issue in connection with one of the really hard cases—gay Catholics who stay in the Church. In other words, how do they preserve their identity as Catholics while remaining in a Church that pathologizes their lifestyle? Dillon maintains that pro-change Catholics such as gays solve the problem of identity by means of "a critical, reflexive, collectively contested activity whereby the plurality of symbols and traditions within Catholicism are reappropriated and reinterpreted in multiple ways."

Pro-change Catholics stay because they retain a strong attachment to the Mass and the symbols of Catholicism and have a strong feeling for the universality of the Church and its himself a bishop on the Internet, but a storm erupted as people protested Rome's action—including even the president of the French bishops' conference, Joseph Duval, who joined in the protest, declaring, "This an authoritarian act that can't be accepted in society, not even by the Church. People want consultation and dialogue. Authoritarian gestures on the part of Rome have multiplied in recent days: the Catechism of the Church Universal, the encyclical on morality *(Veritatis Splendor)*, the ban on ordaining women, the impossibility of giving Communion to divorced and remarried persons. These acts make the Church look like a rigid, closed organization."[33]

One year later the French bishops issued a booklet about HIV in which it was argued that condoms can be a "necessity," a position totally rejected by the Vatican. Surprisingly, the Dutch cardinal Adrianus Simonis of Utrecht, a well-known traditionalist, even came out in favor of the liberal position as a "lesser evil."[34]

Underlying so much of this polarization in the Church is the issue of democracy: How much democratization is possible in the Church? The Church had a traumatic experience trying to accommodate itself to the new democratic political order after the French Revolution and spent much of its energy wrestling with it like Laocoön with the snakes.[35] Pius IX condemned some of the main principles of democracy in the *Syllabus of Errors.* Now the scenario seems to be repeating itself as liberals in the Church push their democratic agenda. Broad-based opposition movements have appeared, buttressed by huge lists of signatures under the banner "We are the Church." "What concerns everyone should be decided by everyone," they cry.

The phenomenon, widespread throughout the Catholic world, reached a peak in Austria, where over 140 liberal Roman Catholic groups linked through the Internet wrote to every cardinal calling on them to elect a Pope who would be a "collaborative" leader, one who would let bishops, priests, and laypeople share in decision making. They also wanted a Pope who would

---

continuity over two thousand years with the Apostles. They are optimistic about the future and believe the Church can become a more inclusive and pluralistic community. They are also encouraged by surveys such as the one of Catholic theologians drawn at random from two major U.S. centers of Catholic theology in which it found that the theologians agreed to a large extent with their pluralistic understanding of Catholicism. See Michele Dillon, *Catholic Identity: Balancing Reason, Faith, and Power* (New York: Cambridge University Press, 1999).

[33] Bernstein and Politi, *His Holiness,* p. 509.

[34] Ibid.

[35] This ancient Greek statue is in the Vatican Museum.

be sensitive to the "awakening of women's consciousness" and would welcome to the priesthood qualified candidates, whatever their gender, marital status, or sexual orientation.

Women's role in the Church has thus remained one of the most polarizing issues. It was taken up courageously by bishops in Australia who met in conference on November 22, 1999. Their report "Woman and Man: One in Christ Jesus," incorporated the largest research project yet undertaken by the Church there, which indicated widespread frustration about the roles allowed to women. "Pain, alienation and often anger resulted from a strong sense of women's marginalisation, struggle, disenfranchisement, powerlessness, irrelevance and lack of acknowledgment within the Church." In his comments on the report, Cardinal Edward Clancy, archbishop of Sydney, spoke of how many of the women present at the conference, though sharply critical, still manifested a deep love for the Church. But, he noted, they saw their tasks allotted to them as "secondary, ancillary and even menial and hence felt hurt, angry and alienated."

At the conference the polarity was sharp. Some participants stressed traditional teaching and obedience to the hierarchy, the authority of Church documents, and traditional roles of women. On the other side were those who spoke of the vision of the Gospels, the spirit of the Second Vatican Council, theological scholarship, and the increasingly varied contribution of women to society. Many of the angry and frustrated—both women and men—were evidently still making a great effort to stay in the Church, according to the coordinator. Cardinal Clancy declared that as the Church universal contends with this issue, this report will prove to be a basic resource that none will be able to ignore.

One of the strongest polarizing voices for reform in the Church is the "Wir sind Kirche," "We are Church," movement in Germany. In a statement issued on November 23, 1999, the leaders of the movement declared that it deeply regretted Pope John Paul II's criticism of Church reform groups in a recent address to the German bishops. The group's demands include the ordination of married men, allowing remarried divorcées to receive Communion, and the ordination of women. These demands, it claimed, were now shared by many committed Catholics all over the world. Similar reforms have been urged by the American group Call to Action.

A Gallup poll reported on June 19, 1992, showed that two thirds of Roman Catholics in the United States favored opening the priesthood to women, an increase of 20 percentage points over one taken seven years before.[36]

THE POLARIZED PARISH

The way this polarization in the Church plays out in various U.S. parishes is colorfully depicted by Charles R. Morris in his book *American Catholics.*[37] He contrasts parishes in two dioceses, one in Lincoln, Nebraska, headed by Bishop Fabian Bruskewitz, and one in Saginaw, Michigan, headed by Bishop Kenneth Untener. Bishop Bruskewitz, the head of possibly the most conservative diocese in the country, hews to a hard line. He has excommunicated pro-abortionist Catholics and threatened Catholics members of Call to Action with the same penalty.

The key words to describe the tenor of the Lincoln diocese are strict orthodoxy and obedience. According to the good bishop, John Paul's model parish is one where the people obey the pastor and the pastor obeys the bishop and the bishop honors and obeys the Pope. Off limits is dissent or any toying around or muffling the neuralgic issues tormenting the Church today—birth control, women's roles, homosexuality, pedophilia. Clerical protocol is followed faithfully. "Father Jones is not Tom Jones and nuns dress," as they say there, "like nuns." One thing is clear about the success of such tight conformity to traditional teaching and policy: The recruitment rate of priests is far above the national average. One of the brightest stars in the diocese, Monsignor Kalin, responsible for the flood of vocations, says, "If the priesthood isn't an elevated position, if you're just a spiritual coordinator and social director, why would you give up marriage, family, and all the rest?" But replicating such a model? Lincoln is a very small diocese in a very conservative setting.

Juxtaposing the Lincoln model with the liberal diocese of Saginaw, Michigan, tells you a good deal about the polarization in the American Church, says Morris. At a liturgy in the Saginaw cathedral the pastoral administrator, Sr. Honora Remes, took a prominent role. Standing by the priest at the altar and delivering the homily, she projected the image of a woman in charge, while Fr. Groh, the celebrant brought in from the chancery, appeared as a kind of deus ex machina. Sr. Honora, in fact, is one of some 20,000 paid

---

[36] *The New York Times,* June 19, 1992.
[37] New York: Random House, 1997, pp. 382–394.

pastoral administrators, 80 percent of them women, who have become an important part of parish life in the United States, where they run some three hundred parishes.

The contrast between the liturgies in Lincoln and in Saginaw underscore the sharp differences between the two. The interior of the Saginaw Cathedral has the feel of a secular meeting hall or, as Morris says, like the renovated Washington train station, with its lack of the traditional Catholic iconography and the semicircular arrangement of chairs instead of pews. One hears also the catchy tunes of the latest in hymns. The attitude toward the Eucharist in the Saginaw liturgy seemed to accentuate most of the differences between the two current styles of liturgy although in most parishes I suspect there is more of a mix of the two styles. The coin-shaped white host favored in Lincoln was replaced in the Saginaw Cathedral by a kind of Syrian flatbread. The consecration was performed in a matter-of-fact, rather unritualistic way. The message was clear: The worshipper was reminded by these and other subtle differences that the old wine of the Roman liturgy with its aura of awe and the sacred as well as its individualistic slant has been replaced by the new wine of Vatican II, which calls for a work-a-day kind of liturgy befitting a real community at prayer. However, the impact of this enormous transformation on worshippers' belief in the Real Presence is beginning to raise alarms.

ARCHBISHOP WEAKLAND VS.
THE "REFORMERS" OF THE REFORM

In fact, concern about declining Catholic belief in the Real Presence is one of the motives of those in the Church and especially the Curia who, Archbishop Weakland believes, are trying to reform the "reform." Known for his willingness to roil the waters. the archbishop of Milwaukee recently took on these restorationists, as he calls them, in a long article in *America* magazine.[38] It is not surprising, he says, that the Vatican Council's reform of the liturgy has drawn criticism, and he admits that the changes were made hastily and clumsily. But now a new wave of criticism in a very polemical spirit has surfaced, one that he claims has taken a "restorationist" approach—in the words of some of the leaders, a "reform of the reform." This seems to be the approach behind the recent decisions of the Congregation for Worship and the Discipline of the Sacraments in its *Liturgiam authenticam* (March 2001) and the

---

[38] *Commonweal,* January 11, 2002.

new version of *Institutio Generalis Missalis Romani* (General Instruction of the Roman Missal). In Weakland's view they betray a definite restorationist approach in their intense concern for orthodoxy and their insistence on more literal translations, as well as their directives restricting lay participation in the liturgy.

A key to this restorationist approach, Weakland says, can be found as early as 1985 in "The Ratzinger Report," in which Cardinal Ratzinger found fault with certain interpretations of Vatican II which he thought reflected an overly optimistic approach toward an agnostic and atheistic world. It was time for a change of direction, he concluded.

Weakland strongly disagrees, though he admits the need for some improvements in the liturgical renewal. The Kiss of Peace is perhaps wrongly placed. The amount of banal, trite music is surely a problem. But he rejects the restorationists' claim that the new liturgy lacks a sense of continuity with the past. It is not easy to decide which elements of a complex tradition should be preserved in the interests of continuity, he maintains.

But the biggest bone the restorationists have to pick with the reform comes from the conciliar document *Sacrosanctum concilium* itself—specifically, its demand that the texts and rites should be short, simple, and intelligible so that the laity "should be able to understand them with ease and to take part in them fully, actively, and as befits a community."[39]

Does this insistence on simplicity and intelligibility reflect the rationalistic temper of the Enlightenment, as the restorationists claim (they cite this passage as proof)? In fact, Weakland knows from personal experience that these words are hardly more than a paraphrase of a passage from the work of the great liturgical scholar Edmund Bishop. In his monumental study *Liturgica Historica* (Oxford, 1918), Bishop said, "The genius of the native Roman rite is marked by simplicity, practicality, a great sobriety and self-control, gravity and dignity."

Weakland believes that at the core of restorationist thinking stands a generally negative evaluation of modern culture as secular and lacking a sense of the transcendent. For his part, Weakland prefers to frame the problem in terms of the general alienation of artists from the Church. The Christian community, he believes, shares the blame for this, for "despite its many laudable efforts

[39] "Constitution on the Sacred Liturgy," in *Documents of Vatican II,* Walter Abbot, S.J., ed. (New York: Guild Press, 1966), p. 146.

to preserve traditional morality and the social fabric, [it] has abdicated its stewardship of culture and, more importantly, has frequently chosen ideology rather than imagination when approaching the challenges of the present."[40]

Weakland also wonders why the restorationists downplay a very important concern of *Sacrosanctum concilium,* its call for full participation of the laity. For instance, the restorationists put much emphasis on the hierarchical nature of the liturgy while at the same time they subordinate the role of the people to their pre–Vatican II liturgical position, so much so that one wonders whether one of the worst aspects of modern culture—its deep-seated individualism—has not left its mark.

No doubt, the driving forces of the "reformers of the reform" is their perception of tendencies toward doctrinal error that have crept into the Church since the reform. The restorationists especially point to dwindling devotion, or even disbelief in the Real Presence. But to lay the blame for this solely on the liturgical reform, Weakland says, ignores such factors as poor catechesis, the inaccuracy of the surveys, and certain implications of modern physics that create confusion, especially in young people's understanding of the Real Presence. However, no doubt, the desire to reinforce belief in the Real Presence is behind the newly prescribed measures affecting the placement of the tabernacle, gestures of adoration (kneeling during the whole Eucharistic prayer), and renewal of perpetual adoration. Weakland has problems with this strategy of altering the "inner laws of liturgy" for the sake of catechesis.

The blurring of the role of the priest is also a concern of the restorationists, hence the Vatican's new directives about restricting lay distribution of Communion and more clearly demarcating the sanctuary. But will this mean putting the priest on a pedestal again as a member of a superior caste? Weakland asks.

Where is the Pope in all this? In spite of his positive statements about the fidelity of the reformed liturgy to tradition, John Paul has sent out some ambiguous signals by opening the door to the Tridentine usage.

Weakland deplores the strategy of liturgical pluralism, which he believes has been adopted pragmatically by the restorationists to bide their time while attempting to increase the appeal of the Tridentine usage with certain modifications. Eventually, they hope to swing the whole Church back to its

---

[40] *Commonweal.* January 11, 2002.

pre–Vatican II position. But Weakland believes the chances of success for such a maneuver do not seem very good, especially in the absence of a clear theology to justify such a change. He hopes for a more balanced approach based on a consensus of the whole Church as to what is beneficial in the renewal and what needs to be improved. For, as he says, "Paul VI saw the *Novus Ordo* [New Regulations] as a renewal of the Roman rite in its totality and not the creation of a new rite."

Another move by the "reformers of the reform" occurred when the American bishops learned that their English-language version of the 1975 Roman Missal had to be revised again. In the works for a decade, the new translation ran afoul of Rome's new tighter rules on translation into the vernacular. The new rules, promulgated in the recent Roman document *Liturgiam authenticam*, rejected such changes as those designed to eliminate sexist language. "Man" would not be replaced by "Everyone," for instance. But did Rome exceed its authority here? It seemed so, since Vatican II had conferred on the national conferences of bishops the responsibility for producing and approving vernacular ritual texts. In spite of considerable frustrations voiced by the American bishops' committee on translations, so far Cardinal Jorge Medina Estevez, prefect of the Congregation for Divine Worship, has stood firm along the lines of the old adage *"Roma locuta, causa finita"* (Rome has spoken, the case is closed).

THE PRIESTHOOD IN TROUBLE

One of the most agonizing issues facing a polarized Church is the shrinkage of the priesthood. In the previous chapter, we noted the gravity of the crisis.[41] But an interesting report by the Center for Applied Research at Georgetown University noted that the number of men studying for the priesthood at the graduate level has risen to its highest level in five years, although the numbers are still not enough to replace priests who retire or die each year. There were some 3,386 men in the United States enrolled in graduate-level theological studies for the priesthood in 1999—up 228 for the previous year.[42] However, in Africa and southern Asia, where the Catholic population is growing rapidly, there has been a much larger increase. Europe, on the other hand, shows

[41] Chapter 34, p. 378.
[42] *The New York Times,* April 17, 1999.

only a continuing decline in recruitment. Meanwhile, enrollment at the Pontifical North American College in Rome is at its highest level in a quarter century.

It was also found in a poll of more than five hundred religious and diocesan priests ordained since 1995 that half the priests still serving after five years are "very satisfied" with obligatory priestly celibacy. But guess what—93 percent of those who resigned from the priesthood were not. (About 15 percent of priests in the United States resign within five years of ordination.) More than three quarters of those who resigned from the priesthood complained of loneliness, lack of privacy, and unsettling proximity to work. But the priests who remain said that for the most part they were satisfied with these aspects of priestly life.

In Italy the shortage of priests in some areas, particularly in the north, has inspired major changes in how local parishes function. An article in the *New York Times* relates the experience of Rev. Luigi Gugliemetti, one of few priests left in Sermenza Valley, in the remote Valesia region, where he serves an aging and shrinking population that was once was served by six priests. He now is helped by four nuns, including three missionaries from Africa and India.[43]

A survey commissioned by the National Conference of Catholic Bishops noted that the nationwide shortage of Catholic priests is due to smaller families, more plentiful career choices, pedophilia scandals, and stressful work. More than half the parents surveyed admitted they did nothing to encourage children to enter the priesthood; some said they could not encourage their sons to enter a vocation that offered little advancement, demanded material sacrifices, and would not accept their daughters. It was also noted that many of the priests now entering retirement had few alternatives available when they entered the seminary, a situation vastly changed today.

Somewhat offsetting the dearth of young seminarians is the growing number of men entering the clergy and becoming priests in midlife after years in the secular workplace. They seek greater fulfillment in nurturing the spiritual needs of others. This is reflected in the increase of the average age of seminarians, from twenty-five in 1966 to thirty-two in 1993. The new seminarians are far more conservative and tradition-bound than the previous generations, according to surveys. They are rejecting the liberalism and rebellion of the 1960s and '70s. But some Church leaders worry about the gap between

---

[43] Ibid., November 8, 1997.

the young priests and the majority of no longer conforming American Catholics.

A bombshell hit when Father Donald Cozzens, the rector of a theological seminary in Cleveland, published his study of the priesthood, "The Changing Face of the Priesthood: A Reflection on the Priest's Crisis of Soul," in 2000. He posits a major shift in the "identity" of the priest from a "cultic" model to a model of the "servant leader." He identifies five other areas of change that are transforming the face of the priesthood: the relationship between priests and bishops, the shortage of vocations, the gay ascendancy, the crisis of authority, and the crisis of intellect. Father Cozzens also expressed grave concern about the sexual orientation and the quality of today's seminarians. According to Cozzens, an inordinate number of candidates for the priesthood are homosexual. Altogether, Cozzens has helped ignite a debate that will no doubt go on for a long time.

PEDOPHILES AND PRIESTS?

In his much admired book *American Catholics*, Charles Morris registers the huge change in public perception of the Catholic priest. The glamorous Spencer Tracy or Bing Crosby image of the pre–Vatican II Church was transformed as the Church entered into a period of Sturm und Drang. Catholics began to see the priest as hardly more than an ordinary slice of humanity, often as troubled as his troubled flock. But even this change was mild compared to the change that occurred when the so-called pedophile priest scandal erupted in the 1980s.

The average priest would now be tarred by the revelations that some of his brethren were involved in the sordid offense of child sexual abuse (pedophilia.) The numerous revelations began with the Gauthe case in the diocese of Lafayette, Louisiana. Father Gauthe was revealed in court as a molester and forcible abuser of more than one hundred boys and girls in a series of parishes from 1972 to 1984. The diocese had to pay some $20 million in damage awards. During the next four years, some forty Catholic priests were charged with acts of molestation and outright rape. A flood of new revelations followed. The shock to the Catholic community was all the more painful, since such offenses had previously been kept undercover by the officials with the help of a generally compliant police and press.

The most sensational incident occurred in late 1993 when a lawsuit was filed for damages against Cardinal Bernardin of Chicago by a former seminarian, Stephen Cook, who stated that in a recovered-memory session he remembered that he had been sexually molested by Bernardin. In a press conference, the cardinal, visibly shaken, emphatically asserted his innocence before a huge crowd of reporters. As the newspapers continued to investigate, a break occurred when Cook's psychologist, William Wester, revealed that the notes he had kept of his interviews with Cook during the period of the alleged abuses indicated no such problems. The tide of public opinion, which under the influence of the number of scandals involving clergy was running against Bernardin, then shifted abruptly when Cook admitted that he might have imagined the episode. Further developments occurred when it was found that the hypnotist who had "uncovered" Cook's suppressed memories of the affair was found to be unlicensed and controversial. Cook's lawyers abandoned their suit and Cook recanted. Bernardin visited the young man and in a touching ceremony of reconciliation embraced the youth and prayed with him. The Catholic clergy, harried by the stream of sordid revelations besmirching their estate, heaved an enormous sigh of relief that echoed around the country.

The scandal caused by multiple cases of pedophilia in the priesthood began to taper off as the new millennium began but was rekindled when a sensational trial opened in Boston in January 2002. Father Geoghegan was accused of molesting some 150 children during his various assignments at Boston parishes. Cardinal Law and the officials of the diocese were then targeted by the *Boston Globe* and other media for having moved Geoghegan from parish to parish after serious allegations had been made of his abuse of children. Reports of similar cases reports began to proliferate around the country: Priests accused of child abuse had been reassigned to ministries that put them into renewed contact with children. The abuse issue has been called the gravest moral crisis for the Church in centuries, and terms like "ecclesiastical Watergate" a "meltdown," "the S and L disaster of the Catholic church" have been bandied about in the press.

One expert who has studied the pedophilia scandals in the United States for some twenty years has a different opinion, however. Philip Jenkins, distinguished sociologist and professor of history and religious studies at Pennsylvania State University, throws a different light on this whole problem of clerical abuse of minors.[44] He calls the priest pedophile crisis a classic example of a *socially constructed problem*. As he puts it, such a "problem may have at its

---

[44] *Pedophiles and Priests* (New York: Oxford University Press, 1996). Jenkins is an Episcopalian.

heart an objective condition that can be observed, examined, and quantified, but the exact interpretation will depend on subjective factors, the perception that the condition is harmful, threatening, and worthy of attention. The social construction of the problem depends on the ideologies and assumptions of a particular society at a given historical moment and the rhetorical work of the various interest groups and individuals who make and establish claims about issues."

As Jenkins says, the scholar who calls a social problem "socially constructed" does not mean he denies the existence of a real problem or denies the harmful consequences that might be caused. But he finds it necessary to question why some behaviors rather than others come to be seen as so uniquely harmful in certain societies and historical periods. He also asks why the question of child abuse should have been so fundamentally reformulated during the 1970s and 1980s, whereas in the two previous decades a much more tolerant attitude toward nonviolent molesters and other sex deviants had prevailed. Another question is why, for instance, the drug problem was seen as a national menace during the 1980s or why by the early 1990s clergy abuse was perceived as so ubiquitous and pernicious a threat.

He traces this phenomenon to the media's need when reporting an event to give it some meaning and place it in a frame of reference that will be familiar to the assumed audience. This process involves what he calls identification and contextualization by which events are made to *"mean"* by the media.

He points out how this framing has occurred in regard to the "pedophile priest" crisis. Since the early 1980s, there have been hundreds and probably thousands of cases in which clergy of various denominations have been accused of sexual involvement with minors and indeed have been found guilty by the civil courts. The frame given to these events has been "pedophile priests," the term regularly employed.

There are several problems with this "frame." "Pedophile priests" limits the phenomenon to Catholic priests. Also, the term "pedophile" is used beyond its strict clinical meaning. A pedophile is a man sexually attracted to children below the age of puberty, but the vast majority of recorded instances of clergy abuse or misconduct involve an interest in teenagers of either gender. Often these cases belong in the category of homosexual offenses, behavior that is blameworthy in terms of ecclesiastical and moral codes (and where minors are involved, they are obviously illegal) but is not clinical pedophilia.

They are more properly grouped under the term *ephebophilia ("epi hebe")*, or the love of pubescent boys or girls. Official psychiatric manuals define pedophilia as "sexual activity with a prepubescent child." The difference can be important, since true pedophiles are more difficult to treat or control than offenders who direct their attention to older targets.

HOW THE MEDIA CAME TO FOCUS ON CLERICAL ABUSE AS A PECULIARLY CATHOLIC PROBLEM

Any number of programs or articles in the mass media assumes that the problem of clerical sexual abuse is specifically a Catholic one. Hence there is much talk about what there is about the Catholic Church and the priesthood in particular that makes sexual misconduct so prevalent. Actually, Jenkins says Catholic clergy are not necessarily represented in the sexual abuse phenomenon at a rate higher than or even equal to their numbers in the clerical profession as a whole.

The question Jenkins then seeks to answer in his book is why the problem of clerical sexual abuse has been constructed as a peculiarly Catholic problem—the problem of the pedophile priest? He finds a number of reasons:

- The very size of the priesthood, more than 45,000 priests currently active, which is larger than the total membership of many denominations.
- No comparative quantification of the abuse rate relative to other religious groups is available.
- Misconduct in the Catholic Church has been studied much more intensively than in other churches, largely because of the assumption (unproven) that a celibate group would likely have a higher rate of sexual deviancy.
- As more attention was focused on the Catholic clergy, more possible victims were encouraged to report incidents and begin litigation.
- The disproportionately high level of reported scandals is explainable by the fact that the Catholic Church is highly centralized and bureaucratized and dossiers on its parish clergy are efficiently maintained and are rather easily subpoenaed by attorneys. On the other hand, the second-largest church, the Baptists, prizes congregational autonomy. Baptists are much less open to the kind of in-

vestigation of the records that can be used to show a systemic problem. The same is true in varying degrees of the other Protestant churches.[45]

- Modern perceptions of clergy abuse also need to be placed in the much longer historical context of anti-Catholic and anticlerical imagery and rhetoric.

- Ironically, it is the Catholics themselves who are perhaps most responsible for making the widespread problem of pedophilia a "Catholic problem." Led by the priest novelist and TV pundit Andrew Greeley and the *National Catholic Reporter,* the Catholic dissenters, of both the left and right, have found the issue a godsend for pressing their reform agendas. Abortion rights advocates, Catholic activists, gay rights advocates, those calling for abolition of clerical celibacy, advocates of a radical change in the Church's sexual code, and an end to the ban on contraception, those calling for an end to the patriarchal autocratic structure of the Church—all of these found the issue of clerical abuse most helpful in gaining attention and support for their views.

- On the other hand, conservatives and traditionalists who stand opposed on most of these issues and believe that the post–Vatican II reforms have gone too far also find the issue useful for their cause. Clergy abuse, they believe, was a natural outcome of liberal and Vatican II excesses, specifically the infiltration of homosexuals into the clergy who were morally contaminated by liberal opinions. Led by *The Wanderer,* a Catholic weekly, they have aimed especially at the liberalism of bishops such as Hunthausen, Weakland, Ferrario, and the late Cardinal Bernardin. Malachi Martin, the ex-Jesuit TV novelist now deceased, spoke of a "self-protective network of gay Church officials which covers up for other homosexual and child sex offenders in the priesthood."

- To sum up, the extremely polarized state of the Catholic Church

[45] The prestigious British periodical *The Economist* said (April 6, 2002) that the spotlight should be trained into many other corners. Sex offenders teach in schools, coach sports teams and run scout troops and day-care centers. Carol Shakeshaft, a professor at Hofstra University and the author of a forthcoming book on sexual violence in schools, has found that 15 percent of pupils are sexually abused by a teacher or staff member between kindergarten and high school graduation and that up to 5 percent of teachers sexually abuse or harass students.

has been an enormous contributing factor in the genesis of the "crisis."

Jenkins also suggests that there has been extreme exaggeration of the number of priest pedophiles. Numbers have been thrown around recklessly. Actually, according to the best records, 1,000 to 1,500 out of 150,000 active priests have been reported for molesting youth over a period of forty years.[46] Even assuming all charged were guilty, it suggests an offense rate of less than 2 percent. The only systematic review of a large cohort of clergy was commissioned by Cardinal Bernardin, who had the personnel files of the Chicago Archdiocese between 1952 and 1991 studied. In that time span 1.7 percent of priests were justifiably charged with sexual abuse. Unfortunately, on a national talk show Andrew Greeley miscalculated and stated the figure of 5 percent and this became the basis of further media comment on the matter. Another reliable study by the authoritative St. Luke Institutes concluded that 0.3 percent of the Catholic clergy were guilty of abuse of minors. In fact, according to Jenkins it would be quite justifiable to argue that "it is rare to find a true pedophile in the priesthood or religious life,"[47] using "pedophile" in the strict sense.

Jenkins makes another interesting point: It was at this time that the discovery of pedophilia as a national problem occurred and put the spotlight on the hierarchy, who were now blamed severely for their tolerant treatment of offenders. In fact, the hierarchy had treated delinquent priests in a way that at that point seemed naïve but actually was in accord with the liberal attitudes prevailing prior to the mid-1980s. Liberal mainstream psychiatric and criminological opinion held that adult sexual activity with children was quite a rare phenomenon and merited therapy rather than punishment. "But by 1985 those who believed in the magnitude of a sex-abuse problem had succeeded beyond all expectation in establishing as plausible quite far-reaching notions about the scale and seriousness of the issue, and the incurably predatory nature of sex offenders."[48]

As the press juggernaut rolled on, the amount of money the Church had to expend on settling the cases rose to enormous proportions—already by some estimates over a billion dollars. The archdiocese of Santa Fe even an-

[46] Jenkins, *Pedophiles and Priests,* p. 80.
[47] Ibid, p. 82.
[48] Ibid., p. 93.

nounced in December 1993 that it might have to declare bankruptcy because of the dozens of sexual molestation accusations against its priests. (Santa Fe was in an unusual situation because a treatment center for priest offenders from around the country was located nearby. Some of them were given employment in the diocese after treatment.) Each parish was asked to contribute cash and property, rather than have its assets seized by the courts. To add to the mess, the Archbishop himself, Robert F. Sanchez, had to admit to relationships with three young women who gave interviews to the television program *60 Minutes.*

Another particularly unsavory case also involved a bishop, Patrick Ziemann of Santa Rosa, California, who admitted to a "consensual" relationship with a priest, Jorge Salas, who had sued him for sexual abuse. Ziemann resigned his post but denied the charge that the sex was forced. Salas was removed for embezzling church money.

Perhaps the most disconcerting scandals were reported later in Africa, where numerous cases of sexual abuse of nuns by priests were reported over a seven-year period. Much of this was due to the AIDS epidemic, which supposedly caused priests to turn to nuns for sex instead of to prostitutes out of fear of contracting AIDS.[49] About seventy demonstrators gathered outside the United Nations on July 14, 2001, to call for greater efforts by the Vatican and the Pope to combat sexual abuse of nuns in Africa and around the world. Detailed accounts were given of nuns being forced to have sex with priests and in some cases being forced to have abortions after becoming pregnant.[50]

LAITY ON THE MOVE

Amid the discouragement provoked by the pedophilia scandal and the shrinkage of the clergy, one of the encouraging signs was the emergence of educated, informed, loyal, and active Catholic laypeople, especially in the United States. It is a generation like no other in history. And as the shortage of priests worsens, bishops are more and more turning to the laity for help in running parishes and special ministries.

Women in particular are assuming pastoral, liturgical, and administrative responsibilities in growing numbers. Laywomen and sisters serve as theologically educated professional hospital chaplains, campus ministers, directors of

[49] *The New York Times,* March 21, 2000.
[50] Ibid., July 15, 2001.

religious education, professors in colleges and seminaries, spiritual directors and heads of retreat centers, chancellors of dioceses, parish associates, and even pastors of parishes without full-time priests. Nor is this just a North American phenomenon. Women are prominent in the leadership of Latin America's base communities and catechetical circles. In France 3,000 Sunday assemblies are without priests, but there are 13,000 designated leaders of which 70 percent are women.

A new angle was introduced in November 12, 1995, when an influential group of experts in canon law concluded that ordaining women as deacons would be in keeping with Catholic theology and past practices. The Canon Law Society of America gave cautious endorsement of such a step, terming it "desirable."

The United States Catholic Conference released a profile of the American men and women currently entering religious orders. Nearly half of them live in a band of eight contiguous states along the Great Lakes and Atlantic Ocean.[51] They are highly educated, many of them well into their thirties with master's degrees and experience in secular careers. The new nuns take the same vows as women in the 4th century but live them in very different ways. Some of them have experienced the trauma of divorce, struggled with addictions, or raised children. Typically they devote themselves to the social problems of their communities, caring for crack babies or ministering to convicts on death row. They wear everything from blue jeans to business suits on the job.

They enter the ranks of orders that in the United States have suffered a more than 40 percent decline in membership since 1962. This decline of the orders' membership occurs at a time when the Catholic population has grown by nearly 40 percent. Reasons for the decline include lack of strong leadership, growing individualism, and a deep distrust of the Catholic hierarchy and the Vatican. In Europe, however, the contemplative orders are thriving, although hundred of convents and monasteries continue to close.

IS SMALLER BETTER?
While traditional religious orders continue to decline, new forms of lay religious communities are springing up. A growing number of laymen and -women are seeking a form of community more intense than that offered by the average parish.

[51] *The New York Times,* January 31, 1998.

Already, the Synod of Bishops in 1974 recognized the increasing interest in smaller communities—some having a form of life in common, others with less structure whose members meet for prayer and Bible study. Pope Paul VI referred to this movement when he noted that the Church must address her message to the communities of the faithful, which are scattered amid the multitudes. Analyzing the different types of small communities, he said that the groups that unite themselves to the Church and foster her growth will be a hope for the universal Church."[52]

Later, on November 9, 1976, Jean Jadot, the Apostolic Delegate to the United States, spoke to the issue at a general meeting of the National Conference of Catholic Bishops. Noting the problem of parishes that failed to meet the expectations of many Catholics, he suggested that one solution might be to form new patterns of parochial organizations so that a parish might become a community of small communities.

In fact, small church communities are emerging all over the Catholic parish landscape. They seem to meet a need to offset an individualistic and consumerist culture. American Catholics are finding them a means of uniting themselves more intimately with God, one another, and the larger common good.

The global spread of these small communities is one of the more significant developments of the last several decades. As Ian Fraser of the Iona Community said at a meeting in Cochaamba, Bolivia, they are the result of "the spontaneous combustion of the Holy Spirit all over the world." In the United States there are 50,000 of them, according to current estimates.[53] The basic pattern is simple. The members meet at least monthly—often enough to create a relational structure that provides a framework for sharing their faith experience. The meetings will usually include reading and discussion of Scripture and prayer.

At the Cochaamba meeting, Bishop Ottenweller said they might especially appeal to young people today who are searching for a group in which they can find a true communion of faith, of worship, and of commitment. Often suffering from loneliness, they feel a need to identify with others who share their yearning for a more communal life. They seek a truly spiritual community that will have Christ as its center and the Church as its frame-

---

[52] *"Evangelii Nuntiandi,"* n. 57.
[53] *America,* May 7, 2002.

work. According to a nationwide poll taken in July 1998, their Catholic faith apparently consists of a few core beliefs and a dedication to helping the poor.[54]

DYNAMIC LAY COMMUNITIES

Some of the new independent communities of laypeople have drawn considerable attention because of their extraordinary radius or unusual activities. One of the most dynamic is the Sant'Egidio Community of Rome, which meets nightly for prayer and has branch groups in at least forty other countries. Besides their ministries to the poor, they have been active in mediating international conflicts and in the year 2001 they won the UNESCO peace prize for brokering a 1992 peace accord in Mozambique, and the group recently sponsored a conference of Christians and Muslims. One of the speakers, Yusuf al-Qaradawi, director of the Sunna Research Center in Qatar, caused a stir when he explicitly tied recent terrorist attacks to the treatment of the Palestinians in Israel. This led some Jewish observers to ask whether the conference had turned into an anti-Jewish affair. But the founder of the community, Andrea Riccardi, pointed to Sant'Egidio's long history of dialogue with Jewish groups and noted that they would soon have a special event commemorating the killing of the Jews in Rome during World War II.

Another of these mushrooming lay communities, the Focolare, promotes a new lifestyle, an innovative spiritual itinerary to draw people together as sisters and brothers. It had a most interesting origin amid the death and devastation of World War II in Italy. The founder, Chiara Lubich, told of growing up in Trent, as the air raids gradually destroyed the persons and things she and her friends held most dear. "Vanity of vanities," she and her friends began to realize. They began to ask themselves, "Is there an ideal in life that no bomb can destroy, in which we can give ourselves wholeheartedly?" The answer they found was God. They decided to make God the ideal of their lives. But who was God? God is Love. God is our Father. They found the reason for living they were looking for—God, who is Love.

But what kind of life would this entail, they asked themselves. Turning to the life of Jesus as their model, they found that this meant giving a generous response to the will of the Father. While forced to run constantly to the air-raid shelters, they carried the Gospel with them and began to read it as if it

---

[54] *The New York Times*, July 18, 1998.

were completely new. Putting into practice the command of love, they has-tened to help those in need. Ignoring the bombs, they brought succor to the elderly and the invalid. "Give," they read, "and it shall be given to you." The more they gave away—food, clothing, firewood—the more they received. Death was always near as the bombs fell and their creaky air-raid shelter shook, but if they had to die, they wanted it to be while pleasing God. And reading Jesus' words "no greater love than this to lay down one's life for one's friends" (John 15:12–12), they looked each other in the eyes and said, "I am ready to give my life for you." These experiences of love in the midst of death, of sharing their material possessions, their spiritual insights, their joys and suf-fering, were so real, so powerful, so joy-giving and fostered such inner peace that they were able to understand life in an entirely new way. The suffering they experienced in the turmoil and terror was accepted in the spirit of Jesus' words: "Unless the grain of wheat falls to the earth and dies, it remains just a grain of wheat." After only a few months, about five hundred people of all ages and social backgrounds joined their movement.

The movement continued to spread and today involves millions of peo-ple in 182 nations. As it spread, the members began to establish relationships of mutual understanding and dialogue with the great religious traditions of humanity. They learned how much those sacred texts and teachings matched their own—above all the centrality of the love command in both the Jewish and Muslim faiths. They began to forge close links around the world with both Jews and Muslims. Chiara Lubich recently ended a talk urging her lis-teners to "love everyone without distinction, just as God does. Don't make distinctions between the people of your own country and foreigners or be-tween Africans and Asians or between Jews and Muslims or Christians and Hindus. Love not with words but with deeds."

IS THE CHURCH TOP-HEAVY? KASPER VS. RATZINGER

While some question the adequacy of the current parish structure, others question the existing power structure of the universal Church. Specifically, a number of bishops believe the church is top-heavy, with too much power con-centrated in Rome and the Curia. After all, they point out, one of the classic doctrines of the Church's social philosophy is subsidiarity, meaning that, the upper levels in a state should not take over what the lower are capable of do-ing, a doctrine which they believe should be applied, *ceteris paribus,* to the

Church. For instance, they would like lower levels to have a better-defined role in the nomination of bishops.

This issue came to the fore at the time of the Hunthausen crisis (see previous chapter) when Archbishop Hunthausen was disciplined by Rome without any effort to consult with the American bishops. The case revealed the tensions between some of the three hundred American bishops and the Vatican and the difficulty of defining the proper balance of power between the Vatican and the various national bishops' conferences. These conferences have played an increasingly important role in the Catholic Church since the Second Vatican Council in the mid-1960s emphasized collegiality—the idea that the bishops have a collective responsibility in the governance of the Church.

In June 1995 more than forty American bishops endorsed a twelve-page statement that criticized the weakening of the role of the bishops' conferences and the Vatican's practice of issuing binding decrees on a billion Catholics without prior consultation. "There is a widespread feeling," the American bishops said, "that Roman documents of varying authority have for some years been systematically reinterpreting Vatican II documents so as to present the minority positions at the Council as the true meaning of the Council."[55]

No doubt they had in mind Cardinal Ratzinger, who has continually downplayed the importance of the national bishops' conferences. Recently he has been challenged by the German bishops Karl Lehmann and Walter Kasper. Kaspar has argued that restorationists in the Curia are working to restore the centralism which the majority at the Second Vatican Council clearly wanted to overcome." Kaspar said, "The progressive interpretation of Vatican II as a criticism and overturning of the centralism of Vatican I is being thwarted." And he points to the issuance in 1992 by Ratzinger's office of the document "The Church as Communion" as "more or less in effect a reversal of the Second Vatican Council."

Ratzinger apparently favors even greater centralization, which he says is all the more needed in the present age of globalization. He goes on to justify it theologically by a rather abstruse distinction between the "universal Church" and the local churches. According to him, the universal Church (embodied in Rome) has priority over the local church both ontologically (by its very nature) and historically. Historically, he maintains, the distinction was al-

[55] Bernstein and Politi, *His Holiness*, p. 511.

ready present in the New Testament, where the expression "the Church" meant the Church conceived as a kind of transcendent reality, as opposed to the local churches. Thus, this "universal Church" was called the heavenly Jerusalem (Gal. 4:26) or "our mother and the assembly of the first-born" (Hebrews 12:22–23). In other words, the "universal Church" was something distinct from and over and above the individual local churches. And it is this "universal Church" that is today, he maintains, embodied in Rome and the papacy.

Kasper aimed a direct challenge at this view and holds that, historically and ontologically, the local Church came first. He claims that in the *Acts of the Apostles,* Luke saw the Jerusalem Church as both universal and local and universal only insofar as it was in communion with the local Churches existing at the time. Ratzinger, Kasper claims, holds that the "universal Church" somehow preceded the local Church and then stealthily "identifies this one universal Church with the Roman Church and thus the Pope and the Roman Curia." Thus, the Church understood primarily as a communion of churches disappears, and it is this understanding, Kasper says, that provides Ratzinger with an important weapon in his attempt to restore and maintain Roman centralism in spite of Vatican II's move away from it.

While seemingly academic the distinctions argued about are of significance in the current debate over the authority of Rome vis-à-vis the local churches. Lurking behind their "friendly" erudite argument were some concrete issues they had already crossed swords about regarding the issue of Roman centralism. One hot potato had to do with the attempt of Kasper and other German bishops to allow divorcées under certain conditions to receive Communion. Another was Kasper's dismay at the monkey wrenches he said Ratzinger kept throwing into ecumenical dialogue. As president-to-be of the Council for Promoting Christian Unity, Kasper was dismayed especially at two recent moves by Ratzinger: his brusquely critical comment on the joint Lutheran-Catholic declaration on the doctrine of justification and the other was the more recent CDF document "Dominus Jesus," which dismissed Christian denominations as "not Churches in the proper sense."

THE DEBATE'S IMPACT ON ECUMENISM

Kasper's criticism of Roman centralism thus has a direct bearing on the ecumenical venture, for he believes the ultimate aim of the ecumenical movement to be the formation of not one uniform united Church but "one Church in reconciled diversity." Kasper believes that if we are to move forward ecumenically, we must show how we ourselves have reconciled our unity with diversity, that is, how the universal Church and the local Church are related as unity in diversity and diversity in unity. He believes that identifying the universal Church so closely with Rome would jeopardize the whole enterprise.

Kasper insists that the local Church is not a province or a department of the universal Church. It is, rather, the Church in that particular place. The bishop is not a delegate of the people but rather a representative of Jesus Christ: He enjoys his own sacramentally based individual responsibility.

Kasper maintains that the relationship between the universal and the local Church has become unbalanced, which, he says, is "is not just my own experience but the experience and complaint of many bishops around the world."[56] He could cite the similar views of such dignitaries as Cardinal Koenig, the retired archbishop of Vienna, and Cardinal Martini, the archbishop of Milan. Kasper traces this situation in part to Ratzinger's theology of the "universal Church" as a reality embodied in the Roman Church, which is ontologically and temporally prior to every individual Church."

This debate is extraordinary for several reasons. First, it is being carried on in public; and second, Ratzinger's opponent, Kasper, was made a cardinal in February 2001, in spite of his challenge to the reigning orthodoxy upheld by Ratzinger.

Cardinal Koenig, the retired archbishop of Vienna, weighed in with an assertion that the current centralism had been inflated contrary to the intent of Vatican II. To correct it, the competence of local and regional bishops as Church leaders must be acknowledged not only in theory but in practice. This means among other things that bishops must have a say in episcopal appointments.

This is not only called for by the Council's doctrine of collegiality, Koenig says, but other weighty reasons also call for strengthening the link between the Pope and the bishops. First, as he says, the Catholic Church has now become in fact a world Church. There is therefore a need for a more graduated structure of authority, which can better deal with the diversity this global respon-

---

[56] Walter Kasper, "On the Church," *Stimmen der Zeit,* December 2000.

sibility entails. Also the reality of decision making shared by Pope and bishops would defuse the charge that the Pope is a dictator. Moreover, linking papal primacy in a visible way to the episcopal college would foster the cause of Church unity. For "unless the episcopal college is made responsible in conjunction with the pope, neither the Orthodox nor the Anglicans nor the Protestants will consider any practical steps towards unity."

In other words, a new model of exercising papal authority is needed, Koenig says, in a world that is increasingly averse to the present patriarchal, authoritarian, and ethnocentric one. We need to project the model of the Church as a communion of communions. But for this to take place, a practical, day-to-day exercise of collegiality is indispensable.

Another prominent voice joined in the discussion. In an address at Oxford University on June 30, 1996, Archbishop John R. Quinn called for major reforms in the operation of the papacy. He would shift power to the world's Roman Catholic bishops and away from the Vatican bureaucracy. He also called for a new ecumenical council of bishops to usher in the millennium and discuss the questions left unresolved by the Second Vatican Council.

The increasing centralism of the Church was also a topic at the general assembly of the Synod of Bishops in Rome, which opened on September 30, 2001. Few topics surfaced as often as the balance of power between Rome and local churches. The president of the Brazilian bishops' conference, Jayme Henrique Chemello, delivered one of the more impassioned treatments. He called the way bishops are chosen, with papal ambassadors funneling secret recommendations to Rome, a "source of constant suffering." He noted how good candidates could be derailed for "circumstantial or ideological" reasons. There is no doubt that Chemello's comments carried special weight in view of the fact that Brazil, with 137 million Catholics, is the largest Catholic nation in the world. He offered four examples in which local churches should have more authority: translations of liturgical texts; nominating witnesses for marriages; dispensations from ordained ministry; and annulment of marriages. A number of bishops questioned the tight control of Rome over liturgical translations in view of the Second Vatican Council's concession of responsibility for these to the national bishops' conferences.

One source said that tough language inside the hall on decentralization of Church power had been weakened in the final propositions. "Still, 250 bishops heard more than 50 of their members talking about the need for redressing the exaggerated centralization of the Church's style today and that will have some effect."[57] However, where the rest of the 4,300 bishops of the world stood on the issue was not apparent. But there is no doubt that the issue is a serious one. Certainly, the question of "collegiality" (the technical term for decentralization) will play a critical role in the next conclave.

It is interesting to speculate also as to the effect of a proposition calling on the bishops to embrace a lifestyle of poverty in solidarity with the poor.

But can the Vatican reform itself? History does not encourage optimism. Reform has been stymied time after time and has only occurred under the pressure of external forces and political events.

Actually, recent actions by the Pope have tightened Rome's grip over the 108 bishops' conferences around the world. In a directive in July 1998, the Vatican severely limited the bishops' conference freedom to issue binding statements on public-policy topics such as nuclear weapons or the status of women that diverge from the Vatican view.

Moreover, John Paul showed the same approach at the synod on May 24, 2001, which brought together all 134 cardinals eligible to vote in a papal conclave. They spent four days in discussions designed to chart the future of the Church (as well as in campaigning delicately to succeed him, no doubt). Some cardinals took aim at the power of the Vatican bureaucracy and expressed the need for more democracy within the billion–member community. They called for more power sharing and frank discussion. But the papal response was unequivocal: "The existing systems are effective," John Paul asserted.

The Pope recently gave Bishop Karl Lehmann of Mainz his red cardinal's hat; at the same time, he handed him a letter sharply criticizing the Catholic Church in Germany as liberal and weak. While praising its strong organizational structure and the array of social services it offered to the public, he said he thought the German Church was lacking in faith and inner strength. He urged the cardinals to stress the Church's uncompromising stance against contraception, the refusal to allow divorcées to receive Communion, and the need to uphold the traditional view of marriage as a indissoluble union between a man and a woman.

---

[57] *National Catholic Reporter,* November 9, 2001.

SHAPING THE FUTURE?

In January 2001, the Pope named 37 new cardinals, bringing to 128 those eligible to vote for his successor and of these, 118 were his appointments. Presumably sharing his vision, they will shape the future direction of the Church. The choice also expressed the Church's growing strength in developing areas of the world and the Pope's continuing effort to internationalize the Catholic Church as well as exert influence on political events in some of the world's hot spots. Latin America will now have 26 voting cardinals, the largest representation of any continent. There are also four Asians and one African. One of the newly chosen is Giovanni Battista Re, head of the Congregation of Bishops, who is close to the Pope and must now be reckoned one of the *papabile* Italian cardinals. The Archbishop of Lima, Juan Luis Cipriani Thorne, is the first open member of Opus Dei to be made a cardinal. Also notable is the number of appointments to Latin America, where about 40 percent of the world's Catholics live. Two of the new cardinals are from the United States and one is from Britain and one, from Ireland. Cardinals from developing countries make up 41 percent of the college today, up from 38 percent in 1978.

By means of changes he has made in the rules for papal elections, the Pope seems to have gone even further in securing his conservative legacy than by his cardinal appointments. This little-noticed but important change in the method of electing a Pope was put in force by John Paul in February 1996. It provides for election by a simple majority instead of the basically two-thirds rule, which has been in effect for eight hundred years. The apostolic constitution "Universi Dominici Gregis" ("Of the Lord's Whole Flock") requires a two-thirds majority (unless the numbers present are not divisible by three, in which case an additional vote must be held).

Now, however, if no one has received a two-thirds vote after three days of voting, the voting is to be suspended for a day of prayer and discussion. If additional days of prayer and discussion followed by voting do not resolve the deadlock, then the cardinals may suspend the rule and allow for election by an absolute majority (just one more than half). This could allow a hard-line authoritarian conservative—or the hardly likely alternative, a hard-line liberal—to be elected. In the past, if the cardinals were deadlocked or polarized, it was often necessary to find a compromise candidate in order to achieve the two-thirds vote needed. But now those with an absolute majority of the votes could hold on until the additional time ran out and elect their candidate, who might possibly be unwanted by almost half the cardinals.

Two of the cardinals appointed in early 2002—Walter Kasper and Karl Lehmann—caused a sensation. Lehmann had taken a position on the pregnancy counseling centers in Germany at odds with the position of Cardinal Ratzinger, prefect of the Congregation for the Doctrine of the Faith, whose rulings he challenged. Lehmann had also provoked criticism from the Curia by suggesting that John Paul might one day consider resigning. As noted, Walter Kasper had also crossed swords with Ratzinger over the issue of Curial centralization. And both Lehman and Kasper had suggested that the Church could be more lenient in allowing divorced and remarried Catholics to receive Communion, even if they do not have an annulment.

APPARITIONS GALORE

Although Church attendance in Europe continued to decline catastrophically throughout Europe, pilgrims are flocking to Catholic shrines across the continent. It was reported in October of 1993 that Lourdes, the most popular, had not had so many pilgrims since the apparition of the Virgin Mary was first reported there in 1858. An increasing number of reports describe people witnessing animated religious icons and effigies weeping and bleeding. These invariably are seen by Orthodox or Catholic Christians, either in their churches or shrines or in private homes. The Catholic Church is usually wary about giving such visions an endorsement, wariness justified by the frequency of fraud involved. One of the most sensational apparitions of the Virgin Mary occurred in Clearwater, Florida, on December 26, 1996, when a thirty-foot-tall breathtakingly beautiful iridescent image of a hooded Madonna appeared on the glass windows of the Seminole Finance Corporation. Soon the usual confluence of people arrived, clogging traffic and requiring extra police. Explanations by the skeptical were not lacking. One person produced similar iridescent images by mixing oil and water on glass while the less agnostic deposited flowers and offerings on a ledge nearby as vendors hawked souvenirs.

One of the most noteworthy apparitions is claimed to have occurred at Medjugorje in western Herzegovina, a place that has become not only a spiritual shrine but a focal point of Croatian nationalism. Six Croatian children claimed to have first seen "Gospa" ("the Virgin" in Croatian) at this spot on

June 24, 1981. Since then, tens of thousands of pilgrims have flooded into the village on a daily basis. Praying the rosary in assorted languages, they climb through thorn bushes up the difficult slope from the village of Medjugorje to the jagged rocks and wait for the Virgin Mary to appear. They leave offerings—miniature crucifixes and crosses, flowers, flags from every continent—and requests. "Dear Mary, please bless my sick husband, John," or "I come to you on my hands and knees, a sinner, an alcoholic. Please, Mary, wash over me. Help me be clean." They cry: "Please, Mary, show us a sign." Father Rookey, a healing priest from Chicago, lays his hands on a middle-aged man in a stretcher. Many mourn the third anniversary of the civil war that took their sons and husbands.[58]

Controversy has not been lacking. Two Yugoslav commissions of psychologists, bishops, scientists, and theologians assigned to investigate the Medjugorje phenomenon in the early 1980s concluded that there was no proof of any of the claims of supernatural interventions. The bishop of Mostar has remained an unyielding skeptic and called the visions a hoax perpetrated by the Franciscans. Meanwhile, psychiatrists who tested the visionaries diagnosed them as sane. By 1995 only two of the six visionaries were still active at the shrine, Vicka Ivankovic and Ivan Dragixevic. Vicka conducts healing prayers from the veranda of her parents' modest home and takes bundles of messages from the pilgrims, which she promises to pass on to Gospa. Ivan holds his encounters with the Virgin Mary daily at 6:40 P.M. in a crowded choir loft at St. James Church. Sporting a Hawaian shirt, he kneels before a painting of the Virgin Mary for some twenty minutes, motionless before the silent onlookers.

One of the principal actors in this spiritual drama is Father Jozo, a Franciscan who was initially skeptical and suspected the children were being used by the Communists to undermine the Church. But after hearing a voice he became the childrens' protector, for which he suffered imprisonment and torture by the Communists. His witness authenticated the "miracles" and added a new page to the history of the Franciscan heroes, who since the fifteenth century, have kept the faith alive there in the face of persecution by the Turks and have been rewarded by tremendous loyalty from the Herzegovinan Croats. The charismatic Father Jozo holds forth at Masses, where many pil-

---

[58] Elizabeth Rubin, "Souvenir Miracles," *Harper's,* February 1995.

grims are "slain in the spirit," an act of fainting and rebirth. In his sermons, he tells how Medjugorje shook the foundations of Communism and began the movement that "changed the world."

The question of whether the shrine should be approved by the Church as a public cult has brought to the fore some questionable assertions of the visionaries. These include their claim of having visited hell in the company of the Virgin and of having seen a neighbor wearing horns, of a visit of the Virgin to the Pope on his sickbed after he was shot, and a notice they received from the Virgin that she had changed the date of her birthday.[59] There is also the vilification of the local bishop by associates of the visionaries.

CHARISMATIC MOVEMENT

Will the increasingly popular ministry of healing—the Charismatic Movement—become part of the daily life of the Church? Charles Whitehead, currently chairman of Catholic Evangelisation Services in Britain, said it would be "wonderful if after Mass on a Sunday morning, when anyone wanted prayer for a difficulty in their life—whether a physical problem or a family situation—there would be a few people who could spend just five minutes praying with them."[60] The ministry of healing is especially popular among Hispanic Catholics, who are attracted by the warmth and intimate character of the services. A prayer service to celebrate the twenty-fifth anniversary of the Charismatic Renewal held in St. Patrick's Cathedral on February 22, 1992, drew more than a thousand people. Enthusiasts point to the meeting of John Paul II with leaders of the movement from around the world in 1981 as proof of his approval of the Charismatic Movement.

But warnings against rousing emotions, mass hysteria, and other "excesses" were expressed in a document issued by the Congregation for the Doctrine of Faith (CDF) and Congregation for Divine Worship in December 2000. The fears behind this document seemed to be confirmed when Archbishop Milingo, one of the star healers of the Charismatic Movement in his native Zambia, took part in a bizarre ceremony presided over by the Rev. Sun Myung Moon of the Unification Church. The archbishop married a much younger Korean woman, but after a short interval of married bliss, Milingo

---

[59] *The Tablet,* June 2, 1990, p. 701.
[60] *The Tablet,* November 24, 2001.

had second thoughts and left his bride, who then started a fast in St. Peter's Square, accusing the Vatican of kidnapping him. The denouement of the affair came a few weeks later, in August 2001, when a repentant Milingo bade farewell to his wife in a tearful ceremony after patching up his relationship with the Church.

The strange goings-on by Milingo did not seem to adversely affect the Catholic Charismatic Movement. At a three-day meeting in November 2001, the leaders of the movement got a welcome boost from Cardinal J. Francis Stafford, head of the Council of the Laity, who said that the healing ministry was "a manifestation of the new forms of evangelisation which the Holy Father has called for." At the same time, he noted that it would take time for the hierarchical Church to understand it.

REVISION OF THE RITE OF EXORCISM

In January 1999 the Vatican reaffirmed that the devil exists and is at work in the world. But no doubt in a nod to liberal Catholics, it urged those performing exorcism to take pains to distinguish between possessed people and those suffering from forms of mental and psychological illnesses.

The Church's best-known exorcist is the Rev. Gabriele Amorth in Rome who says he sees about ten people a day for demonic possessions, obsessions, and other milder problems. His book *An Exorcist Tells His Story* has been reprinted seventeen times. While throwing a punch at the incredibly popular Harry Potter series because of the danger it poses of enticing children into supernatural adventures, he thinks that the evil Lord Voldemort of the Potter stories is a rank amateur compared with Satan himself. "Wars," he says, "are mostly caused by the devil. Certainly Hitler was consecrated to Satan as was Stalin." He thinks most of the people seeking his professional help need a psychiatrist and he won't see them until they do. People who are possessed are not evil themselves but are victims of a spell, he maintains. His career included taking part in the Italian resistance and working as a deputy to Giulio Andreotti, Italy's recent prime minister. After entering the clergy, he undertook exorcism at the request of his bishop and his experience has taught him that the Church is too easygoing about the possibility of possession. And he is especially critical of the new rite of exorcism, which, he complains, forbids talking to the devil and allows exorcism only when possession is a certainty. He feels the movie *The Exorcist* shows the way it should be done.

SECULARIZATION

An oft-debated issue is the extent of secularization, a loss of the sense of the sacred, in the world today. There is no doubt that organized religion has lost ground in many parts of the world, but this does not necessarily mean that secularization has increased. The Jesuit sociologist John Coleman argues that we simply can't say whether there has been a diminution of a sense of the sacred in modern society. Moreover, even though the decline of the influence of the Church on morality and political, social, and economic behavior is a fact, this does not mean that religion has lost its indirect influence on individuals. It is clear, however, that, as Coleman says, "authoritarian religion based on rigid doctrinal or moral orthodoxy finds an inhospitable climate in the modern situation."[61]

One country where the decline of religion is most obvious is England, which has often been called the most secularized country in Western Europe. The status of the Catholic Church reflects this picture clearly. According to the Catholic Directory statistics for the Church in England and Wales published in 1999, the Church's membership reached its peak in the mid-sixties and has declined ever since. One might think this was due to the influence of the Second Vatican Council, but since membership in other churches also declined in this period, there must be other reasons. Nevertheless, the Catholics have suffered the highest rate of decline of any religious group in the United Kingdom in the period since 1985. Only the Charismatic Evangelicals registered growth. No doubt, the decline can be traced in part to the onset in the sixties of an individualism spurred by the "sex, drugs, and rock 'n' roll" culture. The number of ordinations, Communions, and baptisms as well as the figures on attendance at Mass have declined by nearly 50 percent in England and Wales. At the same time, the number of marriages within the Catholic Church has slumped much more disastrously, from 45,592 in 1964 to 14,705 by 1997.

A 1999 British poll shows that only a minority of Britons now believe in the tenets of Christianity. Less than half believe that Jesus was the Son of God and 22 percent think he was just a story. This decline of belief in the role of Jesus has occurred dramatically over the last forty years. However, just over half the population still believe that there is life after death, a number hardly

[61] John Coleman, *Theological Studies* 39 (December 1978), pp. 601–32.

changed in the last forty years. While the majority of people (65 percent) still believe in God, only 28 percent believe in "a personal God." Slightly less than 50 percent say they belong to any particular religion. This is a rapid decline since 1990, when the majority of Britons (58 percent) claimed adherence to a particular religion. Hardest hit by the rapid decline was the membership of the Church of England, which fell from 40 percent of the national population in 1990 to 27 percent in 1999. Catholics, on the other hand, have remained constant at 9 percent of the total population.

In spite of this decline, a quarter of the population still claim that they go to church at least once a month and nearly half the population (48 percent) say they attend religious services at least once a year.[62] But the fact remains that the churches were unable to halt the decline during the 1990s, in spite of their intention to make that decade a time of renewed evangelization.

The rapid decline of the Catholic Church in the U.K. is reflected throughout Europe. A poll taken in 1995 by the Italian bishops' conference found that only 23 percent of Italians regularly attend Mass and 60 percent never go to confession. However, in Africa and Asia, the Church is rapidly growing.

As to the situation in the United States, where alienated Catholics are numerous, Andrew Greeley maintains that at least 85 percent of those who are born Catholics remain committed to the Church. He believes the reason is in the way the Catholic religious sensibility appeals powerfully to the whole person. Other statistics bear up Greeley's contention, showing that Church attendance has held steady over the last decades after a drop of nearly one third in the late 1960s and early 1970s.

The rite of the Christian initiation for adults has proved very effective in drawing converts to the Church, as many thousands yearly complete their conversion to Roman Catholicism through the rite.

The communal approach has enabled the Church to market itself more effectively to Americans, who shop around and tend to change their religion easily. In the 90 (of 189) U.S. dioceses for which figures were available, 63,000 people became Catholics on April 22, 2002, during the solemn Easter vigil, the holiest time of the Church's liturgical year.[63] Catholic membership patterns more closely resemble the gains of Evangelical churches, which

[62] *The Tablet*, December 18, 1999.
[63] *America*, May 6, 2000.

gained 6.4 million new adherents between 1970 and 1997. The nine major Protestant denominations, however, lost 22 percent of their membership between 1970 and 1997, a decline of 5.8 million.

One of the most difficult sectors of the American population to convert to Catholicism has been African Americans. There are many reasons for this. One sociologist, Sam Dennis, traces the problem back to the Church's maintenance of slavery, its acceptance of segregation, and its failure to develop African American clergy. Many African Americans still view the Church as racist institution, according to Jacqueline Wilson, former president of the National Association of Black Catholic Administrators.

During the past fifteen years, the United States hierarchy has issued an impressive number of documents that recognize the importance of African Americans to the Church and of the contributions of black culture. Organizations have been set up and programs launched, but the slow leakage of African Americans from the Church continues.

It was especially good news, therefore, when Bishop Wilton D. Gregory was elected the first black President of the United States bishops' conference in November 2001. One of his memorable addresses had occurred several years before at a meeting of the National Black Catholic Congress before more than a thousand representatives of the nation's 2 million black Catholics. He proclaimed his joy at the heavy emphasis on African identity at the Congress.

In Africa, the Church continues to grow in both absolute numbers and as a percentage of the population. A synod of 300 African bishops in Rome in May 1993 was held to set Africa's 95 million Catholics on course for Christianity's third millennium. Some synod participants underscored the dilemma Africa has always posed for the Church, for they said, it is difficult for Africans to make the exclusive commitment that the Church demands of them.

Figures released in September 1998 show that during John Paul's papacy (which began in October 1978) the number of baptized Roman Catholics rose from 750 million in 1978 to almost 990 million in 1995, with a slight drop in the proportion of the world's population that is Catholic, from 17.8 percent to 17.4 percent.

EPILOGUE

When the Pope goes to his reward, he may leave the Church still in the throes of one of its greatest crises, equal to the major ones of the past: the great persecution by the Roman Empire, the fall of Rome and the Barbarian invasions, the capture of the Church by the feudal magnates, the Great Schism (three Popes), the Protestant Reformation, and the French Revolution.

At least it is safe to say that the challenges he will bequeath to his successor are formidable indeed—above all, a Church polarized between those who want to move forward on what they call the progressive lines laid down by Vatican II and those who wish to adhere more faithfully to the certainties of Church traditions.

When he took office, John Paul II made it immediately clear that he stood with the latter party. He showed little taste for venturing into the unknown, at least doctrinally and theologically. He was determined to reunify a Church in disarray and hold the line on further change. As he saw it, the crisis was a crisis of identity. The changes introduced by Vatican II had shaken the "unchangeable" Church to its roots and caused a huge exodus of its clergy and religious from their stations and left the laity dazed and demoralized. His answer was to insist on tradition and authority. He would be a superbishop, a shepherd who would, as Timothy was admonished to do by Paul, "convince, rebuke and encourage" his worldwide flock through his personal visitations.

The charismatic Pope communicated a sense of authority and continuity by stressing the strength of the Catholic tradition as he called for total conformity to the Church's teachings. Cafeteria, or pick-and-choose, Catholics were admonished and dissenting theologians were punished.

He planned to challenge not only the Church but modern society as well by targeting the liberal assumption that religion should be relegated to the private sphere. He had no qualms about insisting on the Church's role as the fount of civilization and witness to an ethic based on fundamental human rights and values. He moved the project out to the world stage. As Giancarlo Zizola says, "He opened up new geopolitical areas both to the universal requirements of evangelisation and to the ethical and political demands of Christian charity. This was a dynamic interpretation of Catholicism, according to the original meaning of Catholic in the Greek, *kata-holon*," "for all."[64]

And he also strove to make the Church a power through a worldwide social and ethical role. A basically fundamentalist morality would be communicated by satellite TV. The power would also be exerted through Vatican diplomacy, which was greatly expanded. In 1978 there were 89 nunciatures

[64] *The Tablet*, October 3, 1998, p. 1429.

and 21 apostolic delegations. There are now 167 Vatican representatives in as many countries.

John Paul II is a complex personality baffling to many observers. On the one hand, he has called on the other churches for help in remodeling the Petrine office to remove the historical encrustations of absolutism from its exercise and return it to its essential functions. On the other, he has increased its area of infallibility to include even the operations of the ordinary magisterium.

On the one hand, in *Orientale lumen,* he has spoken of the pluriform Church and of his respect for the different theological, liturgical, and disciplinary traditions of all churches and their necessary autonomy. On the other, he has shown little sympathy for diversity within the bounds of the Roman Communion and has opposed the issuance of national catechisms by the different bishops' conferences while imposing an extremely conservative catechism on the universal Church.

He could stand forth before the world as the champion of Polish democracy as he galvanized the Polish people to shake off the yoke of Communism and its herd mentality. But was there a lesson for this within his own Church? If so, he didn't seem to see it. On the other hand, though, there is the remarkable statement he made to the bishops of the countries of the Maghreb during a visit to Tunisia on April 14, 1996, when he stressed the need to be open to others. Such an attitude, he said, was "in some way a response to God, who acknowledges our differences and wants us to know each other more deeply." He suggested that "the different religions, at their root, all agree on the acceptance of differences and on the benefit to be drawn from looking critically at each other and seeing how other people formulate their faith and live it out."[65]

One central question: Will his successor carry on the Pope's ecumenical thrust and the dialogue with the other great religions of the world?[66] Will he be able to resist the increasing pressures to revise the Church's teaching on the ordination of women, contraception, etc. Will he continue to reinforce the centralization of power in the Church or will the implications of Cardinal Kasper's

---

[65] Ibid.

[66] Cardinal Ratzinger speculated recently in the German newspaper *Die Welt* on the possibility of an African Pope. In an interview on his seventy-fifth birthday he noted that Africa had some "truly great figures, fully of stature for the job." He thought such a development would be a good sign for the whole of Christianity.

vision of the Church as a communion of communions be realized? If recruitment to the clergy continues to decline, will he bite the bullet and open the door—already slightly ajar—to a married priesthood?

One of the most promising developments of the post–Vatican II era has been the emergence of an energetic, informed, mature laity that could play an enormous role in the transformation of the Church into what it could become—truly a world Church, pluralist, capable of inspiring a world poised for self-destruction, with its message of hope, its well-tested and worked out social justice agenda, and its doctrine of human rights. Or will it hold on to the last vestiges of medievalism that Vatican II failed to dislodge? Will it fail to fulfill its great spiritual potential to be a Church truly Catholic and truly a light to the Gentiles?

One thing is glaringly obvious: The weight of the papacy has become impossible for one man to bear without adequate reforms (as Giancarlo Zizola has said).[67] Perhaps the image of infirmity the Pope projects as he shuffles around the altar and mumbles his sermons is a fitting sign of a future reformed, more humble papacy, more on the model of Peter than of Gregory VII. Perhaps this more humble papacy would not fear re-examining some of the positions John Paul has upheld so staunchly. The reforms proposed by some of the best minds in the Church can hardly be delayed without huge losses.

The idea of a Church with many centers and shapes, "pledged to inculturate the truths of the faith in different parts of the world," hangs in the balance. A tragic optimist, as an intelligent Catholic should be, would only say, "Wait, pray, and see."[68]

---

[67] Giancarlo Zizola, "The Power of the Pope," part 1, *The Tablet,* October 17, 1998, p. 1352.
[68] Giancarlo Zizola, "Poured Out in Service," *The Tablet,* October 31, 1998, p. 1429

APPENDIX: THE CARDINALS CLASSIFIED

Exercising suitable caution about the difficulty of classifying the cardinals—since parties as such technically do not exist in the college of cardinals—John Allen, the author of *Conclave* (Doubleday Image Books, 2002) nevertheless goes ahead and groups them under several headings of his own invention. First there are those he calls the "Border Patrol party," who believe that relativism and secularization are the main threats to the Church from the world. They fear that Catholics will lose their identity and will gradually be assimilated by the surrounding culture. The remedy these cardinals favor is doctrinal clarity. They also have strong views on the need to pull back from the reform of the liturgy, which they think has gone too far. (See the section on Archbishop Weakland's response to this "reform of the reform.") The leader of this party is Cardinal Joseph Ratzinger, head of the Congregation for the Doctrine of the Faith. Others who fit in here include Jorge Medina Estevez of Chile, Giacomo Biffi of Bologna, Jan Schotte of Belgium, Christoph Schonborn of Vienna, Bernard Law and Francis George of the United States, Johannes Degenhardt of Paderborn, Ivan Dias of Bombay, Desmond Connell of Ireland, Aloysius Ambrozi of Canada, Marian Jaworski of Ukraine, and Jozef Tomko, a Curial official.

Allen calls the second group the "Salt of the Earth party"; it consists of those who believe that the social order should reflect as far as possible the teachings of the Church, especially on such issues as contraception, childless marriages, homosexual marriages, and artificial insemination For them intra-Church disputes over such issues as the placement of the tabernacle are a waste of time. The right wing of this party, whom Allen calls "integralists," are those who favor a position that has some affinities with the old pre–Vatican II doctrine on the union of Church and State. They include Camillo Ruini, the Pope's Vicar of Rome and head of the Italian bishops' conference; Angelo Sodano, Secretary of State; and Jozef Glemp of Poland, Norberto Rivera Carrera of Mexico, Juan Luis Cipriani Thorne of Peru, Maria Rouco Varela of Spain, and Alfonso Lopez Truijillo of Colombia.

On the left wing of the "Salt of the Earth party" are cardinals who whose concerns tend to lie in the realm of social and economic justice, with such issues as debt relief, globalization, and racial justice. They call for efforts to find the root causes of and remedies for poverty, hunger, illiteracy, disease, and racial prejudice. Rather than insisting on traditional Catholic arguments, they tend to favor the widest coalition possible with those of similar concerns. Among these cardinals are Theodore McCarrick of Washington, Medardo Mazombwe of Zambia, and Oscar Rogdriguez Maradiaga of Honduras. Maradiaga has been especially visible on the issue of debt relief for the impoverished nations of the free world. Also in this group are Paulo Evaristo Arns and Aloisio Lorscheider of Brazil, Jaime Sin of the Philippines, Julius Riyadi Darmaatmadja of Indonesia, and Wilfrid Napier of South Africa.

The left wing of the "Salt of the Earth party" were involved in the G-8 summit in Genoa in July 2001, where a "Catholic Manifesto for Social Change" was presented to the G-8 leaders. Calling for a wide range of political and economic reforms, Genoa's Cardinal Dionigi Tettamanzi gave it a ringing endorsement. (Tettamanzi can also seem like a "Border Patrol" type, depending on the topic.)

Finally there is the "Reform party," which favors internal reform along progressive lines, including greater collegiality, or decentralization, greater tolerance of diversity and experimentation, and a reform of the Roman Curia. Included in the "Reform party" would be Karl Lehmann and Walter Kasper of Germany, Carlo Martini of Milan, Godfried Danneels of Belgium, Roger Mahony of the United States, and Edward Cassidy of Australia. Some of them even favor the convocation of a Third Vatican Council. (See section on Walter Kasper's debate with Cardinal Ratzinger, pages 514–16.) They would like to turn the Roman Curia into a servant of the local churches, a kind of clearinghouse of information. None of the "Reform" cardinals openly supports the ordination of women or homosexual marriage, but they are by instinct men who believe in discussion and debate. They believe that the season of reform launched by Vatican II was for various reasons prematurely cut short during the pontificate of John Paul II. One of their concerns has to do with the Congregation for the Doctrine of the Faith, the former Holy Office. They believe it should be a teaching instrument such as they claim Paul VI wanted, rather than a watchdog agency. Instead of promoting good theological work in the spirit of Paul VI's wishes, they see it as being fixated on correcting abuses.

To wind up his study Allen ventures a list of *papabili*—cardinals with a good chance of being the next Pope—while admitting it is educated guesswork. His choices (in alphabetical order): Francs Arrinze of Nigeria; Dario Castrillon Hoyos of Colombia; Godfried Danneels of Belgium; Roger Etchegara of France; Claudio Hummes of Brazil; Lubomyr Husar of Ukraine; Walter Kasper of Germany; Karl Lehmann of Germany; Nicolas de Jesus Lopez Rodriguez of the Dominican Republic; Jean-Marie Lustiger of France; Carlo Maria Martini of Italy; Wilfrid Fox Napier of South Africa; Jaime Lucas Ortega y Alamino of Cuba; Giovanni Battista Re of Italy; Norberto Rivera Carrera of Mexico; Oscar Andres Rodriguez Maradiaga of Honduras; Christoph Schonborn of Austria; Dionigi Tettamanzi of Italy; and Miloslav Vlk of the Czech Republic.

ANNOTATED BIBLIOGRAPHY

BASIC REFERENCE WORKS

Conciliorum Oecumenicorum Decreta. Giuseppe Alberigo et al., eds. Basel: Herder, 1962. The
    decrees and canons of the early Councils.

Encyclopedia of Theology: The Concise Sacramentum Mundi. Karl Rahner, S.J., ed. New York:
    Seabury Press, 1975.

The New Catholic Encyclopedia. 17 vols. New York: McGraw-Hill, 1967–79.

The Oxford Dictionary of the Christian Church. 3rd.ed. F. L. Cross and E. A. Livingston, eds.
    New York: Oxford University Press, 1997.

Quasten, Johannes. *Patrology.* 4 vols. Westminster, Md.: Newman Press, 1962–63.

Stevenson, James. *A New Eusebius: Documents Illustrative of the History of the Church to A.D.
    337.* London: S.P.C.K., 1957.

van der Meer, F., and C. Mohrmann. *An Atlas of the Early Christian World.* London: Nelson,
    1958.

Vatican Council II: The Conciliar and Post Conciliar Documents. Austin Flannery, O.P., ed.
    Collegeville, Minn.: Liturgical Press, 1975.

PERIODICALS ESPECIALLY USEFUL FOR THE ENGLISH-SPEAKING STUDENT

The Catholic Historical Review. Washington, 1915 seqq. [CHR]

Church History. New York–Chicago, 1932 seqq. [CH]

Journal of Ecclesiastical History. London, 1950 seqq. [JEH]

Revue d'histoire ecclésiastique. Published by the faculty of the University of Louvain. One does
    not have to be francophone to make use of its bibliography—the most comprehensive
    available for the whole field of ecclesiastical history. [RHE]

GENERAL WORKS

Duffy, Eamon. *Saints & Sinners: A History of the Popes.* New Haven: Yale University Press,
    1997. A prestigious Church historian turns his historical telescope on the papal millen-
    niums and puts a heavy emphasis on historical accident in the evolution of the papacy.

Hastings, Adrian. *A World History of Christianity.* Grand Rapids, Michigan: W. B. Eerdmans, 1999.

La Due, William J. *The Chair of Saint Peter: A History of the Papacy.* Maryknoll, N.Y.: Orbis, 1999. A reviewer in *Theological Studies* considers this work to be a valuable contribution to ecumenical dialogue because of its attention to the context and contingencies that have promoted or curbed papal power and influence. The author, like many historians, believes that events in the nineteenth century gave a "papalist tilt" to the Church, one that continues despite the more balanced ecclesiology of Vatican II.

McManners, John, ed. *The Oxford Illustrated History of Christianity.* New York: Oxford University Press, 1992. A splendid overview by the best scholars in the field.

van der Meer, F. *Early Christian Art.* Chicago: University of Chicago Press, 1967. Notes how the basilica as it was designed after 313 was a latent creation of genius perfectly suited to meet the needs of a universal Church.

SPIRITUALITY

No one chapter is solely devoted to this important aspect.

Ignatius of Loyola, Saint (1491–1556). *Monumenta Ignatiana. Series secunda: Exercitia spiritualia S. Ignatii de Loyola et eorum directoria.* Nova editio. Jose Calveras, SJ, and Candido de Dalmases, SJ, eds. Rome: Institutum Historicum Societatis Iesu, 1969.

Ignatius of Loyola, Saint (1491–1556). *The Spiritual Exercises of St. Ignatius of Loyola.* Trans. from the autograph of Father Elder Mullan. New York: P. J. Kennedy & Sons, Printers, 1914. A modernized adaptation by D. L. Fleming, S.J. of *A Contemporary Reading of the Spiritual Exercises.* St. Louis: Institute of Jesuit Sources, 1980.

Bremond, H. *A Literary History of Religious Thought in France.* Trans. K. L. Montgomery. 5 vols. London: n.p., 1928–36. London: Society for Promoting Christian Knowledge; New York, Macmillan Co., 1928.

Dupre, L., and D. Saliers, eds., in collaboration with John Meyendorff. *Christian Spirituality: Post-Reformation and Modern.* New York: Crossroad, 1989.

McGinn, B., and J. Meyendorff, eds. *Christian Spirituality: Origins to the Twelfth Century.* New York: Crossroad, 1985.

J. Raitt, ed., in collaboration with B. McGinn and J. Meyendorff. *Christian Spirituality: High Middle Ages and Reformation.* New York: Crossroad, 1987.

PART ONE: THE CHURCH TRIUMPHS OVER PAGANISM, A.D. 30–600

GENERAL WORKS

Barry, Colman, O.S.B., ed. *Readings in Church History.* Vol. 1. Westminster, Md.: Christian Classics, 1985.

Baus, Karl. *From the Apostolic Community to Constantine* (Vol. 1 of *History of the Church,* Hubert Jedin and John P. Dolan, eds.). New York: Crossroad, 1982.

Brown, Peter. *Society and the Holy in Late Antiquity.* Berkeley: University of California Press, 1982.

Cadoux, Cecil J. *The Early Church and the World: A History of the Christian Attitude to Pagan Society and the State*. Edinburgh: T. & T. Clark, 1955. A monumental study.

Carrington, Philip. *The Early Christian Church*. 2 vols. Cambridge: University Press, 1957.

Chadwick, Henry. *The Early Church*. New York: Penguin Books, 1988.

The Christian Centuries. 5 vols. Louis J. Rogier et al., eds. New York: Paulist Press, 1978.

Danielou, Jean, and H. Marrou. *The First Six Hundred Years* (Vol. 1 of *The Christian Centuries*). New York: Paulist Press, 1983.

Duchesne, Louis. *Early History of the Christian Church*. 3 vols. London: John Murray, 1907. A great ground-breaking study that was put on the *Index* at the time of the Modernist crisis for reasons beyond the ken of the historian.

Dunn, James D. *Unity and Disunity in the New Testament: An Inquiry into the Character of Earliest Christianity*. Philadelphia: Westminster Press, 1984.

Eusebius. *The Essential Eusebius*. New York: New American Library (Mentor-Omega Book), 1966. Eusebius (c. 260–c. 340) is often called the Father of Church History. His *Ecclesiastical History* is the principal source for the history of Christianity from the Apostolic Age till his own day. Although poor in style, it contains an immense number of extracts from earlier writers, which he sometimes misinterprets because of his lack of critical judgment.

Frend, W. H. C. *The Rise of Christianity*. Philadelphia: Fortress Press, 1984.

Greenslade, Stanley L. *Schism in the Early Church*. New York: Harper & Brothers, 1953.

Hughes, Philip. *A History of the Catholic Church*. 3 vols. New York: Sheed & Ward, 1935–47.

The Imperial Church from Constantine to the Early Middle Ages. Vol. 2: *History of the Church*. New York: Crossroad, 1980.

Kidd, James Beresford. *History of the Church to A.D. 461*. Oxford: Clarendon Press, 1922.

La Porte, Jean. *The Role of Women in Early Christianity*. New York: E. Mellen Press, 1982.

Lot, Ferdinand. *The End of the Ancient World and the Beginnings of the Middle Ages*. New York: Harper Torchbooks, 1961.

Markus, Robert. *Christianity in the Roman World*. New York: Scribner, 1974.

Pelikan, Jaroslav. *The Emergence of the Christian Tradition (100–160)*. Vol. 1: *A History of the Development of Doctrine*. Chicago: University of Chicago Press, 1971.

Vasiliev, Alexander. *History of the Byzantine Empire, 324–1453*. Rev. ed. Madison, Wis.: University of Wisconsin Press, 1972.

Wand, J. W. C. *A History of the Early Church*. London: Methuen (distributed by Harper & Row in U.S.), 1974.

Werner, Martin. *The Formation of Christian Dogma: An Historical Study of Its Problem*. New York: Harper & Brothers, 1957.

Wiles, M. F. *The Making of Christian Doctrine: A Study in the Principles of Early Doctrinal Development*. New York: Cambridge University Press, 1975.

1. JESUS

Badia, Leonard. *Jesus: Introducing His Life and Teaching*. New York: Paulist Press, 1985.

Bornkamm, Gunther. *Jesus of Nazareth*. New York: Harper & Brothers, 1960.

Bowker, John W. *Jesus and the Pharisees*. London: Cambridge University Press, 1973.

Bultmann, Rudolf. *The History of the Synoptic Tradition*. Oxford: Basil Blackwell, 1968.

Cook, Michael. *The Jesus of Faith*. New York: Paulist Press, 1981.

Dodd, Charles H. *The Founder of Christianity.* New York: Macmillan, 1970.

Fiorenza, Elizabeth Schussler. *In Memory of Her: A Feminist Theological Reconstruction of Christian Origins.* New York: Crossroad, 1985.

Flusser, David. *Jesus.* New York: Herder & Herder, 1969.

Fuller, Reginald. *The Formation of the Resurrection Narratives.* New York: Fortress Press, 1980.

Grant, Michael. *Jesus.* London: Sphere Books, 1978.

Grant, Robert. *A Historical Introduction to the New Testament.* New York: Harper & Row, 1963.

Jeremias, Joachim. *The Eucharistic Words of Jesus.* Translated by N. Perrin. Philadelphia: Fortress Press, 1977.

Klausner, Joseph. *Jesus of Nazareth: His Life, Times and Teaching.* New York: Macmillan, 1929. The Jewish point of view in a pioneering work.

Küng, Hans. *On Being a Christian.* Garden City, N.Y.: Doubleday, 1976.

Meir, John P. *A Marginal Jew.* 3 vols. New York: Doubleday, 1991–2001.

Noth, Martin. *The History of Israel.* London: S.C.M., 1983.

Perrin, Norman. *Rediscovering the Teaching of Jesus.* New York: Harper & Row, 1976.

Streeter, Burnett H. *The Four Gospels: A Study of Origins.* Rev. ed. New York: Paulist Press, 1983. A classic work and still foundational.

Synopsis of the First Three Gospels. A. Huck and H. Lietzmann, eds. English version edited by F. L. Cross. New York and London: G. E. Stechert & Co., 1936. The Greek text—an essential tool for study.

Tambasco, Anthony J. *In the Days of Jesus: The Jewish Background and Unique Teaching of Jesus.* New York: Paulist Press, 1983. Richard A. Lebrun calls this work a superb introduction to the results of recent New Testament scholarship.

Also see the various commentaries on the Gospels by such scholars as C. H. Dodd on John, E. Trocmé on Mark, A. R. C. Leaney on Luke, and the collaborative work on Matthew by G. Bornkamm, G. Barth, and H. J. Held.

2. THE CHURCH SPREADS ACROSS THE EMPIRE

Barnard, L. W. *Justin Martyr.* New York: Cambridge University Press, 1967.

Brown, Raymond E. *The Churches the Apostles Left Behind.* New York: Paulist Press, 1984.

Conzelmann, Hans. *History of Primitive Christianity.* Nashville: Abingdon Press, 1973. A great scholar's view. The traditional story of early Christianity was taken from the Acts of the Apostles: The early community spread out from Jerusalem and expanded its mission beyond the Jewish people to include the Gentiles. The twelve Apostles directed this expansion. Paul was the one who gave the impetus to the Gentile mission. But C. points out inconsistencies in this account. What happened to the Twelve? Could they simply have been the organizers of the Jerusalem Church whom later Christians pictured with a special relation to the historical Jesus? Acts is unreliable about Paul's role, seeing him as the original force behind the Gentile mission. Rather it came from the Godfearers who were close to the synagogue but uncircumcised. He points out how as A.D. 100 drew near, a structured early Catholicism with emerging tradition and doctrinal positions evolved out of primitive Christianity.

Cullmann, Oscar. *Early Christian Worship*. London: S.C.M., 1953.

———. *Peter: Disciple, Apostle, Martyr*. Philadelphia: Westminster Press, 1962.

Davies, William D. *Paul and Rabbinic Judaism*. New York: Harper & Row, 1965.

Dunn, James D. *Unity and Disunity in the New Testament: An Inquiry into the Character of Earliest Christianity*. Philadelphia: Westminster Press, 1977.

Frend, W. H. C. *Religion Popular and Unpopular in the Early Christian Centuries*. London: Variorum Reprints, 1976.

Grant, Robert. *Augustus to Constantine: The Thrust of the Christian Movement into the Roman World*. New York: Harper & Row, 1970.

Harnack, Adolph von. *The Mission and Expansion of Christianity in the First Three Centuries*. New York: Harper & Row, 1962. The fundamental work on this period.

Karrer, Otto. *Peter and the Church: An Examination of Cullmann's Thesis*. New York: Herder, 1963.

Küng, Hans, *The Church*. Garden City, N.Y.: Doubleday Image Books, 1976.

Meeks, Wayne A. *The First Urban Christians: The Social World of the Apostle Paul*. New Haven: Yale University Press, 1983.

Neill, Stephen. *A History of the Christian Missions*. Harmondsworth, England: Penguin Books, 1986. Considered the best one-volume treatment of missionary activity traced from the earliest days of the Church.

Richardson, Peter. *Israel in the Apostolic Church*. London: Cambridge University Press, 1969. Shows the long process involved in the Church's assumption of the heritage of Israel and how it came to consider itself as the true Israel, a third race. As time passed and as the Jews refused to recognize Jesus as the Messiah, the Church became more aware of its own identity and its independence vis-à-vis the Jewish rites as well as its right to the promises, thanks to the death of Christ and the new covenant he instituted.

Stark, Rodney. *The Rise of Christianity: A Sociologist Reconsiders History*. Princeton, N.J.: Princeton University Press, 1996. How did a tiny, obscure, messianic movement from the edge of the Roman Empire displace classical paganism and become the dominant faith of Western civilization? Stark challenges conventional explanations. Instead of being a movement among the downtrodden, Christianity, Stark argues, had its strongest base among the privileged classes. Otherwise it could easily have been uprooted by the power of Rome. He also points out that an important factor was the role of women in Christian growth. Among Christians, girl babies were much more often allowed to live, unlike among the pagans, where infanticide of females was rampant. Hence the ever-rising birthrate in the Christian community. Moreover Christian women frequently married pagan men. Such marriages often resulted in the conversion of the male spouse. Finally, the Christians' uniquely effective and compassionate response to the misery, chaos, fear, and brutality of Graeco-Roman civic life helped to revitalize urban life and gain converts.

Toynbee, J., and J. Ward Perkins. *The Shrine of St. Peter and the Vatican Excavations*. New York: Longmans, Green, 1956.

Tyson, Joseph B. *The New Testament and Early Christianity*. New York: Macmillan, 1984. Recent scholarship testifies to the great variety of early forms of Christianity. Tyson distinguishes six kinds: (1) *Primitive:* characteristic of the first three or four decades after death of Jesus. (2) *Pauline:* tributaries of Paul's great stream. (3) *Johannine:* formed almost exclusively by John's Gospel. (4) *Jewish:* the Jewish Christian community in Palestine devoted to Old Testament law and in tension with Gentile Christianity. (5) *Gnostic:* A powerful challenge to "Proto-Catholic" Christianity. Recent study has shown it to be rooted in a movement prior to and independent of Christianity. It gave rise to a great variety of sects. (6) *Early Catholicism:* Dominant by the third century, it cherished unity, clarity, and order, and sought to propagate one single form of Christianity.

3. A CHURCH WITH AUTHORITY

Batiffol, Pierre. *Primitive Catholicism.* New York: Longmans, Green, 1911.

Campenhausen, H. von *Ecclesiastical Authority and Spiritual Power in the Church of the First Three Centuries.* Palo Alto: Stanford University Press, 1969. He sees office and charism in an uneasy relationship from the beginning and already in Clement I and Ignatius a trend toward office as the exclusive authority.

Danielou, Jean. *Origen.* New York: Sheed & Ward, 1955.

Documents in Early Christian Thought, M. Wiles and M. Santer, eds. New York: Cambridge University Press, 1976.

The Fathers of the Primitive Church. Herbert Musurillo, S.J., ed. New York: New American Library (Mentor-Omega Books), 1966.

Grant, R. M. *Gnosticism and Early Christianity.* New York: Columbia University Press, 1950.

Haenchen, Ernest. *The Acts of the Apostles: A Commentary.* Philadelphia: Westminster Press, 1971. Haenchen is a good antidote to Conzelmann and Kasemann's claim of a "sharp break" in Lucan material between the time of Jesus and the time of the Church.

Hanson, Richard P. *Origen's Doctrine of Tradition.* London: S.P.C.K., 1954.

———. *Tradition in the Early Church.* London and Philadelphia: Westminster Press, 1962.

Kelly, John. D. *Early Christian Creeds.* New York: Longman, 1981.

Knox, John. *Marcion and the New Testament.* Chicago: University of Chicago Press, 1942.

Lawson, John. *The Biblical Theology of Saint Irenaeus.* London: Epworth Press, 1948.

The Lost Books of the Bible. New York: Bell Pub. Co., 1979. Translations of many early Christian writings that were excluded from the New Testament canon.

Moule, Charles F. D. *The Birth of the New Testament.* New York: Harper & Row, 1962.

Pagels, Elaine. *The Gnostic Gospels.* New York: Penguin Books, 1982. A sympathetic, highly praised account of the Gnostics.

Wilson, Robert M. *The Gnostic Problem.* London: AMS Press, 1958.

4. CONSTANTINE FAVORS THE CHRISTIANS AND INAUGURATES A NEW ERA OF CHURCH HISTORY

Baynes, Norman H. *Constantine the Great and the Christian Church.* New York: Gordon Press, 1974.

Frend, W. H. C. *Martyrdom and Persecution in the Early Church.* Grand Rapids, Mich.: Baker Book House, 1981.

Gager, Roger. *Kingdom and Community: The Social Role of Early Christianity.* Englewood Cliffs, N.J.: Prentice Hall, 1975.

Jones, Arnold H. M. *Constantine and the Conversion of Europe.* Toronto: University of Toronto Press, 1978.

5. WORSHIP, FAITH, AND LIFE IN THE EARLY CHURCH

Ancient Christian Writers. St. Cyprian: The Lapsed. Westminster, Md.: Newman Press, 1957.

Brown, Peter. *The Cult of the Saints: Its Rise and Function in Latin Christianity.* Chicago: University of Chicago Press, 1982.

Campenhausen, Hans von. *The Fathers of the Greek Church.* New York: Pantheon, 1959.

———. *Men Who Shaped the Western Church.* Palo Alto: Stanford University Press, 1972.

Cross, Frank L. *The Study of St. Athanasius.* Oxford: Clarendon Press, 1945.

Danielou, Jean. *Gospel Message and Hellenistic Culture.* Philadelphia: Westminster Press, 1973.

Dix, Gregory. *Shape of the Liturgy.* New York: Seabury Press, 1984.

Duchesne, Louis. *Christian Worship—Its Origin and Evolution: A Study of the Latin Liturgy up to the Time of Charlemagne.* London: S.P.C.K., 1956.

The Fathers of the Church. St. Cyprian: Letters. Washington, D.C.: Catholic University Press, 1964.

Fortman, Edmund J. *The Triune God: A Historical Study of the Doctrine of the Trinity.* Grand Rapids, Mich.: Baker Book House, 1982.

Gregg, Robert C. *Early Arianism: A view of Salvation.* Minneapolis: Fortress Press, 1981.

Gwatkin, Henry M. *The Arian Controversy.* Eugene, Ore.: Wipf & Stock, 2001.

Hanson, R. P. C. *The Search for the Christian Doctrine of God: The Arian Controversy, 318–381.* Edinburgh: T. & T. Clark, 2000.

Hippolytus, *Church Order,* 31, 11:21, F. X. Funk, ed (trans. *Cambridge Ancient History,* X, II). New York: Cambridge University Press, 1956.

Jedin, Hubert. *Ecumenical Councils.* New York: Paulist Press, 1961. The standard work on the history of the councils.

Jungmann, Josef. *The Mass of the Roman Rite.* Westminster, Md.: Christian Classics, 1980.

Kelly, John N. D. *Early Christian Doctrines.* New York: Harper & Row, 1978.

Klauser, Theodor. *A Short History of the Western Liturgy: An Account and Some Reflections.* New York: Oxford University Press, 1979.

Knowles, David. *Christian Monasticism.* New York: McGraw-Hill, 1969.

Lawrence, Clifford Hugh. *Medieval Monasticism: Forms of Religious Life in Western Europe in the Middle Ages.* New York: Longman, 1989. Richard Lebrun calls this an excellent study.

Noonan, John. *Contraception.* New York: New American Library (Mentor Books), 1967.

Pollard, T. E. *Johannine Christology and the Early Church.* New York: Cambridge University Press, 1970. Sees John and the Logos concept in his prologue as the chief influence on the diverse and one-sided interpretation of the Christian message as "word theology." The controversy over Marcellus of Ancyra's theology (he was deposed in 336) was the crossroads where four theologians of the Trinity—each having his own interpretation of John—came into collision: Marcellus, Arius, Eusebius of Caesarea, and Pseudo-Athanasius. The last is seen as the only one who did justice to the original intent of John. Pseudo-Athanasius' focal point is soteriology, and his regulative concept of Jesus is not as Logos but as Son. His is the common faith of East and West and is found in the Nicene Creed.

Poschmann, Bernhard. *Penance and the Anointing of the Sick*. New York: Herder & Herder, 1964.

Prestige, George Leonard. *God in Patristic Thought*. London: S.P.C.K., 1936. A very fine analysis of the Trinitarian disputes.

Russell, Jeffrey B. *The Devil: Perceptions of Evil from Antiquity to Primitive Christianity*. Ithaca, N.Y.: Cornell University Press, 1987.

Stevenson, James. *A New Eusebius: Documents Illustrative of the History of the Church to A.D. 337*. London: S.P.C.K., 1957.

Wagner, Walter H. *After the Apostles: Christianity in the Second Century*. Minneapolis: Fortress Press, 1994. Brings together events, ideas, and people in the second century, which was so critical for Christianity. Many important questions had to be faced such as who created the world, what is the destiny of humans, who was Jesus and what is the role of the Church. Five thinkers are chosen who met these challenging questions in a variety of ways: Ignatius of Antioch, Justin Martyr, Clement of Alexandria, Tertullian, and Irenaeus of Lyons. A fine introduction to historical theology that places each author within his social context.

Walker, G.S.M. *The Churchmanship of St. Cyprian*. London: Lutterworth Press, 1968. Argues that Cyprian held that Peter's primacy was purely temporal. His apostolate, unique in origin, was extended to the college of bishops and his office of pastor was perpetuated in the college of bishops. This work was favorably reviewed by M. Bevenot in *Revue d'histoire ecclésiastique* 66 (1971). But as W.H.C. Frend (*The Rise of Christianity*, p. 400) says in the West, Matthew 16:18 was being literally interpreted as the Lord's will and Peter's see was regarded by Cyprian as the origin and seat of episcopacy with which communion must be maintained. He never went back on this principle, even in the heat of the Rebaptism controversy. But recognition of Rome as the "leading see" (principalis) did not imply juridical rights.

Wiles, M. F. *Archetypal Heresy: Arianism Through the Centuries*. Oxford: Clarendon Press, 1996. Earlier writers held that philosophical concerns were paramount in the origin of Arianism, but recent studies view theological concerns as primary, namely, the need to distinguish the divinity of the Father from that of the Son in order to express the Incarnation in a way that did not ascribe the limitations of the Incarnate Son to the full divinity, which they attributed uniquely to the Father.

6. THE FINAL VICTORY OVER PAGANISM

Jones, Arnold H. M. *The Later Roman Empire, 284–602 A Social, Economic and Administrative Survey*. 3 vols. Oxford: Blackwell, 1964.

MacMullen, Ramsay. *Christianizing the Roman Empire, A.D. 100–400*. New Haven: Yale University Press, 1986. This eminent historian concludes that the Christian sweep of the ancient world owed more to political and economic causes and the appeal to miracle than to a "rising tide of Christian piety." W. H. Frend calls it "a landmark in research into the social history of early Christianity," in *The Catholic Historical Review* 71 (1985), p. 449.

Momigliano, Arnoldo. *The Conflict Between Paganism and Christianity in the Fourth Century*. Oxford: Clarendon Press, 1970.

7. JEROME

Katz, Solomon. *The Decline of Rome and the Rise of Medieval Europe.* Ithaca, N.Y.: Cornell University Press, 1955.

Kelly, John N. D. *Jerome: His Life, Writings and Controversies.* New York: Harper & Row, 1975. The latest study of this restless, cantankerous spiritual genius.

Rousseau, Philip. *Ascetics, Authority, and the Church in the Age of Jerome and Cassian.* New York: Oxford University Press, 1978.

The Satirical Letters of St. Jerome. Paul Carroll, trans. Chicago: Henry Regnery, 1956.

Williams, Stephen, and Gerard Friell. *Theodosius: The Empire at Bay.* New Haven: Yale University Press, 1995. Treating a pivotal period in Roman relations with the Germanic peoples, the authors dispute the view that Rome's decline after the death of Theodosius in 395 was due to the quality of its armies, which were staffed with many ethnic Germans. Rather, they say, it was the loss of the preponderance of force previously used to overawe the barbarians. A major mistake of Theodosius was in failing to train his sons to succeed him. Hence, Alaric's ability to exploit the ensuing rivalries between East and West. As to the authors' Gibbonesque treatment of Christianity's role in the decline and fall, the reviewer in the *Journal of Early Christian Studies* (vol. 4, Winter, 1996), thinks it is a caricature.

8. AUGUSTINE

Bentley-Taylor, David. *Augustine: Wayward Genius.* Grand Rapids, Mich.: Baker Book House, 1981.

Bonner, Gerald. *St. Augustine of Hippo: Life and Controversies.* Norfolk, England: Canterbury Press, 1986.

Brown, Peter. *Augustine of Hippo: A Biography.* Berkeley: University of California Press, 1967. Still the best in English.

Campenhausen, Hans von. *The Fathers of the Latin Church.* Palo Alto: Stanford University Press, 1969.

Deane, Herbert A. *The Political and Social Ideas of St. Augustine.* New York: Columbia University Press, 1963.

Dudden, Frederick Homes. *The Life and Times of St. Ambrose.* Wilmington, Del: International Academic Pub., 1979.

Frend, W.H.C. *The Donatist Church: A Movement of Protest in North Africa.* New York: Oxford University Press, 1985.

McLynn, Neil B. *Ambrose of Milan: Church and Court in a Christian Capital.* Berkeley: University of California Press, 1994. A re-evaluation of standard views of Ambrose, whom McLynn calls a "bellicose saint" and evidently dislikes. Ambrose's election was "an improvised response to a botched coup," not the result of overwhelming popular demand. He lied on behalf of the emperor Valentinian on his embassy to Maximus at Trier in 383 and nudged the empire toward civil war by his sermon at Valentinian's funeral. McLynn's verdict: Ambrose was an extremely manipulative though courageous man. The reviewer in the *Journal of Early Christian Studies* (vol. 5, no. 2, Summer 1997) thinks the study is sometimes unfair and not the "whole story."

Merdinger, J. E. *Rome and the African Church in the Time of Augustine.* New Haven: Yale University Press, 1997.

O'Donnell, James J. *Augustine.* Boston: Twayne Publishers, 1985.

Pagels, Elaine. *Adam, Eve, and the Serpent.* New York: Random House, Vintage, 1989. In a number of works, Pagels has emphasized the great influence Christianity has had on our civilization. In the case of Augustine she sees this influence as baleful. She blames the sage of Hippo for propagating an extreme version of original sin, viz. an aboriginal calamity that destroyed the human capacity for free moral decision. Enemies of human freedom ever since, she maintains, have found much support in his writings.

Smith, Warren Thomas. *Augustine: His Life and Thought.* Atlanta: John Knox Press, 1980.

Trout, Dennis E. *Paulinus of Nola: Life, Letters, and Poems.* Berkeley: University of California Press, 1999. Today it is the conversion of Augustine that is given much attention, but the conversion that made headlines at the time was that of his contemporary Paulinus of Nola (c. 352–431). The governor of Campania and headed for an illustrious career among the senatorial elite of the Roman Empire, Paulinus, after meeting Martin of Tours, suddenly renounced the world and shortly afterward, in 394, was ordained a priest.

9. POPE LEO I WINS A GREAT VICTORY FOR PAPAL PRIMACY AT CHALCEDON

Barraclough, Geoffrey. *the Medieval Papacy.* New York: Norton, 1979.

Bowden, John, trans. *Christ in Christian Tradition.* By Aloys Grillmeier, S. J., 2 vols. 2nd rev. ed. Louisville, Ky.: Westminster John Knox Press, 1975.

The Cambridge Medieval History. New York: Cambridge University Press, 1936.

Dvornik, Francis. *The Idea of Apostolicity in Byzantium and the Legend of the Apostle Andrew.* Cambridge: Harvard University Press, 1958. The author shows how at first political rather than theological principle was invoked to determine the importance of a see, but while the Orient remained attached to the political principle, Rome began to base its claim to primacy on petrine apostolicity and therefore claimed to be the "apostolic see" par excellence. This divergence appeared in the twenty-eighth canon of Chalcedon, which was not aimed at Rome but at Alexandria. However, it wounded Rome's susceptibilities and led to a series of tragic misunderstandings culminating in schism.

Grillmeier, A. *Christ in Christian Tradition: From the Apostolic Age to Chalcedon (451).* New York: Sheed & Ward, 1965.

Jalland, Trevor. *The Life and Times of Saint Leo the Great.* London: S.P.C.K., 1941.

Kidd, James B. *The Roman Primacy to A.D. 461.* New York: Macmillan, 1936.

Papal Primacy and the Universal Church. Paul C. Empie and Austin Murphy, eds. Minneapolis: Augsburg Publishing House, 1974. An ecumenical dialogue that registered surprising agreement between Catholics and Protestants vis-à-vis the historic and unique claims of the papacy.

Religion in the Middle East: Three Religions in Concord and Conflict. 2 vols. A. J. Arberry, general ed. New York: Cambridge University Press, 1969. Brings out how it was the welter of certain fractious groups—Monophysites in Syria, Armenia, and Ethiopia; Nestorianism in Persia—and their mutual hostility to Constantinople and each other that made possible Islam's conquest of the Near East.

Richards, Jeffrey. *The Popes and the Papacy in the Early Middle Ages, 476–752.* London: Routledge & Kegan Paul, 1971. Richards's treatment of the papacy in the seventh and eighth centuries opposes the view of Walter Ullmann on the continuity of papal claims from Gelasius on.

Sellers, Robert Victor. *The Council of Chalcedon: A Historical and Doctrinal Survey.* London: S.P.C.K., 1961.

Twomey, Vincent. *Apostolikos Thronos: The Primacy of Rome as Reflected in the Church History of Eusebius and the Historico-apologetic Writings of Saint Athanasius the Great.* Münster: Aschendorff, 1982. Twomey tries to prove that the doctrine of the Roman primacy was firmly and unambiguously present in the churches of the fourth century, but he has failed to win much scholarly support.

Walker, G. S. M. *The Churchmanship of St. Cyprian.* London: Lutterworth Press, 1968. The author agrees with the Catholic scholar Maurice Bevenot that Cyprian saw Peter's primacy as a temporary commission. The Church was built on Peter, but his unique unrepeatable apostolate was extended to the college of twelve, and his office of pastor perpetuated in the multitude of bishops. For Cyprian schism was the gravest of sins.

Ullmann, Walter. *A Short History of the Papacy in the Middle Ages.* London: Methuen (distributed by Harper & Row in the U.S.), 1974.

PART TWO: THE MAKING OF CHRISTENDOM, A.D. 600–1300

GENERAL WORKS

Bloch, Marc. *Feudal Society.* Chicago: University of Chicago Press, 1961.

Cantor, Norman. *The Civilization of the Middle Ages.* New York: HarperCollins, 1993. In this scholarly and readable study Cantor offers many fascinating insights. The points he makes about what he says is the greatly misunderstood Inquisition are of special interest: (1) Innocent III, who greatly expanded the Inquisition, had no alternative if he was to cut the cancerous sore of Catharism out of the body politic of Christendom. Not to do so would have been not only weak and foolish but in his mind a betrayal of the Lord. (2) Contrary to attempts to link the Inquisition with the Nazi holocaust or Stalinist purges, the Inquisitors were not psychotic sadists but well-trained canon lawyers who were eager to welcome dissenters and schismatics as well as Jews back into the Roman community. Some of the early Inquisitors were converted Jews who had joined the Dominican Order. The number who actually died at the hands of the Inquisitors over its active period was relatively small. (3) As to the treatment of the Jews, Cantor notes the increasingly threatening image they presented as associated with other enemies of the Church: heretics, magicians, and witches. The anxiety they caused was not a paranoid delusion but grounded in reality (pp. 423–28).

Davis, Ralph H. C. *A History of Medieval Europe.* New York: Longman, 1957.

Dawson, Christopher. *The Making of Europe.* New York: Macmillan, 1932.

Einhard. *The Life of Charlemagne.* Trans. Samuel Epes Turner. Ann Arbor: University of Michigan Press, 1960.

Heer, Friedrich. *The Medieval World.* New York: Praeger, 1969.

Herrin, Judith. *The Formation of Christendom.* Princeton: Princeton University Press, 1987.

Knowles, David, and Dimitri Oblensky. *The Middle Ages.* New York: Paulist Press, 1983.

Morris, C. *The Papal Monarchy: The Western Church from 1050 to 1250.* New York: Oxford University Press, 2001.

Readings in Church History. Colman Barry, O.S.B., ed. Westminster, Md.: Newman Press, 1960.

The Shorter Cambridge Medieval History. Charles Previte-Orton, ed. Cambridge: Cambridge University Press, 1975.

Southern, Richard W. *Western Society and the Church in the Middle Ages.* Harmondsworth, England: Penguin Books, 1985. Very helpful in getting a general picture of the period.

Ullmann, Walter. *The Individual and Society in the Middle Ages.* Baltimore: Johns Hopkins University Press, 1966. Shows the roots of modern Europe and its unity.

Ullmann, Walter. *The Growth of Papal Government in the Middle Ages.* 2nd ed. London: Bradford & Dickens, 1962.

10. THE POPES AND FRANKS JOIN FORCES TO CREATE A NEW UNITY: CHRISTENDOM

Brooke, Christopher. *Monasteries of the World.* New York: Crescent Books, 1982. Benedict's rule reflected the peculiar Roman genius for governing in its brevity, flexibility, and moderation. The rule gave great authority to the abbot (elected for life), who nevertheless was encouraged to seek to be loved rather than feared. As David Knowles says, Benedict's rule was never "imposed by authority and made its way slowly by virtue of its excellence."

The "economic implications of their attitude towards work were important. Idleness was the enemy of the soul." Time was set aside for manual labor, which contributed to the idea of the dignity of labor. The monasteries were self-supporting and they contributed to "capital accumulation and so to long-term growth of the European economy."

The salvaging of ancient culture was another great contribution of the monks. Since they had to read to be able to pray the divine office, they needed schools, books, and libraries. They devoted much time to copying manuscripts since it was the only way of reproducing books before the age of printing; moreover, copying was considered a form of manual labor. Without their assiduous labor, it seems, we would have lost most of classical Latin literature.

Bullough, D. *The Age of Charlemagne.* London: ELEK, 1973.

Dudden, Frederick H. *Gregory the Great, His Place in History and in Thought.* New York: Russell & Russell, 1967.

Early Medieval Society. Sylvia L. Thrupp, ed. New York: Appleton, Century-Crofts, 1967.

Ganshof, François Louis. *Frankish Institutions Under Charlemagne.* Providence, R.I.: University Press of New England, 1968.

———. *Feudalism.* New York: Harper & Row, 1964.

Hanson, R. P. C. *Saint Patrick: His Origins and Career.* New York: Oxford University Press, 1968. A reassessment of J. Bury's monumental life written at the turn of the century. Holds Bury placed too much faith in Old Irish Annals and believed in the late Irish tradition of a High-King in Ireland at the time of Patrick. Hanson also rejects the long-held view that Patrick was educated in Gaul and was a monk there. The Latin of Patrick's *Con-*

fessions and *Letter to Coroticus* he views as an archaic Vulgate Latin of Britain and not Gaul. No reason in fact for believing Patrick ever spent time in Gaul.

Lehane, B. *The Quest of Three Abbots.* New York: Viking Press, 1968. Three founders of Irish monasticism: Brendan in Scotland and Wales; Columba in Ireland and Scotland; Columbanus in Gaul, Belgium, and Italy, and elsewhere.

Markus, R. A. *Gregory the Great and His World.* New York: Cambridge University Press, 1997. This major scholar notes that the great work of Dudden has been in many respects outdated by the last ninety-three years of scholarship. As the reviewer in the *Journal of Early Christian Studies* (vol. 7, no. 3, fall 1999) points out, one of the leading ideas of Markus (further expanded in *The End of Ancient Christianity)* is that a major intellectual and spiritual shift occurred in the Latin West between A.D. 400 and 600 that forever separated the Christianity of St. Augustine and John Cassian from that of Gregory the Great. "The basic change had to do with a contraction of the intermediate realm of the 'secular,' the realm of religious neutrality that separates the 'sacred' from the 'profane.' " Thus Augustine and Gregory lived in two different worlds, thanks to an emphasis on the ascetic in Gregory's time that depreciated the ancient, non-Christian culture that had so much influence on Augustine's thought.

Noble, Thomas F. X. *The Republic of St. Peter: The Birth of the Papal State, 680–825.* Philadelphia: University of Pennsylvania Press, 1984. Noble says that Pepin had nothing to do with the foundation of the state, for the foundation process was long since complete by Pepin's day. In fact, the papal states emerged in the process, led by the popes, by which Italy disconnected itself from Byzantium.

Oakley, Francis. *The Medieval Experience: Foundations of Western Cultural Singularity.* Toronto: University of Toronto Press, 1988.

Richard, Jeffrey. *The Popes and the Papacy in the Early Middle Ages, 476–752.* Boston: Routledge & Kegan Paul, 1979.

Southern, Richard W. *The Making of the Middle Ages.* New Haven: Yale University Press, 1967.

Wallace-Hadrill, J. M. *The Frankish Church.* New York: Oxford University Press, 2001.

11. HILDEBRAND'S REVOLUTION MAKES THE POPES SUPREME IN CHRISTENDOM

Barlow, Frank. *Thomas Becket.* Berkeley: University of California Press, 1990.

Berman, Harold J. *Law and Revolution: The Formation of the Western Legal Tradition.* Cambridge: Harvard University Press, 1983. According to Berman, the Gregorian Reform was the first and the most "radical" and pervasive of the major revolutions that have shaped our civilization. (The other five are, supposedly, the Russian, the French, the American, the English [1640–90], and the German [Protestant Reformation]). "Revolution" is defined as a fundamental, rapid, violent, and lasting change in the whole social system, which produces a new code of law. This Papal Revolution (1075–1122) enabled the papacy to shake itself free from the dominance of the secular monarchs and become an autonomous, transnational power. Canon Law, its main weapon in the struggle, provided the groundwork for all modern Western legal systems.

According to Berman, the Western legal code was rooted in Germanic folk law and classical Roman law, but it only became a coherent system of its own with the development of canon law in the eleventh and twelfth centuries. Our Western legal tradition, as he points out, derived some of its notable features—such as greater recognition of women's rights and a more humane treatment of slaves—from Christian theology.

The development of secular law was much influenced by the effort of the monarchs to consolidate and expand their authority. In doing so they often found common law an obstacle.

Secular law, though it developed as a counterpoise to canon law, borrowed many of its assumptions and, more important, its structure and methodology.

"In his profound and searching conclusion, Berman criticizes the theories of law advanced by Max Weber and Karl Marx as too unidimensional. They see law as an instrument of domination designed to impose the will of the lawmakers, but it is more than that. Law is also an expression of moral standards as understood by human reason, and it is 'an outgrowth of custom, a product of the historically rooted values and norms of the community'—the result of many generations of trial and error. Thus it has in it both elements that serve and elements that protect against the interests of the ruling class. It both grows upwards from the customs and experiences of a whole society (and of earlier societies) and moves downward from the values and intentions of the current rulers of that society. Law can help to integrate the two and to bring into being a new resolution of antithetical forces. Thus it can embody, ameliorate and codify the monumental clashes—the revolutions—of Western history." Dean M. Kelley's review in *The Christian Century,* 11/14/84, pp. 1071–72.

Bridge, Antony. *The Crusades.* New York: Franklin Watts, 1982.

Brundage, James A. *The Crusades: Motives and Achievements.* Boston: Heath, 1964.

Cowdrey, Edward John. *The Cluniacs and the Gregorian Reform.* Oxford: Clarendon Press, 1970.

The Investiture Controversy: Issues, Ideals and Results. Karl F. Morrison, ed. Huntington, N.Y.: R. E. Krieger, 1971.

McDonald, J. *Hildebrand.* Merrick, N.Y.: Richwood, 1976.

Morris, C. *The Papal Monarchy: The Western Church from 1050–1250.* New York: Oxford University Press, 1991.

Tellenbach, Gerd. *Church, State and Christian Society at the Time of the Investiture Contest.* Oxford: Basil Blackwell, 1940.

Tierney, Brian. *Crisis of Church and State, 1050–1300.* Toronto: University of Toronto Press, 1976.

Winston, Richard. *Thomas Becket.* New York: Knopf, 1967. A short, critical, accurate account fair to all parties and free of absurd theories about the archbishop's conversion or character. Becket portrayed as able, compelling, sincere, but a difficult personality at odds with an efficient, energetic, not unreasonable, but overimpetuous king.

12. THE PAPAL MONARCHY AT ITS ZENITH

Boase, Thomas. *Boniface VIII.* Wilmington, Del: International Academic Publishers, 1979.

The Cambridge Medieval History. Vol. VI. New York: Cambridge University Press, 1936.

Pennington, Kenneth. *Popes and Bishops: The Papal Monarchy in the Twelfth and Thirteenth Centuries*. Philadelphia: University of Pennsylvania Press, 1984.

13. THE EASTERN SCHISM

Attwater, Donald. *The Eastern Churches*, Vol. 2. Milwaukee: Bruce, 1962.

Hussey, J. M. *The Orthodox Church in the Byzantine Empire*. New York: Oxford University Press, 1990. A superlative treatment.

Dvornik, Francis. *Byzantium and the Roman Primacy*. New York: Fordham University Press, 1966. Probably the best general treatment of the issues involved in the schism between the Eastern and Western churches.

———. *The Photian Schism: History and Legend*. Cambridge; Cambridge University Press, 1948.

Lossky, V. *The Mystical Theology of the Eastern Church*. Greenwood, S.C.: Attic Press, 1973. As Kallistos Ware says, "The most precious gift that Orthodoxy has been able to make to the Christian West in our own time has certainly been its tradition of mystical theology— its understanding of silence and the prayer of the heart" *(Oxford Illustrated History of Christianity*, p. 159). One might add that the spirit of mystical prayer is credited in large part with sustaining the faith of the Greek Orthodox during four centuries of Turkish oppression.

The Philokalia: The Complete Text. Compiled by St. Nikodimos of the Holy Mountain and St. Makarios of Corinth. Boston: Faber & Faber, 1979– (5 vols. when completed). This book played a great role in fortifying the faith of the Greek Orthodox during the Turkish period.

Meyendorff, John. *Byzantium and the Rise of Russia: A Study of Byzantine-Russian Relations in the Fourteenth Century*. Crestwood, N.Y.: St. Vladimir's Seminary Press, 1997. A scholarly study. Russian Orthodoxy acceded to the hegemony of Orthodoxy after the fall of Constantinople.

Obolensky, D. *The Byzantine Commonwealth: Eastern Europe, 500–1453*. Crestwood, N.Y.: St. Vladimir's Seminary Press, 1982.

Runciman, Steven. *Byzantine Civilization*. London: Arnold Press, 1975.

———. *The Eastern Schism: A Study of the Papacy and the Eastern Churches during the XI and XII Centuries*. New York: AMS Press, 1983.

Sherrard, P. *Athos: The Mountain of Silence*. New York: Oxford University Press, 1988. The first monastic settlement of which there is reliable evidence is the monastery of the Lavra, founded by St. Athanasius in 961 on Mount Athos. There are now twenty virtually autonomous monasteries on the Chalcidice Peninsula. The author of this book visited Mount Athos in 2001 and marveled at the dedication and spirituality of the monks. But as a Roman Catholic he was definitely treated as a Christian "in error" and in one monastery was segregated from the residents in various ways. The monks are definitely not enamored of current ecumenism.

Ware, Kallistos. *The Orthodox Church*. New York: Viking Press, 1984.

14. CHURCH AND SOCIETY IN WESTERN CHRISTENDOM

PART I: MEDIEVAL ART

A world in itself and a glorious chapter of medieval history, but beyond the scope of this book. The new architectural style called Gothic originated in the middle of the twelfth century in the Île-de-France at the Abbey of St. Denis under its abbot, Suger. In the following century a number of great bishops of northern France vied with each other in erecting vast cathedrals at Chartres, Paris, Orléans, Amiens, Sens, and other sites. The new style featured wide portals, high clerestories, soaring buttresses, pointed arches, ribbed vaulting, rose windows, and magnificent facades teeming with sculpted images that revealed the whole panoply of medieval life and culture. In the contest to erect larger and higher edifices, the bishops strained the resources of their sees and drove the architectural ingenuity of Europe to the limit. These great buildings in the shape of a cross embraced the largest amount of interior space ever seen in the West. The new French style swiftly spread to other parts of Europe, even to Italy, which had originated the earlier Romanesque style. Nothing so eloquently conveys a sense of the spiritual hopes and dreams of the medieval soul than these mighty buildings, which often took centuries to complete and which required an incredible outlay of money and labor. Medieval artisans poured the very best of themselves into the creation of these miracles of beauty.

Several excellent introductions:

Gimpel, Jean. *The Cathedral Builders.* London: Cresset Library, 1988.

Panofsky, Erwin. *Gothic Architecture and Scholasticism.* Reprint, New York: New American Library, 1994.

Temko, Allan. *Notre Dame of Paris.* New York: W. W. Norton: 1994.

Wilson, K. Christopher. *The Gothic Cathedral: The Architecture of the Great Church, 1130–1530.* New York: Thames & Hudson, 1990.

PART II: GENERAL WORKS

Brundage, James A. *Law; Sex, and Society in Medieval Europe.* Chicago: University of Chicago Press, 1987.

Cohen, Jeremy. *Living Letters of the Law: Ideas of the Jew in Medieval Christianity.* Berkeley: University of California Press, 1999. An excellent overview of the changing position of the Jew in Western Christendom in the fourteenth century. "It contributes greatly to our understanding of the medieval growth of Western anti-Judaism" *(CHR:* Shofar: An Interdisciplinary Journal of Jewish Studies; Vol. 20; Winter 2001).

Deansley, Margaret. *A History of the Medieval Church.* London: Methuen, 1954.

Frassetto, Michael, and David Blanks, eds. *Western Views of Islam in Medieval and Early Modern Europe: Perception of Other.* New York: St. Martin's Press, 1999. The editors claim that the European Christian understanding of the Islamic world was more complex than is often recognized.

Hamilton, B. *Religion in the Medieval West.* London: Edward Arnold, 1986.

Histoire d'l'Église, Augustin Fliche and Victor Martin, eds. Paris: Bloud & Gay, 1959.

Le Goff, Jacques. *The Birth of Purgatory.* Chicago: University of Chicago Press, 1984. Argues that the idea of purgatory only took real hold in the West in the second half of twelfth century.

Lewis, C. S. *The Discarded Image: An Introduction to Medieval and Renaissance Literature.* Cambridge: Cambridge University Press, 1967.

Minorita, Nicolaus. *Chronica: Documentation on Pope John XXII, Michael of Cesena and the Poverty of Christ with Summaries in English: A Source Book.* Edited by Gedeon Gall and David Flood. St. Bonaventure, N.Y.: Franciscan Institute Publications, 1996. An account of the conflict that rent the Franciscan Order in the fourteenth century. The problem of how absolute the poverty of the order should be pitted the "Spirituals" against the more moderate members. In 1317 Pope John XXII decided against the Spirituals, many of whom defied the ruling and were executed by the Inquisition. The controversy arose again in 1321 over the question of whether Christ and the apostles held property. The general of the order, Michael Cesena, opposed the Pope's affirmative answer to the question and fled into exile with William of Ockham. These sterile polemics gravely weakened the order during that century. Henceforth the Franciscans have gone through a number of similar crises but have had many periods of renewal that have made them a great spiritual force in the Church.

Mollat, Michel. *The Poor in the Middle Ages.* New Haven: Yale University Press, 1986.

Moorman, John Richard. *A History of the Franciscan Order from Its Origins to the Year 1517.* Oxford: Clarendon Press, 1968. The best general history in English of the early Franciscan centuries.

Oakley, Francis. *The Medieval Experience: Foundations of Western Cultural Singularity.* Toronto: University of Toronto Press, 1988. While general opinion sees Ockham's effect on theology as "devastating," Richard Lebrun points out how Ockham's approach provided the philosophical foundations of modern empirical science, which is based on observation and experiment rather than deduction.

Powers, Eileen. *Medieval People.* New York: Methuen, 1963.

Read, Piers Paul. *The Templars.* London: Weidenfeld & Nicolson, 1999. Popular history in the best sense. It relies on secondary sources but the author uses his own insights as a novelist to interpret the conflicting judgments of historians. He begins with the foundation of the Templars, whose rule was drafted, it seems, by St. Bernard. The Templars played a prominent part in the Crusades, which they carried out with religious fervor. The Crusades are sometimes presented as early examples of unprovoked imperialist aggression by the West, but Read points out that they were a response to the aggressive Muslim expansion, which had swallowed up the Holy Land, the North African coast, and most of Spain, as well as threatening the survival of the Byzantine Christian empire in the East. Read notes that the real reason for the Templars' destruction by Philip the Fair was their wealth and their independence.

Shinners, John, and William J. Dohar. *Pastors and the Care of Souls in Medieval England.* Notre Dame, Ind.: University of Notre Dame Press, 1998.

Tellenbach, Gerd. *Church, State and Christian Society at the Time of the Investiture Contest.* Translated by R. F. Bennett. Oxford: Basil Blackwell, 1940. A solid study that has stood the test of time.

Tawney, Richard. *Religion and the Rise of Capitalism.* London: John Murray, 1926.

15. THE ARISTOTELIAN INVASION

Brooke, Christopher. *The Twelfth-Century Renaissance.* New York: Harcourt, Brace & World, 1973.

Chenu, Marie Dominique. *Nature, Man, and Society in the Twelfth Century: Essays on the New Theological Perspectives in the Latin West.* Chicago: University of Chicago Press, 1968.

————. *Toward Understanding St. Thomas.* Chicago: Regnery, 1964.

Ferruolo, Stephen C. *The Origins of the University: The Schools of Paris and Their Critics, 1100–1215.* Palo Alto: Stanford University Press, 1985. This has been called an important contribution to the history of ideas.

Gilson, Étienne Henry. *A History of Christian Philosophy in the Middle Ages.* New York: Random House, 1956

Haskins, Charles Homer. *The Rise of the Universities.* Ithaca, N.Y.: Cornell University Press, 1969.

Kenny, Anthony. *Aquinas.* Notre Dame, Ind.: University of Notre Dame Press, 1980.

Knowles, David. *The Evolution of Medieval Thought.* New York: Random House, 1964. A masterpiece by one of the masters of our time.

Leff, Gordon. *Medieval Thought: St. Augustine to Ockham.* Atlantic Highlands, N.J.: Humanities Press, 1983.

Pelikan, Jaroslav. *The Growth of Medieval Theology (600–1300).* Chicago: University of Chicago Press, 1978.

Semaan, Khalil I., ed. *Islam and the Medieval West: Aspects of Intercultural Relations.* Albany, N.Y.: SUNY Press, 1980. Roundtable discussions and essays by an international group of scholars, including Muslims.

Strayer, Joseph R. *On the Medieval Origins of the Modern State.* Princeton, N.J.: Princeton University Press, 1970.

Wieruszowski, Helene. *The Medieval University.* Princeton, N.J.: Van Nostrand, 1966.

PART THREE: THE UNMAKING OF CHRISTENDOM, A.D. 1300–1650

GENERAL WORKS

Acton, John E. D. *Lectures on Modern History.* Gloucester, Mass.: Peter Smith, 1975.

Dawson, Christopher. *The Dividing of Christendom.* New York: Sheed & Ward, 1965.

Ferguson, Wallace F. *Europe in Transition, 1300–1520.* Boston: Houghton Mifflin, 1962.

Green, Vivian Hubert. *The Renaissance and Reformation, 1450–1660.* New York: St. Martin's Press, 1964.

Guide to Historical Literature. Board of editors: George Howe, chairman. New York: Macmillan, 1961. A new version of a most useful work.

Hsia, R. Po Chia. *The World of Catholic Renewal, 1540–1770.* New York: Cambridge University Press, 1998. A long overdue study filling the gap of three decades of research and praised by the reviewers. Some regretted, however, its date of 1540 as the beginning of renewal. But it lays Dicken's work to rest.

Leff, Gordon. *Heresy in the Later Middle Ages: The Relation of Heterodoxy to Dissent, c. 1250–1450.* New York: Barnes & Noble, 1967. The heretics felt a conflict between the evangelical values and the morals of the traditional Church; their heresies were not the fruit of incredulity but the desire for reform. Neither Wycliffe nor Hus wanted to do away completely with the visible Church.

Miskimin, H. A. *The Economy of Early Renaissance Europe, 1300–1460.* Englewood Cliffs, N.J.: Prentice-Hall, 1969. A demographic crisis, intensified by the Black Death, ended the economic boom of the commercial revolution soon after 1300. The ensuing decline lasted until 1500, when another upsurge was generated. During the years of stagnation, profits in agriculture declined. The rural cultivators no longer had the cash to purchase the commodities of craftsmen; in addition, the manufacturing sector succumbed to the temptation to reap large profits from the luxury trade. While the Black Death enriched the survivors with increased per capita wealth, a live-for-the-day mentality drove them to conspicuous consumption rather than investing in business.

Morrall, John B. *Political Thought in Medieval Times.* Toronto: University of Toronto Press, 1980.

The New Cambridge Modern History. Cambridge: Cambridge University Press, 1947f.

Nichols, James H. *Corporate Worship in the Reformed Tradition.* Philadelphia: Westminster Press, 1968.

Readings in Church History. Colman Barry, O.S.B., ed., Westminster, Md.: Newman Press, 1965.

Tuchman, Barbara W. *A Distant Mirror: The Calamitous Fourteenth Century.* New York: Knopf, 1978. This is popular history at its best.

Young, Karl. *The Drama of the Medieval Church.* Oxford: Clarendon Press, 1967 (1933).

16. THE DECLINE OF THE PAPAL MONARCHY

Boase, Thomas R. *Boniface VIII.* London: Constable 1933.

Houseley, Norman. *The Italian Crusades: The Papal-Angevin Alliance and the Crusades Against Christian Lay Powers, 1254–1343.* New York: Oxford University Press, 1982. Argues against the common opinion that these crusades damaged the papacy's moral authority and constituted a factor in the decline of its influence. His study is based on a careful examination of the papal registers, where he found few expressions of indignation at the papal policy nor any weakening of the spiritual authority of the papacy.

Oakley, Francis. *The Western Church in the Late Middle Ages.* Ithaca, N.Y.: Cornell University Press, 1979.

Runciman, Steven. *The Sicilian Vespers: A History of the Mediterranean World in the Later XIII Century.* New York: Cambridge University Press, 1982. Runciman sees the temporal politics of the papacy as the "progressive suicide of the grandest conception of the Middle Ages—the universal papal monarchy." The Sicilian Vespers marked one of the grand turning points of history: the papacy humiliated, the empire of Constantinople consolidated, the king of Aragon installed in Sicily, the way opened for new humiliations—and more profound ones—for the Holy See.

Strayer, Joseph R. *On the Origins of the Modern State.* Princeton, N.J.: Princeton University Press, 1970.

Thomson, John A. F. *Popes and Princes, 1417–1517; Politics and Polity in the Late Medieval Church.* Boston: Allen & Unwin, 1980.

Tierney, Brian. *Religion, Law and the Growth of Constitutional Thought, 1150–1650.* New York: Cambridge University Press, 1982. Traces the origin and development of the theory of government by consensus in the writings of the main thinkers, Marsilius and Ockham. The tardy Latin translation of Aristotle's *Politics* provided a major stimulus, and by the fourteenth century the theory of consensual government was well established. Tierney analyzes the ways governmental powers were limited. The Great Schism and the conciliarist movement generated some new ideas, while Nicholas of Cusa saw the Church as a kind of ecclesiastical federation. Modern constitutional theory, according to Tierney, is founded upon the debate over the nature of Church government, while he sees the theory of a mixed constitution with three forms of government rooted in Aquinas.

Trexler, Richard C. *The Spiritual Power: Republican Florence under Interdict.* Leiden: Brill, 1974. Historians generally claim that by the beginning of the fourteenth century, papal censures such as excommunication and interdict were rapidly losing their force. But the author shows how the papal interdict imposed on Florence from March 1376 to July 1378 (when Cardinal Albornoz's campaign to restore papal authority in the papal states met with Florentine resistance) caused Florence severe economic problems and moreover produced in its citizens a serious crisis of conscience and resulted in intense anxiety and guilt.

Van Cleve, Thomas Curtis. *The Emperor Frederick II of Hohenstaufen, Immutator Mundi.* New York: Oxford University Press, 1972. Basically in agreement with the fundamental work of Ernst Kantorowicz. For both, Frederick was a true genius excelling not only in statecraft but also in scholarship and patronage of the arts, while the villains of the story were the Popes Gregory IX and Innocent IV who opposed Frederick's "world empire" with equally ruthless schemes for world dominion based on their claim to *"plenitudo potestatis"* (total power).

17. THE PAPACY SURVIVES THE GREAT SCHISM AND PUTS DOWN CONCILIARISM

Filastre's Diary. L. Loomis, ed. New York: Columbia University Press, 1961.

Gill, Joseph. *The Council of Florence.* Cambridge: Cambridge University Press, 1959.

McFarlane, Kenneth B., *John Wycliffe and the Beginnings of English Non-conformity.* Mystic, Conn.: Lawrence Verry, 1952. The Lollards originally were followers of Wycliffe, though eventually the term encompassed anyone seriously critical of the Church who accepted the Bible alone as authority and rejected transubstantiation, celibacy, and indulgences. The authority of the priest depended on his morality. The Lollards were heavily persecuted but they paved the way for the English Reformation.

Partner, Peter: *The Lands of St. Peter: The Papal State in the Middle Ages and the Early Renaissance.* Berkeley: University of California Press, 1972.

Pernoud, R. *Joan of Arc.* New York: Grove Press, 1961.

Renouard, Yves. *The Avignon Papacy, 1305–1403.* Hamden, Conn.: Archon Books, 1970.

Spinka, M. *John Hus: A Biography.* New York: Princeton University Press, 1998. Hus, the rector of Charles University and a devoted disciple of Wycliffe, was excommunicated by John XXIII in 1412 and appealed to the Council of Constance against the Curia. At Constance, his safe conduct from Emperor Sigismund was disregarded and he was burned at the stake in 1415, becoming a national martyr. The Hussites violently protested and laid down a program of reform which anticipated the Reformation. The movement left a lasting legacy in Bohemia and Moravia.

Tierney, Brian. *Foundations of the Conciliar Theory.* London: Cambridge University Press, 1968.

———. *Ockham: The Conciliar Theory and the Canonists.* Philadelphia: Fortress Press, 1971.

———. *Origins of Papal Infallibility, 1150–1350.* New York: E. J. Brill, 1988. Throws considerable light on the present debate about papal infallibility.

18. THE CHURCH FAILS TO REFORM ITSELF IN TIME

Gilmore, Myron P. *The World of Humanism, 1453–1517.* New York: Harper & Row, 1952.

Huizinga, Johan. *The Waning of the Middle Ages.* London: Penguin Books, 1955. The classic study of the Renaissance.

Lambert, Malcolm D. *Medieval Heresy: Popular Movements from Bogomil to Hus.* London: E. Arnold, 1977.

Pernoud., R. *Joan of Arc.* New York: Grove Press, 1961. During the Hundred Years' War between England and France and the civil war between the House of Orléans and Burgundy, Joan (1412–31), a peasant girl, felt called by celestial visions to save France. She was able to persuade the yet uncrowned Charles VII of the House of Orléans to allow her to lead an expedition to the besieged city of Orléans. Inspired by her leadership, the troops relieved the city and Charles was crowned at Reims on July 17, 1429, with Joan at his side. But captured by the Burgundians and sold to the English, she was tried by the Bishop of Beauvais, Pierre Cauchon, for witchcraft and heresy and was burned at Rouen. She was rehabilitated by Pope Callistus in 1456 and was declared a saint in 1920.

The Medieval Church: Success or Failure? Bernard S. Bachrach, ed. New York: Holt, Rinehart and Winston, 1972.

Ozment, Steven. *The Age of Reform, 1250–1550: An Intellectual and Religious History of Late Medieval and Reformation Europe.* New Haven: Yale University Press, 1980.

19. LUTHER SPLITS CHRISTENDOM

Bainton, Roland H. *Erasmus of Christendom.* New York: Scribner, 1969.

———. *Here I Stand: A Life of Martin Luther.* Göttingen: Vandenhoeck & Ruprecht, 1980. One of the classic studies but somewhat outdated.

Cameron, Euan. *The European Reformation.* Oxford: Clarendon Press, 1991. According to the reviewer in *CHR* this work sets a new standard for one-volume surveys of the Protestant Reformation and should drive all others from the field. Using extremely rich documentation the author discusses every issue with the best scholarship available and concludes that "the medieval church was neither monstrously decadent nor arrogantly unresponsive to the needs of the people." It was just too bureaucratically bloated to respond to a myriad of critics who attacked it on every front. It faced two formidable forces: popular anticlericalism and the secular powers that wanted to bring the church under control. The study highlights the paradoxes of a "reformation" that began by attacking ritual codes of piety and ended up installing a more severe, rational, and demanding code of conduct than ever expected by the medieval Church; it began by tearing down the exalted status of the priesthood but ended by creating a more evenly professional, highly quali-fied dedicated body of religious missionaries than had been heretofore seen; it began by attacking an elaborate, recondite theology in the name of "the simple Gospel" and ended by creating a complex body of teachings even more doctrinaire than medieval Scholasti-cism. In the final analysis Cameron believes the Reformation was the first instance of the use of mass politics to bring about change on the basis of a simple ideology. The reform-ers took a single core idea, propagandized it through public discussion, then tore down the whole fabric of medieval religion by subjecting it to the solvent power of this one idea. They first simplified then completely rebuilt the structures of Western Christianity.

Chadwick, Owen. *The Reformation.* Harmondsworth, England: Penguin Books, 1986.

Dickens, Arthur G. *Reformation and Society in Sixteenth Century Europe.* New York: Harcourt Brace Jovanovich, 1979.

Documents Illustrative of the Continental Reformation. B. J. Kidd, ed. Oxford: Clarendon Press, 1911. A most useful collection.

Erikson, Erik H. *Young Man Luther: A Study in Psychoanalysis and History.* New York: Nor-ton, 1958.

Haile, Harry Gerald. *Luther: An Experiment in Biography.* Princeton, N.J.: Princeton Univer-sity Press, 1983.

Hillerbrand, Hans J. *Men and Ideas in the Sixteenth Century.* Chicago: Rand McNally, 1969.

Lecler, Joseph, S.J. *Toleration and the Reformation.* New York: Association Press, 1960. A solid ecumenical study of Christendom's struggle to unburden itself of its unholy practice of persecution.

Lortz, Joseph. The Reformation in Germany. 2 vols. New York: Herder & Herder, 1968. Lortz was one of the pioneers in forging a Catholic ecumenical interpretation of Luther.

Luther's Works. Helmut Lehmann and Harold Grimm, eds. Philadelphia: Muhlenberg Press, 1957.

Mackinnon, J. *Luther and the Reformation.* 4 vols. New York: Longmans Green, 1925–30.

McSorley, Harry. *Luther: Right or Wrong?* New York: Newman Press, 1960.

Oberman, Heiko Augustinus. *The Harvest of Medieval Theology: Gabriel Biel and Late Me-dieval Nominalism.* 3rd ed. Durham, N.C.: Labyrinth Press, 1983.

Pfürtner, Stephan. *Luther and Aquinas on Salvation.* New York: Sheed & Ward, 1964.

Reardon, Bernard. *Religious Thought in the Reformation.* New York: Longman, 1981.

The Reformation: A Narrative History Related by Contemporary Observers and Participants. Hans J. Hillerbrand, ed. Grand Rapids, Mich.: Baker Book House, 1978.

Rupp, Gordon. *The Righteousness of God.* London: Hodder & Stoughton, 1953.

Spitz, Lewis W. *The Protestant Reformation, 1517–1559.* New York: Harper & Row, 1985. Praised by reviewers as ecumenical.

Tavard, George. *Justification: An Ecumenical Study.* New York: Paulist Press, 1983.

Todd, John M. *Luther: A Life.* New York: Crossroad, 1982. Given high marks by reviewer Jared Wicks, S.J., in the *Catholic Historical Review* 69 (October 1983), p. 603. But Wicks notes how Todd overlooks the importance of Luther's two small catechisms of 1529 and his Smalkald Articles.

Wicks, Jared, S.J. "Roman Reactions to Luther: The First Year (1518)." *Catholic Historical Review* 69 (October 1983), pp. 521–62. Very helpful in explaining why Luther was willing to submit to the Pope in January of 1518 but unwilling by November 1518. Rome's inept handling of the affair was a crucial factor.

20. CALVIN MAKES PROTESTANTISM AN INTERNATIONAL MOVEMENT

Bossy, John. The *English Catholic Community 1570–1850*. Oxford, 1976. A landmark study that challenged the long-standing thesis of David Matthew's *Catholicism in England, 1535–1935: A Portrait of a Minority, Its Culture and Tradition* (London, New York: Longmans, Green, 1936). Against Matthew's idea of a continuity with pre-Reformation tradition, Bossy contended that post-Reformation Catholicism was built around a totally new, separated "minority sect," gathered by Jesuits and other missionaries around gentry households concentrating on the sacramental life. But then Christopher Haigh (see below) challenged Bossy's view and argued from an examination of Lancashire that a recusant, consciously separated community fostered by Marian priests was in place well before the arrival of the Jesuits and Seminarists. Haigh's revision of Bossy's argument has been a byproduct of revisions of the English Reformation itself, no longer presented as an awesome sweeping force but more hesitant, encountering much resistance—a view that has been buttressed by Eamon Duffy's work (see below)

Calvin, John. *Institutes of the Christian Religion*. Trans. Henry Beveridge. 2 vols. Grand Rapids, Mich.: Wm. B. Eerdmans, 1957.

Chambers, Raymond W. *Thomas More*. London and New York: Harcourt Brace & Co., 1935.

Culkin, Gerard. *The English Reformation*. London: Paternoster Publications, 1954.

Davies, Horton. *Worship and Theology in England: From Cranmer to Hooker 1534–1603*. Princeton, N.J.: Princeton University Press, 1970.

Dickens, A. G. *Lollards and Protestants in the Diocese of York: 1509–1558*. London: Hambledon Press, 1983.

Duffy, Eamon. *The Stripping of the Altars: Traditional Religion in England c. 1400–1580*. New Haven: Yale University Press, 1992. Called a mighty and momentous book, it has forced scholars to rethink their view of the Reformation. Based on an exhaustive study of archival, archaeological, and other primary sources, it demonstrates that late medieval Catholicism was not at all in decay but a strong and vigorous tradition.

Elton, G. R. *Reform and Reformation: England 1509–1558*. Cambridge, Mass.: Harvard University Press, 1977.

Haigh, Christopher. *English Reformations: Religion, Politics and Society Under the Tudors*. Oxford: Clarendon Press, 1993. Argues that Catholics who conformed nevertheless assisted the survival and continuity of the Marian faith by keeping alive Catholic traditions and practices (altars, images, holy water, rosary beads, and signs of the cross), thus preparing a body of potential recusants who could gravitate toward the separated community once missionaries began their revival. He also faults the Jesuit missionaries for concentrating on the gentry around London and neglecting the richer opportunities in the north, where recusancy was flowering.

Hughes, Philip. *The English Reformation*. 3 vols. New York: Macmillan; 3rd vol., London: Hollis & Carter, 1954.

————. *A Popular History of the Reformation.* Garden City, N.Y.: Hanover House, 1957.

An Introduction to Mennonite History: A Popular History of the Anabaptists and the Mennonites. Cornelius J. Dyck, ed. Scottdale, Pa.: Herald Press, 1981.

McDonnell, Kilian. *John Calvin. The Church and the Eucharist.* Ann Arbor, Mich.: University of Michigan (Microfilm Books on Demand), 1967. Argues that Calvin's conception of the Eucharist formed the core of his concept of the Church. His opposition to Roman Catholic doctrine was largely a function of his dissatisfaction with Roman Eucharistic theory and practice.

McGrath, Patrick. *Papists and Puritans Under Elizabeth I.* New York: Walker, 1967. It was the Acts of Uniformity and Supremacy of 1559, the author says, that definitively rejected allegiance to the Holy See. The Anglican Church was thereby established over a people the majority of whom were still Catholic in sympathy and in practice, while a flaming minority of extremists, formed at Zurich and Frankfurt, hoped to move Elizabeth's church toward the Geneva model.

McNeil, John T. *The History and Character of Calvinism.* New York: Oxford University Press, 1954.

Walsham, Alexandra. *Church Papists: Catholicism, Conformity and Confessional Polemic in Early Modern England.* Rochester, N.Y.: Boydell Press, 1993. Walsham focuses not on the Catholic gentry but on the poorer rural Catholics who had to solve their conscience problems without the easy access to the priests the conforming Catholic gentry enjoyed. She thinks subsequent research might reveal further evidence of the stubbornness of the "old religion."

Wendel, François. *Calvin: The Origins and Development of His Thought.* Durham, N.C.: Labyrinth Press, 1987.

Williams, George Hunston. *The Radical Reformers.* Philadelphia: Westminster Press, 1962. An important study.

21. THE CATHOLIC CHURCH RECOVERS ITS SPIRITUAL ÉLAN

Bangert, William. *A History of the Society of Jesus.* St. Louis: Institute of Jesuit Sources, 1972.

Bireley, Robert. *The Refashioning of Catholicism, 1450–1700: A Reassessment of the Counter Reformation.* Washington, D.C.: Catholic University of America Press, 1999. Argues, like O'Malley, that this period of Catholic renewal was not a mere reaction to Protestant challenge. Goes beyond institutional change to show the importance of lay piety in the renewal.

Brodrick, James, S.J. *The Origins of the Jesuits.* Chicago: Loyola University Press, 1986.

Burns, Edward McNall. *The Counter Reformation.* Princeton, N.J.: Van Nostrand, 1964.

The Catholic Reformation: Savonarola to Ignatius; Reform in the Church, 1495–1540. John C. Olin, ed. New York: Harper & Row, 1969. A fine collection of documents.

Daniel-Rops, Henri. *The Catholic Reformation.* New York: Dutton, 1962.

Delumeau, Jean. *Catholicism Between Luther and Voltaire: A New View of the Counter-Reformation.* Philadelphia: Westminster Press, 1977.

Dicken, E. W. Trueman. *The Crucible of Love: A Study of the Mysticism of St. Teresa of Jesus and St. John of the Cross.* New York: Sheed and Ward, 1963. Regarded as one of the best studies in English on the subject.

Dickens, Arthur G. *The Counter Reformation.* New York: Norton, 1979.

Evennett, Henry Outram. *The Spirit of the Counter-Reformation.* Notre Dame, Ind.: University of Notre Dame Press, 1975.

Garstein, Oskar. *Rome and the Counter Reformation.* Oslo: Universitetsforlaget, 1980.

Hallman, Barbara McClung. *Italian Cardinals, Reform, and the Church as Property.* Berkeley: University of California Press, 1985. This fascinating study of 102 Italian cardinals between 1492 and 1563 tells how they accumulated and alienated the wealth of the Church. Cardinals needed large sums of money to pay for the various expenses associated with their way of life. Most of their income came from ecclesiastical benefices (defined as a sacred office, without the care of souls to which a perpetual income is attached), which meant that any reform of the benefice system would directly affected the personal finances of the very men to whom the labors of reform were entrusted. Two factors made it necessary for the cardinals to circumvent the efforts of reformers to shut down the spigots of Church monies: the pomp and luxury central to life at the Roman court and the social needs of cardinalate families. Roman families had to build huge palaces. A tool called the regressus allowed the prelate to regain control of a benefice he had resigned when it again became vacant and thus continue the traffic in bishoprics so scandalous to the reformers. Nepotism and patronage played a large role in the alienation of Church wealth by means of a last will. Nearly 90 percent of the cardinals from 1520 to 1549 provided relatives with ecclesiastical benefices, creating 32 abbots, 148 bishops, and 20 cardinals. Men like Cardinal Savelli, who thought it would have been an evil thing if he had fathered children, saw nothing amiss about leaving large sums of Church property and money to their families. Sons of priests were banned from obtaining any benefices from their fathers, but cardinals seem to have gotten around the ban easily. A primary goal of many Italian cardinals was to found a rich legacy for the lay heir of the family. From the fifteenth century on, Church office enabled new families to emerge and intermarry with the ruling classes to form a new nobility, and patronage—the support of large numbers of servants and retainers—required big sums of money. But apparently such practices of the Church such as nepotism and patronage were regarded much differently than they would be today. The Tridentine decree seems to have had little application at the Roman court. The notion that Church office, including sacred office, was primarily a source of income was still pervasive. The pressures of this mentality deflected the reform efforts of the cardinals away from material matters, and focused them upon things spiritual: defining correct doctrine and repression of error, seeing after the education of priests, giving support to the new religious orders, founding charitable hospitals, and leading pilgrims through the holy city— and glorifying the true faith by embellishing Rome with palaces, fountains, and churches.

Hollis, Christopher. *The Jesuits. A History.* New York: Macmillan, 1968.

Janelle, Pierre. *The Catholic Reformation.* Milwaukee, Wis.: Bruce Publishing Co., 1971.

Jedin, Hubert. *A History of the Council of Trent.* London: Nelson, 1963. A monumental study by one of the great historians of the century.

O'Connell, Marvin R. *Blaise Pascal: Reasons of the Heart.* Grand Rapids, Mich.: William B.

Eerdmans, 1997. Shows that the proper context for understanding Pascal is post-Tridentine Catholicism.

John W. O'Malley. *Trent and All That: Renaming Catholicism in the Early Modern Era.* Cambridge, Mass.: Harvard University Press, 2000. In a tour de force of scholarship, the author shows how the terms "Reformation," "Counter-Reformation," "Tridentine Age," and "Age of Confessionalization" have been used as weapons in a great battle of the books that went on for four centuries. Protestant historians were victorious in being able to fasten the term Counter-Reformation in a pejorative sense on the Catholic movement after Trent. A positive view of the Catholic reform did not get a wide hearing until Hubert Jedin arrived on the scene in midcentury with his monumental *History of the Council of Trent.* Since then, interest in the period has shifted away from sterile polemics about terms and a focus on reform movements to the overall social history of the period.

Osuna, Javier. *Friends in the Lord: A Study in the Origins and Growth of Community in the Society of Jesus from St. Ignatius's Conversion to the Earliest Texts of the Constitutions. (1521–1541).* London: The Way, 1974.

Il Processo Inquisitoriale del Cardinal Giovanni Morone—Edizione Critica. Vol. I: *Il Compendium.* Massimo Firpo, ed. Rome: Istituto Storico Italiano per l'Eta Moderna e Contemporanea, 1981. The first of a multivolume publication of all the documentation on the amazing case of Giovanni Cardinal Morone, who was prosecuted by the Inquisition for heresy though he was the most able papal diplomat of his time and later led the Council of Trent to a successful conclusion. The case throws much light on the struggle within the Church between the early reformers like Morone (the evangelicals) and their more dogmatic opponents who made the Inquisition the premier congregation of the Counter-Reformation Church. Though Morone was exculpated by Pope Pius IV (1559–1565), the next Pope, Pius V, drew up this Compendium which without a trial stigmatized Morone as a heretic whose ideas must be expunged. Such an attitude set the style of Catholicism for the next four centuries.

Roth, Cecil. *The Spanish Inquisition.* New York: Norton, 1964.

Schmitt, Paul. *La Réforme catholique: Le Combat de Maldonat (1534–1583).* Paris: Beauchesne, 1985. Maldonado offers an interesting life for students of the period since his teaching and writing was contemporaneous with the triumph in Catholicism of Counter-Reformation intransigence, which succeeded in excluding the biblical humanism promoted by Erasmus, as well as the experiential element in faith, and the Protestant assertion of personal religiosity over a variety of mediating authorities and determination of norms by the hierarchy. Maldonado fell afoul of church authorities by denying revelatory status to the doctrine of the Immaculate Conception. Jared Wicks, S.J., explains his plight by the fact that Maldonado was a "product of a new style of doctrinal reflection, cultivated in Salamanca and formulated in Cano's *De locis theologicis* (1563) which fostered a refined sense of doctrinal warrants and proper instances of definition *(CHR* 73 [1987], pp. 607–9).

Searle, Graham W. *The Counter-Reformation.* Totowa, N.J.: Rowman & Littlefield, 1974.

Treasure, Geoffrey. *Mazarin: The Crisis of Absolutism in France.* New York: Routledge, 1995. Rehabilitates Mazarin.

PART FOUR: THE CHURCH IN A STATE OF SIEGE, A.D. 1650–1891

GENERAL WORKS

Brinton, Crane. *The Shaping of Modern Thought.* Englewood Cliffs, N.J.: Prentice-Hall, 1950.

The Cambridge History of the Bible: The West from the Reformation to the Present Day. S. L. Greenslade, ed. New York: Cambridge University Press, 1963.

Chadwick, Owen. *From Bossuet to Newman: The Idea of Doctrinal Development.* Cambridge: Cambridge University Press, 1957.

Readings in Church History. Colman Barry, O.S.B., ed. Westminster, Md.: Newman Press, 1965.

The Rise of Modern Europe. Walter Langer, ed. New York: Harper & Row, 1962. A multivolume study.

22. THE CHALLENGE OF THE NEW THOUGHT

Allison, H. E. *Lessing and the Enlightenment: His Philosophy of Religion and Its Relation to Eighteenth-Century Thought.* Ann Arbor, Mich.: University of Michigan Press, 1966. Generally speaking both the deists and their theological opponents agreed that the truth of revealed religion hinged on the validity or invalidity of the historical evidence for such things as miracles, prophecies, and the resurrection of Christ. In Lessing's mature thought, however, and for the first time in the eighteenth century, the validity of Christian doctrine was judged to be independent of the truth or falsity of the historical statements contained in the Bible. However, he only saw Christianity as the highest expression of religious consciousness up to that time.

Brandmüller, Walter. *Galilei und die Kirche oder das Recht auf Irrtum.* Regensburg: Verlag Friedrich Pustet, 1982. This well-known church historian focuses on Galileo's relationship to the Church. Brandmüller argues that the Church in a sense had the right to be wrong at the time in view of Galileo's failure to prove his thesis of a helio-centered universe. Indeed the arguments Galileo used were actually invalid. He admits that the Church took too literal an approach in interpreting Scripture at the time, but he argues that in exercising its God-given authority as guardian of the deposit of faith, the Church will inevitably at times adopt what some later regard as excessively conservative positions. But the Church cannot afford to take the chance of corrupting the faith by too hastily adjusting its doctrine to the changing theories of science.

Butterfield, Herbert. *The Origins of Modern Science.* New York: Macmillan, 1957.

Cattolicesimo e Lumi nel Settecento Italiano. Mario Rosa, ed. *(Italia Sacra. Studi e Documenti di Storia Ecclesiastica,* 33.) Rome: Herder Editrice e Libreria, 1981. These are papers from a congress on ecclesiastical history held at Warsaw in 1978. They show how the Catholic *Aufkärung* (Enlightenment) originated in the early eighteenth century as a movement to revive Tridentine principles of ecclesiastical organization and a "solid and truly Christian piety" based on Muratorian historical scholarship and the works of the Church Fathers, which were being edited with increasing frequency.

The reformers aimed to reconcile Christianity and the Enlightenment, but faced with incomprehension on the part of ecclesiastical authorities, they were forced to turn to the civil governments. "Equating jurisdictionalism with disloyalty and committed to maintaining the primacy of the papacy, the hierarchy thereupon renounced its five-centuries-old alliance with the culturally creative classes of Italy. It struck a new alliance with all those who preferred the rousing sermons of Paul of the Cross to the ponderous tomes of St. Augustine, the charming stories of Alfonso de' Liguori to the inelegant research reports of the Muratorian historians, *santini* to saints. It thus ushered in a wholly new epoch in the history of the Church, one which was to last, at least in the realm of the arts and letters, for another two centuries" (Eric Cochrane in *CHR* 70, no. 3 [July 1984], p. 469).

Chadwick, Owen. *The Popes and the European Revolution.* New York: Oxford University Press, 1981. An authoritative account.

Church and Society in Catholic Europe in the Eighteenth Century. W. J. Callahan and D. Higgs, eds. New York: Cambridge University Press, 1979.

Cragg, Gerald R. *The Church in the Age of Reason (1648–1789).* Harmondsworth, England: Penguin Books, 1974. An Anglican historian surveys this crucial period.

Drake, Stillman. *Galileo at Work.* Chicago: University of Chicago Press, 1981.

The Enlightenment. Frank Manuel, ed. Englewood Cliffs, N.J.: Prentice-Hall, 1965.

Gay, Peter. *The Enlightenment.* New York: Knopf, 1967.

Hall, A. Rupert. *The Scientific Revolution 1500–1800.* Boston: Beacon Press, 1962.

Hazard, Paul. *The European Mind:* Cleveland, Ohio: World Publishing, 1963.

Langford, Jerome J. *Galileo, Science and the Church.* Ann Arbor, Mich.: University of Michigan Press, 1971.

Laski, Harold. *The Rise of European Liberalism.* London: Unwin Books, 1962.

Livingston, James. *Modern Christian Thought.* New York: Macmillan, 1971.

McMullin, Ernan, ed. *Galileo: Man of Science.* New York: Basic Books, 1967.

Nicolaus Steno and His Indice. Gustav Scherz, ed. Copenhagen: Munksgaard, 1958. A seventeenth-century scientist and convert Catholic who after a trailblazing career as a geologist was ordained a bishop and died in the odor of sanctity.

Palmer, Robert R. *Catholics and Unbelievers in Eighteenth-Century France.* Princeton, N.J.: Princeton University Press, 1970. One of the classic treatises.

Phillips, Henry. *Church and Culture in Seventeenth-Century France.* New York: Cambridge University Press, 1997. Against idea that Descartes et al. were hostile to the authority of the Church, Phillips holds that the authority of the Church was made an issue in the area of science and philosophy because Descartes et al. challenged the authority of Aristotle, which the hierarchy considered vital to the maintenance of church authority.

Ravitch, Norman. *Sword and Mitre: Government and Episcopate in France and England in the Age of Aristocracy.* The Hague: Mouton, 1966.

Reston, James. *Galileo. A Life.* New York: HarperCollins, 1994.

Science and Religion. Ian Barber, ed. New York: Harper & Row, 1968.

Stolpe, Sven. *Christina of Sweden.* New York: Macmillan, 1966. A fine study of the amazing seventeenth-century queen who abdicated her powerful throne to become a Catholic.

Tackett, Timothy. *Priest and Parish in Eighteenth-Century France: A Social and Political Study of the Curés in a Diocese of Dauphin, 1750–1791.* Princeton, N.J.: Princeton University Press, 1977.

Van Kley, Dale. *The Jansenists and the Expulsion of the Jesuits from France, 1757–1765.* New Haven: Yale University Press, 1975.

Ward, W. R. *Christianity Under the Ancien Regime, 1648–1789.* New York: Cambridge University Press, 1999. With more attention to Protestantism than to Catholicism, this author of many books on the period argues that the secular Enlightenment did not cause a Christian retreat. The forward march of science and reason was accompanied, he claims, by a renewed vigor of evangelical Protestantism through its intensely personal expressions of faith and its new organized bonds. All of this was helped by the spread of literacy and the development of the printing press, which also contributed to the advance of the Enlightenment.

23. THE CHURCH TORN BY INTERNAL STRIFE:
JANSENISM AND GALLICANISM

Abercrombie, Nigel. *The Origins of Jansenism.* Oxford: Clarendon Press, 1937.

Gres-Gayer, Jacques M. "The *Unigenitus* of Clement XI: A Fresh Look at the Issues." *Theological Studies* 49 (1988), pp. 259–82. Gres-Gayer discusses the fundamental studies of Lucien Ceyssens and Bruno Neveu, who in a number of articles and books in French have recently renovated the research on Jansenism and Gallicanism. Ceyssens, he explains, holds that the conflict between the Jansenists and anti-Jansenists amounted to an irreducible opposition between two visions of the Church and the world. Ceyssens has discovered that Francesco Cardinal Albizzi, a ferocious anti-Jansenist, committed a forgery to prove that the five condemned Jansenist propositions were actually in Jansen's work *Augustinus.*

The original dispute over grace was soon overshadowed by the clash between Gallican and Ultramontane principles. "Ceyssens and Neveu concur in assessing the condemnation of Jansenism/Quesnelism as a way for Rome to resolve another and more crucial question: papal authority under challenge by the Gallicans. The condemnation emphasized the personal power of the Roman pontiff," especially in regard to the question of whether a papal decree had to be "received" by the bishops in order to be authoritative.

The opposition of the bishops to *Unigenitus* was due to the fact they were convinced it contained errors and they felt the theologians who drafted it were ultra-Roman and by no means impartial. They felt that by attempting to impose it on the Church in spite of its errors, the Pope was putting personal interest above the welfare of the Church. They appealed to patristic and historical evidence in their favor, whereas the Roman view stressed the authority of the papacy, whose official pronouncements were declared to be the last word on the matter since they represented the living tradition. Ceyssens shows that the Pope was captive to two extremists, Cardinal Fabroni and Father Le Tellier, and later regretted following their advice in issuing the ill-fated bull. No doubt *Unigenitus* was pivotal to the development of Catholicism between the Council of Trent and the French Revolution.

Hazard, Paul. *European Thought in the Eighteenth Century, from Montesquieu to Lessing.* New Haven: Yale University Press, 1954.

Reynolds, Ernest E. *Bossuet.* Garden City, N.Y.: Doubleday, 1963.

Sedgwick, Alexander. *Jansenism in Seventeenth-Century France: Voices from the Wilderness.* Charlottesville, Va.: University Press of Virginia, 1977.

24. THE FRENCH REVOLUTION SHATTERS THE CHURCH OF THE OLD ORDER

Altholz, Josef L. *The Churches in the Nineteenth Century.* Indianapolis: Bobbs-Merrill, 1967.

Church and Society: Catholic Social and Political Thought and Movements, 1789–1950. Joseph N. Moody, ed. New York: Arts, Inc., 1953. A very comprehensive collection of studies and documents; obsolete in parts but still valuable.

Dansette, Adrien. *The Religious History of Modern France* London: Nelson, 1961.

Hales, Edward E. Y. *The Catholic Church in the Modern World: A Survey from the French Revolution to the Present.* Garden City, N.Y.: Doubleday Image Books, 1961.

———. *Napoleon and the Pope: The Story of Napoleon and Pius VII.* London: Catholic Book Club, 1962.

———. *Revolution and Papacy, 1769–1846* Notre Dame, Ind.: University of Notre Dame Press, 1966.

McManners, John. *French Ecclesiastical Society Under the Ancien Regime: A Study of Angers in the Eighteenth Century.* Manchester: University of Manchester Press, 1960.

———. *The French Revolution and the Church.* London: S.P.C.K., 1969.

Maier, Hans. *Revolution and the Church: The Early History of Christian Democracy, 1789–1901.* Notre Dame, Ind.: University of Notre Dame Press, 1969.

O'Dwyer, Margaret. *The Papacy in the Age of Napoleon and the Restoration—Pius VII, 1800–1823.* Lanham, Md.: University Press of America, 1985. The first complete scholarly biography of Pius VII since 1836.

Palmer, Robert R. *Catholics and Unbelievers in Eighteenth-Century France.* Princeton, N.J.: Princeton University Press, 1939.

Ravitch, Norman. *Sword and Mitre: Government and Episcopate in France and England in the Age of Aristocracy.* The Hague: Mouton, 1966. The 130 bishops at the time of the French Revolution were aristocrats to a man, fiscally independent, indifferent to the needs of their priests, and unwilling to identify with the interests of the nation.

Thompson, James Matthew. *The French Revolution.* New York: Oxford University Press, 1969.

Vidler, Alec. R. *The Church in an Age of Revolution.* Baltimore: Penguin Books, 1974.

Walsh, Henry H. *The Concordat of 1801: A Study in the Problem of Nationalism in the Relations of Church and State.* New York: AMS Press, 1967.

25. PIUS IX SAYS NO TO THE LIBERAL CATHOLICS

Acton, John E. D. *The History of Freedom and Other Essays.* London: Macmillan, 1922.

Altholz, Josef. *The Liberal Catholic Movement in England. The Rambler and Its Contributors.* London: Burns & Oates, 1962.

Aretin, Karl Otmar von. *The Papacy and the Modern World.* New York: McGraw-Hill, 1970.

Artz, Frederick. *Reaction and Revolution.* New York: Harper & Row, 1963.

Aubert, Roger. *The Church in the Age of Liberalism.* New York: Crossroad, 1981.

———. *Le Pontificat de Pie IX (1846–1878).* Paris: Bloud & Gay, 1963.

Brown, Marvin L., Jr. *Louis Veuillot: French Ultramontane Catholic Journalist and Layman, 1813–1883.* Durham, N.C.: Moore, 1977.

Carr, J. *St. Clement Mary Hofbauer.* London: 1939. A Redemptorist from 1784, St. Clement labored with great success in Warsaw among the German-speaking population, devoting himself to the care of souls and to educational and charitable activities. Later, in Vienna, he exerted a powerful influence over all sectors of society and greatly counteracted the effects of Josephinism and the Enlightenment.

The Church in a Secularized Society. Roger Aubert, ed. New York: Paulist Press, 1978. A fine survey by the foremost Catholic historian of this period.

La Condamnation de Lamennais. M.J. LeGuillou and Louis LeGuillou, eds. Paris: Editions Beauchesne, 1982. These documents provide a great amount of indispensable material for an understanding of this tragic story. The prophets of the past are well represented here with their arguments for the Church's dependency on the established social order and its preference at the time for absolute monarchy, aristocracy, hierarchy, and all that it implied, including control of the press and restrictions on religious freedom. As Edward Gargan says so well in his review in *CHR* 70, no. 3, p. 488: "Reflective historians will be led to wonder how men sincerely devoted to the Church had so little confidence in its capacity to survive in a changing world. This collection is of paramount significance for the understanding of how men of good will are able to injure one another and all that they love."

Eichner, H. *Friedrich Schlegel.* New York, 1970. Schlegel (1772–1829) was a leader of the Romantic movement. A convert to the Church in 1808 with Clement Mary Hofbauer, he sought to restore the national life of Germany and Austria on a Catholic basis. Despairing of this, he looked to literature and philosophy for a renewed Catholicism.

Fleischmann, K. *St. Clement Mary Hofbauer.* Graz: 1988.

A Free Church in a Free State? The Catholic Church, Italy, Germany, France, 1868–1914. Ernst Helmreich, ed. Boston: Heath, 1964.

Geiselmann, Rupert. *Die katholische Tübinger Schule.* Freiburg im Br.: Herder, 1964. Until this study, Möhler was the only German theologian of that period known in wider circles. Drey, the founder of the Catholic Tübingen School, invented a powerful new theological method to meet the challenge of the Kantian and post-Kantian philosophy.

Hales, Edward E. Y. *Pio Nono: A Study in European Politics and Religion in the Nineteenth Century.* Garden City, N.Y.: Doubleday Image Books, 1962.

Hayes, Carlton H. *A Generation of Materialism.* New York: Harper & Row, 1963.

Holmes, J. Derek. *The Triumph of the Holy See; A Short History of the Papacy in the Nineteenth Century.* Shepherdstown, W. Va.: Patmos Press, 1978.

Lebrun, Richard Allen. *Throne and Altar: The Political and Religious Thought of Joseph de Maistre.* Ottawa: University of Ottawa Press, 1965. A specialist's study of one of the diehard Catholic reactionaries.

Le Guillou, L. *Les Discussions critiques: Journal de la crise mennaisienne.* Paris: A. Colin, 1967.

Liberalismus in der Gesellschaft des deutschen Vormarz. Wolfgang Schieder, ed. Göttingen: Vandenhoeck & Ruprecht, 1983. On May 17, 1832, some twenty to thirty thousand Germans gathered in the town of Neustadt, where with flags of black, red, and gold and a banner proclaiming GERMANY'S REBIRTH, they marched to the castle ruins near Hambach. Henceforth known as the Hambacher Fest, the meeting was "German liberalism's first great demonstration and a clear indication that the age of participatory politics had dawned in Central Europe."

As the book shows, the movement drew on a most diverse collection: Protestants and Catholics, free traders and protectionists, radical agitators and well-placed bureaucrats. Indeed, this proved to be one of the factors in its downfall.

Maistre, Joseph de. *The Pope*. New York: H. Fertig, 1975. The bible of the nineteenth-century Catholic reactionaries, which contained de Maistre's famous aphorism: No morality without religion, no religion without Christianity, no Christianity without Catholicism, no Catholicism without the Pope.

O'Connell, Marvin R. *The Oxford Conspirators: A History of the Oxford Movement*. New York: Macmillan, 1969.

O'Ferrall, Fergus. *Catholic Emancipation: Daniel O'Connell and the Birth of Irish Democracy*. Atlantic Highlands, N.J.: Humanities Press International, 1985. An important contribution to the literature on the great Irish emancipator and liberal Catholic.

Vanden Heuvel, Jon. *A German Life in the Age of Revolution: Joseph Gorres, 1776–1848*. Washington, D.C.: Catholic University of America Press; 2001. As a youth a supporter of the French Revolution, Gorres became disillusioned and turned to religious studies inspired especially by German Romanticism. In 1814 he started the great German newspaper, *Rheinische Merkur*, which eventually fell afoul of the reactionary Prussian government. When he stood up for the Catholic Church's freedom, he had to flee to Strasbourg. In 1824 he formally returned to the Church and as professor at the University in Munich he became the center of a circle of famous Catholic scholars, including J. J. I. von Doellinger. In 1838, with his tract *Athanasius*, he rallied all Catholic Germany to the defense of the Church, which was suffering persecution by the Prussian government. His contribution to the spread of Catholic ideas in modern Germany was considerable.

Savon, Hervé. *Johann Adam Mohler: The Father of Modern Theology*. Glen Rock, N.J.: Paulist Press, 1966. A good introduction to the work of one of the founders of the Catholic intellectual revival after the French Revolution.

Schwedt, Herman H. *Das römische Urteil über Georg Hermes (1775–1831): Ein Beitrag zur Geschichte der Inquisition im 19. Jabrbundert*. Rome, Freiburg, and Vienna: Herder, 1980. Another depressing account of the reactionary Curia under the pontificates of Gregory XIV and Pius IX. Hermes's work was given short shrift by Roman censors who were poorly informed and doctrinally and culturally prejudiced. They took propositions out of their context and presented them in translation higgledy-piggledy so it was never really clear just which works of Hermes were condemned. The papal decree of 1835 condemned Hermes's *books*, but the Roman authorities never specified which doctrines were erroneous. Perhaps they couldn't. Later Pius IX used Hermes as a whipping boy to show that he was not liberal on doctrine and as part of his strategy to prevent the formation of a German national Church.

Vidler, Alec R. *Prophecy and Papacy: A Study of Lamennais, the Church, and the Revolution*. New York: Scribner, 1954. A very well written study of this fascinating and tragic priest-prophet.

26. THE *SYLLABUS OF ERRORS* SQUELCHES THE LIBERAL CATHOLICS

Acton, John E. D. *Essays on Church and State.* London: Hollis & Carter, 1952.

Blakiston, Noel. *The Roman Question. Extracts from the Despatches of Odo Russell 1858–70.* Wilmington, Del.: M. Glazier, 1980. Russell's accounts of his conversations with Pius etch a most fascinating portrait of this key Pope of modern Catholicism.

Ker, Ian. *The Achievement of John Henry Newman.* Notre Dame, Ind.: University of Notre Dame Press, 1990.

McElrath, Damian. *The Syllabus of Pius IX: Some Reactions in England.* Louvain: Bibliothèque de l'Université, 1964. Tells of the turmoil in England and how Newman, who considered the *Syllabus* a heavy blow, worked out a solution (applauded by all), arguing that Catholic obedience to the Pope is not superior to conscience while limiting the civil domain in relation to the religious domain.

Norman, Edward. *The English Catholics in the Nineteenth Century.* New York: Oxford University Press, 1984.

Trevor, Meriol. *Newman.* 2 vols. London: Macmillan, 1962.

27. PIO NONO CARRIES ULTRAMONTANISM TO A GRAND TRIUMPH AT VATICAN I

Binkley, Robert. *Realism and Nationalism.* New York: Harper & Row, 1963.

Butler, Cuthbert. *The Vatican Council, 1869–1870.* Westminster, Md.: Newman Press, 1962. A classic account by a participant.

Hasler, August B. *How the Pope Became Infallible: Pius IX and the Politics of Persuasion.* Garden City, N.Y.: Doubleday, 1981. A controverted study of alleged shenanigans indulged in by Vatican officials (including the Pope) in order to secure the definition of infallibility. Hasler was a German priest who used hitherto unexploited documents he found in the Vatican archives while working there as a member of the Curia. Slanted, but the documentation is solid.

Hennessey, James, S.J. *The First Council of the Vatican: The American Experience.* New York: Herder & Herder, 1963. Underlines the politically liberal and pragmatic orientation of the American bishops, a good number of whom were also opposed to the definition of infallibility.

Sperber, Jonathan. *Popular Catholicism in Nineteenth-Century Germany.* Princeton, N.J.: Princeton University Press, 1984. This study focuses on the area of North Rhine–Westphalia in describing popular religious life between 1830 and 1880. It shows how the secularization of the first half of the century was reversed in the two decades after 1850 and the revival of the people's loyalty to the Church helped greatly in establishing political Catholicism. Urbanization and industrialization may actually have strengthened popular piety.

PART FIVE: THE STATE OF SIEGE IS SLOWLY LIFTED, A.D. 1891—

GENERAL WORKS

The Church in the Industrial Age. Roger Aubert et al., eds. (vol. 9 of *History of the Church,* Hubert Jedin and John Dolan, eds.) New York: Crossroad, 1981.

Daniel-Rops, Henri. *A Fight for God: 1870–1939.* London: Dent & Sons, 1965.

Latourette, Kenneth S. *Christianity in a Revolutionary Age.* 5 vols. New York: Harper & Brothers, 1958–61.

The New Cambridge Modern History. Vol. 12.: *The Era of Violence, 1898–1945.* David Thomson, ed. New York: Cambridge University Press, 1960.

Readings in Church History. Vol. 3. Colman Barry, O.S.B., ed. Westminster, Md.: Newman Press, 1965.

28. SOCIAL CATHOLICISM AND CHRISTIAN DEMOCRACY

Anderson, Margaret Lavinia. *Windthorst: A Political Biography.* New York: Oxford University Press, 1987. Based on recently uncovered documents, it proves its subject to have been a brilliant parliamentarian of the Center Party who successfully opposed Bismarck's attempt to resuscitate a "national" church.

Arnal, Oscar L. *Ambivalent Alliance. The Catholic Church and the Action Française, 1899–1939.* Pittsburgh, Pa.: University of Pittsburgh Press, 1985. As reviewer Joseph N. Moody says, while the Vatican did not manifest consistent hostility to threats from the Right, the core of the Catholic Right was balanced by countervailing forces by the beginning of the mid-twenties.

Bokenkotter, Thomas. *Church and Revolution.* Garden City, N.Y.: Doubleday Image Books, 1998. Signaled by Roger Aubert *(RHE* 95, no. 2) for making an original contribution to the history of Social Catholicism.

Brand, Mary V. *The Social Catholic Movement in England; 1920–1955.* New York: Pageant Press, 1963.

Buchanan, Tom, and Martin Conway. *Political Catholicism in Europe, 1918–1965.* New York: Oxford University Press, 1996.

Calvez, Jean-Yves, and Jacques Perrin. *The Church and Social Justice: The Social Teachings of the Popes from Leo XIII to Pius XII (1878–1958).* Chicago: Regnery, 1961.

Camp, Richard L. *The Papal Ideology of Social Reform: A Study of Historical Development, 1878–1967.* Leiden: E.J. Brill, 1969. A critical but generally positive view by a non-Catholic scholar of the Popes' witness for social justice.

The Church Speaks to the Modern World: The Social Teachings of Leo XIII. Etienne Gilson, ed. Garden City, N.Y.: Doubleday Image Books, 1954.

Fogarty, Michael P. *Christian Democracy in Western Europe, 1820–1953.* Westport, Conn.: Greenwood Press, 1974.

Gargan, Edward T. *Leo XIII and the Modern World.* New York: Sheed & Ward, 1961.

The Great Encyclical Letters of Pope Leo XIII. New York: Benzinger Bros., 1903.

Jemolo, Arturo. *Church and State in Italy, 1850–1950.* Philadelphia: Dufour Editions, 1961.

Langer, William L. *Political and Social Upheaval: 1832–1852.* New York: Harper & Row, 1969.

McClelland, Vincent. *Cardinal Manning.* London: Oxford University Press, 1962.

Paul, Harry. *The Second Ralliement.* Washington, D.C.: Catholic University of America Press, 1967.

Social Wellsprings: Fourteen Epochal Documents by Pope Leo XIII. Joseph Husslein, ed. Milwaukee, Wis.: Bruce Publishing, 1940. Includes the text of *Rerum Novarum.*

Vaillancourt, Jean-Guy. *Papal Power: A Study of Vatican Control over Lay Catholic Elites.* Berkeley: University of California Press, 1980.

Vidler, Alec. *Social Catholicism.* London: S.P.C.K., 1964.

Wallace, Lillian P. *Leo XIII and the Rise of Socialism.* New York and Durham, N.C.: Duke University Press, 1966.

Whyte, John H. *Catholics in Western Democracies: A Study in Political Behavior.* New York: St. Martin's Press, 1981. Finds two types of contemporary political Catholicism: "closed" and "open." Shows how decisive a role European Catholics played in the democratic reconstruction of Europe after World War II. The emancipation of the Christian parties from Church tutelage after World War I is viewed as a historical process of great import.

29. THE MODERNIST DEBACLE

Barmann, Lawrence F. *Baron Friedrich von Hügel and the Modernist Crisis in England.* London: Cambridge University Press, 1972. By one of the leading experts on the movement.

Chadwick, Owen. *Secularization of the European Mind in the Nineteenth Century.* New York: Cambridge University Press, 1975.

Daly, Gabriel. *Transcendence and Immanence; A Study in Catholic Modernism and Integralism.* New York: Oxford University Press, 1980.

Heaney, John J. *The Modernist Crisis: von Hügel.* Washington, D.C.: Corpus Books, 1968.

Kurtz, Lester. *The Politics of Heresy: The Modernist Crisis in Roman Catholicism.* Berkeley: University of California Press, 1986. A study of the crisis by a sociologist who places it in the perspective of previous efforts to reconcile Catholicism with modern critical thought. His ascription of political motives to the Popes in their pursuit of modernists has been questioned.

Lagrange, Père. *Personal Reflections and Memoirs.* Translated by H. Wansbrough. Mahwah, N.J.: Paulist Press, 1985. Account by perhaps the most important Catholic pioneer in the historical method and biblical criticism of the struggle to reconcile dogma with these approaches.

Loisy, Alfred. *My Duel with the Vatican.* New York: E. P. Dutton, 1924.

Loome, Thomas M. *Liberal Catholicism, Reform Catholicism, Modernism: A Contribution to a New Orientation in Modernist Research.* Mainz: Matthias Grünewald Verlag. 1979. While generally recognized as an important contribution to the question, in the July 1982 *Downside Review,* a number of writers note its principal weaknesses: its perspective, which is theological rather than historical; its oversimplification of the history of modern Catholicism by reducing it to two currents—the liberal and conservative; the way it minimizes what was original in Catholic Modernism in relation to liberal Catholicism, i.e.,

Modernism's challenge to the authority of the magisterium and its evolutionary view of doctrine, and finally the exaggerated role Loome attributes to German Catholicism.

McCool, Gerald. *Catholic Theology in the Nineteenth Century.* New York: Seabury Press, 1977. The author shows how the failure of the Roman Thomists to move beyond Liberatore, Kleutgen et al. had tragic consequences for the Church. Their ignorance of history and the historical sciences as well as their hostility to modern philosophy created a gulf between modern thought and the Church and ruined Leo's hope for a brilliant revival of Thomism.

McCready, Douglas. *Jesus Christ for the Modern World: The Christology of the Catholic Tübingen School.* New York: Peter Lang, 1992.

Poulat, Emile. *Catholicisme, Démocratie et Socialisme. Le mouvement catholique et Mgr Benigni de la naissance du socialisme à la victoire du fascisme.* Paris: Casterman, 1977. No one has done as much as Poulat to deepen our understanding of Modernism. Benigni he sees as a tragic figure: The organizer of a system of secret denunciations and espionage for Pius X, he died a lonely outcast from papal circles and a friend of the Fascists. Benigni shared Pius X's total opposition to the Modernists' search for ways of integrating the Church into a new pluralist society largely motivated by nonreligious values. (Insofar as the Modernists' approach also involved accepting pluralism in the Church as well, the issue is obviously far from settled.)

Ranchetti, Michele. *The Catholic Modernists: A Study of the Religious Reform Movement, 1864–1907* New York: Oxford University Press, 1969.

Ratté, John. *Three Modernists: Alfred Loisy, George Tyrrell, William L. Sullivan.* New York: Sheed & Ward, 1967.

Roman Catholic Modernism. Bernard M. G. Reardon, ed. Palo Alto: Stanford University Press, 1970. A very useful collection of excerpts from some of the Modernists and the papal condemnations.

Root, John D. "The Final Apostasy of St. George Jackson Mivart." *Catholic Historical Review* 71 (1985), pp. 1–25. Relates the sad story of an English convert, a distinguished man of science and zealous apologist for the Catholic faith, who at the end of his life turned violently against the Church. Although given to intemperate expressions at times (one of his famous articles tried to prove there could be "happiness in hell"), his real tragedy was thinking that the obscurantists in the Roman Curia and the English hierarchy would have mercy on a layman who upheld such dangerous and "heretical" views as development of Catholic doctrine, evolution of the human *body,* and that the Church should accept the secure findings of biblical criticism. Mivart was one of the first victims of the purge of liberal Catholics in England, which reached its peak in the English bishops' Joint Pastoral of December 1900.

Vidler, Alec. *The Modernist Movement in the Roman Church.* Cambridge: Cambridge University Press, 1934.

———. *A Variety of Catholic Modernists.* London: Cambridge University Press, 1970. By a long-time student of the movement, written as one would expect con brio.

Zalar, Jeffrey T. " 'Knowledge Is Power': The Borromäusverein and Catholic Reading Habits in Imperial Germany." *Catholic Historical Review* 86 (January 2000). Notes how the history of Catholicism in imperial Germany (1871–1918) reveals the difficulties of the Church in coming to terms with modernity. Although Catholics were 37 percent of the population in 1871, they played a very minor role on the intellectual scene. Looked down on by the dominant Protestant neighbors as culturally incompetent and politically dangerous, they retreated behind the walls of clerical authority. Silent in the great conversation over scientific advance, they made only feeble contributions to literature, painting, architecture, and music. The editors of the *Borromäus Blätter*, a periodical begun in 1902, essayed to change this situation by exposing Catholics to the best in contemporary culture. To share in the burgeoning German identity, they said, Catholics had to undergo an intellectual reorientation from what was perceived as superstition and myth to demonstrated fact. To this end they registered considerable success in getting Catholics to read and acquire the great Western literary and scientific classics. The *Borromäus Blätter* became an important forum where Catholic doctrine came to face with the claims of modern science. It also helped to foment a Catholic form of nationalism that made German Catholics finally feel like true sons and daughters of the fatherland—an attitude very apparent by 1914, for weal or woe. (Note: Donald Dietrich in *CHR* [April, 2002] notes how German Catholicism was influenced by this myopic patriotism in their response to the political and ethical issues they faced in the first half of the twentieth century.)

30. THE CHURCH MOVES OUT TO THE WHOLE WORLD

Boxer, Charles R. *The Christian Century in Japan, 1549–1650*. Berkeley: University of California Press, 1974.

Caraman, Philip. *The Lost Paradise: An Account of the Jesuits in Paraguay, 1607–1768*. London: Sidgwick & Jackson, 1975. Those who saw the film *Mission* will especially appreciate this study of the famous Jesuit "reductions."

Cronin, Vincent. *The Wise Man from the West: Matteo Ricci and His Mission to China*. London: Fount Paperbacks, 1984.

Hay, Malcolm. *Failure in the Far East: Why and How the Breach Between the Western World and China First Began*. Philadelphia: Dufour Editions, 1957. Finds the Jansenists and the Roman Curia the culprits in causing the tragic failure of the Jesuit missions by their refusal to accept the Chinese rites.

King, Noel Q. *Christian and Muslim in Africa*. New York: Harper & Row, 1971.

Krahl, Joseph, S.J. *China Missions in Crisis: Bishop Laimbeckhoven and His Times, 1738–1787*. Rome: Gregorian University, 1964. The good bishop conformed scrupulously to the disastrous condemnation of the Chinese rites, which ruined a good chance of converting China.

Minamiki, Georg, S.J. *The Chinese Rites Controversy from Its Beginnings to Modern Times*. Chicago: Loyola University Press, 1985. Concentrates on the events in China, Japan, and Manchuko that finally brought a change in Church policy.

Neill, Stephen. *A History of Christian Missions*. New York: Penguin Books, 1986. Recognized as the best survey.

Picken, Stuart D. B. *Christianity and Japan: Meeting, Conflict, Hope*. New York: Harper & Row, 1983. The tale is told largely through pictures, but is a worthwhile contribution.

Rowbotham, Arnold H. *Missionary and Mandarin: The Jesuits at the Court of China*. New York: Russell & Russell, 1966.

31. THE AMERICAN CHURCH

Abell, Aaron. *American Catholicism and Social Action.* Westport, Conn.: Greenwood Press, 1980.

Ahlstrom, Sydney E. *A Religious History of the American People.* 2 vols. Garden City, N.Y.: Doubleday Image Books, 1972.

Broderick, Francis L. *Right Reverend New Dealer: John A. Ryan.* New York: Macmillan, 1963. Ryan is no doubt the person most responsible for fixing American social Catholicism in a progressive mold.

Catholicism in America. Philip Gleason, ed. New York: Harper & Row, 1970.

The Church in a Secularized Society. Roger Aubert, ed. New York: Paulist Press, 1978. Fine chapters on the United States by John Tracy Ellis and on Canada by Paul E. Crunican.

Coles, Robert. *Dorothy Day: A Radical Devotion.* Reading, Mass: Addison-Wesley, 1987. A fine study of the "sweetheart" of all socially conscious American Catholics.

Cross, Robert D. *The Emergence of Liberal Catholicism in America.* Cambridge: Harvard University Press, 1958. A very highly regarded study of the Americanist controversy.

Dolan, Jay. *The American Catholic Experience: A History from Colonial Times to the Present.* Garden City, N.Y.: Doubleday, 1985.

Ellis, John T. *American Catholicism.* Chicago: University of Chicago Press, 1969. The dean of American Catholic historians condenses a lifetime of reflection on the American Church's experience.

———. *Documents of American Catholic History.* Wilmington, Del.: M. Glazier, 1987.

———. *The Life of James Cardinal Gibbons.* 2 vols. Westminster, Md.: Christian Classics, 1987.

Guilday, Peter. *A History of the Councils of Baltimore, 1791–1884.* New York: Macmillan, 1932.

Handy, Robert T. *A History of the Churches in the United States and Canada.* New York: Oxford University Press, 1979.

Hennessey, James, S.J. *American Catholics.* New York: Oxford University Press, 1983. A basic, very readable account.

Jaenen, Cornelius J. *The Role of the Church in New France.* New York: McGraw-Hill Ryerson, 1976. Good brief treatment.

McAvoy, Thomas. *A History of the Catholic Church in the United States.* Notre Dame, Ind.: University of Notre Dame Press, 1969.

McShane, Joseph, S.J. *"Sufficiently Radical." Catholicism, Progressivism, and the Bishops' Program of 1919.* Washington, D.C.: Catholic University of America Press, 1986. Tells the story of the "Bishops' Program," a pivotal document. In issuing it the bishops abandoned their previous policy of masterly inaction on social issues and entered the mainstream of American reform efforts. Its main author, John A. Ryan, united American progressivism and the social Catholicism of Leo XIII.

Morris, Charles. *American Catholic. The Saints and Sinners Who Built America's Most Powerful Church.* New York: Random House, 1997. In a vividly written, well-researched account, Morris notes how the huge Irish immigration provided the Church with members who had an intense devotion to the Church, acceptance of celibacy, and deference to the clergy. This also led to a hierarchy that left little room for intellectualism. But he highlights the remarkable bishops who, against powerful forces of bigotry, built a Church that by the 1950s appeared as the pre-eminent American church. He also notes the strong current of social activism that lent luster to its image. But the triumphal-era Catholicism with its bewitching ritual and strong discipline came to a crashing end in the 1960s: The institution was awash in change, its subculture was broken down, and it had been overtaken by extreme polarization. Its clergy was in flight and those remaining had been riven by scandal. Add to that a disillusioned laity, and the whole shebang possibly seemed ready to go the way of mainstream Protestantism. But the good news is that the loyal and active American Catholics are, he claims, like no other generation in the history of the Church: educated, literate, informed, and interested in their religion.

Moynihan, James H. *The Life of Archbishop John Ireland.* New York: Harper & Brothers, 1953.

O'Brien, David. *American Catholics and Social Reform.* New York: Oxford University Press, 1968.

Pastoral Letters of the United States Catholic Bishops. 4 vols. Hugh H. Nolan, ed. Washington, D.C.: United States Catholic Conference, 1984.

Reeves, Thomas C. *America's Bishop: The Life and Times of Fulton J. Sheen.* San Francisco: Encounter Books, 2001. A basically positive view of the best-known priest in the United States in the mid-twentieth century. As a man he had his share of contradictions, combining a love of great luxury with ambitious spiritual aspirations. As America's most popular TV preacher he was sometimes careless with the facts. But the message he brought so eloquently to millions gave them renewed hope and spiritual enrichment.

Walsh, H. H. *The Church in the French Era.* Toronto: Ryerson Press, 1966. First volume of a three-volume ecumenical history of the Canadian Christian churches.

32. THE POPES OF THE TWENTIETH CENTURY

Blet, Pierre, S.J. *Pie XII et la Seconde Guerre Mondiale d'après les archives du Vatican.* Paris: Perrin, 1997. As John Jay Hughes has pointed out in *CHR* (vol. 85, no. 2, pp. 268–70), Blet shows that the Pope's wartime policy was not neutrality but impartiality—judgment based on the demands of justice and truth. However, the Pope did push this policy to the limit by secretly informing the British in 1940 that a group of German generals was ready to replace Hitler if they could be assured of an honorable peace. His plea in his 1942 Christmas address for "those hundreds of thousands who [because] . . . of nationality or race are marked for death" (words repeated in 1943 in a speech to the cardinals) is often criticized as being much too tame. But as he said, he had to weigh every word carefully to spare the victims further suffering. Flaming public protests would have been counterproductive—as the Dutch bishops learned to their sorrow.

Chadwick, Owen. *Britain and the Vatican During the Second World War.* New York: Cambridge University Press, 1986. Quotes D'Arcy Osborne, British minister to the Holy See from 1935 to 1947, who was on very close terms with Pius XII. The Pope "would have been ready to give his life to save humanity from the consequences of the war."

Cianfarra, Camille M. *The Vatican and the Kremlin.* New York: Dutton, 1950.

Dietrich, Donald J. *Catholic Citizens in the Third Reich: Psycho-Social Principles and Moral Reasoning.* New Brunswick, N.J.: Transaction Books, 1988. Citing exhaustive research, the author argues that Catholics did offer some local opposition to Hitler's Final Solution, but the bishops failed to mobilize them as a body in part because they themselves were divided, had little inclination to do so, and, even if they had, would have had reason to suspect they would lose.

Falconi, Carlo. *The Popes in the Twentieth Century: From Pius X to John XXIII* Boston: Little, Brown, 1968.

Graham, Robert A. *Vatican Diplomacy. A Study of Church and State on the International Plane.* Princeton, N.J.: Princeton University Press, 1959. Basic.

Harrigan, William. "Nazi Germany and the Holy See, 1933–1936: The Historical Background of *Mit brennender Sorge.*" *Catholic Historical Review* 51 (1965), pp. 457–86.

Hellman, John. *Emmanuel Mounier and the New Catholic Left, 1930–1950.* Buffalo: University of Toronto Press, 1981.

Holmes, J. Derek. *The Papacy in the Modern World, 1914–1978.* New York: Crossroad, 1981.

Lewy, Guenter. *The Catholic Church and Nazi Germany.* New York: McGraw-Hill, 1965. Lewy accuses the Church of capitulating to the Nazi regime.

The Mind of Pius XII. Robert C. Pollock, ed. London and New York: Crown, 1955.

Morley, John F. *Vatican Diplomacy and the Jews During the Holocaust, 1939–1943.* New York: Ktav, 1980. Using archival material, Father Morley argues that the Vatican could have done more to assist the Jews. He criticizes the excessive reserve and prudence shown by the Pope and Secretary of State Cardinal Maglione in not using the full weight of their diplomatic position as representatives of a great moral power. Their devotion to the institution, he maintains, got in the way of the higher claims of human brotherhood.

Rhodes, Anthony. *The Vatican in the Age of the Dictators, 1922–1945.* New York: Holt, Rinehart & Winston, 1974.

Zahn, Gordon. *German Catholics and Hitler's Wars: A Study in Social Control.* New York: Sheed & Ward, 1962. Not very pleasant reading for Catholics.

33. THE RESURGENT LIBERAL CATHOLICS RING DOWN THE CURTAIN ON THE POST-TRENT CHURCH AT THE SECOND VATICAN COUNCIL

The Documents of Vatican II. Walter M. Abbott, ed. New York: Guild Press, 1966.

Hales, E. E. Y. *Pope John and His Revolution.* Garden City, N.Y.: Doubleday Image Books, 1966.

Hebblethwaite, Peter. *John XXIII: Shepherd of the Modern World.* Garden City, N.Y.: Doubleday, 1985.

Horton, Douglas. *Vatican Diary 1963: A Protestant Observes the Second Session of Vatican Council II.* Philadelphia: United Church Press, 1964–66.

Ratzinger, Joseph. *Theological Highlights of Vatican II.* Paramus, N.J.: Paulist/Newman Press.

Rynne, Xavier. *Vatican Council II.* 4 vols. New York: Farrar, Straus & Giroux, 1968. A blow-by-blow account.

Trevor, Meriel. *Pope John.* Garden City, N.Y.: Doubleday Image Books, 1968.

34. THE SOUND AND FURY OF RENEWAL

Chirico, Peter. *Infallibility: The Crossroads of Doctrine.* Wilmington, Del.: M. Glazier, 1983. An innovative approach to a grand old problem.

The Crisis of Religious Language. Johan Baptist Metz and Jean-Pierre Jossua, eds. New York: Herder & Herder, 1973.

Dulles, Avery. *Models of the Church.* Garden City, N.Y.: Doubleday Image, 1974. A fine application of the "new" theology to questions about the nature of the Church. A tour de force.

Gilkey, Langdon. *Catholicism Confronts Modernity: A Protestant View.* New York: Seabury Press, 1975. Very helpful for understanding the challenges Catholicism faces with renewal.

Küng, Hans. *Infallible? An Inquiry.* Garden City, N.Y.: Doubleday, 1970.

Nichols, Peter. *The Pope's Divisions: The Roman Catholic Church Today.* New York: Penguin Books, 1982.

Noel, Gerard. *The Anatomy of the Catholic Church: Roman Catholicism in an Age of Revolution.* Garden City, N.Y.: Doubleday, 1980.

O'Collins, Gerald. *Has Dogma a Future?* London: Darton, Longman and Todd, 1975. Helpful introduction to historical theology.

Toffler, Alvin. *Future Shock.* New York: Random House, 1971.

35. THE BARK OF PETER IN A STORMY SEA (1976–1989)

Authority in the Church and the Schillebeeckx Case. Leonard Swidler, ed. New York: Crossroad/ Herder & Herder, 1982.

Berryman, Phillip. *The Religious Roots of Rebellion.* Maryknoll, N.Y.: Orbis Books, 1984.

Bigo, Pierre. *The Church and the Third World Revolution.* Maryknoll, N.Y.: Orbis Books, 1977.

Bühlmann, Walbert. *The Coming of the Third Church: An Analysis of the Present and Future of the Church.* Maryknoll, N.Y.: Orbis Books, 1977.

The Church in Anguish: Has the Vatican Betrayed Vatican II? Hans Küng and Leonard Swidler, eds. New York: Harper & Row, 1987.

Cox, Harvey, *The Silencing of Leonardo Boff: The Vatican and the Future of World Christianity.* Oak Park, Ill.: Meyer-Stone Books, 1988.

Cullmann, Oscar. *Unity Through Diversity.* Philadelphia: Fortress Press, 1988.

Cuneo, Michael. *The Smoke of Satan: Conservative and Traditionalist Dissent in Contemporary American Catholicism.* New York: Oxford University Press, 1997. Focuses first on the conservative Catholics led by the century-and-a-half-old *The Wanderer,* which beats the drum for a Catholic political and religious conservatism while making hay out of the sexual peccadilloes of the "liberal" clergy and acting as a major rallying point for anti-abortion activists. Cuneo goes on to describe the various pockets of a Catholic underground of traditionalists stemming from Lefebvre's Pius X Society. A schism within its ranks begat the Pius V Society, which in turn in another schism begat the Mount St. Michael's Community. Then there are the Mystical Marianist apocalypticists. One of these, the Infinite Love Community, has its own Pope Gregory XVII (directly chosen by God). Like the traditionalist groups they reject the authority of the Second Vatican Council and the Popes of the council but, strangely, do not feel bound to the traditions of the preconciliar church (for example, they allow clerical marriage). The most sensational of the Marianist apocalypticists was the unsavory Veronica Lueken of Bayside Queens, who transmitted messages from the Virgin Mary that spoke insistently of doom. Veronica even asserted that Pope Paul VI had been poisoned and an imposter installed in his place by Curial conspirators.

Curran, Charles E. *Tensions in Moral Theology.* Notre Dame, Ind.: University of Notre Dame Press, 1989.

De Kadt, Emmanuel. *Catholic Radicals in Brazil.* London: Oxford University Press, 1970.

Dillon, Michelle. 1999. *Catholic Identity: Balancing Reason, Faith, and Power.* Pp. x, 289. New York: Cambridge University Press. See ppx, 289. In *Slouching to Gomorrah* Robert Bork laments the fragmentation of our society and the rejection by many of God, reason, the laws of history, and moral or natural law. Communitarian sociologists such as Amitai Etzioni think the remedy for this social anarchy is in a return to core values. But others, including Ms. Dillon, find the recovery of such "universalism" unrealistic. However, the advent of cultural diversity need not, she thinks, mean the proliferation of subcultural groupings disconnected from a broadly shared tradition. As an instance of this possibility, she offers this study of pro-change Catholics, showing how the they have managed to craft their own identity while remaining connected to the broad Catholic tradition.

Dulles, Avery. *The Reshaping of Catholicism.* San Francisco: Harper & Row, 1988.

Fries, Heinrich, and Karl Rahner. *Unity of the Churches: An Actual Possibility.* Philadelphia: Fortress Press, 1985. A set of bold proposals that didn't get even faint praise in the Curia.

Gallup, George, Jr., and Jim Castelli. *The American Catholic People.* Garden City, N.Y.: Doubleday, 1987.

Gannon, Thomas M. *World Catholicism in Transition.* New York: Macmillan, 1988. Consists of twenty-two essays mainly from a sociological viewpoint. Its study of a Church that is nearly as varied and confusing as the world itself makes some interesting points. For instance, it shows how the Tridentine model of Church and society still hangs on in some very secularized parts of Europe. On the other hand where the Church is a minority and frequently a much beleaguered one at that, Catholicism has become an ally of the protesters and dissenters.

The progressive Catholics among the authors display their unhappiness with the reactionary direction of the present papacy. The Jesuit progressive John Coleman believes the Catholic Church in the United States must loosen its ties with Rome and take on a more thoroughly American and democratic character. Others see the democratizing and secularizing model of liberal Protestantism as a dangerous temptation for Roman Catholicism.

Groen, Bert, and Will van den Bercken, eds. *Four Hundred years: Union of Brest (1596–1996): A Critical Reevaluation.* Leuven: Peeters, 1998. Articles marking the four hundredth anniversary of the union of the Orthodox Metropolitanate of Kiev (encompassing today's Belarus and Ukraine) with the Roman Church. The possibility of the Ukrainian Greek-Catholic Church's becoming the center of a reunited Catholic-Orthodox communion is broached. However, there is a discouraging note in the "absolutist" type thinking of the Moscow Patriarchate displayed *(CHR* 86 [2000], p. 127). But others see the Union of Brest as a "perfect model of a provisional and growing koinonia between two sister Churches."

Gutierrez, Gustavo. *A Theology of Liberation.* Maryknoll, N.Y.: Orbis Books, 1988.

Haight, Roger. *An Alternative Vision: An Interpretation of Liberation Theology.* New York: Paulist Press, 1985. A sympathetic analysis.

Hennelly, Alfred. *Theologies in Conflict.* Maryknoll, N.Y.: Orbis Books, 1979.

Kelleher, Steven S. *Divorce and Remarriage for Catholics?* Garden City, N.Y.: Doubleday Image Books, 1976.

Kennedy, Eugene. *The Now and Future Church: The Psychology of Being an American Catholic.* Garden City, N.Y.: Doubleday, 1984.

———. *Tomorrow's Catholics, Yesterday's Church.* New York: Harper & Row, 1988.

Knitter, Paul. *No Other Name? A Critical Survey of Christian Attitudes Toward the World Religions.* Maryknoll, N.Y.: Orbis Books, 1985.

Lernoux, Penny. *People of God: The Struggle for World Catholicism.* New York: Viking Press, 1989.

Mahoney, John. *The Making of Moral Theology: A Study of the Roman Catholic Tradition.* New York: Oxford University Press, 1987.

McDonnell, Kilian. *The Charismatic Renewal and Ecumenism.* New York: Paulist Press, 1978.

McGovern, Arthur F. *Marxism: An American Christian Perspective.* Maryknoll, N.Y.: Orbis Books, 1980.

Novak, Michael. *Will It Liberate? Questions About Liberation Theology.* Mahwah, N.J.: Paulist Press, 1987.

Quebedeaux.R. *The New Charismatics: The Origins, Development, and Significance of Neo-Pentecostalism.* Garden City, N.Y.: Doubleday, 1976. Tells the story of the movement of renewal that began in California in the late 1950s and has had an important influence on the churches, including the major denominations.

Ratzinger, Joseph. *The Ratzinger Report: An Exclusive Interview on the State of the Church.* San Francisco: Ignatius, 1986.

Sacred Congregation for the Doctrine of the Faith. *Instruction on Certain Aspects of the "Theology of Liberation."* Boston: Daughters of St. Paul, 1985.

Smart, Ninian. *The Phenomenon of Christianity.* London: Collins, 1979. Describes lucidly the varieties of Christianity today.

Suenens, Leon Cardinal. *Co-responsibility in the Church.* New York: Herder & Herder, 1968.

Theology in the Americas. Sergio Torres and John Eagleson, eds. Maryknoll, N.Y.: Orbis Books, 1976.

Van Beeck, Frans, S.J. *Catholic Identity After Vatican II.* Chicago: Loyola University Press, 1985.

Williams, George H. *The Mind of John Paul II: Origins of His Thought and Action.* New York: Seabury Press, 1981.

36. ON THE THRESHOLD OF THE NEW MILLENNIUM

Arinze, Francis Cardinal. *Religions for Peace: A Call for Solidarity in the Religions of the World.* London: Darton, Longman & Todd, 2002.

Fox, Thomas. *Pentecost in Asia: A New Way of Being Church.* Maryknoll, New York: Orbis Books, 2002.

Formicola, Jo Renee. *Pope John Paul II: Prophetic Politician.* Washington, D.C.: Georgetown University Press, 2002.

Froehle, B., and M. Gautier. *Global Catholicism: Portrait of a World Church.* Maryknoll, New York: Orbis Books, 2003.

Gy, Pierre-Marie. *The Reception of Vatican II: Liturgical Reforms in the Life of the Church.* Milwaukee, Wisconsin: Marquette University Press, 2003.

Jenkins, Philip. *The Next Christendom: The Coming of Global Christianity.* New York: Oxford University Press, 2002.

McInerny, Ralph. *The Defamation of Pius XII.* South Bend, Indiana: St. Augustine's Press, 2001.

Sanchez, José M. *Pius XII and the Holocaust: Understanding the Controversy.* Washington, D.C.: Catholic University of America Press, 2001.

Thorn, William, Phillip Runkel, and Susan Mountin, eds. *Dorothy Day and the Catholic Worker Movement: Centenary Essays.* Milwaukee, Wisconsin: Marquette University Press, 2001.

INDEX